LABOR IN THE UNITED STATES

Third Edition

SANFORD COHEN

Professor of Economics

University of New Mexico

Charles E. Merrill Publishing Company
A Bell & Howell Company
Columbus, Ohio

International Standard Book Number: 0-675-09369-4

Library of Congress Catalog Card Number: 70-104060

2 3 4 5 6 7 8 9 10—77 76 75 74 73 72 71

Printed in the United States of America

PREFACE to the First Edition

In his provocative book, *The House of Intellect,* Jacques Barzun describes the professional's fallacy as the failure to distinguish between knowing the subject and knowing the craft. Several decades of mass education in economics at the college level have apparently produced no mass sophistication in the field of economics, and certainly part of this failure must be attributed to the professional's fallacy. Much of the educational effort has consisted of a training in craftsmanship for an audience that has not aspired to journeyman status. As a result, many students leave their classrooms knowing neither the subject nor the craft.

The purpose of this book is to start the reader on the road to knowledge of the subject and an intelligent understanding of labor issues in the United States. Throughout, the needs of the interested layman and professional in the field have been kept in mind. I have placed much emphasis upon background knowledge because I believe, and here too I concur with Barzun, that preoccupation with the contemporary distorts perspective. A decade of university teaching experience has convinced me that the major deficiency of the American undergraduate student of the social sciences is a lack of historical perspective and that an overemphasis upon contemporary events and theories produces an ephemeral knowledge that evaporates as events move on and theories change.

This is not, however, a history book but rather a book that approaches the subject partly through the past, partly through disciplines that border upon economics, and partly through economics. The approach, in short, is interdisciplinary, and I have drawn heavily from the fields of history, sociology, and political science. The treatment of wages is essentially economic, and for this part of the book I have assumed that the reader will have had some knowledge of economic principles.

Paul Johnson of Purdue University, Glenn Miller and Herbert Parnes of Ohio State University, and David Roberts of Butler University read substantial parts of the manuscript and made many helpful comments. The fact that none of these persons read the entire manuscript or saw the work in its final form should be sufficient to establish the sole responsibility of the writer for all errors of omission or commission. My wife Julia's academic background and practical experience in the labor relations area proved to be exceptionally helpful as were her editorial and typing talents.

SANFORD COHEN

iii

PREFACE to the Second Edition

In the labor area, the years since 1960 have been unusually eventful. Perhaps a good indicator of the pace of events is the extent to which a book published in 1960 has become obsolete less than half a decade later. Because of the many developments, the revision of the first edition of *Labor in the United States* required more comprehensive treatment than statistical updating and references to new legislation. In the second edition, two new chapters have been added and more than half of the chapters in the original edition have been substantially revised. An attempt was made—with some but not total success—to retain the basic framework and orientation of the first edition.

A number of persons, some of them personally unknown to me, were kind enough to submit comments on the first edition, and these proved to be most helpful in my revision.

SANFORD COHEN

iv

PREFACE to the Third Edition

This revision was undertaken primarily to bring up to date those sections of the Second Edition affected by the numerous recent developments in the areas traditionally examined under the headings of labor economics and industrial relations. The necessity of updating the various materials, however, has provided an opportunity to expand the discussions of certain subjects and to incorporate some entirely new materials. The treatment of public employee unionism, for example, is more comprehensive in the present edition as is the description of unionization in the agricultural sector. Similarly, the chapters concerned with the labor market have been expanded and phrases such as "active manpower policy" and "human capital" appear for the first time.

I continue to be grateful to the many persons who have made suggestions for improving *Labor in the United States* and I hope that a few of them, at least, will find the evidence of their influence in the pages that follow.

SANFORD COHEN

Contents

PART THREE

COLLECTIVE BARGAINING

PART FOUR

WAGE ANALYSIS

PART SIX

THE PROBLEM OF ECONOMIC SECURITY

PART ONE

THE LABOR FORCE IN THE UNITED STATES

CHAPTER 1

Sources of Labor Supply in The United States

THE HISTORY OF THE AMERICAN WORK FORCE IS A COMPLEX AND FASCI-
nating story of the men and women who provided much of the physical and
mental power essential to the development of the highly productive economy of the United States. It is a story that must include characters as
diverse as the early slave laborers and modern-day clerical workers, indentured servants and semi-skilled factory operatives, migrant farm workers
and tightly organized building tradesmen.

The phrase "labor supply" usually brings to mind occupational categories such as factory operatives or clerical workers. The total labor supply
is much more comprehensive than this, of course, and includes corporation
executives, movie stars, professional athletes, and others who are not
usually thought of as workers. The broad concept of labor supply will be
used in this text, although the bulk of our attentions will be centered upon
factory operatives, service and retail trade employees, agricultural workers,
lower echelon white collar workers, clerical workers, and government employees.

The number of workers within an economy will depend upon the size
of the total population and the "labor force participation rate" or the degree to which persons of working age engage in labor force activity. In
this chapter we shall be concerned primarily with immigration and population growth and other population characteristics that are significant from
the standpoint of labor supply. Labor force participation rates will be
analyzed in the chapter that follows.

Our analysis will start with a brief consideration of the work force in colonial America. Why go back this far? Primarily for the perspective that is provided by an early starting date. The colonist worked under conditions that differed fundamentally from those of the present day. It is possible that equally fundamental changes will occur in the next century and a half. Perhaps an appreciation of the degree of change that has occurred will make it easier to comprehend the forces that are responsible for change in the contemporary world of work.

THE COLONIAL PERIOD

The tremendous amount of work involved in making a new continent habitable and the sparsity of population in the colonies resulted in an early condition of labor scarcity. This condition continued to exist for many years. Evidence of this fact can be found in the frequent references to and complaints about high wages in the colonies. In his *Wealth of Nations*, published in 1776, Adam Smith noted that wages of labor were much higher in North America than in any part of England. Much earlier, John Winthrop, first governor of the Massachusetts Bay Colony, had written that:

> The scarcity of workmen has caused them to raise their wages to an excessive rate, so as a carpenter would have three shillings the day, a laborer two shillings and sixpence, etc.; and accordingly those who had commodities to sell advanced their prices sometime double to what they cost in England. . . .[1]

In the face of this labor shortage, attempts were made in a number of colonies to regulate wages, but these appear to have met with indifferent success. Winthrop noted that the wage regulations caused workers to "remove to other places where they might have more" or "to live by planting and other employments of their own."[2]

Apart from the device of wage regulations, attempts were made to adjust to a labor scarcity by a variety of economies in labor use. It was a common practice to plant corn among the standing trunks of dead trees instead of thoroughly clearing the fields. The building of one fence around the "common fields" in New England towns instead of erecting a fence around each individual landholding was, at least in part, a laborsaving device. As several writers have suggested, the major source of farm labor in the early

---

[1] John Winthrop, *The History of New England from 1630 to 1649* (Boston: Little, Brown and Company, 1853 ed.), I, 138.
[2] *Ibid.*, II, 29.

settlements was the farm family itself. This labor supply consisted of the children and adult female members of the family as well as the adult males.[3]

UNFREE WORKERS

The larger part of the labor force during the colonial period consisted of unfree workers. The two categories of unfree workers were slaves and bound or indentured servants. Although the attribute of freedom was denied to both, there were important legal and economic differences between indentured servants and slaves.

The Indentured Servant

Roughly stated, an indentured servant had all rights except those denied by law, while a slave had no rights except those granted by law. A most important difference was the fact that an indentured servant became a free man at the expiration of his term of service.

As far as compensation went, the indentured servant did not receive money wages. His—or her—payment consisted primarily of food, clothing, and lodging. At the end of the term of service, the servant usually received "freedom dues."[4]

Before considering various aspects of the master–indentured servant relationship, however, it is necessary to look briefly into the source of these laborers.

In the seventeenth and eighteenth centuries there were economic as well as other currents that both pushed and pulled potential workers toward the colonies. Many early colonial settlements represented a financial investment by enterprisers, speculators, and landlords. The original hope of discovering deposits of precious metals was eventually replaced by an interest in the development of the natural resources of the area. The satisfaction of this interest rested to a large extent upon the possibility of recruiting a labor force from England and the continent.

The forces that were pushing immigrants to the colonies stemmed from the prevailing economic and political conditions in Europe. In England, the

---

[3] Percy W. Bidwell and John I. Falconer, *History of Agriculture in the Northern United States, 1620–1860* (Washington, D.C.: Carnegie Institution of Washington, 1925), p. 34.

[4] The exact content of freedom dues and the degree of legal obligation of the master to provide such dues varied from colony to colony and over time. Typically, the ex-indentured servant received a year's supply of clothing and frequently tools and a supply of provisions. Freedom dues on occasion included a grant of land, although this was not the usual practice. There are recorded instances of the master meeting his legal obligation by granting money payments, although, again, this was unusual.

enclosures of the common lands meant that many agricultural workers and independent farmers were being torn from the soil that represented their source of livelihood. Features of the English poor laws and the general confusion that accompanied a fundamental economic change created a body of persons who could be expected, in one way or another, to emigrate to a strange and untamed continent. Members of many religious sects such as the Pilgrims, Quakers, Puritans, and Huguenots migrated in an attempt to escape religious oppression.

Different specific circumstances surrounded the transfer to the colonies of persons who were to become part of the unfree white labor supply. There were persons who bound themselves for two to seven years of labor —usually four years—in return for passage to the new continent. Redemptioners agreed to pay for their passage by selling their labor upon arrival in the colonies. If they failed to consummate an agreement, the shipmaster could then undertake to sell them. A second group consisted of those who entered into contracts before departure from Europe. On occasion the cost of transportation was underwritten by the future employer in the New World, and at times this was done by merchants who specialized in the traffic of indentured servants.

British convicts constituted another source of bound labor. Successive English statutes starting with an order by James I in 1615 authorized the transportation to the colonies of persons convicted of a wide variety of crimes. Kidnapped persons were also a source of labor supply for the colonies, although the significance of this source is a matter of dispute.[5] There is no doubt, however, that there were many active spirits who by the liberal use of liquor, force, or other devices managed to induce or force victims aboard ship to be transported to America and then sold into servitude. The word "kidnapper" was apparently coined in the seventeenth century as a derogatory term used in reference to recruiting agents.

The Master-Servant Relationship

Possibly a quarter of a million persons labored under the indentured servant status in the pre-Revolutionary War period. Servants were used primarily as agricultural field hands although some mechanics and professionals signed articles of indenture. It has been asserted that two-thirds of the schoolmasters employed in Maryland just prior to the Revolution were indentured servants or convicts.[6]

While the bulk of the colonial labor force in the seventeenth century and through the middle eighteenth century consisted of indentured servants, the

---

[5] Richard B. Morris, *Government and Labor in Early America* (New York: Columbia University Press, 1946), p. 337.

[6] Marcus W. Jernegan, *Laboring and Dependent Classes in Colonial America, 1607– 1783* (Chicago: The University of Chicago Press, 1931), p. 53.

incidence of their use varied widely among the colonies. New England relied mainly on free labor, whereas the middle and southern colonies depended heavily on the use of unfree white labor. Eventually the institution
of indentured servitude was to die out, first in the South, where it was to
be replaced by Negro slave labor, and finally in the middle colonies. Indentured servants were still used in fairly large numbers in Pennsylvania as
late as 1831.

Thus much of the colonial labor force consisted of persons who were not
free but who had hopes of becoming free. Upon completion of their periods
of servitude, some of the ex-servants became mechanics and artisans in the
towns; more eventually became small landholders.

Slave Labor

Although a cargo of twenty Negroes was sold to a group of Jamestown
settlers as early as 1619, the institution of slave labor in the colonies developed slowly for a time. At the middle of the seventeenth century there
were only 300 Negroes out of a total Virginia population of 15,000. By
1670, the colony's slave population had increased to about 2,000.[7] In the
Carolina area, the rapid importation of slaves did not begin until the start
of the eighteenth century; and the number of slaves in the northern colonies
by this date was negligible.

From the standpoints of supply and demand, however, factors were
operative that accelerated the slave traffic and the use of slave labor. The
breakup of the monopoly of the Royal African Company in 1698 meant
that the slave trade was to feel the invigorating effect of free competition.
In the area of international relationships, the coveted "assiento"—the right
to supply the Spanish slave markets—was awarded to the English in the
Treaty of Utrecht in 1713. The slave trade was ready to become a full-
blown capitalistic venture. Capital began to flow into the trade, specially
outfitted ships were constructed, and the inevitable system of middlemen
appeared. Local African chieftains participated in the regularization of the
chain of supply, and it was not unusual for the chieftains to sell their own
tribesmen into captivity. The slave trade was at all times highly speculative,
since mutinies, epidemics, and suicides frequently decimated the human
cargoes. The profits of a successful trip were enormous, however, and were
quite tempting for the investor with uncommitted capital.

On the demand side, the plantation system of southern agriculture
required a larger labor supply than could be provided by the natural population increase. Indentured white servants were first used, but these were
eventually replaced by Negro slaves. The mere fact of a constant supply of

---

[7] Ulrich B. Phillips, *American Negro Slavery* (New York: Appleton-Century &
Appleton-Century-Crofts, 1918), p. 75.

slaves in the eighteenth century as compared to the sporadic supply of the seventeenth was a stimulus to slave use, but there were more important economic considerations underlying the replacement of indentured by slave laborers. At the start of the eighteenth century, the term of an indentured servant could be obtained for approximately one-half to two-thirds of the price of an adult slave. Slave labor, however, was purchased for life, while the servant ordinarily regained freedom after about four years. Furthermore, the offspring of a slave mother became the property of the plantation owner. Although more difficult to train as a field hand, the slave, once trained, was probably as efficient as a white servant. Women slaves could be used as field hands, while women servants were not ordinarily so used. No freedom dues would have to be paid to the Negro slave, and it was somewhat more difficult for the slave to escape. All in all, as a plantation laborer, the slave had marked economic advantages over the white servant.[8]

Within the plantation labor force there was some specialization of labor, the basic division being that of house and field servants. Among the field slaves the top position was that of the "driver," who exercised immediate charge of the hands and had a combination of powers including some power to discipline. Larger plantations would have slaves specializing in certain skilled tasks, such as carpenters, blacksmiths, and coopers. At the occupational bottom were the field hands. Jobs such as nursing, cooking, water carrying, and gardening were found for the young and the aged.

In the towns, slaves were employed in a variety of occupations. Most were used as domestic servants, however; and it is the opinion of one student that the use of slaves in the town trades was a by-product of the presence of domestics. Almost all slave mechanics were husbands or sons of cooks and other household servants.[9] Whereas a plantation could always use another hand, this was not the case in a household. The town dweller was frequently obliged to sell or hire out those slaves who did not fit into his domestic establishment.

Although use of slave labor within New England was comparatively moderate, slaves were brought into the region throughout the colonial period.[10] By the 1770's slaves constituted about 2.5 per cent of the total New England population of approximately 660,000 persons. In the diversified New England economy, Negro slaves were used on the farms and as skilled and unskilled workers in industries such as shipbuilding, lumbering, and distilling. If the New England farmer owned any slaves at all he was unlikely to have more than one or two. In a few areas such as Rhode Island

---

[8] For an excellent analysis of the relative merits of slave and servant labor see Lewis C. Gray, *History of Agriculture in the Southern United States to 1860* (Gloucester, Mass.: Peter Smith, 1941), I, 361–371.

[9] Phillips, *op. cit.*, p. 404.

[10] Lorenzo J. Greene, *The Negro in Colonial New England, 1620–1776* (New York: Columbia University Press, 1942), p. 72.

or eastern Connecticut where larger estates existed, there were somewhat larger slaveholdings. In colonial New York, slaves constituted about 10 per cent of the population and according to one student of the subject performed much of the menial and unskilled work in that colony.[11]

In the North as well as the South, then, the slaves working at a wide variety of jobs constituted an important segment of the labor force. Of the 500,000 Negroes in the colonies at the time of the Revolution, about 75,000 were in the northern states. As in the case of the indentured servant, there were forces at work encouraging a diminution in the use of slave labor. The increasing number of free workers, the hostility of skilled white workers toward slave labor competition, and the necessity of maintaining the slave during periods of enforced idleness resulted in a considerable decline in the use of slaves in the North. In the South, the economics of the plantation system and especially the invention of the cotton gin offset the effects of these forces and perpetuated a controversial social and legal relationship.

FREE LABOR IN COLONIAL AMERICA

The colonial labor force was engaged largely in agrarian pursuits. In the year 1770, only five cities—Philadelphia, New York, Newport, Boston, and Charleston—had populations of more than 8,000 persons. Together, these cities had only 84,000 people or slightly less than 4 per cent of the total population. There were few large concentrations of labor, and most of these were on plantations engaged in industrial as well as agricultural activity. As already indicated, the plantation labor force consisted mainly of unfree labor. Outside of the plantations, industries such as furnace and forge, shipbuilding, textiles, and lumber were modest in size. Apart from employment in industries such as these, free workers were engaged as artisans in the towns or as hired hands in agriculture.

The free colonial labor force, the size of which cannot be determined with any accuracy, consisted of immigrants, former indentured servants, free persons born in the colonies, and freed Negroes.

Originally all skilled workers had to be drawn directly from Europe.[12] Despite constant attempts to induce skilled workers to migrate to America, the continuing scarcity of such workers appears to have been a contributing

---

[11] Samuel McKee, Jr., *Labor in Colonial New York, 1664–1776* (New York: Columbia University Press, 1935), pp. 114, 115.

[12] Clark has distinguished five definite migrations of skilled workers to New England in the colonial period. The skills transported included shipbuilding, iron work, textile work, the arts, and flaxwork. Artisans from Germany, Holland, Portugal, and Ireland contributed to the success of early American manufacturing enterprise. See Vincent S. Clark, *History of Manufactures in the United States* (New York: McGraw-Hill Book Company, 1929), I, 152–155.

cause to the slowness of industrial progress during the colonial period. Once in the colonies, many skilled workers left their occupations and turned to agriculture. This dearth of workers, while detrimental to industrial growth, did result in higher wages and a higher standard of living than could be earned for equivalent employment in Europe.

Various devices were used to counteract the shortage of skilled labor. In the early colonial period laws were enacted requiring workers to remain at their trades, Negro slaves were trained for skilled work, skilled workers were exempted from taxation in several of the colonies, and a number of attempts were made by employers to lure workers from other colonial areas.[13]

In a number of ways, Negro slaves were able to acquire freedom, and by 1790 there were almost 35,000 freed slaves in the South alone.[14] Free Negroes were outcasts in southern society, however, and were subject to many social and economic disabilities. Most earned their living at unskilled labor or from the soil. Free Negro mechanics had an additional disadvantage in that skilled whites were sensitive to Negro competition and overtly hostile. Despite these disabilities, Negroes did somehow manage to work at a variety of skilled trades. In the North, there was a similar situation. Handicraftsmen vigorously opposed the employment of both slaves and free Negroes in the skilled trades.

IMMIGRATION

The United States in 1900 was vastly different from the United States in 1800. A small nation of seaboard states with a population of 5 million engaged mainly in agricultural activity had grown to a nation of over 75 million persons; and an industrial system, still not fully matured by 1900, was threatening to assume giant proportions. Industrialization and territorial expansion and the consequent economic opportunity were both cause and effect of labor force growth. Available labor supply is a necessary attribute of an expanding economy, but the existence of economic opportunity or even the belief in its existence is somewhat like a magnet attracting people who want something better than what they have.

Indentured servitude and slavery, the institutional arrangements that prevailed during the eighteenth century, did not, of course, disappear auto-

---

[13] Morris, *op. cit.*, pp. 30–33.

[14] Manumission of slaves was not uncommon, and frequently the will of a master provided that his slaves be freed. A few Negroes in the fortunate position of being able to earn money incomes were able to buy their freedom. On occasion, Negroes were granted freedom because of exceptionally meritorious service or heroic deeds.

matically with the advent of a new century; but the former was already on its way out,[15] and importation of slaves was prohibited after 1808. Unfree labor, the backbone of the work force before the Revolutionary War, diminished in importance and finally disappeared with the emancipation of the slaves.

With the beginning of the factory system, labor needs could be met in part by long working hours. In an economy where agriculture prevailed, it was not unusual that factory operators should insist upon sunup to sundown as a normal working day. Factory labor was at first recruited from the women and children in the towns and villages surrounding the factory areas. The first persons employed in the Slater mills, for example, were seven boys and two girls between the ages of seven and twelve.[16] In the Massachusetts mills, the general policy was to employ female operatives who were boarded at company houses and subjected to considerable company control insofar as conduct was concerned. Such employments, significant as they might have been, were a "drop in the bucket" in terms of labor requirements. The explanation of labor force growth in the nineteenth century is closely related to the history of the population growth that occurred. An important element in the population growth was the tide of immigrants who came to the United States in increasing numbers until government policy discouraged large-scale immigration after the first world war.

Mass migration of persons from one nation to another is a result of a complex combination of many factors. Compelling reasons must be present to induce persons to break forever the sentimental and other ties to their native lands. Not only must there be a nation willing and able to receive immigrants, but there must be a hope, realistic or otherwise, that life in the new location will be an improvement over life in the homeland. In addition, transportation facilities must exist to accommodate the migrants. In the nineteenth and early twentieth centuries, these necessary conditions were met; and the result was a migration of staggering proportions from Europe to the United States.

In a brief summary it is impossible to do justice to a description of the many causes of this intercontinental migration of persons. The differential

---

[15] The redemptioner trade continued in some volume during a few periods in the 1800's primarily because those who were engaged in the traffic found that servants were taken off their hands quickly in periods of acute labor shortages. Thus, many Irish migrated as redemptioners in 1818 in response to demand for common labor in the agricultural, construction, and shipping industries. Economic distress in 1819, however, resulted in sharp losses for those engaged in the redemptioner traffic. These economic losses were important contributing factors in the decline of the system. See Marcus L. Hansen, *The Atlantic Migration, 1607–1860* (Cambridge, Mass.: Harvard University Press, 1940), p. 105.

[16] Clark, *op. cit.,* I, 397.

between economic opportunities in Europe as Europeans knew them and opportunities in the United States as they imagined them was sufficient to attract millions to a new life. The economic causes, however, were often bolstered by political and religious persecutions suffered by particular groups.

On the United States side of the Atlantic Ocean, the demand for labor was a major stimulant to immigration. Turnpikes, canals, and railroads were built largely with immigrant labor. In prosperous periods, word of job availability spread swiftly to the European continent. Ship captains spread the word at European ports, contractors sent recruiting agents abroad, and those immigrants who fared well in the New World wrote to their Old World relatives and friends and frequently sent remittances to pay for their passages to the United States. A number of states enacted legislation to encourage immigration.

How many persons migrated to the United States? Table 1 shows immigrant aliens admitted between 1820 and 1967. In the decade starting in 1820 when government statistics on immigration were first collected, an annual average of 15,000 persons arrived. Thereafter the average rose swiftly, declining only during the Civil War years and certain depression periods. The movement reached its height in the period 1903–1914 when approximately 1 million persons entered the country each year. All in all, more than 40 million aliens entered the nation after the end of the Revolutionary War.

Where did the immigrants come from? Students of immigration distinguish between the "old" and the "new" migrations to this country. Until well toward the close of the nineteenth century, almost all immigrants had come from northwest Europe and particularly from Ireland, England, and Germany. After 1880 the proportion coming from southern and eastern Europe increased steadily. The new immigration was different from the old in a number of significant respects. A larger proportion was made up of unmarried men. Few moved into agricultural labor. Instead, the migrants congregated mainly in the larger cities in the East. Nationalities tended to group together in these cities and thus to assimilate less rapidly into American life. Many were birds of passage—migrants who stayed in the United States only long enough to accumulate a certain amount of wealth before returning to their native lands. Following the discovery of gold in California, the Chinese began to arrive, and by 1890 there were slightly more than 100,000 Chinese in the country, most of them living on the West Coast. After 1890, the Japanese began arriving in large numbers. Following World War I, the numbers of persons entering from Canada and Mexico increased. Immigrants from these countries constituted only 4 per cent of all immigrants in the period 1901–1910 but constituted 30 per cent in

TABLE 1

UNITED STATES IMMIGRATION, 1821–1967

PERIOD OR YEAR	NUMBER

Decades, 1821–1900:

1821–1830	143,439
1831–1840	599,125
1841–1850	1,713,251
1851–1860	2,598,214
1861–1870	2,314,824
1871–1880	2,812,191
1881–1890	5,246,613
1891–1900	3,687,564

Five-Year Periods, 1900–1954:

1900–1904	3,255,149
1905–1909	4,947,239
1910–1914	5,174,701
1915–1919	1,172,679
1920–1924	2,774,600
1925–1929	1,520,910
1930–1934	426,953
1935–1939	272,422
1940–1944	203,589
1945–1949	653,019
1950–1954	1,019,035

Annually, 1955–1967:

1955	237,790
1956	321,625
1957	326,867
1958	253,265
1959	260,686
1960	265,398
1961	271,344
1962	283,763
1963	306,260
1964	292,248
1965	296,697
1966	323,040
1967	365,972

Source: Annual Reports of the Immigration and Naturalization Service of the United States Department of Justice.

1931–1940. Since 1940, the number of persons migrating to the United States from elsewhere in the Americas has increased significantly. In 1966 and 1967 there was a substantial increase in the number of immigrants entering from Asia as a result of changes in government immigration policy enacted in 1965.

Government Policy and Immigration

Government policy concerning the admission of aliens is based upon many factors other than labor supply considerations. At the same time, the nature of this policy cannot fail to have a serious influence upon the size and character of the labor force. Since most migrants are of labor force age, a liberal immigration policy will ordinarily result in an unusually rapid labor force growth. A tight policy, on the other hand, means that the economy must depend upon the natural population increase for its manpower potential.

The question of appropriate government immigration policy has rarely been free of controversy in the United States. At all times there have been proponents of both restrictive and liberal policies. Despite this controversy there was little regulation of alien entry until 1882. In the period 1783–1830, with minor exceptions, there was no control by any government agency. Between 1830 and 1882 there was some limitation of immigrant entry by state legislation, particularly by those states situated on the eastern seaboard. At the same time, however, a number of the interior states were encouraging migrants. Since 1882, immigration has been limited in important ways by national law.

The era of federal regulation can be separated into two basic periods, with the end of World War I marking the dividing point. Before this time, control of immigration was effectuated by setting up standards of admission and excluding specific classes of aliens. The year 1882, for example, saw the passage of the first general immigration regulation law. Paupers, criminals, and those afflicted with specified disease conditions were excluded. In the same year a Chinese exclusion act was passed.

The intellectual climate after World War I was favorable for the growth of a fundamentally different type of restriction. A skepticism of all things foreign resulted in the growth of isolationist attitudes. The fear of massive immigration was accentuated by the depression of 1921. The American Legion, The American Federation of Labor, and the National Grange, among other groups, contributed to the successful campaign for restrictive legislation.

Immigration legislation enacted in 1921 reflected the philosophy that there should be a quantitative restriction on the number of annual immigrants and that preference should be shown for immigrants from particular nations. This was accomplished by specifying quotas for different countries.

The computation of the quota was technically complex but the net effect was to favor the northern and western European countries or the sources of the old migration against the southern and eastern areas.[17]

The Immigration and Nationality Act of 1952 (the McCarran-Walter Act) was the first attempt to bring within one statute all laws relating to immigration and nationalization. The quota system was retained but the method of calculating the quota was simplified. The total of immigrant aliens permitted to enter annually (154,657) represented an increase of only several hundred over the earlier maximum. Groups favoring a more liberal immigration policy were disappointed by the 1952 law, and the issue remained a controversial one. The major arguments raised against the law were that the number allowed to enter annually was too small, that it continued an outdated quota system, and that the provisions relating to persons in the Asian-Pacific triangle were especially discriminatory.

Dissatisfaction with the McCarran-Walter Law led finally to new legislation in 1965 that incorporated major reforms in national immigration policy. Under the law, the quota system, designed to preserve the national ethnic composition of an earlier period, was phased out of existence by 1968. Since then, visas have been issued on a basis of priorities with first preferences going to members of separated families, workers possessing skills needed in the United States, and political refugees. Within each preference category, visas are issued on a first come-first serve basis. There is a basic limitation of 20 thousand persons in a single year from any nation outside the western hemisphere and, for the first time, an over-all annual ceiling of 120 thousand on the number of immigrants who may enter from western hemisphere nations.

Under the new law, immigration has increased substantially rising from an annual average of 290 thousand for the 1961–65 period to well over 300 thousand in 1966 and 1967.

As noted above, one of the preference categories is workers with skills needed in the American economy. Prior to 1965, aliens otherwise qualified to enter the United States permanently were generally admitted regardless of occupational skill level. Under the new law, aliens seeking to enter the country for employment purposes may not be admitted until a certification is issued by the U.S. Department of Labor. The purpose of certification is to carry out the legal mandate to give priority to workers with needed skills and to safeguard American workers by giving them the first chance at

---

[17] From 1924 to 1929 the annual quota of each nationality was fixed at 2 per cent of the number of foreign-born residents of such nationality in the continental United States as determined by the census of 1890. An eligible nationality was given a minimum quota of 100. After July 1, 1929, the annual quota for an eligible nationality was roughly one-sixth of 1 per cent of that nationality's representation in the United States population according to the census of 1920. No quota limits were set on immigrants from Canada and from Central and South American countries.

available jobs. An alien with a low-level skill or in an occupation for which there is an abundance of American workers must find an American employer willing to employ him. Even if he is able to do this he will not be certified for entry if workers in the local area are available for a job with the requirements and specifications of the offer made to the alien.

Immigrants and the Supply of Labor

Immigrant contribution to domestic labor supply was especially large in the last quarter of the nineteenth century and the first decade of the twentieth when net migration accounted for roughly one-third of total labor force growth. By 1910 immigrant workers made up more than 20 per cent of the white labor force and together with their children constituted over 45 per cent of the total. From 1910 to 1950, the proportion of foreign-born among the white male workers declined to the extent that they constituted less than 10 per cent of the total in the later year. Since the enactment of restrictive legislation in the 1920's, immigration has ceased to be a major source of labor force growth but it has by no means dwindled into insignificance. In 1967, over 150,000 new immigrants listed an occupation and, presumably, are engaged in work activity in the United States. This number would account for about 10 per cent of the labor force growth in that year. Over 25 thousand were admitted on the basis of occupational preferences or because they possessed skills determined to be in short supply in the United States economy.

POPULATION FACTORS

As long as entry into the United States was relatively unrestricted, the population was swelled by the combined influences of international population movements and the natural rate of increase. Since immigration has been limited by national policy, the natural rate of growth has come to be the single predominating influence. A word of caution is necessary at this point. Whether or not an expanding population is beneficial depends upon many circumstances.[18] In the nineteenth century population growth was obviously beneficial. A large nation had to be sufficiently peopled before

---

[18] In the early years of the nineteenth century, the English economist, Thomas Malthus, developed the theory which has become known as the Malthusian Law of Population. Briefly stated, the law holds that population tends to increase each generation according to a geometrical progression, *i.e.,* 2–4–8–16–32, etc., while at best food supply can only increase in arithmetical progression, *i.e.,* 1–2–3–4–5–6–7, etc. Obviously, then, there must be checks such as vice, war, famine, and pestilence that keep population within the limits imposed by the food supply. The only alternative to these checks according to Malthus is moral restraint, by which he means delayed marriage. Today population students recognize that food supply is only one variable among many affecting population growth and that the Malthusian Law has been tempered by changes in technology that have increased agricultural productivity much beyond the limits of Malthus' pessimistic ratio.

its agricultural and industrial potential could be realized. Today population growth is, in a sense, a challenge. More than a million new jobs have to be created annually to absorb those who reach working age. The economy must be dynamic and expansive to absorb these new workers. It is not good enough to equal last year's performance. From a military manpower stand-point—a different type of consideration—a growing population is quite important. The difficulties faced by many local draft boards during the Korean campaign resulted directly from the low birth rate of the depression years of the 1930 decade.

Table 2 shows population growth in the United States by decade. The rate of growth, never less than 25 per cent per decade until 1890, was sufficient to insure an adequate labor supply for a nation whose economic development was no less phenomenal than its population increase. Even after allowance is made for the effect of immigration, the rapid growth of population must remain a source of amazement.

An impressive feature of the record is the decline in the rate of growth between 1920 and 1940.[19] The sensitivity of the birth rate to economic factors is dramatically illustrated by the sharp drop in population growth during the 1930's. Many persons, faced with unemployment and bleak prospects for the future, delayed their marriages. Others, already married, delayed having families for considerable periods of time.

An offset to the decline in population growth during the 1930's was the resurgence of the rate of growth in the 1940's. Population forecasts made by statisticians and population specialists for 1950 erred on the low side— another example of the experts gone wrong.[20] The return of prosperity and the unusual milieu of the World War II era resulted in a rash of marriages and a rapid increase in the number of births. The population gain recorded between 1940 and 1950 was the highest in the nation's history, but it was 9 million less than the 1950–1960 increase. Signs of a slowdown in the population boom appeared in the early 1960's. The birth rate has declined consistently since 1962 and the natural increase in 1967 was the smallest for any year since the end of World War II.

Population and Labor Force Size

Labor force growth may reflect the volume of immigration, the natural rate of population increase and/or the extent to which persons of working age

---

[19] When measured in absolute terms, the growth by decade has been much larger in the twentieth century than in the nineteenth, of course. Thus, the *rate* of increase in 1840–1850 was 35.9 per cent, whereas the number was 6,122,423. In the decade 1940–1950, the *rate* was only 14.5 per cent, but the number was 19,028,086.

[20] See, for example, Warren S. Thompson and P. K. Whelpton, *Estimates of Future Population in the United States, 1940–2000* (Washington, D.C.: National Resources Planning Board, 1943), p. 48. For one analysis of why the population forecasts went wrong see Joseph S. Davis, *The Population Upsurge in the United States* (Stanford, Calif.: Food Research Institute, 1949), p. 39.

TABLE 2

POPULATION OF CONTINENTAL UNITED STATES, 1790–1969

| | POPULATION | | |
| | | Increase over Preceding Census | |
YEAR	Number	Number	Per Cent
1790	3,929,214		
1800	5,308,483	1,379,269	35.1
1810	7,239,881	1,931,398	36.4
1820	9,638,453	2,398,572	33.1
1830	12,866,020	3,227,567	33.5
1840	17,069,453	4,203,433	32.7
1850	23,191,876	6,122,423	35.9
1860	31,443,321	8,251,445	35.6
1870	39,818,449	8,375,128	26.6
1880	50,155,783	10,337,334	26.0
1890	62,947,714	12,791,931	25.5
1900	75,994,575	13,046,861	20.7
1910	91,972,266	15,977,691	21.0
1920	105,710,620	13,738,354	14.9
1930	122,775,046	17,064,426	16.1
1940	131,669,275	8,894,229	7.2
1950	150,697,361	19,028,086	14.5
1960	179,323,175	27,997,377	18.5
1969	202,250,000	22,926,825	12.7

Source: U.S. Bureau of the Census. The 1960 figure includes the populations of Alaska and Hawaii. The 1969 figure is an estimate of the Statistical Bureau of the Metropolitan Life Insurance Company.

actively participate in the labor market. In his recent study of the interrelationships among population, the labor force, and economic conditions, Easterlin concludes that the growth of both population and the labor force has been characterized by roughly synchronous swings since at least 1870 and that these swings have been related to the condition of the economy.[21] In different periods of American history, however, different variables have responded to changes in the economic climate to dominate as major causal forces. Until 1920, for example, large swings in population and labor force size arose primarily from corresponding movements in immigration. Immigration waves, in turn, were responses to changes in economic conditions within the United States. When labor market conditions were tight, the volume of immigration rose. When they were loose, immigration declined.

With the slacking of immigration, the size of the domestic labor force .has come to be determined primarily by the natural increase in population and the labor force participation rate. The argument that population swings are tied to changes in economic conditions is based upon the experiences

---

21 Richard A. Easterlin, *Population, Labor Force and Long Swings in Economic Growth* (New York: National Bureau of Economic Research, 1968).

of certain periods such as the 1930's when the tie appeared obvious and also upon evidence that the rate of household formation is influenced by labor market opportunities for younger persons. This last point is conjectural and some demographers challenge a purely economic explanation of swings in the rate of population growth.[22] Whatever the reasons, sharp period to period variations in birth rates have occurred in the present century with the result that population growth and consequently labor force growth has been uneven.

The decline in the natural rate of population increase in the 1930's, for example, was reflected in the relatively small increase in labor force size during the 1950's. The net increase in the labor force in the fifties was 8.3 million persons as compared with over 13 million in the 1960's when persons born in the post-1940 population upsurge began to enter the labor market. The projected increase in the labor force for the 1965–1975 period is approximately 15 million.[23]

Such breaks in the rate of labor force growth may be perpetuated in the future by "echo" population effects. The smaller number of potential parents born in the 1930's, thus, may be echoed in a future undersized generation. The reverse is true for the larger number of potential parents born during the baby boom. (The echo effects may be dampened or accentuated by changes in labor force participation rates. Factors affecting these rates will be discussed in the following chapter.)

In addition to its impact upon labor force growth rates, variations in the birth rate affect the age structure of the work force. Fluctuations in the birth rate since 1930 have resulted in a large increase in the relative number of young workers. In the 1955–1965 period, persons in the labor force aged 16 to 24 increased by 34 per cent while the number over 25 years of age rose by 9 per cent. Department of Labor projections for 1965–1975 indicate a further 34 per cent rise in the younger group and a 15 per cent growth in the older one.[24]

INTERNAL POPULATION MOVEMENTS

Migration within a nation is a process by which people adjust to changes in economic opportunities. Sometimes the movement is relatively sudden and dramatic as was the case in the 1930's when the so-called "Okies" and

---

[22] Richard F. Tomasson, "Why has American Fertility been so High," Bernard Barber (ed.) *Kinship and Family Organization* (New York: John Wiley and Sons, Inc., 1966), pp. 327–338.

[23] *Manpower Report of the President,* January, 1969, p. 63.

[24] *Ibid.*

"Arkies" moved in large numbers to the West Coast area. At other times the movement is slow and gradual, since many persons tend to resist movement from localities in which they have close personal and property ties.

A continuing significant population shift is the rural to urban movement. The 1790 population census showed only 5 per cent of the people residing in urban areas. This percentage increased gradually, but it was not until 1920 that the census showed more urban than rural dwellers. Urbanization has continued to the extent that today approximately 70 per cent of the population reside in places classed as urban.[25]

Related to this movement is the change in the farm versus the non-farm population. In the late 1960's, there were fewer than 13 million persons residing on farms as compared to the 32 million in 1910. Thus, both absolutely and relatively, the farm population has declined. Because of the increasing mechanization on the farms, which has raised the farmer's productivity, and because of the manpower pull of the urban situated industries, the agricultural sector of the economy has been a labor exporting area for some forty years. Not all persons who have left farming have moved to urban areas. Many former farmers continue to reside in rural places. In 1920, farmers comprised 60 per cent of the rural population. Today, non-farm rural residents outnumber farmers by about four to one. (Interestingly, the twentieth century outmigration from the farms may be slowing down and perhaps even drawing to a close. Preliminary estimates by the United States Department of Agriculture show no change in the adult farm population between January, 1968, and January, 1969.)

In recent decades large interstate population movements have occurred which overlap, to some extent, the rural–urban movements described above. In 1960, 14 million persons lived in a state other than their state of residence in 1955; and in the single year 1962, over 5.5 million persons, or approximately 3 per cent of the population, moved from one state to another. On the whole there has been a close relationship between these population shifts and the changing geographical incidence of job opportunities with the regions which enjoy large increases in non-farm payroll employment acquiring population at the expense of the others.

The migration patterns between 1950 and 1960 did not change greatly from those of the prior decade. The general direction of the movement was away from the agricultural states of the Middle West, the South, and

---

[25] Bureau of the Census definitions of "urban" and "rural" have changed from time to time. Basically, urban areas are those with 2,500 or more inhabitants. The definition of "urban" was expanded somewhat in the 1950 and 1960 censuses. Under the new definition, 69.9 per cent of the population was classed as urban, whereas under the 1940 definition, 63 per cent of the 1960 population would have been classed as urban. For an explanation of the differences between the old and new definitions see U.S. Bureau of the Census, *Statistical Abstract of the United States* (1963), pp. 1, 2.

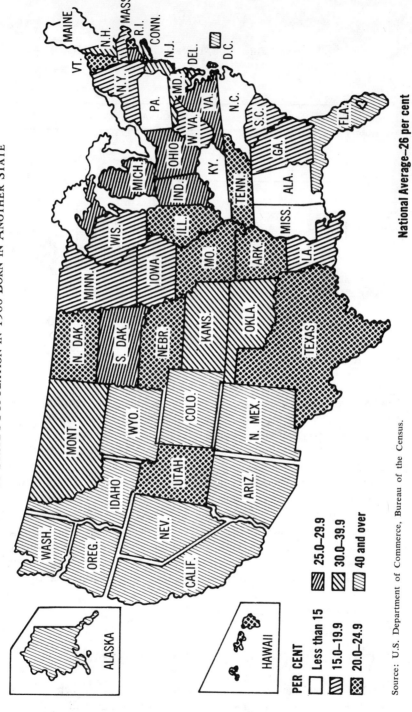

FIGURE 1

PER CENT OF STATE'S POPULATION IN 1960 BORN IN ANOTHER STATE

National Average—26 per cent

PER CENT

Less than 15	25.0–29.9
15.0–19.9	30.0–39.9
20.0–24.9	40 and over

Source: U.S. Department of Commerce, Bureau of the Census.

FIGURE 2

<small>AVERAGE ANNUAL NET OUT-MIGRATION
FROM THE FARM POPULATION</small>

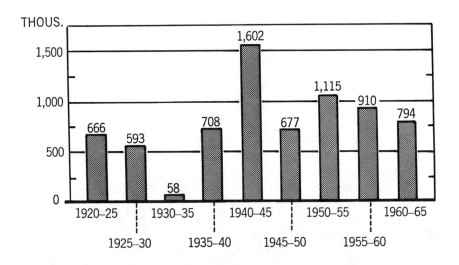

Source: U.S. Department of Agriculture.

the states containing the Appalachian coal region and toward the metropolitan centers of the West. With the exception of Florida, a net out-
migration occurred in all the southern states and ranged from 6.2 per cent
of the 1950 population in Georgia to 22.7 per cent in Arkansas. Outside of
the South heavy population losses from migration were suffered in Pennsylvania, Iowa, and Nebraska. States registering noteworthy gains from
in-migration were Florida, California, Arizona, Maryland, and New Jersey.
With three exceptions (Arkansas, West Virginia, and Mississippi) all states
gained in population between 1950 and 1960, but only twenty-three states
owed part of their increase to an excess of in-migration over out-migration.

In addition to the interstate population shifts, there was considerable
movement within states during the 1950–1960 decade. Four out of every
five counties in the country lost residents through out-migration. Most of
the losers were rural counties, whereas those gaining through migration
were largely urban or suburban.

MOBILITY OF POPULATION SUBGROUPS

Among the population subgroups in the United States, there are a number
that have been unusually mobile in the past several decades. These include

the Negroes, the Puerto Ricans, and a mixed group of migratory farm workers. Each will be considered briefly.

The Negroes. The Negro population in 1960 was 18.8 million, an increase of 3.8 million over the 1950 total. In 1960, 25 per cent of the Negro population lived in the rural South, 35 per cent lived in the urban South, and 40 per cent lived outside the South. By way of contrast, 90 per cent of all Negroes lived in the South in 1900; and, of these, 75 per cent lived in the rural South. The amount of Negro migration that has occurred is suggested by the fact that 2.6 million Negroes born in the South were living in other regions in 1950. Seven of the sixteen southern states actually had smaller Negro populations in 1950 than in 1940, and three had smaller Negro populations in 1960 than in 1950. These losses occurred in the face of a national increase in Negro population of 6 million between 1940 and 1960. The migration of Negroes from the South has been described as the most extensive movement by a single group in American history.[26] As a result the percentage of the total Negro population residing in urban places is now larger than the equivalent percentage of the total white population.

TABLE 3

PERCENT DISTRIBUTION OF THE NEGRO POPULATION
BY REGION

	1940	1950	1960	1966	1968
United States	100	100	100	100	100
South	77	68	60	55	53
North	22	28	34	37	40
Northeast	11	13	16	17	18
North Central	11	15	18	20	22
West	1	4	6	8	8

Source: U.S. Department of Commerce, Bureau of the Census.

The Negro population shift cannot be explained solely by economic factors, of course, but the movement, nonetheless, has been from areas of low economic opportunity to areas of greater opportunity. In the rural South the condition of the Negro farmer has remained poor. The increased mechanization of agriculture, furthermore, has lessened the need for un-skilled and semi-skilled agricultural workers.[27] These factors plus the

---

[26] Dorothy K. Newman, "The Negro's Journey to the City," *Monthly Labor Review,* May, 1965, p. 502.

[27] J. M. Maclachlan and J. S. Floyd have suggested that increased agricultural mechanization during World War II may have been induced by the migration of Negro workers to the war plants. Once established, the level of mechanization constituted a barrier to the return to agriculture by Negroes. *This Changing South* (Gainesville: University of Florida Press, 1956), p. 64.

belief that life is better in the city than on the farm have resulted in a voluntary large-scale movement of Negroes to urban southern and urban non-southern areas. In the 1950's, 1.5 million Negroes left the South, about 70 per cent of them going to the middle Atlantic and east north central states and another 24 per cent going to California. The urban orientation of these movements is suggested by the fact that six northern and western cities—New York, Chicago, Philadelphia, Detroit, Washington, and Los Angeles—contain one-fifth of the total Negro population in the United States. Within the South the rural to urban movement has produced heavy concentrations of Negro population in many southern cities. In Birmingham, Atlanta, and New Orleans, for example, about 40 per cent of the total population is Negro.

The Negro's belief in the economic advantages of the cities is justified to an extent. Apart from sociological considerations, the advantages in urban non-South locations consist of greater ease in finding work, higher wages, and a wider range of opportunities. In the North and West, impressive occupational gains have been scored by Negroes in clerical, service, and semi-skilled occupations. The ratio of nonwhite to white earnings, furthermore, is considerably higher in the North and West than in the South.[28]

All of this, of course, is not to gloss over the labor market disadvantages suffered by black persons in all areas of the nation. Measures such as unemployment rates, median income, and years of education highlight their depressed status. Even these measures of relative disadvantage, however, indicate that the Negro population has enjoyed a significant improvement in economic status within the past decade.[29]

The Puerto Ricans.   Although the movement of Puerto Ricans to the mainland has been going on for some time, large scale migration did not begin until after World War II. Between 1942 and 1951 some 250,000 persons left the island for the United States. In recent years, annual Puerto Rican migration to the mainland has ranged from a high of 52,000 in 1956 to a minus quantity of 5,400 in 1963 when a net out-migration occurred. A fairly close relationship exists between movements of Puerto Ricans to the mainland and the conditions of the stateside labor market. Between 1961 and 1964 when unemployment rates in the United States were high, the total flow from the island was light. With the strengthening of demand for labor after 1964, migration rose to a total of over 25 thousand in 1966 and again in 1967.

---

[28] *Ibid.,* p. 503.
[29] U.S. Department of Commerce, Bureau of the Census, Current Population Series, Series P-23, No. 26, *Recent Trends in Social and Economic Conditions of Negroes in the United States,* July, 1968.

By 1960, 893,000 residents of the continental United States were either born in Puerto Rico or were the children of persons born there. About 70 per cent of these residents live in or around New York City. The economic pull of New York City, in fact, is one of the major factors motivating the movement of Puerto Ricans to the mainland. Most regard that city as a goal, and those in New York who consider the possibility of leaving think primarily of a return to Puerto Rico.

Within the New York City labor market, opportunities open to Puerto Ricans are usually limited to unskilled or semi-skilled jobs. Many of the males find employment as bus boys, laundry workers, or porters, and as assemblers, pressers, and floor boys in the garment industry. The women typically find work as domestics or hospital employees or in the garment trades. The occupational distribution of second generation Puerto Ricans is quite different from that of their parents. The main feature of the inter-generation mobility is a movement out of the blue collar and into the white collar occupations. Fifty-seven per cent of the women and 31 per cent of the men in the second generation are white collar workers.

In recent years, unemployment among the Puerto Ricans has been high, with the rate for this group typically being double the rate for the total work force. Unemployment statistics understate the employment problems of the Puerto Ricans, since many return to the island when they are unable to find work.

The Migratory Farm Workers.   The movements of migrant farm workers differ from those of other migrants in a fundamental respect. Typically the non-agricultural migrant arrives at a destination, takes up residence, and ceases to be a migrant. For the migratory farm worker there are only temporary stopping places. His work life is a movement from one crop planting or harvest to another, a routine interrupted only by the frequent periods of unemployment that are inevitable in the casual agricultural labor market.[30]

Temporary and seasonal farm work in the United States has been performed by a succession of groups: European immigrants, Chinese, Japanese, Hindus, and displaced persons from the dust bowl area of Oklahoma,

---

[30] Large numbers of migrants follow fairly definite patterns of geographical movement. The major paths of migration are: (1) a movement along the Atlantic coast from Florida to New Jersey to work primarily on the potato, bean, and fruit harvests; (2) an eastern fruit migration to pick cherries, peaches, tomatoes, and apples in Michigan, Wisconsin, Indiana, and New York; (3) a sugar beet migration concentrated primarily in Michigan, Nebraska, Colorado, Idaho, and Montana; (4) a wheat migration starting in Texas and moving northward through Oklahoma, Kansas, Nebraska, North and South Dakota; (5) a cotton migration, part of which moves eastward to the Mississippi Delta, part westward to New Mexico, Arizona, and California; (6) Pacific coast movements from one crop to another in California and the Northwest.

Arkansas, Missouri, and Texas. Few persons are migratory workers by choice, and most members of the above listed groups have moved to more stable employments.

In recent years, the migratory labor force consisted, for the most part, of "Texas-Mexicans"; Negroes, many of them ex-sharecroppers; Mexican "wetbacks," who entered the country illegally; and foreign nationals who entered under special contract arrangements. The latter group was made up largely of Mexicans, although aliens from the Bahamas, Jamaica, and Canada were also involved.

Mexican contract workers were imported into the United States for the first time in 1942. What began as a wartime measure to offset farm labor shortages became a more enduring arrangement with the passage of Public Law 78 in 1951. Under the mechanics of the alien labor arrangement, growers' associations and individual employers filed requests at their state employment services. Certificates were issued to employers who claimed that they could not fill their manpower needs from domestic sources. The certificate was then approved by the United States Department of Labor and placed with a United States representative at the foreign recruiting center, which was usually in Mexico.

Public Law 78 was under constant attack by church and labor groups, among others, since the ability of farm employers to supplement domestic labor supplies with alien workers was instrumental in perpetuating what were, perhaps, the worst working conditions in the national labor market. In December 1964, Congress allowed Public Law 78 to expire.

Alien farm labor can still be admitted under provisions of the Immigration and Nationality Act but only in accordance with regulations issued by the Secretary of Labor. These regulations attempt to insure that foreigners will not be admitted when unemployed Americans are available for farm jobs or under circumstances that would depress domestic wage levels.

With the expiration of Public Law 78, seasonal farm labor will have to be obtained primarily from domestic sources. In this respect, there is some evidence that suggests a breakdown of long standing migratory patterns. A study of migratory labor in California, for example, revealed that the gap left by the *braceros* has been filled primarily by short term workers from local and intrastate sources rather than from the interstate migratory stream.[31]

SUMMARY

Where did the American work force come from? The answer depends upon the precise time period being analyzed. The colonial period was charac-

[31] Varden Fuller, "A New Era for Farm Labor?" *Industrial Relations,* May, 1967, pp. 285–302.

terized by an unusually large amount of unfree labor and general labor shortages. The colonial labor force arrangements, however satisfactory they were before the nineteenth century, were too rigid from an economic standpoint and too controversial from a moral standpoint to survive on a permanent basis. Since the start of the nineteenth century the major sources of labor supply have been immigration and natural population increase, with the former becoming relatively unimportant after World War I. The depression decade of the 1930's saw the rate of population growth decrease sharply. The resulting "undersized" generation of the thirties may well cause future labor force problems, but the precise nature of these cannot be known accurately beforehand. The problems for a fully employed economy, for instance, will be different from those of an underemployed economic society. The fear that a continuation of the low birth rate of the 1930's might doom us prematurely to a stagnating population has been dispelled by the upsurge in the birth rate that started during World War II and continued until the early 1960's. Significant population movements have been occurring that will have serious implications in terms of the labor force potentials of various geographic regions. The basic characteristics of these trends are (1) a continuing movement from rural to urban areas and (2) a westward movement of the geographical center of the population.

QUESTIONS

1. The composition of the labor force in colonial America was different from that of the present day in fundamental ways. In your opinion will changes of equal degree occur in the next 150 years? How do you think the labor force at that future time will differ from the present-day labor force?

2. Do you believe present United States immigration policy is too restrictive, too liberal, or just about right? Defend your position.

3. Should the present rate of population growth in the United States be a cause of optimism or pessimism? Explain.

4. Population movements within the United States have shifted the geographical center of the population westward. How do you account for the westward bias of these internal population movements? What are the labor force implications of such movements?

5. Migratory farm workers labor under what are some of the worst conditions in the American labor market. Can you suggest any appropriate public policies for improving these conditions?

CHAPTER 2

The Labor Force Today

IN THE PREVIOUS CHAPTER, A NUMBER OF BASIC POPULATION TRENDS WERE considered. In the absence of more refined labor force data, measures of gross population as indicators of labor force characteristics can be misleading. The fact that an economy has a large population does not necessarily mean that it has a large skilled labor force, nor does it mean that the distribution of workers among the various industries is ideal from the standpoint of economic efficiency. Insights into such questions require a more elaborate statistical breakdown of population data. In this chapter, the labor force of the United States will be examined from various standpoints to illustrate some of its major characteristics.

LABOR FORCE STATISTICS

Before the data are actually presented, however, some consideration of the nature of labor force statistics is necessary. This is an age of statistics. Intellectual curiosity together with a growing realization that intelligent economic policy must rest upon accurate factual knowledge have combined to exert a tremendous pressure for the accumulation of numerical data. Part of the contemporary urge among economists to quantify can also be regarded as a reaction against the overly abstract logic of the classical and neo-classical economists.

It must be kept in mind that the numbers in a statistical table are an end result. Prior to the publication of the information, there are the processes of framing questionnaires, polling respondents, centralizing and sifting the information, and performing the tabulations. At any link of this statistical chain, decisions must be made that can and do condition the end results. Of crucial importance, however, is the original objective or the decision as to what the statistics are supposed to show. In other words, if accuracy in the collection and tabulation of data is assumed, the end results reflect the original conceptual framework that structured the entire statistical endeavor.

Definition of "Labor Force"

The most commonly cited labor force statistics are those collected by the Bureau of the Census and presented by the Department of Labor.[1] These data involve a special definition of "labor force" and a number of corollary decisions to determine when a person is to be statistically included in or excluded from the labor force. Persons counted as being in the labor force include the employed and the unemployed. The employed category includes (*a*) those who are at work and (*b*) those with a job but not at work. Persons in category *a* are defined as those who do *any* work for pay or profit or who work without pay for fifteen hours or more per week on a family farm or business. Category *b* includes persons who have a job from which they are temporarily absent because of vacations, illness, industrial dispute, or bad weather. Unemployed persons actively seeking work are included by the Census Bureau count as among those in the labor force.[2] All civilians sixteen years of age or over who are not classified as employed or unemployed are considered as "not in the labor force."

Certain persons are excluded from the labor force count. Those under sixteen years of age are excluded, although it is known that there are some persons below that age who are working. This exclusion makes for a slight understatement of actual labor force size, as does the exclusion of inmates of institutions.

Persons who report that they have worked at all, during the week of the enumeration, are included in the labor force even though most of the week is spent in non-labor force activity. A housewife who works at a job one or two afternoons a week is counted as a member of the labor force. This approach results in some overstatement of actual current labor force size.

As noted above, if a person performs any work during the week of the

---

[1] Since July, 1959, these statistics have been collected by the Bureau of the Census and published by the Department of Labor. Prior to that time, the Census Bureau performed the job of publication as well as the collection of data.

[2] There are several exceptions to the rule of active work seeking. Even though they are not looking for work, persons are counted as unemployed if they are waiting to be called back to a job from which they have been laid off or if they are waiting to start a new job within the following thirty days.

Census Bureau survey, he is classified as "employed" although he may actually be unemployed for the greater part of the week. This is one of the controversial features of Census Bureau labor force statistics. In a later chapter the statistical treatment of the unemployed will be examined in greater detail.

Several references have been made above to the weekly period of activity. The labor force concept is centered upon the fact of current activity or activity during the week the count is being taken. What the statistics show, then, is more or less a snapshot picture of the labor force. Like any snapshot, this one is limited in the dimensions it is able to reveal. Thus, it is possible to get a picture of how many persons are at work, how many are unemployed, and how many are non-workers, although the special definitions applicable to these categories must be kept in mind. At the same time there are important hidden dimensions, such as the manpower potential that resides in the non-labor force section of the population. How would students and housewives react to a situation of easy job availability and very high wage rates? What sort of response would be achieved by an appeal for more workers based upon a patriotism theme? Would a severe depression increase or decrease the number of job seekers? Some insights into such questions might be acquired by examining a series of the statistical labor force snapshots, but it would be dangerous to reach any conclusions from a report that is based upon activity during one specific week.

Monthly Labor Force Reports

Labor force statistics are presented monthly by the Bureau of Labor Statistics in the Department of Labor and are based upon a sample population survey of 52,500 households.[3] The statistics are referred to as household data, meaning that the information is obtained from persons interviewed in their own homes. In many cases the respondent is the housewife, and the accuracy of the data depends upon the familiarity of the housewife with the details of the employment status of other members of the household. Since the information is based upon a sample, there is always some possibility of sampling variation. The results, therefore, should be regarded as approximations. Once each decade, the decennial population census is taken, and the statistics obtained from this census of the total population can be regarded as a more accurate check on the size and

---

[3] The character of the population sample has been changed several times in recent years. The current sample is drawn from 449 sample areas comprising 863 counties and independent cities with coverage in every state. For a description of the character of the data and the methodology used to derive them see Bureau of Labor Statistics, *Concepts and Methods Used in Manpower Statistics from the Current Population Survey*, Report No. 313, June, 1967.

characteristics of the labor force.[4] Policy decisions, however, often require up-to-date information. Consequently, it is necessary to rely upon the monthly reports as well as a variety of other statistics about labor supply that are available.

Basic labor force data, as shown in Table 4, are released monthly in the Department of Labor publication, *Employment and Earnings and Monthly Report on the Labor Force.* In addition to the classifications shown here, the monthly release presents other breakdowns such as duration of unemployment for the unemployed group and the occupational and industrial characteristics of the active population.

Apart from the household data described above, the main source of employment statistics is a monthly Bureau of Labor Statistics report that is based upon establishment data. Establishment statistics are obtained directly from industrial, commercial, and government establishments rather than households. Each month, the BLS collects employment data from a sample of employer units covering about 47 per cent of total employment. These data are used to prepare national estimates of non-agricultural employment with detailed industrial breakdowns. In a number of respects, the establishment data are not comparable with those derived from household interviews. The former, for example, do not include unpaid family workers, domestics, proprietors, and self-employed persons.

LABOR FORCE SIZE

Before 1940

Historical comparisons of labor force size are extremely difficult to make, since labor force statistics collected before 1940 were based upon substantially different concepts from those collected after that date.[5] Attempts

---

[4] This statement must be qualified. Logically, it would appear that a count of the labor force based upon an enumeration of the entire population would be more accurate than a count based upon a statistical sampling of households. There is an offsetting factor, however. Enumerators who make the monthly sampling are long-time employees of the Bureau of the Census who are qualified by virtue of training and experience. Many of the persons who poll the population in the decennial census are employed only for that special purpose and are hastily trained. Consequently, the labor force classifications made by the latter group are likely to be less accurate than those made by the enumerators during the monthly sampling.

Recent research has shown that the 1960 census missed about 5.7 million persons or 3.1 per cent of the estimated true population. As a result of the undercount, there was a substantial understatement of employment levels and a discrepancy between census labor force data and other statistical descriptions of the labor force. See Denis F. Johnston and James R. Watzel, "Effect of the Census Undercount on Labor Force Estimates," *Monthly Labor Review,* March, 1969, pp. 3–13.

[5] Before 1940, persons were classified as "gainful workers" or "not gainful workers." Gainful worker statistics were based upon questions relating to occupation rather than

TABLE 4

EMPLOYMENT AND UNEMPLOYMENT ESTIMATES

(In Thousands)

EMPLOYMENT STATUS, AGE, AND SEX	JANUARY, 1969	JANUARY, 1968
Total		
Total labor force	83,351	81,386
Civilian labor force	79,874	77,923
Employed	77,229	75,167
Agriculture	3,752	4,003
Non-agricultural industries	73,477	71,164
Unemployed	2,645	2,756
Men, 20 years and over		
Total labor force	49,189	48,538
Civilian labor force	46,131	45,770
Employed	45,231	44,740
Agriculture	2,680	2,931
Non-agricultural industries	42,551	41,809
Unemployed	900	1,030
Women, 20 years and over		
Civilian labor force	26,950	25,810
Employed	25,999	24,802
Agriculture	691	683
Non-agricultural industries	25,308	24,119
Unemployed	951	1,008
Both Sexes, 16–19 years		
Civilian labor force	6,793	6,343
Employed	5,999	5,625
Agriculture	381	389
Non-agricultural industries	5,618	5,236
Unemployed	794	718

Source: U.S. Department of Labor, Bureau of Labor Statistics.

current employment status. Gainful workers were defined as persons reported as having a gainful occupation regardless of whether they were working or seeking work at the time of the census. Some of the more important specific differences between gainful workers statistics and the presently employed "current activity" data are as follows:
1. Seasonal workers not working nor seeking work are not counted as being in the labor force under the present concepts. In 1930 they were counted as gainful workers if they reported an occupation.
2. New workers without experience but seeking work are now included in the labor force, whereas they were not formerly counted as gainful workers.
3. Retired persons and those unable to work are not counted as being in the labor force. In earlier censuses such persons often reported an occupation and thus were counted as gainful workers.
4. Since 1940, labor force statistics have been restricted to persons fourteen years of age and over, whereas gainful worker statistics were secured for persons ten years of age and over.

have been made to develop comparable statistics from the available data, but the accuracy of such adjustments is beyond test.[6] Despite this lack of precise comparability, it is possible to note general tendencies in the characteristics of labor force change. The number of persons in the labor force in 1930 was approximately twice what it was in 1890, growing from 23 million in 1890 to about 49 million in 1930. Labor force growth that occurred in the decade of the thirties was somewhat below what might have been expected on the basis of prior experience. The number of persons in the labor force in 1940, 53 million, represented a decline in the labor force participation rate—the ratio of persons fourteen years of age or over in the labor force to total number of persons fourteen or over.[7]

Several factors appear to be responsible for the unusually small labor force size in 1940. The difficulty of finding work during the depression years may well have discouraged many older workers to the extent that they gave up seeking work and simply regarded themselves as involuntarily retired. Whereas 55 per cent of the male population over sixty-five years of age was in the labor force in 1930, only 43 per cent of this age group was engaged in labor force activity in 1940. Teen-agers who might have gone to work if jobs had been available tended to stay in school for longer periods of time. The labor force participation rate for fourteen- to nineteen-year-old males dropped from 43 per cent in 1930 to 38 per cent in 1940.

The population group consisting of women over twenty years of age increased its labor force activity during the decade. This increase could have resulted from the fact that delayed marriages and delay in starting families made it possible for many women, who otherwise would have engaged in housework, to seek work. A simpler explanation is that many women were forced by economic pressures to try to find jobs. On the other hand it is also probable that many housewives who would have taken jobs if employment had been more easily available did not make any serious attempt to find work because of strong competition for such jobs that did exist.

---

[6] For a good description of the type of adjustments necessary to make earlier statistics comparable with contemporary data see John D. Durand, *The Labor Force in the United States, 1890–1960* (New York: Social Science Research Council, 1948), Appendix A.

[7] The exact size of the decline in the labor force participation rate in 1940 varies depending upon the statistical indicator that one chooses to use. A Census Bureau adjustment of the 1930 gainful workers statistics making them comparable with the 1940 labor force statistics results in a labor force participation rate of 53.2 per cent in 1930 and a rate of 52.7 per cent in 1940. See U.S. Bureau of the Census, *Comparative Occupational Statistics in the United States, 1870–1940*, p. 13. A number of other adjustments of labor force size in these two census years have been made, and most of these indicate a declining labor force participation rate. See, for example, Durand, *op. cit.*, p. 19, and U.S. Bureau of the Census, *Current Population Reports*, Series P-50, No. 42.

The Forties

The depression of the thirties was succeeded by the war prosperity years of the 1940's. As might be expected, this changing economic environment had a substantial effect upon the labor force behavior of the population. Between 1940 and V-E Day, labor force size increased by 10.6 million persons. The most spectacular growth occurred between April, 1942, and April, 1943, when the total of persons in the labor force increased by more than 4 million.[8]

Where did the extra workers come from? Primarily from the population under twenty years of age and from the adult female population, where the greatest proportionate increases occurred in the age group thirty-five to fifty-four. It has been estimated that 3.4 million youths fourteen to seventeen years of age were employed in 1945 compared to 1.1 million in 1940.[9] The importance of teen-age labor in local labor markets during the war period can be illustrated by one experience in Franklin County, Ohio, where the number of first work permits issued by the board of education rose from 1,776 in 1940 to 10,147 in 1943.[10] In the adult female population, the sharpest increase in labor force activity occurred among married women free of the burden of caring for young children. There was not very much change in the employment status of mothers with young children. Older persons of both sexes also contributed to the increase in labor force size. Many of these were persons who had been marginal workers during the competitive labor market situation prior to 1941 but who were able to find full-time jobs during the period of wartime manpower shortages.

The period immediately following V-J Day was one of turmoil in labor developments. Soldiers were discharged by the millions, families were re-united, long-delayed marriages were taking place, and many workers were leaving war centers to go "back home." When the smoke of this manpower demobilization period had cleared, it became apparent that important changes had taken place in labor force composition.

Total labor force size, including members of the armed forces, declined by about 4 million between August, 1945, and August, 1946. This decrease was the algebraic total of a 9.7 million decline in armed forces size and a 5.6 million increase in the civilian labor force. The number of civilian women workers had increased by more than 2 million, whereas the male

[8] Persons in the armed forces are included as being in the labor force. Since over 5 million persons were inducted into the armed services between 1942 and 1943, the civilian labor force declined by approximately 1 million. The significance of a labor force increase of this size is dramatically illustrated by the fact that a withdrawal of 5 million persons of labor force age from the civilian population only diminished the civilian labor force by 1 million.

[9] E. A. Merrit and E. S. Gray, "Child Labor Trends in an Expanding Labor Market," *Monthly Labor Review,* December, 1948, p. 500.

[10] Sanford Cohen, "Teen-Age Student Workers in an Ohio County, 1940–1949," *Monthly Labor Review,* July, 1954, pp. 776–778.

component of the labor force increased by almost 8 million. The number of "extra" workers—those persons who probably would not have been in the labor force except for the unusual job opportunities provided by the mobilized economy of the war years—dropped sharply as shown by the following table:

Date	No. of Extra Workers (In millions)
April, 1945	8.1
August, 1945 (V-J Day)	7.0
April, 1946	3.3
August, 1946	2.5

Source: Leonard Eskin, "The Labor Force in the First Year of Peace," *Monthly Labor Review*, November, 1946, p. 676.

The character of this departure from the labor force is illustrated by the breakdown shown below:

	Decline in Extra Workers April, 1945–April, 1946 (In millions)
Women, 20–34 years of age	1.5
Women, 35 and over	1.6
School age persons (teen-agers of both sexes and men 20–24 years)	2.6
Men, 25 and over	.1

Source: *Ibid.*

A number of important factors influenced labor force size after the war. Many veterans did not go directly into civilian employment. Some took extended vacations, but far more enrolled in schools on a full-time basis. Marriage rates rose sharply, and this accounted for some labor force exodus by members of the female labor force. The continuation of prosperity that so confounded many business trend forecasters meant that jobs were still relatively available and could account for the fact that many women in the thirty-five to sixty-four age group continued to remain in the labor force despite the fact that the patriotic motivation to work was no longer operative.

The Fifties and Sixties

In the early fifties, the civilian labor force remained relatively stable at an average level of about 63 million persons. This reflected, in part, the 1930 birth rate drop and the demands of the military establishments which kept younger persons out of the civilian labor force in both direct and indirect ways. The number in the armed forces increased by about 2 million between 1950 and 1952. Less directly, draft regulations provided some incentive for persons of draft age to remain in universities on a full-time basis. Furthermore, potential draftees frequently found employers disinclined to hire them. It is possible that many of draft age became discouraged to the extent that they were only nominally attached to the labor force.

A sharp expansion in labor force size took place after the middle of 1955. In that year and again in 1956, the civilian labor force grew by almost 1.5 million persons. Almost 40 per cent of the new entries were adult women, and another third consisted of teen-age persons. The labor force gain among adult males was a result of population growth rather than an increase in the labor force participation rate.

Between 1957 and 1962, the net annual increase in the labor force averaged about three-quarters of a million persons. This growth was somewhat below what had been anticipated. With a slackening in the demand for labor, fewer women were added to the work force, and participation by young persons and by men over sixty-five declined. Labor force developments in 1963 reflected the impact of the post-World War II baby boom and improved employment conditions. The first large group of those born after the war reached working age at a time when an economic upturn produced a rise in the demand for labor. The result was a growth in labor force size of 1.3 million persons. Growth of a similar order occurred through 1966, and the civilian labor force reached 75.8 million at the end of that year.

In 1967, the labor force increased by 1.6 million, the largest annual growth in two decades and larger by 300 thousand than the 1966 increment. This unusually large gain resulted from both population growth and an increase in the proportion of women in the labor force. Over one million adult females entered into labor force activity in 1967, a development consistent with the general pattern of recent years although the number of new female entrants was substantially higher. A novel feature of the 1967 labor force growth was the entry of a large number of males aged 20–34. Labor force increases for this age group totaled 500 thousand as against almost no change in 1966. This surge in labor force entry by persons in the young adult male cohort reflected the high birth rates during and immediately after World War II plus the fact that military calls in 1967 were light, leaving more young persons free for civilian labor force activity. Labor force growth in 1968 was approximately equal to that for 1967 resulting in a civilian labor force of almost 80 million persons.

Summarizing developments since 1961 when a sharp acceleration in labor force growth began, we find a gain in labor force size of over 9 million persons between 1961 and 1968. This amounted to an average annual gain of 1.3 million, or more than half again the average increase that occurred in the 1947–61 period. The major components of this recent rise were young workers and married women. In 1965, one in five persons in the labor force was under twenty-five years of age. By 1968 the ratio has

FIGURE 3

ANNUAL CHANGES IN TOTAL LABOR FORCE OF ADULT MEN
AND WOMEN, AND TEENAGERS, 1960–67

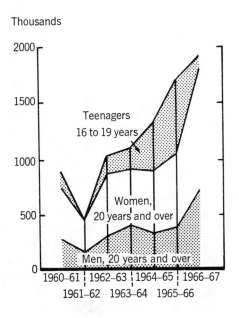

Source: U.S. Department of Labor.

changed to one in four. Working wives, who in 1961 constituted 18 per cent of the total labor force, were 22 per cent by 1968.

Department of Labor projections suggest a civilian labor force of approximately 90 million persons by 1975. The growth that occurs in the years immediately ahead will be conditioned by characteristics of the population structure described in Chapter One. The teen-age population, which was a significant component of labor force expansion through 1966, will grow only slightly in the next few years. Males over twenty years of age who accounted for relatively little of the labor force growth in the recent past will be responsible for a much larger part of the total growth in the next several years.

FLEXIBILITY OF LABOR FORCE SIZE

The brief survey of labor force changes described in the above section would seem to indicate that labor force size in the United States is volatile, moving up and down rapidly as conditions change. Actually the data are not adequate to justify such a conclusion. The issue which concerns us here involves the "short run" labor supply. Basic trends affecting population size and population characteristics such as age, sex, race, and marital status determine the number of potential workers in an economic system. More often than not, however, there is some difference in the number of those who might conceivably be working or seeking work and those who are actually doing so. The question of a short run labor supply revolves about variations in degree of labor force activity in a time period too short for these basic population characteristics to change significantly.

WAGE INDUCED VARIATIONS

A number of generalizations or theories concerning short run labor supply can be found in economic literature. Within broad limits the traditional conclusion of economists is that labor supply will expand as wage rates increase. This expansion results from additional persons being induced to work as the prospects of high earnings overcome their reluctance or aversion to labor; or it might also result from persons, already working, offering to supply more hours of labor as wage rates rise. It is also proposed that, at some very high level of wage rates, the supply of labor will decrease because many workers with high incomes will prefer leisure as an alternative to more work and more take-home pay. This theory, then, makes labor supply a variable factor dependent upon levels of wage rates. For purposes of practical analysis, the approach has a number of weaknesses. Factors other than wage rates that might affect labor supply are assumed to be held constant. This means that a host of dynamic forces that condition economic behavior are ruled out as complicating factors. Another weakness is the fact that even though the logic of the theory is admitted, it is difficult to develop a practical test to show the degree of variation in labor supply that will be associated with given variations in wage rates. Assume, for instance, that at a given wage level all persons who want work are employed. How much would wages have to be increased before additional persons would become workers? It is not likely that an increase in the average level of wages from $2.00 to $2.01 per hour would affect labor supply materially, whereas an upward adjustment to $4.00 per hour might very well result in some additional labor supply. A theory of labor force behavior would have to be immeasurably more precise than this before it would be helpful in dealing with real problems.[11]

---

[11] For comments on the indeterminate nature of the labor supply curve see Giovanni Demaria, "Aggregate and Particular Labour Supply Curves," John T. Dunlop (ed.), *The Theory of Wage Determination* (London: Macmillan & Co., Ltd., 1957), chap. 21.

Nevertheless, because of its emphasis on limits, there is some point in paying attention to this theory of labor supply. Within a given context of economic and social conditions there is some limit to the amount of available labor. When the limit is reached, a further increase in supply is not likely to be forthcoming without an unusual shock such as a large-scale increase in the level of remuneration. Furthermore, a point can be reached in any economy where monetary incentives are incapable of increasing the over-all supply of factors of production. Although traditional economic theory sheds no light on the location of these crucial points, it does call attention to the fact of their existence—a fact so obvious that it sometimes tends to be forgotten. One reason we tend to forget is that the American economy is so unstable. Frequent periods of less than full employment give the impression that there is always some labor surplus that can be drawn upon in the event of expanded economic activity. The possibility of limits in labor supply was illustrated by the World War II experience, however, when after a time, additional monetary incentives would have accomplished little by way of increasing the number of available workers.

Unemployment and Labor Force Size

Many students of the labor force believe that, by and large, there is not much relationship between labor force size and the pay level. The basis for such a conclusion is that most of the people in the labor force have to work of necessity and that this necessity is present regardless of the wage level. It is true that there is a hard core of labor supply and that this hard core accounts for the bulk of the labor force; however, it also appears to be true that there are some variations in labor force size that cannot be accounted for by long run population changes alone. While these variations are small relative to total labor force size, they can become economically important in stress periods.

The "additional worker" and "discouraged worker" hypotheses posit a relationship between labor force participation rates and the amount of unemployment that exists. The major premise of the additional worker hypothesis is that when the household head becomes unemployed, additional members of the family who do not ordinarily work will attempt to find jobs. Hence, during depression periods when unemployment of the household head is not uncommon, there is an unusual swelling of the labor force as additional workers in the family seek to augment the family income. It must be kept in mind, incidentally, that persons who seek work are counted as members of the labor force regardless of the success of their search for employment. The discouraged worker hypothesis alleges that labor force size contracts during periods of high unemployment. Many persons, according to the hypothesis, withdraw from the labor force when they become discouraged over their inability to find work.

The controversy over the additional worker hypothesis has centered upon the question of its verification. Until recently, most labor force students argued that available statistics did not show the existence of a significant number of extra workers during the latter years of the 1930 depression or during the post-World War II recessions.[12] Recent analysis, however, lends support to both the additional worker and the discouraged worker hypotheses. The discouraged worker effect appears to be the dominant one, however. For the period 1953–62, a loss of 100 jobs was roughly associated with a reduction in the size of measured labor force of fifty persons.[13]

"Full" Employment and Labor Force Size

Another hypothesis that warrants some attention in the analysis of labor force characteristics is the reverse of the additional worker theory. This is the notion that a major variable influencing labor force size is the mere fact of job availability. It has already been noted that the number of persons engaged in labor force activity increased notably during World War II. There were many unusual circumstances present during the war, and it is not an easy task to disentangle the web of motivations that pulled persons into the labor force. Undoubtedly there were many who took jobs because of the patriotic feeling that they ought to do something to help the war effort. Very probably many married women went to work because their husbands entered the armed forces. It is also possible that many persons took jobs because it was extremely easy to find employment. For instance, a housewife could put on working clothes, pack a lunch, and head for a factory in the vicinity with the very reasonable expectation of being employed that same day.

A number of case studies appear to substantiate the hypothesis that there is a secondary labor force or a body of non-permanent workers that materializes when jobs are easy to find and moves back into non-labor force status when the jobs disappear. In their study of the Kankakee and "Shoe Town" labor market areas, for example, Wilcock and Sobel found

---

[12] See, for example, Clarence D. Long, *The Labor Force Under Changing Income and Employment* (Princeton: Princeton University Press, 1958), chap. 10.

[13] Kenneth Strand and Thomas Dernburg, "Cyclical Variations in Civilian Labor Force Participation," *The Review of Economics and Statistics,* November, 1964, pp. 378–391. A number of labor force students have taken issue with the details of this study, but there appears to be widespread agreement as to the existence of a significant discouraged worker effect. See Jacob Mincer, "Labor Force Participation and Unemployment: A Review of Recent Evidence," R. A. Gordon and M. S. Gordon (eds.), *Prosperity and Unemployment* (New York: John Wiley and Sons, Inc., 1966), chap. 3; Peter Barth, "Unemployment and Labor Force Participation," *Southern Economic Journal,* January, 1968, pp. 375–382.

that a sudden and sharp increase in the demand for workers drew large numbers of persons into the labor force.[14]

Teen-agers. Some evidence that a condition of extreme job availability influences labor force size can be found in the record of teen-age workers during World War II. For many years prior to 1940, there was a downward trend in the number and percentages of children gainfully employed. The Fair Labor Standards Act of 1938, as well as other federal and state legislation, limited the employment of minors in many ways. The historical increase in the number of persons attending school and college was also an influence in the dwindling of teen-age employment. During the tight labor market period of World War II, however, there was an explosive burst of labor force activity among teen-agers. The number of employed persons in the fourteen to seventeen age group by 1945 was triple the number in 1940 and a national study made in 1945 concluded that the teen-age youth group was one of the most important sources of additional workers during the war.[15]

Since 1947, the general trend in the male teen-age labor force participation rate has been downward. The 1947 rate for eighteen- and nineteen-year-old males, for example, was 80.5 while the 1967 rate was 70.9. (In the same time span, the female rate remained stable.) The declining rate for young men occurred in the face of a large rise in the absolute amount of teen-age employment. The absolute rise, in fact, may have been associated with the drop in the participation rate since the flood of young workers resulted in an intensified competition for the jobs open to youths. Since 1957, teen-age unemployment has generally run two to three times the national average, and this has apparently discouraged many young men from job-seeking activities. The recent record, thus, appears to substantiate the relationship between teen-age labor force participation and the availability of jobs that young persons are qualified to fill.

Women. Married women constitute another group whose labor force activity has been influenced by both long run and short run considerations. Over the years, the burden of the housewife has been lessened considerably by the development of time-saving contrivances ranging from automatic washers to frozen foods. These, together with a decline in average family size and a changed philosophical attitude toward working-girl status, have

---

[14] Richard C. Wilcock and Irvin Sobel, *Small City Job Markets* (Urbana, Ill.: Institute of Labor and Industrial Relations, University of Illinois, 1958). For a statistical study of the relation between manpower supply and changes in the demand for labor see Alfred Tella, "The Relation of Labor Force to Employment," *Industrial and Labor Relations Review,* April, 1964, pp. 454–469.

[15] Lester Pearlman and Leonard Eskin, "Teen-Age Youth in the Wartime Labor Force," *Monthly Labor Review,* January, 1945, pp. 6–17.

combined to exert a long run influence in the direction of a greater inclination among married women to work. In short run periods, conditions of prosperity have opened up avenues for employment. In 1940, 14 per cent of married women living with their husbands were in the labor force. By 1967, this labor force participation rate had increased to 37 per cent. The importance of short run changes in the demand for adult female labor can be illustrated by the post-World War II record. Between 1947 and 1951, an average of 650,000 married women entered the labor force each year. In the first year of the Korean War, the increase totaled a million. In 1953, when economic activity slowed down somewhat, only 350,000 married women entered the labor force. Between March, 1961, and March, 1962, when overall unemployment was high, labor force entry on the part of married women was 32 per cent of the population increase for that group. In the equivalent 1962–1963 period, there was an improvement in the job market and net labor force accessions of married women exceeded the population increase by 18 per cent.[16] In the late 1960's when the labor market was generally strong, wives entered the labor force in record numbers. By 1968 they were 22 per cent of all workers compared with 18 per cent in 1961.[17]

Several aspects of this postwar experience are noteworthy. (1) Almost all of the increase in female employment between 1947 and 1966 resulted from the entry of married women into the labor force. There was relatively little change in the number of unmarried women workers during this period. (2) The largest increases in female labor force participation occurred in the forty-five- to fifty-four-year-old age group. At the present time over 50 per cent of the women who fall within this age bracket are in the labor force. At the turn of the century, incidentally, the average female life expectancy was fifty-one years. Today this is an age at which large numbers of women are committing themselves to full-time labor force activity. (3) Among married women, the highest participation rates are found in the group with the most education. The rate is 29 per cent for those with eight years of education, 40 per cent for high school graduates, and 49 per cent for college graduates. (4) As noted above, the largest increases in the female labor force have occurred among those over forty-five years of age. Since 1960 and especially in the latter years of that decade, labor force statistics indicate an accelerated rise in participation on the part of younger women including those with pre-school age children. Between 1960 and

---

[16] Vera C. Perrella, "Marital and Family Characteristics of Workers," *Monthly Labor Review,* February, 1964, pp. 149–150.

[17] See Gertrude Bancroft McNally, "Patterns of Female Labor Force Activity," *Industrial Relations,* May, 1968, pp. 207–212, for a summary of studies of the impact of changes in aggregate demand on the female labor force.

FIGURE 4

MARRIED WOMEN REPRESENT A GROWING
PROPORTION OF THE LABOR FORCE

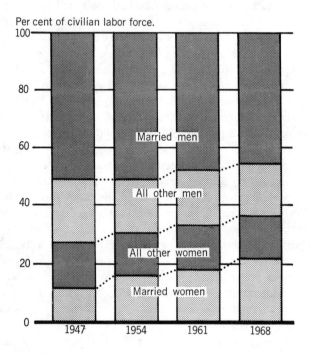

Source: U.S. Department of Labor.

1967, thus, there was a seven per cent increase in the labor force participation rate of married women with children under six years of age. Should this trend continue, the possibility of further large scale increases in the size of the female labor force can be identified since population projections show an increase of almost 40 per cent in the number of younger women (ages 20 to 34) between 1965 and 1975.

A full explanation of the growth in female labor activity would have to consider many factors, but there is little question that the existence of job opportunities must rank high among them. What has apparently emerged is a two-phased working life for women. After high school or college, many take jobs as a matter of course. With marriage and the birth of children there is a sharp drop in labor force activity. The second phase starts when the children reach school age. More and more mothers are returning to the job market when their children enter school and, as noted above, there has been some tendency for a labor market reentry among those with pre-school age children. Many women, however, apparently delay their re-entries until such times when jobs can be found with relatively little difficulty.

Conclusion

What, if anything, can be concluded about short run flexibility of the labor force? First, there is a core of persons, primarily males aged twenty to forty-five, who will either work or seek work under any set of economic and social conditions that is likely to prevail. This core lends a certain stability to labor force size. On the other hand there are groups whose economic behavior is likely to be conditioned by the prevailing degree of prosperity or depression, and these groups make for some variation in labor force size. It should be noted here that part of the problem is a statistical one. An adult male who loses his job is likely to start looking for another one immediately. Consequently, he continues to be counted as a member of the labor force. Housewives who lose their jobs, in many cases, go back to being full-time housewives. They are no longer counted as being in the labor force. A high school student who is fired from his after-school-hours job and who makes no serious effort to find another job will not be counted as a member of the labor force. A different statistical framework—one for instance that would count as "in the labor force," persons who say they would take jobs if jobs were available—would give different results from those shown by "current activity" labor force statistics. For analyzing problems dealing with manpower resources and the size of labor reserves, it is very likely that a set of data based upon concepts other than current activity would be more meaningful.

OCCUPATIONAL AND INDUSTRIAL CHARACTERISTICS OF THE LABOR FORCE

Since the end of World War II, the occupational and industrial characteristics of the labor force have changed significantly, and the end of the economic adjustments that have produced these changes is not yet in sight. Certain aspects of the contemporary labor convolutions are an acceleration of long run secular trends, whereas others reflect the impact of recent technological innovations, a rise in the rate of industrial relocation, and relatively recent shifts in consumer preferences. The depth of the various changes is difficult to gauge, since it is no simple matter to disentangle short run cyclical and frictional influences on labor force size and composition from the more enduring influences of basic structural transformations in the economy. The general character of what is happening seems to be clear, however.

From the standpoint of employment opportunities provided, there has been a decline in the relative importance of the primary industry (agriculture) and the secondary industries (manufacturing, mining, and construction) and a rise in the importance of the tertiary industries (transportation and public utilities, trade, finance, service, and government). These industrial shifts have produced changes in the number of workers needed in different occupations, and within industries the occupational composition of the labor force has been affected by technological and other forces. In broad outline, the shift in labor demand has been away from the farm, manual labor, and factory operative occupations and toward the clerical, sales, technical, and managerial employments. In even more general terms, the move has been away from blue collar and toward white collar work. The details of these industrial and occupational shifts are described below.[18]

The Shift from Farm to Non-farm Employment

In the early period of American history, approximately 90 per cent of all economic effort was centered in the agricultural sector. As late as 1910, farmers and farm laborers accounted for 30 per cent of total employment. By 1960, this occupational group included only 8.1 per cent of the persons in the labor force. Increasing mechanization of farm work and the resulting increase in efficiency has led to a reduction in the agricultural labor force while agricultural output has gone up. In 1910, the farm output for a nation of 91 million persons was produced by some 11 million farmers. In the summer of 1968 about 4 million persons provided sufficient farm products for a nation of 200 million.[19] What is even more astounding is that the smaller number of farm workers manage to pile up surplus products that are costly in an economic sense and embarrassing in a political one. Since the rural population has maintained its historical fertility advantage over the urban population, it has been a population source supplying labor to the urban-situated industrial sector of the economy. Interestingly, in 1968 the adult male population residing in rural areas did not decline, and agricultural employment was approximately the same as in 1967. This was the first time since 1959 that agricultural employment had not fallen by at least 100,000 workers. The significance of this arrest of the long term trend cannot be fully weighed until several more years of experience accumulate. It is possible, however, that farm to city population movement that has continued for over half a century may be levelling off.

---

[18] In the discussions below, employment statistics cited for recent years are annual averages of the monthly surveys of the labor force. Statistics for 1960, consequently, will differ somewhat from the 1960 census data which reflect employment as of a single month. Because of the non-comparability of recent and earlier labor force data, long run comparisons should be regarded as rough approximations.

[19] In the first edition of this book, the above sentence read "In 1950, 6.7 million persons provided sufficient farm products for a nation of 150 million." Since the end of World War II, agricultural employment has declined by about 50 per cent.

FIGURE 5

EMPLOYMENT IN GOODS-PRODUCING INDUSTRIES AND IN
SERVICE INDUSTRIES, 1919–1962
(ANNUAL AVERAGES)

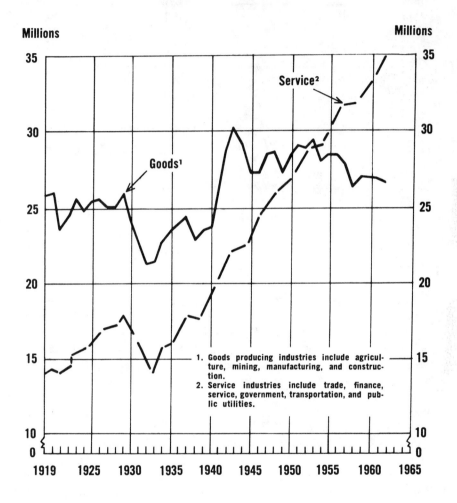

Source: U.S. Department of Labor, Bureau of Labor Statistics.

Changes in the Proportions of Unskilled and Semi-skilled Workers

At an earlier point in our economic history, most of the non-farm employees were probably laborers, workers who loaded, unloaded, dug holes,

FIGURE 6

FARM EMPLOYMENT

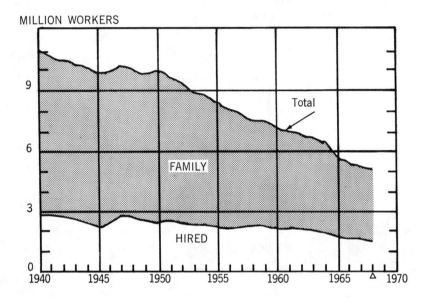

Source: U.S. Department of Agriculture.

or pushed heavy weight around. With the industrialization of the economy, the importance of the laborer declined, and that of the semi-skilled worker increased. Today there are, and for many decades into the past there have been, more persons employed as "operatives and kindred workers" than as members of any of the other major occupational groupings.[20]

The shift in the relative importance of the unskilled and semi-skilled workers can be summarized as the replacement of human brawn by men working with power-driven machinery. Between 1910 and 1950, the percentage of persons in the labor force classified as "operatives and kindred workers" increased from 14 per cent to 21 per cent. This increase was part and parcel of the rapid development of the mass production industries. The moving assembly lines, the development of specialized metal-working machinery, the predominance of a social type of production in large plant units, and the development of efficient transportation facilities to service these production units were among the important factors accounting for the expanded demand for operatives and other semi-skilled workers. The

---

[20] As used by the Bureau of the Census, the occupational classification "operatives and kindred workers" includes such jobs as truck drivers, metal polishers, railroad brakemen, and a variety of semi-skilled jobs in practically every industry.

growth in semi-skilled employment provided job opportunities for the newly arrived immigrant, the farmer moving to the city, and the urban dweller with limited formal education.

The dominance of the semi-skilled worker in the occupational structure is being threatened, however, by an automation technology which is substituting machinery for human workers in the more routinized operations. Within the past decade, large increases in manufacturing industries have occurred with no commensurate increase in manufacturing employment. In the face of a large general rise in the volume of employment, this has meant that the relative importance of the operative and kindred worker group has declined. After a half decade of declining employment in the operative occupations, a sharp upturn occurred in 1963–1964. Even in these years, however, the expansion was less than that which occurred in white collar employment. In the late 1960's, year to year changes in the number of persons employed as operatives have ranged from virtually no change to increases of less than 200,000. Employment in the semi-skilled occupations will continue to grow; but the outlook is for a decreasing rate of growth, and it is quite likely that by 1975 there will be as many persons in the clerical occupations as in the operative and kindred group.

The changes described above can be illustrated by a brief survey of the statistical record. In 1910, approximately one out of every nine persons employed outside agriculture could be classified as a laborer. Fifty years later the proportion was one out of nineteen. According to census data, 3.7 million persons were non-farm laborers in 1960. Projections of occupational employment made by the United States Department of Labor indicate that the number of such workers will remain constant during the next few years and that, as a result, they will constitute 4.1 per cent of the total labor force in 1975.[21]

Although operatives and kindred workers rose from 14 per cent to 21 per cent of the labor force between 1910 and 1950, they dropped to 18 per cent by 1960. Department of Labor estimates indicate a further decline to 16.9 per cent by 1975.

The Growth of the White Collar Occupations

It is not possible to be quantitatively specific about the number of white collar workers. There is no Bureau of the Census classification of white collar workers as such. These occupations are included among the jobs listed in more specific classifications such as "sales workers," "clerical and kindred workers," and "professional, technical, and kindred workers." Under Professor Mills' definitions the three largest occupational groups in the white collar "mass" are schoolteachers, salespeople in and out of stores, and

---

[21] *Manpower Report of the President,* January, 1969, p. 235.

TABLE 5

ACTUAL AND PROJECTED EMPLOYMENT FOR PERSONS 16 YEARS AND OVER, BY OCCUPATION GROUP, 1960 TO 1975

OCCUPATION GROUP	ACTUAL 1960 Number (thousands)	ACTUAL 1960 Percent distribution	ACTUAL 1965 Number (thousands)	ACTUAL 1965 Percent distribution	PROJECTED 1975 Number (millions)	PROJECTED 1975 Percent distribution	NUMBER CHANGE (MILLIONS) 1960–65	NUMBER CHANGE (MILLIONS) 1965–75	PERCENT CHANGE 1960–65	PERCENT CHANGE 1965–75
Total employment	65,777	100.0	71,088	100.0	87.2	100.0	5.3	16.1	8.1	22.7
Professional and technical workers	7,474	11.4	8,883	12.5	12.9	14.8	1.4	4.0	18.9	45.2
Managers, officials, and proprietors	7,067	10.7	7,340	10.3	9.0	10.4	.3	1.7	3.9	23.3
Clerical workers	9,759	14.8	11,129	15.7	14.8	16.9	1.4	3.6	14.0	32.5
Sales workers	4,216	6.4	4,497	6.3	5.6	6.4	.3	1.1	6.7	25.0
Craftsmen and foremen	8,560	13.0	9,222	13.0	11.4	13.0	.7	2.1	7.7	23.1
Operatives	11,950	18.2	13,336	18.8	14.7	16.9	1.4	1.4	11.6	10.5
Service workers	8,031	12.2	8,936	12.6	12.0	13.8	.9	3.1	11.3	34.4
Nonfarm laborers	3,557	5.4	3,688	5.2	3.6	4.1	.1	—.1	3.7	—2.4
Farmers and farm laborers	5,163	7.8	4,057	5.7	3.2	3.6	—1.1	—.9	—21.4	—21.6

Source: *Manpower Report of the President*, January, 1969, p. 235.

assorted office workers.[22] The growth in the number of white collar workers, according to Mills, has given a new character to the American middle
class. Whereas the distinguishing characteristic of the middle class at one
time was property ownership, today the main point of distinction between
middle and other classes is an occupational one.[23]

Various currents have jointed to cause a large-scale growth in the number of white collar workers. Possibly as important as any immediate cause
is the mountain of paper work with which the modern business firm has to
contend. Apart from the records connected with the actual operations of
the firm, there are federal and state tax reports, social insurance reports,
census returns, reports to specialized government agencies, information for
trade associations, requests from private researchers, and so on. The development of more sophisticated accounting procedures and the increasing
use of statistical quality controls and market research compound the burden.
This work requires an array of skills and specialists. With the exception
of the very small firm, the one-girl office is a thing of the past.

The concentration of economic activity in a relatively few large firms
has also given impetus to expanded white collar employment. Big business
requires a large number of lower level managerial employees as well as a
variety of professionals such as research scientists, medical doctors, and
lawyers. Additional factors responsible for the growth in the number of
white collar jobs include the upsurge in government employment, the increased number of teachers as school enrollments go up, and the increased
proportion of persons engaged in sales work as problems in distribution
come to be as complex as those in production.

Some notion of changes in the amount of white collar employment can
be obtained by examining trends in occupational groupings where white
collar workers predominate. In 1960, 6.4 per cent of the active civilian
population were in sales work, as compared to 5 per cent in 1910. Almost
15 per cent were in clerical and kindred work, whereas only 5.5 per cent
were so classified in the earlier year. More than 11 per cent were professional, technical, and kindred workers in 1960, whereas only 4.6 per cent
were in this category in 1910.

As a result of the very rapid rate of growth in white collar employment
since the end of World War II, the number of professional, managerial,
clerical, and sales workers reached and surpassed the number in the blue

[22] C. Wright Mills, *White Collar* (New York: Oxford University Press, 1953),
p. 64.
[23] *Ibid.*, p. 65. Under Mills' system of classification, the majority of the middle class
today consists of managers, salaried professionals, salespeople, and office workers.
Seventy years ago, the great majority consisted of farmers, businessmen, and free
professionals.

collar occupations in 1956.[24] Since that date the numerical gap between the two groups has widened. In 1962, there were 29.9 million persons in white collar jobs, 9.7 million more than in 1947. This increase accounted for 97 per cent of the total employment increase that occurred between the two dates.

Between 1950 and 1960, the fastest growing of all the major occupational groups was the "professional, technical, and kindred worker" category, a classification that includes all the recognized professions plus those working at the technician skill level. Employment in this group increased by 47 per cent, a rate of growth more than three times the average for all occupational groups. In the clerical occupations, the increase was 34 per cent and in sales work 19 per cent. In the "manager, officials, and proprietors" group, employment increased at less than the national average for all occupations between 1950 and 1960. There was a considerable increase in the number of managers and other salaried officials employed by private industry and government, but part of this gain was offset by the large number of small proprietors eliminated by the competition of the supermarket and the discount store.

According to Department of Labor projections, the number of professional and technical workers will grow by 45 per cent between 1965 and 1975.[25] In the same time span, the "managers, officials, and proprietors" group will expand by 23 per cent, clerical workers by 32 per cent, and sales workers by 25 per cent. Growth in all these categories will be higher than the projected 22 per cent increase in total employment.

The Skilled Worker

For the purposes of this section skilled jobs will be regarded as those listed by the census under the heading of "craftsmen, foremen, and kindred workers." Since the turn of the century, the number of skilled workers has ranged from 11 per cent to 14 per cent of the total active population. At the present time the percentage is about 13.

For the skilled group as a whole, the outlook is for stability in terms of its relative ranking within the occupational structure. Should this occur, the number of skilled workers will increase from about 9 million at the present time to slightly over 11 million in 1975.

Within the skilled group of occupations, certain ones are declining rapidly as job sources while others are growing in importance. In the 1950's, for example, two-thirds of the employment growth for skilled workers occurred in the foremen, mechanics, and repairmen occupations. The em-

---

[24] *Manpower Report of the President* (Washington, D.C.: U.S. Government Printing Office, 1963), p. 26.

[25] *Manpower Report of the President,* January, 1969, p. 235.

ployment rise in the latter two classifications was especially large because of the increased demand for maintenance, repair, and installation work in factories and homes. About 25 per cent of all skilled workers are construction craftsmen, and as a group they witnessed only a small increase in the number employed during the past decade. Among the building craftsmen there was a rise in employment for electricians, brickmasons, and operators of excavating machinery but a decline in employment among carpenters and plasterers. Other skilled crafts that have grown rapidly in the past few years are those of the tool and die maker, lineman, and auto mechanic, whereas reduced employment has been suffered by the locomotive engineer, motion picture projectionist, furrier, and paperhanger.

The Rising Importance of Service Work

"Service workers" is a diverse group that includes such occupations as hospital attendants, barbers, bootblacks, cooks, policemen, and waiters. About one out of every eleven workers was in service work at the beginning of the century and today the figure is one out of nine. This long run stability in the relative position of the over-all occupational class, however, is in sharp contrast with changes that have occurred within the class. At the turn of the century over 50 per cent of all service workers were employed in private households. Today less than one-third are so employed. Employment in the category "service workers, except private household" rose twice as fast as employment generally in the 1950's. These increases reflected sharp rises in the demand for hospital and protective services as well as services associated with the vacation industry. In the 1960's, service work continued to be a major source of employment for the expanding labor force. In 1968, for example, the service-producing industries accounted for 1.7 million new jobs or four-fifths of the total employment gain in that year.

Occupational Trends among Female Workers

Today a larger proportion of the labor force consists of women workers than in former years. Along with this growth in female labor force participation, there have been important changes in the occupational patterns of female employment. At the turn of the century, service work, and particularly household domestic service, was the major source of female employment. Today, only about six per cent of all women workers are employed in private households. The most striking gain in female employment has occurred in clerical work. About one out of three employed women is in a clerical job, whereas only one out of ten was so employed 60 years ago. Other occupations in which marked increases in female employment have occurred are sales work and professional and technical work. The proportion of women employed as operatives has remained rather constant over the years, while the number of women laborers, including those engaged in farm labor, has declined both absolutely and relatively since 1910. The major change in the female occupational pattern, then, has been a shift from service to clerical occupations. The probable job of a woman today is office work, whereas the probable job fifty years ago was in domestic or personal service.

The Industrial Distribution of the Labor Force

Table 6 shows the industrial distribution of the non-agricultural labor force for selected years. Estimates of the distribution for the post-1960 years indicate that the trends evident in the table are continuing. The manufacturing figure for 1967, for example, was slightly under 30 per cent while government employment had risen to about 17 per cent.[26] Viewed as a whole, the picture is one of the service-producing industries advancing in relative importance at the expense of the goods-producing industries.

Until 1953, it took more than half the workers in the American economy to produce the food we eat and the goods we consume. Since 1953, it has taken fewer than half. In 1920, it took almost 40 per cent of all non-farm employees to manufacture the goods consumed. Today only about 30 per cent are needed. In coal mining, employment has declined as a result of improved methods of production and the growth of competitive sources of power. Even within the expanding service-producing sector, there have been important changes in the relative amounts of employment provided by the various industries. Largely as a result of the growth of private transportation, the share of total employment provided by "transportation and public utilities" has fallen by 50 per cent. On the other hand, the proportion of persons engaged in selling us the things we want to buy and providing us with the hotel, vacation, medical, engineering, auto repair, amusement, and other services that we want has increased markedly. We also buy more government services. There were fewer than 3 million government employees in 1920. Today there are more than 11 million.

On the basis of present signs it appears safe to project the industrial shifts described above into the future. Although long run projections of the industrial structure of the labor force are necessarily conjectural, the data suggest the need for a vast vocational reorientation of workers. Recent Department of Labor projections indicate that by 1975 the secondary sectors (manufacturing, mining, and contract construction) will provide jobs for 32 per cent of the non-agricultural workers as compared to the present 36 per cent. The tertiary or service-producing sectors will increase

---

[26] U.S. Department of Labor, Bureau of Labor Statistics, *Handbook of Labor Statistics, 1968*, p. 67.

from 64 per cent to provide the remaining 68 per cent. Within the secondary sector, projected employment in manufacturing will decline from 29 per cent of total non-agricultural employment to 26 per cent by 1975.

By way of emphasizing the character of these changes, certain aspects of the structural transformation will be examined below.

Goods-producing Industries.   From the standpoint of industrial output, the years 1957–1963 were good. Output was high and many new products were developed. The employment picture was less bright, however. Despite the output increases, employment in the goods-producing industries was 20.6 million in 1963, a decline of 300,000 from 1957. Although sharp gains in manufacturing employment occurred in 1964, the total remained below the post-war peak reached in 1953. Since 1964, employment in the manufacturing sector has expanded to the extent that fears of massive technological unemployment have been allayed somewhat. The relative importance of the goods-producing sector has fallen, however, since the growth of employment in that sector has not kept pace with the expansion in the service area.

TABLE 6

PER CENT OF NON-AGRICULTURAL EMPLOYMENT,
INDUSTRY DIVISION (SELECTED YEARS)

INDUSTRIAL DIVISION	1920	1930	1940	1950	1960
Goods-producing	46.5	40.4	40.5	40.6	37.6
Mining	4.5	3.4	2.9	2.0	1.3
Contract Construction	3.1	4.7	4.0	5.1	5.3
Manufacturing	38.9	32.3	33.6	33.5	30.9
Service-producing	53.5	59.6	59.5	59.4	62.6
Transport and Public Utilities	14.8	12.6	9.4	8.9	7.4
Wholesale and Retail Trade	17.1	20.8	21.7	21.6	21.0
Finance, Insurance, Real Estate	4.1	4.8	4.5	4.1	5.0
Service and Miscellaneous	7.9	10.6	10.8	11.3	13.6
Government	9.6	10.8	13.1	13.5	15.7

Source: U.S. Department of Labor, Bureau of Labor Statistics.

Part of the decline in the rate of growth of direct production employment has been offset by a sizable increase in non-production jobs such as engineering, research, personnel and executive positions. In 1967, for example, non-production employment in the goods-producing sector expanded by 200,000 whereas there was a slight decline in the number of production workers.

Service Industries.   The importance of the service-producing industries has already been noted. To the extent that these industries continue to expand, the problem of absorbing workers rejected by the goods-producing industries will be diminished. Should the rate of job growth in the service industries drop off, however, serious employment problems can be anticipated. Between 1961 and 1968, employment in the goods-producing industries increased by 3.7 million workers. The gain in the service sector was 10.1 million. Expressed in percentages, the former witnessed a 19 per cent employment growth as compared to a 29.6 per cent growth in the latter. As noted in the section below, a large proportion of the rise in service employment was due to the increase in the number of persons working for government.

Government Employment. Employment in government has grown faster than in any sector of the private economy since the end of World War II. Practically all of this growth has been accounted for by the rise in state and local employment. From 1961 through 1968, state and local governments added about 3 million persons to their payrolls, which in the latter year totaled 9.4 million. Federal employment, 2.2 million in 1961, grew by less than one-half million in the same period. Government employment as a whole expanded by over 40 per cent and accounted for almost 25 per cent of the total increase that occurred between 1961 and 1968.

SUMMARY

In a general way, the size of the labor force has been linked to the basic patterns of population growth in the United States. During certain periods, however, changes in labor force size that cannot be explained by long run population trends have occurred. During the 1930's for instance, the labor force grew at what appeared to be a less than "normal" rate, and there is little doubt that the depressed economic conditions discouraged many would-be workers during that decade. The demands of the war economy of the 1940's, on the other hand, drew many persons who ordinarily were non-workers into the labor force. Since the termination of World War II, labor force size has seemingly been influenced by the degree of prosperity, growing at a somewhat faster than average rate in years of strong economic expansion and at a slower rate when the economy has been depressed.

The groups most responsive to economic stimuli have been married women and teen-aged persons. There has been a long run trend of increasing labor force participation by women, but the rate of female entry into the labor force seems to have been accelerated during the prosperous years since the end of World War II. The trend among teenagers, on the other hand, has been a declining rate of participation; but the rate has diminished, and at times the decline has been reversed in recent periods of heavy demand for labor.

Important changes in the occupational distribution of the labor force have occurred within the present century. Among the significant changes have been the decrease in agricultural employment, the relative decline of the manual occupations, and the growth of employment in the white collar occupations. Among industries, the importance of the goods-producing industries as a source of employment has declined relative to the service industries.

QUESTIONS

1. In your opinion would labor force size expand or contract in the event of a severe depression? What would happen to labor force size in a period of strong prosperity?

2. How do you explain the rise in the female labor force participation rate?

3. Among women in the labor force, the highest labor force participation rates are found in the group with the most education. How would you explain this fact?

4. Would the labor force participation rate for teen-agers be higher if more jobs were available for younger persons?

5. What factors account for the large rise of employment in state and local government work?

SELECTED READING

BOGAN, FORREST A. "Employment of School Age Youth," *Monthly Labor Review,* October, 1968, pp. 33–38.

Manpower Report of the President, Washington, D.C.: U.S. Government Printing Office, Annual.

McNALLY, GERTRUDE BANCROFT. "Patterns of Female Labor Force Activity," *Industrial Relations,* May, 1968, pp. 204–218.

WOLFBEIN, SEYMOUR. *The Emerging Labor Force.* Washington, D.C.: Chamber of Commerce of the United States, 1969.

PART TWO

ORGANIZED LABOR IN THE UNITED STATES

CHAPTER 3

The First Century

"IN ALL INDUSTRIALLY ADVANCED COUNTRIES, THE STORY OF TRADE UNION development is a story of successive adaptations to changing conditions and problems."[1] With this statement, two authorities began their description of nineteenth century American unionism; and if one were limited to a single statement concerning union development in this nation, it is doubtful that a better one could be derived. By the end of the century a particular type of unionism was emerging as a dominant form in the United States, a form strongly influenced by the unique characteristics of the American political and economic system. During the century, however, we find a diversity of movements that range along the ideological spectrum from broad reformism to narrow and relatively conservative economic unionism. In method, we find such varied approaches as communalism and political action as well as economic pressures not unlike those used by present-day unions.

By the end of the nineteenth century, or at least shortly after the start of the twentieth, it had become apparent that the craft-oriented national unions that emphasized trade agreements with employers would probably have a staying power that earlier worker groups had failed to achieve. Why this type of unionism and not some other? Why, for example, did a strong class-conscious proletarian movement fail to materialize? Any answer given to this question will be complex and probably incomplete. The following factors are pertinent, however. In the first part of the century, the aspirations of wage earners were more likely to be oriented toward

---

[1] Harry A. Millis and Royal E. Montgomery, *Organized Labor* (New York: McGraw-Hill Book Company, 1945), p. 12.

property ownership than based upon an assumption of permanent worker status. Given the rapid growth of the economy, the abundance of resources, and the open-class characteristics of the society, these aspirations were not unrealistic. The political protest movements that were generated in this society cut across occupational strata; and in these protests, workers joined with others to oppose the forces that were tending to limit opportunity. In the latter part of the century when the economic environment was a closer approximation to the capitalism described by Karl Marx in *Das Kapital*, the heterogeneity of the work force made things difficult for the development of worker class consciousness. Successive waves of immigration produced a mixture of races and nationalities not easily boiled down into a group from which a pervasive class consciousness might emerge. Whatever the reasons, the American socialist movements were not able to attract the mass followings that were achieved by the indigenous protest movements. No Marxist-oriented movement, for instance, was able to arouse an enthusiasm equal to that engendered by greenbackism, free silver, or the single tax. Possibly the reason was the ineffective leadership of the socialists, inadequate articulation of the socialist appeal, or an inability to frame the appeal in an idiom that could win popularity in the United States. In any event, the latter-century protest movements that flourished, albeit briefly, were essentially middle class appeals against monopolistic tendencies in the economy.

Another basic question centers upon the choice of methods. Why did an economic rather than a political form of unionism emerge? There were workingmen's parties during the nineteenth century, although in their political activities they tended to emphasize citizenship rights rather than economic matters such as wages and hours. The labor historian, John R. Commons, believed that the legislatures and the courts frustrated labor to the extent that workers in this country had to achieve, through collective bargaining, what had been granted by law in other nations. In a more recent study, however, Lloyd Ulman has contended that the subordination of political activity to collective bargaining was due to the effectiveness of bargaining.[2] Possibly a plausible explanation is that at the time that the American economy had crystallized to the extent that a permanent labor movement was likely to emerge, there existed a base of unions with leaders whose personal experiences and ideological orientations led them to a strong advocacy of economic unionism.

The characteristics of economic or business unionism will be detailed at a later point. Whether the nature of this unionism with its emphasis upon

---

2 Lloyd Ulman, *The Rise of the National Trade Union* (Cambridge, Mass.: Harvard University Press, 1955), pp. 577, 578.

collective bargaining grew out of a worker consciousness of scarcity of opportunity and a concomitant desire to "own" and extend the area of opportunity as Perlman averred[3] or whether it reflected a unique combination of opportunity, insecurity, and a high standard of living as Ulman has contended,[4] economic unionism had a sufficient appeal to workers and a sufficient effectiveness as a method to endure in an environment that was still hostile to trade unionism in many ways.

What follows in this chapter might be called an illustrative history of worker movements in the nineteenth century. Emphasis will be placed upon the varieties of approaches, the shifting character of goals, the influence of economic conditions, and the reactions of the government and employers to the organized activities of laborers.

THE FIRST LABOR UNIONS

Concerted activity among workers on the American continent was recorded as early as 1636 when a group of fishermen in what is now Maine protested against their wages being withheld. In 1741, the New York bakers struck against a municipal regulation on the price of bread. During the Revolutionary War there were worker protests against the rise in the cost of living relative to wages. These and other incidents were sporadic in nature, however, and were spontaneous protests rather than continuing group efforts. Such worker organizations as did exist were fraternal or benevolent associations. It was not until the closing years of the eighteenth century that trade unions, as we know them today, appeared on the American scene.

The period in which these first unions existed, roughly from 1790 to 1820, was one of important political and economic changes in the new nation. In these turbulent years, the appearance and experiences of the first labor organizations must be regarded as a minor feature of the nation's history. The circumstances surrounding their brief lives, however, are important as a prelude to a century-long struggle of organized labor groups to exist and function successfully.

Employer-Worker Relationship

These early labor unions—or societies, as they were called at the time— were not formed until economic circumstances caused a cleavage to de-

---

[3] Selig Perlman, *A Theory of the Labor Movement* (New York: The Macmillan Company, 1928), *passim.*
[4] Ulman, *op. cit.,* p. 604.

velop between employer and worker interests.[5] Prior to this time, many of the essential commodities that could not be produced in the home were made by itinerant mechanics or by resident journeymen who were employed by masters in the then sparsely populated urban centers. The master employer frequently doubled as a journeyman worker, and it was not uncommon for journeymen to achieve the status of employer. Production was on a "bespoke" or custom work basis, and prices could be so manipulated as to provide for a reasonable return to both masters and journeymen. Thus, employers and workers producing for local areas that had little by way of alternative sources of supply were able to set work and price standards that satisfied them both. Factors working to inhibit growth of class feeling among workers were the real possibility of achieving master status, the continuation of the scarcity of skilled labor that characterized the colonial period, the opportunities for workers to become propertied farmers, and the ability of the masters to take advantage of the circumscribed market area to strike price bargains that enabled them to pay satisfactory wages.

The tempo of change during these times was rapid, and this employer-worker relationship was soon upset. The newly adopted federal Constitution prohibited the states from levying duties on imports or exports. Internal improvements such as canals and turnpikes resulted in some decrease in the high transportation costs that had been detrimental to the growth of internal commerce.[6] The establishment of the first United States bank and the rapid rise in the number of state banks were important in providing the greater availability of credit essential for long distance commerce.

These factors, as well as others, had the effect of breaking down the localized nature of production. Spatially separated markets came into competition with each other. The merchant-middleman appeared on the scene; and the functions of retailer, employer, and worker—which frequently had been performed by the same person—were differentiated. The merchant-middleman, who might be regarded as the equivalent of the modern day wholesaler, could buy in the cheap markets and sell in the dear ones. Brought face to face with competition from outside areas, the employer was forced to become more cost conscious. In an era when the major cost was labor, this could only result in a separation of employer and employee interests. The stage was set for organized protest by workingmen.

---

[5] There is much that is vague about the formation of the first labor organizations in the United States, and labor historians have yet to work out a totally satisfactory explanation. The discussion here follows what has probably been the most widely accepted hypothesis, the so-called "market theory" worked out by John R. Commons and his associates at the University of Wisconsin. For a summary of the Commons theory and an alternative hypothesis see Ulman, chap. 18.

[6] It has been estimated that by 1824 the cost of moving freight over the turnpikes was around thirteen cents per ton-mile and that the cost over ordinary roads was two or three times as much. Chester W. Wright, *Economic History of the United States* (New York: McGraw-Hill Book Company, 1941), p. 266.

Organization of Craftsmen

The first unions were local organizations of skilled craftsmen. Thus, there were organizations among the shoemakers in Philadelphia, the printers in New York, the tailors in Baltimore, and among other similar groups. As yet there was no unionization among factory operatives.[7]

The demands of these unions have a modern ring. They wanted higher wages, a shorter working day, and what is now called a closed shop. Bargaining usually took the form of the workers' agreeing upon a wage scale and then mutually pledging not to work for employers who paid below scale. To enforce their demands, these unions relied mainly on the "turn out" or strike. Tramping committees, visiting the various establishments to insure that journeymen were not violating the strike, served a function roughly similar to that of the present-day picket line.

To counteract union pressures, the employers formed associations and, in the case of the shoemakers, resorted to the courts. There are on record six pre-1820 cases involving the shoemakers. In effect, these cases established the principle that a combination of workers that exerted pressure upon an employer was a criminal conspiracy.[8] There was political controversy at this time over the applicability of the English common law in the United States. The Federalist party maintained that the law was applicable, whereas the Jeffersonian Republicans held a contrary view. The conspiracy cases which involved an application of the common law caused a considerable furor and created a situation in which workers could never be quite certain which of their pressure activities would be held illegal. Not until the 1842 case of *Commonwealth* v. *Hunt* was the legal situation clarified to an extent, and until that time the common law doctrines of conspiracy were constant threats to the existence of these early labor bodies.

Few of these labor organizations survived the Panic of 1819. Following the conclusion of the War of 1812, American ports were thrown open to foreign imports. Goods overflowing the warehouses in England were shipped to the United States and sold at terms that American manufacturers could not meet. This was a crushing blow to domestic manufacturers and a strong influence toward the enactment of the protective tariff of 1816. The continuing European demand for the domestic staples of the United States, however, maintained the prices of these products for several additional years and sustained a speculation that had developed in western lands. The price level of foodstuffs and cotton broke in 1819 when the

---

[7] It has been suggested that this was because wages being paid to factory workers were equal to those being paid elsewhere. Consequently, the change to factory work did not lower living standards of these employees. John R. Commons and Associates, *History of Labour in the United States* (New York: The Macmillan Company, 1918), I, 111.

[8] The criminal conspiracy doctrine is analyzed in Chapter 16.

European demand dropped sharply. Banks suspended payments, unemployment was widespread, and farmlands declined drastically in value.

These points merit stress because they illustrate a pattern of events that occurred at intervals throughout the nineteenth century. The appearance of unions as economic pressure groups was to stimulate the development of employer techniques to counteract these pressures. In the absence of legislation, legal controversies between employers and workers were to end in the courts where the sympathy of the judges, clothed in one legal doctrine or another, reflected an ideology that consistently favored employer interests. Finally, recurrent depressions were to create a series of economic environments in which unions were unable to survive.

Political Action

Workers may seek to reach their objectives by a variety of techniques. In the United States, contemporary unions have relied largely on so-called economic pressures whereby attempts are made to improve the worker's lot by obtaining wage and other concessions directly from employers. Another approach is to achieve goals through the use of political power. Workers may attempt to influence legislation by lobbying, supporting friendly candidates, forming labor parties, or by attempting to seize the reins of government forcibly. Thus, possible degrees of political action range from the relatively mild to the very radical. In American labor history, there are examples of groups advocating one or another of these forms of political action. The first substantial experience with political as opposed to economic action occurred more than a hundred years ago.

After 1822, business conditions improved, and there was a renewal of activity by labor organizations. Unions were formed by groups such as female factory workers that had not previously been organized. Strikes occurred with some frequency, and it was one such strike—that of building trade workers in Philadelphia for a ten-hour day—that led to the formation of the Mechanics Union of Trade Associations in 1827. This was a central group to which the various labor unions of the city belonged, and it appears to have been the first such city central organization of workers in the world. Formation of this city central led to the subsequent formation of the Working Men's Labor Party which, in 1828, was able to gain the balance of power in the city council. Labor parties soon appeared in many other areas. In New York, Ohio, New Jersey, and Delaware worker groups engaged actively in local and state politics. In New England, the Association of Farmers, Mechanics, and other Workingmen was at the same time a type of industrial union and a political group.

The nature of these movements is best illustrated by the character of their demands. Abolition of imprisonment for debt, reform in the banking system, universal public education, reform of the militia system, and mechanics lien laws were consistently sought by the parties in the various areas. Newly enfranchised in many states, workers were attempting to remove what they regarded as major causes of injustice. Under the existing system of debtors' prisons, persons could be—and were—thrown into prison and kept there for long periods for debts as small as one dollar. The militia system in effect in most states required that all men of appropriate age be called to serve in the militia a certain number of days per year or be subject to fine. Since many of the wealthier men preferred to pay the fine, the burden of actual service fell upon the lower income groups. Such free schools as existed were regarded as charitable institutions for the children of paupers. Labor leaders as well as educational leaders like Horace Mann and statesmen such as DeWitt Clinton were among those who fought for tax supported schools that children of all classes could attend without being stigmatized as charity cases. Mechanics lien laws would give workers a claim on the assets of bankrupt firms. The absence of such laws together with the frequency of business failures meant that many persons were unable to secure back wages. Supervision of banks by the state governments was lax, and safeguards for depositors' funds were inadequate. This situation aroused much bitterness and stimulated the demand for reform of the banking system.

The fight during this particular era was not so much between employer and employees as it was between the rich and the poor, the "haves" and the "have-nots." This was the period of Jacksonian democracy, when the agrarian interests of the West rose in protest against the commercial and moneyed interests of the East. The philosophy and practices of democracy were advancing in new directions, and the laboring groups were caught up in this movement.

These working men's parties were short-lived. By 1833, most of them had disappeared. In instances, as in the case of the Philadelphia party, the labor party was unable to cope with the political tricks of the trade as practiced by the professional politicians. In New York, internal dissension split the party and minimized its effectiveness. One faction, led by Thomas Skidmore, proposed to have all titles to private property eliminated. The property would then be distributed at an auction at which all persons would have equal purchasing power. Another faction was headed by Robert Dale Owen, son of the English reformer, and espoused a system of "state guardianship" in which all children were to be removed from their homes and placed in national schools. Repelled by the extremity of these programs, a third group broke away and formed still another party. On more than one occasion in the future, the American labor movement was to be similarly split by dissension stemming from doctrinaire philosophies.

Apart from these specific causes of failure, general economic and social conditions did not favor a distinctive labor party. An expanding economy and the absence of a class feeling among workers themselves militated against the successful formation of a political alignment that would have to be based upon an assumption of permanent working class status by the workers.

Although the labor parties did not survive, many of the proposed reforms were achieved. Public education was soon to be widespread practice, debtors' prisons disappeared by the middle of the century, and many of the other reforms demanded were eventually realized.

Economic Action

After 1833, labor organizations turned their backs on political activity for the most part and returned to economic action. Unionization took place at three levels as many local unions, city assemblies of the several unions in numerous areas, and a national union came into being. The increasing use of child, female, and convict labor, the quickening tempo of economic competition, and the rapid rise in prices spurred workers to organize in an attempt to preserve living standards.

The first attempt to accomplish a national grouping of unions occurred in 1834 when the National Trades Union was established. At the annual meetings of this body, labor issues were debated, and the union took positions on a number of economic and social problems. The first president was Ely Moore, who was elected to Congress in 1834 and served as an effective spokesman for labor rights.

The ten-hour day was a popular labor demand during this period. Prevailing hours of work were from sunup to sundown, and workers complained that this exhausted physical strength and left little time for the leisure essential for education and other self-improvement. Employers countered with the argument that additional leisure would only lead to vice and debauchery. Although some workers achieved a shorter day at the time, most did not; and the question of the length of the working day was to continue as a major labor issue for many more decades.

As in the case of the earlier unions, employer opposition, unfavorable rulings by the courts in conspiracy cases, and adverse business conditions brought the lives of these unions to a close. The Panic of 1837 brought about a major collapse of the economy. Local unions, city assemblies, and the National Trades Union disappeared rather suddenly as economic depression swept the nation.

REFORM MOVEMENTS

In prosperous times when jobs are plentiful, workers tend to concentrate their group efforts on improvements in wages and working conditions. This has been called "bread and butter unionism." In times of depression workers as well as other groups grope for some solution to the mystery behind the difficulties of society. In such periods, there is an inevitable appearance of crackpot schemes, vague panaceas, and proposals for far-reaching reforms. When something seems to be fundamentally wrong with the economy, as in the case of prolonged depression, proposals for extensive reform have an obvious appeal. Equally appealing are panaceas that promise to end all the trouble by some simple scheme.

The years from 1837 to 1852 have been described as the "long depression." In actuality the period was not one of complete depression, but rather one in which prosperity alternated with a number of minor depressions.[9] For workers, however, the years witnessed an increase in pauperism and a large amount of degradation, especially in the industrial areas. Thus, despite a considerable amount of economic progress and industrial growth, living conditions for many workers resembled those usually associated with depression periods. In these years, American workers were attracted by a variety of novel movements that ranged from the bizarre to the relatively practical.

Fourier

Leaders of one such movement proposed that groups of people set up model communities so organized as to be immune to the elements that plagued society as a whole. American proponents of this "associationist" movement drew their inspiration largely from the French social theorist, Charles Fourier.[10] Albert Brisbane was the first American disciple of Fourier. Horace Greeley, editor of the *New York Tribune*, became an ardent supporter as did a number of other intellectuals who, through writ-

---

[9] The conclusion that the period was one of long depression was reached by the Wisconsin school of labor historians, and this conclusion fitted their thesis that the labor movements swings from a preoccupation with reform movements during depression to trade union activity during prosperity. As Ware and others have pointed out, however, the period under consideration included some of the most prosperous years in American history. See Norman Ware, *The Industrial Worker* (Boston: Houghton Mifflin Company, 1924), Chaps. 1–4. The poor state of the industrial worker was caused by many factors, including large-scale immigration, a decline in real wages, and the general social confusion that has typically characterized the early phases of an industrial revolution.

[10] Fourier's voluminous writings are sparked alternately by the brilliant and the ridiculous. While some of his proposals anticipated social reforms that are now commonly accepted, he also spoke of domesticating beaver and zebra and predicted that some day the aurora borealis would be harnessed to supply heat and light to the Arctic regions. Basically, Fourier felt that social arrangements must be devised that would be compatible with man's passions, which numbered twelve according to his count. His suggestion was that people live in phalanxes where unproductive labor would be eliminated and work made attractive by various devices such as playful competition between working groups. The phalanx would consist of approximately 1800 persons living in an area of one square league. There would be roles for capital, labor, and talent, and a share of the output would go to each. Once the phalanxes were established, the rest of society apparently would be so impressed that ultimately the phalanx would become the basic form of social and economic organization.

ing and lecturing, spread the gospel. The idea of communal life where work and living arrangements would be ordered according to an elaborate blueprint had a certain amount of attraction for workers living in a society where order and hope had been displaced by confusion and fear. A phalanx was set up at Sylvania, Pennsylvania, and some forty others were subsequently established during the 1840's. Most of these experiments collapsed in short order. They were apart from the main stream of American life and were, essentially, sugar-coated efforts to resolve the shortcomings of a complex economy by a method that did not address itself to these complexities.

Producers' Co-operatives

Producers' and consumers' co-operatives enjoyed some popularity during this period. Producers' co-operatives, by opening an avenue for achievement of self-employment, could appeal at once to both the practical and idealistic sides of the worker's temperament. There was a spurt in the number of producers' co-ops established after 1836 when many unions had engaged in unsuccessful strikes. Throughout the forties and early fifties, such organizations continued to be established and were particularly popular among German workers whose recent experiences in the European revolutions resulted in an eagerness to participate in far-reaching reforms. These co-operatives were no more successful than the phalanxes. Inadequate financing, poor management, and employer opposition were among the major causes of failure. Enthusiasm for producers' co-operatives waned only to reappear at a later time in the century.

Consumers' Co-operatives

During the 1840's, interest in consumers' co-operatives also developed. Affecting economies by purchasing through co-operative societies was one answer to the widespread distress of the time. In New England, particularly, this movement prospered; and at one time the Working Men's Protective Association had several hundred separate co-operative purchasing divisions.[11] It is possible that this promising start in consumer co-operation might have led to an enduring co-operative movement in the United States if the confusion of the Civil War period had not upset the existing societies. Despite the numerous attempts made in co-operation in this and later periods, neither producers' nor consumers' co-operatives have been able to flourish in the United States on a scale comparable to some of the European movements.

---

[11] Selig Perlman, *The History of Trade Unionism in the United States* (New York: Augustus M. Kelley, Inc., 1950), p. 34.

Agrarianism

Another reform movement that drew large-scale labor support was "agrarianism." The radical frills of Skidmore's land reform program in the 1820's repelled many workers and were important contributing causes to the breakup of the labor party in New York. George Henry Evans, who had been associated with Skidmore, returned to the public scene in 1844 with an agrarian reform program that was palatable to labor as well as other groups. Briefly, Evans proposed that Congress dispose of public lands by giving free homesteads to actual settlers. Thus, wage earners would have the opportunity to become propertied land owners in the West. To the extent that this land policy drained workers from industrial employment, those remaining in the industrial East would be in a stronger bargaining position with employers.

To accomplish his objective, Evans proposed to ask candidates of existing political parties to pledge to support his program. Those willing to do so would receive labor support. This was a narrower approach to political action than the alternative of creating a new political party and was a forerunner of the "reward your friends, punish your enemies" policy that was to become a major feature of the political philosophy of the American Federation of Labor in later years.

Evans' land reform program was the most successful of the several movements afoot during the period under consideration. In 1862, Congress passed the homestead law which provided for grants of 160 acres to all settlers. It was not a complete victory, however, since the large-scale grants made to railroads ran counter to Evans' idea that land grants should be limited to small parcels.

By 1852 prosperity arrived in the wake of the California gold discoveries. Labor organizations lost interest in broad reform movements and vigorously turned to trade unionism. The Panic of 1857 had the usual effect of driving most of these unions to the wall. Before this occurred, however, a number of local unions had joined forces to form national organizations in specific trades. The printers, locomotive engineers, and hat finishers organized nationally in the early 1850's, and by 1859 the iron molders, machinists, and blacksmiths had also formed national unions. This was a harbinger of things to come.

THE NATIONAL LABOR UNION

While General Grant's divisions were wearing down the Confederate troops of General Lee of Appomattox, more than the Civil War was being brought to a close. An era in American capitalism was ending. The economy, hitherto characterized by the dominant forces of commercial and planter capitalism, was, for the remainder of the century, to be molded by an aggressive industrial capitalism. Profits earned during the Civil War were sufficiently large to provide the initial capital funds for industrial expansion, while a sympathetic Congress and judiciary were to provide a hospitable legal environment.

Industrial Growth

Industrial growth was, indeed, phenomenal. The number of persons employed in manufacturing increased from 1.3 million to 4.5 million in the last forty years of the century, while the number of manufacturing establishments grew from 140,000 to 512,000.[12] Names such as Jay Gould, John D. Rockefeller, and Andrew Carnegie were to be associated with fabulous industrial and financial empires as well as with hard-hitting and often ruthless techniques of business behavior. In oil, meat packing, steel, railroads, as well as in other industries, business was to become *big* business. Technological advances, the corporate form of business organization, a swelling labor supply fed by ever-increasing immigrant arrivals, and ingenious business arrangements such as trusts and pools were among the factors favoring a large-scale growth in business operations.

These developments, of course, had a serious impact on the wage earners of the nation. As the railroad trunk lines merged to form a transcontinental transportation system, a national market came into being. Toward the end of the century the large number of immigrant arrivals from southern and eastern Europe insured the existence of a large, docile labor supply capable of working in the new factories where the process of dividing the jobs into a number of simple operations was eliminating the need for many handicraft skills.

In view of the national scope of industrial competition and the presence of large numbers of unskilled workers who represented a constant threat to already achieved working standards, it is not surprising that the decade of the sixties witnessed a growth in the formation of national unions among the more skilled workers. Between 1864 and 1874, twenty-six national unions were organized.[13] Thus, as industry assumed new forms, labor organizations adjusted, in a structural sense, by attempting to develop forms that would be effective in the changed economic environment. Few of these national organizations, however, were able to emerge immediately as strong,

---

[12] John R. Craf, *Economic Development of the United States* (New York: Mc-Graw-Hill Book Company, 1952), pp. 310–311.

[13] Commons and Associates, *op. cit.*, II, 47. The largest of these national unions was the Knights of St. Crispin, a shoemakers' organization which at one time could boast of a membership of 50,000.

integrated unions. For the most part, the power centers continued to be the local unions and the city trade assemblies.

With this resurgence of trade unionism, the idea of creating an overall national labor organization began to grow in the minds of many labor leaders. As the war prosperity vanished, trade unions were finding it more difficult to win gains by economic action, and this spurred the search for alternative methods of pressing for labor objectives. The demand for an eight-hour day was becoming popular, and this too stimulated efforts to form a national federation.

National Federation

A convention met in Baltimore in 1866, and the National Labor Union came into being. Delegates represented local trade unions, city trade assemblies, national labor unions, and the eight-hour leagues which had been blossoming since 1864. In subsequent years, there were delegates from farmers' organizations, the Woman Suffrage Association, Negro groups, and miscellaneous reform movements. The National Labor Union was a loose federation. At all times it was torn by a certain amount of dissension; this was especially true over the question of whether primary emphasis should be placed upon trade unionism or legislative action. Although the union was to take stands on many questions, its major efforts were exerted in connection with the eight-hour day and the greenback movements.

At first, the National Labor Union centered its attention on the eight-hour day. The driving spirit behind this movement was a Boston machinist named Ira Steward. Essentially a man of one idea, Steward had developed an unusual chain of logic to support the physical fervor which he threw into the fight for a shorter working day. The major assumption in Steward's reasoning was that the worker's standard of living determined the wage level. By decreasing the working hours to eight per day, the worker's leisure time would increase and as a result his wants would multiply. The resulting quest for a higher standard of living would lead to a rise in wages and would stimulate industry in general. This, then, was more than an argument for shorter hours. It was a theory of economic progress.

The popularity of this movement is shown by the rapid growth in the number of eight-hour leagues. Between 1865 and 1877 some eighty local leagues came into existence.[14] In the National Labor Union, agitation was focused on the passage of an eight-hour law for employees of the federal government. Such a law was enacted in 1868, although it was ineffective until its meaning was clarified in 1872. Eight-hour laws were passed in a number of states, but there the victory was illusory. Workers could "will-

---

14 Perlman, *op. cit.*, p. 47.

ingly" contract to work longer hours, and few of the laws had any enforcement provisions.

Greenback Movement

In the National Labor Union, interest in the eight-hour movement had waned considerably by the time the second convention met in 1867. By this time, the members had become engrossed in "greenbackism." Until its demise in 1878, the greenback movement attracted a variety of groups interested for one reason or another in a government policy of easy money. Labor leaders, many of whom had seen their experiments in producers' co-operatives fail because of insufficient capital, proposed that greenback currency be made convertible into government bonds bearing interest at the rate of three per cent. The details of the plan are less important than the ultimate result that supposedly would flow from its achievement. Low interest rates would remove the bankers' stranglehold on available capital. Capitalism, as it existed, would eventually be replaced by a system of worker-owned co-operatives. The evils of the economic system would not be corrected on a piecemeal basis but instead would be bypassed by a fundamental reform financed in the first instance through credit made available by a specific government monetary policy.

By 1872, the National Labor Union was ready to undertake political action to further the greenback cause. Two years earlier, the trade unions, less eager to enter politics than to further the union movement by economic pressures, had withdrawn from the National Labor Union. Such membership as remained held a political convention and nominated Judge David Davis of Illinois for President. Davis, who at first accepted the nomination, later withdrew his candidacy. This served as the union's death blow.

The experience of the National Labor Union must be considered another failure of organized labor to function successfully in politics. Its efforts were pointed toward raising the status of labor as a whole at a time when a developing capitalism was operating strongly to create a permanent group of wage earners. Whatever the merits of its goals, the National Labor Union, like the Knights of Labor at a later time, was incapable of developing the techniques to accomplish them. The clash of interests between trade unions anxious to further the welfare of special groups of workers and a national labor organization with a visionary program to reform society for the benefit of all was to become even sharper in the approaching decades.

DEPRESSION AND VIOLENCE

Enough of the history of organized labor has been reviewed to show the devastating effects of depressed economic conditions on the various labor organizations. Living somewhat precarious lives even in prosperous times, oftentimes confused about goals and uncertain about the appropriate means for attaining them, the early unions generally collapsed when business conditions created hordes of workers hungry for work of any kind at almost any wages. That the Panic of 1873 took its toll of trade union lives, consequently, was neither surprising nor unusual.[15] Nor was the generation of hostile feeling between workers and employers unusual. Earlier history provided many examples of this. What was unusual about the decade, however, was the degree of violence that occurred when an adolescent labor movement and an immature capitalistic spirit collided in the midst of one of the nation's worst depressions.

Panic of 1873

The depression that began in 1873 and lasted until 1879 provided the setting for the labor uprisings. The economic upheaval that accompanied the Civil War foreshadowed a difficult process of postwar readjustment. The large volume of railroad construction—mileage was doubled between the close of the war and 1873—somewhat delayed this process. European funds which had financed much of the construction ceased to flow to the United States; hence, railroad expansion was curtailed. When Jay Cooke and Company, underwriters of the Northern Pacific Railroad, failed, a banking panic ensued.

The depression was severe. This was partly due to the overly rapid railroad expansion. Too much of the mileage, according to one observer, connected nothing in particular.[16] Since railroad construction accounted for such a substantial part of the total investment activity at this time, the depressing effect of curtailment in railroad expansion extended far beyond this industry. The price level dropped sharply, and business failures were common. Confusion in the government's monetary policy also contributed to the severity of the depression.

For the workers, all of this meant unemployment, hunger, and despair. Those who continued to work saw their wages slashed mercilessly. As the effects of the panic spread, thousands of the unemployed gathered in mass meetings to protest the pitiful conditions of their lives. With tension mounting, only a spark was necessary to touch off a social explosion. Unfortunately, more than one spark was provided.

Outbursts by workers took many forms and occurred in widely scattered localities. Many of these outbursts were spontaneous, such as the local disturbance of the Tompkins Square Riot in New York City. Here the

---

15 Total union membership fell from about 300,000 in 1873 to less than 50,000 in 1878.

16 Elmer C. Bratt, *Business Cycles and Forecasting* (Homewood, Ill.: Richard D. Irwin, Inc., 1953), p. 285.

mounted police, learning that radical agitators were going to address a gathering, charged into the crowd and applied their clubs with what the New York Times described as "reasonable but not excessive severity."[17] In the anthracite coal areas of Pennsylvania, the Molly Maguires carried on the practice of terrorism that had characterized the organization in its Irish homeland. Taking matters into their own hands, the "Mollies" sought to rectify low wages and intolerable working conditions by a campaign of deliberate and calculated murder and violence. Order returned to the coal fields only when the Molly Maguire leaders were apprehended and hanged for murder.[18]

Riots of 1877

Serious as these incidents may have been, they were minor in impact compared to the widespread riots in the railroad industry that rocked the nation in 1877. The railroad companies, although heavily overcapitalized, had continued to pay high dividends throughout the depression.[19] The farmers through high freight rates and the workers through reduced wages had borne the burden of sustaining inflated railroad stock values. So deep was the rancor among the workers that little by way of additional grievance was necessary to snap the tension.

On the Baltimore and Ohio, a proposed ten per cent wage cut after two prior reductions set off the chain of protest. At Martinsburg, West Virginia, a strike halted all freight movements and quickly spread to other junctions. When the local militia fraternized with the strikers, federal troops were requested by the governor of the state. These were sent, and they managed to move some trains. Meanwhile, disturbances had broken out in Baltimore. Here the National Guard and federal troops quelled a three day riot only after thirteen were killed and many wounded. Refusing to arbitrate the issues, the company eventually broke the strike with the liberal use of troops.

At Pittsburgh, strife occurred on the Pennsylvania Railroad. Militia from Philadelphia—the mistake of calling the local militia was not repeated —enraged the population by firing into a crowd and killing twenty persons. Twenty thousand infuriated people surrounded these troops, who finally

---

[17] Foster Rhea Dulles, *Labor in America* (New York: Thomas Y. Crowell Company, 1949), p. 116.

[18] This was accomplished largely as a result of the efforts of a Pinkerton detective who worked his way into the group and the gathered the evidence necessary to destroy it. From this time on, the "Pinkerton" was to play an active anti-union role. For a price the agency stood ready to supply labor spies, strikebreakers, and strong-arm men.

[19] Samuel Yellen, *American Labor Struggles* (New York: Harcourt, Brace & World, Inc., 1936), p. 6. The New York Central paid about eight per cent in cash dividends each year.

shot their way to safety. A fire broke out and destroyed some $5 million worth of railroad property. Looters took advantage of the situation to pilfer whatever they could carry, and order was restored only by patrols of citizen volunteers. Meanwhile the strike had spread to other cities, losing none of its violent character. Troop trains with mounted Gatling guns finally moved into Pittsburgh and broke the freight tie-up. On the Erie Railroad, on the New York Central, at Rochester, Syracuse, Chicago, St. Louis, on other railroads, and in other cities strikes flared and, after varying amounts of violence and disorder, were put down.

The railroad riots were spontaneous and poorly organized. If they had had better direction, possibly they would have been less easily quelled and, at least to a small degree, more successful. As it was, mobs of workers turned out to be a poor match against armed troops, hostile government officials, and an inflamed public opinion. The driving capitalistic spirit that motivated the railroad officialdom had no room for accommodation of deeply felt grievances of workers. The inflexibility of the employers—the president of the New York Central refused even to admit that his workers were on strike—their callous disregard of economic poverty, and the inability of the labor organizations to channel the discontent into effective protest created a situation where violence was the most probable result.

THE KNIGHTS OF LABOR

As the century drew to a close, a variety of ideologies competed for the allegiance of American workers. The worker who was attracted to the idea of joining his fellows to exert organized pressure could move in a number of directions. Seeds of socialist philosophies that had originated in Europe fell on American soil. Followers of Marx, Bakunin, and LaSalle in the United States not only inveighed against capitalism but battled ferociously among themselves. Henry George and his single-tax movement provided an indigenous radicalism. For a time, greenbackism, and later William Jennings Bryan's call for free silver, served as media for a political party type of protest. There were narrowly centered trade unions and a broad reform "uplift" union.

From this welter of sometimes competing and sometimes complementary philosophies, an enduring labor organization was to emerge; it was to be one that could find that hitherto elusive but essential ingredient of success —the capacity to survive. Before turning our attention to this successful organization, however, it is necessary to consider the experience of the Noble Order of the Knights of Labor, a group that in many respects represented an approach directly opposed to that of the more durable American Federation of Labor.

Founding

In 1869, a handful of tailors met in Philadelphia and secretly founded the Noble Order of the Knights of Labor. Times had been hard for labor groups. Determined employer resistance and economic depression had destroyed union after union until only a few remained. The secrecy of the order was justified as a necessary means of forestalling persecution by employers. In its early years, the Knights had an elaborate system of ritual, secret handshakes, and passwords which probably reflected, more than anything else, the fact that the leader, Uriah Stephens, was a Mason, an Odd Fellow, and a Knight of Pythias. The Order enjoyed only modest growth at first; and in 1879 Terence Powderly, who was to lead the group during the tumultuous phase of its career, succeeded Stephens as Grand Master Workman. After some controversy, the secrecy of the order was dropped.

Organization

The Knights had a triangular structure of organization. At the base were the local assemblies.[20] These might be mixed, that is, open to all workers, or trade assemblies, open only to members of specific trades. Local assemblies were affiliated with district assemblies, although the locals did have some discretion as to the district with which they might affiliate. The general asembly was at the peak. The problem of how skilled craft workers were to fit into this organizational scheme proved to be a vexing one and eventually was a contributing cause of the downfall of the organization.

"An injury to one is the concern of all." Thus the Knights of Labor stated their slogan. What Powderly visualized was one big union in which skilled workers would stand up for the unskilled; the strong would support the weak; all would behave as though an injury to one was, in fact, the concern of all.[21] In Powderly's philosophy, the villain was the wage system. This was the cause of man's degradation. Under this system, material considerations took precedence over moral ones. The wage system had to be bypassed, but Powderly did not consider a violent class struggle as a solution.[22] His means were to be education, legislation, and reform. The

[20] Local assemblies were to be composed of not fewer than ten workers, of whom three-fourths were to be wage workers. Membership in the Knights of Labor was open to all except persons in specified occupational categories, such as lawyers, doctors, bankers, and saloon keepers.

[21] In his autobiography, Powderly noted wistfully that in the experience of the Knights the concern of one had often been made the occasion of an injury to all. Terence V. Powderly, *The Path I Trod* (New York: Columbia University Press, 1940), p. 62.

[22] Powderly, far from favoring violence, was actively opposed to it. He would not favor a strike unless the cause was just and every reasonable effort had been made to avert the strike. He boasted that he had never ordered a strike and that he was directly responsible for the settlement of 408 labor disputes. *Ibid.,* pp. 105, 106.

ultimate goal was to have an economic system composed of worker-owned co-operatives. In theory, at least, the Knights of Labor was motivated by a long run visionary objective designed to raise the economic and social status of all workers.[23]

Rise and Decline

The fortunes of the Knights of Labor after 1879 can be shown by its membership statistics. In that year there were 9,000 members. After secrecy was dropped, this increased to 42,000 by 1882 and to 100,000 by 1885. Before another year had passed, the membership figure jumped to 700,000.[24] Within two years, membership dropped to 200,000; and by 1893 it had fallen to 75,000.

What was behind this swift rise and decline? Important among the factors accounting for the growth was victory in several important strikes. Although deprecating the strike weapon, leaders of the Knights frequently found units of the order embroiled in bitter disputes. When Jay Gould capitulated to the union's demands in a threatened strike on the Wabash Railroad, the Knights were so swamped by a rush of would-be members that organizers had to suspend formation of new assemblies for a time. Press reports contributed to the notoriety of the union and magnified the potential power of the group. For instance, an article in the New York *Sun* pictured the executive board of the Knights as persons holding the power to grind the economy of the nation to a halt at will. These exaggerated reports undoubtedly impressed many workers at the time. For publicity, however, the Knights did not rely upon the press. Numerous lecturers were sent out to address public meetings and win recruits. To the unskilled and semi-skilled workers, the Knights of Labor represented the only apparently effective labor organization that would welcome them. Rejected by the unions of skilled tradesmen, the unskilled found the hospitality of the Knights especially warm by comparison.

Dissolution

The immediate causes of the dissolution of the Knights of Labor may be distinguished from a number of underlying causes. In an immediate sense, the fortunes of the order took a turn for the worse when a certain cockiness

---

[23] The "First Principles" adopted by the Knights in 1878 listed the following immediate goals among others: direct representation and legislation, the initiative and referendum, establishment of bureaus of labor statistics, taxation of unearned increments in land values, compulsory arbitration of labor disputes, prohibition of child labor, government ownership of the railroad systems, the eight-hour day, and free coinage of silver at a ratio of sixteen to one.

[24] These figures overstate the size of the Knights of Labor, although it is not possible to know by how much. Membership was unstable, and the turnover rate was high.

engendered by the flush of victory led to a series of strikes that were defeated. The earlier victory over Jay Gould was nullified when a strike that began on the Texas and Pacific and spread to other roads ended in complete failure. In the meantime, the reviving national trade unions, joined together in a Federation of Organized Trades and Labor Unions, started to agitate for a general strike to promote the eight-hour day. Powderly issued a secret circular opposing the participation of members of the Knights in this strike. On May 1, 1886, thousands of workers throughout the country went on strike, and many of the Knights of Labor were among them.[25] Very few lasting gains resulted from this strike movement, and the absence of support from the Knights was resentfully regarded by many workers as a contributing cause of this failure. Later during the year, a dispute over the eight-hour day broke out in the Swift and Company Chicago plant and soon spread through the stockyards. The packers' association held fast to the ten-hour day and also announced that members of the Knights of Labor would not be employed in the future. Although the workers appeared to be on the way to victory, Powderly cut the ground from under the strikers by sending a telegram ordering them back to work. This type of inept leadership plus the increasingly adamant resistance of employers turned the tide against the Knights, and the membership exodus began.

Aside from these specific causes of failure, it is probable that their philosophy, ideals, structure, and leadership would have doomed the Knights to eventual extinction. The technical structure, with the general assembly supposedly having complete authority over the districts and locals, was inconsistent with the weak leadership of the group. When bold steps were in order, again and again the leadership proved to be bumbling and inept. Too often, local units took the initiative and created situations with which the general assembly was unable to cope.

Philosophically, the Knights were confused as to the nature of their quarrel with the capitalist class. Eschewing conflict, disdaining violence,

---

[25] The strike was the background for the Haymarket Square affair, one of the important landmarks in the nation's history. Two days after the strike for the eight-hour day, Chicago police killed four strikers at the McCormick Harvester plant. A protest meeting was organized by members of the Black International, a small band of anarchist extremists. The meeting had been peaceful and was on the verge of breaking up when a police detachment arrived and ordered the crowd to disperse. A bomb was thrown into the police ranks. In the ensuing melee, seven police and four workers were killed and more than a hundred persons were injured. The reaction of the nation was one of hysteria and outrage. Eight anarchist leaders were arrested, and seven of these were sentenced to death although there was no evidence to connect these persons with the bombing. Two of the convicted saved their lives by pleading for executive clemency and receiving life sentences. Governor Altgeld pardoned these men six years later, for which act he suffered bitter personal attack. The Knights of Labor joined in the wholesale condemnation of the anarchists and was violent in its denunciation of them. This behavior, however, did not protect the Knights from the strong wave of anti-labor feeling that followed the bomb explosion in Haymarket Square.

anxious to avoid head-on collision with employers, the order, nevertheless, was unable to develop the capacity for settling labor disputes peacefully. Motivated by a visionary program of long run reform, the Knights of Labor rose and declined on the basis of success and failure in the clash for immediates. In the area of activity where fundamental reform was attempted, that of producers' co-operatives, the Knights were no more successful than were former co-operative organizations.

The idealistic belief that all workers had a common cause and that the skilled would support the unskilled proved to be untenable in practice. The Knights were rarely successful in working out techniques to accommodate the skilled workers. These latter workers, anxious to improve conditions in their own trades, frequently found themselves faced with conflicting loyalties. The standards of the skilled were often threatened by the presence of masses of unskilled workers, and when this situation arose it was usually the broader loyalty that was abandoned. The conflict between the Knights of Labor and the trade unions greatly increased; and the relationship between Powderly and Samuel Gompers, who represented the trade union viewpoint, became personally bitter.

The experience of the Knights of Labor might be regarded as the last fling during the nineteenth century of a broad reformist approach to union organization. As such it came into competition with a narrower approach represented by the organized tradesmen; and, in this competition, it was the loser. In the following chapter, we first turn our attention to the group that was to dominate the history of organized labor for many years, the American Federation of Labor.

SUMMARY

Organization by workers took place in one form or another almost since the inception of the United States government. The particular form of these group efforts, however, varied over time and tended to reflect prevailing economic, social, and political conditions. The sensitivity of trade union fortunes to business conditions has been stressed repeatedly in this chapter. The economist Pigou has noted that although business cycles are of the same family, no two are twins. In a similar vein, it can be stated that although trade unions tended to collapse during the depressions of the nineteenth century, the subsequent reactions of workers varied in the different periods. After the Panic of 1819, recovery occurred gradually, and trade union activity revived simultaneously. In the 1840's, utopian notions prevailed. In the 1870's, there were violent social explosions. Even if there is a pattern to this history, the variations are perhaps as significant as the pattern itself.

Labor union structure changed as the character of markets changed. Primarily local in form when the areas of economic relationships were geographically restricted, union structure embraced larger forms as the frontier moved westward and a railroad network welded local and regional product markets into national ones. Institutions adapt to changing conditions slowly, however, and the concentration of power in national organizations as opposed to local or regional entities was not accomplished overnight. At the point we have reached in this history, however, this transfer of power was occurring in discernible proportions.[26] As a rough generalization, it is not inaccurate to state that the character of labor union structure has tended to parallel the scope of the relevant product markets.

The character of labor movements in the nineteenth century was often colored by an ultimate objective that involved a fundamental transformation of the worker's status. Whether the movement involved co-operation, communalism, or political action, the goal, more often than not, reflected a worker desire to be something other than a worker. The presence of a land frontier, the still predominantly agricultural nature of the economy, a philosophical tradition of equal opportunity to all, and the absence of any obvious indicators of the difficulty of rising to a propertied status were forces that could channel the energies of organizations in the direction of fundamental societal reform rather than toward the achievement of immediate needs. If the labor movements in the twentieth century United States are different from those of the nineteenth, one reason is the increasing acceptance by workers of the fact of permanent worker status.

In the period under survey, the legislative branch of the government generally ignored worker organizations; the executive branch, for the most part, was out of sympathy with them; and the courts had a record of hostility tempered only by occasional qualms.

QUESTIONS

1. List the various methods by which workers attempted to improve their living conditions in the nineteenth century. Can you think of any methods used in the present century that were not used in the last one?

2. Does it seem logical to you that labor organizations should have difficulty during depressions and should thrive during prosperity as was generally the case in the nineteenth century? Explain.

---

[26] It would be an oversimplification to regard any point in time as the precise instant in which national labor unions became the dominant bodies. Even today there are union organizations in which the balance of power between national and local headquarters is a precarious balance. Furthermore, particular local unions affiliated with national organizations may carry more weight at national headquarters than other affiliated locals.

3. How do you explain the fact that the co-operative movement has never flourished in the United States as it has in many European nations?

4. Much of the worker degradation in the United States during the nineteenth century was a by-product of the industrial revolution. It has been noted that a similar degradation has accompanied the industrial revolution that has taken place in the present century in the Soviet Union. This has led some observers to conclude that a certain amount of human misery is a price that must be paid for industrialization regardless of the form of the economy. Do you agree?

SELECTED READINGS

DULLES, FOSTER R. *Labor in America*. New York: Thomas Y. Crowell Company, 1949. Chaps. 1–8.

GROB, GERALD N. *Workers and Utopia*. Evanston, Ill.: Northwestern University Press, 1961.

MILLIS, HARRY A., and MONTGOMERY, ROYAL E. *Organized Labor*. New York: McGraw-Hill Book Company, 1945. Chap. 2.

PELLING, HENRY. *American Labor*. Chicago: The University of Chicago Press, 1960. Chaps. 1–3.

WARE, NORMAN. *The Industrial Worker*. Boston: Houghton Mifflin Company, 1924.

CHAPTER 4

The AFL and The CIO

THE HISTORY OF ORGANIZED LABOR IN THE LATE NINETEENTH CENTURY and in the twentieth century encompasses more than the fortunes of the American Federation of Labor and the Congress of Industrial Organization. The important developments with which a broad survey must deal, however, are closely interwoven with the formation and subsequent histories of these major organizations. This chapter, consequently, will deal primarily with these two labor bodies.

SAMUEL GOMPERS

The early history of the AFL is, to a considerable extent, a history of the efforts of Samuel Gompers. Determined, energetic, and resilient in the face of many disappointments, Gompers continued in his efforts to build an organization while oftentimes depriving himself and his family of the most basic needs. Selected as the first president of the AFL after its formation in 1886, Gompers served in that capacity, with the exception of one year, until his death in 1924. Until 1891 he was the only full-time officer of the federation. For a period, his office was the front room of his apartment. Funds were scarce, and even the purchase of a second-hand typewriter involved a major financial decision. From such modest beginnings, the AFL was able to grow into a giant federation. Its early survival can be attributed to a leadership that was determined to foster a specific type of unionism. It was a narrower and less visionary unionism than the one exemplified in the philosophy of the Knights of Labor, but it had the merit of being able to survive in an environment that was as inhospitable to the AFL as it had been to earlier labor groups. Gompers and his fellow leaders built well—perhaps too well. At a later date when new times called for new tactics, the AFL was lacking in a necessary flexibility.

Samuel Gompers was born in London, the son of a Jewish cigarmaker of Dutch extraction. When he was thirteen the family migrated to the United States. For the Gompers family, the move was from East London to the east side of New York City. In an economic sense, life was not much easier in the new country.

Gompers' formal education ended when he was ten. His subsequent education was drawn from such sources as the free night lectures at Cooper Union, debating groups, and discussions with fellow workers in the cigar-making establishments where he worked.[1] He moved into union work at an early age. It was some time, however, before his labor philosophy crystallized. As he put it, he was groping his way through a mass of impressions, impulses, and theories.[2] In time, he developed a strong appreciation for the practical and a contempt for the radical and the utopian. He saw the National Labor Union flounder on the rocks of political action, and this helped him to decide against a politically oriented unionism.

At union meetings, at the shops where he worked, in the back room of Justus Schwab's saloon, he heard socialist thought and socialist plans. In 1879, he helped to draft a local union constitution that contained this clause:

> We recognize the solidarity of the whole working class to work harmoniously against the common enemy—the capitalists. . . . United we are a power to be respected; divided we are the slaves of the capitalists.

In a speech at the 1903 convention of the AFL, Gompers, addressing himself to the socialists present, stated:

> I declare to you that I am not only at variance with your doctrines, but with your philosophy. Economically, you are unsound; socially, you are wrong; industrially, you are an impossibility.

In the years separating these statements, Gompers had apparently grown bitter, first toward the socialists, and then toward socialism. He found the

---

[1] It was not an uncommon practice at the time for the workers to chip in to pay the wages of one who would read to the others while they rolled their cigars. Because his voice was strong, Gompers was often called upon to do this reading. In his biography, he likened these shop discussions to public debating societies. Samuel Gompers, *Seventy Years of Life and Labor* (New York: E. P. Dutton & Co., Inc., 1925), I, 81.

[2] *Ibid.*, p. 103.

constant struggles between the Marxists and the LaSalleans irritating, and he resented the socialists' maneuvers to use the union movement as a tool to achieve ultimate political goals. It is no overstatement to say that, at least in the early years of the AFL history, Gompers' efforts were directed as much toward fighting socialist control of the trade unions as they were toward bolstering the unions against employer opposition. Gompers' difficulties with the Knights of Labor further cemented his attitudes regarding the "correct" type of unionism.

The AFL is often cited as an example of "pure and simple" unionism. The connotation of the phrase "pure and simple" is that primary emphasis is placed upon the achievement of immediate gains, such as higher wages and shorter working hours. Testifying before a congressional committee, Adolf Strasser, president of the cigarmakers' union, claimed that he had no ultimate goal, he worked on a day-to-day basis. This was probably an overstatement. What is important, however, is that idealistic notions of fundamental reform did not deter AFL leadership from doing the hard and often dirty job of building solid, well-knit trade unions that could withstand attack and be effective instruments to improve the worker's lot in an immediate sense.

In practice this type of unionism had various facets, all of them reflecting in one way or another labor experiences of the past. Organization was primarily by craft units; leadership by non-worker intellectuals was resisted; gains were to be won by the economic power of unions rather than by legislative action; strong emphasis on craft autonomy meant that the national unions were to be independent in their internal affairs.

Gompers fought for this type of labor unionism. His philosophy was blended from his personal experiences with socialists, the Knights of Labor, employment conditions in his own trade, the government, and a widespread acquaintance with all manner of men who led or aspired to lead the workers in the United States. In industry, concentration of economic power unfettered by government restraint had been the key to economic success. Gompers proposed to use the same key for the benefit of labor unions.

The different strands of this philosophy will be examined in greater detail in the following section.

AFL CHARACTERISTICS

At all times there were groups affiliated with the American Federation of Labor that were somewhat at odds with the dominant philosophy of the Federation. The description of basic AFL characteristics that follows, consequently, must be read with the understanding that these describe elements of the labor philosophies of an effective majority of the Federation's membership. The implication should not be drawn that within AFL councils there was ever a 100 per cent unanimity as to what constitutes a "correct" type of unionism.

Economic Unionism

As we have seen, in the nineteenth century workingmen were attracted at times to economic unionism and at times to political unionism. In the AFL the die was cast for the former approach. Workers organized in strong unions would be possessed of an economic power that constituted the most effective weapon for achievement of labor goals. When the economic power of employers was matched by the economic power of labor, workers would be in a good position to demand and win benefits for themselves.

The Political Perspective

Did a concentration on economic power preclude any interest in political matters? No, but it did limit the amount and nature of such interest. Political office seekers friendly to labor were to be supported; others were to be opposed. Support for specific pieces of legislation, such as prohibition of child labor and restriction of immigration, was not precluded by a policy of limited political action. On the other hand, suggestions for the formation of a labor political party were opposed on the grounds that such a party would probably fail and an expensive division of the energies of the labor movement would be the necessary consequence of independent political party action.

Some insight into this political philosophy can be derived from Gompers' reaction to anti-trust legislation. Concentration of industry, he believed, was a natural development of economic forces that was stronger than legislative or police powers. He had no faith in the effectiveness of government control of monopoly power and hence was opposed to the Sherman Anti-Trust Act. Control there must be, but it must be worked out by the economic world according to its own procedures and principles of order. Labor unions were important and necessary agencies for the development of this control. What Gompers wanted from the government, essentially, was not help but freedom for unions to do a voluntary job of policing industry for the benefit of their members and, ultimately, for the benefit of all society. This freedom involved, among other things, specific limitations on the right of the courts to issue injunctions against union activities and exemption of unions from prosecution under the anti-trust laws.[3]

---

[3] *Ibid.*, II, 26, *passim.*

Craft Unions

The Knights of Labor attempted to weld all workers into one big union. This attempt failed; and when national unions of skilled workers organized the AFL, in part they were registering discontent with the "one big union" idea. Organization of unions along craft lines was consistent with the Federation's emphasis on economic power. In a period when few workers belonged to unions, this type of power could best be developed by labor unions composed of workers occupying strategic positions in the industrial process. The vast numbers of the unskilled, fed by a continuous stream of immigrants, were not regarded as proletarian partners by the skilled. More often they were thought of as economic menaces against whom protective barriers must be raised. The craft union, with its restrictive membership requirements, constituted such a barrier.

The demand for industrial unionism, in which all workers in an industry are included in the same union regardless of type of work performed, was made frequently during the early career of the AFL.[4] Possibly because this demand came primarily from the socialist elements in the AFL, resolutions favoring organization along industrial lines were consistently defeated at the Federation's annual conventions. The problem, however, did call for attention, and the early solutions were in the nature of minor concessions to a broader type of union organization. In the Scranton Declaration of 1901, the Federation went on record as favoring the amalgamation of closely allied crafts. Formation of departments such as the Building Trade Department provided an organizational unit where unions with common interests could foster some degree of relationship to one another. Despite these efforts and in spite of the fact that certain unions such as the United Mine Workers were organized on an industry basis, the AFL remained basically a craft-oriented labor federation until relatively recent times.

Autonomy of the National Unions

The American Federation of Labor was organized as a voluntary association of national labor unions. National unions were to be autonomous insofar as their internal affairs were concerned. Matters such as dues to be paid by the rank and file of workers, elections of officers, intensity of organizing activity, etc. were to be completely within the provinces of the national unions. The primary power of the Federation rested in its right to grant charters to the nationals. The charter defined the jurisdiction of

---

[4] For a concise description of this early agitation for industrial organization, see Louis S. Reed, *The Labor Philosophy of Samuel Gompers* (New York: Columbia University Press, 1930), pp. 131–137.

the national union; and whenever jurisdictional disputes arose, the Federation supposedly had the power to determine these disputes. Even here, however, the Federation frequently found itself without the power to enforce its decisions. The significance of this type of organizational structure was that the power centers in the AFL came to be the national unions. The Federation can be described as a co-ordinator, advisor, helper, and at times an exhorter. Thus, it was a body that supplemented the power of the national unions affiliated with it.

AFL Objectives

The concentration of the AFL upon immediate goals such as higher wages, shorter hours, and improved working conditions rather than upon ultimate goals such as major social reforms has already been noted. This approach did not deny the existence of a conflict of interest between workers and employers, but it did deny that such a conflict had to have the revolutionary consequences described by the socialists. Within the capitalistic system, according to AFL philosophy, there was room for worker organizations seeking to win the benefits of the system by methods not too unlike those used by the capitalists themselves.

In summary then, in its formative years the AFL was a loose federation of autonomous national labor unions organized primarily among skilled workers with the major objective of winning material gains for these workers.

SOME EARLY EXPERIENCES

The AFL was born at an unpropitious time. The superficial successes of the Knights of Labor aroused a fear of organized labor in many quarters. Anti-labor feeling was at a high pitch because of the Haymarket affair.

The main barrier against successful unionism, however, was a resultant of the economic phase through which the nation was passing. American capitalism was at triumphant heights; and the industrial capitalist, ruthless in his relationship with his fellow businessmen, was not inclined to be receptive to challenges from his employees. Professor Hacker has caught this capitalistic spirit in an excellent passage:

> The ranks of the industrialist-capitalist host were filled with shrewd, energetic, personally frugal (in the beginning) young men who originated for the most part in the petty bourgeoisie, who were distrustful of finance, who managed their own concerns, and who carefully watched and tended their businesses, expanding them by the plowing back of profits. Their personal psychologies were curious: having come up from the ranks they were dangerous and hard bitten antagonists who never yielded an inch to

competitors or workers; adept at in-fighting, they took advantage of every opening, corrupting government officials and rivals' employees according to the rules (or rather, no-rules) of rough and tumble combat. . . .[5]

Representing a conservative type of unionism, the AFL was caught in a curious crossfire of attack. To the employer, it was a threat to his property and his right to conduct his business as he saw fit. To the radical, the AFL amounted to a betrayal of the historical revolutionary mission of the proletariat. The AFL and the unions affiliated with it, consequently, faced not one but a variety of hazards, the nature of which will be summarized briefly.

Attack from the Left

The labor philosophy inherent in the AFL approach could not help but invite attack from the several socialist sects committed to programs of fundamental change in economic society. The tactics employed in the socialist efforts to take over the American labor movement consisted of "boring from within"—working from within the existing unions with the idea of taking them over—and "dual unionism," which involved the establishment of socialist unions to rival the non-socialist labor organizations.

These skirmishes extended over a period of years, and only a few examples will be cited here. At the 1890 convention of the AFL, a charter was refused to the socialistic Central Labor Federation of New York on the grounds that it was a political organization. At the 1894 Denver convention, socialist delegates submitted a program for Federation approval. Controversy centered upon "Plank Ten," which called for collective ownership of the means of production and distribution. By parliamentary maneuvers, the AFL leadership managed to defeat this resolution. In the process, however, Gompers was unseated as president for a one-term period. A Socialist Trade and Labor Alliance was established in 1895 as an AFL rival, but it never managed to develop into a serious threat.

In 1905, the IWW (Industrial Workers of the World) was formed at Chicago. It consisted of the Western Federation of Miners, a conglomeration of socialist groups, and a scattering of dissatisfied AFL locals. In its preamble, the IWW boldly proclaimed that workers and capitalists had nothing in common. Its philosophy envisioned a final overthrow of the capitalist system to be accomplished by organizing workers into militant industrial unions. In all respects—philosophy, tactics, membership, goals—the IWW was the antithesis of the AFL. It appealed to the unskilled, re-

---

[5] Louis M. Hacker, *The Triumph of American Capitalism* (New York: Columbia University Press, 1947 printing), p. 401. (This quotation is reproduced here with the permission of Columbia University Press.)

fused to recognize the sanctity of agreements with employers, and believed that an industrial form of organization was essential for the waging of class warfare. In contrast to the immediate and material goals of the AFL, the IWW visualized an ultimate socialism. Although they engaged in many struggles for immediate benefits, the IWW leaders regarded these struggles primarily as steps to the ultimate goal. In IWW philosophy there was no admission that a strike could be lost. The strike was a positive good in itself in that it was a necessary step toward socialism.

In a stormy career, the IWW waged its fights on battlefronts that ranged from Seattle to Paterson. Before the termination of World War I, it had directed or participated in some 150 strikes plus a number of "free speech" fights that developed when local authorities interfered with IWW organizational efforts.

The appeal of the IWW found its greatest response among the unskilled and casual workers. By 1912 it could boast of a membership of about 100,000. These were mainly migratory agricultural workers, lumberjacks, dockworkers, and textile mill employees. Never characterized by an elaborate formal organization, the IWW suffered from this informality in that it failed to develop some technique for consolidating and stabilizing its membership. The final decline of the IWW had more fundamental causes, however. One cause was the inability of rival factions within the organization to accommodate their differences. Shortly after the formation of the IWW, the powerful Western Federation of Miners withdrew and additional splits occurred several years later as a result of squabbles between representatives of the Socialist Labor party and the Socialist party. The instability caused by internal dissension was compounded by severe government repression. The IWW took an anti-war stand during World War I. As a result, most of its important leaders were sentenced to prison terms. Membership losses to the newly organized Communist party of the United States after World War I ended the effective phase of the IWW in American labor history.

The IWW, thus, did not survive as a rival of the AFL. Nevertheless, the fact that it was able to flourish, even briefly, was partly due to the structural and philosophical weaknesses of the AFL. These same weaknesses were to prove troublesome to the AFL in the years ahead.

Attack from the Right

Average annual membership in American labor unions increased from 447,000 in 1897 to more than 2 million in 1904.[6] Roused into action by this increasing power of labor, organizations of employers engaged in a variety of counter-attacks that seriously hindered the further growth of unions.

---

[6] Leo Wolman, *Ebb and Flow in Trade Unionism* (New York: National Bureau of Economic Research, 1936), p. 16.

In terms of their attitudes toward labor unions, employer associations have been classified as "negotiatory," "belligerent," and "mediatory."[7] The year 1903 marks the beginning of a period of pronounced belligerence by such associations.

Organized in 1895 to promote business interests, by 1903 the National Association of Manufacturers was mainly engaged in promoting the "open" or non-union shop. Among the other groups that moved into the anti-union fight were the American Anti-Boycott Association, The National Metal Trades Association, the National Founders Association, and the Citizens Industrial Association.

Devices used by these associations included the blacklist—agreements not to give jobs to known union sympathizers—lobbying, newspaper advertisements attacking labor unions, use of strikebreakers, and organization of counter unions.[8]

At least in a short run sense, this anti-union drive was effective. The rate of union growth slowed considerably after 1904. Such a foothold as unions had managed to achieve outside of the large urban centers was eradicted, and attitudes generated in small town rural America constituted an almost impregnable barrier against union penetration. By picturing the labor union idea as something alien to the American scene, employers' associations had hit upon a chord that drew public response. This together with the specific devices used, while not eliminating unionism, did contain its growth.

During this period, the one pronounced example of a "mediatory" type of employer association was the National Civic Federation. Employer representatives, professional people, and labor leaders—Gompers was vice chairman for a time—constituted the membership of an association that was ready to bestow some sympathy upon labor unions and even to combat some of the propaganda of the NAM. By participating in this organization, some of the AFL leaders hoped to gain a fair public hearing of their positions; and, to some extent, they did. All in all, however, the net gains for organized labor that could be attributed to the National Civic Federation were modest in character.

Homestead and Pullman

During the 1890's, two events occurred that have since been regarded as highlights in American labor history. In our analysis, we are more concerned with the implications than with the events themselves.

---

[7] Clarence E. Bonnett, "Employers Associations," reprinted in E. Wight Bakke and Clark Kerr, *Unions, Management, and the Public* (New York: Harcourt, Brace & World, Inc., 1949), p. 337.

[8] For a fuller listing of these devices see Robert F. Hoxie, *Trade Unionism in the United States* (New York: Appleton-Century & Appleton-Century-Crofts, 1917), chap. 8, *passim*.

The Homestead Steel strike in 1892 involved the Carnegie Steel Company and the Amalgamated Association of Iron and Steel Workers, once described as the strongest union that the American labor movement had yet produced.[9] Union and management relationships had not been unfriendly, and in 1889 a three-year labor agreement had been signed. Andrew Carnegie had publicly expressed himself in favor of labor unions; but the workers began to have feelings of uneasiness when the management of the company was turned over to Henry C. Frick, a person of known anti-union sympathies. This feeling was justified. Terms of the new contract offered to labor called for a wage reduction and included other unfavorable clauses. During the strike—or more accurately the lockout—that ensued, the company called upon Pinkerton strikebreakers, the state militia, and the local courts for assistance. After a strike of five months, the workers capitulated. Unionism was eliminated at Homestead and in most of the other Pittsburgh area steel mills.

A strong union had clashed with a modern corporation and had been routed. Labor organizations were driven from the steel industry not to return in any strength until the CIO's organizing drives of the 1930's. Not only steel but most of the large-scale factory industries remained impervious to union organization until the New Deal decade. The resources of the giant corporation proved to be more than a match for the degree of power represented by AFL philosophy and organizational techniques.

In June, 1894, employees of the Pullman Palace Car Company struck in protest against a 25 per cent to 40 per cent wage cut and against living conditions in their company-dominated town. Earlier these workers had joined the American Railway Union, an industrial union of railroad workers that had been organized by Eugene Debs when he became dissatisfied with the timidity and caution of the Railroad Brotherhoods. When Debs ordered a boycott against all trains with Pullman Cars, the strike spread in scope. The contest developed into one between the American Railway Union and the General Managers Association, a voluntary association of the managements of twenty-four railroads radiating out of Chicago.

The strike interfered with transportation of the mails, and there was also interference with interstate commerce. On these grounds, the federal government found the necessary justification for moving against the strikers. President Cleveland sent federal troops to Illinois over the protest of Governor Altgeld. More important, however, was the move by federal attorneys to obtain a court injunction restraining the strikers from interfering with the mails or with the flow of interstate commerce. The injunction issued by the circuit court was so sweeping that, literally, any positive action taken by the strikers would have placed them in contempt of the

---

[9] Perlman, *op. cit.,* p. 133.

court order. Debs and other strike leaders were, in fact, sentenced to prison terms for violating the injunction. The combined opposition of the employers and the government was too strong. The strike collapsed, as did the American Railway Union.

For the organized labor movement there were several significant facets in the denouement of the Pullman strike. The circuit court had relied in part upon the Sherman Anti-Trust Act to support its legal logic. When the union leadership appealed its convictions, the Supreme Court avoided a direct ruling on the applicability of the Sherman Act to organized labor activities and sustained the conviction on other grounds.[10] Nevertheless, there was cause for labor to be concerned about possible court attitudes should a direct test of this issue arise. More disconcerting, however, was the facility with which the courts had found it possible to justify the issuance of injunctions against the use of traditional labor weapons in labor disputes. The business interests had found an ally in the courts; and the AFL, which had not been involved in the Pullman strike—Gompers resisted a plea by Debs to have AFL unions engage in sympathy strikes—was hereafter forced to devote a substantial part of its energies to fighting a series of legal battles in front of judges who were more inclined to sympathize with property interests than with labor aspirations.

Organized Labor and the Government

There is no such thing as *a* government attitude toward organized labor. The executive, legislative, and judicial branches and the federal, state, and local levels of government all have opportunities to relate to organized labor in numerous ways. There is no reason to believe that the attitudes of all these governments will be similar in labor or other matters.

In the time period under consideration here, the most antagonistic attitudes were generally expressed by the courts. The federal legislative and executive branches were somewhat less hostile and after 1900 moved slowly in the direction of increased sympathy. President Cleveland had had few qualms about using the power of his office to crush the railroad strike. In the 1902 dispute between the United Mine Workers and the anthracite coal operators, President Theodore Roosevelt, by way of contrast, used his influence to force the owners to submit the issues to arbitration.[11] Reluctantly they did so; and although the award of the President's commission was not a complete victory for the miners, neither was it a complete defeat.

---

[10] *In re Debs,* 158 U.S. 564.

[11] It was during this dispute that George F. Baer, spokesman for the coal operators, made his oft-quoted remark: "The rights and interests of the laboring man will be protected and cared for—not by the labor agitators but by the Christian men to whom God in his infinite wisdom has given control of the property interests of this country. . . ."

One of the first expressions of legislative sympathy with the cause of organized labor occurred in 1898 when Congress passed the Erdman Act. Section 10 of this law prohibited discrimination by interstate railways against workers because of union membership. Prior to this there had been little labor union legislation enacted by legislative bodies.

Restricted by unfavorable court decisions in the matters of strikes, boycotts, picketing, and organizational rights, the AFL attempted to obtain relief by exerting political pressure on the Congress. A Bill of Grievances was submitted to Congress, but this was ignored until the Clayton Act of 1914 was enacted during the Woodrow Wilson administration. Section 6 of this act declared that the labor of a human being was not a commodity. Section 20 seemed to offer labor unions some relief from the hostility of the courts. Labor leaders breathed more easily. Gompers called the act "labor's Magna Charta."

The "victory" lasted only until the relevant issues could be brought to test before the Supreme Court. The type of legal problem faced by organized labor can probably best be illustrated by citing a number of representative court rulings.[12] In a case involving the above mentioned Erdman Act, the court ruled that an interference with the employer's right to fire a worker because of union membership was an arbitrary interference with freedom of contract and a violation of the fifth amendment.[13] In the Danbury-Hatters Case, the court resolved all questions about the applicability of the Sherman Anti-Trust Act to organized labor. A secondary boycott that affected interstate commerce was illegal under the law.[14] In *Gompers* v. *Buck Stove and Range Company*, the court ruled that a listing of the company's name in a "we don't patronize" column of a union newspaper was an illegal secondary boycott.[15] As for Section 20 of the Clayton Act, the wording of this section was sufficiently vague so that in *Duplex* v. *Deering*, the Supreme Court was able to rule, in effect, that the section meant nothing in particular and unions were as much subject to limitations by court injunctions as they had been before the passage of the act.[16]

The attitudes of the different branches of the government showed that the executive and legislative arms were somewhat more influenced by the changing climate of public opinion than were the courts. The literary output of the muckrakers had exposed the sordid side of business operations, and Theodore Roosevelt had fixed his glare upon the monopolistic aspects

---

[12] Many of the court decisions cited here will be examined in greater detail in Chapter 16. The cases are mentioned here to illustrate court attitudes during a special period of union history.

[13] *Adair* v. *U.S.*, 208 U.S. 161 (1908). A similar law enacted by the state of Kansas was declared unconstitutional in *Coppage* v. *Kansas*, 236 U.S. 1.

[14] *Loewe* v. *Lawlor*, 208 U.S. 274 (1908).

[15] 221 U.S. 418 (1911).

[16] 254 U.S. 443 (1921).

of business behavior. It was a progressive era, and society was ready to accept a humanitarian type of limitation on the excesses of laissez-faire. In the courtrooms, however, the judges showed less awareness of the temper of the times. The sanctity of contractual rights and the novel theory that the expectations of business were a form of property that must be protected against damage in the same manner as physical property pervaded the legal decisions that struck down the economic pressure activities of organized labor time and again. Only in the dissenting opinions of Justices Holmes and Brandeis was there an anticipation of the sociological jurisprudence that was one day to characterize the thought of the court majority.

GROWTH OF ORGANIZED LABOR, 1897–1920

Professor Leo Wolman selects 1897 as the year that marks the beginning of the modern period of trade unionism.[17] Although union membership had reached a peak of almost 1 million in 1886, there was a rapid decline after that year, most of which was accounted for by the decrease in the size of the Knights of Labor. After 1897, while increases in the number of persons who belonged to unions were less spectacular than in some earlier years, they were also less ephemeral.

Membership in labor unions increased slowly but steadily between 1897 and 1904. A good part of this growth could be attributed to the increase in the number of labor unions; unions affiliated with the AFL grew in number from 58 in the former year to 120 in the latter. After 1904, increases in union membership were largely a result of expansion in the size of already existing unions. Between 1904 and 1914, the impressive feature of the statistical record is the relative stability in size of union membership. There were years of decline and years of growth; and although there were approximately one-half million more union members at the end than at the beginning of this ten-year period, the rate of growth was markedly below that of the 1897–1904 period. After 1915 there was a rapid increase in unionization as the economic stimulus of World War I created prosperity and a situation of labor shortages. A union membership peak of 5 million was reached in 1920.

As has been the case throughout the nineteenth century, decline in union membership was associated with economic recession. Depressed conditions were at least partly responsible for the membership dips in 1904–1906, 1908–1909, and 1913–1915.[18]

---

[17] Leo Wolman, *Growth of American Trade Unions, 1880–1923* (New York: National Bureau of Economic Research, 1924), pp. 29–33.

[18] *Ibid.*, p. 33.

TABLE 7

LABOR UNION MEMBERSHIP: 1897 TO 1920

YEAR	ALL UNIONS TOTAL MEMBERSHIP (*thousands*)	AMERICAN FEDERATION OF LABOR		
		Number of Affiliated Unions	TOTAL MEMBERSHIP	
			Thousands	Per Cent of All-Union Total
1897	440	58	265	60
1898	467	67	278	60
1899	550	73	349	63
1900	791	82	548	69
1901	1,058	87	788	75
1902	1,335	97	1,024	77
1903	1,824	113	1,466	80
1904	2,067	120	1,676	81
1905	1,918	118	1,494	78
1906	1,892	119	1,454	77
1907	2,077	117	1,539	74
1908	2,092	116	1,587	76
1909	1,965	119	1,483	76
1910	2,116	120	1,562	74
1911	2,318	115	1,762	76
1912	2,405	112	1,770	74
1913	2,661	111	1,996	75
1914	2,647	110	2,021	76
1915	2,560	110	1,946	76
1916	2,722	111	2,073	76
1917	2,976	111	2,371	80
1918	3,386	111	2,726	81
1919	4,046	111	3,260	81
1920	5,043	110	4,079	81

Source: U.S. Department of Commerce, *Historical Statistics of the United States, 1789–1945*, p. 72.

Concentration on statistical totals can frequently give misleading impressions. Growth in union membership was not spread evenly throughout the various industries. About half the 1897–1914 gain, in fact, was accounted for by the United Mine Workers, the building trade unions, and the railroad unions. There was little organization among the unskilled and semiskilled.

World War I created an environment that proved to be ideal for union growth. The government showed an unprecedented interest in labor organizations, and labor representatives served on many of the specially created war agencies. A War Labor Board was established in 1918 with the function of settling industrial controversies that affected the war effort. Recognition by this board of labor's right to organize and bargain collectively was, of course, favorable to the union cause. A sympathetic government and economic prosperity were sharp stimuli to union growth. Even during the war, however, the upturn in union membership was confined to a relatively small group of unions. As might be expected a large part of this growth occurred in industries such as metal, shipbuilding, and machinery that were closely tied to the war effort. Unions in these industries, together with the building, clothing, and transportation groups, accounted for three-fourths of the union membership increase in the 1915–1920 period.[19]

THE 1920's

The 1920's was an unusual decade in many respects, and the fortunes of organized labor took an unusual turn in an economy that, except for the agricultural sector, was a prosperous one. After a sharp economic dip in 1920 and 1921, there was a quick revival, and the years 1922 to 1929 were characterized by prosperity conditions. Contrary to past experience, there was no expansion in the extent and influence of unionism. There was, in fact, a continuing decline in membership. The largest drop occurred between 1920 and 1923 when the number of those belonging to unions fell from over 5 million to slightly more than 3.5 million. Heavy union losses were suffered at this time in industries that had expanded rapidly in the war period. Thereafter there was a moderate annual decline—1927 was an exception—and only 3,392,000 persons belonged to unions in 1930.

A combination of factors worked to retard union expansion. Some were relatively subtle, whereas others were quite apparent. Prosperity is usually characterized by some price inflation with wages lagging behind. The resulting drop in real wages can be a potent spur to organized worker protest. Between 1922 and 1929, however, the price indexes showed remarkable stability.[20] Thus, an economic factor that might have favored unionism was absent.

Clearly detrimental to union expansion was the determined resistance of employers. The time was ripe for an anti-union campaign. A wave of nationalism was sweeping over the country. The United States turned its back on the League of Nations, restrictive immigration laws were passed, Attorney General A. Mitchell Palmer was rounding up alleged radicals by the boatload, and the Ku Klux Klan was soon to extend its influence to the northern reaches of Ohio and Indiana. In such an environment, an obviously effective tactic would be that of identifying unions as un-American

---

[19] Leo Wolman, *Ebb and Flow in Trade Unionism* (New York: National Bureau of Economic Research, 1936), p. 38.

[20] The Bureau of Labor Statistics Consumer's Price Index (1935–1939 = 100) showed a seven point spread between the high and low points during the years 1922–1929. The changes from year to year, however, were quite gradual. See United States Department of Commerce, *Historical Statistics of the United States, 1789–1945*, p. 236.

groups. This was the purpose of the "American Plan." Employer associations led this successful drive to sell the open shop. Union influence was eliminated in many cities, and even such a labor stronghold as San Francisco was for a time turned into an open-shop city.[21]

Within the American economy, the most rapid expansion was taking place in those industries that were least penetrated by unionism. In mass production industries such as automobiles and electrical manufacturing, enthusiasm for "scientific management" and "welfare capitalism" was at a high point. These devices, together with the flowering of company unions and other aggressive anti-union tactics, were successful in warding off such weak thrusts as the unions managed to make toward organizing the factories.

The fact that the mills and factories remained unorganized, however, was not due to employer resistance alone. AFL leadership, tied too closely in principle to the idea of organization by crafts rather than by industries, was unable as a group to adjust its sights to a new situation. The Steel Strike of 1919 is a case in point. Conditions in the industry certainly called for improvement. Wages were low, and a large part of the work force put in a twelve-hour day, six days a week. The organizing committee set up in 1918 under the leadership of William Z. Foster consisted of representatives of *twenty-four* different unions. This was sufficient to doom any attempt to beat the giant United States Steel Corporation. A much greater degree of co-ordination than that possible among so many mutually suspicious unions would have been necessary to organize an industry that was to counterattack by importing thousands of strikebreakers, stirring up racial antagonisms, smashing picket lines, and identifying the strike as one fomented by Moscow-inspired revolutionaries.[22]

Other factors that worked against unionization of workers were the continued hostility of the courts and a conservative temper in the other branches of government. A government that on the whole was not inclined to tamper with the economic mechanism certainly could find no basis for doing so during the "golden" prosperity of the twenties. If the balance of power between workers and management was heavily weighted on the management side, this would have to be corrected by the workings of demand and supply relationships in the market place or not at all. Unions, in short, could expect little help from the forces of organized government.[23]

---

[21] Lewis L. Lorwin, *The American Federation of Labor* (Washington: The Brookings Institution, 1933), p. 203.

[22] The Commission of Inquiry, the Interchurch World Movement, *Report on the Steel Strike of 1919* (New York: Harcourt, Brace & World, Inc., 1920), chaps. 1, 2, 7, and pp. 246–250.

[23] Like most generalizations, this one needs some qualification. The Railway Labor Act was passed in 1926 and can be regarded as a forerunner of the collective bargaining legislation of the 1930's.

Conditions favorable to union growth are usually present during prosperous times. In the 1920's, however, an unfavorable political and social environment cancelled what advantages the labor movement might have derived from the prevailing prosperity. When the decade ended, the workers of the nation were, for the most part, unorganized.

THE 1930's: DEPRESSION BACKGROUND

Between 1929 and 1933, gross national product in the United States fell from $104.4 billion to $55.9 billion. Wages and salaries paid dropped from $50 billion to $28.9 billion in the same period. Unemployed persons were estimated to number as many as 15 million. These bare statistics summarize the tragic plunge from prosperity to depression. Logically it would seem that economic changes of these magnitudes would have been foreseen. This was not the case. In 1928, Herbert Hoover had declared that the conquest of poverty was not a mirage.[24] Eminent economists echoed these sentiments. Americans were assured that they were living on a "permanently high plateau of prosperity." Little men and big men took flyers on a stock market that was soaring to crazy heights. The crash came in October, 1929, but it took several additional years before the more optimistic admitted that this was more than a shaking out of the security markets.

The task of dealing forcefully with economic disaster was too much for an administration that could admit only with great reluctance that disaster had occurred. After 1932, the job of facing up to the economic elements fell to the Democratic party under the leadership of Franklin Delano Roosevelt.

The new administration acted quickly and energetically. The NRA, WPA, PWA, CCC, NYA, and AAA were designations of the more widely known agencies set up to deal with special aspects of the depression; there were many others. Mistakes were made. The economy recovered slowly, and in 1937 there was a serious recession. The harsher edges of a great depression had been softened, however, and the American economic system maintained enough of its vitality to play a crucial role in a second world war.

In a period of uncommon hardship, the government was guided less by strictures of economic philosophy than by the pragmatic facts of life. Old attitudes changed. Economic misfortune that was distributed rather democratically among men who had always been comfortable as well as those who had been poor, among professional people as well as day laborers, among descendants of colonial settlers as well as among new immigrants

---

[24] Dixon Wecter, *The Age of the Great Depression* (New York: The Macmillan Company, 1948), p. 1.

could not be attributed to the failures of individuals. It was a social failure, and the problem called for social efforts. What was anathema in 1925 became common sense in 1935.

All of this created a new social environment, and a key feature of this environment was a new government attitude toward labor unions. Never more than half tolerant of unions before the Great Depression, the branches of government became positively encouraging after 1932.

THE STATE OF ORGANIZED LABOR

By 1933, the number of persons in unions had fallen to slightly less than 3 million, roughly the membership total in 1917. Almost half of the organized workers were in the building construction and transportation unions, and even these groups had suffered serious declines.

Labor spokesmen shared in the general confusion of the times. The substance of AFL President William Green's program for alleviating unemployment was a reduction in the length of the work week to spread the jobs. He also declared himself in opposition to unemployment compensation benefits for workers who had lost their jobs.[25] This last point illustrates the lethargy that had overtaken most of the union leadership. Distrustful of government help because of some bad early experiences and because the idea behind unemployment compensation could not easily be squared with a philosophy that was hostile toward such help, the old guard AFL leadership showed its inability to recognize that a new day had arrived.

The enactment of the National Industrial Recovery Act in June, 1933, provided an opportunity for organized labor. The act stipulated that industry was to agree to codes of fair competition. These codes ostensibly would soften the rigors of competition and create conditions in which business could move ahead with confidence. As a *quid pro quo* to labor, Section 7(a) provided that workers should have the right to organize and bargain collectively free from interference, restraint, and coercion. Furthermore, those seeking employment were not to be required to join company-sponsored unions. Section 7(a) did not guarantee anything to unions, but it did create an opportunity. The administration of this section by specially created labor boards was not very effective, and employer opposition to unions did not vanish into thin air because of a provision in a law. Nevertheless, Section 7(a) served as a stimulus to organized labor. A ground-swell of enthusiasm swept through the workers in many industries. In the

---

[25] This opposition to unemployment compensation was soon to be relaxed, but it is interesting to notice this early opposition in view of the strong AFL support for such legislation in recent years.

coal fields the United Mine Workers campaigned effectively with the slogan "President Roosevelt wants you to join a union." Significantly, the greatest stir occurred in those industries that had been little penetrated by unionism. In automobiles, steel, rubber, and lumber, workers were organized by the thousands.

The AFL proved unequal to the opportunity. Of the factors responsible for this, two might be cited as especially important. The first was the idea that organization should be accomplished primarily by the workers desiring a union. This approach had been somewhat successful among skilled workers, but it was completely ineffective in the mass production industries. Large numbers of semi-skilled workers without craft skills to give them a community of interest or bargaining power were no match for the large corporation. Experienced leadership wise to the ways of union organization was needed, and this leadership could only come from the existing unions. The second factor was the inability of the AFL to exploit the organizational successes that had been accomplished. The old-line leadership stood firmly against attempts to organize along industrial lines. Instead of this, large numbers of federal unions were chartered.[26]

The ineffectiveness of this tactic can be illustrated by an experience in the rubber industry. Several thousand workers in a rubber firm had organized themselves into a single industrial union. When they applied to the AFL for a charter, an organizer was sent from Washington. He proceeded to divide the union into nineteen separate locals.[27] This led to a collapse of the union and necessitated a new organization effort.

This experience was repeated many times. Overly impressed by successes that were now twenty or thirty years old, too many of the top AFL leaders balked at the thought of changing the good old ways. This, then, was the state of the unions—weak, devitalized, unimaginative. But other leaders, more ambitious and aggressive by temperament, were beginning to challenge the old order. The stage was being set for far-reaching developments in American labor history.

UNIONS *V.* UNIONS

There are many examples of inter-union conflicts prior to the AFL-CIO split. The struggles of the AFL with the Knights of Labor and with left

---

[26] Federal unions were local unions chartered by the AFL and directly affiliated with it. This direct affiliation was generally a temporary condition. Once jurisdictional problems were thrashed out, the federal union was assigned to one of the existing national unions or possibly divided up among several.

[27] Herbert Harris, *Labor's Civil War* (New York: Alfred A. Knopf, Inc., 1940), p. 31.

wing unions are among the more noteworthy, but there were others. In no case did earlier conflict result in the eventual strengthening of both factions; oddly enough, this was the long run result of the fight under concern here. The disaffiliation of the most spirited elements within the AFL, rather than wrecking the parent body, served as one of the stimulants of a rejuvenation. This, however, runs ahead of our story.

A fight within an organization may be described in terms of issues, philosophies, and tactics; but social conflict is carried on by men, and it is unusual when the character of the men involved does not have some impact on the nature of the conflict itself as well as the results. The AFL-CIO fight was one between groups of men who reacted differently to an opportunity that stemmed from the combined circumstances of a friendly government, a worker enthusiasm for organization, and a low ebb of business popularity that was inevitable in a period when the business mechanism had stalled so badly.

Labor Leadership

When Gompers died in 1924, rival claimants of the AFL presidency eyed each other suspiciously and then compromised by selecting William Green for the job. Green had worked his way up to become secretary-treasurer of the United Mine Workers and third vice president of the AFL Executive Council. As a state senator in Ohio he had sponsored a workmen's compensation bill that was long regarded as a model for such legislation. As a member of the United Mine Workers, he had, on several occasions, spoken favorably about organization of workers by industry rather than by craft or job. Once in office as AFL president, however, Green did not seek to liberalize prevailing attitudes within the Federation toward political action and industrial unionism. An inveterate compromiser, his inclination was to avoid controversy by placating the dominant power blocs within the AFL. In the face of obvious storm warnings over the issue of industrial unionism, Green sided with those whose organizations and personal careers were closely tied to the narrow conception of unionism that had predominated in AFL circles. When the opposing factions lined up for battle, Green found himself allied with such longtime spokesmen for the craft union viewpoint as William Hutcheson of the Carpenters, Daniel Tobin of the Teamsters, John Frey of the Metal Trades Department, and Matthew Woll of the Photoengravers.

Heading the opposition was John L. Lewis, one of the most dramatic, colorful, and resourceful figures the American labor movement has produced. A coal miner by trade, he had been a local union president, chief statistician, and vice president of the United Mine Workers before he assumed the presidency of that body. During the twenties he had his work cut out for him. His union was weak, disorganized, and under constant attack by the mine operators. Descriptions of union-operator fights in such places as Mingo and Logan counties in West Virginia and the "Little Egypt" area of southern Illinois read like war communiques.[28] Despite employer attack, internal union dissension, and economic difficulties in the coal industry, Lewis managed to hold his union together although membership strength fell from about 400,000 in 1920 to fewer than 150,000 in 1930. Possibly because of his long experience in fighting under unfavorable conditions, Lewis had developed a keen facility for sensing opportunities and coming up with the appropriate tactics to exploit them. Thus, at a time when most of the union leaders were doing little more than they had done during the twenties, Lewis was eager to pounce upon the newly developing opportunities for unionism which he was quick to perceive. Allied with him were Sidney Hillman of the Amalgamated Clothing Workers, Charles P. Howard of the Typographical Workers, Max Zaritsky of the Hat, Cap, and Millinery Workers, and a number of others.

Outwardly, the battle was joined over the issue of whether the workers in the mass production industries should be organized on the basis of the jobs they performed or the industries they were in. Underlying this issue was a seething hostility that stemmed from the suspicions and jealousies of rival leaders. In retrospect, it seems clear that the makeup of the men in the forefront of the fight over craft versus industrial unionism was an important factor that narrowed the possibility of successful compromise. This is not meant to minimize the seriousness of the industrial union issue. Nevertheless, the nature of the conflict and the eventual results cannot be successfully interpreted in terms of craft versus industrial union issues alone.

The Battle of the Conventions

The annual convention of the AFL can be thought of as the Federation's legislative arm. Each national or international union (the international union is one with some local units in Canada) sends delegates on the basis of its membership size. The larger the union the greater the number of delegates and voting power it enjoys. The issue of craft versus industrial unionism was fought out in the first instance on the convention floor. As in the case of most political meetings, the behind the scenes maneuvering and jockeying for position were as important as the sometimes florid oratory that prevailed.

Up to this point, the words "craft" and "industrial" have been used to describe the opposing viewpoints. These words, however, oversimplify the

---

[28] For a good description of the fortunes of the United Mine Workers during the 1920's, see Saul Alinsky, *John L. Lewis* (New York: G. P. Putnam's Sons, 1949), chap. 3.

facts. Membership in a pure craft union is limited to workers with similar craft skills. At the opposite structural pole is the pure industrial union. In this case, all workers in an industry belong to the same union. The dynamics of a rapidly changing technology together with the politics of unionism have contrived to minimize the number of unions that fit into either of these categories. Most unions represent some variation of these basic forms.

The issue at stake, consequently, was not whether the workers in mass production industries should be organized on an industrial rather than a craft basis but whether the workers in these industries who might conceivably fall within the jurisdiction of existing unions should be detached and assigned to such unions. In the automobile industry, for example, should all workers be in one big union or should the electricians, stationary engineers, tool and die makers, skilled machinists, carpenters, etc., be separated from the others and assigned to unions that historically had exercised jurisdiction over such workers?

To substantiate the case for issuing charters on an industrial union basis it was argued that (1) this was the preference of the workers in the industries involved, (2) prior attempts to divide these workers on the basis of occupations always ended up with no one being successfully organized, (3) the facts of modern technology left no practical alternative to organization by industry, (4) the task of organizing the workers would be substantially easier, (5) some fifty years of experience with job-oriented unionism had resulted in failure to organize the factory workers.

On the other side, it was argued that (1) the sanctity of existing jurisdictional rights was a cardinal feature of AFL philosophy; (2) craft-oriented unionism had managed to survive over the years, whereas other types had failed; (3) the basic issue, in any event, was not craft versus industrial unionism but whether majority rule would prevail in the determination of AFL policy.

At the 1934 annual convention in San Francisco, fourteen different resolutions were submitted on the subject of industrial unionism. The debate served to expose the extremes of feelings on the matter. The upshot was a compromise. Charters were to be issued for mass production workers, but the rights of the craft unions were to be safeguarded. It was also recommended that the executive council undertake a campaign of organization in the steel industry. This resolution, which could mean whatever one chose to read into it, somehow or other soothed the ruffled feelings of the delegates.

By the time the 1935 convention met at Atlantic City in October, the ambiguity of the 1934 resolution was quite evident. Nothing had been accomplished by way of organizing the steel industry, and the charters the executive council had offered to the auto and rubber workers were considerably different from those the proponents of industrial unionism had had in mind.

The convention was a lively one. To the delegates assembled, John L. Lewis roared out—"At San Francisco, they seduced me with fair words. Now, of course, having learned that I was seduced, I am enraged and ready to rend my seducers limb from limb. . . ." He spoke of the new unions withering like the grass before the morning sun. High wassail would prevail at the banquet tables of labor's enemies if organized labor let this opportunity slip. Philip Murray struck at the strategy of breaking up the new unions into occupational components. Referring to a specific incident in steel, he described the consequences of having divided a new union into nine parts: "Now they have no organization, they have no charter, they have no independent union, they have no craft union. They are today where they were before they started their campaign eighteen months ago." In rebuttal, Daniel Tobin of the Teamsters spoke of labor's rock of ages: the rock of craft autonomy. The movement toward industrial unionism, he declared, was an attempt to destroy the foundations upon which the Federation had been built.

The debating concluded, the convention voted. The minority report of the Resolutions Committee favoring industrial unionism was defeated by a vote of 18,024 to 10,933. The eloquence of the case for industrial unions had left the Federation's dominant power blocs unmoved.

Shortly after the convention adjourned, nine leaders in the pro-industrial union faction met and organized a Committee for Industrial Organization. The purpose was to "encourage and promote organization of workers in the mass production industries. . . ." The committee's functions were to be "educational and advisory." For two years, there was threat and counter threat, move and counter move between the CIO and the AFL. Despite the counsel of the moderates in both camps, neither side showed an inclination to compromise. An attempt to ward off a complete rupture was made at a meeting in 1937. The AFL offer was that the original CIO unions, earlier suspended from the parent body, were to be readmitted as such. The other CIO unions, grown to twenty-two in number, were to negotiate mergers with the AFL unions in their respective industries. The CIO proposal was that all CIO unions be admitted into the AFL with full membership privileges. Neither side budged, and the negotiations collapsed. Only the formalities of officially acknowledging the split remained. The Federation expelled the CIO unions, and in May, 1938, the Committee for Industrial Organization reconstituted itself as the Congress of Industrial Organizations.

UNIONS *V.* MANAGEMENT

A list of the major American business corporations would be, at the same time, a list of the firms that were least penetrated by unionism up to 1935.

Between that date and 1941, most of the large industrial firms whose names are household words—United States Steel Corporation, Ford Motor Company, General Motors Corporation, Goodyear Tire and Rubber, among others—recognized a union and entered into a collective bargaining relationship with it. When the long history of successful anti-unionism by these firms is considered, the organization of their workers in such a brief time is indeed cause for amazement. It would be erroneous to conclude, however, that the task of organizing was easily accomplished because of the brevity of the time period involved. Management resistance was strong, sometimes vicious, and occasionally the physical flareups matched in intensity anything that had occurred in prior labor history.

Organizational Success

Even with the benefit of some thirty years of hindsight, it is not easy to pick out one of several reasons that are definitive explanations of the union organizational successes in this period. Many composite elements make up the broad canvas of history, and succeeding generations have tended to place the priority of importance on different elements. In the matter of unionization, numerous factors accounted for an over-all result that added up to a marked advance in labor union power.

In part, union victories were due to lucky breaks. It was a stroke of good fortune that the Steel Workers Organizing Committee began its drive on the United States Steel Corporation when production was starting to pick up after many lean years and when choice contracts might have been jeopardized by unstable labor conditions. It was a stroke of good fortune that the "sitdown" strike technique developed rather spontaneously at the time that it did. No one in the union high command invented the sitdown strike. When the workers in the Akron rubber plants voiced their protests by just sitting down at their jobs, it was apparent that this was a tactic that could eliminate some major obstacles to strike success such as wholesale importation of strikebreakers and anti-picket line forays by local vigilantes. Thus, a weapon of doubtful legality—union leaders and sympathizers generally had many qualms about the sitdown strike, and it was eventually outlawed by Supreme Court decision[29]—erupted into prominence, conditioned the results of several crucial strikes, and has since been used sparingly or not at all.

Luck alone could hardly account for all that transpired in the labor-management field. Some measure of labor's success must be attributed to a leadership whose performance was as brilliant as it was determined. Lewis, his first-line lieutenants, and a host of others whose names will be known

---

[29] *National Labor Relations Board* v. *Fansteel Metallurgical Corporation,* 306 U.S. 240 (1939).

in the future only to very close students of labor history had no illusions about the character of the job they faced. They marshalled the money and forces available to them with impressive effectiveness, took gambles when the odds seemed to be right—and sometimes when they weren't—underwent personal and often physical abuse, and kept their sights fixed firmly on the major objective—organization of the unorganized.

In the key areas of steel and automobiles, where success or failure could influence the results in other industries, the union cause was helped substantially by industry's failure to maintain a solid front. When General Motors was being struck, loss of sales to competitors was a strong pressure on the corporation to concede to union demands. Unwittingly, Ford and Chrysler helped to create the conditions that made the organization of their own workers more likely. When the United States Steel Corporation agreed to recognize the steel workers' union, the tactical position of the union in its fight against "little steel" was strengthened immeasurably.

Favorable labor legislation was another factor that worked to union advantage. The National Labor Relations Act of 1935 required that companies recognize unions chosen by workers and bargain with such unions in good faith. The law, however, was slow in its operations. Elections had to be held to determine the workers' choice of union or no union. Charges of violations of the act had to be filed with the National Labor Relations Board. Investigations had to be held. All of this took time, and the law's delays are especially chafing when profound issues are at stake. But slowly or otherwise, the law did operate; and in those cases where management was most determined to hold out against union recognition a day of reckoning with the law of the land inevitably had to arrive. This time, the law worked to the advantage of the unions.

A final reason to be advanced here in explanation of labor's organizational success stems from the feelings of the workers themselves. Rarely have workers needed less convincing of the possible benefits of unionism. Wages were low, the practice of speeding up the tempo of the assembly line had reached a point where work conditions in many firms were intolerable, and spying upon workers had developed into a finely practiced art. In many instances, the petty tyrannies practiced by the shop foreman provided additional matter for worker complaint. Added together, these amounted to a set of working conditions that literally forced employees to seek redress of their grievances. The situation was ripe for the CIO organizing committees to tap the open hostilities of men who had had little first-hand experience with labor unions up to this time.

Management Reaction

In its simplest terms, the issue can be described this way: the CIO affiliates wanted to be recognized by management as bargaining representatives of the workers; management, in most cases, did not want to grant this recognition. As a result of this situation, a wave of organizational strikes swept the nation. Strike statistics for 1937 are a good indication of what was happening. The 4,470 work stoppages that occurred were more than twice those of the previous year. The issue in more than half of these stoppages was union recognition. Over a million workers were involved.

Management reaction to all of this took different forms. As already noted, the United States Steel Corporation decided that its interests were best served by recognizing a labor union and bargaining with it. Other managements chose to fight it out. Employers used all the tactics that had served them so well in the past and added a few new twists. Detective agencies that specialized in supplying plant guards and strikebreakers did a land office business. So did the manufacturers of industrial munitions.[30] Strikebreaking was reduced to a formula—the "Mohawk Valley Formula." This involved a series of carefully staged maneuvers such as publicity barrages, charges of communism, organization of community pressures, fake back-to-work movements, and theatrical plant reopenings.[31] There were many instances of violence, the most notable being the "Memorial Day Massacre." On May 30, 1937, a line of marching pickets was halted by police in front of the Chicago shops of the Republic Steel Corporation. Without apparent provocation, the police opened fire, killing ten and wounding more than a hundred. These examples are sufficient to establish the fact that many of the organizational conflicts were carried on in a context of violence. In most cases, the union drives were successful, and factory employees in the basic industries were organized. The character of the fight, however, left a legacy of distrust and mutual suspicion.

ORGANIZED LABOR AND THE GOVERNMENT: THE 1930's

In the 1930's, the administrative branch of the federal government supported laws favorable to unions, the legislature enacted them, and the courts eventually proclaimed their constitutionality. What turned out to be a period of unusual government friendliness toward organized labor ac-

---

[30] Report of the Senate Committee on Education and Labor, *Violations of Free Speech and Rights of Labor* (76th Congress, 1st Session, Report No. 6), Part 3, p. 46. Twenty firms and employers' associations purchased a total of $375,992 worth of gas munitions. These twenty largest purchasers included seven steel firms, four employers' associations, two rubber firms, one railroad company, one chemical firm, and one purchaser unidentified by industry.

[31] For a description of the Mohawk Valley Formula see David J. Saposs and Elizabeth Bliss, *Anti-Labor Activities in the United States* (New York: League for Industrial Democracy, June, 1938), pp. 19–21. Reprinted in Bakke and Kerr, *op. cit.*, p. 461.

tually had its beginnings before the start of the New Deal era.[32] It was not until the decade was nearly over, however, that the full import of changed government attitudes was apparent. By 1940, there had occurred a virtual revolution in labor law. The two federal statutes that dealt with collective bargaining relationships were the Norris-LaGuardia Anti-Injunction Act of 1932 and the National Labor Relations Act of 1935. The former act provided procedural and substantive protections against the free and easy issuance of court injunctions during labor disputes. The labor relations statute, which declared that equality of bargaining power between management and workers was government policy, marked the start of a new era in the government-labor relationship. Workers, for many years, had had the right to organize and bargain collectively. Management, however, had had the equivalent rights of combating labor organizations and refusing to bargain with them. The revolutionary impact of the law lay in the stripping away of these management rights. Henceforth, the matter of union choice was to rest exclusively with workers. Any management attempt to influence or coerce workers in their exercise of this choice was an "unfair labor practice," and remedies were provided to correct such practices where they occurred.

A big question mark centered upon Supreme Court reaction to the pro-labor legislation of the decade. For years the courts had been striking down a variety of legislation that would have favored organized as well as un-organized labor. The logic of these decisions rested upon a philosophy that would brook little interference with the employer's right to do business. The courts, in short, wrote into the law the economic philosophy of *laissez-faire*. Continued application of this reasoning would have nullified the efforts of the legislative and administrative branches to help organized labor. Court decisions invalidating the Agricultural Adjustment Act,[33] the Bituminous Coal Conservation Act of 1935,[34] and a New York State minimum wage law[35] indicated that the court would remain conservative. The legal merits of these cases varied considerably, but in all the decisions the basis of the rulings gave little ground for hope of a judicial approach that would be more consistent with the will of the other branches of government.

President Roosevelt sought to circumvent this roadblock by reorganizing the federal judiciary. His "court packing" bill was ill-received and ill-fated.

---

[32] In *Texas and New Orleans Railway Company* v. *Brotherhood of Railway and Steamship Clerks*, 281 U.S. 548 (1930) the Supreme Court upheld the legal rights of collective action granted to railroad workers in the Railway Labor Act of 1926. The company's obligation to bargain with unions, furthermore, could not be circumvented by the establishment of a company-sponsored employee-representation plan. The Norris-LaGuardia Act of 1932 is another example of pre-Roosevelt-era legislation favorably disposed toward unions.

[33] *United States* v. *Butler*, 297 U.S. 1 (1936).

[34] *Carter* v. *Carter Coal Co.*, 298 U.S. 238 (1936).

[35] *Morehead* v. *New York* ex rel. *Tipaldo*, 298 U.S. 587 (1936).

Aroused public sentiment, however, apparently had the effect of accomplishing what the President's bill sought. In 1937, the court reversed itself on the minimum wage question.[36] The five to four conservative majority became a five to four liberal majority as a result of Justice Roberts' switch in the minimum wage case. Several weeks later, the constitutionality of the National Labor Relations Act was upheld.[37] The decision had implications much beyond the labor relations field. The liberalized definition of interstate commerce upon which the decision rested amounted to a vast expansion of the powers of the federal government. In a series of additional rulings the court clarified the meaning of the NLRA. It became apparent that the broad purposes of this law as well as other New Deal legislation would not be nibbled away by court interpretation. The pendulum of government attitudes toward organized labor had reached the high point of the arc on the labor side.

Political Action

While the realignment of government attitudes toward labor was taking place, there was also change in labor attitudes regarding the degree of political action that was appropriate for unions. Underlying this latter change were a number of factors. The existence of economic depression made the limitations of economic activity obvious to many workers. Millions of persons were organized into CIO unions with no long tradition of limited political action. The aggressiveness of the drives to organize had enough momentum to carry over into election contests. Furthermore, there was a President and a party that had stirred the hopes of union leaders and the rank and file to the extent that they identified their interests with those of the Democratic party.

Although the supporters of independent—third party—political action were not insignificant in number, organized labor, for the most part, continued to operate in the political field according to the non-partisan pattern established by the AFL; however, the fervor of the effort and the amount of financial aid and personal time devoted by politically minded unionists served to differentiate their activities from many of the earlier political drives of labor. The non-partisanship, furthermore, was such in name only. There was a little-disguised support of New Deal policies and candidates, and the continued ballot-box success of these candidates was a strong point in the arguments of those labor leaders who felt that independent political action was not necessary.

In 1936, international unions affiliated with both the CIO and the AFL formed Labor's Nonpartisan League. With the purpose of promoting labor's

---

[36] *West Coast Hotel* v. *Parrish*, 300 U.S. 379.
[37] *National Labor Relations Board* v. *Jones and Laughlin Steel Corp.*, 301 U.S. 1.

interests in the political arena, the League operated for the most part through the existing political organizations. On occasion, the League entered its own candidates in primary elections, and in New York State the American Labor Party was established. The ALP actually held a balance-of-power position in that state for a time and in 1940 was instrumental in carrying the state for President Roosevelt. Dissension between the left wing and right wing factions soon reduced the potency of the ALP. Similarly, Labor's Nonpartisan League lost some of its effectiveness because of CIO-AFL hostility. By 1938, AFL president William Green was flinging charges of CIO domination and urging AFL affiliates to withdraw.[38]

The exact extent of labor's influence in the elections of 1936 and 1940 is not measurable. The wave of popular sentiment for the New Deal was high. Riding on a winning tide, labor could claim some credit for the victory, and undoubtedly some credit must be accorded. On one point there can be little doubt. Organized labor had acquired a new sense of the importance of meaningful political action.

SUMMARY: THE AFL AND THE CIO

The American Federation of Labor and the national and international unions affiliated with it constituted a type of unionism that was more restrictive in membership than the Knights of Labor, less politically oriented than the National Labor Union, and less class conscious than the several left wing groups that sought to win worker allegiance. Described as "job conscious" and "bread and butter unionism," the AFL managed to make a successful beachhead on the American industrial scene. Efforts to dislodge it were numerous and came from many directions. In one sense these efforts failed. The AFL had the capacity to survive. In another sense, however, they were not complete failures. AFL growth was contained in size and direction. The most dynamic developments in the American economy were occurring in the mass production industries; and in this area, employer resistance plus an unimaginative and sometimes indifferent union leadership stymied the organization of workers.

Restive under an inept AFL leadership, an aggressive CIO broke away from the parent organization and also broke out of what had remained, essentially, a mere beachhead in the industrial world. Unencumbered by time-worn ideas of union structure and organizational methods, the CIO succeeded in organizing millions of factory workers.

---

[38] Officially, the AFL itself was never affiliated with Labor's Nonpartisan League. By 1938, many of the important AFL figures associated with the League had withdrawn or were in the process of doing so.

The AFL was not to be counted out. Levying a special assessment of one cent per member per month to finance an organizing campaign, the Federation enlarged its organizing staff and granted charters to many new unions. Both the AFL and CIO reached out eagerly for new members, and the old distinction between craft and industrial unionism, always somewhat blurred in practice, broke down more than ever.

The organizational campaigns waged simultaneously by rival unions resulted in frequent jurisdictional conflicts. In longshoring, textiles, electrical manufacturing, meat packing, automobile manufacturing, and other industries, rival unions clashed head-on in their race to organize. In 1937, the total CIO membership of 3.7 million actually outstripped AFL membership size by almost 1 million. By 1940, however, the AFL could count over 4 million members, whereas the CIO had slipped back to about 3.6 million. At this time the CIO had forty-two affiliated national and international unions, and the AFL had 105.

Union jurisdictional squabbles were one of several factors that had the effect of alienating some of the public sympathy that had developed for the union cause. The late thirties probably mark the high point of public and government sympathy for unionism. Later, these favorable attitudes receded, slowly at first but with more momentum as the war ended. The nature and significance of these changes will be examined in later chapters.

QUESTIONS

1. How did the American Federation of Labor, the Knights of Labor, and the Industrial Workers of the World differ in the following respects: (a) philosophy, (b) organizational structure, (c) tactics, (d) membership?

2. In its formative years, the American Federation of Labor was under attack from both socialists and capitalists. How do you explain this simultaneous attack from proponents of such diverse philosophies?

3. Historically, labor organizations have enjoyed a growth in membership during prosperous periods. What factors operated during the 1920's—a prosperous period—to inhibit union growth?

4. Since the AFL had always had industrial unions affiliated with it, why did a controversy develop during the 1930's over the structure of the new unions in the mass production industries?

5. The CIO unions enjoyed a phenomenal organizational success in the late 1930's even though management opposition was as intense as ever. What factors explain this union success?

SELECTED READINGS

ALINSKY, SAUL. *John L. Lewis.* New York: G. P. Putnam's Sons, 1949. Chaps. 3–7.

BERNSTEIN, IRVING. *The Lean Years.* Boston: Houghton Mifflin Company, 1960.

DERBER, MILTON, and YOUNG, EDWIN (eds.). *Labor and the New Deal.* Madison: The University of Wisconsin Press, 1957.

DULLES, FOSTER R. *Labor in America.* New York: Thomas Y. Crowell Company, 1949. Chaps. 9–17.

GALENSON, WALTER. *The CIO Challenge to the AFL.* Cambridge, Mass.: Harvard University Press, 1960.

PELLING, HENRY. *American Labor.* Chicago: The University of Chicago Press, 1960. Chaps. 4–7.

CHAPTER 5

Organized Labor in The War and Postwar Periods

As THE 1940's BEGAN, LABOR-MANAGEMENT RELATIONS WERE IN AN UN-settled state. Some of the factors responsible for this have already been analyzed. The labor union penetration into hitherto unorganized industrial territories had been strongly resisted, and many union victories were in the nature of conquests. Unionization of workers, however, did not automatically produce the terms and conditions of industrial peace. The attitude of many in management was that they had lost a battle rather than a war. On the union side, many leaders approached management with suspicion and hostility.

Compounding the difficulty was the fact that large sections of union and management leadership had had little experience in dealing with each other. The position of a management spokesman who bargains with a union official for the first time is not completely unlike that of a newly inducted soldier. The gap between civilian and military life is such that few will not stub their toes at least once while making the transition. Similarly in industrial relations, the company representative must adjust to a new way of life. Powers he once exercised unilaterally must now be shared. The dividing line between his authority and that of the union is not clearly marked. Furthermore, he may be dealing with a local union official who is just as inexperienced in the collective bargaining game as he is. Between them, the two will undoubtedly stumble into trouble that more experienced hands would avoid.

There were other aspects to the unsettled state of affairs in the early forties. The schism in the labor movement did not respond to the several attempts to promote unity between the factions. Far too much energy was being expended in the expression of mutual hostility by prominent CIO and AFL leaders. Frequently, as in the case of jurisdictional disputes, both the employers and the public had to suffer the consequences of internal union warfare. Another complication in the blurred picture stemmed from the new governmental attitudes towards unions. Management spokesmen challenged the "one sidedness" of the National Labor Relations Act, and pressure was exerted to obtain the repeal or amendment of the law. Nor was the National Labor Relations Board, which administered the act, immune from labor attack. The AFL claimed that the board was pro-CIO, whereas the latter organization frequently charged the reverse. Meanwhile the board was finding that the complexities of industrial relations created more and more problems, the resolution of which inevitably embroiled the agency in political controversy.

What was needed, in short, was time for labor and management to adjust to their new relationships, to recognize the new dimensions of their respective powers, and to appreciate the social responsibilities that flowed from the possession of these powers. Time was needed for the government as well as for labor and management to appreciate the full implications of a new legal setting. The time in which these adjustments might have been made ran out, however, as the nation became involved in a war, first by way of increased sympathy and assistance for the western allies, and then, after December 7, 1941, as an active belligerent.

THE WAR SETTING

Depression had been the economic background of the historical events of the thirties. Prosperity appeared rather abruptly in the wake of the defense and war programs. In 1940, 8 million persons were without jobs; but within two years, unemployment had virtually disappeared. Workers were earning larger incomes than they had in a decade, and business firms were earning larger profits. The fear of insecurity that had plagued so many workers was replaced by a variety of new problems. Vast population shifts occurred in response to work opportunities in the mushrooming war centers. Few areas, however, had adequate housing facilities for in-migrants. Many lived in makeshift arrangements or slum conditions. Curtailment of consumer goods production caused much inconvenience and some hardship. As manpower shortages developed, working hours were lengthened and a seven-day work week was not uncommon. This meant higher earnings; but it also meant fatigue, a tendency toward irritation, and a disruption of normal family living patterns. The degradation, frustration, and boredom of unemployment were replaced by the tension, confusion, and clamor of an economic system whipped to a high peak of activity by the demands of war.

The unresolved problems of the labor-management-government relationship had to be considered in this new economic and social context. Ordinarily, union-management differences are resolved by collective negotiations or by strikes and lockouts. A nation engaged in a battle for survival, however, cannot be tolerant of work interruptions that deprive its armed forces of essential military items. Elimination of industrial disputes, then, was a first requirement of the defense program. Another was that of preventing the economy from being wrecked by monetary dislocations. In a war period, the swollen incomes generated by high level prosperity are bidding against a much reduced supply of consumer goods. In this situation, the choices open to a government are (1) to tax these excess incomes away or otherwise neutralize them to prevent inflationary pressures or (2) to prevent incomes from rising to dangerous levels by a system of direct wage and price controls.

The United States government relied on both approaches during World War II. Our interest here is in the implications of the second for labor-management relations. A government policy of preventing strikes and controlling wages is one that contains somewhat inconsistent elements. Unions were asked to give up their traditional weapons and to forego one of their basic goals—improved wage and other income benefits. In a broad sense, such a policy strips unions of one of their major functions and creates a problem of union security. How does a labor union hold on to its membership when it gives up its weapons and accepts an imposed limitation on its economic goals? This question becomes especially acute in a period of economic expansion when many firms expand their labor forces and turnover is likely to be high.

In the arena of labor-management contention, the basic problem for the government during the war became that of getting both parties to accept decisions that were less attractive than those either labor or management might have won by a resort to force. In a democratic society, this problem can be satisfactorily resolved only if all parties concerned recognize the existence of a public problem that transcends in importance the interests of special groups. Both labor and management must also have confidence that neither will gain undue advantage as a result of emergency conditions. Part of the history of organized labor in World War II centers upon the problems involved in maintaining the voluntary compliance of labor and management in the control program. Another part is the story of the growth of government power over unions as well as management. Not all the details of this record can be treated exhaustively here. Instead, selected aspects will be examined to illustrate the nature of the problems and the attempts to resolve them.

THE UNION SECURITY ISSUE

In labor relations terminology, "union security" refers to agreements by employers to help unions get and keep membership. The most extreme form of union security is the closed shop. Employers under closed shop contracts agree to hire only union members. A worker must belong to a union before he can get a job. This type of agreement is widespread in the building trades and other skilled craft occupations. In the factory employments, a more popular type of security clause is the union shop. In this case, the employer has the freedom to hire whomever he chooses, but the new employee must join the union within a specified time to keep his job. The union security question has been a source of labor management controversy for 150 years.[1] In the defense and war periods, it became an issue that stubbornly defied solution for a time and so commanded an unusual amount of attention.

Although the National Labor Relations Act requiring employers to recognize and deal with labor organizations chosen by employees provided a substantial measure of security for unions, this was not enough to quiet the fears of many labor leaders. Industrial firms were expanding rapidly as war orders mounted. Large numbers of newly hired persons had not been through the organizational fights and felt no special allegiance toward labor unions. The core of loyal union members might drift off to other jobs or be swamped by the deluge of new workers. Labor leaders were not convinced that employers would not take advantage of such situations to overturn the still recent union organizational victories. An additional factor accentuated the union thirst for contractual security agreements. AFL and CIO unions were at loggerheads in many industries and were not above raiding each other's memberships. Union security was a type of insurance that offered a protection against challenges from other unions.

On the employers' side, it was argued, as it had been for years, that union security agreements denied the right to work to men who were temperamentally, philosophically, or otherwise opposed to labor unions. Underlying this argument, and indeed beneath the arguments of the unions, was the question of power. An arrangement that guarantees a large union membership means that the power of the union is greater than it otherwise would be. Employers are ordinarily reluctant to enter such agreements and, in the forties, were fearful that widespread surrender to closed or union shop demands would mean an unduly large increase in the power of unions. Labor leaders, on the other hand, were afraid that the war emergency would be used as a guise to prevent them from obtaining the strength that they otherwise might have developed. That the union security question would become a widespread source of disputes

---

[1] Additional details of the union security question will be examined in Chapter 8.

had become evident long before Pearl Harbor Day, and it was also evident that, somehow or other, the problem would have to be resolved.

On March 19, 1941, President Roosevelt, by executive order, established the National Defense Mediation Board. The board's function was to help settle labor disputes that affected the defense program. Board personnel consisted of three public, four employer, and four labor representatives— two each from the AFL and the CIO. When disputes came before it, the NDMB held hearings and recommended settlements. The procedure was an attempt to settle labor troubles by voluntary processes.

Disputes involving union security were the most difficult that came before the board and eventually proved to be the agency's undoing. The issue came to a head in the dispute between the United Mine Workers and the "captive" coal mine operators.[2] Although about 95 per cent of the miners belonged to the union, the UMW demanded a union shop, and the miners walked out of the pits to support the demand. The Mediation Board voted nine to two—CIO members dissenting—against the union demand. A specially appointed arbitration panel soon granted John L. Lewis his union shop, thereby ending the immediate dispute, but it was obvious that the NDMB was dead. The CIO members had resigned, and a ruling in a key case had been circumvented by a show of power.

A successor agency, the War Labor Board, inherited the union security problem. Gradually, in a case-by-case approach, the board worked out a solution that was less than completely satisfactory to labor or management but nevertheless had the merit of being workable. In those instances where a union demanded and an employer refused to grant a closed or union shop, the board, in most cases, awarded "maintenance of membership" to the union. Under maintenance of membership, all employees had the opportunity to accept or reject membership in the union involved. Those who decided against the union during the "escape period" could continue to work as non-union employees. Those who joined had to remain in the union as a condition of their continued employment.

This was clearly a compromise solution, but it had enough appealing elements to win at least grudging acceptance from all parties. Individuals were not forced to join unions, but labor organizations had some protection against the disintegrating forces that arose from the special circumstances of war.

WAGES AND OTHER BENEFITS

Whereas the major dissatisfaction with the maintenance of membership policy was expressed by management, in the wage control program the

---

[2] Captive coal mines are those owned and operated by the steel companies.

complaints were mainly those of organized labor. Through most of the war years, labor lived with a wage policy while disagreeing with and constantly attacking its most important features.

There was no legal control over wage rates until October 3, 1942—some ten months after Pearl Harbor. The large volume of unemployed manpower and productive resources meant that the defense program could be started without any serious curtailment of consumer goods and, hence, without price inflation. The increasing war drain on the economy's resources, however, raised the fear that upward price pressures of dangerous proportions would appear unless there were aggressive efforts to halt the rise.

The authority of the National Defense Mediation Board was limited to the prevention of labor disputes. The board could recommend a settlement that would modify a wage increase, only in those cases where a dispute centered on wages. There was no control over voluntary wage increases, and in a period of manpower shortages and only partial price controls, employers were frequently willing to use the technique of higher wages to attract and keep necessary manpower.

In April, 1942, a general price freeze was ordered by the Office of Price Administration. By the fall of 1942, the government was convinced that a wage freeze was also necessary. Executive Order 9250, issued on October 3, gave the War Labor Board control over changes in wage rates. The order specified that, with some exceptions, wages were to be stabilized at September 15, 1942, levels.

The foundation stone of the wage stabilization program was the Little Steel formula. This permitted an increase in straight time hourly earnings of 15 per cent over January 1, 1941, levels. The logic was that living costs had increased 15 per cent between that date and May, 1942, and that wages should be permitted to catch up to this extent. For a time, wage controls were administered flexibly. Adjustments beyond the Little Steel formula had to be approved by the WLB, but approval could be given for a number of reasons. The most prominent of these were wage increases to correct interplant inequities, to remove substandard living conditions, and to provide for promotions and reclassifications.[3]

---

[3] Interplant inequities were wage disparities between plants in a given area doing similar work. Low-wage plants were generally permitted to bring wage rates up to prevailing area levels. Substandard corrections referred to approval of wage rates to bring them to specified minimum levels. By 1945, the board was approving increases in rates up to fifty-five cents per hour on a substandard basis. Within limits, increases could be granted by employers for promotions and reclassifications. Without the possibility of such increases, ordinary administration of plant wages would break down. Such increases, however, made possible an evasion of wage controls by means of excessively liberal upgrading and reclassifications. Strict policing of all such changes would have been physically impossible.

Despite the wage and price freeze, both wages and prices continued to creep up, and in April, 1943, a hold-the-line order was issued. In effect, the order provided that no additional increases could be made on an inter-plant inequity basis, although this was relaxed somewhat at a later date. With more and more unions finding that they had achieved all wage gains permissible under the limits of the control program, labor leaders turned their attention to fringe items such as paid vacations, paid holidays, and premium pay. Since these benefits involved costs and consequently could be inflationary, the WLB developed standards for the control of fringe items.

Most petitions for wage increases came to the WLB not as dispute issues but as requests for adjustments jointly agreed upon by management and labor. This meant that the purely economic aspect of the labor-management relationship was shifted in large part away from the collective bargaining table to a government agency, one-third of whose membership consisted of labor representatives. In a sense collective bargaining over wages for the entire nation was carried on by a tripartite board operating under anti-inflation policies established by higher echelons of government. Despite its participation, labor did not cease its attacks on the overall philosophy of the control program.

The complaint of labor centered largely upon the relationship between basic wage rates and the cost of living. Living costs had admittedly risen more than the 15 per cent increase in wage rates permissible under the Little Steel formula.[4] Pointing to this fact and to the level of business profits, labor contended that it was shouldering an excessive share of the financial burden of the war.

The answer made to labor's contentions was that although wage rates were stabilized, earnings were not, and when earnings were considered labor had more than held its own.[5] The statistical record seems to bear out this argument. Between January, 1941, and July, 1945, basic wage rates increased 24 per cent. (Urban wage rates increased 32.4 per cent.) Straight time hourly earnings, however, increased an estimated 70 per cent, while cost of living increased approximately 33.3 per cent. Average weekly

---

[4] Spokesmen for organized labor contended that the living standards of workers had deteriorated far beyond that shown by comparison of living-cost and wage-rate changes. Challenging the accuracy of the price data issued by the Bureau of Labor Statistics, labor contended that the BLS index understated the actual rise in living cost by some twenty percentage points. A specially appointed committee headed by economist Wesley Mitchell found that the understatement was more in the nature of 4 or 5 per cent.

[5] Earnings include premium pay for overtime and other additions to pay that are not shown by the basic wage rate.

earnings in manufacturing rose from $26.64 in January, 1941, to $45.45 in July, 1945. The factors accounting for this increase are shown below:[6]

	Amount	Per Cent of Total Increase
Weekly earnings, January, 1941 . . .	$26.64	
Increase due to—		
Changes in basic wage rates	$6.22	33
Liberal administration of merit increases, piece-rate adjustments, changes in output of piece-rate workers	2.17	12
Changes in distribution of workers between regions, occupations, shifts; changes in overtime pay provisions and for work on extra shifts	2.10	11
Changes in distribution of workers as between industries	1.40	7
Extension of workweek	4.85	26
Additional premium payment for overtime work	2.07	11
Total increase	18.81	
Weekly earnings, July, 1945	$45.45	100

As the war drew to a close, labor pressure to relax wage controls mounted. After V-J Day, a new executive order provided that wage increases of any amount could be granted provided such increases were not used as the basis of price increases. By this order, the wage question shifted in part from the government back to the collective bargaining table.

Although neither labor nor management was particularly happy with wage controls, on the whole, the program worked. The cost of living was kept within reasonable bounds, and cost-price relationships were not unduly distorted when the magnitude of the wartime strain on the price system is considered. Whether labor or industry fared better during the war is a controversy that was forgotten before it was resolved. By selecting a 1939 base date, the Nathan Report showed a 275 per cent increase for corporate income before taxes and only a 138 per cent increase in wages and salaries. Industry spokesmen, however, pointed out that selection of a 1941 base date showed an opposite picture.[7] About all that was proved by this controversy was that both labor and management had developed a virtuosity in the use of statistical techniques.

---

[6] U.S. Department of Labor, *Problems and Policies of Dispute Settlement and Wage Stabilization During World War II* (Bulletin No. 1009), p. 174.

[7] *Ibid.*, p. 175.

THE RIGHT TO STRIKE

There was little disagreement over the necessity of curbing work stoppages during the war and defense periods.[8] The practical problem centered upon the achievement of this objective. The basic alternatives open to the government were (1) reliance upon the voluntary co-operation of labor and management, (2) reliance upon compulsion, and (3) reliance upon some mixture of the first two alternatives. Government policy moved through several stages, but basically the third approach was used. As time passed, the element of compulsion became stronger; but at no point, before or during the war, was the right to strike banned by law. On the whole, the government program, which relied heavily upon union and management co-operation, worked. What has been aptly described as a miracle of production could not have been accomplished unless it had. It worked imperfectly, however; and therein lies the story of much of the heat engendered by the government's strike policy. A nation at war is not likely to judge objectively how an anti-strike program works on the whole. Strikes did occur; and when they did there was public uproar, and congressional tempers boiled.

The question might be raised as to why a government should tolerate even the possibility of strikes during war. One answer is that it may have no alternative. Strikes are not the results of whims but are the effects of specific causes. These causes do not disappear because the nation is at war. They may, in fact, be multiplied. A sophisticated policy must be prepared to uproot and deal with these causes. Forced industrial peace—if indeed peace can be achieved by force—might be compared to medicine that relieves pain but doesn't cure illness. Unresolved grievances make for sick industrial relations, and sick industrial relations do not make for the high levels of output that are essential in a war economy.

Organized labor was strongly in favor of a voluntary approach to dispute settlement. Compulsion was opposed, not only because it threw into the hands of third parties the problem of resolving labor-management issues, but also because of the fear that anti-strike legislation might be an entering wedge of a campaign to upset the legal gains that labor had won in the 1930's. There was, on the other hand, strong popular support for drastic strike prohibitions. The support was often accompanied by proposals for extremely punitive measures against strikers.

---

[8] Opposition to the war by American communists was expressed tangibly in the form of left-wing-inspired strikes at a number of defense facilities. After Hitler invaded the Soviet Union in violation of the non-aggression pact, the party line changed, of course. With typical thoroughness, the American Communist Party became most intolerant of interruptions of production regardless of cause.

National Defense Mediation Board

The necessity of doing something about strikes was brought home to the nation when a wave of work stoppages broke out in early 1941. The President responded by creating the tripartite National Defense Mediation Board on March 19. The Board had jurisdiction only over disputes certified to it by the Secretary of Labor.[9] The board's jurisdiction, furthermore, was limited to disputes that threatened to "burden or obstruct the production or transportation of equipment and materials essential to national defense." The President's executive order provided that the board should attempt to resolve disputes by helping the parties settle controversies, by affording means for voluntary arbitration, or by investigating issues in a dispute and making public recommendations.

For eight months this policy of tripartite mediation of disputes in defense industries worked reasonably well. Of the 118 cases certified to the board, eighty-six were closed. In forty-five cases, agreements were obtained by mediation. Formal recommendations were made in forty-one cases, and in thirty-seven the disputants accepted the recommendations. In three of the remaining four cases, the government seized the plant facilities because of either labor or management recalcitrance.[10]

Thus, although the program was voluntary and there was no law to force labor or management to accept board recommendations, an element of compulsion was present in the possibility of plant seizure. Some degree of compulsion also existed in the fact that defiance of a recommendation could run afoul of a public opinion easily aroused in an emergency period.

Success of the NDMB depended upon the general co-operation of labor and management as expressed by the willingness of representatives of these groups to serve on the board. This created a delicate balance that could be shattered by the appearance of a fundamental impasse. This, as we have seen, occurred over the union security issue in the Captive Coal Mine Case.

Succeeding strike crises in 1941 were accompanied by public outbursts calling for tighter controls. In Congress, numerous bills were introduced, some of them quite far-reaching.[11] United States entry into the war set the stage for a new approach to achievement of industrial peace.

---

[9] This meant that the board got the hard disputes that the Conciliation Service of the Department of Labor had been unable to resolve.

[10] Plant seizure was ordered in cases involving the Federal Shipbuilding and Dry-dock Corporation, Air Associates, Inc., and North American Aviation Company. In the first two cases it was management non-compliance that resulted in seizure, whereas in the latter case seizure was necessary because of union behavior.

[11] A bill introduced by Representative Howard Smith of Virginia was passed by the House of Representatives on December 3, 1941. The bill provided, among other things, for a thirty day cooling-off period before strikes or lockouts could be called in defense industries. Strikes were forbidden except after workers approved the strike call by a majority vote, unions responsible for illegal strikes were to be forbidden their

National War Labor Board

On January 12, 1942, the President by executive order established the National War Labor Board. Whereas the duties of the earlier Mediation Board were those of helping parties to reach agreements and, when necessary, recommending solutions and encouraging arbitration, the NWLB was charged with the obligation of *finally determining disputes* by mediation, voluntary arbitration, or arbitration under rules established by the board. Like the NDMB, the War Labor Board was tripartite in composition. Reliance was once again placed upon the voluntary co-operation of labor and management rather than upon anti-strike legislation. The approach, described as voluntary arbitration under government auspices,[12] was an expression of confidence in the no-strike, no-lockout pledge that had been made by prominent labor and industry leaders.[13]

The basic test of the effectiveness of the WLB was the degree to which disputants complied with its rulings. About 20,000 cases came to the board as disputes between January, 1942, and August, 1945. In about one-fifth of these cases strikes occurred either prior to the board's assuming jurisdiction, during the processing of the case, or after a decision was rendered. Only forty-six cases, however, had to be referred to the President because the board failed ultimately to win compliance with its orders. Six of these cases were settled as a result of a telegram from the President. The other forty were handled by plant seizure.[14]

An upturn in the number of strikes in 1943 and, particularly, recurring stoppages in the coal fields, resulted in passage over President Roosevelt's veto of the War Labor Disputes Act of 1943. Described as one of the more quixotic of the wartime labor policies,[15] the act provided that unions give thirty days' notice of threatened work stoppages in plants operated by war

---

rights under the National Labor Relations Act and the Norris-LaGuardia Act, jurisdictional strikes and boycotts affecting defense contracts were to be outlawed, and unions whose officers included members of the Communist party or the German-American Bund were to be denied the benefits of the NLRA. Passed by the House of Representatives in an obvious anti-labor mood, the bill was shelved during the excitement after Pearl Harbor Day.

[12] George W. Taylor, *Government Regulation of Labor Relations* (Englewood Cliffs, N.J.: Prentice-Hall, Inc., 1948), chap. 4.

[13] The President had called a Wartime Labor Industry Conference of twelve labor and twelve industry leaders. The conference was held in Washington, D.C., from December 17 to December 23, 1941. The conferees agreed that there should be no strikes or lockouts, that all disputes should be settled by peaceful means, and that the President should set up a War Labor Board to handle disputes. No agreement was reached on the then lively issue of union security. Seizing upon the agreements of the conference and ignoring the disagreements, the President proceeded to establish the War Labor Board.

[14] About half the seizure cases resulted from labor non-compliance with board decisions, whereas the other half resulted from management non-compliance.

[15] Taylor, *op. cit.,* p. 167.

TABLE 8

WORK STOPPAGES OF CONCERN TO NWLB,*
JANUARY 1942–AUGUST 1945

	STOPPAGES	WORKERS INVOLVED (*thousands*)	MAN-DAYS IDLE (*thousands*)
1942	420	238	818
1943	1,439	1,288	11,302
1944	1,629	961	4,867
1945†	869	837	6,563
Total	4,557	3,324	23,550

* Stoppages which developed in disputes certified to the NWLB either after the stoppage had been concluded, while it was in progress, or before the stoppage had developed.
† Through August.

Source: U.S. Department of Labor, *Problems and Policies of Dispute Settlement and Wage Stabilization During World War II* (Bulletin No. 1009), p. 52.

contractors. After thirty days, the workers were to be polled as to whether or not they wished to strike. To many workers, this seemed to indicate that strikes were permissible after a positive strike vote, which indeed they were from a legal standpoint. The inconsistency of this procedure with a voluntary program for strike discouragement soon became obvious, and many union leaders found that they had to assume the burden of convincing workers that the government didn't really mean that it was all right to strike. On the other hand, union leaders also found that the strike vote was a handy method of putting pressure upon employers. The intended congressional purpose—allowing workers to express themselves on the crucial matter of striking in wartime—was quickly lost. Workers had been handed an additional technique for expression of discontent.

During the war, less than two-tenths of one per cent of the man days spent on war production were lost through work stoppages. This doesn't prove that disputes didn't hurt the economy. A small strike can cause a big bottleneck. When all the aggravating circumstances are considered, however, the statistic cited does show the relative success of the program followed. In a period of rapidly rising union membership, with management in many cases still reluctant to accept the idea of unionism, and in a period of tensions when grievances accumulated more rapidly than usual, the record of achievement is not one to be minimized. The strikes made the headlines, but the real news was the determined efforts of many union and management officials who rose to the occasion and saw to it that a degree of co-operation consistent with the war situation was forthcoming.

SUMMARY: THE WAR PERIOD

Somehow, the unsettled issues in labor-management relationships had to be resolved or at least neutralized so that the best efforts of both groups could be channeled toward an effective prosecution of the war. Labor and management collaboration was obtained by the device of letting representatives of both groups participate in the establishment and administration of wage and dispute controls. Behind this participation, however, was the constant presence of the government. In the case of wage controls, War Labor Board decisions had to be consistent with the larger anti-inflationary program; and, in the case of dispute settlement, board decisions were made with the knowledge that failure to resolve disputes would invite a new government approach that would rely more heavily upon compulsion.

What was the effect of all this upon collective bargaining? The act of bargaining between management and organized labor was not legally limited by wartime controls. There was, however, limitation placed upon the decisions reached by the bargainers and upon the use of ultimate weapons of bargaining such as strikes and lockouts. Thus, bargaining was legally free but practically cramped. Furthermore, the mere existence of a government agency with the power to settle disputes made for a certain inflexibility in bargaining. So long as there was a possibility of getting a favorable decision from a government board, neither labor nor management representatives were inclined to engage in the give-and-take compromise that is essential to successful bargaining. The industrial area in which terms of employment were determined by collective bargaining expanded considerably during the war. Union membership increased to almost 15 million by V-J Day. Existing unions not only grew in size, but many were more firmly entrenched in their respective industries or crafts.

THE POSTWAR PERIOD

The pace of events in the world of organized labor has been fast since the end of World War II. Unification of the AFL and the CIO has been accomplished, but unity brought with it a host of bothersome problems. In the labor-management field the conflict over the right to organize has disappeared in substantial sections of American industry. Among non-union employers, however—and roughly 70 per cent of all non-agricultural workers are not union members—strong resistance to organization continues. By the early 1960's, in fact, total union membership was down by

1 million from the 1956 peak of 17.5 million.[16] In the political area, the favorable climate of the Wagner Act era has been replaced in a number of states by a legal atmosphere that is frankly hostile toward unionism. At the federal level, the Taft-Hartley Law of 1947 and the Labor-Management Reform Act of 1959 superimpose a variety of union restrictions upon the basic framework of the Wagner Act. These developments are described in greater detail below.

UNIONS *V.* UNIONS

On December 5, 1955, unity of the two labor federations was achieved at the first constitutional convention of the AFL-CIO. The road to unification had been a bumpy one, and only a few years earlier the possibility of a merger had seemed hopelessly dim. Discussions centering upon unity had been held by leaders of the rival federations at various intervals since 1937, but such talks had led nowhere. The conditions insisted upon by one or the other of the groups and the lack of enthusiasm for a merger among some labor leaders insured the breakdown of the earlier meetings for unity.[17]

Slowly in some cases and rather quickly in others, important factors that had worked against AFL-CIO unity disappeared or lost their meaningfulness. Thus the outlook for a merger brightened considerably in the year or two before the actual act of unification. What were some of the major obstacles that had impeded unification, and how were they overcome?

First, the basic issue of craft versus industrial unionism, that had originally split the AFL, worked for a time to impede unification. In the organizing drives of the 1930's and 1940's clashes between the old and new unions were frequent. By the time the war ended, however, the phrases "craft union" and "industrial union" had lost much of their fighting connotation. Many of the old-line craft unions had been organizing workers on an industrial basis, and industrial unions found it necessary to make special concessions to skilled workers on numerous occasions. Thus, labor unions, regardless of their traditional craft or industrial allegiances, were organizing new units on the basis of practical considerations rather than on the basis of an ideological preference for craft or industrial types of organization.[18]

---

[16] U.S. Department of Labor, Bureau of Labor Statistics, *Directory of National and International Labor Unions in the United States, 1963* (Bulletin No. 1395), p. 47.

[17] Numerous observers have alleged that John L. Lewis had little taste for a merger and was instrumental in blocking discussions for unity that had been initiated by President Roosevelt in 1939. See Arthur J. Goldberg, *AFL-CIO, Labor United* (New York: McGraw-Hill Book Company, 1956), pp. 52–57.

[18] For a discussion of this point see John Dunlop, "Structural Changes in the American Labor Movement and Industrial Relations System," *Proceedings of the Ninth Annual Meeting of the Industrial Relations Research Association*, 1956, pp. 22–26.

The new pragmatism did not eliminate jurisdictional conflict; but, since practical issues are more amenable to compromise than are ideological ones, it created a more hopeful milieu for an AFL-CIO merger.

Changes in labor leadership that were occurring also heightened the possibility of unity. As long as the persons who were intimately associated with the AFL-CIO rupture occupied prominent positions in the labor movement, merger possibilities were lessened by the old and lingering feelings of personal hostility. In 1952 Philip Murray and William Green died. John L. Lewis, after withdrawing his United Mine Workers from the CIO and then the AFL in fits of animosity, was a relatively isolated figure in the American labor movement. The new federation presidents, George Meany in the AFL and Walter Reuther in the CIO, had not been prominently involved in the schism of the 1930's.

Positive action taken in the federations against communism and corruption answered two of the more prominent charges that CIO and AFL spokesmen had been throwing against each other. The rise of the CIO had taken place under conditions that were fertile for communist infiltration into that organization. Skilled organizers who would do the physically dangerous job of organizing workers at the plant level were urgently needed. The job was a natural one for the devoted communist who is unmindful of personal sacrifice as long as his cause is being advanced. John L. Lewis, who had been ruthless in his treatment of communists within his own union, felt that the radicals could be used but kept in hand. In the newly established unions, the communists came to meetings more often than others, stayed later, walked picket lines, distributed literature, and ingratiated themselves with the rank and file. As a result, communists, although not in control of the CIO, occupied many positions of influence.

The course of international history necessitated some tricky party line shifts by American communists, all of them being faithfully echoed by left wing unionists. From an advocacy of isolationism (during the life of the Russian-German non-aggression pact), to all-out war and no strikes (after the German invasion of Russia), to opposition to the Marshall Plan and support of Henry Wallace as a presidential candidate (during the Cold War), the American Communist party adapted itself to the needs of Soviet policy with a minimum of subtlety.

The uneasy truce between the communist minority and the non-communist majority within the CIO was strained to the breaking point during the early Cold War years when the sympathies of most union leaders were strongly in favor of the Marshall Plan and aid to Turkey and Greece. The open conflict between the factions occurred within individual unions, in state and city industrial union councils, and in the CIO as a whole. Slowly and after hard fights, communists were dislodged from influential positions in the National Maritime Union, the Transport Workers Union, and the

United Automobile Workers Union. Finally, in 1949, the CIO at its annual convention voted to expel the left-wing-dominated United Electrical, Radio, and Machine Workers and the United Farm Equipment and Metal Workers. In the following year, nine other left wing unions were expelled. After a protracted struggle for the allegiance of the rank and file in the expelled unions, the power of most of the leftist organizations was broken. Among the expelled unions, only the International Longshoremen and Warehousemen's Union and the International Union of Mine, Mill and Smelter Workers can boast of sizable memberships at the present time.

Within the AFL the problem was corruption rather than communism. For years, the leadership of that body had used the principle of national union autonomy as an excuse to avoid a direct confrontation with several notoriously corrupt affiliates. Strong pressures from within and without the Federation finally forced a change of stance. In 1953, the AFL revoked the charter of the corrupt International Longshoremen's Association and established a rival organization. (Attempts to break the power of the Longshoremen failed, however.) These actions taken by the CIO and the AFL against communism and corruption removed major causes of reluctance to have mutual relationships and enhanced the likelihood of merger.

Another factor that encouraged efforts to achieve unity was the revelation that competitive practices by rival unions had been relatively fruitless. By the time World War II ended, the momentum of the earlier AFL and CIO organizing drives had disappeared. Organizational efforts by many unions now took the form of inducing workers to leave one union and join another. An analysis of data taken from the files of the National Labor Relations Board revealed how unproductive such inter-union raiding had been. In the two year period, 1951–1952, some 1,200 NLRB cases involved attempts by one union to raid the membership of another. In only 17 per cent of the cases was the petitioning union successful in defeating an incumbent union, and when the totals of changed affiliations were analyzed it became apparent that gains enjoyed by CIO and AFL affiliates nearly cancelled each other. The net change in worker affiliation amounted to less than 2 per cent of the total number of persons involved in raiding efforts.[19]

The deteriorating political position of organized labor impressed upon many labor leaders the necessity of strong and unified political efforts by the unions. The passage of the Taft-Hartley Act in 1947 and the rash of anti-union legislation that had appeared in many states provided AFL and

---

[19] Goldberg, *op. cit.*, pp. 76, 77. See also Joseph Krislov, "Raiding among the 'Legitimate' Unions," *Industrial and Labor Relations Review,* October, 1954, pp. 19–29.

CIO leaders with a common political goal and thus must be regarded as one of the forces that worked in the direction of a formal unification of the two labor federations.

The AFL-CIO Merger

Shortly after his election as AFL president, George Meany gave evidence of a serious intent to bring about labor unity, as did Walter Reuther. The latter had been elected CIO president over strong opposition, and among his supporters were those who had been won to his side by assurances that he would work hard to end the AFL-CIO breach. After Reuther's election rumors circulated to the effect that the Steelworkers' Union might leave the CIO and make a separate peace with the AFL if unification efforts failed. Thus, the possibility of instability within the CIO strengthened the intensity of that organization's efforts to end the labor split.

Determination by the leaders of the two federations was not in itself sufficient to produce the desired result of unity. A host of problems had to be resolved; and among these, the matters of jurisdictional conflict and inter-union membership raiding were especially pressing. In 1951 the CIO inaugurated an Organizational Disputes Agreement which sought to prohibit CIO unions from raiding each other and from competing for unorganized workers. No similar agreement, however, inhibited AFL and CIO affiliates from raiding each other or, for that matter, AFL unions from raiding other AFL unions.

At a meeting in April, 1953, the AFL-CIO Unity Committee agreed that prevention of raiding was a necessary condition of merger. Subsequently a no-raiding agreement was drafted and later approved by the AFL and the CIO at their annual conventions. The agreement was to apply to all unions that signed; but signatures were slow in coming in, and for a time the future of the pact was threatened by a CIO insistence that more of the important AFL affiliates and especially the Teamsters Union become signatories of the agreement. The CIO, however, relaxed this demand; and the pact became operative on June, 1954, for the sixty-five of 110 AFL affiliates and twenty-nine of thirty-two CIO affiliates that had signed.

As unity meetings continued, it became apparent that the problem of the non-signing unions might become an insuperable barrier against merger. Dave Beck of the Teamsters indicated that he would not go along with a unity formula that required his signature on a no-raiding pact, and Meany had also taken a position against a compulsory ban on raiding. Reuther, on the other hand, had been holding out for a universal no-raiding agreement. As the merger talks reached a showdown stage, Reuther retreated from his position, and a compromise was worked out. The final agreement provided that the integrity of each affiliated union should be maintained, that the constitution of the merged federation should contain a declaration for respect by each affiliate of the bargaining relationships of other affiliates, and that proper machinery would be provided to implement these provisions. Thus, mandatory signing of a no-raiding agreement was dropped as a precondition of merger to be replaced by a statement of principle that was sufficiently flexible to allow the merger movement to proceed.

Another problem and one closely related to the raiding issue was the matter of union jurisdiction. In the American labor movement the principle of exclusive jurisdiction has long been upheld as an ideal. The concept of exclusive jurisdiction implies that a single union shall have sole jurisdiction over a specified group of workers and that other unions will recognize and respect such jurisdictional rights. In practice the ideal has failed as a tenable guide on numerous occasions. Technological change, for one thing, has shifted the lines that divide industries and crafts so that work once clearly within the jurisdiction of a given union has assumed characteristics similar to work done by persons in other unions. Thus, products once made of wood are now made of metal, and metal has frequently been replaced by plastics. In certain circumstances jurisdictional lines have always been indistinct. Should the hauling of beer, for instance, be the work of the Teamsters or the brewery workers?

In the 1930's additional factors weakened the concept of exclusive jurisdiction. The Wagner Act of 1935 provided workers with the opportunity of choosing their bargaining representatives. In a majority of cases the choice consisted simply of voting for a single union that was attempting to win bargaining rights or voting for no union. Frequently, however, more than one union sought to win recognition as a bargaining agent; and in such circumstances the employees usually selected their representative in an election conducted by the National Labor Relations Board. The Wagner Act elections, coupled with the AFL-CIO split over craft versus industrial jurisdictions, meant that to an extent the choice of bargaining unit rested with workers. This was inconsistent with a concept of exclusive jurisdiction based upon agreement among unions as to who should do the organizing.

Without some resolution of the jurisdictional conflicts so obviously manifested by the extensive degree of raiding, an AFL-CIO merger would have been meaningless. Here again, a compromise agreement was reached. Each national union was to be admitted to the merger federation with its membership intact. The fact that a union had a given group of workers within its jurisdiction was sufficient to establish the union's jurisdictional rights. As Professor Dunlop has suggested, the rights of possession were to prevail regardless of the merits of any prior claims based upon exclusive jurisdiction. All affiliates, furthermore, were to enjoy the same organizing jurisdictions which they had enjoyed prior to merger. In the many cases of overlapping and duplicate jurisdictions, the hope was expressed that *voluntary* mergers of national unions would occur.

The agreement reached in the jurisdictional issue was illustrative of what George Meany called the "short approach" to unity. The long approach was to resolve all conflicts of interest before merger. The alternative, according to Meany, was to effect the merger and then untangle the large residue of problems. The CIO and AFL negotiators selected the short approach. Tactically, they were correct. Merger, otherwise, would have been delayed, perhaps never to materialize. But the short approach saddled the new labor federation with a host of problems that were not to disappear simply because the AFL and the CIO had merged their identities into a single labor body.

THE POST-MERGER ERA: A MIXED RECORD

With the merger accomplished in 1955, spokesmen for the AFL-CIO looked to the future hopefully and spoke in optimistic tones about doubling union membership within a decade. The first post-merger decade, however, witnessed an actual decline in total union membership; and the hopefulness that pervaded the labor movement in the mid-fifties by the mid-sixties had turned to apprehension and pessimism. A substantial literature, most of it written by persons not unfriendly to organized labor, diagnosed the "decline of the labor-movement" and popularized a number of themes that, with variations, have been repeated by the more candid among the labor leadership.[20]

Actually, the post-merger experience has been a mixture of failure and success. Organized labor has been plagued by a number of problems that obviously were not anticipated in 1955. On the other hand, unions have won gains that did not appear to be imminent ten years ago.

On the positive side, labor can point to a slow but steady growth in total union membership since 1963 and the remarkable gains in wages and working conditions that have been negotiated since the end of World War II. Despite these objective measures of success, many observers believe that the vitality of the labor movement has been sapped by a variety of problems, some generated within the unions themselves and some reflecting external forces. These are discussed below.

---

[20] For representative titles in this literature see Solomon Barkin, *The Decline of the Labor Movement* (Santa Barbara, Calif.: Center for the Study of Democratic Institutions, 1961); Paul Jacobs, *The State of the Unions* (New York: Atheneum Publishers, 1963); Paul Sultan, *The Disenchanted Unionist* (New York: Harper & Row, Publishers, 1963); Sidney Lens, *The Crisis of American Labor* (New York: A. S. Barnes & Co., Inc., 1961); and the entire issue of *The Annals of the American Academy of Political and Social Science* for November, 1963.

Internal Factors Affecting Union Progress

A major problem that has hung over from the pre-merger period is the craft versus industrial union issue. In a labor market where blue collar job opportunities are shrinking, the contest has evolved into a fight over job rights in occupational areas where the claims of one side are frequently as tenable as those of the other. A serious sore spot within the AFL-CIO, for example, has been the antagonism between the construction crafts and the large industrial unions who, for years, have been unable to agree upon a definitive dividing line between craft and industrial union jurisdiction in plant maintenance and repair work.

In 1956, the contending groups, with an assist from the AFL-CIO president, George Meany, agreed that the construction unions would have jurisdiction over new construction whereas the industrial unions would control day-to-day maintenance. The agreement was not implemented, however; and by the time of the 1957 AFL-CIO convention the nineteen building trade unions were threatening to secede. The revolt died out when the construction unions were prevailed upon to remain within the federation, but the underlying causes of inter-union conflict remained unresolved.

Along the same lines, there have been frequent clashes between the craft unions in the Metal Trades Department and the industrial unions in the Industrial Union Department. Developments in automation technology have pushed the skilled metal craftsman into a new prominence and at the same time have blurred jurisdictional lines between craft metal trades unions, such as the Sheet Metal Workers, and several of the industrial unions.

Successive efforts to deal with the problem of internal union disputes led finally to a pact between the industrial and craft groups in 1961. The pact was incorporated into the AFL-CIO constitution as Article 21, Section 3; and it specifies that disputes over maintenance and construction work will be resolved on the basis of the "established work relationship." Thus, where one AFL-CIO affiliate has a clear claim to a set of jobs because its members have customarily performed the work, another affiliate may not contend for these jobs on the basis of alleged inherent jurisdictional rights.

The machinery for implementing the policy expressed in Article 21 provides, first, for mediation of disputes over established work relationships. If mediation fails, an arbitrator is to make a ruling. Appeal from the arbitrator's ruling may be made to the Executive Council of the AFL-CIO.

For various reasons, including the fact that the "established work relationship" criterion is not relevant when a dispute involves new jobs, the 1961 agreement has not eliminated the internal disputes that have wracked the AFL-CIO.[21] The procedural machinery, however, has worked to relieve the Executive Council of a good part of the burden of dealing with disputes which, for a time, absorbed much of the council's energies and prevented that body from dealing effectively with other serious problems facing the AFL-CIO and its affiliated unions.

Although the craft-industrial union fight had traditionally been a conflict among rival unions, certain of the industrial unions have been troubled by internal conflicts growing out of differences in interest between the craft and non-craft sections of their membership. Frequently the main cause of the craft worker's dissatisfaction is that the difference between his wage and that of the less skilled worker has been shrinking. The broader complaint is that the leaders of the industrial unions have neglected the special interests of craft workers, who usually constitute a small minority of the total membership. A number of unions have responded to these complaints by making concessions to the craft workers; but, as one student of the subject has observed, industrial unionism has not provided a final solution to the problem of building a stable alliance among diverse occupational groups.[22]

Labor unions have also been troubled by a rank and file restiveness. A reaction to various discontents, the feeling has been manifested in revolts of varying scale against the union officialdom. Serious attempts to unseat national union officers have been relatively rare; but within the past several years they have occurred in the State, County and Municipal Employees Union, the International Union of Electrical, Radio, and Machine Workers, and the United Steelworkers of America. Unions as different in their officer-member relationships as the United Automobile Workers and the International Longshoremen's Association have been embarrassed by the refusals of their memberships to ratify contracts that the leaders of both unions described as the best ever reached in their respective industries. Membership rejection of bargaining agreements reached by union negotiators, in fact, now occurs with sufficient frequency to constitute a major industrial relations problem. Once a rarity, rank and file refusals to ratify agreements that union leaders consider good enough to accept occurred during the mid-sixties in over 10 per cent of the active dispute cases in which the Federal Mediation and Conciliation Service was involved. The most publicized turndown, perhaps, occurred in the summer of 1966 when 35,000 striking airline mechanics overwhelmingly rejected a proposal for

[21] For an analysis of the limitations of union pacts for resolving disputes over the division of work see Margaret K. Chandler, *Management Rights and Union Interests* (New York: McGraw-Hill Book Company, 1964), pp. 189–203.

[22] Arnold R. Weber, "The Craft-Industrial Issue Revisited," *Industrial and Labor Relations Review*, April, 1963, pp. 381–404.

settlement of a dispute reached with the personal help of President Lyndon Johnson. Reasons for rank and file uprisings against proposed settlements include dissatisfaction with the size of the wage package, political rivalries within unions, and poor communications. The longshore contract referred to above, for example, was accepted after the workers received an adequate explanation of how good an agreement it actually was.

Numerous other examples could be cited to illustrate the character of the strains within the labor movement today. Noteworthy evidence of a different type is the difficulties that many unions have had with their staff-level people.[23] Many prominent staff persons with years of involvement in the labor movement have left their organizations, a development, incidentally, which lends support to the assertion that liberals and intellectuals have less partisan attachment to the labor movement today than they had in the 1930's and 1940's.[24]

If the performance of the unions has stirred some of the rank and file to protest, it has lulled more into apathy. The typical union member of the 1930's was one who had fought for the right to have a union. The typical member today has probably joined because of a union shop requirement. He believes that the union provides him with some protections that are important, but he does not identify closely with it except in crisis situations. He pays his dues, expects some services in return, and that is the extent of his involvement. The arrangement is businesslike, but it is not the setting for dramatic spurts in union growth.

Within the AFL-CIO, differences in leadership style and philosophy have led to serious rifts which are reminiscent of the animosities that plagued American unionism before World War II. The disaffiliation of the Auto Workers Union from the AFL-CIO in 1968 was the result of a long-standing feud between UAW president Walter Reuther and AFL-CIO president George Meany. Dissatisfied with what he regarded as a failure on the part of the Federation's leadership to encourage energetic organizing activity and to involve itself wholeheartedly in major contemporary social problems, Reuther chose to lead his union out of the AFL-CIO after repeated rebuffs of his effort to influence the organization's policies from within. As a result of the split, the two largest unions in the United States—the Auto Workers and the Teamsters—are outside the fold of the AFL-CIO. With a combined

---

23 One of the most publicized cases was the attempt by a group of organizers in the International Ladies' Garment Workers Union to form their own bargaining organization. The effort provoked a severe reaction on the part of a union that has taken pride in its reputation as a benevolent organization. See Jacobs, *op. cit.,* pp. 112–136.

24 See Maurice F. Neufeld, "The Historic Relation of Liberals and Intellectuals to Organized Labor in the United States," *The Annals of the American Academy of Political and Social Science,* November, 1963, pp. 115–126.

membership of 3 million, the two unions account for approximately one-sixth of total union membership in the nation.

Ties between the Auto Workers and the Teamsters were forged in July, 1968, when the two groups joined to form an Alliance for Labor Action. The objectives of the Alliance, as originally announced, were to organize the unorganized and to join with others in assisting the poor and the unemployed. Although the Auto-Workers' withdrawal from the AFL-CIO was not followed by a defection of other unions, an Auto Worker-Teamsters' alliance provides a potential base for the formation of a rival federation.

External Factors Affecting Union Progress

Among the "external" obstacles to union growth are some that are similar to those that the unions have always had to face, whereas others are unique and pose a new order of challenge. No labor movement in the past, for example, has been troubled by a significant change in the ratio of blue collar to white collar workers.

In the past decade many labor unions have had to face stiffening resistance on the part of management. Relatively pliant in the immediate post-World War II decade when cost increases could be shifted forward to consumers, managements have tended to take tougher bargaining stances in recent years. Technological developments which have eliminated many jobs have placed unions in a defensive position, and labor organizations have had to devote an increasing share of their attention to job security matters. In some industries, unions have won notable successes in the job security area; but, as one prominent labor leader has observed, ". . . the gravest danger to collective bargaining is that it may do more and more for less and less to its ultimate undoing. . . ."[25]

Technological change has affected the labor-management power balance in other ways. In certain of the public utility industries, for example, the strike weapon has been blunted by the fact that supervisory personnel are able to operate the facilities for considerable periods of time with little loss of output. High productivity levels in other industries minimize the economic losses suffered by the firm during strikes. General Motors was able to earn record profits in 1964 despite a walkout that idled most of its facilities for a month.

One sign of the exacerbating effect of technological change on the character of labor-management relations is the number of strikes resulting

---

[25] Leonard Woodcock, "New Problems for Collective Bargaining," *Proceedings of the Fifteenth Annual Meeting of the Industrial Relations Research Association,* p. 203.

from disputes over plant administration practices. In recent years such disputes have accounted for approximately 15 per cent of all work stoppages and rank second only to general wage disputes as a cause of stoppages.

The evidence most frequently cited to show that the labor movement is in a declining or advancing state is membership statistics. Such evidence must be interpreted cautiously since union size is not always an accurate measure of union strength. In a general sense, however, membership statistics do reveal something important about the response of workers to the union appeal.

A spectacular rise in union membership occurred between 1936 and 1944. From the latter date to 1956, membership continued to climb but at a slower pace. Between 1956 when some 17.5 million persons were enrolled as union members and 1961, membership dropped by about 1.2 million. The decline was halted in 1963 and subsequent annual increments brought the total to a new high of 17.9 million members in 1966. Measured as a percentage of total labor force, union membership dropped steadily from 25.2 per cent in 1956 to 22.4 per cent in 1965. This decline was reversed in 1966 when the percentage rose to 22.7. Union membership expressed as a percentage of the non-agricultural labor force, however, has dropped steadily from 33.4 in 1956 to 28.1 in 1966.

The character of the problems that challenge the organizational ambitions of contemporary unions is best indicated by moving away from aggregative data and examining more closely the possibilities in areas where the union penetration has been relatively small. In industries such as rail transportation and manufacturing where unions are strongly entrenched, most of the workers are already organized and energetic and expensive efforts would be required to organize the others.

Social, economic, and political barriers have inhibited the growth of unionism in the South. In recent years, nevertheless, the rate of union growth in the South has been more rapid than elsewhere in the nation. Between 1953 and 1964, union membership in southern states increased by 9.7 per cent whereas the increase in the United States other than South was 6.1 per cent. Despite these gains, the percentage of non-agricultural employees in the South who belong to unions is only about half of what it is elsewhere in the nation. Future prospects for unionism in the South are mixed. The growth of manufacturing and government white collar employment are favorable factors particularly since much of the new manufacturing consists of branch plants of nation-wide firms covered by company-wide collective bargaining agreements. Unfavorable factors include the large supply of low income agricultural workers who have often been used as strike breakers, the non-metropolitan location of many plants, racial conflicts within unions, and the ability of many southern employers to avoid their legal obligations to deal with unions through delaying tactics. While it is probable that unions will continue to score gains in the South, the gap

FIGURE 7

MEMBERSHIP OF NATIONAL AND INTERNATIONAL UNIONS, 1930–66*

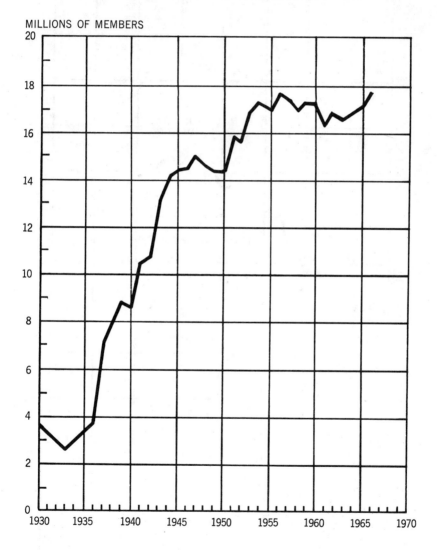

MILLIONS OF MEMBERS

* Excludes Canadian membership but includes members in other areas outside the United States.
Source: U.S. Department of Labor, *Directory of National and International Labor Unions,* 1967.

FIGURE 8

UNION MEMBERSHIP* AS A PERCENT OF TOTAL LABOR FORCE AND OF
EMPLOYEES IN NON-AGRICULTURAL ESTABLISHMENTS, 1930–66

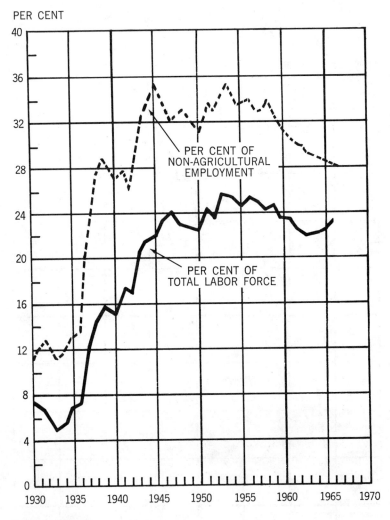

* Excludes Canadian Membership.
Source: U.S. Department of Labor, *Directory of National and International Labor Unions*, 1967.

in the degree of organization between this region and the rest of the nation
is likely to remain large for some time to come.[26]

---

[26] For a summary of the state of unionism in the South, see Ray Marshall, "The
Development of Organized Labor," *Monthly Labor Review*, March, 1968, pp. 65–73.

The agricultural labor force is almost completely unorganized. With the exception of a few recent spurts of unionism, in fact, the industry has remained virtually untouched by the national experience with labor organizations. Formidable obstacles stand in the way of any large scale organization of the farm labor force. These include the seasonal nature of farm work, the large number of farm workers with only partial commitment to either the labor force or farm labor,[27] declining agricultural employment due to mechanization, lack of knowledge about unionism among farm workers, determined resistance by farm employers, and exclusion of farm workers from coverage under the national statutes that protect organizing activity.

A collective bargaining breakthrough in the agricultural sector occurred in 1966 when the United Farm Workers Organizing Committee signed an agreement with Schenley Industries. Since then, the UFWOC has negotiated agreements with a number of other grape growers in California.

The UFWOC, described as a form of "community unionism," is unique in a number of respects.[28] A mixture of job oriented unionism, non-violent philosophy, and ambitious programs of community self-help, the organization, through its own efforts and successful appeals for assistance from others, was able to conduct a sustained drive that eventually led to the achievements noted above. Subsequent efforts to organize farm workers in other parts of the country have not been notably successful. The UFWOC experience, however, suggests that in certain circumstances an agricultural unionism is not an impossibility.[29]

Many of the workers who remain unorganized today have backgrounds and interests sufficiently different from organized blue collar workers to pose a challenge to prevailing techniques of organizing. Whatever the formula for organizing white collar workers, unions, for the most part, have not been able to find it. There are white collar workers in unions, of course—about 14 per cent of total union membership according to Bureau of Labor Statistics data[30]—but organization of the remainder will be beset with numerous difficulties. A large proportion of the persons in the collection of occupations that are grouped in the white collar category are women who regard their employment as a temporary condition and hence are disinterested in the conflict that would attend organization. Male white collar workers have traditionally been more employer-oriented than blue collar workers;

---

[27] About 40 per cent of the farm labor force consists of "casual workers" or persons who engage in less than 25 days of farm work each year. More than half of the migrant workers earn more nonfarm income than they earn from farm work. "The Migratory Farm Worker," *Monthly Labor Review*, June, 1968, p. 11.

[28] Irving J. Cohen, "La Huelga, Delano and After," *Monthly Labor Review*, June, 1968, p. 13.

[29] For a concise analysis of the prospects for unionism in the agricultural sector see Karen S Koziara, "Collective Bargaining on the Farm," *Monthly Labor Review*, June, 1968, pp. 3–9.

[30] Bureau of Labor Statistics, *Directory of National and International Unions in the United States*, 1967, pp. 60–61.

and although some part of this orientation has broken down in recent years, it has not disappeared completely. The bank clerk, the junior accountant, the professional engineer still resist being identified as "workers"; and the type of appeal that has brought blue collar workers into unions has not been particularly successful among white collar employees. As a result of the labor market changes discussed in earlier chapters, white collar jobs are becoming relatively more important in the American economy; and unless unions are successful in shaping an attractive appeal to the white collar group, organized labor will play a less significant role in the future than it has in the past two decades. Since 1956, unions have enjoyed some success in organizing white collar employees in the government, retail trade, communications, and service industries. These gains, however, have been partially offset by membership losses among white collar personnel in manufacturing. A recent development of interest among certain white collar and professional groups has been the use of their professional associations as "near unions" for purposes of negotiating with their employers. This has occurred in the areas of public education and professional athletics.

In addition to the difficulties associated with efforts to penetrate into slightly organized areas, the American labor movement has been troubled in recent years by the problem of a deteriorating image. One reason for this is the acceleration of union activity in the public sector which has produced a rash of strikes by employee groups such as school teachers, refuse collectors, and municipal transit operators. Disruptions of government services touch the public more directly than the typical dispute in the private sector and there has been a growing public impatience with the industrial relations turbulence in government. An image problem of a different character has resulted from the inability of organized labor to communicate effectively with contemporary protest movements. To groups most actively involved in present day protest, organized labor is generally viewed as an irrelevant if not hostile force. The consistently hawkish position on Viet Nam expressed by many prominent labor leaders, the failure to respond quickly or energetically enough to charges of union discrimination against Negroes and Mexican-Americans, and the lack of relevance of labor's traditional goals to the social protests of the young have produced a breach between labor and the "new left." American unionism has been described as having made the transition from "protest movement to going concern."[31] From one point of view this summarizes the progress of organized labor. As an institution it is firmly established in the national eco-

---

31 Jack Barbash, "American Unionism: From Protest to Going Concern," *Journal of Economic Issues*, March, 1968, pp. 45–59.

nomic structure. From the perspectives of the contemporary protest movements, labor as a going concern is part of the "establishment" and, thus, is disqualified as an effective vehicle for change. The gravamen of the charges against labor made by militant groups is not totally unlike that voiced by Walter Reuther when the UAW split away from the AFL-CIO.

SUMMARY: THE POSTWAR PERIOD

Since the end of World War II, the two labor federations have managed to work out a merger; but the fact of merger has not eliminated many of the problems that stand in the way of effective inter-union cooperation. Jurisdictional disputes, personal animosities among the labor leadership, and a lack of the momentum that characterized both the AFL and the CIO in the late 1930's have limited the effectiveness of the AFL-CIO. Organized labor has made many substantial gains through collective bargaining and, in general, management has come to accept the fact of unionism. Total union membership reached an all time high of 17.9 million in 1966 but union membership expressed as a percentage of the non-agricultural labor force has declined. Organizational gains have been scored in the South, among agricultural workers, and among professional and white collar groups particularly in the public sector. The large majority of workers in these areas, however, remains non-union. The public relations position of organized labor has deteriorated somewhat and, among contemporary militant groups, the labor movement is regarded as an ineffective, if not hostile, force.

QUESTIONS

1. What factors in a war economy necessitate a close government concern with the labor-management relationship?
2. How did the government deal with the strike issue during World War II? Would it have been simpler to have followed a policy of declaring all strikes illegal?
3. At the time of the AFL-CIO merger, many persons predicted that the merger would result in a substantial increase of labor union power within the economy. Has this prediction been borne out by the post-merger experience?
4. What have been the major successes of organized labor since World War II? What have been the major failures?
5. Although certain white collar groups have had unions for many years, organized labor has never been able to enroll the bulk of the persons in white collar occupations. Which of the following white collar groups, in your opinion, would be likely to respond favorably to a vigorous union organizing drive and which would not: (a) professional engineers, (b) public school teachers, (c) retail department store clerks, (d) office clerical employees, (e) government employees? Defend your opinion.
6. What special problems are associated with an effort to organize farm workers?

SELECTED READINGS

BARBASH, JACK. "American Unionism: From Protest to Going Concern," *Journal of Economic Issues,* March, 1968, 45–59.

BARKIN, SOLOMON. *The Decline of the Labor Movement.* Santa Barbara, Calif.: Center for the Study of Democratic Institutions, 1961.

DULLES, FOSTER R. *Labor in America.* New York: Thomas Y. Crowell Company, 1966 (Third edition). Chaps. 19–21.

GOLDBERG, ARTHUR. *AFL-CIO, Labor United.* New York: McGraw-Hill Book Company, 1956. Chaps. 1–8.

SEIDMAN, JOEL. *American Labor from Defense to Reconversion.* Chicago: The University of Chicago Press, 1953.

CHAPTER 6

Institutional Aspects of Unionism

THE EXACT NUMBER OF PERSONS WHO BELONG TO LABOR UNIONS IS uncertain. The current estimate is about 18 million. These workers belong to locals which in most cases are affiliated with one of some 190 national or international unions.[1] Most of the nationals, in turn, are affiliated with the AFL-CIO. Some nationals are independent unions. ("Independent" in this sense means that the organizations do not belong to the AFL-CIO.) At the present time, the most prominent among the independents are the United Mine Workers, the Auto Workers, and the Teamsters Unions.

The general structural relationship between the basic units of labor organizations can be pictured in the form of a diagram. What cannot be shown in a diagram, however, are the less mechanical aspects of the relationships between the different levels of organization. Where is the seat of power, who controls the purse strings, what are the functions of the officers at the several levels? Just as a thorough diagram of the structure of the United Nations would fail to show the tensions among member nations, an elaborate diagram of the structure of labor unions would not reveal the pulls and tugs within these organizations. There are, furthermore, important differences among the various national and local unions. Many are modest in size and resources, whereas others have grown to the point where

---

[1] Some labor organizations have locals in Canada and so are international unions. For simplicity in expression, we shall refer here to national unions only. The membership figure cited above does not include the foreign members of the international unions.

they have resources and interests that are not popularly associated with unions.

The independent United Mine Workers is majority stockholder of a large bank in Washington, D.C. The United Automobile Workers has a net worth of over $80 million. A credit union servicing several locals of the Teamsters Union in Cleveland, Ohio, has assets of over $2 million. Some nationals have large staffs of specialists such as educational directors, economists, public relations men, and editors. Certain unions have sufficiently large numbers of employees so that on occasions they are embarrassed by labor trouble. The purpose of this chapter is to examine more closely some of these institutional aspects of unionism.

THE FEDERATION AND THE NATIONAL UNION

Structurally speaking, the AFL-CIO is the top unit in the American labor movement. Most important among its constituent units are the 128 affiliated national unions. Other units directly affiliated with the federation are a number of locals that have not been incorporated into any of the nationals, city and state groupings of local unions, and six trade and industrial departments.

Governmental Structure

The supreme authority of the federation is the biennial convention. All affiliates are entitled to send delegates and participate in the voting. The distribution of voting power is such, however, that the strength lies with the national unions and particularly with the larger nationals.[2] Voting rights for other affiliated units are only nominal.

Between conventions the business of the federation is directed by the officers and by the members of several bodies established by the AFL-CIO constitution. The president, in addition to exercising a general supervision over federation affairs, has the authority to interpret the constitution. His

---

[2] Article 4, Sections 8 and 17, of the AFL-CIO constitution stipulate how the voting strength shall be apportioned among the affiliated units. Section 8 provides that "the number of members of each national and international union, organizing committee, and directly affiliated local unions for the purpose of selecting delegates and for roll-call votes at the convention shall be the average monthly number of which per capita tax is paid for the 24 month period prior to and including the second month preceding the month of the opening date of the convention. . . . The Secretary-Treasurer shall prepare for the use of the convention and submit to it a printed list showing the number of votes and the number of delegates to which each affiliate is entitled."

Section 17 provides that on roll-call votes "each delegate . . . shall be entitled to one vote for every member whom he represents. Each state and local central body and national trade and industrial department shall be entitled to one vote."

FIGURE 9

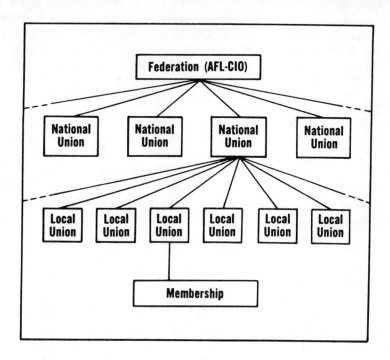

interpretation is conclusive unless reversed or changed by the executive council or a convention.

The executive council is the unit of the federation empowered to carry out policy as determined by the biennial convention. It is also a center of initiative in that its recommendations are not likely to be ignored by the convention. Since the members of the council are, in most cases, the presidents of the stronger national unions, the executive council is the most influential single body in the determination of federation policy. Council membership consists of the president, the secretary-treasurer, and the twenty-seven vice presidents of the AFL-CIO. In addition to carrying out the decisions of the convention, the executive council is empowered to investigate an affiliate when evidence suggests communist, fascist, or dishonest leadership. By a two-thirds vote the council may suspend an affiliate after an investigation, although the suspension may be appealed to the convention. The executive council meets at least three times a year at the call of the president.

Two other bodies complete the top governmental structure of the AFL-CIO. An executive committee consisting of the president, the secretary-treasurer, and six vice presidents selected by the executive council meets every two months to advise and consult with the president and secretary-treasurer on policy matters. The general board of the federation meets at least once a year to decide all policy questions referred to it by the executive officers or the executive council. The membership of the general board consists of all members of the executive council and the chief officers of each affiliated national union and department.

Function of the Federation

The broad job of the federation is to promote the interests of unions and workers. The specific means used to accomplish this are quite varied. One major job is to encourage organization among the unorganized. In its earlier years, the CIO was primarily a giant organizing committee. Today the AFL-CIO is active on the organizational front, in some instances through aid and support of national unions and in others by direct action of organizers attached to the federation staff. The federation, with headquarters in Washington, D.C., is engaged in extensive political activity. Prior to the AFL-CIO merger, the Political Action Committee of the CIO and Labor's League for Political Action in the AFL attempted to swing labor support behind candidates and policies that had been judged favorably by the federations. In the merged federation these functions are performed by the Committee on Political Education (COPE). Top officers of the federation frequently testify before congressional committees in matters that are of interest to labor. The labor lobby, in fact, is quite active during sessions of Congress. In addition to these activities, the federation maintains legal, educational, research, and editorial staffs that provide services to the national unions and otherwise promote the cause of labor by the application of their specialized abilities.

Power Relationship

The question of where the basic power rests is fundamental to an understanding of any organization. One who attempts to understand American government must untangle the federal-state relationship as well as the relationships of the executive, legislative, and judicial branches at both federal and state levels. He will learn that these relationships have not been static ones. There have been, for example, weak and strong Presidents, which is another way of saying that the power of the executive relative to that of the other government branches has varied significantly from time to time.

If one were limited to a single generalization about the federation-national union relationship, the most accurate statement that could be made is that the autonomous national unions are the power centers of the American labor movement. The federation derives its power from the nationals and without their affiliation would be a hollow organizational shell. National unions on the other hand can and have functioned successfully without federation affiliation. National unions are autonomous in several senses. They are, first, their own housekeepers insofar as internal affairs are concerned. Frequency of conventions, manner of selecting officers, dues, assessments, salaries, etc. are matters over which the federation exerts no control. Secondly, short of expulsion, the federation has no power to insist that a national union support such policy as the federation decides upon.

Some qualification of this broad generalization about the power relationship must be made. The AFL was deliberately established as an organization in which the autonomy of the national unions would be jealously guarded. Many of the CIO affiliates, however, owed their existence to the organizational efforts and financial sums expended by the CIO. This resulted in a dependence upon the federation which enhanced its power. The personalities of the federation presidents have had a great deal to do with the exercise of influence upon national union behavior. Cautious and conservative William Green during his long incumbency as AFL president was not likely to challenge anything as fundamental as national union autonomy. On the other hand, the strong-willed John L. Lewis and the highly respected Philip Murray were able to exert a real influence on CIO policy and national union compliance with that policy.

After the deaths of Green and Murray, important changes occurred in the federation-national union relationship in both the AFL and the CIO. George Meany, the new AFL president, gave promise of a vigorous and relatively independent leadership, whereas Walter Reuther, uncertain of his power as CIO president, had to tread lightly. Since the merger, Meany as president of the AFL-CIO has indicated an intention to broaden the functions and power of the federation. It is now clear, for instance, that the autonomy of the national union does not extend to those circumstances where communist domination or corruption are obvious; however, it also seems apparent that expulsion will be practiced infrequently and only then as a last resort.

Apart from the racketeering and communist situations, it is not likely that the basic autonomy of the national unions will be challenged in the near future. For one thing, there is no overwhelming sentiment in the federation to do this. The federation, after all, is made up of representatives whose primary concerns are the interests of their own unions. Several factors are apparently leading to a greater degree of federation influence, however. One is that the vagueness of jurisdictional boundaries has forced the national unions to cede some authority to the federation insofar as the resolution of jurisdictional disputes is concerned. Another important factor is that the growing political role of labor will probably enlarge the federation's job as co-ordinator and leader. While the national union is more

FIGURE 10

STRUCTURE OF THE AFL-CIO

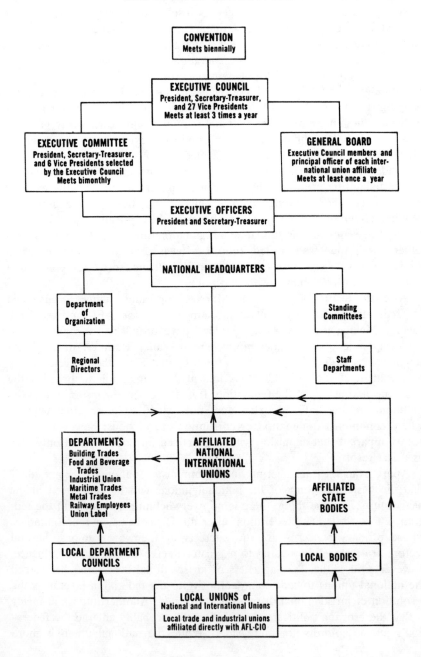

effective than the federation in exerting economic pressure upon employers, a more political-minded unionism will require a centralization of efforts; and here the federation is the logical unit to take the leadership.

THE NATIONAL AND THE LOCAL UNION

There are about 190 national unions in the United States. They vary widely in size, strength, and methods of operation. The Journeymen Stone Cutters Association of North America, The International Alliance of Bill Posters, Billers, and Distributors, and The International Association of Siderographers have total memberships of about 1900, 1600, and 29 respectively. The International Brotherhood of Teamsters, Chauffeurs, Warehousemen and Helpers of America, The United Automobile, Aerospace, and Agricultural Implement Workers of America, and The United Steelworkers of America have memberships of more than a million. In 1966, twenty-four national unions had fewer than ten locals, whereas four had over 2000.

These diversities and others to be noted should occasion no more surprise than the fact that extremely large and very small business enterprises may be organized as corporations. A union may be small because it functions in a small industry, or because it has not successfully organized the greater part of a large industry, or because it has lost out in competition with other unions. As might be expected, the largest unions are found in industries such as steel, automobile manufacturing, and truck transporta-

TABLE 9

NATIONAL AND INTERNATIONAL UNIONS BY SIZE
OF MEMBERSHIP, 1966

NUMBER OF MEMBERS	TOTAL UNIONS	
	Number	Per Cent
Under 1,000	21	11.1
1,000 and under 5,000	33	17.4
5,000 and under 10,000	10	5.3
10,000 and under 25,000	27	14.2
25,000 and under 50,000	28	14.3
50,000 and under 100,000	24	12.6
100,000 and under 200,000	25	13.2
200,000 and under 300,000	6	3.2
300,000 and under 400,000	6	3.2
400,000 and under 500,000	3	1.6
500,000 and under 1,000,000	4	2.1
1,000,000 and over	3	1.6
Total	190	100

Source: United States Department of Labor, *Directory of Labor Unions in the United States, 1967.*

tion, which have huge labor forces. The single fact that an industry is large, however, does not necessarily mean that a large union will be functioning in that industry. In railroad transportation, for instance, there are so many unions representing the various types of workers that no one of the railroad unions is especially large.

Since there is a core of functions and problems that is common to all labor organizations in the United States, there is a certain amount of similarity in their structural, financial, and leadership aspects. Another explanation for this similarity is that newly formed unions have imitated the already established bodies in certain respects. As one writer has pointed out, the appearance of similar provisions in the constitutions of many nationals results, partly at least, from the fact that unions have tended to copy the more attractive constitutional provisions from other unions.[3] Differences among unions are explained by such factors as the technology of the industry, geography of the product market, historical attitudes of employers, competition from other unions, and internal politics within unions.

National Union Officers

So far as formal structure is concerned, most nationals are quite similar. Unions generally have a national president; a secretary-treasurer; an executive council; and a number of appointive officials such as organizers, auditors, international representatives, editors, and educational directors. Underneath this formal similarity, there are substantial differences. In his examination of the constitutions of 115 national unions, Professor Taft found that the presidents in thirty unions have only routine power. In thirty-four unions they have moderate power, whereas in fifty-one others they have considerable power.[4]

Trade union leaders at the national level tend to remain in office for long periods of time. Like any generalization about American labor unions, this one is subject to qualification. Examples of national officer replacement resulting from insurgent movements are not rare and, in recent years, presidents of the Steelworkers Union, the International Union of Electrical, Radio and Machine Workers, and The American Federation of State, County, and Municipal Employees have been defeated for reelection. The general proposition concerning tenure is sound, however. A study of elections held in seven unions between 1910 and 1941 showed that only 17 per cent of the elective offices filled during that period were contested.[5] The

3 Joseph Shister, "Trade Union Government: A Formal Analysis," *The Quarterly Journal of Economics,* November, 1945, pp. 99–100.
4 Philip Taft, "The Constitutional Power of the Chief Officer in America Labor Unions," *ibid.,* May, 1948, pp. 459–471.
5 Philip Taft, "Opposition to Union Officers in Elections," *ibid.,* February, 1944, pp. 246–264.

Brotherhood of Railroad Trainmen had only three presidents from 1909 to 1961; the Carpenter's Union has had only two since 1915 and the Retail Clerks one since 1944. Similar examples of tenure can be cited for many other unions.

This could mean that the officers have been unusually successful and popular with the membership, or it could mean that there are dangers involved in opposing the incumbents. The history of labor unions provides examples of both situations. Union leadership is a career, and it is a rare case when the "in" group is not doggedly determined to stay in. The incumbents have an assortment of advantages over such challengers as may appear. The leader has the prestige that comes with being president. He has avenues of publicity and some patronage to dispense. He can squelch the advancement of a potential opponent. He can become so popular with the rank and file that his own future is beyond challenge. By these and other means, union presidents have managed to hold their offices. Leaders have been successfully challenged, but this is not the usual case.

Most national unions hold conventions attended by delegates from affiliated locals. The usual time interval between conventions is two years, although some unions meet annually and others as infrequently as every four or five years. The significance of the convention varies by union. Some are completely stage managed with the important decisions being made behind closed doors. Others have been the scene of open factional disputes. Whether it is conducted democratically or not, the convention makes it possible for leaders in different areas of the country to know one another, to exchange ideas, and to gain a perspective that is denied to one who never leaves home. Among other things, the convention is a large educational forum.[6]

Functions of National Unions

The major functions performed by national unions are promotion of organization within the industry or trade, bargaining directly with employers in some cases and supervising and assisting local union bargaining in others, lending assistance to strike-bound locals, and maintaining a close watch on legislative and legal developments, especially when these bear directly upon the fortunes of the particular union. Administration of the union health and welfare program is usually handled by the national. Practically all unions publish a journal, and most have some sort of research and education program, although the content and quality of these are quite different from union to union.

---

[6] For a good discussion of the national convention see William M. Leiserson, *American Trade Union Democracy* (New York: Columbia University Press, 1959), chaps. 7–9.

The passage of time has witnessed an increasing centralization of power in the national unions at the expense of their affiliated locals. A number of factors account for this. The spread of industry-wide and regional bargaining enhances the negotiation function of the national and reduces that of the local. Labor leaders have learned that low wage standards in any geographical area result in a competitive advantage to employers within that area and constitute a threat to union standards achieved elsewhere. To prevent this or to eliminate it where it has occurred requires an over-all supervision and policing of all local union contracts with employers. Intelligent bargaining today frequently demands a knowledge of the economics of the industry as well as a first-hand familiarity with technical subjects such as time study, job evaluation, incentive systems, and accounting. Few local leaders are competent in all these matters and consequently must rely upon the national for help. The rapid growth of collective bargaining and the rates of turnover among local union leaders has meant that some inexperienced persons become local officers. In many cases, the intervention of the national has been at the request of the local official who finds himself involved in matters that are beyond his understanding.

The increase in the size and functions of unions has been a force leading to the growth of the national union's role. Many unions handle vast sums of money; and the administration of strike funds, benefit plans, and other special funds is more likely to be efficient when the money is centralized at a national headquarters. The professional staff of the United Automobile Workers Union includes economists; lawyers; social workers; actuaries; and specialists in metropolitan planning, industrial hygiene, older workers, social security, and radio engineering and broadcasting. There are individual corporation departments that specialize in the affairs of the various corporations with which the union deals. Other departments such as Agricultural Implement, National Aircraft, and Foundry and Skilled Trades are organized on industrial or craft lines; and still others deal with the special problems of such groups as women members, retired workers, and veterans.[7] Few unions have such an elaborate service staff, but the trend is toward expanded union services and functions rather than the reverse. Only in rare cases are local unions equipped financially or otherwise to perform these services.[8] As the national union expands its role, it expands its powers simultaneously.

---

[7] Jack Steiber, *Governing the UAW* (New York: John Wiley & Sons, Inc., 1962), chap. 4.

[8] Some large locals provide a rather elaborate set of services for their membership. For examples of this see Maurice F. Neufeld, *Day In, Day Out With Local 3, IBEW* (Bulletin 28 [Ithaca, N.Y.: New York State School of Industrial and Labor Relations, Cornell University, 1955]) and Michael Harrington, *The Retail Clerks* (New York: John Wiley & Sons, Inc., 1962), pp. 46–53.

Control of Locals

The techniques by which the national exerts control over its locals consist of formal constitutional limitations on the local union, intervention by national officers in local bargaining, and the informal exercise of power that is co-ordinate with the process by which an ambitious national leader solidifies his position.

Constitutions of national unions usually specify that locally bargained contracts must be approved by the national and that approval of the national must be obtained before a local can engage in a strike.[9] The executive board of the national union generally has the power, subject to various types of appeal, to suspend the charter of a local union and to oust its officers. In some cases, this power rests with the national president.

As was the case in the discussion of the federation-national union relationship, some qualification of the generalization about the power of the national union must be made. Factionalism is not uncommon within labor organizations; and when a local union lines up with a dissident faction, it is likely to be less amenable to control from national headquarters. A local that is dissatisfied with its treatment at the hands of the national can bolt the parent organization and join another national or simply function as an independent union. So long as this type of organizational mobility is a real possibility, there exists a check against undue autocracy by the national. No matter how closely the national supervises the local, the business of day-to-day unionism such as contract administration, grievance processing, and looking after spontaneous problems must be handled by the local official. In the long run, the success of the union will depend upon the caliber of its local officialdom. Many unions have recognized this as a problem and have established training programs for local officers and potential leaders. As these leaders become more experienced and more able, they are likely to exercise more power. The business of unionism is becoming so complex that national leaders might find themselves quite willing to share some of their burdens. Recent developments in labor law also modify the power of the national over the local. The Labor-Management Reporting and Disclosure Act of 1959, for example, regulates the way in which a national union can set aside local self-government.

Some mention should be made of an intermediate body that exists in many of the national unions. The district or regional office is headed by a director who in some unions is appointed by national headquarters and

---

[9] For a summary of national unions' constitutional provisions regulating the election of local union officers see Office of Labor-Management Policy Development, United States Department of Labor, *Union Constitutions and the Elections of Local Union Officers,* 1965.

in others is elected by representatives of the local unions in his jurisdiction. The director and his staff exercise a general type of supervision over local unions within a defined geographical area. It is the district director who assists local unions with their bargaining and organizational problems and who carries out national union policy within his area. In some labor organizations, the district director does most of the actual contract negotiating.[10]

THE LOCAL AND THE UNION MEMBER

There are about 75,000 local unions in the United States. Most hold charters from national unions, but a number are independents operating without national union affiliation.[11] A third category consists of local unions

FIGURE 11

EXAMPLE OF NATIONAL, REGIONAL, AND
LOCAL STRUCTURAL RELATIONSHIPS

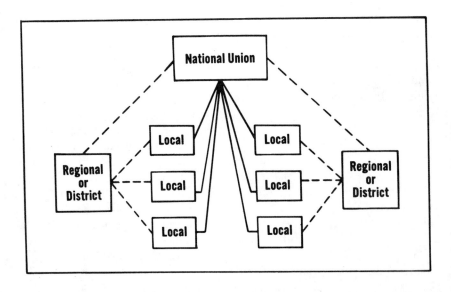

---

[10] For a discussion of the nature and role of the intermediate body see Herbert Lahne, "The Intermediate Body in Collective Bargaining," *Industrial and Labor Relations Review,* January, 1953. See also Jack Barbash, *American Unions: Structure, Government and Politics* (New York: Random House, 1967), chap. 5.

[11] It has been estimated that the number of single firm unions without national union affiliation is 1,400 and that these unions have a total membership of 400,000. See Arthur B. Shostak, *America's Forgotten Labor Organizations* (Princeton, N.J.: Industrial Relations Section, Princeton University, 1962), p. 1.

that are directly affiliated with the AFL-CIO because of the absence of an appropriate national to absorb them. A local union may have only a handful of members, or it may have a membership that runs into five figures. The average local has about 200 to 300 members.

Local unions may take any one of a number of forms. The most prominent types are plant and craft locals. The former is common in manufacturing where production and maintenance workers are frequently members of a single plant local. In an industry such as construction where employees shift from one employer to another and where the typical employing unit is small, all workers of a particular craft within a geographical area will generally belong to the same local. Thus, the carpenters or the bricklayers in a metropolitan area will be members of one local. Locals may be organized on a multi-plant basis. Here, one local will have jurisdiction over workers in several plants. Conversely, workers within one plant may be divided among different locals, each affiliated with a different national union. This type of arrangement is becoming increasingly common. It is not unusual for an employer to find his workers represented by a half-dozen different unions. His production workers may belong to the United Automobile Workers Union, the electricians may be in the International Brotherhood of Electrical Workers, the truck drivers may be in the Teamsters Union, the operating engineers may have their own union, etc. Highly skilled workers or workers in special occupations that are different from those of the main body of production workers often feel that their interests will be better served if they have their own unions. Many of the raids that unions make upon one another's memberships have been designed to pluck small groups of workers away from a plant-wide local. Changes in collective bargaining law have facilitated this "severance" process. The structure of some locals is explained by factors quite different from those that account for the variations described here. This would be the case where local units are organized along racial or nationality lines.

Functions of Locals

In a number of areas, the functions of the local union overlap those of the national. This is especially so in collective bargaining; and, as we have seen, the autonomy of the local in this matter varies from union to union. Functions that are primarily within the local's province include a day-to-day policing of the union-management contract, processing grievances of workers, managing the conduct of strikes, and collecting dues and assessments. Regardless of whether a contract is negotiated nationally or locally, it is the worker who must live with its terms. Local leaders are in the best position to observe employer conformity with the contract and to detect weak or ambiguous provisions. A good portion of the time of the local officer is spent in dealing with the real or fancied grievances voiced by workers. Occasionally a local matter will explode into a big issue that involves eventual action by the national union, but most daily working problems are resolved locally. The burden of conducting a strike usually falls upon the local leadership. Organizing the strike, setting up picket lines, distributing benefit payments, and maintaining striker morale are all parts of the local leader's job. Locals are engaged in other work such as educating the membership about its rights under social security laws, carrying on a program of political action, co-operating with civic groups in community affairs, and promoting social functions for its members. The degree of interest in these and similar matters varies widely from local to local.

Union Officials

Officers of local unions may be part-time officials who receive only token salaries, or they may be full-time officials receiving $15,000 plus automobile and expense account. This depends upon the size and the resources of the local as well as the demands of the job upon an officer's time. In a typical small-plant local, there will probably be a part-time president, a secretary-treasurer who may or may not be a full-time officer, and possibly a scattering of other officials such as a vice president and a sergeant at arms. Several committees will be given special responsibilities. In the plant itself, there will be a chief steward and several department stewards who work at their regular occupations but have some leeway to use working time to look after union business. This business will include recruiting new employees into the union, hearing worker complaints and dealing with them through formal or informal channels, and observing the workings of the labor contract. In large plant locals, most officials will be full-time officers, and even the shop stewards might receive small payments. As the local grows in size, so does the burden of office. The president will meet frequently with the employer to thrash out problems; there will be many—possibly daily—consultations with the stewards; there will be an office that must be managed, internal politics within the union to be watched closely, and regular and special union meetings to be chaired. This is hardly an exhaustive list of the local officer's functions. He is more likely to be overworked than the reverse, and he rarely gets off with an eight-hour working day.

In non-factory industries, where employment is scattered among many small employers, locals will have a business agent who may or may not double as one of the local's officers. The typical business agent is a full-time, comfortably—if not elaborately—remunerated union official. To some extent his functions are similar to those of the shop steward in the factory although his authority is much greater. In a small-scale business such as retail meat sales, it would not be feasible to have a steward at every meat counter in a city. Instead a business agent makes the rounds to check conditions and hear complaints. Because many non-factory jobs are in industries that function in a local market, the local union often has much autonomy in bargaining with employers, and usually it is part of the business agent's job to negotiate the labor contract.[12]

Except for the business agent, who tends to keep his job for a long time, there is a considerable amount of turnover among local union officials. This is especially true among the unpaid representatives, such as shop stewards. They may leave the employment of the plant, be promoted to management jobs, move up to full-time union work, or simply decide that the rewards of the job are not commensurate with the burdens. The recruitment and training of effective stewards is one of the major problems of the local union.

Unionism

The average observer interprets unionism in terms of pronouncements by nationally known labor leaders, spectacular developments in collective bargaining, and major failures in labor-management relationships. He learns what he knows from the newspapers, and the papers publish only what is "newsworthy." To the typical union member, unionism is what is being done to resolve his particular complaint, what kind of a guy the business agent is, how much more money he will earn under the new contract. At the grass roots level of the labor movement, little that occurs is of interest to the city editor. What does occur, however, is the sum and substance of unionism for all but a few of the rank and file of organized labor. The importance of the union-member relationship at the local level is obvious in a society where unionism is widespread, and in recent years many writers have turned their attentions to this relationship.[13] The sense of the various studies is that there are all kinds of union members belonging to all kinds of unions. Although this is hardly a spectacular conclusion, the data underscore the danger of broad generalizations. Unions range from the autocratic to the highly democratic, and member attitudes toward their unions, from hostility and indifference to strong commitment.

The prevailing character of the union-member relationship is frequently a function of union style; and style, in turn, depends in part upon the character of the leadership and in part upon the external forces that dominate

---

[12] For more detailed comment on the business agent and his job see George Strauss, "Business Agents in the Building Trades," *Industrial and Labor Relations Review,* January, 1957, and Jack Barbash, *Labor's Grass Roots* (New York: Harper & Row, Publishers, 1961), chap. 5.

[13] See, for example, Theodore V. Purcell, *The Worker Speaks His Mind on Company and Union* (Cambridge, Mass.: Harvard University Press, 1953); Joel Seidman, Jack London, Bernard Karsh, Daisy Tagliocozzo, *The Worker Views His Union* (Chicago: The University of Chicago Press, 1958).

the attentions of the union. The elaborate welfare programs sponsored by such large organizations as Local 3 (New York City) of the International Brotherhood of Electrical Workers, Local 688 (St. Louis) of the Teamsters, and Local 770 (Los Angeles) of the Retail Clerks bear the marks of an unusually strong leadership. The union-membership relation in these locals is different from that in the Auto Workers local at the Kohler Company where a hostile company-union situation colors all aspects of union life or from that in Ford Local 600 which has carried on a running vendetta against the national union leadership. All of these differ from what is found in the small southern textile union local engaged in a struggle for survival. Unionism—to repeat—is a many-faceted thing, and any general statement about the union-member relationship must be framed cautiously. A situation that is found quite frequently, however—perhaps often enough to warrant the designation of "typical"—is one where the union member pays his dues, receives good services, and has little to do with his union except during crisis situations when his degree of participation increases.

Several aspects of the union-member relationship have aroused concern both within and without the labor movement. At a point in history where the civil rights aspirations of Negroes are being vigorously expressed, it is inevitable that union practices concerning the Negro are being subjected to more searching examination than has been the case in the past. A second area of concern stems from signs that many profess to see of an erosion of democracy within unions. These concerns are discussed below.

Access to Union Membership

A logical first question would be about the possibility of joining a union. For workers generally, the record is quite good in the factories and in some of the service industries. About all that is involved is paying a small initiation fee and keeping up with dues payments. In the skilled crafts, membership is much less open. Craftsmen often fear that too many practitioners will mean not enough work for all; and entrance to the union, which is a prerequisite for practicing the craft, is limited by one device or another. In some building trade locals, apprenticeship training is open only to sons of union members. Certain locals have been notorious for the excessively high initiation fees charged. Some have class *B* memberships with limited rights, and others issue temporary work permits as an alternative to admitting new members when demand for labor increases. From a social standpoint, little can be said in defense of limitations in union membership. From the standpoint of the groups of workers involved, the argument in justification is much the same as that used by the businessman who wants a tariff against "unfair" competition. Both the tariff and union membership limitations are devices to overcome the menace of competition.

On the question of racial prejudice, the record of organized labor is spotty. Some of the railroad unions and an assortment of others, particularly in the crafts, have maintained only thinly disguised policies of discriminating against Negroes. Even the large industrial unions, whose leaders have frequently been active proponents of civil rights, have been troubled by overt discriminatory practices of affiliated locals in the South.

The dilemma of the leadership in certain unions can probably be best explained through reference to the concept of "working class authoritarianism." Persons who can be classified as in the "working class" are usually liberals. A number of studies, however, have drawn attention to a distinction that can be made between economic and non-economic liberalism.[14] Working class persons are generally liberal on such issues as social security, progressive taxation, and public regulation of private enterprises. On non-economic issues such as civil rights for racial minorities, however, they tend to take conservative positions.[15] The reasons for this are complex, but they can be summarized as a working class predisposition to authoritarian attitudes which reflects, among other things, shorter exposure to educational experience and tensions generated by fears of economic insecurity. Working class authoritarianism, incidentally, appears to be a universal rather than a national phenomenon.

There is a cleavage, thus, between the ideals and preachments of some of the union leadership and the situation that is found to prevail in certain of the local unions. In many cases, the leader finds that there is nothing that he can do about the problem.

Although organized labor has been troubled by the racial problem, it should be noted that the official stand of the AFL-CIO has been forthright. Delegates to the 1963 convention of the AFL-CIO adopted, without a dissenting vote, a resolution urging all affiliates to remove "the last vestiges of racial discrimination from within the ranks of the AFL-CIO." Translating the 1963 resolution into practice has been difficult, however, particularly in the area of union apprenticeship programs. Union spokesmen have argued that the absence of Negroes in such programs has been due more to the difficulty of recruiting qualified applicants than to racial discrimination, an argument that receives partial but not total support from a Department of Labor sponsored study.[16] Whatever the reason, there is no dispute over the

---

14 See, for example, Seymour M. Lipset, "Democracy and Working Class Authoritarianism," *American Sociological Review*, August, 1959, pp. 482–501. In these studies, the phrase "working class" is used interchangeably with "lower class" and "poorer class" at some cost in clarity. As used, however, "working class" connotes manual labor, and lower levels on the income and education scales.

15 *Ibid.*, p. 489. The per cent of persons classified as "most tolerant" in one study was highest for college graduates in high level white collar occupations and lowest for those with grade school educations in the low manual occupations.

16 U.S. Department of Labor, Manpower Administration, *Negroes in Apprenticeship*, Manpower/automation research monograph no. 6, August, 1967.

fact that relatively few Negroes have been enrolled in training for skilled craft jobs,[17] and in 1968 the presidents of the 18 AFL-CIO building trades unions adopted a plan to admit more Negroes to apprenticeship training and to work with Civil rights groups to carry out the plan.

Union Membership and the Civil Rights Act of 1964.   Until the passage of the Civil Rights Act of 1964, Congress shied away from the issue of discriminatory membership practices of labor unions. In the Civil Rights Act, however, Congress took a step that it had refused to take in 1959 when it passed the Landrum-Griffin Act which imposed a variety of controls on the internal affairs of labor organizations. Title VII of the 1964 enactment makes discriminatory employer and union practices unlawful. Our concern here is with the unlawful union practices.

Under the "Equal Employment Opportunity" section (Title VII) of the Civil Rights Act, it is unlawful for a labor organization ". . . to exclude or to expel from its membership, or otherwise to discriminate against any individual because of his race, color, religion, sex, or national origin." It is also unlawful for a union to segregate or classify its members so as to limit the employment opportunities of any racial or ethnic group or to use discriminatory practices in apprenticeship or on-the-job training programs.

Enforcement of Title VII is the duty of a newly established Equal Employment Opportunity Commission. The commission is charged, first, to use informal methods to resolve violations. If this fails, an aggrieved person may file a civil action in a United States district court. The Attorney General may bring a civil action in cases where there is a "pattern or practice of resistance." Where a court finds an intentional violation, it may enjoin the unlawful activities and order affirmative corrective action. When an unlawful practice occurs in a state which has a law prohibiting the practice, charges may not be filed with the commission without prior resort to the state procedures.

Democracy in Unions

How democratic are unions? Do they reflect the desires of the members? Are they run by small cliques of bureaucrats? Answers to these questions involve some analysis of the nature of the union. For many years now, students of labor have noted the multi-sided nature of the labor organization. In part, the union is a protest movement fighting to improve the status of its members. In part, it is a business organization attempting to regulate the sale of labor power in an orderly and efficient manner. In part, it is a

---

[17] See *Monthly Labor Review,* August, 1968, p. 70.

political unit marked by the conflicts of rivals who aspire to hold the reins of office.

The union leader must play different roles, a job that is not simplified by the fact that the roles are often inconsistent with one another. In the first phase of a union's life—organization against employer opposition, negotiation of the first contract, realignment of power relationships in the workplace—there is apt to be a high sense of unity between the leadership and the rank and file. They share a common goal, membership participation is high, and communication between leader and member is direct and frequent. Once the union is established, the leader's role as fighter must be tempered by the sobering responsibilities of his office. He cannot go to war with management over every worker complaint. He must turn down some of the demands that the membership makes. As he deals with management, he becomes more sophisticated about the economics of the industry, and he comes to appreciate the problems of management. He must spend time managing an office, making speeches to non-labor groups, and balancing financial statements. As the size of the union grows, he spends less time at the plant with workers and is more involved with the inevitable demands of what has become a bureaucracy. The distance between leader and member widens.

Effective leadership of a union can come only with experience, and experience can come only with continuity in office. Furthermore, after some years in office the thought of returning to the work bench is not appealing to most officers. Thus, the leader must be a politician, maneuvering against opposition and building a machine through patronage. When factionalism becomes strong he is apt to overlook the niceties of democratic procedures. As a general rule, it can be stated that the older a union, the less democratic its operations. There are exceptions, of course, but in practice the inefficiencies of pure democracy are at a disadvantage when matched against the flexibility and experience of a strong leadership.

The gradual evaporation of democracy in unions cannot be attributed solely to the designs of labor leaders. In fairness to the leadership, it should be noted that their power often comes to them by default. Union meetings are poorly attended, and more often than not the member is not overly interested in the workings of his union. As one writer has observed, a democratic union is not obligated to manufacture an opposition.[18]

---

[18] Michael Harrington, *The Retail Clerks* (New York: John Wiley & Sons, Inc., 1962), p. 21. In their study of leadership attitudes among union officials, Miles and Ritchie found that most union leaders believe that rank and file members should be encouraged to participate in decision-making. The same union officials, however, expressed doubt that the actual quality of decisions would improve as a result of greater rank and file participation. Raymond E. Miles and J. B. Ritchie, "Leadership Attitudes Among Union Officials," *Industrial Relations,* October, 1968, pp. 108–117.

A close parallel can be drawn between the attitude of the worker toward his union and that of the citizen toward his government. Few people participate in government, other than at election time, and even then the turnout is not too impressive. Unless an individual has a direct interest in the proceedings he is not likely to attend his city council meeting. His attitude toward the politician is cynical. He is against all taxes but wants more services. Behind this cynicism and indifference, however, there is a loyalty to the government that comes to the fore strongly in crisis situations.

The situation is much the same in the labor union. Union meetings are often dull and are certainly not on an entertainment par with TV, the movies, bowling, or the ball game. The labor leader is a "pork chopper," hardly a complimentary reference. The member expects good service for the dues he pays. In effect, he feels that he is buying and paying for these services. Despite his outward apathy toward his union, however, the member will come to its support when it is attacked. American labor history is replete with evidence that proves this point.

Democracy *v.* Oligarchy

In most unions written constitutions provide a framework for the practice of democracy. Appeal procedures are available to those disciplined for infraction of the rules, and processes are established for the popular election of officers. There might be raised, then, the question of why there is such a discrepancy between the formal guarantees of democratic procedures and the actual practice of control by a small group. As Lipset, Trow, and Coleman have noted in their study of union democracy, almost all private organizations such as labor unions, professional and business associations, veterans groups, and co-operatives tend to be ruled by a one party oligarchy.[19] A number of reasons for this have been suggested above, but perhaps the matter warrants a summary restatement.[20] (1) Bigness requires bureaucratic patterns of behavior. Usually there is an incompatibility between bureaucratization and democratic turnover of office holders. Bureaucracy, furthermore, gives an incumbent administration advantages in the form of control over financial resources and communication media as well as a near-monopoly of political skills. (2) In the modern urban society, few individuals are actively interested in the affairs of their union. Leisure time is spent away from one's vocation, and this absence of participation in union affairs facilitates one-party oligarchy. (3) Democracy involves risks for office holders. They may be defeated for re-election; and such a defeat would involve a move from a position of power, status, and income to a

---

[19] Seymour M. Lipset, Martin A. Trow, and James S. Coleman, *Union Democracy* (New York: Free Press of Glencoe, Inc., 1956), p. 3.
[20] This summary follows the analysis in *ibid.*, pp. 403, 404.

much lower position in all three respects. In a society that emphasizes achievements and status, incumbents in office are under pressure to practice undemocratic tactics if these are essential to the retention of their offices.

According to Point 3, democracy should be more prominent in small local organizations where the status gap between leaders and rank and file is small. As a matter of fact, many local unions are highly democratic, and this tends to substantiate the thesis that the absence of democracy flows from the fact of bigness and attendant bureaucracy. Even within local unions, growth in size carries with it a tendency toward bureaucracy and extended tenure for office holders.

The prevalence of oligarchy does not mean that a union hierarchy is typically unresponsive to the desires of the membership. One-party rule is frequently justified on the basis that an organization characterized by political instability is unable to do a good job of looking after member interests. In a number of unions, furthermore, matters in which members are most keenly interested, such as contract ratification and decisions to strike, are subject to referendum vote. There is no necessary incompatibility between servicing member needs and oligarchic rule; and, in the usual union situation, the strength of the incumbent group rests in part upon an ability to judge what the members want and to act accordingly.

Formal Appeal

Almost all unions impose penalties for infractions of one sort or another. To safeguard the rights of members, unions have established procedures by which disciplinary decisions of local unions may be appealed. The conduct that calls for punishment may consist of a breach of union rules such as working for less than union pay scales or walking through a picket line, or it may consist of a disloyalty to the union that is sometimes described broadly as "conduct unbecoming a union member."

The formal appeal mechanism varies among unions, but in a typical situation the sequence of events would be similar to the following. Charges are brought against a member in his local union. A trial committee hears the charges and reports back to the local meeting where the decision of the committee is affirmed or rejected. The person found guilty may then appeal according to an established process. Frequently, there is a right to appeal to the union president, then to the executive committee, and finally to the national union convention.

How effective are such mechanisms in protecting the "civil rights" of union members? Here again, the situation will vary among unions. In many cases procedural safeguards that the American Civil Liberties Union would regard as basic, such as the right to be defended by counsel and the right to cross examine, are not provided. The trial officer, furthermore, may be personally interested in the disposition of the case and thus be less than objective about the outcome.[21] The appellate machinery within unions, nevertheless, cannot be written off as mere window dressing. Professor Philip Taft, who made an intensive study of appeals in eight important unions, concluded that the penalties imposed were reasonable and that the appeal process offered real protection in most unions.[22]

Democracy and the Organizational Web

Discussion of democracy within unions frequently runs to extremes. Thus, one can find assertions to the effect that unions are, or are rapidly becoming, one party oligarchies as well as defense of the proposition that there is nothing seriously wrong with the condition of representative rule within labor organizations. The discussion below deals with certain of the factors that underly such a polarization of opinion.

The description of union government in this chapter has concentrated upon formal structure and the interrelationships between the levels of government such as federation–national union and national union–local union. As Cook has pointed out, however, unions have two governments.[23] In addition to the formal government which can be described in terms of constitutions, by-laws, etc. there is a second concerned with the functions of collective bargaining and contract administration. The two governments overlap and crisscross, often in confusing patterns. From the standpoint of union democracy, the significance of the political dualism is that one can find situations where the degree of democracy will be more pronounced in one government than in the other. A tightly controlled organization providing no adequate safeguards for a political opposition, for example, may have a shop steward arrangement that is highly responsive to membership opinion in matters of contract administration. In such a case, one may find a flourishing democracy or a cynical one-party rule, depending upon

---

[21] The United Automobile Workers has established a final appeal board composed of prominent persons who are not members of the union. For an analysis of the UAW Public Review Board see Jack Steiber, Walter W. Oberer, and Michael Harrington, *Democracy and Public Review* (Santa Barbara, Calif.: Center for the Study of Democratic Institutions, 1960).

[22] Philip Taft, *The Structure and Government of Labor Unions* (Cambridge, Mass.: Harvard University Press, 1954), p. 180. For a detailed description of union disciplinary procedures see the following articles in the *Monthly Labor Review:* David A. Swankin, "Grounds for Trial of Members and Local Officers," February, 1963, pp. 125–132; Leon E. Lunden, "Trial Powers and Procedures at the Local Union Level," March, 1963, pp. 255–261; Swankin and Lunden, "Selected Due Process Safeguards and Appeals," April, 1963, pp. 378–384; Swankin, "Influence of the LMRDA on Constitutional Discipline Provisions," May, 1963, pp. 491–496. See also Harry R. Blaine and Frederich A. Zeller, "Who Uses the UAW Public Review Board?" *Industrial Relations,* May, 1965, pp. 95–104.

[23] Alice H. Cook, "Dual Government in Unions," *Industrial and Labor Relations Review,* April, 1962, pp. 323–349.

which government is being observed. In unions where the web of organization is an involved crisscross of the two governments at local, intermediate, and national levels, casual observation is not likely to reveal the location of the true power points or the prevailing character of officer-member communications.

Judgment concerning union democracy will also differ depending upon the weight that is placed upon certain types of evidence. Poor attendance at union meetings and infrequent turnover of officers may be signs of an undemocratic organization, but they are not foolproof indicators. Union members may not go to meetings; but they do go to work where, not infrequently, they are part of a "shop society" or an informal social group capable of quite forceful expression about what the rank and file want from their union.[24] Tenure in office can also be a misleading test. In some cases, union officers have held their posts for long times despite active opposition,[25] and lengthy tenure in office has not always meant that the preferences of the officers are slavishly followed.[26]

Finally, many of the arguments concerning the lack of union democracy, though valid, are not applicable to all unions or to all levels within the union hierarchy. There is, undoubtedly, a definite trend toward oligarchy in labor organizations; but it is probably true, as Barbash claims, that very few local unions are oligarchies.[27] In the large majority of locals, as he points out, there are no full-time officers, turnover among such officers is frequent, and there is little social distance between the members and the leaders.

CITY AND STATE FEDERATIONS

To complete the picture of the structural relationships of the units of organized labor several additional groupings must be described. The AFL-CIO is a federation that attempts to co-ordinate certain of the activities of national unions. On the state and city or country levels, similarly, there are bodies that serve as co-ordinators of locals belonging to AFL-CIO affiliated nationals.

The city federations are known by various names. (Before the AFL-CIO merger, city bodies of AFL locals were called trades and labor assemblies, central labor unions, or city federations of labor. The CIO counterparts

---

[24] Herbert J. Lahne and Joseph Kovner, "Shop Society and the Union," *ibid.*, October, 1953, pp. 3–15.

[25] Joel Seidman, *The Brotherhood of Railroad Trainmen* (New York: John Wiley & Sons, Inc., 1962), chap. 4.

[26] Morris A. Horowitz, *The Structure and Government of the Carpenters' Union* (New York: John Wiley & Sons, Inc., 1962), p. 21.

[27] Jack Barbash, *Labor's Grass Roots* (New York: Harper & Row, Publishers, 1961), p. 228.

were called city industrial union councils.) These groups receive their charters from the AFL-CIO and have as members the local unions within a stipulated area. The locals send delegates to meetings which are usually held on a bi-weekly or monthly basis.

One of the important functions of the city central body is to unite the political efforts of local unions. Before an election, the city body will come up with a slate of endorsed candidates. In recent years, there has been active campaigning by many of these groups for selected candidates and issues. The city central usually maintains some sort of informal lobby at city hall, and a spokesman oftentimes presents the labor viewpoint to committees of the city legislature. The interest of the city central is not confined to matters that involve only organized labor. It attempts to make its voice heard in Blue Cross rate determinations, school board policy setting, resolution of public transportation problems, and other civic issues. Interests of the central labor body may also include union educational programs, public relations, and co-operation with others in community fund-raising drives. Individuals or groups who seek the support of local labor bodies usually make their appeals to the city central. In this way, it is possible to reach delegates from many local unions at one time.

The state central labor bodies are chartered by the AFL-CIO. Local unions and the city central bodies within a state constitute the membership of the state organizations. The major function of the state federation is political action. During sessions of the state legislature, the staff of a state federation maintains a constant watch over the progress of bills introduced and applies pressure at strategic points in the legislative process. In election campaigns, the state organizations make strong efforts to deliver the labor vote to endorsed candidates.

Other Organizational Units

Other units that co-ordinate the efforts of local unions are known as joint boards and district councils. These may be composed of local unions within an area that are affiliated with the same national union, or they may be made up of locals of different nationals that have a common trade interest. In some circumstances a local union may belong to both types of groupings. A Teamsters union local of bakery drivers, for example, will belong to a Teamsters district council along with other Teamster locals such as construction industry drivers, department store delivery van drivers, vending machine servicemen, and municipal truck drivers. The bakery drivers local may also belong to an area food council that might include locals from the meat cutters, warehousemen, and bakery and confectionary workers unions. The responsibilities and authority of these bodies vary. In some cases they have the power to settle jurisdictional disputes among members, to negotiate agreements with employers, and to call strikes. In other cases they are mainly advisory bodies.

FIGURE 12

STRUCTURAL RELATIONSHIP BETWEEN CITY AND STATE CENTRAL
BODIES AND OTHER UNITS OF ORGANIZED LABOR

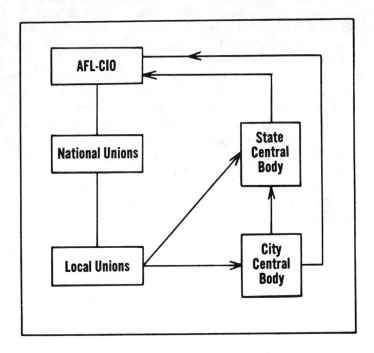

In a survey of the structural organization of the AFL-CIO, at least brief mention must be made of the departments. Five departments affiliated with the AFL had no counterparts in the CIO. These departments were Building and Construction Trades, Metal Trades, Railway Employees, Maritime Trades, and Union Label. In the merged organization these departments retained their identities, and a sixth, the Industrial Union Department, was established. In 1961, a new department composed of unions in the food and beverage industry was organized. Except for the Union Label Department, the general functions of the departments are to co-ordinate the activities of unions whose interests overlap because of common industrial attachments; to seek means of settling troublesome jurisdictional disputes; and, in certain circumstances, to co-operate in collective bargaining.[28]

---

[28] As Barbash notes, the departments, though constitutionally subordinate, lead relatively independent lives and, at times, engage each other as well as the federation in adversary roles. Jack Barbash, *American Unions: Structure, Government and Politics* (New York: Random House, 1967), pp. 120–22. The Industrial Union Department, which served as a base of power for Walter Reuther, will undoubtedly diminish in importance as a result of the UAW's withdrawal from the AFL-CIO.

UNIONS AND MONEY

At one time, labor unions were cubby-hole operations making ends meet on a day-to-day basis. This era is past. It takes money to run a modern labor organization, and no labor leader can afford to be cavalier about his union's financial statement. Unions take in and spend annually about $1.5 billion in dues revenue and have something to say about the administration of three times that much in treasury, pension, and welfare fund reserves.[29] This is a lot of money, but a statement of the gross revenues of labor organizations is likely to give the impression that all unions are swimming in affluence. The actual fact is that a majority of the organizations handle relatively little money. A 1962 publication of the Bureau of Labor-Management Reports entitled *Union Financial Statistics* indicated that 69 per cent of the reporting locals had annual receipts of less than $10,000, and 46 per cent of the national unions had less than $100,000.

Initiation fees and monthly dues paid by the rank and file constitute the basic and most important source of union income. The local union, which is the only unit having direct and continuous contact with the membership, serves as a collection agency for fees, dues, and special assessments. Following the collection, there is a rather elaborate process of splitting the income among the various units in the organizational structure. The local makes per capita payments to the national, and the national makes payments to the federation. City and state organizations, district councils, and joint boards also participate in the division. The process might be visualized as one in which the money flows up through the labor hierarchy while a variety of services flow downward. The national makes payments to the federation and in return receives legal, legislative, educational, and other services. The local makes payments to the national and receives help in organizing, bargaining, and legal, research, and welfare matters. The member pays his dues to the local and is serviced by way of grievance adjustments, contract negotiations, welfare programs, as well as by many informal types of assistance.

Initiation Fee

A person who joins a union will usually find that his first payment is an initiation fee. The amount varies considerably from union to union. If he is a plumber he may pay as much as $300. In the Building Service Employees Union he may pay only $1.00. The constitutions of some national unions specify a flat amount that must be charged by all locals. Some specify maximum initiation fees, others fix the minimum, and still others set no constitutional limit on what the locals may charge. Certain unions tie the

---

[29] A. H. Raskin, "The Unions and Their Wealth," *Atlantic Monthly*, April, 1962, pp. 87–96.

initiation fee to a skill or income classification. The International Airline Pilots Association, for example, has varying charges depending upon the pilot's annual income.

The initiation fees of most unions are modest and reasonable. In some cases, however, they have been set deliberately high to serve as a barrier to membership. A study of initiation fee practices in 3400 local unions found that 50 per cent of the locals charged either no fee or up to $5.00. Thirty-one per cent charged between $5.00 and $20.00. In the remaining locals, about half had initiation fees of between $20.00 and $50.00 and the other half had fees of over $50.00.[30]

The 1947 Labor-Management Relations (Taft-Hartley) Act makes it an unfair labor practice for unions to require members employed under union shop agreements to pay "excessive" or "discriminatory" initiation fees. Very few complaints have been filed under this provision of the law.

Dues

In the matter of dues, some unions specify how much their locals will charge, whereas others set a range and allow locals to charge any amount within the expressed limits. It is hazardous to compare dues of one union with another, since payments often include premiums for insurance and pensions. About 70 per cent of the income of the Carpenters Union, for example, is paid out in pension and death benefits to the members. In unions having jurisdiction over workers with marked differences in skills, as in the case of the International Brotherhood of Electrical Workers, it is not uncommon for dues to be set at one level for the higher income group and at a lower level for the unskilled or semi-skilled members. Recently a large local of the Electrical Workers voted to eliminate all dues payments for workers earning less than $1.25 an hour. Some unions collect no dues at all and apparently support themselves by levying special assessments from time to time. The large majority of locals charge $5.00 per month or less.[31]

Salaries

An important item in the union budget is expenditures for salaries. There has always been some popular feeling that the labor leader is a leech who lives by extracting payment from the hard-earned money of the union members. With the general public becoming more sophisticated about labor unions and the burdens borne by the union official, this feeling has been

---

[30] Leon Applebaum, "Dues and Fees Structure of Local Unions," *Monthly Labor Review,* November, 1966, p. 1237.
[31] *Ibid.*

somewhat dissipated. There is still a degree of suspicion, however, that is attached to any person who earns his living in the business of unionism.

How much do national labor officials earn? Not as much as corporation executives, motion picture stars, or top flight jockeys but considerably more than school teachers, policemen, or rank and file union members. The president of the Teamsters earns $87,000 a year and the president of the National Maritime Union, $79,000. Among the others at the upper part of the range are the presidents of the United Steel Workers and the United Mine Workers, both of whom earn $50,000. The president of the United Auto Workers, the second largest union in the United States, earns only $28,000. In 1963 about 80 per cent of the national unions paid their presidents less than $20,000 a year. The salaries of other top level national union officers such as vice president and secretary-treasurer usually run about 20 per cent less than the president's salary.

A 1954 survey of salaries paid to 1,500 local or district officers revealed that 65 per cent were paid $1,000 or less for their services. Only 11 per cent earned more than $8,000.[32] Though somewhat dated, the validity of this survey was substantiated by a more recent study of salaries paid to officers by 93 locals in Milwaukee. Very few of the Milwaukee unions paid more than $8,000 per year to their highest salaried officers.[33]

Corruption within Unions

A discussion of union finances leads inevitably to the question of racketeering within unions. Racketeers recognize no jurisdictional lines on the scope of their interests, and labor unions have not been free from their attentions. It is as unfair to judge all unions as dishonest as it would be to pass a similar verdict upon banks simply because the banking system produces an annual crop of embezzlers. Recent investigations, however, have shown that the problem of dishonesty among labor leaders is of more substantial proportions than was commonly supposed and that even those persons closely affiliated with the labor movement in the United States were not fully aware of the extent of the corruption.

The history of racketeering in unions goes back at least sixty years. At one time or another racketeers have successfully exploited employers, workers, or both in building construction, the needle trades, Atlantic and Gulf Coast longshoring, and truck transportation, among other industries. The techniques used have been varied, but an important element in most of the American experiences with union-based crime has been a total and ruthless control of the sale of labor in a particular labor market. Such control

---

[32] Taft, *op. cit.*, p. 88.
[33] Leon Applebaum, "Officer Turnover and Salary Structures in Local Unions," *Industrial and Labor Relations Review*, January, 1966, p. 227.

gives those in power a range of opportunities to collect an assortment of payoffs from employers and workers. Industries most vulnerable to underworld control have been those characterized by (1) numerous and relatively small employer units, (2) a highly competitive product market, and (3) a casual or mobile labor force. In the construction industry, for example, contractors who stand to suffer heavy losses from work stoppages are highly vulnerable to extortion. In East Coast longshoring, the combined facts of a casual labor force, an excess of labor supply, and employer collusion made possible the practice of terror that facilitated the collection of worker payoffs to union leaders.

In some cases, corruption resulted from the simple fact that those who rose to union leadership were dishonest people. At the turn of the century, for example, Sam Parks in New York City and Martin "Skinny" Madden in Chicago seized control of the building trades councils and proceeded to amass personal fortunes by extorting employers and dipping into union treasuries. In other cases, corruption was a result of union invasion by mobsters who saw the union movement as nothing more than an opportunity for personal advantage. This invasion occurred on a somewhat systematic basis during and immediately after the prohibition era. Names such as Charles "Lucky" Luciano, Arnold Rothstein, Louis Lepke, and Al Capone—names familiar to even the most casual student of American crime —are prominent among those who were able to use unionism as a base for a variety of plunders. It has been estimated that two-thirds of all local unions in the Chicago area were controlled by Al Capone in the early 1930's.[34] In two instances, those of the Building Service Employees International Union and the International Association of Theatrical and Stage Employees, the underworld seized complete control of the national union. By the end of the 1930's, however, many of the criminal empires within the labor movement had been broken by federal and state prosecutions and by the heroic efforts of honest unionists to rid their unions of criminal elements.

In the postwar world, the labor movement remains plagued by spots of corruption that threaten the fortunes of honest unionism. Some of this corruption is in the nature of the old-style racketeering described above, but several new dimensions have been added. Developments in collective bargaining that created large welfare funds also created new opportunities for dishonesty. A number of these funds have been plundered by malpractices such as kickbacks to union officials from insurance brokers, excessive administration costs, and unusually favorable benefits provided for union officers. In 1955, an investigating subcommittee of the House Labor Committee reported that employers had shirked their duties as joint fund ad-

---

[34] John Hutchinson, "Corruption in American Trade Unions," *The Political Quarterly,* July–September, 1957.

ministrators, that union leaders had used strong-arm methods, and that insurance companies had engaged in irregular practices. The blame in the case of welfare fund maladministration, thus, appears to be widespread.

Another problem in union leadership morality was brought to light in 1957 by the Senate Select Committee on Improper Activities in the Field of Labor and Management headed by Senator John McClellan. The problem, which can possibly be summarized by the word "commingling," is best illustrated by the situation in the International Brotherhood of Teamsters. Teamster leaders, in short, have commingled their personal fortunes with the fortunes of the union. The use of "contacts" to make favorable personal investments, liberal expense accounts, and interest-free loans from the union treasury are devices by which highly placed Teamster officials have prospered coincidentally with the prosperity of the union. It is important to note that the rank and file truck driver has not fared poorly while all this has been going on. Unlike the racketeer who makes no pretense of serving worker interests, Teamster officials in many cases have done an excellent job of winning higher wages and better conditions for the union membership. In fairness, furthermore, it should be noted that in the vast and sprawling Teamsters organization there are many local unions that are as honestly managed and as democratic as any in the American labor movement.

The Counterattack Against Corruption

Organized labor has taken a number of steps in recent years to purge the criminal and the corrupt from the labor movement. In 1953 the International Longshoremen's Union was expelled from the AFL; and at its 1957 convention, the AFL-CIO ousted the Teamsters union, the Bakery and Confectionary Workers, and the Laundry Workers International Union. Other unions were placed on probation, with expulsion being withheld pending efforts by the unions involved to clean up their own organizations.

The expulsions from the AFL-CIO were made pursuant to the constitution of that organization and to the Ethical Practice Codes adopted in 1956 and 1957. Article 2, Section 10 of the AFL-CIO constitution provides that an object of the organization is to "protect the labor movement from any and all forms of corruption." Six separate codes on ethical practices deal with local union charters, health and welfare funds, racketeers and supporters of totalitarian movements, conflicts of interest in the investment and business interests of union officials, financial practices of unions, and union democratic practices.[35]

---

[35] For the full texts of the ethical practice codes see the *Monthly Labor Review*, March and July, 1957.

THE LANDRUM-GRIFFIN ACT AND INTERNAL UNION AFFAIRS

The revelation of malpractices within certain unions created a considerable amount of public indignation. This fact plus the apparent inability of organized labor to find means to clean its own house made some type of legislation inevitable. In September, 1959, the controversial Labor-Management Reporting and Disclosure (Landrum-Griffin) Law was enacted. The titles of the law dealing with internal union affairs are briefly summarized below.

Title I: Bill of Rights of Members of Labor Organizations

Title I contains provisions that are designed to provide union members with a number of rights that are roughly similar to those enumerated in the Bill of Rights of the federal Constitution. Members, according to Title I, are to have equal rights in nominating candidates for office, voting in elections, attending meetings, and participating in deliberations. Members are also guaranteed the right to assemble and speak freely and to vote on increases in dues and assessments and are protected against arbitrary disciplinary actions. These rights may be enforced by civil suit in the federal courts.

Title II: Reporting and Disclosure Requirements

Every labor organization must file two reports with the Secretary of Labor. One consists of a copy of the organization's constitution and by-laws and a variety of other information such as initiation fees, dues, and detailed descriptions of internal union procedures. The second is a financial report describing assets and liabilities at the beginning and end of each fiscal year, all receipts and their sources, payments to all union officers and employees who receive more than $10,000 a year from a union or its affiliated unions, and all loans of more than $250 a year to union members or employees. An additional report must be filed if union officials have certain types of financial dealings with employers of the employees represented by such officials. The purpose of this last report is to deter conflict of interest arrangements involving union officials.

Title III: Trusteeships

A union trusteeship is an arrangement whereby the national officers of a union appoint a representative to assume control over the affairs of a local union. The trusteeship is a legitimate device used to correct corrupt or inefficient practices that crop up in local bodies. The McClellan Committee, however, uncovered numerous instances of abuse of the trusteeship device.

Under Title III, every labor organization which assumes supervisory control over a subordinate body is required to file a report with the Secretary of Labor within thirty days of imposing such control and semi-annually thereafter. The report must state the reasons for the trusteeship and must include a detailed financial account of the body placed under control. Trusteeships may be established only for the following purposes: (1) to correct corruption, (2) to correct financial malpractices, (3) to assure the performance of union contracts, (4) to assure the performance of a bargaining representative's duties, (5) to restore democratic procedures, (6) to carry out the legitimate objects of the labor organization. In any proceeding contesting the validity of a trusteeship, the trusteeship shall be presumed to be invalid after eighteen months unless the labor organization is able to show by "clear and convincing proof" that a continuation is necessary.

Title IV: Elections

Title IV specifies that national unions must hold elections at least once every five years and locals at least once every three years. Such elections must be by secret ballot; and where national officers are elected by convention delegates, such delegates must be chosen by secret ballot. Other provisions of this title deal with the conduct of elections, tabulation of the results, and the procedures for challenging the results.

Title V: Safeguards for Labor Organizations

The fifth title provides a variety of safeguards for labor organizations. One section specifies that union officers and other representatives of labor organizations occupy positions of trust in relation to such organizations. This means that the officers are placed in the legal category of fiduciaries or persons who undertake to act in the interest of others. As fiduciaries they are subject to common and statutory law relevant to the subject; but the precise requirements that the section places upon union officers, other than honesty, is still not clear. Other sections of the title prohibit communists and felons convicted of certain crimes from serving as union officers.

Title VI: Miscellaneous

The sixth title is a catch-all title containing a number of unrelated provisions. One section prohibits extortionate picketing for the purpose of extracting money from an employer against his will or for the personal profit or enrichment of any individual.

OTHER UNION ACTIVITIES AND INTERESTS

In 1955, a $100,000 grant from the Philip Murray Memorial Fund was used to establish a chair of international labor studies at Roosevelt College in Chicago. A grant of equal size from the William Green Memorial Fund is being used to finance annual scholarships at Ohio State University. In St. Louis, the Teamsters union has established a network of union stewards who are to concern themselves with civic projects such as street repair, elimination of racial tension, etc. In Pennsylvania, The Amalgamated Clothing Workers of America has opened a resort with vacation and recreation facilities for its 20,000 union members in the state. These items are mentioned here to illustrate the expanding interests and activities of labor unions.

The scope of what has been described as the "extracurricular activities" of unions extends much beyond the examples cited in the above paragraph. Unions publish newspapers and journals—almost a thousand are distributed on a weekly or monthly basis. Unions carry on research activities. Some of this is general in nature, covering such subjects as the record of Congress or national economic trends. Much of it is geared to provide specific material to buttress a union's arguments in collective bargaining. Unions are interested in community services. Approximately 10,000 union representatives serve on the boards and committees of community social service agencies. Unions conduct educational programs of many types, and the labor institute is becoming a common occurrence on the university campus. Unions have produced educational films and have sponsored radio commentators. Some run their own credit unions. Co-operative housing projects have been developed. The staff of a larger union will include lawyers, accountants, educators, research directors, economists, and journalists.

There is no need to describe these matters in detail here. The important points are that (1) these interests and activities are quite broad and reflect the problems and interests of the large community in which unions function and (2) the techniques used by unions to accomplish their goals are similar in most respects to those generally used by organized groups in our society.

QUESTIONS

1. What are the functions of the AFL-CIO?
2. Where are the centers of power in the American labor movement? Explain the relationship between the AFL-CIO and the national unions affiliated with it.
3. Labor union officers at the national level tend to remain in office for long periods of time. How is this fact explained?

4. Through the years there has been an increasing centralization of power in the national unions at the expense of their affiliated locals. What factors account for this?

5. What factors tend to make the practice of pure democracy difficult in organizations such as labor unions? How would you summarize the prevailing state of democracy within unions?

6. Although most national labor leaders have been outspoken advocates of racial equality, many local unions have followed discriminatory practices. How do you explain this disparity?

7. What are the functions of the city and state federations of labor?

SELECTED READINGS

BARBASH, JACK. *American Unions: Structure, Government and Politics.* New York: Random House, 1967.

ESTEY, MARTIN. *The Unions: Structure, Development and Management.* New York: Harcourt, Brace and World, Inc., 1967.

JOHN HUTCHISON. "The Anatomy of Corruption in Trade Unions," *Industrial Relations,* February, 1969, pp. 135–150.

LEISERSON, WILLIAM. *American Trade Union Democracy.* New York: Columbia University Press, 1959.

PETERSON, FLORENCE. *American Labor Unions.* New York: Harper & Row, Publishers, 1963.

SAYLES, LEONARD R. and STRAUSS, GEORGE. *The Local Union.* New York: Harcourt, Brace and World, Inc., Revised Edition, 1967.

TAFT, PHILIP. *The Structure and Government of Labor Unions.* Cambridge, Mass.: Harvard University Press, 1954. Chaps. 2, 3, 4.

PART THREE

COLLECTIVE BARGAINING

CHAPTER 7

The Participants

IN EVERY SOCIETY THERE ARE CERTAIN BASIC ECONOMIC AND SOCIAL decisions that must be made. What is to be produced; how is the product to be divided; who gives the orders; what is the relationship between those who give orders and those who follow them? In one way or another, these questions must be answered if an economy is to function in an orderly manner. In a completely planned economy, fundamental decisions are made by a top level planning group and are then translated into action by the various levels of bureaucracy. In a primitive society, economic privileges and duties are apportioned by customs and mores. In the model world of free competition that economists sometimes use to illustrate their principles, the entrepreneur is the locus of the decision-making process, but his job is a simple one. He has only to observe the workings of the market place and then to react with common sense to the signals of the market.

The American economy fits none of these molds. The businessman makes most of the basic economic decisions, but he must keep at least one eye on the rules established by the government. He cannot be disdainful of public opinion, and when his workers are organized into unions, he no longer has the right to make unilateral decisions in many of the matters that affect them. In short, we live in a complex economy, an unstable compound of free enterprise, government, organized pressure groups, and a usually passive but sometimes aroused public.

COLLECTIVE BARGAINING

This chapter and the three that follow are concerned with collective bargaining. The concept of bargaining is simple. It is a method of making decisions. Workers, organized into a union, bargain as a group with their employer over matters that affect them. In the absence of collective bargaining the worker bargains with his employer individually; but this turns out, more often than not, to be a one-sided affair. The worker does not have the knowledge or resources to be a strong bargainer and ordinarily accepts the terms and conditions stipulated by the employer. Only when there are general manpower shortages or when the worker has a much needed skill can he bargain from a position of strength. By bargaining collectively, workers pool their strengths and face the employer with a meaningful aggregation of power.

Collective bargaining between employers and workers, then, is a method of making some of the decisions that must be made in any society. Although the concept of bargaining is simple, the subject itself is complex. This is so because the forms, the subject matter, and the strategy and tactics of collective bargaining are quite varied and often quite complicated. Understanding collective bargaining involves an understanding of these varieties and complexities.

We have described collective bargaining as a method of making decisions, but this description is quite broad, of course. In this and the following four chapters various aspects of bargaining will be examined in detail. By way of introduction, however, some basic facts of bargaining might be noted.

Workers Affected

First, how many workers are affected by collective bargaining? This can be answered with only limited accuracy. The 18 million workers who belong to unions are directly affected. Millions of others are affected even though they do not hold union cards. A union certified by the National Labor Relations Board as the bargaining representative of a unit of workers, for instance, must bargain for all the workers in that unit including those who are not union members. Not infrequently, employers adjust the terms of employment for employees outside the bargaining unit along the lines of the negotiated adjustment. In a plant where the white collar workers are non-union, employers often adjust white collar salaries by amounts equal to what has been bargained for the blue collar workers. For various reasons, non-union employers frequently find it expedient to change their wage structures in the face of what has happened in an influential labor-management bargain. Thus, it is obvious that the influence of bargaining reaches far beyond the area of union membership.

Responsibility

Who is responsible for the actual task of bargaining? In some cases local union officers, and in other cases international officers, do the bargaining. Frequently representatives of locals and internationals participate jointly. At the present time there are about 74,000 local unions affiliated with some 189 national unions. From organization to organization the bargaining responsibility is placed differently, but in varying degrees these locals and internationals share the responsibility for negotiating about 125,000 collective agreements with an unknown number of individual employers and more than 5,000 employer associations.

Extent

The extent of bargaining varies considerably within and among major industry groups. In manufacturing as a whole, about two-thirds of all production employees are covered by collective bargaining agreements. In petroleum products, automobile manufacturing, basic steel, and rubber products the percentage covered is more than 80, whereas in textiles, hosiery, lumber, and luggage it is less than 50. In non-manufacturing the proportion of wage earners under union-management agreements is high— over 75 per cent—in activities such as entertainment, local public transportation, longshoring, and construction, whereas it is less than 25 per cent in retail trade, restaurant work, clerical work, and beauticians' work. The importance of bargaining also varies by geographical region and by size of community. In the north central states, for example, more than three-fourths of the production workers are covered by labor-management agreements as compared with fewer than one-half in the southern states.[1] In the larger cities, persons in service occupations such as barbering, cab driving, and hotel work usually work under terms and conditions specified in a labor-management contract, whereas practitioners of the same occupations in rural or small town areas are usually non-union.

These data as well as those in the paragraphs above suggest some part of the tremendous variety that characterizes collective bargaining in the United States. A few contrasts will further emphasize this variety. The character of bargaining in newly organized firms will be different from that in long-established and seasoned labor-management relationships. Negotiations between the United Steel Workers and the major firms in the steel industry take place in the glare of publicity, whereas thousands of small local agreements are consummated annually without public notice. The problems of coal miners and airline pilots or longshoremen and butchers

---

[1] Florence Peterson, *American Labor Unions* (New York: Harper & Row, Publishers, 1963), pp. 149–152.

are different in many respects, and it can be expected that their respective union-management agreements will reflect these differences. Some agreements can be reproduced in five mimeographed pages, whereas others require more than 100 pages of closely printed text. Many other contrasts might be noted, but the point should be clear. The phrase "collective bargaining" covers a great deal; and, as suggested above, an understanding of bargaining requires an understanding of these variations.

In this chapter we shall look at the participants in the bargaining process —those who participate directly and those whose influence is less direct but who nevertheless have some effect on the character and results of the union-management bargaining relationship.

MANAGEMENT

In a broad sense, "management" includes anyone who is engaged in the management of an enterprise. A union will have a management, as will a government agency or an army post. Since our interest here is in the collective bargaining process, our attention is limited mainly to management in the business firm.

Of the 3.2 million companies counted in the Bureau of the Census' 1963 report on enterprises in the United States, 179 thousand had 20 or more employees.[2] Only 551 companies had more than 5 thousand employees, yet these firms accounted for approximately one-third of total employment in the 3.2 million companies. Thus, a relatively small number of firms account for a large proportion of total employment in business.

In the smaller firm, which may be a proprietorship, a partnership, or a corporation, the owner is likely to be the manager as well. His relationship with the union is direct and simple. He may be handed a master contract with little real choice other than signing, or he may hold the upper hand over the union for a number of reasons—possibly because his workers are more employer- than union-oriented. As a small employer, his social background may be similar to that of his workers, and so he may be sympathetic with unionism. On the other hand, as a self-made man, he may fight viciously against any attempt to interfere with the running of his business as he sees fit. There is no particular attitude toward unionism and no specific conduct in bargaining that flows from the fact that a small business is being dealt with. The full range of bargaining experiences that have occurred in larger firms have also occurred in many smaller businesses.

---

[2] U.S. Bureau of the Census, *1963 Enterprise Statistics* (Washington, D.C.: U.S. Government Printing Office, 1968), pp. 160–161.

The substantial difference in the case of the small business is that the complexities introduced by the elaborate formal structure and the informal social groupings in the large corporation are either absent or present only in much modified form.

Management and the Corporation

The corporation is the dominant form of business organization in most types of economic activity in the United States. Only in agriculture, the service industries, and some miscellaneous types of activity is more than 50 per cent of the business done by non-corporate enterprises.

Legally, the stockholders sit at the peak of the corporate hierarchy, and below them are ranged the directors, the layers of managers, and the workers. In theory, the stockholder-owners select the directors, who in turn appoint those who manage the firm in the interests of the owners. In practice the separation between ownership and control has become wide. Ownership of many corporations is diffused among thousands of stockholders. The current corporation prototype, according to one student of the subject, is increasingly that of a corporation with stock widely scattered among individuals, investment trusts, or institutional investors who faithfully vote for the incumbent management and resolutely refuse to participate in its concerns.[3]

The board of directors, which is elected at the annual meetings of stockholders, supposedly exercises a broad supervision and control over the functioning of the corporation.[4] Students of the American corporation, however, generally believe that the board in the typical corporation does not exercise an important part of the leadership function.[5] In many firms, the board majority consists of executives of the corporation, which means that the board of directors is not an independent and separate body. As Professor Gordon has worded it,

> . . . the board as a whole is . . . a not too wieldy body representing a diversity of interests, whose non-officer members, in so far as they are active, function chiefly as advisers. As a formal group, the board takes little part in the leadership function, and the selection of its members

---

[3] Eugene V. Rostow, "To Whom and for What Ends is Corporate Management Responsible?" in Edward S. Mason (ed.), *The Corporation in Modern Society* (Cambridge, Mass.: Harvard University Press, 1959), p. 53.

[4] Except when there are active contests for the control of a corporation, these elections amount to little more than a solicitation by the directors of stockholders' proxies. Most stockholders are not likely to know the names of the directors of their corporations.

[5] Robert A. Gordon, *Business Leadership in the Large Corporation* (Washington, D.C.: The Brookings Institution, 1945), p. 143.

rests much more on the management whom it is expected to supervise than on the stockholders whose interests it is supposed to represent.[6]

Corporations, then, are run by professional managers who typically own very small fractions of the outstanding stock.[7] Since these are the men who establish corporate policies in collective bargaining, it is necessary to take a closer look at the men of management.

The Managers

Any attempt at a generalized description of business executives runs into the frustrating fact that so many exceptions must be made. For one who aspires to leadership in the business firm it is quite helpful to have a successful businessman as a father; yet frequently men have reached the top without such an advantage. A college education seems to be a necessary qualification, but there are not a few executives who do not have a degree. Intelligence, shrewdness, flexibility, foresight, practicality, imagination— these would all seem to be essential traits for the leader of industry; but most sociologists insist that there is no universal set of traits that characterizes all leaders.[8] Businessmen themselves lend implicit support to the sociologists' position by their inability to reach agreement on what makes a business leader.[9]

Although it is difficult—perhaps impossible—to draw a collective picture of the corporation executive, it is possible to gain some insight into executive attitudes about collective bargaining by noting some aspects of the environment in which business leaders function.

1. In the United States, the business executive lives in a society that rewards successful performance most lavishly. The rewards consist not only of money, although the monetary returns are not inconsequential, but of power, prestige, and status as well. The heroic status of the business-

---

[6] *Ibid.,* pp. 144–145. This generalization about the role of the board of directors must, of course, be modified in some cases. For the most part, it is a reasonably accurate picture of the role of the directors in the large American corporation. (The above quotation is reproduced here with the permission of the publisher, The Brookings Institution.)

[7] *Ibid.,* p. 24.

[8] The "trait" theory of leadership seems to be unfashionable today. For a good summary and critique of modern-day sociological thought relative to leadership, see Alvin Gouldner's introduction to *Studies in Leadership* (New York: Harper & Row, Publishers, 1950).

[9] For an interesting—and inconclusive—round table discussion by a number of business leaders, among others, on executive leadership see Eli Ginzberg (ed.), *What Makes an Executive?* (New York: Columbia University Press, 1955). Prevailing thought on the subject of executive performance is probably summarized by Dalton's statement that there are still no generally accepted indexes of competence in office despite mountains of print on the subject. Melville Dalton, *Men Who Manage* (New York: John Wiley & Sons, Inc., 1959), p. 190.

man was diminished somewhat by the depression experience of the 1930's. Still it would be a rare occasion when it would be a disadvantage to introduce oneself as a vice president of General Motors, U.S. Steel, or Swift and Company. In a society that looks kindly upon successful performance, the motivations for success in the business world are strong.[10]

The fact that the top executives of a corporation are not typically large-scale stockholders does not affect their feelings of loyalty for or identification with the firm. The corporation is the vehicle in their drive for success, and neither the junior executive "on the make" nor the senior executive who has arrived is likely to take action inconsistent with the proper maintenance and care of the vehicle. In the large modern organization, as Presthus notes, the demand for conformity is strong.[11] Such organizations tend to resemble churches which need champions to endorse their values and to increase their survival power. There is little room for dissent, and when the corporation is challenged by the union, self-interest is a force leading the executive to rally around the corporate banner.

2. The corporation is, by nature, a bureaucracy.[12] This has important implications. Management must function within a setting that generally is inflexible in adjusting to new influences. The going bureaucracy is usually massive and sluggish. A pattern of performance has been established, and extensive change disrupts the pattern. Although bureaucracy is efficient in dealing with the static and unchanging, sharp and frequent policy changes are capable of upsetting the bureaucratic equilibrium. The lower levels in the hierarchy are not without defense mechanisms when unpopular changes are instituted. Informal groups can co-operate in a program of sabotage, or dissatisfied individuals in strategic positions can disrupt the flow of accurate communications. Sometimes it is more expedient for management to go along with things as they are than to initiate new policies. At the very least, the strategy of imposing change must be studied carefully if change is to be successfully imposed.

---

[10] A good description of how the social order affects the motivations of the businessman can be found in John E. Sawyer, "Entrepreneurship and the Social Order," chap. 1 in William Miller (ed.), *Men in Business* (Cambridge, Mass.: Harvard University Press, 1952).

[11] Robert Presthus, *The Organizational Society* (New York: Alfred A. Knopf, Inc., 1962), p. 168.

[12] By "bureaucracy," we do not mean the popular conception of bureaucracy as an inefficient government unit. We refer, rather, to Max Weber's conception as modified by contemporary sociologists. Bureaucracy is a form of administration characterized by a hierarchy of authority within which hired experts are governed by general rules which make unnecessary the issuance of orders in all individual circumstances. Within the bureaucratic structure, there is a power locus at the top. At each level of bureaucracy there is likely to be an informal grouping of persons whose goals as an informal group may enhance, frustrate, or be neutral toward the policies of the organization. Bureaucracy is a characteristic form of organization in contemporary society.

The union as a force making for change is, in a sense, inconsistent with the bureaucratic processes. The union seeks a voice in policy determination and execution. Many managers see the union as an extraneous unit inserting itself in the power flow of the corporation. By nature, and often by design, the labor organization constitutes a challenge to the established pattern of decision-making and policy-execution in the business firm. It is not difficult to understand why this frequently leads to hostility between the manager and the union organization.

3. The attitudes and behavior of the manager in the corporation are conditioned by the totality of the experiences that marked his ascension to power and by a particular mode of life that goes along with being a corporation executive. There is what Professor Bakke has labeled a group structure of living, and there are strong compulsions for an individual to mold his own way of life along the lines of the group.[13] The manager's world is a composite of many elements that overlap the worker's world in only a few respects. His outlook, values, goals, and philosophies are different from those of the worker. He is a product of different experiences, and he lives in a different economic and social setting. Thus, what the manager sees when he looks at a particular problem is quite likely to be different from what the worker or the union representative sees.

4. For the union, a good contract with the employer is a primary and major goal. The union-employer relationship, thus, is a crucial factor in the union's life. For the corporation, labor relations is only one problem among many. The manager must face up to problems of engineering, sales, finances, stockholder relations, competitor's activities, etc. To the extent that his freedom to make decisions in any one area is limited, his over-all flexibility of action suffers. The manager frequently sees the union as an organization that interferes with his powers of manipulating resources to the best advantage of the corporation.

What this all amounts to is that the manager would ordinarily prefer not to deal with a union.[14] As he sees it, the labor organization intrudes in the management domain, attempts to substitute its goals for those of management, and is generally bothersome. A basic strand in the philosophy of management is that a healthy corporation will mean benefits for everyone,

---

[13] E. Wight Bakke, *Adaptive Human Behavior* (New Haven, Conn.: Yale Labor and Management Center, 1951).

[14] There are exceptions to this. In a very competitive society, it may be in the interests of management to have the union stabilize wages and thus remove labor cost as a factor in competitive advantage. In industries with many small employers, a centralized union hiring hall may be desirable as a device for removing chaos in the labor market. These and other instances are examples of situations where the union is in a position to perform an economic service to employers that is immediately obvious.

including the workers. When a former president of General Motors stated that what was good for General Motors was good for the country, he was not voicing an isolated opinion. Management literature is full of similar sentiments. The existence of a union constitutes a challenge to this philosophy. It is visible evidence of the fact that workers have rejected the idea that management alone is capable of serving as the steward of employee welfare.

Management's over-all feeling about labor unions does not necessarily lead to permanent hostility. A corporation leader may decide that unions are here to stay and that he might as well adjust to this fact by making the best of things. Another possibility is to tolerate the union for the time being and look for an opening for some future offensive. Still another avenue of behavior is to accept the union without reservations and to work out constructive patterns of mutual co-operation. The historical record has examples of all these attitudes—continuing warfare, temporary toleration, resignation, mutual co-operation. The management outlook has a bias against admitting a legitimate role for labor unions. The outlook is broad enough, however, to encompass a number of specific policies toward unionism, ranging from complete co-operation to total hostility.

THE UNION

Sharing the center of the collective bargaining ring with management is the union. The history, structure, and philosophy of unionism have been discussed in earlier chapters, and there is no need to repeat the details here. Some attention must be directed, however, to the union official in his role as a negotiator.

The Labor Leader

Like their counterparts in the corporation, leaders of labor are too diverse in personality, attitudes, and backgrounds to be summarized glibly in a collective portrait. No such portrait will be attempted here. A number of observations will be made, however, to illustrate some important factors that influence the conduct of many union officials during negotiations with employers.

1. At both national and local levels, the labor leader has a multiplicity of roles to perform, and his behavior in any one role cannot be insulated from the demands of the others. As was noted in the last chapter, the union official must be, among other things, a general of an army, a merchandiser of labor power, a boss of a political machine, and an administrator of a bureaucracy. Assume by way of example that the union negotiator becomes

convinced that the employer cannot grant more than a five cent per hour wage increase without courting financial difficulties. As a merchandiser of labor power, his rational course of action would be to accept the five cents. His political position within the union may preclude his acceptance, at least until he makes a vigorous and sometimes sustained protest. The membership may have been led to expect more; a challenger may be breathing down the neck of the union leader; or the rank and file may be restive because of other grievances, and an unsatisfactory wage offer might touch off a spontaneous mass protest. Assume another case now. The union official feels that, with strong pressure, he can squeeze a fifteen cents per hour wage boost from the employer; but he may know that his members are generally satisfied and would resent being pulled out on strike. Consequently, he settles for a lower figure. In collective bargaining, the union leader is out to make the best bargain he can under the circumstances, but the circumstances that influence his conduct often consist of more than the pure economics of the employer's situation.

2. Many union leaders have been in the labor movement for a long time. In a rather large number of labor organizations, the leadership hierarchy at both national and local levels is made up of elderly individuals. This was so marked in the AFL that one observer described that body as a gerontocracy.[15] A younger organization, the CIO had a leadership population that was generally younger than AFL leaders. Even within the CIO, however, the prominent personalities were persons with long experience in the business of unionism.

Insofar as collective bargaining is concerned, the age and long tenure in office of most of the prominent labor leaders are important in several respects. The typical leader is one whose experience goes back far enough so that he has personal recollections of the extremes in employer hostility. The blacklist, labor spies, and organized strikebreakers are not tactics that he has read about in books, but are experiences in his own life. Most of the present-day officialdom have personal recollections of the anti-labor drives of the twenties or the organizational fights of the thirties. These were traumatic experiences for labor leaders. Although the physical warfare type of labor-management relationship has passed out of the picture in numerous industries, many officers still maintain a distrust of employers that stems from their experiences in the days of open warfare.[16]

If the passage of time has not served to erase completely a stereotyped picture of the employer from the mind of the labor leader, it has served to

---

15 C. Wright Mills, *The New Men of Power* (New York: Harcourt, Brace & World, Inc., 1948), p. 73.

16 An influence in keeping this feeling alive is the fact that violence between organized workers and employers occurs with just enough frequency today to instill the fear that employers have really not changed but are just biding their time.

mellow the antagonisms that were once rooted in ideological preconceptions. Look closely at the background of a labor union official, and the chances are good that you will find some trace of socialism, reformism, or an unclassifiable but nevertheless real feeling of idealism. The burdens of office have deradicalized these feelings. There are great pressures on the labor leader to come through with tangible benefits for the membership. The American environment being what it is, the leader has learned, through the years, that the tactics of plain hard businesslike negotiations pay off better than does a disposition to reform everything or anything. Thus the negotiator faces the employer not as a general reformer of society but as a practical man trying to accomplish something that his practical membership will recognize as an improvement.

3. Labor leaders are not a breed apart from other men. They live in a society where people are stratified and accorded status on the basis of the symbols that mark life within the society. The typical labor leader is not a deviant in the free enterprise society. Since he accepts free enterprise in principle, he has no quarrel with the basic forces that motivate men in such a society. On the contrary, he is motivated by these very forces. He wants to be successful. In his case that means that he wants power, prestige, the respect of the people he relates to, and a salary that is large enough to give him status as well as comfort.

In most cases, the labor leader wins his position by hard work. The probable occupation of his father was that of a wage worker.[17] He, himself, has come up from the ranks of the workers. He has survived a rigid process of selection that has winnowed out many would-be leaders. He came into union work at an early age and fought his way against odds to a position of power. He has achieved success according to the American tradition of the self-made man.

The American labor leader, thus, is a man with achievements; but he lives in a society that has not yet bestowed upon him the full measure of prestige and status that he would like. He bargains with a businessman who usually earns more money, gets better press notices, and has a higher social standing than the labor leader enjoys. Some part of the attitude of the union official toward the management man on the other side of the bargaining table must be attributed to these factors. The discrepancy in the social positions of union and management personnel varies in individual situations. It is probably most important as a factor accentuating strains in the labor-management relationship when these develop from other causes.

The above described factors, of course, are not complete descriptions of the forces that have shaped the American labor leader, nor have they produced any particular pattern of leadership. Mere mention of the names

---

[17] Mills, *op. cit.,* pp. 88–90.

of James Hoffa, Harry Bridges, Walter Reuther, and George Meany is sufficient to show how different labor leaders may be in personality and approach. Of all the forces influencing the conduct of the union head, one of the most important is the nature of the immediate problems that he faces. These will not be the same among all unions. Some industries are depressed while others prosper. Some industries are technologically static while others undergo basic changes. Geographical factors are important. The South, for instance, has been inhospitable to labor organizations. Some industries produce for local markets, whereas others operate on a nation-wide scale. Some employers are co-operative; others are antagonistic. This listing could be expanded indefinitely, but the point should be obvious by now. The strategy and tactics of a labor leader are shaped in part by his individual problems, and these to a greater or lesser degree will be different from the problems of his fellow leaders.

THE RANK AND FILE

The worker does not sit at the bargaining table, and yet no one has more at stake in collective bargaining than he has. Decisions are being made that will affect his take-home pay, job classification, seniority rights, pension, and insurance. Few aspects of his work life, in fact, will not be touched upon sooner or later in the bargains struck by his employer and his union representative.

If the worker is not physically involved in bargaining, his presence is felt nevertheless. In an earlier chapter the absence of a town hall type of democracy in unions was noted. There are exceptions to this generalization. Frequent examples can be shown of an active and energetic local union membership that is outspoken when collective bargaining demands are being formulated. Even when such democracy does not prevail, the importance of the rank and file should not be minimized. It has been suggested that in analyzing union policy-making, it is well to distinguish between membership participation and membership influence.[18] Influence may be strong even when participation is weak, and the union leader who wants to maintain his popularity must be sensitive to the grievances and expectations of the rank and file.[19]

Apart from a general type of influence that flows from the facts of union politics, union members in many cases have a direct opportunity to express

[18] Sumner H. Slichter, *The Challenge of Industrial Relations* (Ithaca, N.Y.: Cornell University Press, 1947), pp. 111, 112.

[19] For a recent study that found a strong relationship between union membership pay preference and the leaders' predictions of those preferences see Edward E. Lawler, III and Edward Levin, "Union Officers Perceptions of Members Pay Preferences," *Industrial and Labor Relations Review*, July, 1968, pp. 509–517.

their feelings relative to collective bargaining demands, the negotiated contract, and the calling of a strike. It is common procedure for union officialdom to submit a list of proposed demands to a local meeting for discussion from the floor. Practice varies considerably among unions, but it is not unusual for a certain amount of membership polling to precede the actual formulation of demands. Such polling may be formal, or it may consist simply of informal discussions with union members and lower level officials. In either case, many unions provide opportunities for expression of worker preference.

A study of the constitutions of 73 of the larger national unions has shown that 29 formally require that negotiated contracts be ratified by the union membership.[20] These figures understate the degree to which local union members enjoy the option of accepting or rejecting the agreements reached by labor and management negotiators since a large number of unions follow a practice of submitting such arguments to a membership vote even though there is no constitutional requirement to do so. In many cases such a submission is a formality and ratification follows almost automatically upon the recommendation of union officers. Within the past few years, however, there has been a growing tendency for the rank and file to reject proposed agreements. An analysis of the more difficult cases in which the Federal Mediation and Conciliation Service was involved in the two-year period beginning July 1, 1965, revealed that 12.9 per cent of the tentative settlements were rejected by the union members.[21] In absolute numbers this amounted to 1,937 known cases of membership rejection of proposed contracts that the union leadership had accepted. While this represents a small percentage of the total agreements negotiated over the two-year period, a figure of this size must be regarded as significant in view of the rarity of contract rejection by the rank and file in earlier years.

Strikes

Another dimension of the worker's influence in collective bargaining comes from his willingness or unwillingness to go on strike. As a union member, the worker constitutes the basic element in the union negotiator's bargaining power. Collective bargaining can be likened to diplomacy in the realm of international relations, and the strike can be equated to warfare. The power of the labor leader is closely tied to the size and state of readiness of his army.

The process of calling a strike varies among unions. In many organizations strike votes must be taken. In some, the mere call to "hit the bricks"

---

[20] Herbert J. Lahne, "Union Contract Ratification Procedures," *Monthly Labor Review*, May, 1968, pp. 7–10.

[21] William E. Simkin, "Refusals to Ratify Contracts," *Industrial and Labor Relations Review*, July, 1968, p. 523.

is sufficient. On occasions, the membership must be keyed up to an aggressive state of mind by a propaganda barrage. In other cases, existing grievances insure a good response if and when a strike order is issued. Whatever the situation may be in the individual case, the fact remains that union negotiating strength is frequently tied to the ability of the union to withhold labor power from the employer.

How prevalent is the practice of strike votes? A study of 133 national unions made by the Bureau of Labor Statistics in 1954 found that strike votes are required by the constitutions of about three-fifths of the nationals.[22] In his study of strike vote provisions in 59 local unions, Parnes found that the constitutions of many locals require a strike vote even though the national union constitution does not.[23] In the 59 locals studied, incidentally, it was found that all but a few had taken a strike vote at one time or another, including a number of locals that had never engaged in a strike.

Like contract ratification, strike votes are oftentimes formalities, and approval of a strike usually follows automatically from a submission of the issue to the membership. It is not unusual for a union negotiator to call a strike vote as part of his bargaining tactics. The mere fact that the strike issue must be submitted to the membership, however, is a factor that reduces the independence of the union leader and enhances the influence of the rank and file.

Like the union negotiator, the employer must pay attention to his workers' attitudes. The employer is in business to make money, and money is not made during a strike. It is true that he may take a firm stand that results in a walkout, but this is a risk that he hopes will pay off in time. The worker is an essential factor of production; and, whatever his tactics, the businessman must think in terms of the quantity and quality of labor supply.

Dual Allegiance

Since collective bargaining is frequently a conflict situation, one might pose the question of where the loyalty of the worker lies. His co-operation is obviously essential to both union and management; but does he direct his allegiance primarily to one or the other—and, if so, to which one? This is a question of attitudes that can be answered only by probing the minds of workers.

A number of studies have been made of worker loyalty, and almost all reach the same conclusion. Workers have a dull loyalty; they believe that

---

[22] "Strike Control Provisions in Union Constitutions," *Monthly Labor Review,* May, 1954, pp. 497–500.

[23] Herbert S. Parnes, *Union Strike Votes* (Princeton, N.J.: Industrial Relations Section, Princeton University, 1956), p. 36.

both union and company are interested in their welfare.[24] Dual loyalty does not always occur, of course; and in some work situations we would expect to find a loyalty for the one organization associated with hostility toward the other. It is significant, however, that so many researchers, working independently, have found evidence to support the conclusion that the allegiance of workers to one organization has no apparent effect on the allegiance to the other. Even during conflict situations, many workers, while supporting the union, believe that the union and the company are interdependent organizations having compatible goals. An additional conclusion of several studies merits mention. Among employees surveyed, those who thought that management was disinterested in worker welfare also thought that the local union leaders were doing a poor job. Those who were relatively satisfied with the company thought that the union leaders were doing a good job.

BARGAINING UNITS

Collective bargaining is not a static process carried on in all places and at all times in an unchanging form. Workers, employers, and unions may be grouped in any one of a large number of possible unit types. Historical accidents, the scope of the product market, occupational characteristics of workers, relative strengths of employers and unions, and legal policy are some of the factors that influence the nature of the groupings in collective bargaining relationships. In this section the more prominent of the bargaining forms will be listed and described.

Employee Groupings

The basic types of employee groupings are usually described as craft or industrial units. In the craft group, the bargaining unit consists of workers who constitute a homogeneous group because they are all practitioners of one of the traditional craft skills, such as carpentry, printing, or plumbing. In the industrial unit, workers are banded together not because of the specific job that each performs but because all are engaged in the produc-

---

[24] See, for example, Lois Dean, "Union Activity and Dual Loyalty," *Industrial and Labor Relations Review,* July, 1954, pp. 526–536; Theodore V. Purcell, *Blue Collar Man* (Cambridge, Mass.: Harvard University Press, 1960); Arnold Rose, *Union Solidarity* (Minneapolis: University of Minnesota Press, 1952), pp. 65–69; Ross Stagner, "Dual Loyalty in Modern Society," *Monthly Labor Review,* December, 1953, pp. 1273–1274. For a good discussion of the concept of dual loyalty see Arnold Tannenbaum and Robert Kahn, *Participation in Union Locals* (Evanston, Ill.: Row, Peterson and Co., 1958), pp. 104–109.

tion of a particular product. Thus, in the Chevrolet plant in Indianapolis, all plant workers are members of Local 23 of the Automobile Workers Union, an industrial unit. Included in the unit are plant maintenance personnel and highly skilled toolmakers as well as those in the semi-skilled and unskilled job classes. The United Mine Workers bargains for all the workers in a coal mine regardless of the particular job that each performs.

In practice, many units are hybrid types that do not conform perfectly to either the pure craft or industrial units. A true industrial unit would include the production, maintenance, craft, clerical, and service workers employed by a firm. Few units are so all-inclusive. So long as the mass of the production workers bargain as a group, however, a unit is usually referred to as industrial. Although most bargaining groups are not purely craft or industrial, it is ordinarily possible to classify them as craft-like or industrial-like on the basis of their more prominent characteristics.

The description of a union as industrial or craft or "in between" tells nothing about its jurisdictional area. With whom does the unit bargain? To answer this question it is necessary to consider the possible types of employer groupings.

The Individual Employer

An employer may band together with the fellow employers in his industry to bargain, or he may bargain individually. In the latter case, the area of bargaining may be very narrow or quite comprehensive. Thus, an employer may bargain separately with partial groupings of his employees such as tool and die makers, or electricians, or production workers, or he may bargain with all the workers grouped together in a comprehensive industrial unit.

When the employing firm consists of more than one plant, the possible bargaining arrangements multiply in number. An employer with several plants, for instance, may negotiate on a plant-by-plant basis or with the employees in several plants grouped together in a multi-plant unit. The most comprehensive unit possible so long as the employer bargains individually is that in which the employees in all plants are joined in one bargaining unit. Company-wide units or close approximations to it are now common in the automobile, basic iron and steel, electrical supplies and equipment, rubber, and meat packing industries.

Individual employer bargaining is the most prevalent arrangement in the United States. Although precise statistics are lacking, a common estimate is that 80 per cent of all agreements are for employees of a single company and that two-thirds of all agreements are limited in coverage to employees of a single plant. Collective bargaining agreements between unions and individual employers cover about two-thirds of all persons working under labor-management agreements.

Multiple Employer Units

Although most employer bargaining is carried on by units of individual employers, bargaining by groups of employers is not uncommon. About one-third of all employees under contract are covered by agreements reached between unions and employer associations.

The three main types of multi-employer bargaining units are local or city-wide, region-wide, and industry-wide. Of these, city-wide or local area bargaining occurs most frequently. Local industries in which joint employer bargaining units are commonly found are construction, retail and wholesale trade, hotels, restaurants, printing, publishing, and local trucking. Examples of region-wide bargaining arrangements can be found in the longshore, maritime, coal mining, and clothing industries. Industry-wide bargaining is relatively rare; but examples can be found in the glass container, elevator installation and repair, and pottery industries.

Many forms of multi-employer bargaining are found in practice. In some industries, such bargaining consists of nothing more than a large number of small competing firms signing an identical contract at the insistence of the union. Not infrequently, employers who are organized in no other way will get together for joint negotiations with a union. The most prevalent type of multi-employer bargaining unit consists of employers who are formally associated for negotiatory purposes.

Students of multi-employer bargaining have drawn a distinction between "negotiatory" and "administrative" employer groups. The former type consists of more or less formal groupings of employers who once a year or so associate for the major purpose of bargaining jointly with a union. The administrative type is a continuing organization frequently engaged in the administration as well as the negotiation of contracts and staffed with full-time professional labor relations personnel. One of the best known examples of an administrative grouping is the San Francisco Employers Council. Membership in the council consists of a wide variety of local firms such as those in the trucking, hotel, restaurant, and cleaning industries. Actual bargaining is carried on by trade associations of the individual industries, but the council supplies experts and even negotiators to assist the associations. Strong pressure is exerted on individual firms to hold the line and not break a solid employer front during bargaining; and, on occasion, the council has taken disciplinary action against members that signed separate agreements with unions.

Labor organizations usually seek to expand the scope of bargaining for several reasons. A master agreement negotiated with an employer group results in a standardization of benefits that eliminates the competitive advantage enjoyed by some of the employers. As long as any employers have an advantage because they pay lower wages than others, the security of the union and the benefit level achieved at the higher paying establishments are being threatened. When there are many employers in an industry, group negotiations result in a substantial diminution in the union's bargaining burden. A business agent with 100 individual contracts to negotiate annually would have little time for any other work. Multi-unit bargaining also eases the job of contract enforcement. It is easier for a union official to oversee the administration of a master agreement than it is to police dozens of contracts with widely differing details. An additional advantage to a union that stems from multi-employer bargaining is the protection that such an arrangement affords against a rival union. When a union bargains with an employers' association, a rival union must win the allegiance of workers in many firms before it can successfully intrude into the jurisdiction of the incumbent union.

The advantages of multi-employer bargaining are not limited to unions, and in many cases such bargaining has developed as a result of employer preference. The San Francisco Employers Council, for instance, was organized by employers whose bargaining strength had deteriorated. In a number of industries, employers have pressured unions to expand the bargaining unit to include firms paying low wages, and unorganized firms.

Several different types of advantages accrue to employers who bargain jointly. One of the most important is that it provides a defense against union whip-sawing tactics—the practice of wringing concessions from a single firm and then using such concessions to win similar gains from other firms. Small employers, by bargaining jointly, are in a better position to resist unreasonable union demands. Standardization of wages and other terms of employment within an industry is a usual result of bargaining on a multi-employer basis, and many firms prefer such standardization to a cut-throat type of wage competition. For these and other reasons, thousands of employers in the United States have found joint employer bargaining preferable to individual bargaining.

Trends in Bargaining Structure

In recent years, one set of forces has moved the structure of collective bargaining units in the direction of centralization whereas another has pulled in an opposite way. While the latter has by no means been insignificant the major thrust has been to move the center of decision-making away from the local place of work.

Certain of the forms of centralization have already been alluded to. The practice of multi-plant and multi-employer bargaining has spread to the extent that these forms predominate among the larger employing units. Among such units, multi-plant agreements are apparently the most popular form of centralization in manufacturing while multi-employer contracts dominate in the non-manufacturing sectors.[25]

Centralization, incidentally, can occur independently of changes in the formal structure of bargaining units. In "pattern bargaining," for example, an agreement between a union and a prominent firm in an industry becomes a pattern for other settlements. Patterns may be multi-industry in impact and specific in amount, as was the case in 1946 when the steel industry settlement of eighteen and a half cents per hour was put into effect in plants covering one-fourth of all manufacturing employees; or they may be limited, for the most part to a single industry with considerable deviations from the "key" settlement.[26] Patterns in recent years have been less distinct than they were immediately after World War II. In a number of industries, however, key settlements continue to set patterns.

Within the past several years, much interest has been generated by the efforts of certain unions to further centralize labor-management negotiations through the device of "co-ordinated" or "coalition" bargaining.[27] Co-ordinated or co-operative bargaining efforts among unions are not novel and have been expressed in various ways for at least seventy years.[28] Recent attention has been focused on the subject, however, by the intensive efforts of the AFL-CIO's Industrial Union Department to promote inter-union co-operation in bargaining and also by the fact that coalition bargaining was a major dispute issue during the 1966 negotiations in electrical manufacturing and the 1968 negotiations in the copper industry. Coalition bargaining has taken various forms including efforts by different unions (1) to obtain joint company-wide bargaining within a particular firm, (2) to frame common bargaining demands in order to strengthen the bargaining positions of all unions negotiating with an employer, and (3) to form a formal alliance for bargaining purposes among unions that had previously negotiated individually within an industry. These efforts at interunion co-operation, not all of which have been successful incidentally, can be interpreted as moves to enhance labor's bargaining power in situations where more than one labor organization represents workers in a large multi-plant firm, a condition that has become prominent in a business setting

---

[25] Arnold Weber, "Stability and Change in the Structure of Collective Bargaining," in Lloyd Ulman (ed.), *Challenges to Collective Bargaining* (Englewood Cliffs, N.J.: Prentice-Hall, Inc., 1967), p. 25.

[26] Harold M. Levinson, "Pattern Bargaining: A Case Study of the Automobile Workers," *The Quarterly Journal of Economics,* May, 1960, pp. 296–317.

[27] Herbert J. Lahne, "Coalition Bargaining and the Future of Union Structure," *Labor Law Journal,* June, 1967, pp. 353–359.

[28] Both terms have been used to describe co-operation in collective bargaining on the part of different national unions.

characterized by frequent company mergers and the appearance of the conglomerate corporation.

Counter thrusts to the drive toward centralization have developed from within the unions themselves. The more centralized the bargaining structure, the more difficult it becomes to deal effectively with the concerns of minority occupational groups in the negotiating unit and with the special problems generated by local working conditions. Worker restiveness has led to modification in the bargaining structure of certain unions so as to give special representation to classes of skilled workers and to return local issues to the local union for resolution through plant level bargaining.

NLRB Policy

Government influence on the nature and details of collective bargaining will be examined comprehensively in later chapters. It is appropriate at this point, however, to note briefly how government policy can affect the character of bargaining units. The National Labor Relations Board is empowered by the Taft-Hartley Act of 1947 to determine the scope of the bargaining unit for purposes of union representation. The earlier Wagner Act Board had the same power. Ordinarily, the NLRB will not disturb a unit that the union and management parties have agreed upon. When a dispute arises as to the appropriateness of a type of bargaining unit, the board will make a determination. In making such a determination, the NLRB gives heavy weight to the actual history of bargaining in the particular situation and to the mutuality of interests existing among the employees. Thus, if a firm has several plants, if the workers at all the plants have always been included in the same bargaining unit, and if the work in all plants is similar, the board will be reluctant to establish individual bargaining units at each plant should the employer request such a unit. On the other hand, if one plant is in California and another in New York, if the products are dissimilar, and if the workers have always been in separate bargaining units, a petition for a multi-plant unit by the union is not likely to be accepted. While some counter-tendencies can be found in the administrative history, the long run direction of NLRB policy has been to encourage the establishment of multi-plant units and to make it difficult for workers to withdraw from such units once they are established.[29]

THE GOVERNMENT

Directly and indirectly the government influences the conduct, scope, and results of collective bargaining in many ways. One form of such influence

---

[29] George W. Brooks and Mark Thompson, "Multi-plant Units: The NLRB's Withdrawal of Free Choice," *Industrial and Labor Relations Review*, April, 1967, pp. 363–380.

was noted in the immediately preceding section, and in later chapters the characteristics of collective bargaining law will be examined in some detail. The purpose of the present section is to emphasize the fact that government attitudes toward bargaining are important and to suggest, in a broad way, the dimensions of government influence.

The general legal milieu created by government may encourage or discourage bargaining. A government policy that encourages and stimulates organization of workers is, at the same time, a policy that encourages bargaining. Obviously the reverse is also true. When the government makes it more difficult for organization to occur, labor unions are less able to develop as effective bargaining agents.

Government policy toward unionism has evolved through a number of stages and has not yet reached a final resting place. Over a period of time, policy as manifested by one or another of the branches of government has varied from hostility toward unions to different degrees of friendliness. Through the nineteenth century and the first three decades of the twentieth century, the lack of sympathy or the indifference toward unions expressed by the judicial and legislative branches of the government retarded the growth of collective bargaining. During the 1930's the law actively favored bargaining; and in the post-World War II period, the situation has been one of legal ambivalence, with the law encouraging bargaining in some respects and discouraging it in others. In the 1960's aspects of government policy reflected an uneasiness about the power of labor organizations to negotiate inflationary wage increases. The Kennedy Administration's "Guideposts for Noninflationary Wage and Price Behavior" first presented in 1962, were an effort to contain the economic influence of collective bargaining.[30] While not notably successful they retain significance, nevertheless, as forerunners of probable future efforts to limit collective bargaining through devices outside the framework of the older body of industrial relations law.

In addition to offering general encouragement or discouragement, the law may affect the details of bargaining. Currently, government regulation of the details of collective bargaining is more widespread than at any time in the past. The size of the bargaining unit, the conduct of the negotiators, and the subject matter of bargaining are conditioned by the law to some extent. At the present time, for example, plant guards may not be in the same bargaining unit as production workers, an attempt to change a union-management agreement must be preceded by at least sixty days' notice prior to the agreement termination date, notice of a strike must be given to the Federal Mediation Service, and union and management negotiators must bargain in good faith. This is only a partial listing of legal requirements currently imposed upon those subject to federal labor relations law,

---

[30] Details of the guideposts are discussed on pp. 427 to 430 below.

but it is illustrative of the nature of the controls exerted over the details of bargaining.

What the government does when bargaining breaks down has a significant effect on the bargaining process. The strategies of unions and managements are usually modified when they know that a breakdown in any bargaining may result in plant seizure, compulsory arbitration, or some other type of government intervention.

It is not stretching a point to suggest that the government participates in some way in every negotiation that takes place between labor and management. In a majority of cases the participation is minimal, but not infrequently the processes and results of bargaining bear the marks of direct government influence.

THE PUBLIC

It is no simple matter to define what is meant by "the public"; and, given the present state of knowledge about public opinion, it is impossible to make a very precise statement about how this opinion affects collective bargaining.[31] More and more, however, both labor and management are making the assumption that public attitudes are important; and both are making liberal use of the mass communication media to present their sides of controversial issues. The full-page newspaper ad, for instance, has become a popular medium for leveling charges or refuting ones that have been made by the opposite party.

Two possible ways in which public attitudes might affect the bargaining process will be suggested here. First, in a broad political sense, the electorate, by the voting process, chooses a philosophy of government as well as office holders. It is not necessary to have a crystal clear knowledge of the difference between Republican and Democratic party philosophies to know that the election of Roosevelt over Hoover or Landon made a difference from the standpoint of legislative consequences. The nation did not express itself specifically on the matter of labor legislation, but it did choose an administration that was more likely to enact laws favorable toward unions than was the Republican party. Similarly, when the Republicans won control of the Eightieth Congress, the electorate returned to power those more likely to restrict aspects of union activities. The expression of prevailing attitudes in a national election gives a philosophic point of view an opportunity to be expressed in the details of legislation.

---

[31] For a description of the difficulties involved in pinning down a definition of "public opinion," see Avery Leiserson, "Public Opinion as a Factor in Labor Disputes," *Proceedings of the Fifth Annual Meeting of the Industrial Relations Research Association* (1952), pp. 26–30.

In the narrow matter of bargaining relationships between specific union and management groups, the second effect of public attitudes demonstrates itself as a mild influence on the behavior of leaders in both camps. One student has suggested that management and labor leaders are not likely to follow courses of action that they believe will outrage the public and set pressures in motion that will rebound disadvantageously.[32] Although public attitudes do establish limits on the bahavior of labor and management, these are fluctuating limits. The public relations policies of both labor and management are designed to influence the dimensions of the limits.

When labor-management relations are cordial, there is no particular reason for the bargaining parties to pay much attention to public attitudes which, in fact, are not likely to be crystallized over anything that happens between a friendly union and management. It is during conflict situations that both sides appeal for public sympathy almost as a matter of course.

SUMMARY

It is no more possible to identify *a* management attitude toward labor unions than it is to identify *a* labor attitude toward management. In the ranks of both management and labor there are persons of widely different backgrounds, education, philosophy, and personality. Despite this qualification, it is probably safe to say that among managers there is a bias against recognizing a legitimate role for the union. As an outside group seeking to insert itself into the power structure of the business firm, the union interferes with the ability of management to manipulate company resources for the accomplishment of company goals as these goals are defined by the managers. Although the management outlook has a bias against recognizing a legitimate role for labor unions, the outlook is broad enough to encompass a variety of specific policies toward unionism ranging from complete co-operation to total hostility.

Similarly, there is much in the background of labor leaders to make them distrustful of management. The behavior of a particular labor leader, however, is likely to be strongly influenced by the nature of the immediate problems he faces such as the prosperity of the particular industry, the geographical characteristics of the product market, the rate of technological change, and the receptiveness of employers in the industry to unionism.

Although only management representatives and union officials participate directly in bargaining, the indirect participants are not without influence. This is especially true in the cases of the rank and file worker and the government. The precise influence exerted by public attitudes is vague.

---

[32] *Ibid.*, p. 31.

Both labor and management have been impressed by the power of public opinion, however; and in serious conflict situations, both will make an appeal for public sympathy.

QUESTIONS

1. Within the United States, there are some in management who are actively in favor of labor unions, some who are willing to bargain in good faith because "unions are here to stay," and some who are actively opposed to labor unions. How would you explain the variations in attitudes toward unionism that are found among those in management?

2. The large corporation and the large union are bureaucratic. Does this fact have any significance in the collective bargaining relationships between union and management?

3. Typically, the backgrounds of business executives are quite different from those of labor leaders. How might this fact color the nature of the collective bargaining relationship?

4. Since the worker does not participate directly in collective bargaining he is a pawn whose fortunes are being decided by business and labor leaders over whom he has no control. Do you agree with this statement? Explain your position.

5. The trend in the United States is toward a centralization of authority in collective negotiations. What factors account for this trend? Are there any forces working in an opposite direction?

6. Do public attitudes influence the bargaining process? If so, what is the nature of this influence?

SELECTED READINGS

BARBASH, JACK. "Union Leadership," *The Practice of Unionism.* New York: Harper & Row, Publishers, 1956. Chap. 15.

CHAMBERLAIN, NEIL W., and KUHN, JAMES. "The Bargaining Unit," *Collective Bargaining.* New York: McGraw-Hill Book Company, 1965. Chap. 10.

CHERNISH, WILLIAM N. *Coalition Bargaining.* Philadelphia: University of Pennsylvania Press, 1969.

DUBIN, ROBERT. "Bases of Management's Labor Decisions," *Working Union-Management Relations.* Englewood Cliffs, N.J.: Prentice-Hall, Inc., 1958. Chap. 2.

MILLS, C. W. *The New Men of Power.* New York: Harcourt, Brace & World, Inc., 1948. Chaps. 5, 8.

WARNER, W. LLOYD, and ABEGGLEN, JAMES C. *Big Business Leaders in America.* New York: Harper & Row, Publishers, 1955.

ULMAN, LLOYD (ed.). *Challenges to Collective Bargaining.* Englewood Cliffs, N.J.: Prentice-Hall, Inc., 1967. Chap. 1.

CHAPTER 8

The Bargaining Contract

THE PURPOSE OF UNION-MANAGEMENT NEGOTIATIONS IS TO REACH AGREE-
ment on the terms of the collective bargaining contract. The bargaining
sessions that occur immediately after a firm has been organized by a labor
union usually produce a brief document dealing with wages and other of the
more important matters that affect the parties involved. Over a period of
time, the agreement tends to expand. As the union becomes firmly entrenched more and more of the matters that were decided unilaterally by
management become subject to joint determination. Often provisions in a
contract prove to be ambiguous, and clarification makes the insertion of
additional clauses necessary. Thus, each bargaining session is likely to
produce a contract bulkier than the one being replaced. The Ford–United
Automobile Workers' collective bargaining agreement booklet, for example,
grew from twenty-four pages in 1941 to 330 pages in 1961. Although new
matter is very likely to be inserted during negotiations, rarely are old
provisions thrown out in their entirety. In some establishments, contracts
have become so involved that unions find it necessary to hold special classes
to explain the agreement to their stewards. Management does the same for
the foremen.

Despite the detailed nature of many contracts, they cannot deal with
every issue that might conceivably arise in the workplace. The world of
work is far too complex for all of its facets to be dealt with in a twenty- to
fifty-page booklet. Some of the non-contractual understandings, furthermore, might be as important to the workers as matters that have been
decided by the bargaining process. There may be a common understanding

that the informal group leader will work on the machine nearest the window, or that the worker with the greater seniority will drive the newest truck, or that only so many units of work will be turned out each hour. In establishments where there is a well developed pattern of discrimination against a minority group, the discriminatory practices will not be specified in the bargaining agreement.

Not only does the contract fail to deal with the totality of the working environment, but it also does not say everything that might be said about the contractual provisions. The most tightly drawn clauses relating to overtime payments or the order in which workers will be released will fail to deal with the unusual situations that inevitably seem to develop. Many provisions in an agreement represent compromises between the parties; and when there is ambiguity in the wording, the union understanding of a particular provision may be different from management's conception. A contract is something that must be lived with in the year or two that elapses between bargaining sessions, and in this time span it will have to be interpreted on numerous occasions.

Issues that cannot be clearly settled by referring to the contract can be treated in a number of ways. They can be ignored and thus left to smolder as issues. They can be resolved by a show of force. They can be dealt with by an arrangement established specifically for such purposes. The latter method is referred to as a grievance procedure, and the typical contract includes some provision for grievance processing. The usual grievance arrangement provides that levels of union and management representatives, starting with the union steward or business agent and the foreman, take a turn at resolving a grievance. Most contracts provide for arbitration or a final decision by an outside party when a problem passes through all the steps in the grievance procedure and still remains unsolved.

In the thousands of existing labor-management agreements there is an almost infinite variety of detail. Certain major headings turn up in the tables of contents rather consistently, however, although not always in the same order. After a general introductory clause which names the parties and states the date and duration of the agreement, there are sections dealing with union recognition, types of security granted to the union, wages and other remuneration matters, hours of work, seniority, working conditions, grievance procedure, and union and management rights. (This last provision is less nearly universal than the other named.) Occasionally, a complete scale of wages for all job classifications is appended to the agreement. Insurance and pension benefits are described within the contract in some cases and detailed under separate cover in others.

In this chapter, some of the major sections of the contract will be examined. Since wage determination will be discussed more fully in later chapters, the present section will simply describe the nature of the wage agreement. Other contract matters will be described and also discussed as issues.

WAGES

The man on the street with no trade union experience probably thinks of the labor-management contract as primarily a wage agreement. In actuality, not more than 25 per cent of any contract is likely to be devoted to wage matters, and in many cases the percentage figure will be even smaller. The number of pages devoted to an item is not necessarily an accurate measure of its importance, however. With some notable exceptions, the wage section has been the most highly publicized part of the union-management agreement. It is one in which the workers are keenly interested, and that part of the contract in which the wage scales are presented is usually more heavily thumbed through than any other.

In addition to the level of wages, there are several basic decisions that any establishment—union or non-union—must make. There is, first, the major question of how work is to be measured for payment purposes. Should wages be paid according to the amount of time an individual spends on the job; or should they be tied, in one manner or another, to the worker's performance? Once the decision is made as to whether the payments will be based upon "time," "incentive," or some combination of the two, there are further questions of detail to be settled.

Time Payments

A wage structure that is built upon time payments may take one of three basic forms. These are (1) single rates, (2) rate ranges, and (3) random rates. The single-rate system is one in which there is one wage rate for a specified occupation or group of employees. An example of a single-rate system as it might appear in a labor-management contract is shown below:

	Job Classification	*Rate per Hour*
Assembler	C	$2.00
	B	2.15
	A	2.25
Automatic Machine Feeder	B	2.05
	A	2.15
Grinder	B	2.10
	A	2.20
Drill Press Operator	C	2.10
	B	2.20
	A	2.30

Occasionally, in a single-rate system, there will be a starting rate that is slightly below the regular job rate. After a certain amount of service that might be as short as one week or as long as six months, the beginner is advanced to the regular job rate. There are advantages to a single-rate system. It is simpler to administer; and, since all who perform a given job are being paid at the same rate, it minimizes favoritism. The one big disadvantage is that it is difficult to reward the worker for good performance or long service except by promotion.

In a rate range system, there is a range of wages for all job classes, as follows:

	Job Classification	*Rate per Hour*
Assembler	C	$2.00–2.15
	B	2.15–2.25
	A	2.25–2.40
Automatic Machine Feeder	B	2.05–2.15
	A	2.15–2.25
Grinder	B	2.10–2.20
	A	2.20–2.30
Drill Press Operator	C	2.10–2.20
	B	2.20–2.30
	A	2.30–2.45

When rate ranges are used, some plan must be devised to govern the progression of employees within the ranges. The usual progression methods are known as "merit" or "length of service" plans. Frequently, a combination of the two plans is used. When an employee is rated according to merit, the labor-management agreement will usually specify intervals at which the individual's record is to be reviewed. Ordinarily, management reserves the right to judge an employee's merit, although, as might be expected, the matter of grading performance sometimes leads to controversy. In a length of service plan an employee is automatically granted an increase when a specified period of service is completed. Thus, a class C assembler in the example given above might start at $2.00 per hour, move to $2.05 after six months, and reach the range maximum of $2.15 after two years of service. When a combination of merit and length of service is used, the worker usually is granted automatic progression to some point within the range and advanced by merit thereafter. A common method is to provide for automatic progression to the range midpoint and then to advance the individual by merit from that point onward. When such plans are used, the rate range is generally much wider than those shown in the examples above.

A random rate structure is a non-systematic arrangement in which payments to those who hold similar jobs may differ in amount and bear no apparent relationship to each other. Existence of a random rate structure shows that management has not paid much attention to its wage system or that favoritism has been practiced. When a union organizes a plant where random rates are in effect, it usually attempts to install a more orderly system. This is no simple task. Under a random structure many rates are out of line. A semi-skilled worker, for instance, may be receiving a higher hourly rate than some of the skilled workers. When random rates are replaced by single rates or rate ranges, there is usually a large residue of "red circle" rates. This means that workers who had been receiving wage payments clearly out of line with others doing the same job continue to receive the same high rates even though the new system calls for a lower payment. Red circle rates can be gradually eliminated over time as quits, retirements, or promotions occur. Despite the obvious irrationality of random rates, a surprisingly large number of establishments, some of them unionized, have operated in recent times with such wage structures. This was revealed during the wage control programs of World War II and the Korean War when applications for approval of wage increases had to be accompanied by a description of the firm's wage structure.

Incentive Payments

In an incentive system, the worker's pay is dependent upon his output. Incentive payments are not workable for some types of jobs. Where spoilage must be kept to an absolute minimum because raw materials are expensive or where the rate of output is controlled by the speed of a machine, payment methods other than incentive systems are more appropriate. The ideal setting for incentive pay plans exists when the work process is repetitive, when variations in the rate of output are due primarily to worker exertion, and when the units of work are identifiable and easily counted. Many ingenious incentive plans have been developed, however, that apply to productive processes in which conditions are in some respects different from these.

A confusing variety of incentive plans are currently being used. They vary from simple piecework plans whereby a specified amount of money is paid for each piece produced to very elaborate standard hour plans whereby standard or "normal" production is first determined and employee pay is then tied to production beyond standard as determined by one of many measuring systems. Incentive plans may be individual—that is, based upon the work record of the individual employee—or they may be group plans whereby payment is geared to the productive efforts of a unit of workers.

When an establishment uses an incentive system of payments, the collective bargaining agreement may deal with many aspects of the system. The goal of the union is to have a greater voice in the determination of the details of the system. Provisions of the agreement will usually reveal the extent of the union's progress toward achieving this goal. The following is a list of types of items relating to incentive pay that might be found in a wage contract:

1. *Establishment of Standards.*   Basic to all incentive systems is the idea that superior performance is to be rewarded. This implies that some standard must be developed as a basis of measurement. The standard might be derived from time studies, historical experience, or plain haggling during negotiations. Whatever the method used, the union will usually make some attempt to spell out its rights to participate in the standard-establishing process.

2. *Minimum Wage Guarantees.*   Many incentive systems provide that in no event will pay fall below a certain guaranteed level.

3. *Down-time Payments.*   "Down-time" refers to those periods when an employee is unable to work at his regular incentive-rated job for reasons such as machinery breakdowns. A contract might specify that while on down-time the worker will be paid on the basis of his average earnings, at the rate for the temporary job to which he is assigned, or his guaranteed minimum.

4. *Incorporating Wage Changes into the Incentive Plan.*   When a firm grants a general wage increase, there always arises the question of how the increase will be incorporated into the incentive system. The increase may be granted as a "tack-on," which means simply that the amount of the pay boost will be tacked on to whatever incentive earnings happen to be. The other possibility is to incorporate the increase into an incentive base rate. The advantage of the first alternative is that it is the simplest method of making an adjustment in a complicated incentive plan. The advantage of the second possibility, to the worker at least, is that it might make larger incentive earnings possible. This would be the case where the system is designed to make it possible for employees to earn a specified percentage above the base rate.

5. *Changes in the Incentive Plan.*   A bargaining agreement will often spell out the procedures that either management or the union must follow when changes in the plan are sought. Such changes might consist of re-timing certain operations, modifying a base rate, or placing additional jobs under the incentive plan.

6. *Settlement of Grievances.*   A complex incentive plan can be a prolific source of grievances. Usually a contract will contain some provision relating to the settlement of such grievances, and not infrequently the provision will call for final arbitration of disputes that cannot be settled by the bargaining parties.

Recent Developments in Incentive Pay and other Practices

There has always been some range in both management and union attitudes toward incentive pay plans. Before 1940, however, managements tended to favor such pay arrangements, and unions generally opposed them. A common management viewpoint was that an incentive plan was an effective method of stimulating effort and rewarding superior worker performance. Unions, on the other hand, were suspicious of an arrangement which they regarded as a way of pitting worker against worker and of getting more work for less pay.

Some change in these traditional attitudes has apparently occurred since the end of World War II. In an improper industrial relations setting, an incentive system can break down quite easily, and this has happened to the extent that a certain amount of management disenchantment with incentives has developed. Many firms have found themselves saddled with "demoralized incentive systems" and have been moved either to abandon or to revise their plans.[1] At the same time, a number of local unions have found incentive work to be an effective way of fattening the pay envelope and have resisted management efforts to abandon incentive plans.

As a result of the experiences described above, there has been a considerable amount of adjustment in methods of payment, with some firms eliminating incentives, others revising their systems, and still others extending them in novel ways. These changes have apparently not modified significantly the proportion of manufacturing employees paid on an incentive basis,[2] but they have produced some collective bargaining turmoil. Bargaining contracts reflect these developments in a number of ways. Clauses relating to wage incentive revisions, for example, are now more carefully drawn; and arbitration of incentive grievances, once generally opposed by management, has become an accepted procedure.

Changes in technology and work processes have had an important impact upon the character of incentive plans in many establishments. In the past, standardized jobs, measurable output, and a direct link between worker effort and amount of output have been regarded as necessary conditions for the successful implementation of an incentive plan. Thus, in establishments using incentives one would usually find the work divided into incentive and non-incentive jobs, the latter category including such occupations as janitoring, maintenance work, and machine set-up for which

[1] For a discussion of the "demoralized incentive plan" see Garth L. Mangum, "Summary of Wage Incentive Practices in American Industry," *Studies Relating to Collective Bargaining Agreements and Practices outside the Railroad Industry* (Appendix Volume IV of the Report of the Presidential Railroad Commission [Washington, D.C., February, 1962]), pp. 247–252.

[2] L. Earl Lewis, "Extent of Incentive Pay in Manufacturing," *Monthly Labor Review,* May, 1960, pp. 460–463.

incentive pay methods were regarded as inappropriate. In recent years, industrial output has come to depend, more and more, upon the pace of the machine rather than the effort of the worker. This development would appear to argue for an abandonment of incentive pay methods, since the basic conditions for incentive work are lacking.

In practice, there seems to be little relationship between the character of plant technology and the use of incentives.[3] Frequent examples can be found of the application of incentives to machine-paced tasks, although the traditional measurement methods have been replaced by such concepts as "utilization time" or "attention time." Pay, in other words, is no longer tied to production beyond some measured standard but is based, instead, on the degree to which expensive equipment is utilized. The "incentive" worker can earn no more than a maximum amount stipulated, but he can earn less when utilization time drops. Under these arrangements, historical distinctions between incentive and non-incentive jobs have broken down, and there has been a movement in the direction of incorporating maintenance and other "non-production" work into incentive plans.

In addition to the changes in the character of incentive plans described above, other recent developments in wage payment methods reflect new efforts to reconcile labor's concern with equity and management's interest in efficiency. Arrangements such as profit sharing, productivity bargaining, cost reduction plans, and long run wage guarantees have been scrutinized with more openmindedness on the part of union and management negotiators than had hitherto been the case, and bargaining contracts in certain industries already show the marks of this examination.[4]

Fringe Benefits

Before World War II the typical worker received money wages in payment for time worked or output produced, and this constituted the whole of his remuneration. Today it is unusual when the worker does not receive benefits in addition to his money wages. Such benefits have been variously described as "non-wage benefits," "supplementary pay," and "fringe benefits," with the latter appellation having the widest usage. Most supplementary pay items fall into one of the following categories: (1) pay for time not worked such as holidays, vacations, sick leave, or jury duty; (2) premium pay for overtime, work performed on holidays, and late shift

---

[3] Summer H. Slichter, James J. Healy, and E. Robert Livernash, *The Impact of Collective Bargaining on Management* (Washington, D.C.: The Brookings Institution, 1960), p. 533.

[4] For a description of these arrangements and an analysis of the background factors that have generated interest in them see Robert B. McKersie, "Changing Methods of Wage Payments," in John T. Dunlop and Neil W. Chamberlain (eds.) *Frontiers of Collective Bargaining* (New York: Harper and Row Publishers, 1967), chap. 7.

work; (3) legally required employer payments for social insurance; (4) private welfare plans such as pensions and health and accident insurance; (5) Christmas, year-end, and a variety of other bonuses.

In the first category, the most prominent of the items are paid vacations and holidays. Relatively rare before 1940, provisions for paid vacations and holidays now appear in the large majority of collective bargaining agreements. By early 1963, nearly all office and plant workers in metropolitan areas were receiving paid holidays and were covered by some type of paid vacation plan.[5] Vacation plans vary considerably in detail; but prevailing practice for plant employees appears to be one week of paid vacation after one year of service, two weeks after two to three years of service, and three weeks for ten to fifteen years of service. Seven paid holidays is the national average for plant employees in establishments providing paid holidays, although provisions for eight or more are not uncommon.

In recent years there has been a movement in the direction of liberalizing vacation benefits for long-tenure employees. Twenty-two per cent of plant employees in metropolitan areas received four or more weeks of vacation in 1960 after twenty-five years of service. By 1967, the percentage had increased to fifty-three. Recent contracts negotiated between the United Steel Workers and eleven major basic steel producers have provided especially liberal vacation benefits. Employees in the top half of each company's seniority list receive a thirteen week vacation (including their regular annual vacation) once in every five years. Employees in the lower half of the seniority list receive three weeks, in addition to their regular annual vacation, once in five years. One-fifth of the senior workers and one-fifth of the junior workers receive their extended vacations each year.

Private welfare plans have proliferated since the end of World War II, and 98 per cent of all plant workers in metropolitan areas are now covered by some form of insurance or health plan. Since 1960 there has been a rapid growth in the popularity of major medical insurance as a supplementary pay item.

Estimates of the costs of fringe benefits currently granted vary because there is no general agreement about what should be included among the fringe items. Some studies, for example, include premium pay practices such as shift differentials, extra pay for holidays worked, and extra pay for weekend work. Others include the cost of employer contributions to social insurance programs. The usual estimate, however, runs to somewhere between 20 per cent and 25 per cent of total payroll. A National Chamber of Commerce study of fringe benefits paid by 102 companies showed that the cost of fringes in these firms increased from 15 per cent of payroll in

---

[5] "Supplemental Wage Benefits in Metropolitan Areas, 1962–63," *Monthly Labor Review*, May, 1964, pp. 536–542.

1947 to over 23 per cent in 1957.[6] More recent studies by the Department of Labor indicate that supplementary pay items expressed as a percentage of gross payroll amount to 20.2 per cent for factory workers; 22.5 per cent for employees in finance, insurance, and real estate; and 25.6 per cent for mine workers.[7] In the basic steel industry, supplementary items for production workers represent 27.1 per cent of total compensation. Between 1950 and 1965 when straight time pay for steelworkers doubled, hourly expenditures for pay supplements quadrupled.[8]

The spread of wage supplements has been rapid, and the outlook is for a continuing liberalization of the fringe or non-wage items. Although employers in many cases have not opposed the idea of these benefits, the main pressure for expansion has come from labor organizations. This raises the question of why so much stress has been placed upon the fringe items. Anything granted as a fringe benefit can be translated into a money equivalent and granted to the workers as a straight wage increase. For a variety of reasons most unions have preferred a "package" that includes supplements to money wages. Students of collective bargaining have not as yet worked out a full explanation for the rapid spread of fringe benefits, but the following factors are partly responsible:

1. Wage controls imposed during World War II allowed more leeway for adjustments of fringe benefits than for wage increases. As firms exhausted the wage grants that were permissible under the control program, both management and unions turned their attention to wage supplements. Management, at this stage, frequently relied upon a package of liberal fringe benefits to recruit manpower in a period of severe labor shortages.

2. The popularity of fringe items did not subside after the termination of hostilities. What had happened was that a vast and virtually untouched area had been opened to bargaining. The sociology of collective bargaining is such that when new matter is allowed at the bargaining table, the possibilities provided thereby are likely to be exploited quickly. When traditional pattern setters such as the bargains in steel, automobiles, and coal mining established precedents in the health and welfare field, it became highly likely that similar benefits would be bargained out in other industries. The pressures on labor leaders not to be outdone by others, the prevailing prosperity which minimized the intensity of employer opposi-

---

[6] *Fringe Benefits, 1957* (Washington, D.C.: Chamber of Commerce of the United States, 1958), p. 28.

[7] "Supplemental Remuneration for Factory Workers, 1959," *Monthly Labor Review,* January, 1962, pp. 30–37; "Pay Supplements in Finance, Insurance, and Real Estate," *ibid.,* March, 1964, pp. 305–312; "Supplementary Remuneration for Mine Workers," *ibid.,* June, 1962, pp. 654–661.

[8] William M. Smith, "Compensation of Workers in Basic Steel," *Monthly Labor Review,* July, 1968, p. 47.

tion, and federal court decisions that upheld the bargainability of health and welfare items were factors that contributed to the growth of fringe benefits.

3. Certain practical considerations have been involved in the recent union drive for fringe benefits. The employer, for instance, who provides pension and hospitalization benefits to his workers can derive tax advantages that are denied to workers who provide such benefits for themselves. In a period of inflation and high personal income taxes, furthermore, many of the fringe benefits are more attractive than their money equivalents. A paid holiday for the $2.00 per hour employee costs a total of $16.00 if we assume an eight-hour day. In take-home pay this might come to about $12.00. Twelve dollars spread out over fifty-two paychecks amounts to twenty-three cents per week, which is much less attractive than an additional paid holiday. Given prevailing prices and tax rates, anything less than a substantial wage boost does not amount to very much and looks much better when converted to one of the fringes.[9]

4. More leisure time has been an historical objective of labor unions, and many of the modern-day fringes are old objectives in new guises. Prior to World War II, the drive for more leisure time was defined primarily in terms of shorter hours and a shorter work week. To these objectives there has been added a new goal of a work year made shorter by holidays, vacations, and a host of other items. Up to a point, leisure time is a mark of status in our society, and the leisure currently enjoyed by workers is one of the numerous ways in which the distance between the wealthy and the not so wealthy has been narrowed. Fringe benefits, in other words, have symbolic as well as economic significance.

SENIORITY

In the typical bargaining agreement, a number of important clauses will be devoted to problems involving job rights of workers. Questions about job rights may arise in connection with layoffs, recalls, promotions, and transfers. In a non-union shop or in the absence of a bargained agreement, discretion in such matters rests with employers. When a firm is newly organized, the union will usually seek to temper the employer's discretion, and a major result of the American bargaining experience has been the substitution of joint for unilateral determination of many of the problems involving the job rights of workers.

---

[9] For a summary of several studies showing that workers prefer increases in benefits as against monetary compensation see Richard A. Lester, "Benefits as a Preferred Form of Compensation," *The Southern Economic Journal*, April, 1967, pp. 488–495.

The seniority rule has become the most prominent principle in the settlement of conflicts over job rights. "Seniority" can be broadly defined as the rule of "last man hired is the first man laid off." This description refers, of course, to layoffs where the seniority rule enjoys a wide application. In job right questions generally, seniority implies that the most advantageous alternatives accrue to persons with the lengthiest service. As we shall see, straight seniority—that is, seniority not modified by qualifications of one sort or another—is applied in relatively few situations. Ordinarily, the labor-management agreement will condition the seniority principle by requirements such as ability to do a job or by limiting the area of the firm in which a given worker's seniority applies.

Before discussing various facets of seniority, it is necessary to note that seniority is only one of many ways in which job rights might be protected. Restrictions which unions impose on layoffs, for instance, may range from the relatively mild requirement that the employer give advance notice of a prospective reduction in force to a guarantee of annual wages for regular employees.

Many unions do not stress seniority at all because of its unworkability in their industries or trades. When employment fluctuates sharply because of seasonal or other factors, a strict application of the seniority rule would divide the work force into an older group of high seniority workers and a younger group of low seniority workers who would bear the brunt of unemployment within an industry. The conflict of interest between high and low seniority workers in such a situation could result in a challenge to union authority. In seasonal industries such as the needle trades, labor-management agreements usually provide for some sort of work sharing rather than the application of the seniority rule.

A wide variety of work-sharing arrangements are found in practice. The clauses listed below illustrate some of these variations:

> There shall be an equal and equitable distribution among the workers of the shop at all times. There shall be no reduction in the regular working force at any time whatsoever, and all available work shall at all times be divided among the employees as above stated. (*Cap and Uniform Manufacturers of Chicago and the United Hatters, Cap and Millinery Workers International Union.*)

> At all times work shall be distributed to the members of the union as equally as possible. During the slow season whatever work there is shall be equally distributed to members of the union in each branch of the shop so as to enable each one to work an equal number of hours. (*Children's Cotton Dress and Sportswear Contractors Association and International Ladies Garment Workers Union.*)

> When there is not sufficient work for all regular employees, temporary or probationary employees with less than 90 days' seniority shall be laid

off and then said remaining work shall be as nearly equally divided as possible among remaining regular workers regardless of seniority in order to avoid discrimination between workers. (*Wholesale Furniture Manufacturers of Illinois and Michigan and Upholsterers International Union of North America.*)

Some Details of Seniority Clauses

The seniority clause in the collective bargaining agreement may be a simple one or two paragraph statement of intent, or it may be a many-paged section with excruciatingly fine details. The following example, taken from an actual contract, is about as simple a seniority clause as one can find:

> As to layoffs and rehiring, the principle of seniority shall apply. Seniority shall be determined on the length of service of the employee with regard to his ability to perform the work. All circumstances being reasonably equal, length of service shall be the controlling factor.

This clause may be workable in a small establishment where there are few job classifications, but it would raise more questions than it would resolve in larger firms with many departments, large work forces, and dozens or even hundreds of different job classifications. The basic principle of seniority—the employee with the longest service will be the last laid off and the first rehired—is difficult to administer because of the complex departmental structure of many firms and also because no set of seniority rules will make everyone happy. Once a firm has become committed to the principle of seniority, union and management officials must iron out a host of complicated details. Some of these are described below:

1. *The Dimensions of the Seniority Unit.* One of the most perplexing seniority questions involves the scope of the seniority unit. A seniority unit may be company-wide, plant-wide, department-wide, or occupation-wide. It is not uncommon for a unit to be a combination of two or more of these possibilities. In a company-wide unit, the oldest employee, from a length of service standpoint, will retain his job even if it involves transfer from one plant location to another. In the plant-wide unit—more prevalent than the company unit—the single plant is the unit for seniority purposes. When layoffs occur, a senior employee may "bump" any junior employee in the plant whose job he is qualified to hold. In departmental or occupational units, the seniority rights of employees are limited to the boundaries of departmental or occupational divisions in the plant.

Agreement on the general principles of seniority provides no ready-made answer as to the appropriateness of the different possible units. Much depends upon the nature of the work process. If the essential skills are interchangeable, a broad unit is at least feasible. If the plant departments are highly specialized, inter-departmental transfers may be exceptionally disruptive. Older employees usually prefer a broad seniority unit, since this enlarges the base of younger workers whom they might displace. Younger workers, conversely, prefer a narrow unit. Employers generally prefer narrow units because they prefer to minimize the breakup of work units where efficiency has been achieved.

Job or departmental units are apparently the most common. A Bureau of Labor Statistics study found that over 60 per cent of the agreements surveyed provided for job or departmental seniority, whereas only 6 per cent provided for plant units.[10] In a number of firms the unit varied with such factors as the nature of the employee's job, length of service, or the nature of the layoff. Some agreements stipulated that separate seniority lists were to be maintained for each sex. This arrangement is fairly common in the food industries and in firms manufacturing transportation equipment.

2. *Measurement of Seniority.*   The problem of measuring seniority overlaps the question of the dimension of the seniority unit in some respects. A worker may be a junior member of a department and, at the same time, have more plant service than anyone else in the department. Conversely, the senior member of a new department may have been in the plant a relatively short time. The possible combinations of plant, departmental, job class, or occupational seniority are almost endless, and a vast number of arrangements are found in practice. The following examples show how length of employment is measured for seniority purposes in a number of selected agreements:

> In the event an employee is requested by the employer to assume duties in another department and the question of seniority develops, it is agreed that the employee so transferred shall maintain his seniority in the department from which he was transferred. (*Producers Dairy and Local 336, Milk and Ice Cream Drivers and Dairy Employees Union.*)

> When layoffs are necessary because of lack of work, the company will apply the principle of seniority within noninterchangeable occupational groups. (*United Aircraft Corporation and International Union of United Automobile, Aircraft and Agricultural Implement Workers.*)

> It is understood that both departmental and plant seniority shall be taken into consideration in the application of the seniority principle. . . . In instances of layoff where an employee has 1 year or more of plant seniority, the seniority considered shall be plant seniority, but where an employee has less than 1 year of plant seniority, the seniority for layoff purposes shall be departmental seniority. (*Hercules Powder Co. and International Chemical Workers Union.*)

---

[10] Bulletin 1209, U.S. Department of Labor, Bureau of Labor Statistics, 1957.

The Bargaining Contract 221

Measurement of length of service for seniority purposes is further complicated by the problem of how to treat certain breaks in service. Should seniority accumulate during strikes, temporary layoffs, military service, or illness? In the event of layoff, how long should seniority rights remain operative? Different answers to such questions will be found in different agreements. It is not unusual, though, for a contract to specify that the seniority rights of an employee terminate if he is not called back to work within a given time limit.

3. *Limitations and Exceptions.* A completely rigid application of the seniority principle would cause difficulties for the union as well as for management. Most systems, consequently, include some provisions for making exceptions or for otherwise limiting the application of straight seniority. Quite frequently, seniority is limited by considerations relating to ability. Sample clauses incorporating ability criteria are shown below:

> As to layoffs and rehiring, the principles of seniority shall apply. Seniority shall be determined on the length of service of the employee with regard to his experience and ability to perform the work. All circumstances being reasonably equal, length of service shall be the controlling factor. (*Cleveland Food Industry Committee and Local 427, Amalgamated Meat Cutters and Butcher Workmen of North America.*)

> The above seniority is conditioned on the employee having the skill and ability to do the work involved, and should a question arise concerning skill and ability, it shall be settled satisfactorily between the Union and Management. (*Maxwell Company and International Association of Machinists, District 54.*)

Some clauses spell out more specifically the relative weight to be given to ability as against other factors. An agreement between Republic Steel and the United Steel Workers, for example, contained the following provision:

> In recognition of the responsibility of management for the efficient operation of the plants, it is understood that in all cases of decrease of forces or recalls after layoffs, the following factors as listed below shall be considered; however, only when both factors (a) and (b) are relatively equal, shall continuous service be the determining factor:
> (a) ability to perform the work;
> (b) physical fitness;
> (c) continuous service.

In practice, clauses that modify seniority by making it operative only after the employee meets specifications of ability and physical fitness frequently do little by way of actual modification. "Ability to perform the job" is a vague phrase, and its use as a criterion is as likely to lead to a grievance as it is to provide a clear-cut standard in a given case. Although many seniority clauses make mention of equal ability, such clauses are often meaningless unless spelled out in greater detail.

One of the more common exceptions to the application of the seniority principle is the practice of superseniority for union representatives or key personnel. Superseniority means that the particular employee will retain his job regardless of his place on the seniority list. Ordinarily an agreement will specify the categories of union officials who will have superseniority or will limit the extra protection to a fixed number or proportion of officials. An example is shown below:

> Two officers of the local union, eight chief stewards, and regular stewards shall head the list of their occupational groups if they have one year's seniority. Regular stewards' preferential seniority shall not cause an employee with more than five years' seniority to be laid off. (*National Lock Co. and International Union of United Automobile, Aircraft, and Agricultural Implement Workers of America.*)

Workers with special skills or training are sometimes exempted from the operation of plant-wide seniority provisions, and in some instances management retains the right to select a specified number of persons who may be kept on the job even though their seniority rankings are below those of workers being laid off.

4. *The Scope of Seniority.*   Seniority is usually regarded as a principle that is applied during the processes of layoffs and recalls. Actually, evidence of the principle can be found in other sections of the labor-management agreement. It is not uncommon, for instance, for the agreement to specify that job vacancies are to be posted on a bulletin board. Workers then bid for the opening with the understanding that the job is to be awarded to the qualified person with the most seniority. Automatic wage increases granted pursuant to a progression plan in a rate range system involve the application of seniority. Vacations and other non-wage benefits frequently become more liberal as the worker accumulates service time. The benefits that accrue with lengthy service have become more and more extensive in the past several decades.

Seniority: Pros, Cons, and Problems

Elaborate sets of arguments for and against the seniority principle have been developed. The major arguments in favor of seniority are that it eliminates favoritism and protects older workers from the harsh consequences of an overly strict application of the efficiency criterion. Against seniority, it is alleged that it is biased against the more able worker and that it inhibits the efficient operation of a plant by interfering with management's ability to advance and retain workers on the basis of productivity.

There is merit to the contentions of both sides; but, carried to extremes, neither position is tenable. Straight seniority applied without qualifications and without consideration for the basic interests of plant efficiency can and has produced some intolerable situations. Total management discretion, on the other hand, frequently leads to favoritism and even corruption and may work heavy hardship on older workers. Practiced with intelligence and tempered with qualifications that may be required in different types of employment, seniority probably has more merits than demerits. In essence, it places the burden of adjusting to work shortages on the shoulders of the youngest workers who, when all things are considered, are better able to bear the burden.

Few seniority systems will be free of problems, and in the long run the union organization may be the chief victim of an inherent weakness of seniority—it pits workers against each other. In periods of extensive layoffs, widespread dissension may develop. A case study revealed the elaborate process of gerrymandering that occurred in one plant as workers jockeyed to improve their seniority positions.[11] One technique was to "dead end" a job—that is, remove it from a ladder of promotion. This meant that no one occupied a job immediately above the one in question and that consequently no downward bumping could occur. This and similar practices reflected the interests of the stronger political groups within the union. Some were able to secure seniority advantages by manipulating union power in their own interests, but these gains were at the expense of other workers.

In recent years, new types of seniority problems have been raised by the frequency of plant shutdowns and company mergers. When a multiplant firm closes one of its plants, the employees affected may be offered job opportunities at one or more of the company's other facilities. At that time, it must be decided whether transferring employees will carry their total company service with them for seniority purposes or whether seniority will be based upon the date of entry into the new job. The general practice in the automobile industry has been for the employee to get date of entry seniority for layoff and recall purposes, whereas total company service applies in the determination of pension, vacation, and other fringe benefit entitlements. Different practices have been followed in other industries, however.

When two companies merge, a perplexing problem of integrating seniority lists may result. Numerous methods, some of them quite complicated,

---

[11] Leonard R. Sayles, "Seniority: An Internal Union Problem," *Harvard Business Review,* January–February, 1952.

have been used in working out such integrations.[12] Straight length of service integration is the simplest procedure, but not infrequently "ratio integration" has been applied. Ratio integration means, basically, that factors other than length of service are taken into consideration. Assume, for example, that company A with 200 employees merges with company B which has 100 employees. Under a ratio integration, the two senior A employees might be placed at the top of the seniority list to be followed by the senior B employee, with the same pattern being continued until the two lists are fully integrated. When seniority list integration involves factors such as departmental seniority and skill differentals, ratio integrations can become very complex.

UNION SECURITY

In most collective bargaining contracts, a clause near the beginning specifies that management recognizes the union as sole collective bargaining agent for all employees in the employment unit involved. This may or may not be followed by a "union security" clause. When it agrees to some form of union security, management assists the union by participating in one of several possible arrangements that makes it easier for the union to enroll and retain workers within union ranks. Challenges to the existence of a union may come from employers, the workers, a rival union, or a government body. Directly in some cases and indirectly in others, a union security agreement strengthens the position of the union against any of these challenges.

Goals of unions are sometimes differentiated into "union-oriented" and "membership-oriented" goals. The union, in other words, has survival and other problems that are different in character from the ultimate purposes of unionism, which center upon the wages and working conditions of the worker members. In the United States, many labor organizations have placed heavy emphasis upon the goal of union security. This is explained in part by the historical experiences of unions and in part by certain features of the economic and social structure of the nation.

Until relatively recent times, few American employers conceded that unions had a legitimate role to perform. The long history of determined employer opposition plus the high mortality rate suffered by labor organizations impressed many labor leaders with the need for contractual arrange-

---

[12] For discussions of this issue see Mark L. Kahn, "Seniority Problems in Business Mergers," *Industrial and Labor Relations Review*, April, 1955, pp. 361–378; Dan H. Mater and Garth L. Mangum, "The Integration of Seniority Lists in Transportation Mergers," *ibid.*, April, 1963, pp. 343–365; Slichter, Healy, and Livernash, *op. cit.*, pp. 130–136.

ments to enhance the survival possibilities of their unions. Apart from employer opposition, the real opportunities for moving out of working class status and the melting pot characteristics of the labor force deterred the development of a worker solidarity that is essential for the firm establishment of unionism. In Europe, by way of contrast, opportunities to move out of the working class are limited, and workers within a nation constitute a relatively homogeneous economic and social group. These facts have contributed to a greater feeling of class solidarity among European workers, and it is significant that the union security issue has never been as vital in the European nations as it has been in the United States. Other factors that have threatened the existence of unions in this nation from time to time, and thus have accentuated the demand for the protection provided by a union security clause, include the hostile legal climate that prevailed for so many years and competition for membership by rival unions. In employments where labor turnover is high, union security has been sought as a protection against the indifference of transient or temporary workers.

The exact number of persons covered by union security agreements is not known. Studies of major collective bargaining contracts published in 1955 and 1960 by the Bureau of Labor Statistics show that approximately 75 per cent of these contracts provided for some form of union security.[13]

Various forms of union security agreements are found in practice. The meaning of "union security" can be clarified by defining the more prevalent types of such agreements.

1. *The Closed Shop.* The closed shop is the strongest form of union security. Under a closed shop agreement, all employees must be members of the union before they can be hired by the employer. Employees must continue to be union members in good standing as a condition of keeping their jobs. In effect the union is the hiring agent. In many instances where the closed shop exists, the employer obtains his labor by hiring through the union hall.[14]

2. *The Union Shop.* In a union shop arrangement the employer is free to hire whomever he chooses, but all employees must join the union within a specified period. They must also continue to be members of the union in good standing so long as they work in the establishment where the union shop exists. An example of a union shop clause as it might appear in a labor-management agreement is shown below:

The Company agrees that all employees of the Company covered by this agreement shall be members of the Union. The Union agrees that the Com-

---

[13] *Monthly Labor Review,* June, 1955, p. 61, and January, 1960, p. 26.

[14] Under the Taft-Hartley Act of 1947, a worker who is denied employment because of a closed shop contract may file unfair practice charges against employer and union.

pany may hire non-Union members, provided that if these workers are employed by the Company more than thirty (30) days, they shall join the Union, it being understood that every employee hired by the Company shall become a member of the Union thirty (30) days after the date of employment and maintain a good standing in the union for the duration of this contract.

3. *Maintenance of Membership.*[15] A maintenance of membership clause is similar to a union shop in some respects and different in others. It is different in that the employee has an option that is absent in the union shop. After the effective date of a labor-management agreement, the employee has a certain amount of time—usually fifteen days—to decide whether or not he wants to be a union member. He may decide against joining the union, and in this case he can continue to hold his job without penalty. His employment cannot be terminated simply because he has not joined the union. For those who elect union membership, union shop conditions prevail. They must remain members of the union in good standing for the duration of the labor agreement. Under a maintenance of membership clause, the option must be expressed during the "escape period." A worker, for instance, cannot decide to join the union and at some later date change his mind without assuming the risk of being discharged. Workers hired after the effective date of the labor agreement have a specified period in which to make up their minds about union membership. An example of a maintenance of membership clause as it appeared in some of the contracts negotiated in the steel industry is shown below:

> Each employee who on July 1, 1954 is a member of the Union in good standing . . . and each employee who becomes a member after that date shall as a condition of employment maintain his membership in the Union in good standing for the duration of this agreement; provided, however, that this provision shall not apply to any employee who within fifteen days next preceding the end of this agreement . . . shall withdraw from membership in the Union.

4. *The Check-off.* As a form of union security, the check-off differs in character from the three types discussed above. Under a check-off agreement, the employer agrees to deduct the union dues and initiation fees from the paychecks of the employees and to transfer these amounts directly to the union. For the union, this facilitates the process of collecting dues, minimizes the problem of delinquency, and simplifies the bookkeeping. More important than any of these, it guarantees the union a financial security as a result of the continuing and steady payment of dues obligations.

---

[15] The World War II background of the maintenance of membership type of union security clause is discussed in Chapter 5.

A check-off clause may exist concurrently with other union security provisions, or it can stand by itself as the only type of union security recognized by the labor-management agreement. The following example illustrates the nature of a check-off provision:

> The Employer shall, for the term of this agreement, deduct initiation fees and union dues from the first pay of each month of employees who are members of the Union and who individually and voluntarily certify in writing authorizations for such deductions. The Employer shall remit all sums deducted in this manner to the Union before the fifteenth (15th) day of the month for which the initiation fees and dues were collected.

5. *The Agency Shop.* Under the agency shop arrangement, an employee need not join the union as a condition of employment, but he must pay to the union an amount that is usually equal to the prevailing dues. The agency shop form of union security has been used primarily as a device to circumvent the limitations of state right-to-work laws which prohibit union-management agreements that make union membership a condition of employment.

The Union Security Argument

The pros and cons of union security have been debated for many years. For a long time the controversy centered about the closed shop. In recent years, the union shop has developed as one of the most prevalent forms of union security, and the idea of the union shop has been drawn increasingly into the vortex of the continuing debate. The antagonists, it should be noted, are not split solidly down the middle with the labor unions on one side and management on the other. Some labor officials have spoken out against the abuses of the closed shop, and quite a few will admit that peripheral types of security clauses such as the check-off have had a long run effect that works to the disadvantage of the union. Their reasoning is that such clauses make the labor leader's job too easy. The union shop gets the workers into the union; the check-off collects their dues; and the minor union official, as a result, has the greater part of his work done for him. He becomes soft, loses his drive, and sinks into the protective folds of union bureaucracy. On the other hand, many in management have had years of practical experience with union security and are satisfied with the results. Having come to terms with whatever problems are involved in union security clauses, they are uninterested in carrying on a fight over issues that do not concern them. The battle over union security has been a noisy one, but there are many in labor and management who have not participated in the shouting.

As is often the case in a long-standing debate, the pro and con arguments have become fairly standardized. Terminology and emphasis have changed somewhat, but whenever the controversy erupts anew the same basic contentions reappear. The major arguments usually made in justification of union security contractual agreements are as follows:

1. *The Free Rider Argument.*[16]   The person who reaps all the gains of unionism but refuses to contribute his share toward achieving these gains by becoming a union member is a "free rider." The labor union, the argument goes, has managed to win benefits for workers only after hard work and many tribulations. In accepting the benefits won while refusing to make his own contribution through union membership, the non-unionist is riding on the coat-tails of others. It is not contrary to sound ethics or to the principles of democracy to require such an individual to belong to a union by means of a union security agreement. Furthermore, under existing collective bargaining legislation, a labor organization has the obligation to represent the interests of *all* workers in the bargaining unit regardless of union membership. This fact further justifies a labor-management agreement that makes employment conditional upon union membership.

2. *Union Security Promotes Union Responsibility.*   So long as a labor union has to worry about the security of its existence, it is less able to assume the responsibilities and burdens of industrial statesmanship. Once security is achieved, union officials can concentrate upon developing a labor-management co-operation that will benefit all concerned. Such concentration is impossible when so much of the union's energies are absorbed by a struggle for survival. Management frequently insists that unions be responsible for the behavior of workers in accordance with the terms of the bargaining agreement. It is inconsistent, the unions claim, for management to insist on the one hand that unions be responsible for the acts of their members and, on the other hand, to deny the membership conditions that would make such responsibility possible. When union security is an actuality, the union is in a much better position to control the membership so as to minimize spontaneous outbursts that disrupt production and circumvent orderly procedures for ironing out differences.

3. *The Employer Benefits from Union Security.*   In addition to the general advantages derived from dealing with a responsible union, specific benefits accrue to the employer as a result of union security. The firm is less likely to be the scene of union jurisdictional rivalries; and, in industries characterized by a use of casual labor such as the maritime industries, the existence of a union hiring hall provides a labor market stability that would otherwise be absent.

---

[16] For a statement of the free rider argument framed in terms of the theory of collective goods see Allan G. Pulsipher, "The Union Shop: A Legitimate Form of Coercion in a Free-Market Economy," *Industrial and Labor Relations Review,* July, 1966, pp. 529–532.

4. *Union Security Is Not Undemocratic.* Union security, especially of the union shop and maintenance of membership types, can continue to exist only if the majority of the union members are in sympathy with the idea of union security. It is no more undemocratic to insist that the minority join the union than it is to insist that citizens pay taxes for purposes they oppose. Since the union has the legal obligation to look after the welfare of all the workers in the bargaining unit, it is consistent with democratic practices to insist that the minority pay its "taxes."

5. *The Right to Work Is Not Involved in the Argument.* Those who oppose union security claim that such agreements deny the right to work to persons who refuse to join a union. The absence of a closed or union shop does not guarantee anyone the right to work. The individual must find a job before he can work, and this is sometimes difficult. He must also meet whatever qualifications the employer insists upon. No one enjoys an inalienable right to work. It is a conditional right, and the condition that a worker join a union before he can work at a specific job is only one of the many conditions that exist in our economic society.

The following are prominent among the arguments made against union security agreements:

1. *Union Security Agreements Violate Democratic Principles.* Closed or union shops do deny a worker the right to work if he is opposed to unionism in general or to the particular union involved in his circumstances. The right to work without joining a union is as basic as any existing American right.

2. *The Closed Shop Leads to Union Autocracy.* A closed shop arrangement vests too much power in the hands of labor leaders. They can limit entrance to a trade by charging exorbitant initiation fees or by simply refusing to admit new members. In many instances, the closed shop has led to the control of the union by autocratic and corrupt officials who have fattened their pockets at the expense of both workers and employers. Because these officials have the power to deprive a man of his livelihood by the device of terminating his union membership, they cannot be held accountable for their misdeeds in office.

3. *Unions Should Sell Themselves to Workers.* Labor union officials should stand on their own feet and sell unionism to workers instead of relying on union security agreements to do a recruiting job for them. If the benefits of unionism are as obvious as they are claimed to be, they should have no difficulty in doing this. By insisting upon closed or union shop, labor leaders admit their own failure to convince workers that the labor union is an organization essential for employee welfare. Under exist-

ing law, closed or union shop agreements are not essential for union security. The main purpose of such agreements today is to force workers into membership.

Behind all these arguments, there are the hard facts of the labor-management power struggle. When union membership is compulsory, the labor organization is in a better position to drive hard for improvements in wages and working conditions. There is explicit recognition of this fact in many southern areas where the absence of unionization is held forth as a lure to attract new industries. In other regions the economic argument is played down to an extent, and the union security debate is conducted mainly on moralistic and philosophic grounds.

The Legislatures and Union Security

In recent years union security has been kept alive as a social issue by the passage of the so-called "right-to-work" laws in a number of states. As a background to this development it is necessary to refer first to the National Labor Relations Act of 1935. This law provided that workers were to have the right to organize unions of their own choosing and were to be free from interference or coercion while they expressed their preferences. Agreements requiring union membership as a condition of employment, however, were not to be construed as violations of the law.[17] Union security agreements, thus, were fully legal under the National Labor Relations Act.

The Taft-Hartley Act of 1947 amended the union security features of the 1935 Wagner Act in several respects. The closed shop was virtually outlawed, and the union shop could become a subject of collective bargaining only after a majority of the employees in a bargaining unit voted in favor of a union shop. After several years of experience with union shop authorization elections, the voting requirement was removed in 1951. The elections had turned out to be little more than expensive formalities. Given an opportunity to express themselves on the union security issue, workers time and again responded by voting overwhelmingly in favor of the union shop.

Another legal limitation placed upon union security agreements was the stipulation in the Taft-Hartley Act that "Nothing in this Act shall be construed as authorizing the execution or application of agreements requiring membership in a labor organization in any state or territory in which such execution or application is prohibited by state or territorial law."[18]

---

17 *National Labor Relations Act of 1935,* Sec. 8 (3).
18 *Labor-Management Relations Act of 1947,* Sec. 14 (b).

This provision made it possible for the states to enact more stringent restrictions upon union security than the federal government had done without being in conflict with federal law. Eleven states enacted "right-to-work" laws in 1947, and by 1965 there were nineteen states with such laws on their statute books. The details of the laws vary among the states but the basic specification is that no person can be denied, or excluded from, employment because of membership or non-membership in a labor organization.

TABLE 10

STATE RIGHT-TO-WORK LAWS AS OF 1969

STATE	DATE OF ADOPTION
Alabama	1953
Arizona	1947
Arkansas	1947
Florida	1944
Georgia	1947
Iowa	1947
Kansas	1958
Mississippi	1954
Nebraska	1947
Nevada	1952
North Carolina	1947
North Dakota	1947
South Carolina	1954
South Dakota	1947
Tennessee	1947
Texas	1947
Utah	1954
Virginia	1947
Wyoming	1963

Until 1957, only southern or predominantly agricultural states had passed laws against union security agreements. In that year, however, Indiana enacted a right-to-work law and attempts to pass similar legislation in a number of other industrial states were defeated only through the determined political efforts of organized labor. The legislative tide turned against union security limitation in 1958. Right-to-work measures appeared on the ballots in six states and were rejected by the electorate in all but Kansas. In 1965, the Indiana law was repealed. By the middle of 1965, no major industrial state had a right-to-work law.

MANAGEMENT RIGHTS

Are there any boundaries to the entire matter of collective bargaining? Are there any management prerogatives upon which the union may not legitimately encroach? These questions go to the heart of a fundamental issue in labor-management relations. If the growth of unionism can be visualized as a horizontal movement extending to more and more of American industry, then the union penetration into the domain of "management rights" might be regarded as a vertical movement that has continuously fed new matters to the bargaining table as food for collective bargaining. The two movements have gone together. The spread of unionism has resulted in the development of stronger unions that have been able to insist successfully that the scope of bargaining be broadened. This latter success has raised the inevitable question of limits. How far do the unions have a right to go?

The general answer of management is that there is a clear and definable line that separates issues that are proper for bargaining and those that lie solely within the discretion of management. The union reply is that at any given time there are functions being performed solely by management and that labor has no interest in interfering with these functions. Labor leaders, however, usually refuse to acknowledge the existence of a specific boundary to union interests. They allege that many of the matters now admitted by management to be bargainable were once regarded as exclusive management rights. Labor consequently has been reluctant to admit that any management functions should be accorded the permanent status of non-bargainable issues.

When World War II ended, President Truman called a conference of high ranking business and labor representatives to discuss problems and to attempt to settle differences in the common interest. One area in which no agreement was reached was that of management's right to manage. In a separate report the management spokesmen listed the following functions as part of the management responsibility and not subject to collective bargaining:

1. The determination of products to be manufactured or services to be rendered to customers by the enterprise; and the location of the business including the establishment of new units and the relocation or closing of old units.

2. The determination of the lay-out and the equipment to be used in the business; the processes, techniques, methods, and means of manufacture and distribution; the materials to be used (subject to health and safety measures) and the size and character of inventories.

3. The determination of financial policies such as accounting procedures, pricing of goods or services, and customer relations.

4. The determination of the management organization of each producing or distributing unit, and the selection of employees for promotion to supervisory and other managerial positions.

5. The determination of job content and size of the work force; selection of employees; establishment of quality standards; maintenance of discipline and control and use of plant property; the scheduling of operations, and the number of shifts.

6. The determination of safety, health, and property protection measures where legal responsibility is involved.

Management also contended that where prompt initial decisions were necessary to insure the effective operation of an enterprise, as in cases involving discharge for cause and application of seniority provisions, management should have the right to take such prompt initial action subject to later review through grievance procedures.

In their own report the labor members of the committee expressed their philosophy by making the following points, among others:

1. It would be unwise to build a fence around the rights and responsibilities of management on the one hand and the unions on the other. Experience has shown that the responsibility of one party today may become the joint responsibility of both parties tomorrow.

2. Management and union prerogatives cannot be sharply defined without either side constantly attempting to invade the forbidden territories, thus creating much unnecessary strife.

3. There is a need for an understanding of the significance and importance of the management function, but this will follow rather than precede the development of sound industrial relations.

4. Labor and management must come to a realization that both can function most effectively when each enjoys the confidence and has the consent of the other.

The statements issued as a result of the Labor-Management Conference illustrate sharply contrasting positions. Management insisted that it had functions and responsibilities upon which labor should not encroach. Labor countered by pointing out the inadvisability of erecting barriers between management and union rights.

Collective Bargaining

More than twenty-five years have elapsed since the conference; and, in that time interval, there has been no broad philosophical resolution of the management rights issue. In a dynamic economy characterized by equally dynamic industrial relations it is not likely that substantial sections of both labor and management will simultaneously reach a meeting of minds on a proper division of functions. The widely different conditions in industries and individual firms also constitute barriers to any conclusive social agreement on prerogatives. A workable division of functions in one firm may not be appropriate elsewhere.

Union Penetration

Chamberlain, who studied the degree of union penetration into managerial areas in the automobile, steel, rubber, electrical equipment, meat packing, and public utility industries, found that the deepest penetration had been made in the personnel area.[19] In one or more of these industries, unions had won the right to participate with management in making decisions relative to type of personnel to be employed, the size of the work force, hiring practices, layoff procedures, work sharing, allocation of workers, disciplinary control, and, of course, wages and hours. In the production area, the union influence was large in matters of job content and rate of production. Chamberlain found that none of the unions had opposed technological improvement, but all insisted that changes in technology should not operate as threats to job security. The unions have shown interest in procurement, distribution, product lines, plant location, and research and development; but in these areas there have been no planned union programs to share authority. Occasional union forays into these fields have been rebuffed by management; and when this has occurred, the labor organizations have withdrawn.

Chamberlain's findings, although drawn only from the six industries studied, are probably accurate descriptions of the prevailing situation in the greater part of American industry. Union penetration of the management domain, thus, has been closely tied to matters that directly and visibly affect worker welfare. In areas one or more steps removed from direct worker concern, labor organizations have shown interest but, in general, have exerted little influence.

It is possible, of course, for a union to take an extreme position and claim that every management decision has some effect upon worker welfare and that therefore no management function is beyond the pale of collective bargaining. This approach, in fact, is implicit in a union philosophy that

---

19 Neil W. Chamberlain, *The Union Challenge to Management Control* (New York: Harper & Row, Publishers, 1948), chap. 4.

refuses to specify limits to bargainable matters. In practice, however, such extremity has been rare. There has been little union invasion or attempted invasion of such management functions as product design, sales, product promotion, pricing, and finance.

The question of how far unions will or should go in assuming a right to participate in decisions now made by management alone will be decided by the facts of the future rather than by contemporary debate. Few American labor leaders presently envision a co-determination type of relationship in which union personnel sit on the boards of directors and share in the top level decision-making process of the corporation. Collective bargaining has been fruitful, and so long as it remains so the American labor movement is not likely to participate in a far-reaching about face. Control over the terms and conditions of employment is the basic interest of unions in the United States. Interest in the direct control over all corporate policies will develop, if it develops at all, when collective bargaining ceases to be effective as a technique for protecting worker income and status.

In the areas where unions have "penetrated," the scope of managerial discretion has been limited in significant ways by both the terms and the administration of the labor-management contract. In their intensive study of collective bargaining practices, Slichter, Healy, and Livernash concluded that the union-management contract limits managerial discretion in three main ways.[20] These are (1) through requirements that management follow rules in such matters as layoffs, transfers, promotions, overtime assignments, and establishment of production standards; (2) through requirements that management take only "reasonable" or "fair" actions or that certain actions be taken only after consultation with the union or with the consent of the union; and (3) through prohibition of certain types of conduct such as "excessive overtime." Within an establishment, the character of managerial control over employees is determined as much, or more, by the way a contract is administered as it is by the language of a contract. Identical contract clauses can result in widely divergent results among firms in the same industry or even among different plants of the same firm. Unions and managements may be reasonable or pugnacious in the process of contract administration, contractual rights may be asserted frequently or infrequently, and the contract might be interpreted literally or loosely. The precise meaning of a contractual clause—and, thus, the specific character of management rights—is usually hammered out in the give and take of an industrial relations setting which is affected by the variables listed above and many others. Managerial discretion, finally, is limited by the arbitration process. About 90 per cent of all agreements provide for binding arbitra-

---

[20] *Op. cit.,* p. 948.

tion of contract interpretation disputes. In these agreements, management has conceded that controversial matters of contract interpretation will be resolved by the judgments of neutral arbitrators.

The current phase of the management rights dispute is being fought, to a considerable extent, over work assignment and subcontracting questions. In general, management has the right to assign work to an employee. Challenges to managerial discretion are frequently raised, however, when attempts are made to shift jobs from one seniority district to another, when changes are made in work loads or crew sizes, or when overtime assignments do not adhere rigidly to job classification lines. Disputes over such matters are not novel, but they have been intensified by the inroads of a changing technology upon old production routines.

The issue of management's right to subcontract work provides an excellent example of the differences in the approaches of labor and management. Subcontracting has been defined as "the action of a company in arranging with another and outside company or individual to make goods or perform services for it which could be performed with the company's own bargaining unit employees using the company's own facilities."[21] Since many labor-management contracts are silent on the matter of subcontracting, the fight, essentially, has been over the significance of the silence. The management position is that matters not mentioned in the contract are unilateral management functions. This line of thought has been called the "reserved rights theory." Unions counter the argument by citing the "implied limitations theory" which is that other provisions in the contract imply limitations upon management's right to subcontract if subcontracting violates the letter, spirit, or intent of the total contract.

The conflict over subcontracting has been, in the first instance, a clash over the arbitrability of subcontracting disputes. Arbitrators have tended to side with the union on the basis of the implied limitations theory. A number of such decisions were challenged in the courts; and, until recently, the large majority of courts ruled against the position of the arbitrators. A Supreme Court decision, however, has held that doubts about the arbitrability of subcontracting grievances should be resolved in favor of their coverage under the labor-management agreement.[22] Although unions have won on the issue of arbitrability, they have generally lost on the issue of management's right to subcontract. Most arbitrators have ruled that an employer may contract out his work when there is no specific provision

---

[21] G. Allan Dash, Jr., "The Arbitration of Subcontracting Disputes," *Industrial and Labor Relations Review*, January, 1963, p. 208.

[22] *United Steelworkers of America* v. *Warrior and Gulf Navigation Company*, 363 U.S. 574 (1960).

in the agreement prohibiting such action and when the employer bases his decision on economic criteria without the intent of undermining the union.[23]

SUMMARY

In this chapter, selected parts of the labor-management agreements have been analyzed in order to suggest the nature of the agreement as a whole. The sections selected for analysis were (1) the wage section, which is of major concern to all involved; (2) the union security section, which contains matters that are primarily of interest to the union organization; (3) the seniority section, which describes protections and procedures that are of greatest interest to the employees; and (4) the management rights section, where management is the beneficiary of whatever rights are delineated. It oversimplifies matters somewhat to describe the various sections in terms of who gets the benefits specified. Actually all parties are involved to some degree in all clauses of the agreement. The material in the several sections, however, can be described in terms of surface orientation; and, from this standpoint, there are sections that are of greater concern to one or the other of the parties. An exhaustive analysis of the bargaining contract would have to deal with many additional items such as hours of work, overtime and other premium payments, and working conditions. Enough has been presented, however, to illustrate the nature of the agreement and to describe the character of some of the important issues that arise during the bargaining process.

QUESTIONS AND PROBLEMS

1. Obtain a collective bargaining agreement from a local union or a local business establishment. Summarize the agreement by describing the following characteristics:

a. The type of wage system in effect

b. The types of fringe benefits in effect

---

[23] See Marcia L. Greenbaum, "The Arbitration of Subcontracting Disputes: An Addendum," *Industrial and Labor Relations Review,* January, 1963, pp. 231–234. For an interesting recent study on the issue of management rights expressed in the context of the subcontracting question, see Margaret K. Chandler, *Management Rights and Union Interests* (New York: McGraw-Hill Book Company, 1964). The usual discussion of management rights has been in terms of an "erosion theory"; that is, management's right to manage is seen as an eroding quantity. Mrs. Chandler approaches the issue as a problem in industrial sociology and concludes that (*a*) there are pressure groups within management that come into conflict over subcontracting questions and (*b*) management has generated challenges to its rights because of lack of information about the total ongoing process within the firm.

c. The clauses relating to union security

d. The provisions relating to seniority

e. The "management rights" clause

2. Anything granted as a fringe benefit can be translated into a money equivalent and granted to workers as a straight wage increase. What advantages accrue to (*a*) employers and (*b*) workers from having a substantial part of the wage package consist of fringe benefits?

3. The "union security" issue raises some rather complex social issues. Do you believe that legislation is warranted? Do you believe that the philosophy expressed by the so-called "right-to-work" laws is satisfactory from the standpoint of resolving whatever issues are raised by union security agreements?

4. Summarize the pros and cons of seniority clauses in the labor-management agreement. What are some of the practical problems raised by such clauses?

5. Are there areas of management rights that should be permanently barred from the collective bargaining table? What arguments do unions raise against the specification of such permanent bars?

6. Under the reserved rights theory, management has argued that when the collective bargaining agreement is silent on a particular matter, there are no limits to managerial discretion in dealing with that matter. Unions have argued that other provisions of the labor-management agreement may imply the existence of limits upon managerial discretion even over matters not mentioned in the agreement. Which of these positions would you defend as the more tenable?

SELECTED READINGS

DAVEY, HAROLD W. "Managerial Authority and the Scope of Collective Bargaining," *Contemporary Collective Bargaining*. Englewood Cliffs, N.J.: Prentice-Hall, Inc., 1959. Chap. 8.

KUHN, JAMES W. "Right-to-Work Laws—Symbol or Substance?" *Industrial and Labor Relations Review,* July, 1961, pp. 587–594.

MEYERS, FREDERIC. *Right to Work in Practice.* New York: The Fund for the Republic, 1959.

REES, ALBERT. "Seniority," *The Economics of Trade Unions.* Chicago: The University of Chicago Press, 1962. Chap. 8.

SLICHTER, SUMNER H.; HEALY, JAMES; and LIVERNASH, E. ROBERT. *The Impact of Collective Bargaining.* Washington, D.C.: The Brookings Institution, 1960. Chaps. 5, 10, 17, 20, 31.

WORTMAN, MAX S., JR., and RANDLE, C. WILSON, "Concepts of Seniority," *Collective Bargaining: Principles and Practices.* Boston: Houghton Mifflin Co., 1966. Chap. 20.

CHAPTER 9

The Bargaining Process

We have now examined the collective bargaining participants and the collective bargaining contract. In this chapter, the process by which the bargainers reach the agreements that are embodied in the labor-management contract will be analyzed.

THE BROAD CHARACTER OF THE BARGAINING PROCESS

Marketing Theory

Over a period of time, students of labor-management relations have advanced different theories or general explanations of the bargaining process.[1]

---

[1] For a summary of prominent earlier theories see Neil W. Chamberlain, *Collective Bargaining* (New York: McGraw-Hill Book Company, 1951), chap. 6. More recent collective bargaining models have been influenced by the literature on conflict strategy and general bargaining theory under conditions of uncertainty. See Bevars D. Mabry, "The Pure Theory of Bargaining," *Labor Relations and Collective Bargaining* (New York: The Ronald Press Co., 1966), chap. 9. and J. Pen, *The Wage Rate under Collective Bargaining* (Cambridge, Mass.: Harvard University Press, 1959). Most of the models cited in the references above are variations of what has been called the distributive bargaining model. This model assumes a fixed sum-variable share character in the bargaining payoff, that is, the parties are attempting to maximize their respective shares of a fixed sum. While these models contribute to an understanding of the bargaining process, they are fragile in that they do not deal with considerations outside of distributive bargaining. An effort to integrate the distributive bargaining model with other relevant variables is made in Richard E. Walton and Robert B. McKersie, *A Behavioral Theory of Labor Negotiations* (New York: McGraw-Hill Book Co., 1965).

The idea that collective bargaining is basically a means of establishing the price of labor has been called the "marketing theory," and this explanation follows the typical conception of what is involved in the bargaining process. In its original and primitive form in the United States, collective bargaining was, essentially, a method of marketing labor. Groups of workers posted lists of the rates at which they would work, and employers had the alternative of accepting or rejecting the proferred rates. If the employers rejected the rates, the matter became a test of strength between them and the workers. As collective bargaining grew in amount and complexity, it became evident that important aspects of bargaining were left unexplained by a simple marketing theory. Two explanations that attempt to incorporate some of the complexities are the so-called "governmental" and "managerial" theories.

Governmental Theory

The former theory suggests that collective bargaining is, in essence, a form of industrial government. The basic bargaining agreement is visualized as a type of constitution; and management, charged with carrying out the agreement, is likened to the executive branch of government. The negotiating committees which amend or elaborate the contract constitute the legislative branch, and the grievance procedure is the judicial branch.

The governmental theory focuses attention upon the facts that the bargaining relationship is a continuing one and that sovereignty in the workplace is shared by management and the representatives of the workers. As is the case in any representative government, problems must be resolved within the procedural framework and according to the rules that have been established. Efforts to resolve them by a show of force can be regarded as breakdowns in the processes of orderly government.

Managerial Theory

The managerial theory describes collective bargaining as a method of management, "a procedure for making business decisions."[2] The act of collective bargaining necessarily involves a union invasion of management prerogatives and necessarily involves union officials in the business of management. Decisions about wages and conditions of work *are* management decisions regardless of whether they are made unilaterally by management officials or collectively by labor and management representatives. The truth of this assertion is not denied by the fact that union officials do not think of themselves as managers or by the fact that the union participates only in a sector rather than in the entire domain of management.

---

[2] *Ibid.,* p. 130.

The managerial theory, thus, visualizes collective bargaining as a sharing of management. It calls attention to the fact that bargaining involves a basic change in the management institution and that final directive authority, as well as limited administrative authority, is exercised mutually in certain of the decision-making areas within the corporation. By detailing the nature of the union penetration of management prerogatives, the managerial theory emphasizes the fact that property ownership is no longer the sole basis of authority within the business enterprise.

In an earlier chapter, collective bargaining was described as a method of making decisions. Applying this concept to the three theories described above, it can be seen that the marketing explanation concentrates upon price decisions and thus has an economic orientation. The governmental theory attempts to explain the political character of bargaining decisions while the managerial theory concentrates upon the decision-making process in the business firm where ultimate authority is shared by management and labor in certain areas. The three theories are not inconsistent; and, in fact, there is much similarity in the governmental and managerial approaches although they differ in terminology and emphasis. All these explanations provide useful insights into the bargaining process and, because they supplement each other, provide a reasonably comprehensive picture of the broad character of the process.

TYPES OF BARGAINING RELATIONSHIPS

Whether bargaining is a marketing method, a political process, a form of management, or some combination of all of these, the actual conduct of bargaining will be colored by the attitudes of the bargaining parties toward each other. The possible attitudes can be likened to a spectrum with absolute hostility at one end and complete co-operation at the other. The nature of industrial conflict and its possible resolution will be analyzed in the following chapter. The concern here is with how the attitudes of management and labor affect the bargaining process.

In most United States establishments, collective bargaining is a relatively new practice, having its start sometime after the mid-1930's. Thus, what occurred during the organizing drive when the union sought to substitute joint negotiations for unilateral management discretion remains alive in the memories of many present-day management officials, union leaders, and employees. As Selekman has noted, the drive for unionization is frequently "psychologically and socially unsettling."[3] Both union and management

---

[3] Benjamin M. Selekman, *Labor Relations and Human Relations* (New York: McGraw-Hill Book Company, 1947), p. 14.

make strong emotional appeals, the former attempting to show the "boss" in the worst possible light while management in turn tries to undermine worker confidence in the union. At some time during the controversy, a work stoppage is likely to occur, and possibly there will be some violence. Should all this culminate in a final acceptance of the union by management, there is the further complication that old lines of authority have been shattered while the new ones, as yet, are indistinct.

The character of the organizing campaign, then, tends to create a legacy of distrust and mutual suspicion. In those cases where the union is accepted without serious management protest, collective bargaining will have a more auspicious beginning. In a series of case studies of the "Causes of Industrial Peace" sponsored by the National Planning Association, a theme that re-appears in many of the studies of firms characterized by friendly and co-operative labor-management relations is the initial absence of management opposition to worker organization.[4]

Once collective bargaining is inaugurated, the labor-management relationship will fall into some point on the hostility–co-operation spectrum mentioned above. The precise point will be determined by many factors such as the state of the product market, ideological beliefs of union and management officials, caliber of the bargaining representatives, experiences during the union organizing campaign.

The extent to which a co-operative bent or lack of it affects the final outcome will vary depending upon circumstances. Except for those cases where destruction of the union is a primary goal of the company or where a militant union is less interested in bargaining than in militating, the ease with which settlements are reached and the generosity of the final settlements are not necessarily functions of bargaining attitudes. Many of the firms in mass production industries were—some still are—in what has been described as an armed truce type of relationship with labor unions.[5] Still, these firms have agreed to a number of generous settlements in the post-World War II period. Conversely, it may be noted that high degrees of union-management co-operation are frequently found in marginal situations where the firms involved are in financial straits and the parties will soon have little left to fight about if they fail to pull together.[6]

Although the results of bargaining are frequently conditioned as much by the economic health of the firm and the internal politics of the union and management organizations as they are by the fact that the bargainers like or don't like each other, the matter of union-management co-opera-

---

[4] *Causes of Industrial Peace under Collective Bargaining,* Case Studies 1-14 (Washington, D.C.: National Planning Association, 1953).

[5] Frederick H. Harbison and John R. Coleman, *Goals and Strategy in Collective Bargaining* (New York: Harper & Row, Publishers, 1951), chap. 2.

[6] See, for example, A. Howard Myers, *Crisis Bargaining* (Boston: Northeastern University, 1957).

tion merits some examination. Co-operation, in the sense used here, implies a continuous searching for the sources of labor-management compatibility and an experimental attitude regarding the resolution of apparent impasses. It means a reluctance to throw one's weight around simply because one happens to have some weight. When the degree of co-operation is high, in other words, the parties are more likely to resolve their differences if resolution is at all possible.

Harbison and Coleman have developed a classification of the various types of labor-management relationships which, though somewhat broad, is useful as a device for summarization.[7] The classes will be described below and some possible qualifications noted:

1. *The Armed Truce.* In this situation, management believes that, at best, unions are necessary evils. The parties have fundamental disagreements over the proper scope and content of collective bargaining; they maintain a rivalry for worker loyalty and are aware that the upper hand in bargaining will go to the side in the best position to exercise its power. The basic difference between this condition and one of open conflict is that both labor and management would prefer to contain their conflict and work out of a livable collective bargaining agreement. This preference may be the resut of the ruinous cost of past conflict or a fear that future conflict may prove to be excessively expensive. Whatever the reason, the desires to reach agreement are honest ones.

The armed truce relationship exists when the union is too strong to be eliminated by the company but not strong enough to insist that management accept all the important elements of the union's bargaining philosophy. In negotiations, management will attempt to limit the scope of bargaining, whereas the union will fight hard to expand it. Union security will be a live issue. Each side will be ingenious in the exercise of pressures while the bargaining process is going on. The union may covertly initiate "agitation" strikes to prove that the workers are becoming restless over management "stalling." Management will try to put union officials on the spot by appealing directly to the employees with attractive proposals that differ in important aspects from those the union has demanded.[8] Another popular management tactic is to make its offers to the workers depend upon the union leader accepting some personally disadvantageous condition.

2. *Working Harmony.* Further along in the conflict–co-operation continuum is a fairly common type of relationship based upon management's full acceptance of the idea of collective bargaining and the existence of the

---

[7] Harbison and Coleman, *op. cit., passim.*

[8] A variation of this technique has been called "Boulwarism" after Lemuel Boulware of the General Electric Company who developed the approach. Boulwarism is discussed in Chapter 11.

union. Faced with no threat to its existence from the direction of management, the union is in a position to appraise some of its objectives in terms of the company's well-being. The possibility of conflict is not absent, and both parties are aware of this. There is a greater spirit of mutual accommodation, however, and compromises are more easily reached.

In this relatively harmonious setting the union security question will not be a major problem, if it is a problem at all. There will be some tendency for the scope and content of collective bargaining to broaden out, and the negotiators will have sophisticated insights into the institutional problems of their adversaries. The management negotiator, for instance, will patiently sit out a long harangue that the union spokesman is making solely for the record. The union-management relationship in this stage of bargaining has been described as a problem-solving approach characterized by factual bargaining and intimate trading.

3. *Union-Management Co-operation.*   No union-management relationship is ever likely to be completely free of conflict. Occasionally the parties come close to such a relationship, especially in firms or industries that are economically depressed. A fight over the division of spoils makes no sense when there are no spoils to be divided. When the firm faces extinction and the workers face the prospect of seeing their livelihoods disappear, collective bargaining will ordinarily be quite different than in the case where there is a healthy profit to fight over.

In the context of economic hardship, the concern of both parties during negotiations might be centered upon matters of company finance. There will be little fight over union security or management prerogative. These questions will be of little importance. Lowering unit labor costs, eliminating output restrictions, improving company sales, and similar questions will preoccupy the negotiators.[9] Bargaining, in fact, may center upon the terms of a union loan to the company. In the situation pictured, organized labor and management join hands to save themselves from extinction.

A number of situations can be identified that do not fit easily into any of the three types described above. One such situation might be called over-acceptance of the union by management. This occurs when a firm is tempted to take the easy way out of its labor difficulties by being overly receptive to unreasonable union demands. Over a period of time, such concessions can compound into a situation that will breed the very conflict

---

[9] Many examples could be cited to illustrate this type of negotiation. Only one will be used here to show a possible outcome of such negotiations. In 1955, the United Hatters, Cap, and Millinery Workers signed an agreement with the employers in the industry allowing employers to set aside funds for promoting the industry in lieu of increasing contributions to a pension fund. The agreement called for a payment of 1 per cent of the payroll into a special fund to be used for millinery shows, television, and other promotion activities.

that management seeks to avoid. When completely unworkable systems of seniority, work assignments, or incentive pay evolve from a firm's docile compliance with union demands, the ultimate result is likely to be worker dissatisfaction and financial difficulties for the firm. The fact that over-acceptance has occurred usually does not become apparent for some time. Outwardly the picture might be that of a model relationship, since there are few strikes or grievances. Sooner or later, however, the firm is forced into an awareness of the untenable condition of its industrial relations. After this occurs, there is likely to be a long drawn-out reappraisal and readjustment that will probably be punctuated by work stoppages.

Another situation that is not adequately covered by the Harbison-Cole-man classification scheme is that which has been aptly described by Profes-sor Lloyd Reynolds as "collective bludgeoning." This occurs when a small and relatively weak employer faces a strong union. In this instance, bar-gaining may consist of little more than the employer's signing the contract the union hands to him. A variation of this procedure is found in the situa-tion where a union uses the leverage of a strong bargaining position to force acceptance of its demands in areas where its bargaining position is weak.[10]

In classifying types of labor-management relationships, caution should be expressed against drawing the inference that the stages are successive and that a stage of unsatisfactory relationships will eventually be replaced by one of satisfactory relationships. In any given plant situation, labor-management relations may improve or worsen. Ordinarily the more mature type of relationship is found where joint bargaining has been practiced for some time, but improvement over a period of time is not an inevitable development.

BARGAINING PROCEDURES AND CONDUCT

Apart from a few government regulations, there are no set rules covering the bargaining process.[11] In any given situation, the nature of the process will depend upon the personalities of the negotiators, the financial condition of the employer, the degree of union acceptance by management, the nature of the product market, the relative strengths of union and employer, and

---

[10] See Ralph and Estelle James, "Hoffa's Leverage Techniques in Bargaining," *Industrial Relations,* October, 1963, pp. 73–93.

[11] The Taft-Hartley Act and the administrative rulings of the National Labor Re-lations Board provide a few basic standards for bargaining conduct. Bargaining, for example, must be in good faith, certain time requirements must be met in providing notice to the opposite party of a desire to change the agreement, agreements when reached must be put into writing if one party so desires. Some of the administrative rulings have established fairly elaborate criteria for testing compliance with govern-ment-imposed standards. When all is considered, however, few negotiators find their bargaining styles cramped by government regulations.

other factors. A generalized description of the bargaining process, consequently, is difficult to make. The details are too many and diversified. Some of the major questions that are present at the various stages of bargaining can be noted, however, and the more prominent practices can be described.

Preliminaries to Bargaining

Both management and union must make a number of decisions before they meet face-to-face in negotiations. Who will be the spokesmen for each side? Will the conference room be crowded or will there be only a handful of selected negotiators present? Who will formulate the demands to be made? What strategies and tactics will be used? There are no right and wrong answers to these questions. An approach that works well under one set of conditions may fail when the situation changes. In this section some of the important pre-bargaining questions will be examined.

An obvious first question that a union must answer is what it will try to win from management. Collective bargaining is based rather firmly upon the assumption that there will always be matter for bargaining. To date this has been a valid assumption. Unions have rarely been frustrated by an absence of demands to pose. Demands in bargaining can come from management as well as from unions, and in some cases management does come to the conference table with a fairly elaborate set of demands. In the typical union-management relationship, however, the union is the aggressor in the sense that it seeks change, whereas management plays the role of defending the agreement against large-scale change and in some instances against any change at all. It falls to the union in most cases, consequently, to prepare a specific set of demands.

Demands. Where do the demands come from? In practice, demands are usually formulated by the union leadership subject to different degrees of approval by the rank and file. The criteria of pure democracy would be better satisfied if demands stemmed directly from the union membership, but this is no more feasible in collective bargaining than it is in the political legislative process. Some unions do a certain amount of membership polling, and the results of such polls may be incorporated to an extent in the union proposals. With the increasing centralization of authority in the hands of the national unions and with the increasing complexity of collective bargaining issues, there has been a tendency for union bargaining demands to be formulated in a specific sense by higher levels of union officials.

What guideposts do the unions use in formulating their demands? Part of the answer has already been given. The feelings of the rank and file can be a guide to the labor official as to what he should stress in bargaining. In the long run the union leader must come fairly close to expressing vocally the latent and often silent feelings of his membership. Should he fail in this respect he will have to face the consequences of a dissatisfied body of members. This is not a complete answer, however. As we shall see, the bargaining goal of the labor spokesman is compounded of many elements. He may feel that he has to match or surpass what other unions have won. He may have to match what others have merely promised. He may be pointing slowly toward a long run goal such as the elimination of regional wage differentials. He may have to face the fact that he is dealing with an employer in financial distress. Since collective bargaining is frequently a matter of trading concession for concession, the union's first proposals may include a substantial number of demands that may be considered relatively frivolous.

To summarize: union demands may be formulated at any level of the union organizational structure, although increasingly it is at the higher levels that the major proposals are developed. The specific demands reflect the multi-sided nature of the political and economic contexts within which a union functions as well as the particular employment problems of the union membership. Finally, union demands are often premised upon the belief that in the bargaining process some part of the union proposals will be whittled away by management arguments or traded away for management counter-offers.

While not a great deal is known about what management does to prepare for bargaining, a recent study has shown that it does typically engage in a considerable amount of preparatory activity.[12] A first phase in management's preparation involves the collection and analysis of various types of data. Responsibility for this work is usually lodged with an industrial relations unit. In the second phase, decisions are made relative to management's bargaining goals. These decisions are ordinarily made at the top level of the organizational hierarchy although personnel from numerous departments will have been consulted before these decisions are finalized.

Negotiators. Another pre-bargaining question involves the choice of negotiators. Ordinarily the union is represented by a committee rather than by an individual. When bargaining is done on a local basis, the committee may be elected by the membership or by the union stewards or chosen directly by the union officers. Usually, at least one officer will be on the committee. Oftentimes, as one writer has noted, the committee will be all officers, with no rank and file representation.[13] It is common for a district

[12] Meyer S. Ryder, Charles M. Rehmus, and Sanford Cohen, *Management Preparation for Collective Bargaining* (Homewood, Illinois: Dow Jones-Irwin, Inc., 1966).

[13] Neil W. Chamberlain, *Collective Bargaining Procedures* (Washington, D.C.: American Council on Public Affairs, 1944), p. 27.

or a national representative to sit in when bargaining is conducted locally. In certain phases of bargaining, especially in those areas where the national union insists upon uniform contract clauses, the international representative might take an active part in the local negotiations. Occasionally, negotiators are selected by a highly informal process. This writer knows of several situations where a particular business agent bargains with certain employers simply because he has always gotten along with them better than have the other business agents in the union. When negotiations are conducted nationally, the bargaining committee will usually consist of the national officers reinforced possibly by members of the executive board and selected local officials.

On the management side, negotiation may be conducted by a line officer—such as the vice president in charge of production—or by a staff officer—such as the director of industrial relations. Other possible negotiators are company attorneys, attorneys retained specially for bargaining, bargaining experts supplied by employer associations, or committees drawn from the membership of a trade association. In the smaller firm, bargaining is frequently done by the proprietor or the firm's president if the establishment is a corporation.

The question of who should do the negotiating is not unimportant. The ablest of negotiators will fail to reach an agreement when the basic conditions for agreement are absent. In the contrary situation, however, inept bargainers can botch up negotiations and create impasses that more qualified persons would avoid. A certain amount of bargaining expertness, then, is an essential qualification for the negotiator. Except in the cases of a few exceptional individuals, this qualification can only be developed when bargaining experience is added to the other abilities of the would-be negotiator.

The student of collective bargaining will find that from union to union and from firm to firm, negotiations are conducted by persons bearing different titles and having different standings within their organizations. This is part of the rich variety in American collective bargaining experience. The basic bargaining positions of labor and management are established within each organization by the processes set up for that purpose. The selection of the negotiators is usually accomplished by different processes, although quite frequently the person negotiating will have had an important role in the formulation of the position his side holds. With the accumulation of bargaining experience and with the widespread acceptance of the legitimacy of organized labor's role in bargaining, both sides are taking more care in the preparation of their bargaining positions. Positions carefully prepared are not likely to be long entrusted to unqualified and inexperienced negotiators. As the bargaining process becomes more institutionalized, the selection of negotiators will likewise tend to be made by more systematic and efficacious methods.[14]

Other bargaining preliminaries can be described briefly. Some decisions must be made relative to the actual bargaining conference. How many representatives, for instance, should be present from each side? The argument for a large representation, for the labor side at least, is that the interests of more persons will be watched directly if representatives of relatively small groups of employees are present at the conference. On the other hand, it is usually alleged that the presence of too many persons can create an unwieldy conference. This is especially so in the necktie awry, shirt-sleeves rolled up stage of bargaining when decisions are sometimes made by top negotiators during a trip to the water cooler or in a coatroom chat. Other matters that require pre-conference decision are the time and place of meetings, the degree of formality that will ostensibly mark the proceedings, the extent to which progress in negotiations will be publicized, the extent to which the proceedings will be recorded.

Labor and Management at the Bargaining Table

What is the job that faces the negotiators when they finally meet across the bargaining table? To answer this question, let us indulge in some role-playing. Assume that you are a negotiator—labor or management, take your choice. As a labor representative your job is to convince management that it ought to agree to your proposals. Your job is complicated by the fact that your position is not completely fixed and that, so far as you know, neither is that of management. There are some items in the labor proposal about which your side feels quite strongly. These are musts—at least for the time being. Other of your demands are less important, and some are completely expendable. As a management negotiator you may have a definite figure in mind beyond which the company will not go in granting a wage increase. You hope, in fact, that you will not have to go even that far. On other issues you have predetermined positions, some more flexible than others.

This is the situation at the start. Neither protagonist is sure about the other's true position. Occasionally some of the doubt about proposals is removed by pre-conference publicity given to a demand that is to be made. There was little doubt, for instance, that the United Automobile Workers

---

[14] A study based upon interviews with union representatives found that many of these representatives believe it impossible for untrained local union personnel to conduct negotiations successfully. This belief is based largely upon the increasingly technical nature of bargaining subjects. Robert R. France, *Union Decisions in Collective Bargaining* (Princeton, N.J.: Princeton University, Industrial Relations Section, 1955), p. 15.

were going to make a serious bid for more liberal pension benefits in their 1964 negotiations with the major automobile producers. Even in this case, however, the companies could not be sure how much of a fight the union would wage over some of the details of the proposal.

Bargaining. After each side has had an opportunity to study the original proposals and counter-proposals, bargaining starts in earnest. As a negotiator you have an array of techniques at your disposal. You may rely upon your powers of oratory, you may buttress your case with carefully prepared factual and statistical materials, you may threaten, plead, or shout. From what has been stated above it should be obvious that bargaining is an art rather than a science. Books have been written and manuals of instruction have been prepared to guide labor and management negotiators—different manuals for each side, of course. A close reading of the manual will not necessarily produce an ace negotiator. Artists are not produced by do-it-yourself kits. Skill in negotiations requires patience, wisdom, knowledge, and experience. Some persons never become good negotiators. Others pick up the art in a relatively brief time.

Shake-down Stage. Sooner or later, bargaining reaches a shake-down stage. Now comes a period of trading one concession for another, retreating from some positions, and holding fast to others. In a poker game a player must show his entire hand when called. In bargaining, the "players" usually reveal their hands by degrees.

Some observers of the bargaining process have been critical of what has here been called the shake-down stage. Professor George Taylor, for example, believes that the "out of this world" type of demand is a barrier against effective and efficient bargaining. It takes too long, he holds, to whittle down the extreme positions, and the parties often fail to get down to brass tacks before the strike deadline date arrives. When extreme positions are given wide publicity, it becomes difficult for the proposer to back down without losing face. Ridiculous proposals cause trouble during collective bargaining, which is unfortunate since no one was really serious about the extreme items in the first place. Taylor has recommended that the parties hold pre-negotiation conferences where they can review the economic factors they will consider during bargaining. They can then begin the actual bargaining sessions with positions that are less far apart and thus easier to reconcile.[15]

The fact that the starting positions of labor and management are typically far apart may cause trouble during the bargaining process. The extreme demand, even when the bargaining party is not serious about it,

---

[15] George W. Taylor, "Ground Rules for the Use of Statistics in Collective Bargaining," *Proceedings of the Fifth Annual Meeting of the Industrial Relations Research Association* (1952), pp. 14, 15.

does serve certain functions, however; and only when bargaining reaches a stage of maturity where these functions are meaningless is labor or management likely to forego use of this tactic. Politically speaking, it is necessary for union and management spokesmen to listen to many voices within their organizations. It is oftentimes more diplomatic to incorporate someone's pet idea into a set of proposals than to risk giving offense by challenging the idea. An unusual demand, furthermore, may simply be a signal that the same demand will be made in a more serious vein the following year. It may also be a style of communication. The demands of the steel workers union in the 1959 steel industry negotiations added up to a cost of more than $2.00 an hour; but, as one industry official noted, this was the union's way of asking for some type of job guarantee. Finally, the padded set of proposals does make it easier for the parties to hide their true positions a little longer and also provides trading material when bargaining reaches the swapping stage. Only rarely will the parties enter negotiations with stated positions that do not contain at least a little water.[16]

Strike Deadline. It is common practice for unions to set a strike deadline after which date the workers may be called out on strike if no agreement has been reached. Negotiations, of course, may be concluded long before the deadline is reached. A surprisingly large number of agreements are last minute settlements, however. The growing possibility of a strike puts heavy pressure on the bargainers. Faced with an imminent strike, labor and management negotiators must reappraise their positions. They must weigh the possible gains from holding fast to their positions against the costs of a work stoppage. At this time extraneous demands usually melt away. Hurried conferences, off the record meetings by the top negotiators from each side, and package offers and counter-offers are characteristic of this crisis stage in bargaining. During this period it usually becomes possible for the negotiators to determine if there is any compatibility between their respective hard core positions. Agreement is achieved, or the bargaining relationship moves into a stage of more forceful pressure.

---

[16] In his model of collective bargaining strategy, Stevens points out that the alternative to playing the "negotiation game" is to play the "take it or leave it game." Unions and managements generally prefer the negotiation game because it is a way of avoiding the "uncomfortable tensions" of dealing with the opposite number on a take it or leave it basis. Stevens argues that this explanation of why the parties elect to negotiate is also an explanation of the large initial demand. The only rule for starting negotiations that is consonant with subsequent negotiations is that the initial demand must permit "room for bargaining." The major alternative to a large demand as a tactic for starting negotiations is the "minimum demand" or "maximum offer"—that is, an initial bargaining proposal which is virtually identical with the least favorable terms to himself upon which a party is willing to settle. This bargaining technique is essentially what is involved in Boulwarism; and, as Stevens notes, Boulwarism is a technique for converting the negotiating game into the take it or leave it game. Carl M. Stevens, *Strategy and Collective Bargaining Negotiation* (New York: McGraw-Hill Book Company, 1963), pp. 32–35, 60–67.

The peculiar function that the strike weapon serves in collective bargaining should be noted at this point. Precisely what is it that makes the bargainers actually bargain to the extent that agreement is the usual end result of positions that seem hopelessly irreconcilable at the start? The law, in most cases, requires representatives of the union and management to bargain in good faith; but it does not require that they reach agreement. There is, however, a strong force that keeps bargaining going so long as it appears that there is some hope for a meeting of the minds. This force is the power that each side has to work economic hardship upon the other. Widespread popular opinion to the contrary, very few people enjoy a strike or a lockout. The firm loses business, the workers lose wages, the union officers have a package of unpleasant problems dumped into their laps. It is, consequently, the possibility of a strike that jars the collective bargaining participants into the flexible states of mind that are the first essentials for reconciling conflicting positions.[17]

The Significance of the Bargaining Conference

In any labor-management relationship, the bargaining conference will be a highly significant institution if the final agreement is shaped by what happens in the conference. Thus, if either party is impressed by the persuasive or the coercive powers of the other during negotiations, the conference itself can be regarded as very significant. On the other hand, if the parties enter negotiations with firm predetermined positions, the function of the conferees is limited to discovering the compatibility of decisions already made.

How much of the bargaining in the United States is bargaining in fact and how much is a ceremonial prelude to the revelation of hard and fast decisions made outside the conference cannot be determined from available data. There is evidence, however, that hard and fast decisions are made outside the conference and occasionally before negotiations begin in more than a few cases. A study of collective bargaining between sixteen medium-sized corporations and nineteen local unions in the Cleveland, Ohio, area, for example, indicated that decisions of a relatively firm nature were made in half the corporations before the formal bargaining process took place.[18] A number of unions also reported that they made firm decisions in the pre-negotiation period.

It is probably a bargaining rarity when the conference is totally without negotiatory significance. Bargaining is frequently concerned with hundreds

---

[17] In some bargaining relationships, the negotiators do not need to be jarred into bargaining realistically. In very few cases, however, do the bargainers lose sight of the fact that ultimately there must be agreement or a strike.

[18] Paul Johnson, "Decision-making under Collective Bargaining," *Monthly Labor Review*, September, 1957, pp. 1059–1063.

of items, and it is unlikely that a union or a management will have fixed positions on all the items prior to negotiations. Enough decision-making occurs outside the conference, however, to suggest that the actual act of bargaining is not significant in some cases and that not all important decisions are made under the pressure of a strike deadline.

Pressures on Bargainers

After the United Automobile Workers obtained supplementary unemployment benefits in the Ford and General Motors settlements of 1955, the following headline appeared in the *New York Times:* "Reuther's Contracts Spur Rival Union Leaders."[19] One of the most pronounced pressures on the more prominent labor leaders is their felt necessity to outstrip each other in collective bargaining accomplishments. One observer has likened this interunion rivalry to the annual major league pennant race.[20] For a variety of reasons, strong feelings of animosity exist among a number of top level labor leaders. As a matter of saving face and also as a part of the jockeying for positions of power in the labor movement, it has become important to these leaders that they not be outdone at the bargaining table. Another type of interunion bargaining rivalry has its roots in jurisdictional conflicts. In the electrical manufacturing, meat packing, and maritime industries as well as in others, rival unions have competed directly; and one dimension of this competition is the gains that the competing unions are able to make through the bargaining process.

Apart from these external pressures on labor negotiators, there are internal pressures that come from within their own organizations. Labor leaders have learned that it is hard to make everyone happy. A generous wage settlement might disappoint the skilled workers because their relative share of the gain is too small, or because they think it is. Workers in one section of the country might be disappointed because not enough progress has been made in eliminating the geographical wage differential. Leaders of rival factions within the union will deride the settlement no matter how good it is. For political reasons, the labor leader cannot afford to lose sight of the demands of the various interest groups within his organization. As if the pressures exerted by management were not enough, the labor negotiator frequently comes to the bargaining table burdened by many other pressures that fly at him from all directions.

On the management side, the negotiator knows that his performance is being watched by stockholders, bondholders, bankers, trade associations, employer associations, customers, and suppliers. The bargaining concessions he makes will affect all these interest groups in some way. Like the labor

---

[19] June 19, 1955, p. 6E.
[20] *Ibid.*

leader, he too is burdened by the weight of many forces that converge upon him.

The bargaining conference, thus, is the locus of forces that move the negotiators sometimes in ways contrary to their preferences. Labor and management press each other for concessions. Each, in turn, is pressed by forces that mold the character of the concessions sought and influence the degree of doggedness with which the negotiator pursues his objectives. The character of bargaining is often shaped by persons far removed from the bargaining conference.

Contract Administration

Up to this point, the bargaining process has been discussed in terms of contract negotiation. Although the negotiation of a contract may consume only a small part of a year, workers, management, and union must relate to each other for the full year. The fact that collective bargaining has been peacefully concluded does not mean that new problems will not arise. In most firms where workers are organized, some process has been established for dealing with the problems that occur between bargaining sessions. The process is usually referred to as the grievance procedure.[21]

There is a basic similarity in the mechanisms of grievance-handling systems although the details vary from firm to firm. As a usual first step a worker with a grievance informs his union steward of the facts of the situation. The steward discusses the matter with the foreman and, between them, they try to settle the matter on the spot. If they fail to agree, the grievance moves to a second stage in the procedure. Now the next higher ranking person in the union echelon within the plant considers the matter with his company counterpart. If the problem remains unsettled, it moves up for consideration by higher levels of union and management authority. At some ultimate step in the process, such officials as the industrial relations director of the firm and the international representative of the union might be involved in the attempt to settle the problem. Most labor agreements today provide for arbitration of disputes that defy solution at all lower steps.

A formal description of the grievance procedure such as one might find in a collective bargaining agreement will usually reveal very little about the actual operation of the process at a given firm. In some cases, the process is highly informal, with the aggrieved bypassing the specified steps and going directly to higher level authority; or the informality may consist simply of settling disputes by arguments between such persons with au-

---

[21] For a description of the mechanics and the scope of grievance procedures see U.S. Department of Labor, Bureau of Labor Statistics, Bulletin No. 1425-1, *Grievance Procedures* (Washington, D.C., U.S. Government Printing Office, 1964).

thority who happen to be around. Elsewhere the formalities are rigidly maintained, sometimes to the extent that they appear to be more important than the function they ostensibly serve. In some firms the grievance procedure works well, in others poorly, a fact that is not always revealed by counting the number of grievances filed. (A small number of grievances may indicate the absence of worker dissatisfaction, but it may also indicate that the workers are afraid of being classed as troublemakers by the company or that they have no confidence in their union officers.)

Like the actual bargaining process, grievance processing varies so widely in practice that a generalized description going beyond the mechanics is difficult to make. A basic purpose of the grievance procedure is to insure continuity of production as problems are being thrashed out. Some technique to insure such continuity is indispensable in the organized workplace, a fact that can be established simply, perhaps, by noting that 20,000 first-stage written grievances were filed by Ford Motor Company employees in 1954. The potential value of the grievance procedure extends beyond production insurance between collective bargaining sessions, but whether the potential is developed depends upon the over-all character of the union-management relationship. At best, the grievance procedure can be used by a co-operative union and management to uncover contract inconsistencies, to locate unsatisfactory work conditions, to find the roots of morale problems, and to get to the bottom of specific troubles such as low productivity or low earnings on incentive work. At worst, the grievance procedure provides another site for the expression of hostility between union and management. These aspects of the grievance procedure will be examined in another context in the following chapter.

SUMMARY

The collective bargaining process has been described as a method of marketing labor, a form of industrial government, and a method of management. These descriptions are not inconsistent with each other, and taken together they provide a reasonably comprehensive picture of the bargaining process.

The attitudes of labor and management toward each other during bargaining may range from total hostility to complete co-operation, and the character of the bargaining process will be conditioned by the attitudes that prevail in a given situation. The results of bargaining, however, are frequently conditioned more by economic factors than they are by the fact that the bargaining parties like or resent each other.

Prior to bargaining both labor and management must make a number of decisions concerning the selection of spokesmen, the number of negotiators, strategy and tactics to be employed, and demands to be presented. After an original presentation of proposals and counter-proposals, bargaining begins in earnest. Although negotiations may be concluded long before the time of the strike deadline, many settlements are reached when the pressure of the deadline forces both parties to reappraise their positions and search for compromise solutions. During bargaining, both parties are subjected to a variety of pressures, some of them from persons or groups far removed from the bargaining conference.

Most labor-management agreements have established a procedure for dealing with problems that arise after a contract has been negotiated. At best, a formal grievance procedure can make a substantial contribution to the successful administration of a labor-management agreement. At worst, the grievance procedure provides another locus for the labor-management power struggle within a firm.

QUESTIONS

1. Collective bargaining demands are frequently formulated by union officials, subject to varying degrees of approval by the rank and file. In your opinion should the demands stem directly from the union membership?

2. The original proposals and counterproposals of labor and management, in many cases, include items that are injected primarily to strengthen the tactical bargaining positions of the respective parties. Do these items impede the bargaining process? Do you agree with the proposal that the bargainers hold pre-bargaining conferences with the objective of agreeing upon the economic factors they will consider during bargaining? Would such conferences, in fact, reconcile positions that are far apart?

3. It has often been asserted that collective bargaining would not be possible if unions were not free to strike and management were not free to practice the lockout. Do you agree? What is the reasoning behind the assertion?

4. What are the basic functions of a grievance procedure? Explain the mechanics of a hypothetical grievance procedure. Would the filing of an unusually large number of grievances indicate that the procedure is working well or poorly?

5. Occasionally, labor and management negotiators will remark, "I am having more trouble with my own people than with the other side." Describe some circumstances in which this might actually be the case.

SELECTED READINGS

CHAMBERLAIN, NEIL W., and KUHN, JAMES W. *Collective Bargaining.* New York: McGraw-Hill Book Company, 1965. Chaps. 3, 6.

DAVEY, HAROLD W. *Contemporary Collective Bargaining.* Englewood Cliffs, N.J.: Prentice-Hall, Inc., 1959. Chaps. 5–7.

DUNLOP, JOHN T., and HEALY, JAMES J. "The Collective Bargaining Process," *Collective Bargaining, Principles and Cases.* Homewood, Ill.: Richard D. Irwin, Inc., 1953. Chap. 4.

KUHN, JAMES W. *Bargaining in Grievance Settlement*. New York: Columbia University Press, 1961.

SLICHTER, SUMNER H., HEALY, JAMES J., and LIVERNASH, E. ROBERT. *The Impact of Collective Bargaining on Management*. Washington, D.C.: The Brookings Institution, 1960. Chaps. 23, 24.

STEVENS, CARL M. *Strategy and Collective Bargaining Negotiation*. New York: McGraw-Hill Book Company, 1963.

WALTON, RICHARD E., and McKERSIE, ROBERT B. *A Behavioral Theory of Labor Negotiations*. New York: McGraw-Hill Book Company, 1965.

CHAPTER 10

Industrial Conflict

WHEN ALL THE PRESSURES THAT BESET THE BARGAINERS ARE COUPLED with the complexities of the bargaining process itself, the wonder is not that there is so much industrial conflict but that there is so little. The vast majority of labor-management negotiations end in peaceful agreement. Some do not, however; and it is this failure to achieve mutual accommodation that provides the raw material for a consideration of industrial conflict.

The number of persons who belong to unions is greater than in past eras. Unions, furthermore, are active in industries that are strategic in an economic as well as a military sense. The significance of these facts is that industrial conflict has a greater potential for disturbing life than it had in former days. When unionism was a small-scale affair and when the economy was less integrated than it now is, labor-management conflict primarily affected the immediate parties to disputes. Today we depend heavily upon one another. If there is an extended strike in steel, automobile manufacturing, railroad transportation, electrical manufacturing, or coal mining, many persons will be deprived of goods, services, and incomes even though they have nothing to do with the dispute.

Few would disagree with the proposition that industrial peace is a desirable social goal. There is less agreement as to what should constitute the conditions for peace and how these conditions should be maintained. Let us note some of the problems that attend the process of prescribing for industrial peace.

First, the causes of industrial conflict are usually involved and difficult to untangle. Although it is possible that complex social problems will respond to simple remedies, it is more likely that they will not. A simple proposal for the termination of all industrial conflict should be questioned. It is not at all clear, furthermore, that a total termination of conflict would be desirable. Conflict has constructive as well as destructive dimensions. The contemporary workplace is a fertile breeding ground for discontent and tensions; and, in certain circumstances, a strike may be a relatively healthy outlet for grievances that must be expressed. Not infrequently, a strike may serve as a purgative that clears away past misunderstandings and sets the stage for a new start toward labor-management co-operation. From a broad social standpoint, there are situations in which industrial conflict is preferable to a peaceful agreement. If, for instance, excessive inflation or deflation would result from a series of key labor-management agreements, these results might be more harmful than the possible consequences of strikes. Thus, although industrial peace is usually preferable to industrial conflict, it is not always so.

Another problem in prescribing for industrial peace stems from the difficulty of proving conclusively that either labor or management is right or wrong in a given situation. In issues such as "union security" or "seniority" versus "merit," the bargaining parties are disputing problems that can be resolved only when one party defers to the value judgments of the other. It might be supposed that when disputes are over economic issues, such as wages, a more rigorous social verdict could be rendered as to the merits of the dispute. Usually this is not the case, however, since there is no yardstick available with markings sufficiently fine to make the measurements that would be necessary. Economics has not arrived sufficiently as a science to provide precise predictions of the consequences of alternative modes of action. The objective economist hedges his analysis with the "ifs" and "buts" that are required by a scientific approach. As soon as he does this, there is an analytical vacuum into which rush the less objective economists who have fewer qualms about ignoring the qualifications. In the typical dispute over wage-price relationships, it is the analyses of these less objective economists that crowd the airwaves. After all, it is not too interesting to listen to someone who says that he doesn't really know the answer.

There is a looseness in the conclusions of economic analysis that precludes it from being the decisive factor in disputes over deeply felt interests. Economic decisions made by collective bargaining as well as those made by other group pressure processes in our economy undoubtedly fall short of an ideal that might be reached if we had perfect knowledge. But decisions have to be made in some manner, and it is not usually possible to prove that those made as a result of force exerted by a bargaining party are less wise than those that might have been reached by any realistic alternative process.

Perhaps enough has been said by way of introductory comment to establish the point that industrial conflict is not easily resolved. In the remainder of this chapter there will be a consideration of the causes and possible solutions of industrial conflict.

THE LABOR-MANAGEMENT RELATIONSHIP AND THE USE OF FORCE

Industrial conflict is not necessarily a result of the villainy of employers or the ambitions of labor leaders. Conflict has occurred in establishments led by the most far-sighted of management men, and entirely reasonable labor leaders have found it necessary to call strikes from time to time. Why this should be so may puzzle those who believe that sweet reasonableness is a sufficient condition for the resolution of social differences, but the fact remains that the potential for conflict pervades the labor-management relationship. As a first point, it might be noted that the worker-employer relationship is a dynamic one. The amount of power that the employer wields in controlling workers and, conversely, the workers' power for both defensive and offensive purposes have changed materially over the years. If "power" is defined simply as the ability to get what one wants, it is readily seen that the power relationship in the workplace has not been static.

A realignment in the relative capacity to coerce, however, is not a total explanation of conflict. Over a period of time, expectations of both employers and workers change, and a failure of the opposite party to anticipate or to agree with the new expectations creates the possibility of collision. When technological change occurs, for instance, the employer's new interpretation of a fair day's work may differ from the worker's view of it. Furthermore, as one writer has noted, even in a static situation the expectations of both parties to the labor contract may be unclear.[1] Workers agree to supply labor power in exchange for a wage; but questions such as the amount of work, the intensity of work, and the direction of work are frequently specified in only vague ways, and the original expectations of the parties may not materialize in practice.

The ultimate economic philosophy of American labor unions is often summarized simply as "more and more." Such a philosophy, when applied tangibly to a bureaucratic management structure that eschews change imposed from without the structure, can be a source of conflict. New times lead unions to reappraise old goals; and, in an increasingly productive economy, the specific dimensions of "more" are likely to be more liberal than those management considers reasonable.

---

[1] Alvin W. Gouldner, *Wildcat Strike* (Yellow Springs, Ohio: Antioch Press, 1954), p. 163.

The goals of workers, unions, and management, in short, may be different at any given point of time; and before final rapprochement is achieved changes in technology, politics, economic conditions, and social philosophy may lead to a reappraisal of expectations that reintroduces the possibilities of conflict and the use of force. The above is not a total explanation of the causes of conflict, but it is sufficient to show why the process of collective bargaining breaks down on occasions and is replaced by more forceful pressures.

When collective bargaining breaks down, the actual techniques that the bargaining parties may use to coerce each other are many and varied, of course. It may be taken as axiomatic that humans will be resourceful in devising weapons to use against each other. No detailed description of the various tactics of industrial conflict will be given here, since our concern is more with the causes and prevention of industrial warfare than with the character of the warfare itself. In passing, however, the more prominent of the weapons of force will be listed. To protest a management action, the union may resort to a strike, picket line, boycott, slowdown, sitdown, sabotage, or rough-house tactics. The company can resort to a lockout; it can blacklist troublesome employees, fire union ringleaders, import strike-breakers, and use strong-arm men for one purpose or another.

All of this must take place within certain "rules of the game" established by one or another of the levels of government. Physical violence, for instance, is subject to the same legal limitations that are placed upon violence that occurs outside the labor-management context. Specific legal limitations have been placed upon picketing, boycotts, importation of strikebreakers across state lines, sitdown strikes, and many of the other weapons identified above. The role of government, in fact, has had a dynamic quality of its own. Historically, the government has not been neutral and, more often than not, the rules established have favored one side against another. The law of industrial relations will be examined independently at a later point, but in the present context it is necessary to note that the law itself has been a center of labor-management dispute that on many occasions has lent a political cast to the contentions of the bargaining parties.

APPROACHES TO INDUSTRIAL PEACE

Although it is unlikely that any technique can be developed that will guarantee industrial peace, people of optimistic bent feel that there are many things that can be done to minimize conflict. Collective bargaining is essentially a conflict situation, and nothing short of a drastic change in the structure of interest groups in our society can change this fact. Conflict can be expressed in different ways, however, and not all of these are destructive. There is little to be lost and much to be gained by attempts to channel the conflict of labor-management interests along mutually constructive lines. Various approaches are available for use in preventing conflict. None is foolproof. A society that wants freedom must be willing to run some risks. A society that wants to maintain freedom, however, must address itself seriously to the problems that stem from clashes of interest.

In the United States, a number of approaches have been used in dealing with industrial disharmony. They range from mild to relatively severe interference with free bargaining. For summary, these approaches will be divided into two categories: (1) efforts that involve parties outside of the immediate dispute and (2) approaches that depend basically upon the efforts of the immediate parties.

Mediation and Conciliation

In practice the terms mediation and conciliation are used interchangeably, and they will be so used here. Some students insist that there is a meaningful difference between the concepts that is worth preserving, but the predominant feeling is that the differences are not consequential. In conciliation, an outside party attempts to keep collective bargaining from breaking down by persuading the parties to continue bargaining. Mediation involves more active intervention by a third party. The outsider in this case tries to guide the parties to a mutually acceptable agreement. In the event a strike has already occurred, he attempts to persuade the disputants to resume bargaining. The main task of the conciliator, in short, is to keep bargaining going. The mediator may suggest compromises and solutions.

The mediator has no power to force labor and management to agree. He does not render a decision, nor does he ordinarily lay blame. As a neutral party he does what he can do to help the bargainers resolve their differences. If his efforts fail he has no power to prevent open conflict. Mediation, then, is a mild form of outside intervention in the bargaining process.

How effective can mediation be? Since the mediator has no power other than that which may flow from his personal prestige, what can he do in a situation where the bargaining parties themselves have been unable to find a basis for agreeing? The answer depends upon the character of the impasse in a particular bargaining situation. In many cases the mediator can do nothing. In others, there are possible approaches that may lead to a resolution of the difficulties. The following are examples of the possibilities:

1. The mediator might be able to offer the bargainers a way out of a tight spot. In the bargaining process, a negotiator can get himself out on a limb from which there is no possibility of retreat without loss of face. The extreme position can be gracefully abandoned, however, at the sug-

gestion of the mediator. If a strike has occurred, the mediator can call the parties together for further negotiations at a time when both are afraid to make the suggestion because it might be interpreted as a sign of weakness.

2. The mediator can serve as the source of an acceptable recommendation. There may be a solution to a problem that labor or management is unwilling to accept simply because it has been suggested by the opposite party. The mediator can make the solution acceptable by posing as its author.

3. The mediator can help the parties explore various solutions. After a certain amount of fruitless bargaining, positions sometimes tend to become fixed. By suggesting new solutions for exploration the mediator injects possibilities about which positions have not yet become fixed. The parties, thus, have an opportunity to circumvent the jam into which their efforts have led them.

4. The mediator might be able to draw the attention of the bargainers back to the real issues from which they have departed during the heat of bargaining.

These examples suggest the nature of the contribution that the mediator might be able to make. There are many instances on record where potential conflict situations have seemed to respond to the efforts of mediators. On the whole, however, there does not seem to be any evidence that the mediation process has been especially effective in reducing the over-all volume of industrial conflict. As Professor Clark Kerr has concluded: "Strikes seem to go their own way, responsive to other more persuasive forces."[2]

In the United States, a number of government agencies currently provide mediation services. The Taft-Hartley Act of 1947 created the Federal Mediation and Conciliation Service as an independent agency. Before this time, the United States Conciliation Service had been part of the Department of Labor. Under the Taft-Hartley Act's provisions, the Conciliation Service must be notified of a dispute at least thirty days before the termination date of a bargaining agreement. The Conciliation Service may or may not assume jurisdiction over a case. By law it is directed to avoid disputes that have only a minor effect upon interstate commerce. Once jurisdiction is assumed, a commissioner is assigned to the case. So long as the parties appear to be making progress toward an agreement, the com-

---

[2] Clark Kerr, "Industrial Conflict and Its Mediation," *The American Journal of Sociology,* November, 1954, p. 242. For an optimistic appraisal of mediation see David L. Cole, "Government in the Bargaining Process: The Role of Mediation." *The Annals of the American Academy of Political and Social Science,* January, 1961, pp. 42–58.

missioner does not actively participate in the negotiations. If the negotiators appear to be in trouble, he takes the initiative and meets with them. Disputes not settled by the regional offices may be referred to the national office in Washington.

Two other federal agencies provide mediation services in special situations. The National Mediation Board mediates certain types of disputes in the railroad and airline industries, and the Atomic Energy Labor Relations Panel mediates disputes that occur in atomic energy plants.

At the state level, forty-two states have facilities for mediating labor disputes. A number of cities have also developed plans for dealing with local disputes.

Arbitration

Arbitration is a procedure whereby disputes are referred to outside parties for final determination. The difference between arbitration and mediation should be stressed. The mediator tries to help the parties arrive at a satisfactory resolution of their differences, but it is the parties themselves who finally agree or disagree. The arbitrator, on the contrary, makes a decision.[3] After determining the facts of a case, the arbitrator renders an award or decision that is binding on the parties. Arbitration is similar in many respects to judicial proceedings, with which it is often compared.

Arbitration may be voluntary or compulsory. In voluntary arbitration, labor and management agree that an outside person should make a decision for them, and they also agree to accept his award. When arbitration is compulsory, the government appoints an outsider to make a binding award regardless of whether the parties want the dispute to go to arbitration. Our discussion will start with a consideration of voluntary arbitration as an approach to industrial peace.

The subject matter of disputes provides the basis for a useful classification of voluntary arbitration cases. Such cases may involve disputes over rights or over interests. In slightly different terminology, a case may center upon a contract interpretation dispute or a contract negotiation dispute.

Interpretation. When the dispute is over the interpretation or application of the labor-management agreement, the arbitrator can study the

---

[3] A controversy has raged between schools of arbitrators over whether a person called in to arbitrate a case should also practice mediation. One group holds that it is always preferable for the parties to reach their own agreements and that if a person called in to arbitrate sees an opportunity for mediation he should make use of it. The other opinion is that the processes are distinct and that a person hired to do arbitration has no mandate to mediate. They hold, further, that a failure in mediation might destroy an individual's value as an arbitrator. The argument is one over the techniques of dispute settlement and does not affect the fact that mediation and arbitration are basically different processes.

clause in question and ponder its meaning. He can question the parties about their intentions when they wrote the clause. He can study the way the clause has been applied in practice up to the date of the dispute. If the case involves a worker's grievance, he can match the facts of the grievance against the relevant contract clause and decide in his own mind who is right and who is wrong. Because both labor and management have been willing to rely upon the judgments of outsiders in questions of contract interpretation, the practice of going to arbitration with disputes over rights is widespread. Approximately 90 per cent of all labor-management agreements provide for the arbitration of disputes that arise over the interpretation or application of an agreement.[4]

Interests.   The story is quite different in disputes over interests primarily because these disputes by nature are less arbitrable. To illustrate this proposition let us consider a dispute over a seniority clause in two sets of circumstances. In the first, management and union have agreed in negotiations to apply seniority by departmental unit, but they disagree about its application to a few workers who are not directly associated with any of the regular departments. Management claims these workers have super-seniority, whereas the union believes they can be bumped by anyone qualified to perform their jobs. An arbitrator called in to settle the dispute can gather all the available evidence and then decide how the workers in question fit into the seniority scheme. The important point for this analysis is that the dispute is over the precise meaning of a seniority clause to which both parties have agreed.

Now consider a dispute over the seniority unit as such. The union wants seniority by plant, whereas management wants a department-wide unit. To hand this problem to an outsider would amount to commissioning him to

---

[4] The emergence of grievance arbitration as an important part of the labor-management relationship has been associated with a sequence of controversial issues about the nature and scope of arbitration. One of the most recent of these has centered upon the scope of the arbitrator's authority. The language of many collective bargaining agreements provides that arbitration shall be over grievances involving the interpretation and application of the terms of the agreement. Quite commonly, there is also a statement to the effect that an arbitrator shall have no authority to add to, subtract from, or amend any part of the agreement. In the absence of language more specific than this, many arbitrators have held that a union is entitled to be heard on a grievance, even though the contract is silent on the subject involved, if the union can establish that the grievance, in one way or another, involves an interpretation of the agreement.

In a court contest initiated by a union suit to compel arbitration, the Supreme Court upheld this point of view. See *United Steelworkers of America* v. *Warrior and Gulf Navigation Co.*, 363 U.S. 574 (1960). In an earlier case, the Supreme Court had held that a grievance arbitration provision in a collective bargaining agreement could be enforced by way of Section 301(a) of the Taft-Hartley Act which provides for suits by and against labor organizations for contract enforcement. See *Textile Workers Union* v. *Lincoln Mills*, 353 U.S. 448 (1957).

write part of the contract. Neither side is likely to entrust a responsibility of this magnitude to a third party. Since basic interests are in conflict, neither labor nor management will want to take the issue to arbitration unless it is convinced that it is likely to do better under arbitration than under collective bargaining or open conflict.

Submission of interest-type conflicts to arbitration is, in fact, relatively rare. The most common of the interest disputes is probably the wage disagreement, and here it has been estimated that no more than 2 per cent of all general wage changes in peacetime collective bargaining are arrived at through arbitration.[5]

Compulsory Arbitration.   Under compulsory arbitration, strikes are prohibited by law, and disputes, if otherwise unresolved, must be decided by a specified arbitration process. The idea of compulsory arbitration has a great deal of surface appeal. Actually, it is fraught with dangers and problems. The major argument for compulsion is that it is a relatively effective method of stopping strikes that for one reason or another must not be allowed to occur. The arguments against it challenge the workability as well as the alleged value of the process.

One of the most difficult problems of compulsory arbitration is similar to the problem of an arbitrator in a voluntarily submitted dispute over interests. This is the absence of any generally accepted criteria for making judgments when interests are in conflict. How does one determine the merits of a dispute over wages, for instance?

Let us examine the possibilities of compulsory arbitration in a wage dispute. Assume that a firm has offered its workers a general wage increase averaging five cents per hour, whereas the union has demanded a wage increase of twenty cents per hour. Each side holds firmly to its position, and the matter is referred to arbitration in accordance with the procedures of the compulsory arbitration law. The arbitrator must make a decision, and he must base his decision upon something. In his study of wage arbitration, Bernstein found that arbitrators picked the following criteria: comparisons, cost of living changes, the firm's ability to pay, differential features of the work, the presence of substandard wage conditions, productivity changes, regularity of employment, general economic conditions, and manpower considerations.[6] The answer to the dispute question we are considering will be quite different depending upon which of these criteria is chosen. The validity and fairness of the choice will depend upon personal points of view, but some type of choice can be made. It is quite likely, however, that the selected standard will be one that was rejected by one of the parties during negotiations.

---

[5] Irving Bernstein, *Arbitration of Wages* (Berkeley: University of California Press, 1954), p. 14.

[6] *Ibid.*, p. 207.

Since one of the most commonly used standards in voluntary wage arbitration is comparison, we shall continue this analysis on the assumption that our hypothetical arbitrator has decided to use this standard in making his award. He will compare the wages at the plant with wages elsewhere. The problem now becomes that of deciding whose wages will serve as the basis for comparison. Will comparisons be made with other firms in the industry or other firms in the area? Will a comparison be made with a modal wage, a mean wage, or a median wage? What type of comparison can be made if the firm has an historical record of being a wage leader or if bargaining is on an industry-wide basis?

Should all these problems be resolved, there is the residual problem of translating the conclusions drawn from a comparison into a specific cents per hour figure. There are important technical problems involved in comparing wages in one establishment with those of another.[7] Similar job titles in different firms do not mean that job content is similar. To make a complete comparison, furthermore, the value of fringe benefits, the amount of premium pay earned in overtime employments, and the regularity of work in the respective firms might have to be considered. Perhaps enough has been said to illustrate the difficulties of compulsory wage arbitration, but the analysis will be pushed a little further to show possibilities of additional ramifications.

The wage award might affect the competitive position of the firm. It might unsettle the labor market in which the firm is located. It might have price effects of far-reaching nature. It might affect the stockholders of the firm. The wage award, in short, will affect the interests of many groups who might translate their discontent into political pressures for some kind of relief. Whether the wage control that would result from extensive compulsory arbitration is compatible with an uncontrolled price system is questionable. The least that can be said is that there would be economic problems of serious consequence.

Another argument against compulsory arbitration is based upon the effects of this process on free collective bargaining. When an arbitration tribunal is in existence, neither labor nor management will be inclined to bargain seriously if it believes that it will be able to get more from arbitration than it would from bargaining. Compulsory arbitration introduces an inflexibility into bargaining. In the typical bargaining process the parties work out their own version of a compromise. When arbitration is mandatory, however, there is a great pressure for both sides to hold fast to their positions.

Other arguments against compulsory arbitration are that it has not been notably successful where it has been tried, as in Australia and New Zealand,

---

[7] Technical difficulties of a similar nature would be present if the arbitrator had selected one of the other possible criteria.

and that the arbitration tribunal would be subjected to undesirable political control.

Successive outbreaks of strikes have apparently dimmed the appeal of the arguments detailed above, and support for compulsory arbitration seems to be stronger than it has been for some time. There is a limit to public patience; and when prolonged industrial conflict occurs, it can be anticipated that popular opinion will jell in favor of an imposed settlement. Some relaxation in a long-standing total opposition to compulsory arbitration can also be discerned among professionals in the field of industrial relations.[8] This statement is not meant to suggest the existence of a wave of enthusiasm for compulsory arbitration but only that there is now more of a willingness to consider its possible use in occasional and special situations. Precedent for such action exists in the 1963 act of Congress which imposed a requirement of arbitration in a stubborn railroad industry work rules dispute.[9] Congress was reacting to a special set of circumstances which may not be duplicated in other industries, but the experience has undoubtedly made some dent in congressional aversion to compulsory arbitration.[10]

Miscellaneous Government Pressures

There are numerous other ways in which the several branches of the government can seek to influence labor and management to by-pass open conflict and settle their differences by other means. The executive branch with its relative flexibility and capacity for quick action is well situated to take some type of action when a serious dispute threatens or occurs.[11]

---

[8] See, for example, Orme W. Phelps, "Compulsory Arbitration: Some Perspectives," *Industrial and Labor Relations Review,* October, 1964, pp. 81–91.

[9] PL 88-108.

[10] The dispute was initiated in 1959 when most of the nation's major railroads demanded the right to make sweeping work rule changes which would have eliminated thousands of jobs. The operating railroad unions, their membership already seriously affected by large declines in railroad industry employment, rejected the demands. The dispute continued from 1959 to August, 1963 despite the best efforts of three separate fact-finding groups, mediation by the Secretary of Labor, and Presidential recommendations of voluntary arbitration. In August, 1963, when there seemed to be no alternative to a strike short of compulsory arbitration, Congress provided for the establishment of a seven man arbitration board to resolve controversies over the size and make-up of train crews and the proposal to eliminate 32,000 firemen's jobs.

The arbitration board ruled that 90 per cent of the diesel locomotive firemen jobs in freight and yard service work were unnecessary and stipulated procedures for reduction in force which relied primarily upon attrition to accomplish the reduction. The issue of manning crew size was referred back to the parties for local negotiation. The award was made effective as of January, 1964, and, under the act of Congress, was to remain in force for two years. For a description of the provisions of the 1963 Railroad Arbitration Act see *Monthly Labor Review,* October, 1963, pp. 1187–1188. For the text of the arbitration board's award see *ibid.,* January, 1964, pp. 36–43.

[11] Reference here, of course, is to action that will end a dispute rather than to action maintaining peace and order. The latter type of action is a function of the police power and raises different and sometimes serious problems.

Examples will be given here of techniques that have been used by the executive branch.

1. A simple form of executive pressure occurs when the chief executive officer—local, state, or national—intervenes personally. This is nothing more than a form of super-mediation that has a potentiality for effectiveness because of the prestige of the mediator's office. Mediation by a political executive can be especially effective if the labor and management bargainers are anxious to find some way out of an impasse without giving the impression of making concessions directly to the opposite party. A settlement can sometimes be "sold" to the rank and file of the union or the officers of a firm on the basis that the mayor or governor personally requested or suggested such a settlement.

For the executive there are some dangers involved in becoming a mediator. If the mediator's attempt fails, the prestige of the executive office is somewhat tarnished. The wise executive will not expose his office to unnecessary rebuff. The executive post, furthermore, is an elective office; and the incumbent must keep his eye on the next election. He cannot afford to step casually into situations where his behavior might cost him votes and prestige.

2. Appointment of a fact-finding board with the power to make recommendations is another form of executive intervention in labor disputes. Specially appointed fact-finding boards have some advantages over the regular mediation processes. When a board of prominent persons appointed by the President issues recommendations, it is very probable that public opinion will exert a strong pressure on labor and management to accept the terms recommended. The creation of a board in connection with a specific dispute is highly ceremonial. The spotlight of publicity is turned upon the board's efforts, and this tends to create a general expectation that the board will be able to achieve results. The bargaining party that ignores the recommendations of a fact-finding board runs the risk of being branded the villain of the particular dispute.

Some objections to fact-finding procedures have been raised. If used too frequently, labor and management may develop the habit of avoiding serious bargaining until they have a go at the board. This is similar to what occurs when compulsory arbitration is practiced, and it has been noted that the fact-finding process is similar, in respects, to compulsory arbitration. Another shortcoming of fact-finding is that the recommendations of boards may have unintended and far-reaching economic consequences. This is the case when the recommendations made establish collective bargaining patterns that become influential in other industries. The function of a fact-finding board is to settle a labor dispute rather than to make economic decisions that affect the entire economy. The latter result is quite possible, however, when the dispute is between prominent corporations and unions.

Despite the dangers attached to fact-finding procedures, they are a technique that can be highly effective in some situations. Between 1945 and 1950, federal fact-finding boards were appointed on sixteen occasions.

3. Government seizure of private property for the purpose of settling labor disputes has been primarily a wartime phenomenon in the United States. During the World War II period, seizure was practiced fifty-nine times in disputes that threatened to interrupt production of essential war goods. The various pressures that are present in a war emergency combine to make seizure especially effective at such a time. Possibly because of its wartime success, suggestions have been made that some type of business seizure and government operation be practiced in peacetime when serious labor disputes occur in critical industries.

The exact legal basis for property seizure in peacetime is vague at the present time. The Supreme Court has ruled that the President has no inherent power to seize and operate a private firm.[12] Assuming that the constitutional questions can be resolved, by statutory authorization perhaps, the remaining questions center upon the possible effectiveness and wisdom of seizure.

Seizure can be practiced in two different contexts. In one case, property is taken over by the government when labor or management balks at accepting the ruling of a government agency. This was the type of seizure that occurred during World War II. When a union or a business firm held out adamantly against compliance with a War Labor Board order, the government took over and kept the facility in operation. The other case occurs when the government steps in and operates the firm as a neutral party until labor and management negotiate their way to a peaceful settlement. This latter type of seizure has been referred to as a holding action, in contrast to an enforcing action.

The main experiences with government seizure in the United States have stemmed from enforcing actions. Its effectiveness as a holding action to force labor and management to bargain has not been proved.[13] It is quite possible that peacetime seizure under dramatic circumstances in a critically important labor dispute might have the effect of forcing the bargaining parties to reappraise their positions sufficiently so as to make some sort of agreement possible. Frequent use of the seizure technique, however, will create many problems that can be shrugged off in the occasional case. If

---

[12] *Youngstown Sheet and Tube Co., et al.* v. *Sawyer*, 343 U.S. 579, 1952.

[13] For different attitudes about the "holding" type of seizure see Frank M. Kleiler, "Presidental Seizures in Labor Disputes," *Industrial and Labor Relations Review,* July, 1953, pp. 547–556, and Ludwig Teller, "Government Seizure in Labor Disputes," *Harvard Law Review,* September, 1947.

resorted to frequently, the seizure process would have to be standardized, the status of workers and management would have to be defined, some decision about disposition of profits would have to be made, and undoubtedly many unforeseen details would have to be ironed out. It is not easy to forecast the ultimate effects of a mechanical type of seizure upon collective bargaining or free enterprise. It could easily have significant effects upon both of these systems.

Apart from the three techniques discussed above—executive mediation, fact-finding, and government seizure of property—proposals for government action to curb labor disputes have included enforced cooling-off periods, various combinations of mediation and arbitration, strike votes, and methods short of seizure for keeping workers on the job while labor and management grope their way to agreement.[14] A frequently heard recommendation is the "choice-of-procedures" approach. Under this approach, an executive official would have the option under law of using one or any sequence of all the traditional techniques of dispute settlement. In a given dispute, thus, the executive might try mediation, appoint a fact-finding board, halt a strike temporarily with a court-ordered injunction, seize the struck facility, attempt to convince the parties to resort to voluntary arbitration, or impose compulsory arbitration. The arguments for choice-of-procedures are that the element of flexibility would increase the effectiveness of the government's efforts at dispute settlement and that uncertainty about what the government might do would have a restraining effect upon the willingness of the bargaining parties to undergo a work stoppage.

Grievance Procedures

Satisfactory relations achieved by labor's and management's own efforts are ordinarily preferable to imposed peace. If labor and management are able to work out their own problems, the social concern with industrial relations will be much less intense. In this and the next two sections the discussion will deal with approaches to industrial peace that depend largely upon the efforts of labor and management.

Few workplaces are so fortunate as to be completely immune from worker dissatisfaction. A mechanism that roots out and eliminates the sources of trouble will obviously contribute to the achievement of an environment conducive to industrial peace. Grievances left to smolder do not just disappear. The resentment aroused by an unanswered gripe

---

[14] For an example of the last proposal see Stephen H. Sosnick, "Non-Stoppage Strikes: A New Approach," *Industrial and Labor Relations Review,* October, 1964, pp. 73–80.

shows up sooner or later in a form that militates against the achievement of satisfactory industrial relations.

The grievance procedure is a valuable instrument for uncovering the causes of worker discontent. The number of steps in the procedure, the titles of the persons who deal with the grievances at the various steps, and the authority of these personnel will vary from system to system as will the exact character of the final arbitration process. The mechanics of grievance handling, however, are less important than the attitudes of union and management. The most elaborately devised structure for handling grievances will fail to eliminate dissension if labor or management regards the process primarily as another field of battle. The grievance procedure can be used to win victories, or it can be used to eliminate the causes of disputes. In the terminology of Professor Selekman, the approach to grievances and the grievance machinery can be legalistic or clinical.[15] In the former approach, the parties argue over who is right. In the latter they attempt to discover what is wrong. The differences are significant. If a grievance system is to make a maximum contribution to industrial peace, it must be used to eliminate a breeding ground of labor-management conflicts. It is ideally suited for this purpose, since it provides a means of communication whereby dissatisfactions can be brought to the attention of those with sufficient authority to deal with them. If, however, the grievance process is used primarily to fight for worker or management rights as these are defined by the wording of the contract, the procedure might easily have the net effect of intensifying, rather than eliminating, conflict.

Proponents of strong grievance machinery are in general agreement on a number of maxims such as (1) grievances should be dealt with quickly; (2) if possible, grievances should be settled in the early steps of the procedure; (3) foremen and stewards should have adequate authority to settle run of the mill grievances and should be encouraged to do so; (4) the objective of the grievance procedure should be sound and fair settlements, rather than winning cases; and (5) some method such as arbitration should be provided for final determination of disputes.

The grievance system that does this much does a lot. To expect even the best of grievance procedures to serve as a cure-all for all labor-management conflicts, however, would be placing too heavy a burden upon a single technique. Industrial conflict is generated, in part, by causes outside the plant. Furthermore, the most clinically minded union and management personnel might fail to agree on the proper course of action in disputes where value systems clash sharply. A good grievance system will not

---

[15] Benjamin M. Selekman, *Labor Relations and Human Relations* (New York: McGraw-Hill Book Company, 1947), chap. 5.

eliminate all industrial conflict. It can make a strong contribution to industrial peace, however, if the bargaining parties allow it to do so.

The Human Relations Approach

Workers and managers are not merely factors in a productive process. They are human beings with emotions, fears, ambitions, frustrations, likes, and dislikes. This, of course, is only stating the obvious, which can be seen without the help of sophisticated sociological or psychological analysis. In the past decade or so, however, a number of students who have approached the study of industrial relations from the sociological side have placed greater stress upon the human relations aspect of the work process. The workplace has been viewed as a social system, and many studies have been made of the interrelationships of people within this system. These studies have shed much light on the social structure of the workplace, the existence and functions of informal groups, the motivations of worker and boss, the tensions that develop because of boring and repetitive work processes, and the social effects of sudden changes such as the introduction of new machinery and the initial impact of union organization.

The implicit, if not the explicit, conclusion of the human relations approach is that high productivity, high morale, and satisfactory industrial relations can only follow from a better understanding of the forces that make people feel and behave the way they do. A corollary to the implication, of course, is that knowledge of what is responsible for tensions, irritations, and resentments will be a clue to what the intelligent management and union ought to do to create a social environment that is satisfactory to worker, management, and union.

From this standpoint, the grievance procedure is as much a means of communication with the function of bringing problems to light as it is a system for resolving specific grievances. The personnel department's aptitude test is geared not only to test manual skills but social qualities as well. An important requisite for successful performance by union and management negotiators in their collective relationship is that they understand the personal and institutional factors that make the opposite party behave the way he does. Above all, there must be a nearly continuous probing process to determine the real causes of worker dissatisfaction. Failure to locate such real causes often results in the treatment of the wrong ailment. Workers, for instance, may express their hostilities by striking for higher wages when the real cause of their resentment is the behavior of an unpopular foreman. Even though they win the increase, the problem that created the unsatisfactory conditions still remains a problem. It is necessary, then, that union and management leaders be clinically minded and experimental in temperament. Given these attitudes, causes of industrial conflict can be located and treated.

There can be little quarrel with the human relations approach as such. The entire approach is a rather elaborate way of saying that there is more to industrial conflict than meets the eye and that, with adequate understanding and wisdom, the sub-surface irritants can be eliminated. The controversy over the validity of "human relations" centers upon its adequacy as an exclusive approach to the problems of industrial conflict. One may grant the contention sometimes made that in the past too much of the analysis of labor relations was couched in economic terms to the neglect of sociological and psychological considerations. This admission, however, does not prove that economic considerations have no importance at all. The most human of human relations might fail to eliminate conflict if unsatisfactory conditions are present in the product market or the labor market. Other factors external to the operations of a plant, furthermore, such as institutional problems of the union or the corporation, might be responsible for unsettled conditions within a plant. The total social environment of the workplace is a compound of out-plant and in-plant factors, and it is not clear that the human relations approach can make much of a contribution when the former factors are primarily responsible for unsettled conditions. The conclusion that may be drawn is much the same as was made about grievance procedures in the last section: the human relations approach will not resolve all industrial conflict, but in many cases it can make a strong contribution to industrial peace.[16]

Responsible Leadership

A popularly voiced hope by many who are devoted to the maintenance of free collective bargaining is that union and management leaders will develop a strong feeling of social responsibility. In the sense used, "responsibility" means an ability to rise above narrow group interests and to consider the impact of a given line of conduct upon the larger community. Specifically, the hope is that those responsible for the course of collective bargaining will identify their welfare with that of groups larger than the union and the corporation involved in a specific bargaining relationship and that they will be willing to act against the interests of the smaller group when this becomes necessary to promote the more general welfare.

The bulk of American labor and management leaders are not irresponsible people. They do not plunge lightly into actions that are likely to receive strong community condemnation. Strikes that cause much inconvenience and some hardship do occur, however; and it is this fact that leads to charges of social irresponsibility against unions and managements.

---

[16] For a description and critique of recent thought in the "Human relations" area see George Strauss, "Human Relations—1968 Style," *Industrial Relations*, May, 1968, pp. 262-276.

In certain situations, workers and the officers of business firms are quite aware of the capacity they have to inflict harm by virtue of their own conflicts. In public utility industries, atomic energy plants, or munitions-producing facilities during wartime, most persons involved know that a strike or lockout can have far-reaching and possibly disastrous consequences. In industries such as steel production, coal mining, and railroad transportation, unions and management alike know that an extended strike could conceivably grind the entire economy to a halt. Since neither labor nor management leaders are inherently irresponsible, can we not expect that such knowledge will force them to use their power sparingly and cautiously? Can we not, in short, expect labor and management to be mature and responsible in their mutual relationships?

One answer to these questions is that we can expect that these leaders will not be deliberately irresponsible and that the labor-management relationship will probably be conducted on higher and higher planes of maturity as time goes by. The concept of social responsibility, however, is much too vague to serve as an effective and precise guide for behavior in any given dispute. By itself, it provides no answers to the issues under dispute, nor does it suggest any foolproof path to arrive at these answers. The matter might be phrased this way: collective bargaining conflicts are conflicts over interests that do not become automatically resolved simply because the bargainers are far-sighted and responsible individuals. Labor, furthermore, is as biased towards viewing its own interests as identical with those of the community as is management. Since each side regards the other as being at fault in a dispute, each will regard the other as being socially irresponsible and at the same time be quite confident about the responsibility of its own behavior. "Social responsibility" is a vague concept, and its ultimate meaning depends too much upon who is defining the term.

The hope for responsibility among labor and management leaders is a hope that these individuals will become less the leaders of their immediate groups and more the industrial statesmen of the social order. This is probably too idealistic. More realistically, attitudes of greater social responsibility might result in more intensive searches by labor and management for ways out of their bargaining impasses. This could minimize the amount of conflict and shorten its duration, but it would not necessarily eliminate it.

THE EMERGENCY STRIKE

Labor-management disputes may respond to one or another of the approaches described above, but they also may not. This creates a dilemma. As a nation we believe that free collective bargaining is the preferred method for determining the wages and working conditions of organized workers. Collective bargaining can be free and effective only if unions are free to strike and managements are free to say "no" to union demands. If a necessary condition of collective bargaining is forceful pressure, however, there is always a possibility that strikes may occur. We can have free collective bargaining and accept the attendant danger of industrial conflict or we can eliminate conflict—perhaps—by sacrificing collective bargaining and making certain economic decisions in some other manner. It is not apparent that we can have free bargaining without some conflict.

Happily the social and economic fabric of the nation is strong enough to withstand the wear of the typical strike. In the case of most strikes, it is not necessary to face up to the perplexing social question of how to end the dispute, because the consequences of the strike are not sufficiently serious to warrant fundamental policy-making.[17]

This narrows the big social problem to those strikes that might inflict upon society a cost greater than that which society feels that it can afford. There is the danger that from some strikes grave emergencies will arise. What kinds of strikes are these, and what should we do about them?

First, what do we mean by emergency strikes? The phrase "national emergency" as applied to strikes is relatively new, dating back only to the strike wave that followed V-J Day. Several factors might be responsible for the linkage of the concept of an emergency with the effects of certain strikes. One is the increasing social awareness of the problems that flow from the inherent instability of our economic system. The Great Depression of the 1930's and the post-World War II monetary maladjustments are responsible for a lack of confidence in the power of the economic system to adjust to large-scale disruptions. A sizable strike could cause the economy to be so unbalanced that it would be vulnerable to collapse. Hence, there is some fear about the economic effects of strikes. Another factor that has caused worry about the emergency implications of strikes is the state of international political relationships. The world-wide tensions that have been summarized as a cold war have produced a novel environment for the American people. We are not at war, but neither are we at peace. While there is uncertainty about how much industrial conflict the nation can afford, there is widespread opinion that conflicts in basic or strategic industry will weaken our capacity to fulfill our international role, vague as it may sometimes appear to be.

Policy development is made difficult by the fact that not all disputes in basic or strategic industries create emergencies. A strike by bituminous coal miners when there are large coal stocks above ground has a much different impact from a strike that occurs when stocks are low. A strike by

---

[17] All strikes are serious in the sense that some persons will suffer serious deprivation. Most strikes, however, do not cause or threaten to cause disaster either to the nation or the local community. In this sense they are not socially serious. The fact that most strikes do not raise the problem of how strikes as such can be prevented does not mean that the community cannot attempt to end the dispute by mediation, arbitration, or some other means.

employees of a munitions facility could be an emergency if there were no other suppliers but might be relatively unimportant if many other firms were producing the same product. Another complicating element is the time factor. A strike in the basic steel industry might have relatively little effect upon the economy up to a certain point and have rapidly mounting effects after some critical point is reached.

Apart from the problem of identifying emergency disputes, there is the very practical question of what to do about them. In recent considerations of policy for emergency strikes, three lines of thought can be distinguished. One is concerned with the need to improve existing techniques for dealing with such disputes, whereas the other two reflect opposed evaluations of the seriousness of the problem.

The question that inevitably emerges from discussions of techniques for handling major strikes is whether an *ad hoc* approach would be preferable to a single preordained procedure. A strong argument against a preordained procedure has been made by W. Willard Wirtz in his comment on the emergency strike section of the Taft-Hartley Act: "There is a growing feeling that there has been committed here the old mistake of assuming that since the language offers a single phrase to label a set of troubles, there must be a single remedy available to cure them."[18] Different emergency disputes can be dissimilar in every respect other than that they have been adjudged emergencies. A policy that works well in one case will not necessarily be effective in another. Other arguments made against preordained solutions are similar. Compulsory arbitration and seizure procedures replace, rather than encourage, collective bargaining. The elements of give-and-take bargaining that are so essential to bargaining disappear when the possibility of a successful appeal to a government board is present.

The argument against a preordained policy, thus, is essentially an argument for the choice-of-procedures approach discussed above. The responsible executive agency, it is contended, should not be hamstrung by set procedures but should have alternatives and combinations of techniques that could be adjusted according to circumstances. Other points usually stressed are that executive flexibility enhances the risks to management and labor and, thus, directs them away from the government and towards voluntary settlements and that *ad hoc* boards do not establish precedents for themselves.

Some observers have argued that the national emergency strike exists more in public opinion than in economic fact.[19] Historical evidence is used

---

18 "The Choice of Procedures Approach to National Emergency Disputes," in Irving Bernstein, Harold Enarson, and R. W. Fleming (eds.), *Emergency Disputes and National Policy* (New York: Harper & Row, Publishers, 1955), pp. 149–150. (Quoted here with the permission of the publishers.)

19 John P. Horlacher, "A Political Science View of National Emergency Disputes," *The Annals of the American Academy of Political and Social Science,* January, 1961, pp. 85–95.

to support this conclusion. In the basic steel industry, for example, five work stoppages occurred between 1946 and 1959; and, in retrospect, it does not appear that any of these disputes seriously crippled the economy. The 1952 dispute was regarded as especially calamitous at the time because of the Korean War situation, and President Truman justified his attempt to seize the mills as a measure necessary to avoid national disaster. After the Supreme Court invalidated the seizure,[20] a fifty-five day strike occurred, but the campaign in Korea was not visibly affected by a lack of supplies. The 1959 steel strike dragged on for 119 days, but the economy absorbed the damage with a surprising facility. A conclusion that has been drawn from these experiences is that many labor-management disputes have been transformed into national emergencies by the *belief* that the national welfare is being seriously threatened. When the belief becomes widespread, the pressure for political intervention becomes irresistible. The prevailing inclination toward finding a national emergency in any large-scale dispute, thus, threatens the right and weakens the power of labor and management to work out private solutions for their differences.

An opposing position, based upon a pessimistic view of the state of industrial relations, argues for public authority to impose a settlement in those situations where large-scale disputes do not respond to milder forms of intervention. Although expert opinions differ on whether there has been any secular change in the volume of industrial conflict, it is undoubtedly true that the level of public tolerance toward such conflict has been dropping. More and more people have come to regard continuous labor-management discord as irrational, and more and more have grown skeptical about the possibility of achieving an acceptable degree of labor peace without direct government involvement. Evidence of this situation can be found in the fact that proposals for compulsory arbitration no longer evoke the strong and almost unanimous opposition that they once did.

The Taft-Hartley Approach to Emergency Disputes

Current policy for dealing with national emergency-type disputes is set forth in Title II of the Taft-Hartley Act. The essential parts of the title are summarized below:

1. When the President believes that an actual or threatened work stoppage will imperil the national health or safety, he may appoint a board of inquiry to inquire into the dispute issues. The duty of the board is to report on the dispute, but the report is to contain no recommendations.

2. Upon receiving the report, the President may direct the Attorney General to petition the appropriate district court of the United States to enjoin a strike or lockout.

---

[20] *Youngstown Sheet and Tube Company* v. *Sawyer*, 343 U.S. 579.

3. The court is empowered to enjoin an actual or threatened strike or lockout if, in the opinion of the court, such a dispute affects an entire industry or an essential part of an industry engaged in interstate commerce and if the dispute threatens to imperil the national health or safety.

4. After the court has issued its order, the parties are to make every effort to adjust their differences with the assistance of the Federal Mediation and Conciliation Service. Neither party is under a duty to accept any proposal of settlement made by the service.

5. When the court injunction is issued, the President is to reconvene the board of inquiry which had previously reported the facts of the dispute. After sixty days (unless the dispute has been settled by that time) the board shall report to the President the current position of the parties, the efforts made for a settlement, a statement by each party of its position, and a statement of the employer's last offer of settlement.

6. Within the next fifteen days, the National Labor Relations Board shall take a secret ballot of all employees involved in the dispute on the question of whether they wish to accept the employer's last offer. The results of the vote are to be certified to the Attorney General within five days. (Thus, eighty days may elapse after the date of issuance of the injunction: the sixty day period before the last offer ballot, the fifteen days during which the employees are to be polled, and the five days for certification of the results to the Attorney General.)

7. When the results are certified to him or when a settlement is reached (whichever happens sooner) the Attorney General shall move the court to discharge the injunction. Under the law it is mandatory for the court to grant the motion and remove the injunction.

8. After removal of the court injunction, the President is required to submit a report to Congress including the findings of the board of inquiry and the results of the last-offer ballot. The President may also recommend for congressional consideration such further action as he believes appropriate.

As is true with other features of the Taft-Hartley Act, much controversy has been engendered by the national emergency section. Organized labor has regarded the specified procedures as inherently biased against unions and was originally fearful that the injunction would be used frequently as a device to destroy the strike weapon. Almost two decades of experience with the emergency provision have weakened these criticisms. The national emergency title of the law has been called into play infrequently; and in those situations where it has been used, the bargaining power of labor has not been seriously affected. Present-day criticisms of the emergency section are not so much that it favors either labor or management but that it is not a particularly effective instrument for dealing with serious disputes.

The general disfavor into which the Taft-Hartley emergency strike section has fallen is illustrated by the 1959 steel strike experience. The President delayed appointing a fact-finding board as long as he possibly could, and the board, once appointed, manifested an obvious distaste for the injunction procedure. When the board under Chairman George Taylor attempted to mediate the dispute, no protest was voiced even though the letter of the law gives the board no mandate to attempt mediation. Finally, and only after mediation had failed, the board prepared the report that led to an injunction.

Although there is a strong consensus that the national emergency title of the Taft-Hartley Act needs overhauling, there is little agreement about what should replace it. Once compulsory settlement is ruled out as a possibility, the suggested alternatives all end up as roughly similar to what is now being done under the Taft-Hartley Act. Although it is usually argued that a choice-of-procedures approach would introduce more flexibility than the current law provides, it is noteworthy that "choice-of-procedures" has, in effect, been followed in several recent disputes with little success. In the 1962–1963 East Coast longshore dispute, for example, a variety of procedures were used at one point or another by the following public representatives: the President, the Secretary of Labor, an assistant Secretary of Labor, the director and the deputy director of the Federal Mediation and Conciliation Service, fifteen FMCS mediators, a Taft-Hartley board of inquiry, the Attorney General, the federal district court, the mayors of several port cities, and a special board under the chairmanship of Senator Wayne Morse. Despite all of this attention, the dispute lasted for a year. It is doubtful, then, that any amount of tailoring of the Taft-Hartley Act will be effective if the bargaining parties are in fundamental disagreement. Short of compulsion, there is no procedure that can guarantee that disputes will not occur in sensitive areas of the economy.

Dispute Procedures in the Railway Industry

Dispute procedures established for the railway industry by the Railway Labor Act of 1926, as amended, consist primarily of mediation and voluntary arbitration. Like the Taft-Hartley Act, the law provides for a waiting period and special investigation when an emergency threatens. Unlike the Taft-Hartley Act, however, the law places no reliance upon court-issued injunctions; nor is there a "last offer" vote by employees.

Under the Railway Labor Act, carriers and employees are required to give at least thirty days' notice of any intended change in pay rates, rules, or working conditions. Should the bargaining parties fail to reach agreement over such matters, the National Mediation Board attempts to mediate the dispute. If mediation is unsuccessful, the board attempts to induce the parties to agree to voluntary arbitration. If arbitration is refused and if the dispute, in the judgment of the National Mediation Board, threatens to create a transportation emergency, the board is required to notify the President. The President is empowered to appoint a special emergency board to investigate the dispute and issue a report within thirty days. During this period, and for thirty days after the report has been issued, neither party may change the conditions which gave rise to the dispute except by mutual agreement. The parties, however, are free to engage in a strike or lockout after the expiration of the waiting period.[21]

For a time, the Railway Labor Act was regarded as a model law, and numerous observers believed that the formula of mediation, voluntary arbitration, and mild government pressure should be applied to all industries. This optimism has been tempered considerably in recent years. Since 1940 the dispute procedures of the act have proved to be ineffective on a number of occasions, the most notable failure being in the work rules dispute which began in 1959 and ended four and one-half years later only after Congress imposed a requirement of arbitration of the major issues.[22]

THE OUTLOOK FOR INDUSTRIAL PEACE

It is possible to work up a strong feeling of cynicism about the prospects for industrial peace simply by setting one's sights too high. If industrial peace is defined as the absence of all conflict, there is no hope for such peace in this or in any other society that provides opportunities for expression of discontent. The socialist society, like the free enterprise one, has people who give orders and those who take them. Both societies require decisions concerning income distribution. Both are characterized by technological change rendering old skills obsolete and creating the need for new ones. Both have social stratifications and elite groups. These are all conflict-producing situations, and others can be identified. If modern industrial society produces a staggering volume of material goods, it also

---

[21] The Railway Labor Act provides for compulsory arbitration of disputes involving the interpretation of agreements that have been reached through collective bargaining. If such disputes are not resolved by the regular grievance procedures provided in the bargaining agreement, the disputes go to the National Railroad Adjustment Board. Decisions of the Adjustment Board are final and binding.

[22] Questions have been raised about whether the dispute is, in fact, settled and whether free collective bargaining can be re-established in the railroad industry if the right to strike is not permitted. See J. J. Kaufman, "The Railroad Labor Dispute: A Marathon of Improvisation and Maneuver," *Industrial and Labor Relations Review*, January, 1965, pp. 196–212.

creates a bewildering variety of discontents. In the socialist society, discontent may be slightly different in form and manifestation, but the planned society that is wisely planned will reserve at least one panel of experts for the problems of industrial conflict.

Industrial conflict has various dimensions, and any answer to questions of conflict will be conditioned by the dimension that is singled out for analysis. Workers might be unhappy because their jobs do not provide one or more satisfactions that are essential for contentment. The work may be boring and overly simple and thus provide no psychological feeling of accomplishment. The income derived from the job might be too low to provide a desired standard of living, or the job might be generally regarded as menial work that stamps the worker with a low social status.

Apart from the fact of the job itself, social aspects of the workplace can be a prolific source of discontent. Jealousies between workers, personal disappointments, the disorder that characterizes many workplaces, ineffective systems of communication—the list could be extended almost indefinitely—all create a social setting in which conflict becomes more probable than its alternative.

Much broader as a source of conflict than either the job or the workplace is the character of the world in which we live. Economic depressions, wars, tightrope diplomacy, and a continuing industrial revolution have created social ruptures and have necessitated continuous social adaptations to change. In the process there has been large-scale disenchantment. Much that gave meaning to life in the past has been squashed, and in our gropings for new values we have managed so far to produce only a "lonely crowd" of people who have not mastered the art of living in a wealthy if insecure society. From this standpoint, industrial conflict is just one of the methods by which people express a discontent that is rooted in something much broader than industrial relations.

Apart from the conflict-generating forces identified above, it must be recalled that we live in a society that has always extolled the virtues of economic conflict. The early philosophers of free enterprise saw economic conflict as an invisible hand that inevitably would lead to superior economic performance by business units. They did not see with sufficient clarity, however, that elements of conflict could also impede the economic process in the absence of some technique of conflict moderation. It was inevitable that a Karl Marx would build a competing philosophical system that emphasized the conflict rather than the adjustment processes of capitalism. For reasons that have been analyzed elsewhere in this volume, American workers have been more impressed by the rhetoric of capitalism than by the rhetoric of Marxism. Like the entrepreneurs, many workers have come to believe that they can win economic victories by dint of energetic efforts. Increasingly, these efforts have been expressed through the medium of organized group pressure rather than by the laborious and uncertain process of working one's way to the top.

This brings us to the labor union. Essentially, it is an instrument that coalesces discontent into an effective power unit. Although it is true that the union itself can be a cause of labor-management conflict, it does not follow that the absence of a union will remove all causes of industrial discontent. Indeed, if there is any validity at all to the above analysis, the seeds of conflict are not to be found in the existence of large and strong unions but in the totality of the economic and social milieu. The union contribution to conflict stems from the ability of an organized unit to exert a power that has direction and momentum and so collides intentionally with other power aggregates. Labor unions, as we know them, could not exist in a world in which there were no angry people; but, given sufficient numbers of angry people who have freedom to act, some type of protest organization will be formed.

If conflict is all-pervasive in our society, can there be any hope for industrial peace? The outlook on this score is mixed. Certain signs point toward an improved industrial relations setting, whereas others suggest that in the short run, at least, there will be no significant drop in the volume of conflict. A number of relevant considerations on both sides of this question are presented below:

1. In a dynamic society, social change is inevitable, and such change does not occur without conflict. As Professor Dubin has suggested, however, conflict can be institutionalized, and collective bargaining is the great social invention that has institutionalized industrial conflict.[23] In providing a stable means for resolving conflicts, bargaining becomes a method by which social change can occur systematically and with a minimum of overt conflict. Collective bargaining, thus, does not eliminate conflict; but it does operate as a social device for bringing conflict to a successful resolution.

2. A close observation of industrial relations leaves the broad impression that worker-management relationships have improved significantly. This conclusion cannot be verified statistically, nor can it be stated as a scientific fact. Still there are many signs that outwardly, at least, indicate that progress has been made. The bloodletting type of conflict is relatively rare today; unions are accepted without serious management protest in most of the important industries; and, as previously stated, most collective bargaining relationships are carried on without resort to the forceful pressure of the strike. Since the end of World War II, the viability of free collective

---

[23] Robert Dubin, "Constructive Aspects of Industrial Conflict," in Arthur Kornhauser, Robert Dubin, and Arthur M. Ross (eds.), *Industrial Conflict* (New York: McGraw-Hill Book Company, 1954), p. 44.

bargaining has been tested by the emergence of many novel issues, and the over-all record of labor and management adjustment to a changing industrial relations setting has been good.

Certain types of disputes have been eliminated, to a large extent, by the use of legal processes or by resort to procedures that have been accepted voluntarily by labor and management. Approximately 15,000 strikes were called between 1935 and 1939, and a large proportion of them were over the right of workers to have unions of their own choosing. Today the organizational strike is relatively rare. Disputes over union recognition are usually resolved by invoking the election procedures established by the Wagner Act and carried over into the Taft-Hartley Act with some modifications. Strikes over worker grievances have also diminished in frequency. Most bargaining agreements establish grievance procedures with final arbitration for those problems that cannot be settled by labor and management officials. The institutionalization of the process of handling worker complaints has also contributed to the marked diminution in the occurrence of the unsanctioned and spontaneous wildcat strike.

3. Important leaders of labor and management are interested in improving the state of industrial relations and have been willing to experiment with procedures that supplement the traditional bargaining process. From the recent history of collective bargaining, we can cite the Human Relations Committee in the basic steel industry, the National Glass Container Labor-Management Committee, joint study committees in the automobile industry, and the Armour Automation Committee as examples of fresh approaches toward a resolution of the problems of the workplace.[24] Numerous other examples can be cited to illustrate an active desire by union and management leaders to move labor relations to a more satisfactory plane. The specific ideas voiced are not necessarily sound and over time may prove to be untenable in practice. What is more important, however, is that highly placed officials in both camps believe that improved relations are possible, and they are not absolutely hostile to some experimentation with a view to accomplishing the improvement.

4. Industrial conflict does not occur anywhere and everywhere with the same intensity and frequency. Kerr and Siegel have shown that some industries are strike-prone and others are relatively strike-free.[25] Within industries some firms are much more plagued by labor trouble than are others. Ross, who has carried the analysis of differential strike experience

---

[24] For descriptions of the background and functions of the arrangements cited see James J. Healy (ed.), *Creative Collective Bargaining* (Englewood Cliffs, N.J.: Prentice-Hall, Inc., 1965). Discussion of several of these developments will be found in the following chapter.

[25] Clark Kerr and Abraham Siegel, "The Interindustry Propensity to Strike—An International Comparison," chap. 14 in Kornhauser, Dubin, and Ross, *op. cit.*

further, has identified eight "center of conflict" industries where a large proportion of total strike activity is concentrated.[26] These industrial centers of conflict—textiles, apparel, automobiles, basic steel, coal mining, construction, electrical equipment, and machinery—account for only about 18 per cent of non-agricultural employment, but they were responsible for 60 per cent of all man-days of idleness due to strikes during the 1927–1960 period. According to Ross' analysis, the centers of conflict are characterized by periods of belligerency preceded or succeeded by periods of quiet relations. He argues that the belligerent cycles have terminated in the apparel, automobile, coal mining, and textile industries, leaving only basic steel, construction, electrical equipment, and machinery as active conflict areas. With the exception of steel industry strikes, however, the active cycles have not been as important as those that have terminated. The general outlook, then, is for a reduced level of conflict—if no new cycles of belligerency are generated.

Differentials in industry strike experiences suggest that the entire field of industrial relations might be fruitfully investigated for clues to what makes for labor-management harmony. There have been, in fact, many investigations. In the past several decades, many economists, sociologists, psychologists, and political scientists have been drawn to the study of industrial relations, with the net result that our knowledge of the field has been greatly expanded. Some part of this knowledge has already worked its way into personnel and collective bargaining practices.

If the academicians have stepped into the world of labor relations, labor and management have also stepped into the world of academics. The next generation of labor and management leaders will have more formal education than the present leaders. This fact alone should warrant a feeling of optimism among those who believe that the long run solution of intranational conflicts depends ultimately upon a greater diffusion of educational opportunities.

5. In a number of industries and for various reasons, the strike has lost some of its effectiveness as a means of coercion.[27] The rationale underlying a strike, of course, is that the economic damage inflicted upon the opposite party will force the opponent to reconsider his position in the matter under dispute. In certain industries labor and management have devised methods of hedging against strike losses and of otherwise offsetting the adverse economic effects of a strike. On balance, the management position appears to have been strengthened more than that of the union by these developments.

[26] Arthur M. Ross, "The Prospects for Industrial Conflict," *Industrial Relations,* October, 1961, pp. 57–74.

[27] James L. Stern, "Declining Utility of the Strike," *Industrial and Labor Relations Review,* October, 1964, pp. 60–72.

In the airline, railroad, newspaper publishing, and Hawaiian sugar plantation industries, employers have co-operated in the establishment of strike insurance funds which offset part of the revenues lost as a result of strikes. The union counterpart is the strike fund to disburse benefits to members idled by work stoppages. In some communities, needy strikers have been able to draw upon public welfare programs for relief. Apart from these direct offsets to income loss, a number of firms have found that by utilizing standby capacity a significant part of the output lost during a strike can be made up by increasing production before and after a work stoppage. Employees benefit by the same arrangement, since the overtime pay received cancels out part of the wages lost during the time of idleness. In technologically advanced industries such as aerospace, petroleum refining, and telecommunications, it is becoming increasingly difficult for a union to launch an effective strike because of the high ratio of supervisory to non-supervisory employees. By utilizing supervisory personnel, management can continue operations at close to capacity levels and for a considerable time.

If the strike is losing some of its effectiveness, there may be less reliance upon it in the future. The other side of the coin should be noted, however. In those situations where labor and management are able to hedge against the loss of income, the result may be longer rather than fewer strikes. Considerations that argue against the probability of a decline in the volume of industrial conflict include the following:

1. It is difficult to deduce evidence of a long run secular decline in the volume of conflict from available statistics of work stoppages. (See Figure 13.)

2. An analysis of the causes of strikes shows that there has been a succession of dispute-producing issues. Wage disputes have always been prominent among the causes of work stoppages, but the importance of other causes has varied over time. In the late 1930's a wave of organizational strikes occurred. Between 1945 and 1960 the number of work stoppages involving union security or efforts to strengthen the bargaining position of unions increased significantly. At the present time, disputes over job security and plant administration matters such as work rules, discipline, and discharge have become major causes of work stoppages. In 1963, 23 per cent of all work stoppages resulted from job security and plant administration disputes. The emergence of new issues, thus, has an exacerbating effect upon labor-management relationships and tends to induce a rise in the level of industrial conflict.

3. The tendency for management to take tougher stances in collective bargaining and the many bargaining issues being created by technological and economic change support a prediction of a short run rise in the amount

FIGURE 13

TRENDS IN WORK STOPPAGES
[*Semilog scale*]

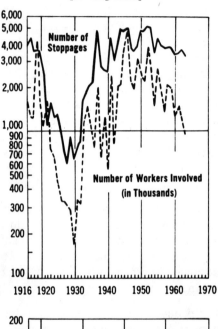

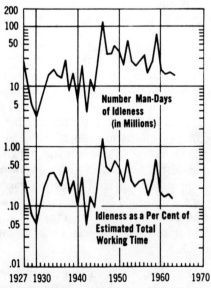

Source: Bureau of Labor Statistics, *Analysis of Work Stoppages*
(Bulletin No. 1420, 1963).

of industrial conflict. Long run predictions are hazardous, of course; and although some writers have spoken of the "withering away of the strike,"[28] the possible emergence of new centers of conflict cannot be ruled out. Public employees, for example, have manifested an unusual degree of restiveness in recent years; and sporadic strike activity has occurred among school teachers, social workers, and hospital employees. It would not be overly bold to predict a rise in the number of strikes by such employees and by other white collar groups and previously placid service groups. Finally, a certain amount of industrial conflict can be anticipated as a consequence of the drive of minority racial groups for equality of economic opportunity.

Can anything at all be concluded about the prospects for industrial peace? If we can assume that our society will not be disrupted by war, business depression, or the impact of large-scale technological change, a fairly strong case might be made for the probability of diminished industrial warfare. The rub, however, is that unstabilizing forces cannot be assumed out of the picture without losing touch with reality. What happens in industrial relations will depend to a large extent upon what happens in the nation as a whole.

If we assume that strong forces will make for social instability in the future, two different attitudes relative to industrial peace are possible. It can be argued that the participants in the bargaining process will develop more mature relationships as time passes and will learn to accommodate conflict situations to the mutual advantage of labor and management. Or one might believe that the dynamics of social change will create new conflicts that will continually upset such equilibria as labor and management have been able to achieve. Should the latter forecast prove to be the more accurate, there will have to be increasing reliance upon the various approaches to industrial peace discussed earlier in this chapter.

SUMMARY

A certain amount of industrial conflict is inevitably associated with the practice of collective bargaining. Various techniques can be used to minimize conflict, however. These include relatively mild intrusions into the bargaining process such as mediation, voluntary arbitration, and government-appointed fact-finding boards as well as more drastic measures such as compulsory arbitration and plant seizure. Frequent use of the latter two

---

[28] Arthur M. Ross and Paul T. Hartman, *Changing Patterns of Industrial Conflict* (New York: John Wiley & Sons, Inc., 1960).

techniques, however, would make serious inroads into the free practice of collective bargaining.

Fortunately, most strikes in the United States do not pose threats to the economic and military security of the nation and can be tolerated if they do not respond to the milder forms of dispute settlement methods. Present policy for dealing with disputes serious enough to create national emergencies is set forth in Title II of the Taft-Hartley Act. In essence, the policy consists of compulsory postponement of a strike or lockout, during which time the parties are subjected to a variety of pressures to resolve their differences. Should the conflict remain unresolved aftcr eighty days, the compulsory postponement ceases to be effective and the parties are free to resume the conflict. Although there has been much criticism of the Taft-Hartley provision, there is little consensus on what should replace it other than that a new procedure should provide for more flexibility in approach.

QUESTIONS

1. Would the total termination of industrial conflict be a desirable social goal?
2. What is the function of a mediator? In your opinion, can mediation be an effective technique for moderating labor-management conflict?
3. Would you favor a law providing for compulsory arbitration of labor disputes? Defend your position.
4. What suggestions would you make to improve the emergency strike provisions of the Taft-Hartley Act?
5. In your opinion, what is the outlook for industrial peace?
6. It has been argued that the racial conflict that broke out in the 1960's is similar, in many ways, to the industrial conflict that occurred during the organizing drives of the 1930's. What similarities and/or differences do you see in the two situations?

SELECTED READINGS

COLE, DAVID L. "Government in the Bargaining Process: The Role of Mediation," *The Annals of the American Academy of Political and Social Science,* January, 1961, pp. 42–58.

CULLEN, DONALD E. *National Emergency Strikes.* Ithaca, New York: New York State School of Labor and Industrial Relations, 1968.

HORLACHER, JOHN PERRY. "A Political Science View of National Emergency Disputes," *Annals of the American Academy of Political and Social Science,* January, 1961, pp. 85–95.

KORNHAUSER, ARTHUR, DUBIN, ROBERT, and ROSS, ARTHUR M. (eds.). *Industrial Conflict.* New York: McGraw-Hill Book Company, 1954. Chaps. 3, 7, 11, 21, 22, 23.

SOSNICK, STEPHEN H., STERN, JAMES L., PHELPS, ORME W. "Discussion: The Strike, The Non-Strike, and Compulsory Arbitration," *Industrial and Labor Relations Review,* October, 1964, pp. 60–91.

CHAPTER 11

Some Recent Developments in Collective Bargaining

SINCE 1958, DISTINCTIVE APPROACHES TO COLLECTIVE BARGAINING HAVE been attempted in a number of industries, the bargaining process has been tested by the special demands of a rapidly changing technology, and certain occupational groups that have not hitherto relied upon collective negotiations to any significant extent have demonstrated a strong interest in the possibilities of collective bargaining. This chapter will include discussions of these developments.

RESPONSE TO PRESSURES: CONFLICT AND COOPERATION

Power positions in the union-management relationship shift over time, reflecting changes in the economic and political environment as well as the many other variables which influence the relative strengths of the bargaining parties. In the late 1950's, unemployment and intensification of product–market competition replaced the more benign economic climate of the immediately preceding years. Responses to the new environment ranged from tougher bargaining stances on the part of some firms to novel and imaginative union-management problem-solving efforts.

The most publicized assault upon traditional bargaining methods came to be known as "Boulwarism" (after Lemuel Boulware, former vice president of the General Electric Company and formulator of Boulwarism). The essential characteristic of Boulwarism is that the management offer during negotiations is made on a "take it or leave it" basis. The offer, derived from a sincere appraisal of what the employees want, is adhered to even in the face of a strike unless the union can supply factual data to warrant a change. The firm, but not ungenerous, offer is one part of the Boulware formula. The other is an elaborate and energetic program of direct communication with employees. The strategy is not subtle. If the company has done a reasonably good job of gauging its offer, the union is in the position of either sanctioning a unilateral management determination of the conditions of employment or generating rank and file enthusiasm for a strike against a wage and benefit package that would probably be acceptable to most of the employees. Boulwarism, thus, is an effort to circumvent rather than to modify the traditional methods of bargaining.

Because of its spectacular nature, a good deal of attention was drawn to Boulwarism, probably more than its importance warrants. More typically, "hard line bargaining" was manifested in an emboldened management approach to sensitive issues such as work rules, job assignments, seniority matters and production standards. Through aggressive stances at the bargaining table, more rigorous administration of the contract, and increased willingness to take a strike, management sought to recapture some of the prerogatives lost in the ten-year period following the end of World War II.[1]

The hardening tone of industrial relations described above stands in sharp contrast to the several experimental efforts to break out of traditional and time worn bargaining methods in order to surmount challenges to bargaining generated by rapid changes in products, market characteristics, and production processes. An arrangement that attracted a good deal of attention but which failed to survive over time was the Human Relations Committee in the basic steel industry. Established after the end of a long, bitter, and inconclusive strike in 1959, the committee was composed of an equal number of union and company representatives. (The companies involved were the eleven basic steel producers who had bargained jointly in 1959). The task of the Human Relations Committee was to conduct studies and recommend solutions for problems involving wages, job classifications, seniority, medical care, and other topics that might be referred to it from time to time. In 1963, the industry and the union agreed that committee recommendations for changes necessary to eliminate disputes and to protect the interests of the union, the companies, or the employees would be placed into effect immediately upon approval of the parties. The work of the committee is now generally credited with having contributed to the

---

[1] For discussions of hard line bargaining see George Strauss, "The Shifting Power Balance in the Plant," *Industrial Relations*, May, 1962, pp. 65–96; Herbert R. Northrup, "Management's 'New Look' in Labor Relations," *ibid.*, October, 1961, pp. 9–24; Jack Barbash, "Union Response to the Hard Line," *ibid.*, pp. 25–38.

relatively smooth course of negotiations in 1962 and 1963. In the former year, a painstaking report on seniority was instrumental in facilitating labor-management accord on that issue; and in the latter, deliberations within the committee led to a novel vacation plan for high seniority employees.

The Human Relations Committee had a promising start, and prominent union and company officials commented upon its contribution to the bargaining process. Conflict between staff and line levels of authority within the union, however, was generated by the heavy reliance of the committee upon staff level technicians. As a consequence, the committee was disbanded in 1965 when a change in union administration occurred.

Another example of a new approach to industrial relations problems is provided by the experience of the Kaiser Steel Corporation. In the 1959 steel industry negotiations, Kaiser broke away from the joint bargaining front of the other producers and arrived at a separate settlement with the United Steelworkers Union. A unique feature of the settlement was the establishment of a Long Range Committee, to recommend a plan for the equitable sharing of the fruits of the company's progress. Unlike the Human Relations Committee, which consisted of company and union representatives, the Long Range Committee is tri-partite in nature with three neutral, three company, and three union members.

The Kaiser committee has addressed itself to the problem of improving local plant relationships and has been active during contract negotiations. The 1962 contract empowered the committee to review the status of negotiations thirty days before the expiration of the contract and, if necessary, to take various actions such as mediation, issuing a private report to the parties with recommendations, or releasing a public report in order to facilitate a settlement.

The most notable achievement of the Long Range Committee is the Long Range Sharing Plan which went into effect at the company's Fontana plant in 1963. The basic idea of the plan is simple, but the design is complicated. The general goal is to circumvent the usual power plays associated with wage adjustments by providing an equitable basis for employee sharing in the firm's progress. The plan attempts to do this through monthly allocations to employees of about one-third of the savings in labor, materials, and supply costs of steel production based upon a 1961 cost standard. (A small fraction of the workers' share is put into a reserve fund from which the company may draw, if necessary, to match or to help match whatever wage and benefit improvements are negotiated by the steel union and the basic steel industry. Under the contract, Kaiser is obligated to match the industry increase.)

Another feature of the Long Range Sharing Plan provides protection against technological displacement. Employees whose jobs are eliminated go into a work reserve until they are reassigned to new jobs. When unemployment is caused by a drop in production, layoffs are made in accordance with the provisions of the seniority system.

One of the problems associated with a cost reduction plan of the Kaiser type is the establishment of an equitable norm for the measurement of cost savings. Over time a standard cost formula will become obsolete and the process of establishing a new norm contains a potential for labor-management friction. This test was passed successfully in the Long Range Sharing Plan through modifications of the 1961 formula made effective in 1966.

The Armour Automation Committee, established in 1959 by agreement between Armour & Company and two meat packing unions is a third example of new bargaining approaches. As a result of plant closings and large-scale employee displacement, the job security issue was prominent in the 1959 negotiations. A company proposal, incorporated into the union-management contract, was to establish a company-financed automation fund. The agreement also created a committee composed of four management representatives, two representatives from each of the unions involved, and a neutral chairman. A second neutral was later added as the committee's executive director.

The committee authorized a number of studies dealing with various displacement problems, and these were conducted by industrial relations experts recruited from universities. The studies provided valuable information on the economic plight of displaced workers as well as data for serious discussions of proposals to transfer displaced employees to other company plants. The committee also sponsored direct efforts to help former employees through a retraining program and assistance in finding new jobs. These efforts were relatively unsuccessful and further underscored the problems of middle-aged and older workers without jobs.

As a result of Automation Committee recommendations, a number of changes were written into the 1961 contract. The company agreed to give longer notice before closing plants, provision was made for transferring employees from closed plants to so-called "replacement plants," and the Automation Fund was to pay relocation costs as well as "technological adjustment pay" for displaced workers awaiting transfer. Improved severance pay and early retirement pay provisions were also negotiated.

The work of the Armour Automation Committee was not wholly a success, and the job security issue has continued to be an irritant in the labor-management relationship. Among the factors responsible for this have been the financial straits of the company which placed constraints upon the firm's ability to undertake more effective measures, complications created by differences between the two unions involved, and a long-standing union-management distrust which colored the deliberations of the committee. The recommendations of the Armour Automation Committee, nevertheless, eased some of the hardships of displacement; and the labor-management effort to deal with the problem was probably more fruitful than it would have been in the absence of the committee's work.

Other examples of new approaches to collective bargaining can be drawn from the recent history of industrial relations; but these, for the most part, are variations of the procedures described above. In these experiments that are attempting to modernize the bargaining process, one or more of the following are usually involved:

1. Continuing efforts to resolve the problems of the workplace
2. The use of special committees to deal with difficult issues
3. A willingness to utilize the talents of third party neutrals
4. Use of fact-finding or special study arrangements to provide the data essential for a serious consideration of technically difficult problems

In 1966 and the years immediately ensuing, the economic pressures that had weighed upon the bargaining process abated and collective bargaining tended to revert to its "normal" forms. By the end of the 1960's, relatively little was heard about hard line bargaining and the enthusiasm generated by the continuous bargaining arrangements had become subdued. These developments have prompted some observers to conclude that both hard line bargaining and the novel problem solving approaches were responses to specific problems rather than fundamental turns in American industrial relations. It may be too early to render final judgment on the bargaining history of the period that extended roughly from 1958 to 1965. Perhaps the most significant lesson of the period is that the bargaining parties showed a capacity to reach out for new ways to surmount challenges. The mixed record, however, provides quotable data for those who are pessimistic as well as those who are optimistic about the future of collective bargaining in the United States.

AUTOMATION AND COLLECTIVE BARGAINING

Automation of a facility will usually result in at least one of the following: (1) a sharp drop in the number of employees needed to perform an operation or to produce a given quantity of output, (2) a change in the types of skills needed to perform the work, (3) a restructuring of the way in which work is organized, and (4) a geographical relocation of the production or service facility. The general character of the employment impact of automation, thus, is similar to the impact of earlier types of technological change. There is a significant difference in degree, however.[2] The number

---

[2] The employment problems created by technological change will be discussed in Chapter 23.

of employees displaced by automated equipment, the frequency of plant closings, and the suddenness of occupational obsolescence have produced unusually severe wrenches in going patterns of industrial relations and are challenging the workability of collective bargaining. The more pessimistic opinion is that collective bargaining, like the old plant and the old occupation, is obsolescent and that labor organizations must look for political solutions to the problems facing workers.

The long run effectiveness of collective bargaining in facilitating a necessary accommodation to a new technology will be established, of course, by the experience of the future rather than the debates of today. It is already apparent, however, that the processes and the contents of bargaining have been influenced by automation in significant ways.

In the usual bargaining situation, the union seeks to liberalize wages and other benefits through contractual change while management plays the defensive role of holding the line. Automation has led to a certain amount of switching in these traditional roles. The installation or prospective installation of automated equipment frequently forces long-standing labor-management contentions over work rules and featherbedding practices to the surface.[3] Management, preoccupied with questions of efficiency, tends to see work rules as a sort of debris that must be swept aside in order to exploit fully the potential of a new technology. Unions, alarmed by the threat to job security, are more concerned with hedging about and controlling the employment impact of automation. In the work rules confrontation, thus, management is on the offense while unions are forced, by the nature of the issue, into a defensive role.

Even apart from the fact of a management offensive, automation, not infrequently, creates a conflict-prone work environment. Disputes over such matters as seniority rights, severance pay practices, supervisory responsibilities, and production standards tend to increase both in volume and intensity. As noted in the last chapter, the number of work stoppages caused by "plant administration" disputes has risen, and a further rise is anticipated.

To a considerable extent, the supplements to traditional bargaining practices discussed in the last section are a response to the conflict engendered by a changing technology. Bargaining under strike deadline pressures and with limited data has obvious defects as a method of dealing with the complexities and the volume of issues raised by drastic changes in the work process. The continuing bargaining arrangements and specialized *ad hoc* committees are, in essence, devices to facilitate labor management accommodation by adjusting the bargaining process so as to improve its

---

[3] Briefly, "work rules" can be defined as prevailing practices which limit management discretion in matters of plant administration. "Featherbedding" refers to the situation wherein employees are paid for unnecessary work or for work not performed.

efficiency in dealing with the special characteristics of "automation induced" problems.

Insofar as the content of collective bargaining is concerned, the most pronounced impact of automation is found in the growing emphasis upon job security and income protection provisions. A recent Bureau of Labor Statistics report listed the following approaches that have been used to protect against the effects of a new technology: (1) guarantees against job or income loss and in some cases against loss of supplementary benefits for varying periods, (2) compensation for employees who lose their jobs, (3) guaranteeing income for workers required to take lower-paying jobs, (4) provisions for retraining, (5) provisions for transfer to other plants and payment of relocation expenses, (6) agreements to provide workers with notice of plant closings or other major changes.[4]

The Mechanization and Modernization Agreement signed in 1960 by the Pacific Maritime Association and the International Longshoremen's and Warehousemen's Union has been one of the most publicized of the labor-management efforts to adjust to technological change.[5]

In return for a relatively free hand to eliminate restrictive work practices and to introduce more mechanization, the employers agree that no class *A* longshoreman will be subject to layoff due to changed cargo-handling methods.[6] Various guarantees are provided against income loss when reduced working time is attributable to mechanization, and provisions are made for early retirement benefits as well as lump sum payments to those who continue to work until normal retirement age.[7] For financing the various employee benefits, the plan provides for annual employer payments of $5 million for five and one-half years to a special trust fund.

Several features of the agreement are noteworthy. First, it followed from a union recognition that its choice was to continue an increasingly ineffective guerrilla-type resistance against mechanization or to accept mechanization and to attempt to "buy" benefits through such an acceptance. The acceptance of technological change was consistent with the approach that the larger number of American unions are following. Out and out opposition to technological innovation is relatively rare in the contemporary situation. Most of the labor organizations, instead, are seeking arrangements to cushion the shock of labor displacement or, as in the

---

[4] United States Department of Labor, Bureau of Labor Statistics, *Recent Collective Bargaining and Technological Change* (BLS Report No. 266, March, 1964).

[5] Strictly speaking, the agreement here was for adjustment to mechanization rather than automation. The technical nature of automation is discussed in Chapter 23.

[6] Fully registered or *A* men have first preference for all work on the docks. Partially registered *B* men are those working to become fully registered. "Casuals" are those who work on the docks occasionally and have last call on available work. Only the *A* men hold union membership.

[7] For details of the agreement see Lincoln Fairley, "The ILWU-PMA Mechanization and Modernization Agreement," *Labor Law Journal*, July, 1961, pp. 664–680.

case of the longshoremen, are seeking to get something in return for a receptivity to mechanization or automation.

An interesting aspect of the agreement is that part of the employers' contribution is explicitly identified as a payment to "buy out" restrictive work practices. The difference between this approach and that followed in the Kaiser Long Range Sharing Plan should be noted. In the latter plan, the special employee payments are regarded as the workers' share of the company's progress. The decision to use a "buying" rather than a "sharing" approach in the longshore case was made in view of the unusual difficulties involved in measuring productivity gains in longshoring work and the interest of the employers in instituting the plan without prolonged delay. Liberalized severance payments found in other collective bargaining contracts can be thought of as payments to buy out the employee's right to a job, although it is rarely admitted that this is what is involved. The "buying out" approach has led to interesting, if inconclusive, debates over whether the employee enjoys a property right in his job.[8] The important fact, though, is that certain types of adjustment to technological change, in fact, treat the job as a form of employee property.

A final point to be mentioned here concerns a broader implication of adjustments to technology through collective bargaining. Although it is difficult to read a pattern into what is a fluid situation, the longshore agreement is similar to many others in its job security characteristics. The employer, in return for union acceptance of new production methods, guarantees job security to regular full-time employees. The problem of surplus workers is met gradually through normal attrition. The employment effect of automation, thus, is made to incide less upon job holders than upon the job seekers.

COLLECTIVE BARGAINING IN PUBLIC EMPLOYMENT

Since the end of World War II, employment in government has grown faster than in any sector of the private economy. About 9.5 million persons now hold local, state, or federal jobs, and together they account for over 15 per cent of total non-agricultural employment. The upsurge in public employment has been associated with a growing interest in collective bargaining on the part of those who work in the public sector. This development has led to a re-examination of long-standing ideas concerning the

---

[8] William Gomberg, "The Work Rules and Work Practices Problem," *Labor Law Journal,* July, 1961, pp. 643–657; Simon Rottenberg, "Property in Work," *Industrial and Labor Relations Review,* April, 1962, pp. 402–405. See also the comment and the reply on Rottenberg's article in *ibid.,* January, 1963, pp. 279–288.

feasibility of collective negotiations in the absence of a private employee-employer relationship.

Growth in union membership among public employees has been rapid in recent years. By 1966, 1.7 million belonged to national or international unions, double the number of a decade earlier. About 645 thousand of the total were state and local public employees. Over one-third of the 2.7 million federal employees belong to employee organizations with the heaviest concentration of members being in the Post Office Department. Exclusive of postal workers, 21 per cent of the classified federal employees belong to labor organizations which have won exclusive bargaining rights within various government agencies. Prominent among the unions representing non-federal public employees are the International Association of Firefighters, The American Federation of Teachers, and the American Federation of State, County, and Municipal Employees. The latter is the largest of the unions representing non-federal employees. One of the fastest growing unions in the United States, the AFSCME with 400 thousand members is, at the time of this writing, the eighth largest affiliate of the AFL-CIO. In addition to these unions which are all affiliated with the AFL-CIO, there are a number of independent organizations of public employees as well as locals affiliated with unions such as the Teamsters, the International Brotherhood of Electrical Workers, and the Communications Workers of America.

Can the methods of collective bargaining be effectively utilized by public employee organizations such as those mentioned above? Opinions differ, and those who are skeptical usually ground their arguments in legal considerations and in the nature of management in the public agency.

The legal status of bargaining in the federal service was clarified—and, incidentally, bargaining was encouraged—by Executive Order Number 10988 signed by the late President Kennedy in 1962. The order specified that employees of the federal government shall have the right to form, join, and assist any employee organization or to refrain from any such activity without fear of penalty or reprisal. Three types of recognition for employee organizations are provided. Under *informal recognition*, an organization may be permitted to present its views to appropriate officials on matters of concern to its members. An agency, however, is under no obligation to consult with the organization. Informal recognition, thus, amounts to little more than the long prevailing practice in many agencies of receiving employee views and giving them such consideration as the agency heads may choose to give. *Formal recognition* is accorded to employee organizations that have "a substantial and stable membership of no less than 10 per centum of the employees in the unit." With formal recognition, an organization is entitled to be heard by an agency on personnel and working condition questions, and the agency must consult with the organization from time to time on such matters. An employee organization is accorded *exclusive recognition* when it has been designated by a majority of employees in a unit as their bargaining representative. The exclusive representative is entitled to negotiate an agreement covering all the employees in the unit, and such an agreement may include provision for "advisory arbitration." Bargaining is subject to a number of constraints including prohibition of strikes and various provisos concerning the content and administration of agreements. All agreements, for example, must conform to existing or future federal laws as well as the standards of the Civil Service Commission. This means that subjects such as salaries, hours of work, and vacation benefits are excluded from bargaining.

Among the states, legal policies vary considerably. A few prohibit organization of public employees, and a few others prohibit negotiations between public employers and their employees. Fourteen states, on the other hand, specify by statute that public employers must recognize and negotiate with organizations chosen by their employees.[9] In most other states, employees have been granted the right to organize as well as the right to present proposals and grievances through their organizations. Certain of these laws, however, limit such rights to special occupational groups such as firefighters, policemen, and transit system employees. Almost all relevant statutes prohibit strikes by public employees. At the state and local level, then, the law has been increasingly receptive to collective bargaining by public employees although the situation is spotty and a number of states maintain formidable barriers against bargaining.

Another strand of the argument that collective bargaining is poorly suited for public employment stresses the differences between management in the public and private sectors. Since the management of a public agency lacks the authority to make binding commitments on salary and other major terms of employment, questions have been raised about how meaningful collective bargaining can be.

Despite the considerable legal and technical barriers, a substantial amount of bargaining on behalf of public employees has occurred. Hundreds of agreements are currently in force, a number of them providing for exclusive recognition, grievance procedures, binding arbitration, and union security. Strikes by public employees, furthermore, have occurred in the face of the legal proscriptions. Actual bargaining practice, as Wildman has noted, has moved ahead of formally expressed policy in providing public

---

[9] For a summary of the more comprehensive state laws dealing with recognition and bargaining rights of public employee unions see Joseph P. Goldberg, "Labor-Management Relations Laws in Public Service," *Monthly Labor Review,* June, 1968, pp. 54–55.

employees with many of the major features of bargaining in the non-public sector.[10]

The manager of a public agency, of course, lacks the authority of the private manager to make agreements or commitments on economic issues. In many cases, however, a degree of discretion is present in the allocation of budgeted funds, and within the range of discretion, public employee organizations have enjoyed some success in influencing the allocative decision. A board of education, for example, might have the option of spending part of its budget for higher salaries, library additions, visual aids, or an experiment in teaching methods. A teacher's union in this case might be able to exert persuasive pressures in favor of increased expenditures for salaries. Even when the possibility of achieving economic gains through agency level negotiations is non-existent, pressures and threats applied at the bargaining table can be effective supplements to appeals directed primarily to legislative bodies or the general public. It is not completely persuasive, in other words, to argue that public employee bargaining is meaningless because of the limits of managerial authority in the public agency.

The experiences of the unions of public employees are still too brief to support any conclusions about how successful these organizations will be in adapting the collective bargaining method to the special circumstances of public employment or in supplanting the organizations that have traditionally spoken for the public servant. Enough has occurred, however, to challenge the generalization that bargaining methods are totally inappropriate. In the federal services where there are severe limits upon bargaining over economic issues, employee organizations will continue to rely mainly upon time honored lobbying procedures to exert pressures for economic gains. The Presidential executive order, however, will undoubtedly encourage the development of formal grievance procedures in a number of agencies; but it remains to be seen how effective these procedures will be.[11]

One of the most perplexing problems generated by the rise of public employee unionism has been the resort to the strike weapon by organizations of government employees. Although all relevant statutory and common law has declared such activity to be illegal, there has been an increasing use of strikes by public employee unions.

The usual arguments against extending to public employees the same

---

[10] Wesley A. Wildman, "Collective Action by Public School Teachers," *Industrial and Labor Relations Review,* October, 1964, pp. 4, 5.

[11] See Harry R. Blaine, Eugene C. Hagburg, and Frederick A. Zeller, "The Grievance Procedure and Its Application in the United States Postal Service," *Labor Law Journal,* November, 1964, pp. 725–735.

striking rights enjoyed by those in the private sector rest, mainly, on the grounds of sovereignty and the essentiality of many government services. Lawmakers responsible to an electorate, according to the first argument, possess the ultimate authority to set the terms and conditions of public employment. The direct challenge to the processes of representative government which is inherent in a strike, consequently, must not be permitted. In addition to this point, it is contended that certain government services are essential, not available through alternative sources of supply, and must be provided without interruption.

These arguments are not air tight. As Hildebrand has noted, once public employees are conceded the right to bargain collectively over terms of employment, the sovereignty of the lawmaker, by that fact, has already been dented.[12] In the matter of the essentiality of government services, not all services are on a par. The consequences of a strike by file clerks in an auto license bureau or tennis instructors in public parks are of a quite different order from strikes by policemen, firemen, or refuse collectors. These differences have led to suggestions that the right to strike be accorded to certain public employees but denied to others. It is doubtful, however, that such a division would be feasible, and the observation that a breach in the no-strike principle for public employees would invite its total destruction is probably correct.[13] Whatever the merits of the various arguments, the experience of the past several years has produced no groundswell of opinion favoring a repeal on the legal ban of public employee strikes. At the same time, no effective methods have been devised to deal with the strikes that occur or to resolve the bargaining impasses that lead to strikes.[14]

Experience with punitive measures has revealed the shortcomings of the very harsh approach—public officials are reluctant to invoke penalties against strong unions because of the danger of political reprisal. The common penalty in public employee anti-strike legislation, furthermore— termination of the striker's employment—is not a practical remedy when large numbers of employees in an essential service are involved.[15]

---

[12] George Hildebrand, "The Public Sector," in John T. Dunlop and Neil W. Chamberlain (eds.), *Frontiers of Collective Bargaining* (New York: Harper and Row Publishers, 1967), p. 139.

[13] A. H. Raskin, "The Revolt of the Civil Servant," *Saturday Review,* December 7, 1968, p. 30.

[14] A Gallup poll published on January 13, 1969, showed 65 per cent of the respondents opposed in principle to strikes by policemen and 60 per cent opposed to strikes by public school teachers.

[15] New York State's Condon-Wadlin Act as originally passed in 1947 provides a good example of the punitive approach. The law stipulated that striking employees were to be automatically released, were to be reemployed only under conditions that prohibited pay increases for three years, and were to remain on probationary status for five years. Although applied in several cases in upstate New York, the law was never invoked in New York City which has been so beset by public employee work stoppages. It is significant, however, that the milder Taylor Law which replaced Condon-Wadlin has not been an effective strike deterrent in New York City.

Compulsory arbitration is a popular proposal for resolving impasse situations but this approach runs into the problem of a clash of authority between the arbitrator and the lawmakers. In fact, when all the dispute settling techniques discussed earlier are reviewed in the context of the public employee stoppage, it becomes evident that there is no magic formula. While speculation is hazardous, what will probably develop over time is a complicated system of mediation and fact-finding procedures with special adaptations required by the unique characteristics of public employment. If experience in the private sector is any guide, this will prevent some stoppages and forestall others. But it is not likely to be totally effective.

THE CASE OF THE MILITANT TEACHER

In 1960, a student of the subject concluded that the foremost fact about teachers' organizations was their irrelevance in the national scene.[16] Seven years later, the superintendent of a large school system observed that collective bargaining in education was here to stay.[17] In this remarkably short time span, school teachers changed from one of the more passive to one of the most militant employee groups in the public sector and upset long standing notions about the reluctance of professional persons to use the methods of trade unionism.[18]

Underlying the spectacle of teachers organizing, striking, and negotiating are important developments that have occurred in the area of public education. Swollen enrollments have turned many school systems into educational assembly lines. At the same time, public preoccupation with formal education has intensified, and communities are demanding more from their schools. In the affluent suburbs, where large percentages of the students go to college, teachers are expected to prepare even the academically sluggish for successful college careers. In the city slums, teachers with no special training for the task are expected to educate children who are poorly prepared for formal schooling. Caught in a crush between community expecta-

---

[16] Myron Lieberman, *The Future of Public Education* (Chicago: The University of Chicago Press, 1960), p. 179.

[17] Lester B. Ball, "Collective Bargaining: A Primer for Superintendents," *Saturday Review of Literature,* January 21, 1967, p. 70.

[18] Self-employed professionals such as physicians and lawyers have been able to exert significant control over admission to the profession and the behavior of the practitioner. In the case of employed professionals, direct control over these matters tends to pass into the hands of administrators. Employed professionals, consequently, have tried to develop new techniques of job control such as lobbying and imposition of sanctions. While this veers toward unionism, the employed professional tends to disavow any relationship between his behavior and that of traditional trade unionism. As will be noted below, the confrontation between labor unionism and the professional association in the area of public education has had the effect of moving the latter toward a union-like behavior which it has disdained in the past.

tions and the paucity of resources allocated to education, teachers have lost a good part of their psychic income—in their case the general satisfaction that comes from performing an important task for society—and have turned more aggressive in their demands for higher money income.

Contributing to the growing militancy of teachers is the fact that more men are entering the teaching profession. By the mid 1960's, women were 65 per cent of the teaching population. Forty years earlier the percentage had been 83. Male teachers are now the majority in the senior high schools and are moving more and more into the junior highs and elementary schools. The new breed of teachers, that is, those who have entered the teaching profession within the past decade or so, has been described as better educated, less dedicated, and more pragmatic than its predecessors.[19] Resentful of the burdens of nonprofessional duties, threatened by educational demands that they have not been trained to meet, and intensely dissatisfied with the economic status of their profession, teachers have shown themselves as ready to embrace the methods of trade unionism for protection against the pressures that weigh upon them and for offensive action to improve their economic condition.

Complicating the labor relations situation in public education and also contributing to the militant state of mind among teachers is the rivalry of two organizations competing for the allegiance of the school teacher. The larger and more firmly established is the National Education Association, a professional organization of teachers and school administrators with a membership of about one million plus another 600 thousand who belong to state or local affiliates of the NEA. The American Federation of Teachers, a labor union affiliated with the AFL-CIO, had, at the start of 1969, a membership of about 150 thousand. Though relatively small, the AFT has more than doubled its membership since 1961.

In the contest between the AFT and the NEA certain of the differences between the organizations have eroded away and, at the school district level especially, many NEA affiliates have been behaving very much like labor unions. The rivalry has been described as less a contest between competing ideologies or between "professionalism" and "trade unionism" than a jurisdictional fight similar to the earlier contentions between the AFL and the CIO in the private sector.[20]

While it is true that the NEA has become more aggressive in its representation of teachers, it is premature to conclude that it has become just

[19] James Cass and Max Birnbaum, "What Makes Teachers Militant," *Saturday Review,* January 20, 1968, p. 56.

[20] Robert E. Doherty and Walter E. Oberer, *Teachers, School Boards and Collective Bargaining: A Changing of the Guard* (Ithaca, New York: New York State School of Labor and Industrial Relations, 1967), p. 41.

another type of union. The NEA has always been strongly influenced by its state affiliates and these, in turn, have been dominated to a considerable extent by school supervisors with rural and small town biases. While this situation is changing, the rates and degrees of change vary considerably among the states. It is noteworthy that the major successes of the AFT have been scored in the larger urban centers. Whereas the NEA has usually emphasized the mutuality of interests among teachers, supervisors, and school boards, the AFT has tended to stress a conflict of interests. Membership in local NEA affiliates is generally open to both teachers and supervisory personnel while membership in the AFT is usually restricted to classroom teachers. NEA pressures for improvements in teaching conditions have been focused, for the most part, at the state level of government whereas the AFT has tended to concentrate upon the school district. As noted above, these distinctions have been whittled away, to an extent, by the inter-organizational rivalry. At the time of this writing, however, it is difficult to forecast the ultimate impact of the rivalry upon the NEA, a complex organization made up of numerous semi-autonomous departments and loosely affiliated state associations.[21]

Whether represented by an NEA affiliate or an AFT local, teachers have demanded and won the right to negotiate collectively with local school boards in scores of communities across the nation. Although the most prominent demand has been for higher salaries, negotiations in various school districts have dealt with such matters as class size, curriculum, textbook selection, extracurricular duties, and even parking lot facilities. Certain of the agreements negotiated, such as the one between the Board of Education of the City of New York and Local 2 of the AFT are as detailed and comprehensive as most of the agreements found in the private sector.

Since the collective bargaining experience in public education is so young, many of the questions raised cannot be answered at the present time. School districts are dependant upon state financial support to a greater or lesser degree and where the dependance is high it is not clear that local level bargaining can be very productive in the absence of simultaneous and effective political pressure upon the state government. The subject matter of local level bargaining is also restricted in many areas by state control over the employment conditions of teachers. Since school districts are so varied in population size, income, and degree of dependance upon non-local

---

[21] The NEA's more aggressive stance on behalf of teachers dates back to 1961 when the New York City local of the AFT won representation rights for the teachers in that city. Subsequent AFT election victories in Philadelphia, Detroit, Chicago, Boston, and Cleveland shocked the NEA into a more militant posture and in 1965 it changed its policy of forbidding strikes by teachers.

sources of revenues, it is predictable that a considerable amount of variation will characterize the negotiating procedures that develop in the years immediately ahead.[22]

As in other areas of public employee unionism, the work stoppage problem in the schools has generated much public concern. Public schools were the most frequently struck government service in 1967 when 89 stoppages involving 96 thousand employees occurred.[23] These totals were approximately double those for 1966, and the latter year, in turn, witnessed more strikes in the public schools than had occurred in the previous ten.

The legal proscription of teachers' strikes has obviously been ineffective particularly in the larger metropolitan areas. Mass resignations and sanctions, furthermore, are other pressure techniques available to teachers which can be differentiated from strikes but, nevertheless, may be similar in impact.[24]

The problem of developing appropriate policy for strikes by teachers is similar to the problem already discussed in connection with public employee unionism. Whether the final answer will be found in the invention of new procedures, application of old techniques such as elaborate mediation or compulsory arbitration, toleration of strikes to the same extent as in the private sector, or some combination of these approaches remains to be seen.

What will be the ultimate nature of the emerging industrial relations system in the public schools? Here too it is only possible to speculate. Garbarino suggests that teachers' organizations will do their best to look and sound like professional societies but, if necessary, they will act like unions.[25] Recent experience indicates a diminishing reluctance to look and sound like unions.

---

[22] For a more detailed discussion of these issues see Michael H. Moskow, *Teachers and Unions* (Philadelphia: Industrial Relations Research Unit, Wharton School of Finance and Commerce, University of Pennsylvania, 1966), chap. 2.

[23] James T. Hall, Jr., "Work Stoppages in Government," *Monthly Labor Review,* July, 1968, p. 53.

[24] The "sanction" which is the NEA's preferred method of withdrawing or withholding services, may take any one of several forms. The mildest is the issuance of an "advisory" which informs NEA members that unsatisfactory conditions exist in a particular school system. The advisory does not include a request that members refuse to accept positions in the affected school district. A second form is an NEA request that members employed elsewhere not seek or accept positions in a school district until certain conditions are corrected. Beyond this form is the request that members already employed in the district as well as those teaching elsewhere not accept employment in the ensuing school year in the absence of corrective action by the district. An ultimate form, rarely employed by the NEA, is to associate the above request with a statement that members ignoring the request may be judged as guilty of unethical conduct and subject to censure or expulsion from the NEA. For a detailed description of professional sanctions see T. M. Stinnett, Jack H. Kleinman, and Martha L. Ware, *Professional Negotiations in Public Education* (New York: The Macmillan Co., 1966), chap. 6.

[25] Joseph Garbarino, "Professional Negotiations in Education," *Industrial Relations,* February, 1968, pp. 93–106.

QUESTIONS

1. Is collective bargaining a feasible method of dealing with employee-employer problems in the public sector of the economy?

2. It has been argued that high seniority employees have what amounts to a property right in their jobs and that they are justified, consequently, in demanding some type of payment when their jobs are eliminated. Do you agree with this proposition?

3. Is collective bargaining as traditionally practiced an obsolete technique for resolving the problems of the workplace?

4. Although strikes by public employees are illegal, they do occur. What policy options are available to public authorities for dealing with public employee strikes?

SELECTED READINGS

BARBASH, JACK. "The Impact of Technology on Labor-Management Relations," in Somers, Gerald G., Cushman, Edward L., and Weinberg, Nat (eds.). *Adjusting to Technological Change.* New York: Harper and Row, Publishers, 1963. Chap. 3.

DOHERTY, ROBERT E., and OBERER, WALTER E. *Teachers, School Boards and Collective Bargaining: A Changing of the Guard.* Ithaca, New York: New York State School of Labor and Industrial Relations, 1967.

HEALY, JAMES J. (ed.). *Creative Collective Bargaining.* Englewood Cliffs, N.J.: Prentice-Hall, Inc., 1965.

HILDEBRAND, GEORGE H. "The Public Sector," in Dunlop, John T. and Chamberlain, Neil W. (eds.). *Frontiers of Collective Bargaining.* New York: Harper and Row, Publishers, 1967. Chap. 5.

MACDONALD, ROBERT M. "Collective Bargaining in the Postwar Period," *Industrial and Labor Relations Review,* July, 1967, pp. 553–557.

PART FOUR

WAGE ANALYSIS

CHAPTER 12

The Wage Theory Problem

THIS CHAPTER AND THE THREE THAT FOLLOW WILL DEAL WITH WAGE problems. In this volume much stress has been placed upon the complexity of many labor issues, and it might be well to reiterate this emphasis here. The problems that center upon wage determination and wage levels have been debated at length by economists. In part this controversy can be traced to a lack of precision in the definition of the issues. More important, possibly, have been some fundamental disagreements over the explanatory significance of the orthodox theory of wages.

Part of the disagreement that arises almost naturally in the wage area stems from the fact that wages or the price of labor is payment for human factors of production rather than for inert factors such as raw material or capital equipment. Spokesmen for and sympathizers with labor have long resented having labor regarded or analyzed as a commodity. By legislation and by other means the transactions through which labor power is sold are hedged about with restrictions that reflect a concern with the human aspect of labor use. Nevertheless, so long as labor power is bought and sold on a relatively free market, this power remains a commodity to some extent, regardless of whether or not people would have it so. At any rate, the controversial elements in wage theory touch upon more subtle problems than whether labor can be regarded as a commodity. This chapter will be devoted essentially to a consideration of the difficulties that surround the development of a workable general explanation of the processes of wage determination.

EARLY WAGE THOUGHT

The employer-employee wage relationship has stimulated the production of a wage literature that dates back to the earliest years of the modern epoch. A good part of this literature is polemical and was or is designed to support the wage philosophies of various interest groups.[1] The special-pleading type of wage analysis, in fact, antedates the theoretical literature which for all practical purposes may be said to have begun with the rather eclectic theory in Adam Smith's *Wealth of Nations*.[2]

In his wage analysis, as in his treatment of other subjects, Smith anticipated the theoretical formulations of later economic writers. His observation, for example, that "Masters are always and everywhere in a sort of tacit, but constant and uniform combination, not to raise the wages of labour above their actual rate," was a forerunner of bargaining power wage theories that were developed in detail at a much later point in time.[3] Elsewhere Smith noted that although employers could not reduce wages below a subsistence level, in all but the growing economies high wages would eventually be forced by the growth of population back to "this lowest rate which is consistent with common humanity."[4]

Adam Smith's wage analysis was part of his effort to discover the laws of natural value of commodities. He believed that if he could uncover the natural value of the factors of production, including labor, he would have found the answer to the problem of commodity values. Later writers, however, among whom David Ricardo was the most prominent, were preoccupied with the economic laws which determine the distribution of output among the laboring, capitalist, and landlord groups.[5] In their hands, the subsistence theory of wages was elaborated into the formal proposition that wages in the long run would tend toward that level necessary to support a worker and his family. This conclusion was based upon the assumption that wage levels above subsistence would result in larger families among the working classes. The increased labor supply would then force wages back to the old level. When wages were below the subsistence level, labor supply would be reduced by starvation and disease, and this, in turn, would

---

[1] Much of the wage literature produced by the writers in the era of mercantilism, for instance, was essentially a special plea for a particular type of wage policy. See Edgar S. Furniss, *The Position of the Laborer in a System of Nationalism* (Boston: Houghton Mifflin Company, 1920).

[2] The historian of economic ideas can show, of course, that the basic strands of classical wage theory are to be found in writings that appeared earlier than the *Wealth of Nations*. See, for example, Michael T. Wermel, *The Evolution of Classical Wage Theory* (New York: Columbia University Press, 1939).

[3] Adam Smith, *An Inquiry into the Nature and Causes of the Wealth of Nations* (Modern Library ed.; New York: Random House, Inc., 1937), p. 66.

[4] *Ibid.*, p. 71.

[5] David Ricardo, *The Principles of Political Economy and Taxation*, 1817.

force the wage upward until it again became adequate for the support of life.

The subsistence theory, or iron law of wages, amounted to an application of Malthusian population theory to the question of income distribution. The share of the national product going to labor was that amount necessary to support the laboring classes at a subsistence level and, in the long run, could never vary substantially from this amount. Changes in the demand for labor could have no enduring effect upon the level of wages.

FIGURE 14

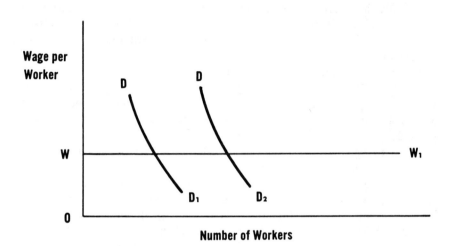

The basic proposition of the subsistence theory can be presented in simple diagrammatic form. (See Figure 14.) OW is the wage necessary to provide a worker and his family with a subsistence scale of life. WW_1 is the long run supply curve of labor. A change in the demand for labor (the movement of the demand curve from DD_1 to DD_2) might produce a temporary rise in OW, but the population cycle would always move it back to the subsistence position.

With a certain amount of elaboration and modification, a subsistence theory of wages can be used to analyze some types of problems in the underdeveloped nations. Because of its broad character and preoccupation with long run forces, however, it sheds little light on the determination of actual wage rates even in these countries. In what are now regarded as the developed economies, the subsistence theory lost its relevance through its failure to recognize the many factors other than food supply that might affect population growth. Ricardo's admission, furthermore, that habit and custom could influence the package of goods essential for worker subsistence was an important crack in the theory. If it is admitted that a subsistence wage is more than that necessary for the bare necessities of life, the theory becomes indeterminate as an explanation of wage levels, since it is consistent with any point within a range of possible levels.

In Volume I of *Das Kapital*, published in 1864, Karl Marx used a modified version of the subsistence theory. Marx was trying to show that exploitation of the working class was inevitable in a system of capitalism. His argument, though long and involved, can be summarized briefly. Commodities derived their value, according to Marx, from the amount of socially necessary labor time expended in their production. Under the capitalistic distributive system, however, only part of the value produced was returned to the worker in the wage payment. The worker, consequently, was being exploited. The difference between the total value of the product and what labor received in wages was "surplus value" or the amount by which labor was exploited.

What determined the actual wage paid to the worker? Marx' answer was that it depended in part upon bargaining power, and here he felt that all the advantage was with the employer, but that in greater part it depended upon the cost of a day's labor. This latter amount was a wage sufficient to enable the worker to perpetuate himself by raising a family.

This, of course, is a subsistence theory of wages; but it differs from earlier versions in that Marx explicitly rejected the Malthusian population theory. Acceptance of the Malthusian propositions, in fact, would have been disastrous for the Marxian analysis, because if population pressures operated as Malthus indicated they did, a socialistic economy could promise the laboring class no better fate than the dismal prospects described by the classical economists.

To explain the excess of labor supply that drove wages to the subsistence level, Marx relied upon the concept of an industrial reserve army. This was a group of jobless workers whose ranks would be swelled over time by technologically displaced industrial workers as well as by the small businessmen and farmers driven into the proletariat by the ruthless competition of the large capitalists.

Marx' analysis of wages was the most elaborate that had yet appeared. Like all subsistence theories, however, it understated the role of demand in the wage determination process, a point pressed home by later critics of the Marxian analysis.

Most of the subsistence theorists recognized that what they were propounding was a statement of long run tendencies toward a "natural wage." Shorter term demand and supply conditions admittedly might cause the market wage to vary from the natural wage, and an early explanation developed for the market level of wages was the "wages-fund" theory. The first statements of the theory appeared at the start of the nineteenth century.

A supplement to, rather than a replacement of, the subsistence theory, the wages-fund theory was advanced by numerous writers, and not all versions were consistent with each other. The discussion below will deal with the basic propositions rather than the details of the theory.[6]

"Wages not only depend upon the relative amount of capital and population, but cannot, under the rule of competition, be affected by anything else." This precise statement by John Stuart Mill in his *Principles of Political Economy* (1848) contains the essence of the wages-fund theory. At any given time it was assumed that there was (1) a capital stock of a given size designated for the payment of wages and (2) a wage-earning population also of a given size. The wage level, consequently, could be determined by the simple process of dividing capital stock by the number of workers.

Wages-fund theorists were not always clear about what they meant by "capital stock," and different writers defined such stock differently. Some regarded it as a supply of money which employers were prepared to spend on wages; others thought of it as a stock of consumption goods available for distribution, and still others, as fixed capital. In all the writing, however, there was agreement that the amount of capital available for wage payments was a firmly fixed quantity.

In the wages-fund theory, demand for labor assumed a more important role in wage analysis. Since the size of the wage-earning population could be regarded as stable over short periods of time, labor demand which depended upon the size of the wages fund could be regarded as the active variable in wage determination.

Like the subsistence theory, the wages-fund theory had important policy implications. According to the wages-fund premises, the level of wages could rise only if there were favorable changes in the size of the working population or the amount of capital stock in the wages fund. In the absence of such changes, efforts by workers to improve their incomes were doomed to failure. Particular groups of workers, through trade union power perhaps, might manage to win pay raises; but this could only be at the expense of other workers. Efforts by the working class to raise the total share of the national output going to labor would be self-defeating although the wages-fund theorists were never completely clear about why the share going to wages could not be increased at the expense of profits or rents.

As might be expected, the conclusions drawn from the wages-fund theory were unpalatable to many people; and after the midpoint of the nineteenth century there was prolonged debate over the theory's validity. Ultimately the debate resulted in the rejection of the theory by most of the prominent economic writers.

---

[6] The best full length treatment of the wages-fund theory is F. W. Taussig, *Wages and Capital* (New York: D. Appleton and Company, 1896).

The basic attack against the wages-fund notion focused upon the idea of capital as a fixed stock. If the amount of consumption goods available for distribution was a flow or the product of current production rather than a fixed stock accumulated from past production, there would be no basis for assuming rigidity in the amount available for distribution. If labor, for example, worked harder or longer in period *B* than in period *A*, there would be an increase in the size of the goods flow, and more would be available for distribution.

The major flaw in both the subsistence and wages-fund theories was in the narrowness of their orientations. Out of the totality of forces affecting wages in both the long and short run time periods, subsistence and wages-fund theorists concentrated upon selected aspects. What they presented as immutable economic laws, consequently, were really explanations of possibilities that might eventuate in special circumstances.

Viewed from this less embracing perspective, both theories are not without some analytical utility even in the contemporary period. Something roughly akin to a wages-fund notion, for example, can be used to explain the relationships between present consumption and future output. Visualize in this respect a self-contained agricultural community with a single staple crop. Depending upon how much is consumed and how much is saved for seed, output next year will be larger, equal to, or less than present output. If all of the current harvest is consumed, there will be no crop next year. At some level, in other words, current consumption can have adverse effects upon future output. In underdeveloped countries preoccupied with their rates of economic growth, this is an important fact that poses difficult problems for income distribution policy. From the standpoint of economic growth, it would be advantageous to treat increases in output as part of a capital stock to be devoted to still further increases in output; but where the level of consumption is extremely low, it is difficult to deny the working groups some share of the larger output even though this will limit the rate of future growth.

The examples cited above hint at the fact that subsistence and wages-fund notions have more relevance in the underdeveloped economies than in the modern and highly industrialized ones. The remainder of this chapter will concentrate upon the problems associated with wage analysis in the modern economies.

WAGE DETERMINATION BY MARKET FORCES

As suggested above, it would be stretching matters somewhat to suggest that there is a prevailing wage theory generally accepted by economists. The most widely discussed theoretical formulation is a set of postulates subsumed under the heading of "marginalism." The greater part of the recent discussion, however, has consisted of a variety of challenges levelled against the validity and the meaningfulness of the marginal approach. The purpose of the description and comments that follow is not primarily to debate the merits of marginalism but to illustrate the type of thinking that economists have done or are doing about wage theory and to stress the difficulties attached to the problem of developing a general explanation of wage determination.

A long-standing debate among contemporary economists centers upon the extent to which wages are market-determined and the extent to which they are influenced by institutional forces such as labor unions, legislation, and custom. By "market determination" we mean, essentially, that the interrelationships of the demand for and supply of labor are the important determinants of wages and that the wage, in turn, is important in the processes by which labor power is allocated among the various users of labor.

The prevailing market-place theory of wages is part of the body of neoclassical economics developed in the late nineteenth century and elaborated in the twentieth. In the former century economists, following the lead of David Ricardo, were preoccupied with the problem of distribution. Since it was assumed that full employment of economic resources was a normal condition and unemployment a self-correcting and temporary deviation from normality, major attention of the "orthodox" economists was directed toward the questions of how the economic product was distributed and whether the distribution was equitable. Out of this body of analysis, there eventually emerged an explanation of wage determination that with refurbishments and refinements continues to be the "market-force" explanation of wages at the present time.

The twin pillars of the market-oriented explanation of wages are the forces of demand and supply. The price of labor (wages) is determined, as are all prices, by the interaction of demand and supply pressures. Thus, in a labor market where workers are many and jobs few, wages will be low because of the competition among workers for the scant employment opportunities. On the other hand, where jobs are plentiful and workers few, wages will be high because of employer competition for workers. At some wage rate, the amount of labor supplied will be exactly equal to the demand; and when this rate prevails, the market will be in equilibrium—that is, no forces will be operating to force wages up or down. At any given time, wages might be above or below the equilibrium rate, but the latter rate is the norm about which wages tend to oscillate.

In Figure 15, the above discussion is summarized diagrammatically. *DD* is the labor demand schedule showing the demand for labor at all possible wage levels. *SS* shows the supply of labor offered for sale at all wage levels.

FIGURE 15

Labor Demand and Supply Schedules

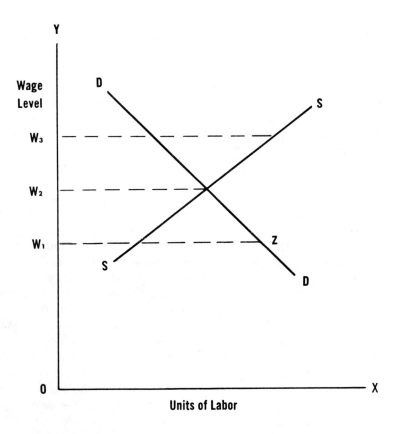

Units of Labor

At level W_1 the demand is greater than the supply. In analyzing what occurs in such a situation, it is important that a basic property of the demand schedule be kept in mind. The schedule is cumulative. At point Z, for example, those demanding labor consist of all who would be willing to pay a higher wage if necessary plus those who will hire only if wages are at W_1 or lower. Since there is not enough labor available to satisfy total demand at wage level W_1, employers will compete among themselves for what is available and in the process bid up the price of labor. In other words, at any level of wages below W_2 competition among employers will force the wage up. The same analysis can be applied to the supply schedule to show that at any wage above W_2 competition among workers will force the wage down. It should be clear, then, why W_2 is the equilibrium wage. At that point, the only buyers and sellers who have not made a bargain are workers who will work only for a higher wage and employers who will hire only at a lower wage. Neither of these groups can affect the prevailing wage level.

The Marginal Productivity Theory of Wages

In an earlier section of this chapter, it was noted that the subsistence theory of wages was built upon a base of certain assumptions about labor supply whereas demand assumed a more prominent role in the wages-fund theory. In modern economic analysis weight is assigned to both demand and supply forces. Until rather recently, what were regarded as the important characteristics of supply were summarized in a few bare propositions, whereas a quite elaborate theoretical structure was developed to explain the demand side. Increasingly, the casual treatment of supply has been called to question; and within the past few years there has been much empirical probing of various labor supply characteristics. Although it will be necessary to touch upon some aspects of labor supply in the present chapter, the main treatment of the subject will be found in the one that follows. The discussion below will concentrate upon the role of demand in the wage determination process.

The marginal productivity theory of wages consists of a body of propositions that purport to explain the employer's demand for labor. The demand for labor by the individual firm can be determined if three factors are known. These are (1) the supply of labor that is available at all possible wage rates (the labor supply schedule), (2) the product selling price, and (3) the net contribution to output by additional workers when all non-labor factors of production are held constant. We make one basic assumption about the employer's behavior: his goal is to maximize profits. Under the marginal analysis, the point of maximum profitability can be identified with reasonable precision.

If a unit of labor can be hired at a total cost of $1.50 per hour to the firm, and if the product of an hour's labor can be sold for $2.00, additional labor should obviously be hired because of the large gap between costs and selling price. In theoretical terminology, the *marginal revenue* exceeds *marginal cost*, and when this condition obtains, it is to the advantage of the employer to hire more labor. ("Marginal revenue" is the increment in the firm's income that results from the sale of the last or marginal unit produced. "Marginal cost" is the increment in cost that occurs when another unit of product is produced.) In the example cited above, the output of an hour's labor is worth $2.00, and as long as an hour's worth of labor time can be purchased for less than $2.00, the profit position of the firm can be improved by adding more labor.

Thus, the profit-maximizing employer hires workers as long as marginal revenue exceeds marginal cost. As he adds more and more workers, however, both cost and physical output are affected so as to narrow the difference between marginal revenue and marginal cost. Eventually a level of employment is reached where the two become equal; and at this point, it is no longer to the advantage of the employer to add more workers.

What causes the equality described above? For one thing, the effort to employ more workers might be associated with an increase in the average cost of a unit of labor power. To attract additional workers, the employer might find it necessary to offer higher wages; and if the rate paid to the marginal worker is higher than the rate being paid to workers hired earlier, the entire wage structure will probably have to be elevated. Marginal cost, in other words, will rise as the firm's work force grows in size. Marginal revenue will also be affected by the employment expansion because of the operation of the principle of diminishing returns. With a constant amount of capital equipment and entrepreneurship, the contribution to physical output by additional workers will eventually be less than proportionate. By this we mean that an increase in the size of the work force will not result in an output increase equal to that which resulted from a prior work force expansion of the same size. When "diminishing returns" set in, total output may be increasing, but it will be increasing at a decreasing rate. Another way to word this is to note that after a point the marginal physical product or the increment in output that is associated with the last worker hired will fall off, and a decline in physical output will result in a decline in marginal revenue.

Visualize in this connection a factory with a fixed and small number of machines. As the very first workers are hired, output will increase quite rapidly and in all probability at a greater rate than the increase in employment. As employment grows from, say, five to ten workers, output will probably more than double because the last five workers, in addition to manning the machines, can supplement the efforts of the original workers in many ways so that everyone is working more effectively. It is possible that output will continue to increase at an increasing rate if a few more workers are hired even after all machines are manned. The last or marginal workers might carry materials to and from the machines, relieve the machine tenders occasionally, and perform other services so that every machine is operated at maximum efficiency throughout the work day. Some point will be reached, however, when the contribution to physical output by additional workers will be less than proportionate to the production increments of workers hired earlier. At this point diminishing returns have set in, and as physical productivity falls off, so does marginal revenue. When the marginal revenue associated with a worker falls below the cost of employing that worker, the firm can no longer increase its profits by expanding employment.

So far the analysis has been carried on under the assumption that capital equipment is fixed in amount and labor quantity is capable of being varied. For the short run this is a reasonable assumption. In many firms, the amount of capital cannot be expanded or decreased with facility. Over the long run, however, the entrepreneur who wants to adjust his output has a choice. He can vary the amount of capital, the amount of labor, or both. If a firm is in disequilibrium—that is, if it can improve its position by changing the proportions and amounts of the factors it employs—the entrepreneur can apply the marginal principle when he chooses between capital and labor. The precise amount of substitution will be indicated by the relationships between prices and efficiencies of capital and labor. If $100 worth of labor will add x amount to the physical product and $100 worth of capital will add $2x$ amount, it is obviously to the firm's advantage to add additional units of capital and to substitute capital for labor.

The firm that is in long run equilibrium is one that can make no improvement in its economic position by substituting one factor of production for another or by adding more units of any factor.[7]

Wage Determination under Perfect Competition

By way of elaborating upon the marginal productivity theory of wages, we shall examine the character of labor demand in different market situations, starting with a perfectly competitive market. Although perfect competition is more in evidence in economic textbooks than in the real world, a competitive model is a useful analytical device for clarifying some basic relationships.

The firm operating in competitive product and labor markets can sell as much as it can produce at the going price and hire as much labor as it

---

[7] So long as the firms within an industry are in the process of adjusting proportions and amounts of productive factors or are experimenting with scales of output, the industry is not in long run equilibrium. Under the assumptions of competition, however, market-place competition is the great adjuster that pushes the industry toward equilibrium. Competition also explains the single industry–total industry relationship. Marginal adjustments accomplished by the mobility of capital and labor direct the entire economy toward a state of equilibrium in which relative advantages of one industry over another tend to disappear. The pure theory of marginalism, in other words, purports to explain the totality of the economic adjustments that tend to be taking place under the stimulus of demand and supply pressures.

The treatment given above of the marginal productivity theory of wages presents only the basic elements of the theory unfurbished by refinements. A number of more thorough descriptions are available for the reader who is interested in details. Readable accounts can be found in Harry A. Millis and Royal E. Montgomery, *Labor's Progress and Problems* (New York: McGraw-Hill Book Company, 1938), chap. 4, and in Paul Douglas, *The Theory of Wages* (New York: The Macmillan Company, 1934), chaps. 2, 3. A highly abstract but readable account by an early marginalist can be found in J. B. Clark, *Essentials of Economic Theory* (New York: The Macmillan Company, 1907), chap. 8. A good analysis of the theory can be found in Allan M. Cartter, *Theory of Wages and Employment* (Homewood, Ill.: Richard D. Irwin, Inc., 1959), Part 1.

wants at the going wage. This follows from the definition of the competitive market. Each firm produces so small a part of total output and uses so small a share of total labor supply that its variations in output and labor usage have no impact upon prices or wages.

In these circumstances, the wage in the relevant labor market—we shall assume here that it is a market for a particular industry—is determined by total industry demand and supply. The single firm, then, must hire on the basis of a going wage rate, and whatever the single firm does by way of hiring or not hiring cannot affect this wage. The marginal cost of labor, thus, is identical to the going wage rate. If this wage is $2.00 per hour, the firm can hire as much labor as it desires at that price, and the increment in total cost (marginal cost) associated with each employment expansion will remain a constant $2.00 per hour.

In the earlier analysis of the marginal productivity theory, we established the proposition that the employer would add labor up to the point where marginal revenue equals marginal cost. (Marginal revenue is the increment in output associated with the use of additional labor multiplied by the product selling price. We shall refer to this value as the marginal productivity of labor.) If marginal productivity is larger than marginal cost (the going wage rate), the firm should add labor, since the cost of the added labor is less than the revenue coming into the firm from the resulting expansion in output. If marginal productivity is less than marginal cost, the firm of course, could enlarge its profits by eliminating some part of its labor supply.

The importance of the principle of diminishing returns should be noted at this point. Assuming fixity in the non-labor factors of production, the increase in physical output associated with the use of a given amount of additional labor will, at some point of production, be smaller than the increase that occurred when there was an earlier expansion of the labor factor of the same magnitude. When this smaller output multiplied by the product selling price is equal to the going wage rate, the firm cannot improve its profit position by expanding or contracting employment.

The relationships discussed above are shown in Figure 16. *DD* shows the firm's demand curve for labor and is also a representation of labor's marginal productivity. If the going wage rate is $2.00 per hour, the firm should hire *OL* quantity of labor in order to maximize its profits. If the firm is using less than *OL* quantity, it can increase its profits by expanding employment. Beyond *OL* the cost of hiring labor is more than the revenue the firm receives from the sale of the increased output.

In the competitive market, then, the marginal productivity theory is an explanation of how much labor the firm will employ. Under the special assumptions of such a market and barring the possibility of a change in the physical productivity of labor, a higher wage will result in reduced

FIGURE 16

DEMAND FOR LABOR BY THE FIRM IN A COMPETITIVE MARKET

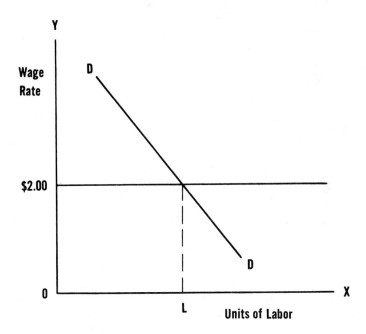

employment, whereas the contrary will occur if the wage is lowered. The amount of reduction or expansion will depend upon the elasticity of demand for labor which is a measure of the employment rise (fall) associated with a reduction (increase) in wages.

Demand for labor as pictured in Figure 17*a* is less elastic than in 17*b*. With a drop in the wage rate from $3.00 to $2.00 there is a relatively small expansion of employment in Figure 17*a* and a much larger expansion in 17*b*. Elasticity of demand depends upon many factors. In the competitive situation being discussed here, it would depend upon the rate at which marginal physical product is declining with the addition of labor inputs.

A caveat or so should be thrown in at this point lest too much be made of the conclusions concerning wages in the competitive market. First, we have been discussing a highly simplified version of the real world. Second, even within the limits of this discussion, conclusions about the wage rate–employment relationship must be tempered. Assume, for example, that there is a sudden increase in labor supply within an industry which forces

FIGURE 17

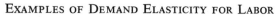

Examples of Demand Elasticity for Labor

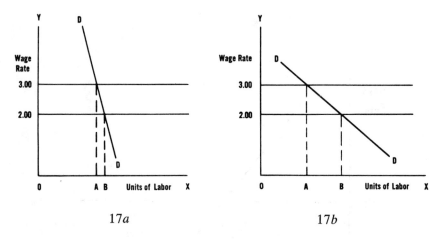

17a   17b

the wage down. The competitive model indicates that this will be associated with an increase in employment; but it will also result in an increase of total industry product output, and in order to sell the larger output it will probably be necessary to lower the product selling price. This, in turn, will affect the marginal productivity of labor; and the end result, depending upon the elasticities of demand for the product and for labor, may be little if any increase in employment.

Monopolistic Competition

In the early 1930's, books written by Edward H. Chamberlain and Joan Robinson were grasped eagerly by an economic profession hungry for a more realistic analysis of price determination.[8] Before this time the theory of price had been built up laboriously around a preconception of pure and perfect competition. Deviations from competition were treated as temporary aberrations or as incidental to the main body of theory. In a world where perfect competition was obviously less in evidence than non-competitive market conditions, the success of a reasonable analysis of "monopolistic competition" was assured.

Our concern here is solely with the implications of the theory of monopolistic competition for wage determination. The competitive analysis of

---

[8] Edward H. Chamberlin, *The Theory of Monopolistic Competition* (Cambridge, Mass.: Harvard University Press, 1933); Joan Robinson, *The Economics of Imperfect Competition* (London: Macmillan and Co., Ltd., 1933).

wages, as we shall see, was fitted rather easily into the new analytical models. Before approaching this wage theory, however, some essential differences between price determination under competitive and less than perfectly competitive conditions must be noted.

When competition is perfect, the output of a single firm is a small fraction of total industry output. What the firm does by way of expanding or contracting output, consequently, has no price effect. It is possible for the firm to sell as much as it can produce at the prevailing price. Should an attempt be made to sell at above market price, however, sales would fall to zero. This results from the fact that all firms produce identical products, and the consumer is indifferent to all considerations other than price.

FIGURE 18

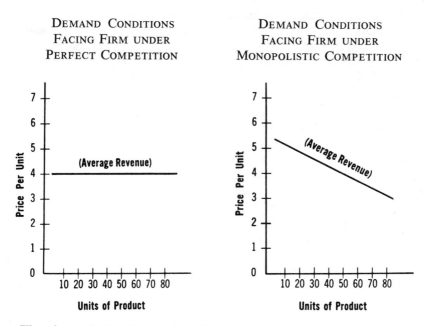

The demand situation facing the firm under perfect competition is shown in Figure 18. The price at which each unit can be sold is constant for the entire range of the firm's technical output capacity.

When competition is less than perfect, the demand curve for the firm's product has a slope. (See Figure 18.) This means that the entrepreneur has some discretion in pricing his product. He can sell more units at a lower price per unit or fewer units at a higher price. Unlike his counterpart in the case of perfect competition, he will not lose all his sales if he increases price, since price is no longer the sole consideration in consumers' preferences.

Some consumers will continue to patronize the firm even if the price is higher than that of similar products because in one way or another the product has been differentiated from others. Products, in other words, are no longer regarded as perfect substitutes for one another.

In both the competitive and the monopolistically competitive cases the employer is presumed to follow the same pattern of conduct. His goal is to maximize profits or to minimize losses. Optimum output is indicated by that point where marginal revenue becomes equal to marginal cost or where the net value of the marginal unit produced is just equal to the additional cost incurred by producing that unit.

The difference in the theory of wage determination under competitive and monopolistically competitive market conditions lies in the different relationships between wages and selling price that develop in the two cases. In the competitive situation the value of each unit added by the marginal worker is equal to the units produced by non-marginal workers. Thus, if fifty workers produce 100 units that sell for $5.00 per unit (total value of output equals $500.00) and a fifty-first worker produces an additional unit that sells for $5.00, the value of the marginal physical product is $5.00. The marginal revenue or the amount added by the marginal worker is equal to the value of the marginal physical product. As we saw in the analysis of wage determination under perfect competition, employers will continue to hire workers so long as the wage rate at which workers can be hired is slightly less than (or possibly just equal to) the value of the marginal product. Another way of describing this is to note that under competitive conditions, the marginal worker can take his pay and, if he chooses, purchase the product he has produced.

When the product market is not perfectly competitive, the entrepreneur can sell a larger output only if he lowers selling price (Figure 18). Because of this fact there is a divergence between the value of the marginal product and marginal revenue. In order to determine the net amount of incremental revenue that the firm derives from the efforts of the marginal worker, it is necessary to consider the effect of the lower selling price necessitated by the attempt to sell the larger output. Returning to the example in the paragraph above, if it is necessary to lower the price to $4.00 per unit in order to dispose of 101 units, the total revenue becomes $404. The value of the marginal physical product is $4.00, but marginal revenue is $-96.00 ($404. – $500.). It is obvious that an additional worker will not be hired in this case.

Let us now assume a less extreme slope to the firm's demand curve. If 101 units can be sold at a price of $4.98 per unit the firm's total revenue becomes $502.98. The value of the marginal physical product is $4.98, but marginal revenue is only $2.98 ($502.98 – $500.00). The contribution to the income of the firm that can be attributed to the marginal worker is

$2.98, and this becomes the maximum wage rate for the pertinent amount of labor time that the firm will pay. In this case it should be noted that the worker's wage is no longer equal to the value of the product he produces.

The marginal productivity theory of wages was, in part, the academic economists' answer to the Marxian thesis that workers were exploited under a system of capitalism. Under competitive market conditions, the last worker hired, or the marginal worker, earns enough to buy back the product he produces. Since, under an assumption of homogeneity of labor, any worker can be considered the marginal worker, no exploitation can be said to exist, because any worker receives wages equal to the value of what he produces. When the market is not perfectly competitive, however, the wage is no longer equal to the value of the marginal product, and some wage analysts have described this situation as "exploitation."

This is highly abstract interpretation of exploitation, as was the earlier argument that no exploitation existed under competitive conditions. A cursory examination of wage structures, for instance, will show that the highest wages are earned and the highest living standards enjoyed by workers in those industries characterized by non-competitive product markets. Where produce markets are highly competitive, on the other hand, workers generally fare the poorest. The sharp divergence between exploitation as defined by economic theory and exploitation as defined by prevailing standards of economic welfare has resulted in a stripping away of the ethical connotations of wage theory. Once highly steeped in matters of ethics and equity, wage theory has become almost exclusively a tool for description and analysis.

Monopsony

Numerous combinations of product and labor markets can be identified. On the product side the usual classification distinguishes among many sellers of undifferentiated products (competition), many sellers of differentiated products (monopolistic competition), few sellers (oligopoly), and a single seller (monopoly). On the labor market side, there may be one, few, or many firms seeking labor, and labor may be supplied competitively or under some degree of control through either legislation or union organization.

Our analysis of the competitive and monopolistically competitive markets can be applied with little or no change to most of the possible competitive combinations that can be derived from the product and labor markets identified above. Let us assume, for example, that there is competition in the product market but monopoly on the labor supply side, a situation sometimes encountered when a strong union is present in an industry made up of many small employers. If the union insists upon a wage that is higher than what would result from the interaction of free demand and supply pressures, employment in the industry would decline. (Diagrammatically, this can be shown very simply. Return to Figure 16 and insert a horizontal labor supply schedule at a rate higher than $2.00 per hour.)

In most of the market situations, an artifically imposed wage increase, everything else remaining equal, would produce a reduction in employment. There are, however, several situations in which this might not be the case. One, the oligopolistic product market, will be analyzed in the latter part of this chapter. Another, the monopsonistic market, is discussed below.

Monopsony is that situation where there is only one buyer in the market. Pure monopsony in the labor market is relatively rare, but approximations can be found in the one-company town where workers who do not want to move have little choice other than to work for the only large-scale employer in the area.

In the case of labor market monopsony, the labor supply curve for the firm is identical to the aggregate labor supply curve. If the employer, thus,

FIGURE 19

LABOR DEMAND IN THE MONOPSONISTIC MARKET

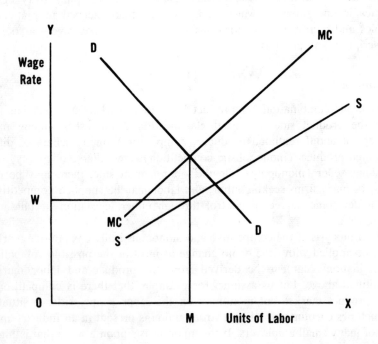

reduces his demand for labor, competition among workers for the available jobs will drive the wage down. To expand the labor force, on the other hand, the employer will have to raise his wage offers to attract additional labor.

Since an increase in the supply of labor is associated with rising wages, the marginal cost of labor lies above the labor supply curve. Profits are maximized at the point where marginal cost intersects the employer's demand curve for labor and in the monopsony case this means that there is a gap between the wage and the value of labor's marginal product. These relationships are pictured in Figure 19. *DD* is the labor demand curve and shows the value of labor's marginal product. The intersection of *MCMC* and *DD* identifies the point where the value of the marginal product equals marginal cost. The firm maximizes its profits by using *OM* units of labor at a wage rate of *OW*.

Assume now that a labor union succeeds in organizing the workers and proceeds to bargain for a higher wage. This situation is usually referred to as bilateral monopoly, because there is now a single buyer and a single seller of labor. The precise wage that is negotiated will depend upon the relative bargaining strengths of the employer and the union. We shall assume here a final settlement at wage level W_2 in Figure 20. S_2 is the new labor supply schedule for the firm. It can hire all the labor it needs at that price but none at a lower price. S_2 is also the marginal cost curve, and the point of intersection between S_2 and *DD* is the point where the value of the marginal product equals marginal cost. As a result of union pressure, then, both the wage rate and employment will have risen. If, under the new labor supply conditions, the employer is using less than OM_2 units of labor, he is not maximizing profits, since he is operating at a point where the value of the marginal product is higher than marginal costs. Only if the negotiated wage is higher than the point of intersection between MC_1 and *DD* will employment be less than it was under the pre-union situation.

Market Forces in the Long Run and Short Run Time Periods

The marginal productivity theory is an attempt to explain how entrepreneurs, seeking to achieve the most advantageous combination of factors of production, vary the units of all factors employed until the cost resulting from the hire of the marginal units is just equal to the income added when that unit is hired. The price paid for the marginal labor unit is a variable that depends upon labor supply and labor demand. Demand in turn depends upon marginal productivity as explained above.

The description so far has concentrated upon wage determination by the individual firm; and, as we shall see shortly, it is here that the market

FIGURE 20

<small>EFFECT OF UNIONIZATION IN THE MONOPSONISTIC MARKET</small>

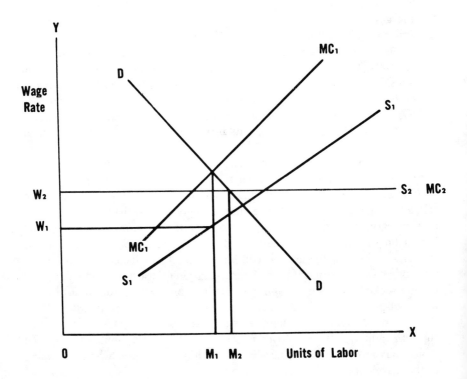

force explanation is least satisfactory. In the short run time period and within the individual firm, many factors that cannot be easily incorporated into a demand and supply explanation appear to be important in the processes of wage determination. The basic demand and supply propositions, however, can be applied to a longer run analysis; and, so applied, the theory can be helpful for certain types of wage analysis.

Over the long run, for instance, a pure demand and supply analysis provides a reasonably good explanation of the direction of the flow of labor throughout the economy. As we shall note in the following chapter, there are many impediments and frictions that hinder the job-to-job movement of workers. If we step back from short run observations to get a long run perspective, however, the general direction of worker movement over time has been away from the low productivity and low wage employments and toward the more productive and remunerative jobs. The market force explanation of wages would suggest that such a movement would lead to some wage improvements for the relatively unskilled workers; and, in fact, there has been a long run compression of the unskilled-skilled wage differential. There are several reasons for the compression, but the secular readjustments in labor demand and supply conditions cannot be written off as inconsequential. The inter-regional movement of labor has also been toward areas of greater economic opportunity or, in the terminology used here, toward the geographical areas where the marginal productivity of labor tends to be higher. These labor supply changes have not eliminated geographical wage differences, and an explanation of persisting differentials must be found in a host of dynamic factors that are not easily incorporated into a theory based upon static assumptions. An understanding of demand and supply pressures, however, will provide useful insights into the long run mobility characteristics of the work force.

The marginal productivity theory is also helpful as an analytical tool for identifying possible methods of raising the general wage level over time. Assume, as some versions of the theory do, that capital is fixed in amount, that the product is competitive, that competitive pressures have equalized wages in all employments, and that throughout the economy a prevailing wage rate is equal to the value of the marginal product. In these circumstances, the general level of wages can be increased only if the supply of labor is reduced or the productivity of labor is increased.

To put the above in terms of a concrete example, let us assume that the value of the marginal product of labor is equal to $1.50 per hour and that this is also the prevailing wage rate. If by collective bargaining or, perhaps, by minimum wage legislation a wage of $1.60 per hour is imposed upon employers, a reduction in employment would necessarily occur, since some workers would be contributing less to their firm's revenues than the cost of their hire. As workers are discharged, marginal physical productivity will rise. (This follows from the operation of the principle of diminishing returns.) When a point is reached where the hourly physical output of a marginal worker is worth $1.60, the employer will cease discharging workers. As corollary propositions it can be stated that if capital equipment is fixed in amount, an increase in the supply of labor will tend to lower the general level of wages, whereas a decrease in supply will tend to raise the level. (An intuitive understanding of these propositions, incidentally, explains why some labor organizations have opposed mass immigration in the past and why some highly skilled craft groups have tried to restrict the number who might practice certain skills.)

If, because of the intensification of worker effort, improvement of capital equipment, or better management, or for any other reason, the productivity of labor increases, an increase in wages becomes possible. Returning to the example used above, if something happens that raises the value of the marginal product of labor to $1.60 per hour, a wage rate of that amount can be imposed without unemployment effects.

Applied to the economy as a whole, the marginal productivity theory suggests that there are limits to the share of national income that can be distributed to labor, that the share is tied to the productivity of labor, and that an effort to go beyond the limits will have consequences such as unemployment. The theory rests upon assumptions, and to the extent that the assumptions fail to mirror reality the description of the consequences may be inaccurate. If, for instance, the economy is characterized by substantial areas of monopoly or monopsony, it may be possible to force wages upward without running into unemployment. The fact that the pressures of the market may be modified or offset to an extent does not establish the fact that the pressures are inoperative. Market forces, in short, cannot be ruled out as important determinants of the share of the national income that goes to labor and of the allocation of labor among the various employments.

THE CRITIQUE OF THE MARKET FORCE EXPLANATION OF WAGES

Many economists have expressed dissatisfaction with the marginal productivity theory of wages. Economic literature has become quite crowded with "disproofs," and numerous guideposts to a new theory of wage determination have appeared. There is little quarrel with the contention that market forces are significant over a long run time period, although the predictive value of a market force explanation even in the long run is blurred by the dynamic economic changes that are constantly affecting the characteristics of both labor supply and demand. The main attack upon an explanation of wages that depends primarily upon a demand and supply analysis, however, is that such an explanation has serious shortcomings as a short run wage theory. Some students even venture to say that we come perilously close to having no short run theory at all. The literature on the subject is extensive, and in this section some of the prominent arguments that have been made in the recent past will be summarized.

Employers Do Not Behave That Way

One strand of the criticism of marginalism places heavy emphasis upon the contention that the theory paints an unrealistic picture of entrepreneurial behavior. Businessmen, it is held, do not go about making calculations of marginal costs and revenues before adjusting output and employment levels. According to this argument, business behavior is best explained on grounds other than marginalism.

Professor Richard Lester has been one of the more ardent proponents of this point of view.[9] Basing his opinion, at least partly, on the results of a questionnaire survey of fifty-six southern firms, Lester has argued that the level of wage rates is given little or no weight by employers when they consider the size of their work forces. The answers given by the executive officers of the firms surveyed suggest that labor demand depends less upon the wage level than upon expected sales volume.

Lester has also challenged several other facets of the marginal theory. Businessmen, he holds, do not react to a wage increase by curtailing employment because they tend to associate a reduction in output with an increase in the variable cost per unit of output. Under the marginal analysis, it will be recalled, a reduction in output supposedly results in a decrease in average variable costs because of the less than proportionate contribution to output by the marginal worker. Most of the firms questioned by Lester, however, reported decreasing unit variable costs up to a range of 70 per cent to 100 per cent of capacity. Business firms, furthermore, are not likely to be in a position to substitute capital for labor with the facility implied by the marginal theory. Most industrial plants are designed and equipped for a certain output requiring a work force of a certain size. Under these conditions, management does not think in terms of adding or subtracting small units of labor except when it is a question of expanding plant and equipment or redesigning the plant.

The type of criticism described above, which incidentally has been made by others besides Professor Lester, is based upon an analysis of the subjective state of mind of the businessman.[10] Precisely what does the businessman think about when he adjusts his employment and output? The marginalist approach strongly implies that the businessman hopes basically for optimum

---

[9] See, for example, "Shortcomings of Marginal Analysis for Wage-Employment Problems," *American Economic Review,* March, 1946, pp. 63–82.

[10] There are other versions of the "businessmen don't behave that way" thesis. Reder argues, for instance, that not all entrepreneurs attempt to maximize profits. The following are cited as examples of non-profit-maximizing behavior: (1) the owner-manager of a small business desires to avoid managerial activity in order to spend less time at his business; (2) corporation executives are reluctant to disturb existing routines of colleagues and subordinates and thus hesitate to institute improvement; (3) management will sometimes tolerate inefficiency so long as the profit and loss statement is satisfactory. M. W. Reder, "A Reconsideration of the Marginal Productivity Theory," *The Journal of Political Economy,* October, 1947, pp. 450–458. Some economists have suggested that it would be more accurate to describe the firm as a "satisficing" rather than a maximizing organization. See Herbert A. Simon, "Theories of Decision-making in Economics and Behavioral Science," *American Economic Review,* June, 1959, pp. 262–264.

Hall and Hitch have suggested that a large proportion of businesses make no attempt to equate marginal revenue and marginal cost in any way that is reasonably close to the economists' description of the process. Businessmen, they allege, have a strong tendency to fix price on a "full cost" basis by which they mean that a conventional amount such as 10 per cent is added to the sum of fixed and variable costs. R. L. Hall and C. J. Hitch, "Price Theory and Business Behavior," *Oxford Economic Papers,* May, 1939, pp. 12–23.

income that would follow from the achievement of certain cost-price relationships. Given certain statistical data or sensing the nature of cost-price relationships when data are skimpy, the businessman, it is contended, will respond by varying his input factors in order to accomplish what he believes to be a profit maximization. The attack upon this analysis purports to establish that the businessman takes other factors—sales volume in Lester's example—as basic data for making employment decisions. The evidence cited by Lester can hardly be regarded as conclusive, but there is a similar paucity of evidence to substantiate the marginalist case. The contention of the marginalists is that the achievement of certain cost-selling price relationships is, in fact, an optimum position for the firm, and it is logical to expect the businessman to move in the direction of the optimum. The counter argument is that a demonstration of the logic of marginalism is no proof that a businessman *must* behave according to the logic.[11]

Employers Cannot Behave That Way

The argument that businessmen cannot make output and employment decisions on the basis of marginal calculations, except perhaps in a very rough fashion, has been based upon a variety of considerations. Among those frequently stressed are (*a*) the complex organizational structure of large business firms and (*b*) institutional or technical factors that impede the implementation of decisions that would follow from marginal calculations.

1. The firm pictured in the typical description of traditional economic theory is a highly simplified organism. Decisions are usually described as emanating from a businessman. The wage schedule implicitly consists of a single rate or a simple structure of rates. Selling price is pictured as a series of alternatives simple enough in nature to be graphically plotted as a continuous line. This is a misrepresentation of the large corporation where basic policy decisions are made by groups, tailored by other groups, and placed into effect by still other groups. The wage structure might consist of hundreds of job classifications—some carrying day rates, others piece rates, and some combining both types of remuneration. Labor cost, furthermore, also depends upon a host of fringe benefits. The cost to the company of some of these, such as paid sick leave, cannot always be calculated in advance. Selling price which might be expected to be a simple datum is often an elusive item. Frequently, list price is meaningless and true price is a complicated compound of discounts and special arrangements. Add to

---

11 H. M. Oliver, "Marginal Theory and Business Behavior," *American Economic Review,* June, 1947, p. 378. A more important point of the marginalist's argument is that the type of evidence cited by Lester is irrelevant; see pp. 340–342 below.

all this the complexities introduced by selling costs, such as advertising, and the joint costs incurred in a multi-product firm, and the precise calculation of anything resembling marginal cost and marginal revenue becomes impossible. Even a broad calculation becomes extremely difficult.[12] A business firm can be complex and still make employment decisions on the basis of some sort of input cost–output price relationship. An examination of the details of the corporate organizational structure suggests strongly, however, that the marginal analysis provides little sophisticated insight into the manner by which cost and price data exert their influences on employment and output decisions.

2. The influence of marginal productivity upon the wage level has been very much modified by the existence of a powerful and aggressive trade union movement. Those who argue along this line do not contend that unions somehow are responsible for a total divorce between wage rates and employment levels. The usual contention, instead, is that union practices create a range of indeterminacy in which there is considerable room for wage jockeying without the unemployment hazard.[13] Labor unions restrict the employer's right to make unilateral decisions in matters such as tempo of work, hiring, and firing and even to modify the rate at which capital can be substituted for labor. Seniority provisions, for instance, prevent an employer from promoting, discharging, or paying a worker on the basis of productivity alone. Thus, instead of the relatively fluid pattern of adjustments visualized in the model theory of the firm, the presence of a union introduces a set of rigidities that modify the wage pattern that would evolve from an application of the marginal productivity theory.[14]

Unions, as Belfer and Bloom point out, not only seek to make labor more expensive to the employer who uses it but also seek to make it expensive for the employer not to use labor.[15] Through featherbedding practices or dismissal wages, unemployment itself can become costly to an employer. Whatever the effect of these rules in the long run, they do becloud the process of wage determination and the effect upon employment of a given wage level in the short run time period.

A quite different illustration of the difficulties that attend the practical application of marginalism has been provided by Wilford J. Eiteman.[16]

[12] For an elaboration of these points see National Bureau of Economic Research, *Cost Behavior and Price Policy* (New York, 1943).

[13] See, for example, Nathan Belfer and Gordon F. Bloom, "Unionism and the Marginal Productivity Theory," in Richard A. Lester and Joseph Shister (eds.), *Insights into Labor Issues* (New York: The Macmillan Company, 1948).

[14] *Ibid.*, p. 249.

[15] *Ibid.*

[16] Wilford J. Eiteman, "The Equilibrium of the Firm in Multi-Process Industries," *The Quarterly Journal of Economics*, February, 1945, pp. 280–286.

The example that follows is taken largely from his statement of the argument.

A basic assumption of the marginal analysis is that the association between output and input is so close that an increase in output can be reasonably imputed to the increment in the variable factor. Although this might be an accurate representation of what occurs in industries such as mining, farming, or logging, it is questionable as a description of the multi-process industry.

Assume, for instance, that three men working in department A of a plant complete in one full day the first step on twelve products. Two men in department B work on these products for another day before the output moves to department C where one man finishes the work on all twelve products in one day. It can be seen from this example that the effect on production of withdrawing a marginal man depends upon which input unit is withdrawn. Removal of one man in department A causes a loss of four output units. In department B the loss is six units, while the removal of the single worker in department C results in the loss of total output. Putting a second man in department C would cause no expansion in output, since A would still produce only twelve units per day. Adding or subtracting a worker in any department or in combinations of departments will reveal a situation that is hopelessly complex. Eiteman concludes from this that an attempt to increase revenue by varying the number of employees so as to equate marginal cost and marginal revenue is not likely to be considered in the multi-process industry where the problems of departmental synchronization dwarf considerations of marginal efficiency.[17]

Analytical Limitations of Marginalism

Part of the recent economic literature of wage theory purports to demonstrate inadequacies of the marginal theory as an apparatus for analyzing certain real situations faced by business firms. Examples of specific and general shortcomings of marginalism in this respect will be described below:

1. The producer who operates in anything other than a perfectly competitive market can only guess what the demand for his product will be at prices different from the going price. The demand curve, in other words, is imaginary; and if a producer should change his selling price, the resulting sales might or might not meet his expectations.

A common relationship among sellers in the United States is what the economist calls an oligopoly. In this relationship there are a few rivals who sell products that are similar or that differ only slightly from each other in some respect. The seller in an oligopolistic market is aware of his sales

---

[17] *Ibid.,* p. 286.

volume at the prevailing price, but prospective sales at alternative prices are conjectural. An important unknown is the reaction of rivals to any price change that he puts into effect. If seller *A* raises his price, his rivals may refuse to follow suit. This might result in his losing customers to the rivals. On the other hand, if *A* lowers his price, competitors might match his price cuts rather than risk desertion by their customers. The possible result in this case is that *A* gains no new customers. Thus, an increase in *A*'s price might result in a loss of business (demand being elastic at any price above current price), and a decrease in price might result in no rise in sales (demand being inelastic at any price below current price). This situation is pictured in Figure 21. *DD¹* is the demand curve facing the oligopolist. *P¹* is the prevailing price and is located at the "corner" of the demand curve. The demand curve is kinked and characterized by different elasticities above and below the kink.[18]

FIGURE 21

DEMAND SITUATION FACING SELLER
UNDER OLIGOPOLY CONDITIONS

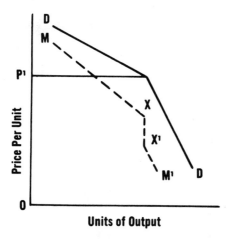

When there is a sharp change in the slope of the demand curve, there is a discontinuity in the marginal revenue curve. (In Figure 21, *MM¹* is the

---

[18] For a more thorough discussion of the kinked demand curve see Paul M. Sweezy, "Demand under Conditions of Oligopoly," *The Journal of Political Economy,* August, 1939, pp. 568–573; George Stigler, "The Kinky Demand Curve and Rigid Prices," *ibid.,* October, 1947, pp. 432–447.

marginal revenue curve. XX^1 shows the range of the discontinuity.) At any price below P^1, a sharp decrease in price will result in very little sales or revenue increase. Marginal cost, thus, might intersect marginal revenue at any point in the range of discontinuity without affecting the firm's price and output equilibrium. The *MC-MR* relationship does not pinpoint a unique employment-output level that represents an economic optimum.

An important implication that can be drawn from the analysis of demand under oligopolistic conditions is that a policy of price stability by the seller makes a good deal of sense. Instead of facing the uncertainties of a flexible price policy, the producer might prefer to leave price unchanged and attempt to push sales by non-price devices such as advertising or special services.

In these circumstances the number of persons to be employed will depend largely upon the sales volume achieved. Within limits, wage changes will have little effect upon employment. In contrast to the elastic demand for labor suggested by the marginal analysis (demand for labor increasing when wages are reduced), demand for labor under oligopolistic conditions might be relatively inelastic.

FIGURE 22

HYPOTHETICAL LABOR SUPPLY CURVE FOR THE FIRM

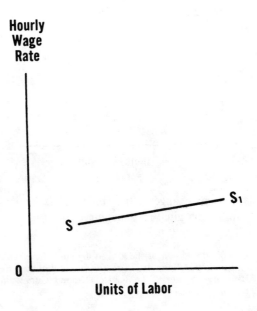

2. Another challenge to the analytical value of marginal theory is based on an examination of certain aspects of the labor supply curve.[19] The supply curve of labor is usually pictured diagrammatically as sloping upward and to the right. The vertical axis of the graph shows various hourly wage rates, and the horizontal axis shows different quantities of labor supply (Figure 22). The shortcoming of such a presentation is that the hourly wage rate does not show the real cost of labor to the employer, nor does it picture the measure of income in which the worker is primarily interested. The worker is concerned with take-home pay, whereas the employer is interested in labor cost per unit of output. Neither of these quantities is accurately described by hourly wage rates, since both take-home pay and unit labor cost can vary independently of hourly rates.[20] Take-home pay and unit labor costs, furthermore, can vary independently of each other.

The assumption that a unique labor supply is associated with each specific wage rate is also questionable, since it ignores some important realities of the working world. Rather large changes in output can occur with no change in the number of workers as a result of the labor force's working with greater or lesser intensity.

To underline the significance of these facts let us return briefly to a basic proposition of the marginal theory. The employer, it is assumed, will attempt to maximize profits by varying his output to achieve an optimum cost-price relationship. An equilibrium position—once achieved—can be upset by numerous factors such as changes in demand, changes in basic hourly wage rates, and changes in production techniques. In addition to these upsetting factors, the above analysis suggests that labor costs can change as a result of subtle changes in labor supply.

If a firm is to move—or to have a tendency to move—in the direction of equilibrium output it must be prepared to adjust output whenever these subtle cost changes occur. This means, for instance, that an increase in cost due to a decreased intensity of effort by the labor force should be followed by an output adjustment to re-equate marginal cost and marginal revenue. If the firm is to follow the necessary paths of instantaneous adjustments, these cost changes must become known to the firm as soon as they occur, and there must be an expectation that the new cost situations will continue indefinitely. If, however, the new costs do not become evident immediately and there is uncertainty about their duration, there is no reason to expect the firm to adjust output instantaneously. As a net result, the firm can

---

[19] An extended discussion of the argument that follows can be found in Lloyd Reynolds, "Toward a Short Run Theory of Wages," *American Economic Review*, June, 1948, pp. 289–308.

[20] Take-home pay, for instance, can be affected by changes in withholding tax rates, union dues, check-off arrangements, and premium pay for overtime work. Unit labor cost can be affected by such items as amount of absenteeism and various bonuses or premiums that are not constant but vary with the work circumstances.

adjust to upsetting factors over periods of time and by various paths. It might, for example, absorb the higher costs out of profits until the nature of the cost changes is more clearly understood. The firm may attempt to offset the higher costs by administrative efficiencies or try to raise product selling price. The marginal analysis, in such situations, loses its explanatory significance for short run adjustments.

3. An interesting case in which the marginal productivity theory does not indicate a unique equilibrium position for the firm can be described as the "economy of high wages" situation.[21] Under the assumptions of the marginal productivity theory, a firm that is forced to pay a higher wage will reachieve an equilibrium position by reducing its labor complement. In the case of workers living under very depressed conditions, however, higher wage incomes may result in substantial improvements in health. This in turn may so raise the productivity of workers that the firm suffers no increase in unit labor costs despite the higher level of wage rates. In underdeveloped nations or in certain sweated industries in the developed ones, there may be more than one equilibrium position for the firm because of the interrelationships between wages, productivity, and employee health.

THE DEFENSE OF DEMAND AND SUPPLY

In this chapter, demand and supply theory—or, more specifically, marginalism—has been presented as the most widely discussed theory of wage determination. Critical reactions to this approach have been detailed under broad headings that might be summarized as attacks upon the realism and the workability of the marginal theory. Spurred on by these attacks, defenders of the marginal analysis have responded with various arguments. Examples of these arguments are given below together with some comments on the merits of the respective positions:

1. One of the responses to the anti-marginalist arguments denies that any of the logic or facts set forth are inconsistent with the basic propositions of marginalism.[22] As long as it can be assumed that the business firm is engaged in a revenue maximization process, business behavior can be explained in marginal terms. The businessman will not follow a course of action when he believes that the resulting costs will be greater than the resulting revenues. Contrariwise it can be assumed that he will do those things that he believes will cause increments in revenue to be greater than

---

[21] See K. W. Rothschild, *The Theory of Wages* (Oxford: Basil Blackwell, 1956), pp. 19–21.

[22] Fritz Machlup, "Marginal Analysis and Empirical Research," *American Economic Review*, September, 1946, pp. 519–554.

increments in costs. There is nothing in the facts of monopoly or oligopoly that cannot be incorporated into the marginal framework of analysis. Even if businessmen explain their behavior in other terms, they must act in accordance with the propositions of marginalism if there is any rationality to business behavior at all.

Against the contention that the businessman does not have the information to equate marginal costs and marginal revenues, it is answered that "marginal analysis of the firm should not be understood to imply anything but subjective estimates, guesses, and hunches."[23] On the matter of employment levels, it is alleged that "there is nothing very exact about this sort of estimate. On the basis of hundreds of previous experiences . . . the businessman would 'just know' whether or not it would pay to hire more men."[24]

This defense of marginalism leaves the theory in a much attenuated form. Wage determination depends less upon the real relationships between costs and revenues than upon subjective guesses and hunches. Omitting the theoretical complications involved in considering the non-pecuniary motivations of businessmen,[25] there can be little quarrel with this presentation of "gross marginalism." It is not clear, however, exactly what is explained by so broad a definition of marginalism other than that, all things considered, the businessman prefers making money to losing money, and he will act to maximize revenues according to directives derived from his own subjective insights. Marginalism, in other words, can be defined broadly enough to be consistent with most of what goes on in the business world; but defined this broadly, it explains very little.

2. Critics of marginalism have made much of the fact that the theory is based upon unrealistic and oversimplified assumptions. Defenders of the theory have, in turn, attacked this line of argument.[26] The basic proposition in this attack is that a theory should be judged by its predictive value rather than by the realism of its assumptions.[27] Thus, the relevant question about marginalism is whether businessmen act *as if* they were seeking to

---

[23] *Ibid.*, p. 522.

[24] *Ibid.*, p. 535.

[25] The businessman, of course, might not be motivated by revenue maximization considerations. He might prefer the easy life and simply coast along in preference to busying himself with earning more money. Such factors can be incorporated into profit maximizing by taking the position that this is the way the particular businessman maximizes. Machlup notes, however, that "if *whatever* a businessman does is explained by the principle of profit maximization—because he does what he likes to do, and he likes to do what maximizes the sum of his pecuniary and non-pecuniary profits—the analysis acquires the character of a system of definitions and tautologies and loses much of its value as an explanation of reality." *Ibid.*, p. 526.

[26] Milton Friedman, *Essays in Positive Economics* (Chicago: The University of Chicago Press, 1953), chap. 1, "The Methodology of Positive Economics."

[27] *Ibid.*, p. 14.

maximize their returns and *as if* they had the necessary cost and demand data.[28] It is not necessarily a disproof of the theory to show that, in fact, businessmen do not have such data or even that they themselves describe their behavior in ways that are inconsistent with marginal theory.

This criticism merits serious consideration. No hypothesis can ever pretend to be completely realistic. The real world is sufficiently complex so that any hypothesis that attempts to incorporate all of reality will break down of sheer weight. Abstraction is an essential attribute of theorizing, and the process of abstracting involves making assumptions that will not accord perfectly with reality.

Carried to an extreme, however, the proposition that a theory should be judged by its predictive potentialities rather than by its outward realism can become absurd. If sufficient numbers of statistical correlations are made it might be found, for instance, that wage movements in the steel industry correlate more closely with mean monthly rainfall in western Europe than with any other statistical series. This farfetched example is cited to suggest that the substance of a hypothesis is rarely divided in toto from reality, and a matter of judgment is involved as to when assumptions are pertinent to the phenomena being analyzed. Furthermore, as has been pointed out, extreme assumptions by themselves do not guarantee a significant theory.[29] This brings the argument back to the basic point under consideration. How significant is the marginal productivity theory of wages?

One answer is that it depends upon the questions under consideration. The evidence cited in this chapter suggests strongly that in many instances marginalism is relatively useless as an explanation of short run wage movements. The specific patterns of behavior that are implied by marginal theory cannot be followed because of real or fancied impediments, and the specific consequences that are presumed to result when such impediments are present simply do not occur in many cases. Although these facts may not disprove marginalism, they do show that short run changes in wage rates cannot always be explained by the marginal apparatus.

There are, on the other hand, numerous situations in which economic phenomena are more adequately explained by demand and supply factors than by anything else. The most obvious explanation of the low wages that prevail in India as compared to those in the United States, for instance, is the relative abundance of labor and scarcity of capital in the former nation.

The basic shortcomings of the marginal analysis, perhaps, is that it provides few insights into the complexities of wage determination. As a very broad generalization it can be stated that demand and supply exert an influence on all wage bargains. When the process of wage determination

---

[28] *Ibid.,* p. 21.
[29] *Ibid.,* p. 14.

is observed closely, however, many other factors appear to have an important influence, and it becomes difficult to generalize from one wage experience to another. The future task of the wage theorist is to develop an analytical framework into which all the important variables that affect wages can be fitted. Such a system would make it possible to derive more meaningful generalizations about wage determination than can be derived from the analytical framework of marginalism.

BARGAINING POWER AND RANGE THEORIES OF WAGES

Two other approaches to a general explanation of wage determination have been featured in recent economic literature. In a sense these approaches are less wage theories than they are broad descriptions of some important elements that characterize the process of wage setting. Neither is completely inconsistent with marginalism, although both can be interpreted as attacks upon a narrow version of the marginal productivity theory.

Bargaining Power and Wage Determination

The bargaining power explanation of wages has as its central thesis the proposition that wage rates depend to an important extent upon the relative bargaining strengths of workers and employer. This is, of course, a fundamental strand of trade union wage philosophy. The idea that the individual worker is helpless when matched against the resources of the employer has been long used by union organizations attempting to sell themselves to potential members.[30]

The concept of power is quite subtle, and statements of the power theory are not always explicit as to the precise dimensions of the power concept involved. In one sense, the marginal productivity theory is a power theory. In the case of perfect competition, at least, it is the power of impersonal market forces that operates to inhibit employers from paying less or workers from receiving more than is warranted by the value productivity contributions of labor. The contention inherent in the bargaining power theory, however, is that *men, rather than the market,* bear a good deal of the responsibility for wage rates being what they are.

If there is validity to the bargaining power theory, there must be some degree of invalidity to the marginal productivity theory as a short run wage

---

[30] For the classic descriptions of how the totality of economic forces bears down to depress workers' wage rates, and hence their living standards, see Sidney and Beatrice Webb, "The Higgling of the Market," *Industrial Democracy* (London: Longmans, Green and Co., 1902), Part 3, chap. 2.

explanation. In this respect, the bargaining theory has the support of some of the critical analyses of marginalism that were described in previous sections.

A number of situations are frequently cited as illustrations of how power can be exerted meaningfully over wage rates. One example is the collusion of employers to refrain from competing for labor. If such collusion exists it may be possible for employers to depress wages below the level warranted by worker productivity. Should this occur, incidentally, it would be to the firm's advantage to hire more labor, since the additional output associated with another worker could be sold for more than its marginal cost. Even if it is assumed that more labor is available to the firm, however, this latter possibility may not materialize for some time. In the short run, plant size may constitute a physical limitation to the number of workers hired even though the economic limit imposed by wage costs has not been reached. Other situations in which bargaining power can be exerted meaningfully are the oligopolistic and monopsonistic market cases discussed earlier in this chapter.

Another example, and one frequently cited, is the case of the inefficient employer. If a firm has tolerated inefficiencies, production costs will be higher than they have to be. A wage increase in such a situation can be "afforded" if the inefficient firm, saddled with new wage costs, is shocked into eliminating inefficiencies.

The examples cited purport to show that there is "room" in many existing wage structures for forced wage changes. The consequences that supposedly follow a forceful change in a competitive labor and product market need not occur if the market is non-competitive in some significant aspect. According to the bargaining theory, there is considerable play in the wage structure of the firm, and wages will be higher or lower depending upon whether the employer or the workers enjoy the superior bargaining power position.

No version of the bargaining theory of wages contends that wages can be raised or lowered limitlessly. There is obviously some limit to how high wages can be forced, and when this limit is passed there may be severe economic consequences. Possibly the most fundamental difference between the marginalist and bargaining-power explanations is a disagreement over the boundaries of these limits.

Range Explanations of Wage Structures

There is no highly formalized analysis of wages that can be summarized as a range theory. There are, however, several analyses of wage structures that focus attention upon the wide spread in rates paid to workers in similar occupations within labor market areas. The data collected to administer the wage stabilization programs of World War II and of the Korean War showed amazing variations in the amounts paid for similar jobs within geographical limits that were believed to be labor market areas. Demand and supply pressures, which supposedly work to narrow the variations in amounts paid for similar work, apparently fail to eliminate gross inequities or irrationalities.[31]

One explanation of these variations is the fact that an employer has a great deal of discretion as to the precise level at which he can establish his wage structure, especially if his workers are unorganized. The maximum rate that a firm can pay is one that would fall just short of threatening the financial base of the business. The minimum is the rate just sufficient to draw the quantity and quality of labor that the firm must have.[32]

A concentration upon the maximum and minimum limits of wage possibilities within a firm does not explain the actual position of wages within these limits. It does serve to emphasize the probabilities of differences in wage levels among various firms, even within the same labor market area. The exact position of a wage rate within a range might be explained by degree of competition, employer psychology, custom historical accident, or any other influence that can be noted. Whatever the reason, variations in wage rates do exist, and the range approach suggests that these differences can be explained only by empirical study of the factors that influence the wage policy decisions of the firm. This does not negate the influence of demand and supply forces, but it does appear to deny that these forces must necessarily operate to eliminate rather wide wage rate differences that exist from firm to firm.

Job Clusters and Wage Contours

Professor John Dunlop has argued that the marginal productivity theory of wages, like the earlier wages-fund theory, appeared at a particular point of history and reflected the prevailing concerns of the times. By the latter part of the nineteenth century there was evidence of a rise in living standards, and the pessimistic cast of earlier economic thought was disappearing. The central theoretical problem of economics was still distribution, but attention was now focused upon distribution to factors of production rather than social classes. In an economy with a rapidly growing output, questions were raised about the consequences of trade union actions and social welfare legislation; and, of course, the Marxian challenge to the equity of the distributive process under capitalism hovered in the back-

[31] Richard A. Lester, "Wage Diversity and Its Theoretical Implications," *The Review of Economic Statistics,* August, 1946, p. 152.
[32] Lloyd Reynolds, *Labor Economics and Labor Relations* (Englewood Cliffs, N.J.: Prentice-Hall, Inc., 1954), p. 552–555.

ground. The marginal productivity theory was a useful tool for the analysis of such questions.

Whatever the analytical merits of the marginal productivity theory, Dunlop contends that it has collapsed as an explanation of how wages are determined. There are two basic reasons for this. One is that the price of a factor of production depends upon supply as well as demand, and since marginal productivity deals only with the demand side it cannot explain particular wages or the general wage level. The other is that it would be a hopeless task to apply the marginal analysis to modern wage structures made up of thousands of different wage rates.

Dunlop proposes that a contemporary wage theory be reconstructed around the concepts of "job clusters" and "wage contours." A job cluster is defined as a stable group of job classes within a firm so linked together by technology, the production process, or custom that they have common wage-making characteristics. A wage contour is a stable group of firms linked together by similarity of product markets, labor markets, or custom to the extent that they have common wage-making characteristics. Wage-making forces are visualized as those which affect key wage rates in the job clusters. These key rates also exert influence beyond the firm and constitute the focal points for wage setting among firms in the wage contours.

The complexities of contemporary wage structures, thus, are regarded as central in the construction of a new wage theory. Demand and supply forces must be analyzed in terms of impacts upon key rates in the job clusters and key firms in the wage contours. Demand and supply forces, however, should be treated as more than immediate and transitory market pressures. They should incorporate, among other things, the historical sequence of growth in wage structures, the different product market competitive conditions, and rates and patterns of industrialization within an economy. The Dunlop approach, thus, does not discard demand and supply but envisages, rather, an intensive probing of both short run market pressures and long run historical patterns to determine what lies behind demand and supply and how the totality of these influences works through existing clusters and contours to determine actual wage rates.[33]

CONCLUSION

By way of conclusion we shall return once more to the matter of marginalism and anti-marginalism to note some basic differences between the contending positions.

---

[33] For a more detailed development of this approach see John T. Dunlop, "The Task of Contemporary Wage Theory," *The Theory of Wage Determination* (London: Macmillan & Co., Ltd., 1957), pp. 3–27.

In part, the difference of opinion is over what the marginal productivity theory explains. The marginal productivity approach is basically an attempt to explain an important factor that conditions the employer's demand for labor. As an explanation of specific wage rates it is, at best, a loose theory of tendencies and long run possibilities. These limitations of the explanatory value of the marginal analysis are not always made clear, and this accounts for some of the confusion. The anti-marginalist (who is likely to be a labor economist) is more interested in the development of a theory that will explain why wages are what they are for given occupations in given industries at various periods of time. The demand and supply emphasis of the marginal productivity theory only goes part of the way in explaining these phenomena, and this is a cause for dissatisfaction among wage specialists.

QUESTIONS

1. It has been alleged that the marginal productivity theory of wages is more an explanation of the level of employment than of the wage determination process. According to the marginal productivity theory, what is the relationship between wage costs and the amount of employment offered by a firm?

2. In a purely competitive market the marginal worker receives wages that enable him to buy back the increment to total production that is associated with his employment. How does this differ from the situation in a market described as one of "monopolistic competition"?

3. The marginal productivity theory is based upon unrealistic assumptions. Does this fact negate the value of the theory?

4. Describe the criticisms of marginalism made by (*a*) Lester, (*b*) Eiteman, and (*c*) Reynolds.

5. Summarize the nature of Machlup's defense of marginalism.

6. In what circumstances would it be possible for a firm to grant a wage increase without reducing employment?

SELECTED READINGS

CARTTER, ALLAN M. *Theory of Wages and Employment*. Homewood, Ill.: Richard D. Irwin, Inc., 1959. Part 1.

DUNLOP, JOHN T. "The Task of Contemporary Wage Theory," *The Theory of Wage Determination*. London: Macmillan & Co., Ltd., 1957. Chap. 1.

LESTER, RICHARD. "Shortcomings of Marginal Analysis for Wage Employment Problems," *American Economic Review*, March, 1946, pp. 63–82.

MACHLUP, FRITZ. "Marginal Analysis and Empirical Research," *American Economic Review*, September, 1946, pp. 519–554.

PIERSON, FRANK. "An Evaluation of Wage Theory," *New Concepts in Wage Determination*. New York: McGraw-Hill Book Company, 1957. Chap. 1.

REYNOLDS, LLOYD. "Toward a Short Run Theory of Wages," *American Economic Review*, June, 1948, pp. 289–308.

ROTHSCHILD, K. W. *The Theory of Wages*. Oxford: Basil Blackwell, 1956.

CHAPTER 13

Factors in Wage Determination

THE DIFFICULTIES OF UNDERSTANDING WAGE DETERMINATION ARE DUE as much, perhaps, to a surfeit of knowledge as to a lack of it. Today wage statistics are more plentiful than ever, and much is known of the influence of custom, legislation, and worker and employer psychology. Explanations of a phenomenon do not emerge by themselves from piles of data, however. It is essential that the researcher sift the available data to see whether there are uniformities from which explanatory statements can be derived. As available knowledge becomes more voluminous, the sifting problem grows in complexity, and the problem of assigning weight to the variable factors becomes crucial. In the last chapter it was noted that much of the wage controversy among professional economists stems from a disagreement over the weight that should be assigned to the non-economic rather than to the economic forces. In this chapter some of the real factors that appear to have a bearing upon wages will be examined.

THE LABOR MARKET

A market is the institutional mechanism through which the acts of buying and selling are performed. Since labor power is a commodity that is bought and sold, we can speak of a *labor* market. It is obvious at once that this market is different from other commodity markets in that the seller cannot sever himself from his product. He must deliver himself in order to deliver the labor power that the employer wants to buy. Labor power can be treated analytically as a commodity, but complications arise because of the relationship between the seller and his product.

The farmer who wants to sell his wheat will sell to the highest bidder. The worker who wants to sell labor power will sell on the basis of price alone only when he considers non-pecuniary considerations to be irrelevant. This is rarely the case. The importance of the wage rate—the price of labor—in the allocation of labor among those who want to buy labor power is one of the important questions that concerns us here.

To illustrate the character of the question, let us compare two types of market situations. In market A, workers sell and employers buy labor solely on the basis of price considerations. Thus, if employer X is willing to pay ten cents per hour more than employers Y and Z, employees in the last two firms will quit their jobs and seek to work for X. Employer X, finding that he is able to get more labor than he needs, will lower his wage offers, whereas Y and Z will increase theirs in order to retain workers. The market will be in equilibrium when wage rates are so balanced that there is no movement of workers from firm to firm. In market B, employers X, Y, and Z all pay different rates for essentially the same type of work. These differentials have existed for a considerable period of time and the workers at the lower paying firms have shown no tendency to move. All three firms appear to be able to hire additional workers in the necessary numbers.

Labor power is allocated on the basis of price alone in market A, whereas the role of price in market B is vague. To know what wage rates will be in the former market it is necessary to know only the relevant demand and supply factors. In B, however, an understanding of wage rates requires additional information. Our question is one of degree. Are labor markets in the United States typically closer to the situation pictured by the A or by the B model? To approach this problem we shall first examine some characteristics of the labor market itself and, in the following section, some attributes of labor supply.

Geographical Characteristics of the Labor Market

Waitresses in Seattle, Washington, do not compete with waitresses in Akron, Ohio, for jobs. Despite the essential similarity of the services supplied in both areas, there is no significant labor market relationship between the two groups of waitresses. Engineering firms in both areas, however, could conceivably be in competition with each other when they attempt to hire recent graduates of engineering schools. This hiring competition can prevail even though the firms compete in no other way. These examples illustrate the difficulty of defining the geographical dimensions of labor markets. Such dimensions vary widely within both occupation and industry.

Within occupations there may be significant differences in the scope of the labor market for different practitioners of an occupational skill. The labor market for well known musicians is a national market. For a select number of musical artists the market is international. On the other hand, there may be little call for the services of a small string quartet outside of the local area in which it has acquired some reputation.

The widely different natures of labor markets can be further emphasized merely by listing a few of the many varieties of work that are performed. Agricultural harvesting, elevator operating, bricklaying, atomic energy research, and coal mining are obviously quite dissimilar in their labor market characteristics from the standpoint of the geographical as well as other dimensions.

In a sense, the worker determines the boundaries of his own labor market when he decides how mobile he will be. If the waitress in Seattle is willing and able to travel, her labor market is virtually the whole of the United States. If, because of family or other ties, she is unwilling to leave Seattle, her labor market is circumscribed by an attitude toward residence changes. Within Seattle the boundaries of her labor market might be further circumscribed by preferences for certain neighborhoods, certain restaurants, or certain hours of work.

Most workers are bound to a particular locality by ties such as home ownership, family, sentiment, or just plain inertia. In ordinary circumstances they expect to work relatively near their residences. The typical employer, too, expects to hire the bulk of his work force from among these residents. From the standpoint of total labor supply and demand in any area, it is permissible to think of, say, a Cleveland, a Pittsburgh, or a Memphis labor market area. In many respects, however, the metropolitan labor market is not an operational concept. Not all the workers in an area are candidates for all the jobs, nor can they be considered as parts of the same labor supply except in a gross or total sense. The concept of a metropolitan labor market area tends to hide the actuality of many smaller labor markets that overlap in numerous respects.

As an example, let us consider the case of a medium sized manufacturer of automotive parts who is located in a city with a population of 500,000. The plant is situated in an industrial-residential part of the city and draws its semi-skilled and unskilled workers from the immediate neighborhood. The residential area is a working class neighborhood and over the years the families in residence have naturally gravitated to the plant for employment purposes. The labor market, then, appears to consist of the plant site and the immediately surrounding territory. The plant management finds, however, that in order to hire adequate numbers of clerical and stenographic help it is necessary to canvass the city as a whole. Although the plant does not compete on a city-wide basis for the bulk of its operatives, it does compete with many other employers for office personnel. There is also a distinct market for skilled workers such as tool and die makers. A cluster of machine shops and tool and die shops is situated in the general area of the plant, and these employers actively compete for the highly skilled laborers. During a peak production season that lasts for two or three months, the plant in question expands employment by some 100 workers. For the past ten years the seasonal employment needs have been satisfied by a seasonal influx of out-of-state job seekers.

It should be clear that the firm operates not in one but in several quite distinct labor markets. In time, the geographical characteristics of all these markets might change. Because of educational advantages, the children of the neighborhood workers might become dissatisfied to some extent with the opportunities offered by employment in the plant. Their employment horizons expand, and they no longer drift to the jobs their fathers held. The same educational advantages might qualify more of the young women in the neighborhood for office jobs. The location of a new industrial plant some several hundred miles away might change the mobility patterns of the in-migrants. Other possibilities and their labor market consequences can be supplied by the reader. The point is that a geographical labor market is by nature a rather vague and elusive concept. The dimensions are shaped by the many-sided characteristics of labor supply and demand and by the interrelationships of these factors.

The Efficiency of the Labor Market

A market is efficient if the time and expense involved in bringing buyers and sellers together is negligible. The New York Stock Exchange can be taken as a model of efficiency. All offers and bids are quickly centralized in one location. The seller in New Orleans does not have to search out the buyer, who might happen to be in Boston.

In the labor market there is no equivalent of the "big board." A worker who is discharged Friday evening will not find a central source of information to which he can turn on Monday morning. The closest equivalent is probably an office of his state employment service, but neither employers nor job seekers have developed the habit of extensive reliance upon the public employment service. The private, fee-charging agency is a possible source of information, but the private agencies usually specialize in particular types of jobs, and the fees are high. The worker who sets out to find employment very likely goes through a process of chasing down vague rumors or leads and knocking on the employment office doors of firms that employ workers with his qualifications. Apart from this personal canvassing procedure he may have no way of getting accurate knowledge about job openings. On the side of the firm there is a similar inefficiency. When an opening occurs, a satisfactory employee may not be found instantaneously. The labor market operates with frictions. Occasionally, knowledge of job openings is widespread, and buyers and sellers of labor find each other with a minimum of difficulty. All too frequently, however, the buyers and sellers, blindfolded by a lack of knowledge, simply grope about until they bump into each other.

Another characteristic of an efficient market is that demand and supply prices are easily known. Returning to the stock market analogy, in a matter of minutes anyone who is interested can learn the latest price at which any listed stock sold. Wage rate information cannot be obtained with the same facility, and job seekers often—though not always—have little knowledge of what is being paid by the various potential employers. The lack of such information often makes shopping for a satisfactory job a two phase project. First, it is necessary to learn where job openings exist; then the wage advantages of the available jobs must be compared. Such comparisons are not always easily made. Wage structures may be very complex, especially where incentive or commission work is involved.

Summary

Two basic points have been made in the discussion of the labor market. (1) The concept of a labor market is subtle. Its dimensions are not always obvious; and these dimensions, whatever they are, may in time undergo fundamental modification. (2) The labor market is not a well oiled mechanism that operates without frictions. Frequently it takes time for the available workers and the available jobs to be matched.

Both points have significance in an analysis of wage determination. Demand and supply forces supposedly work to establish a wage that reflects the relative abundance or scarcity of jobs and workers. If, however, the dimensions of the labor market are not easily recognized, it will be difficult to judge the ultimate effects of demand and supply pressures. Since the labor market is characterized by frictions, it might be expected that going wage structures will differ somewhat from those that would result in a perfect market. The mechanical characteristics of the labor market, in other words, can have an independent effect upon the level of wage rates.

In the discussion of wage theory in the last chapter, it was noted that most employers function in imperfect product markets and that this fact influences the nature of the demand for labor. In this chapter, the imperfections of the labor market have been noted. In the next section, characteristics of labor supply will be examined in order to determine whether there are any peculiarities on the labor supply side that are significant in wage analysis.

MOBILITY OF LABOR

The marginal productivity theory analyzed in the last chapter is basically a theory of labor demand. Worker productivity and product selling price make specific levels of employment possible at various wage rates. The exact level of employment that will prevail depends upon the wage preferences of workers which are summarized theoretically in the labor supply curve. Labor supply in a sense is outside the analytical apparatus of the marginal productivity theory. Supply affects wages in that it sets limits to the employer's choice regarding the number of workers that can be profitably employed. It is a datum that the employer considers along with other data in determining quantity to be produced and number of employees to be hired.

The supply of labor available to the single firm will depend upon many factors such as over-all labor supply conditions, mobility of labor, supply conditions in particular occupations, and the presence or absence of a labor union. In the first two chapters of this book, factors affecting aggregate labor supply were analyzed. In this section, job mobility characteristics of workers will be considered.

The importance of mobility should be underscored. In a dynamic economic system some plants, companies, and industries will be expanding; others will be declining; and new ones will come into being as technological changes occur. These changes may be accompanied by important shifts in industry location. Unless labor as a factor of production can adjust to such developments with some facility, disruptive consequences may offset some part of the benefits that flow from technical improvements. If workers refuse to move to the employments where they are most needed and insist upon remaining where they are least needed, the absence of a necessary mobility will impede the achievement of the efficiency that has become physically possible.

In a perfectly competitive market, it is assumed that over time, workers will respond to wage differentials by leaving low-wage jobs and moving up to high-wage jobs. Since under perfect competition high wages reflect high value productivity and low wages reflect the reverse, this mobility has the effect of removing workers from the least productive employments and placing them where they are most productive.[1] A perfect mobility would not result in the eventual equality of all wages. Some occupations are more unpleasant than others, some require longer training periods, some are physically dangerous. In a perfect market equilibrium, conditions are such that differences in wage rates can be wholly accounted for as compensations for variations in pleasantness, risk, skill, and other similar factors.

No one has ever pretended that worker mobility begins to approach the degree implied by the perfect market model. As long ago as 1776,

---

[1] An assumption of the marginal productivity theory is that under competitive market conditions and over time, the movement of workers will equalize marginal productivity of all workers in similar jobs within a labor market area. So long as wage rate differences reflecting productivity differences exist, it is to the economic advantage of workers to leave the low productivity employments for jobs in the higher productivity firms, and it is to the advantage of the latter firms to hire them.

Adam Smith noted that ". . . a man is of all sorts of luggage the most difficult to be transported." The practical question is not whether there is perfect mobility but whether job-to-job movement that is motivated by wage differentials is sufficient in amount to affect wage rate levels.

The Amount of Worker Mobility

All relevant data indicate that a considerable amount of job-to-job movement occurs each year. Although the exact number of job changers is not known, various studies indicate that at least 15 per cent and probably more of those in the labor force work for more than one employer during the course of a year.

A direct measurement of mobility made in a special Bureau of the Census study found that 11.5 million persons or 15 per cent of those with work experience had more than one job during 1955.[2] In a less direct measurement, a Bureau of Labor Statistics study revealed that 7 per cent (3.3 million) of the eighteen- to sixty-four-year-old males moved to another county or another state between March, 1962, and March, 1963.[3] Half of the migrants reported work-related factors as reasons for their moves. Another BLS study, measuring mobility in terms of worker movement from one occupation to another, found that 5.5 million persons of the 70 million employed in January, 1966, were working in an occupation different from the one they were practicing in January, 1965.[4]

Mobility studies covering a longer time indicate that it is quite unusual for a person not to make at least one job shift during a work career. About 90 per cent of all male workers in the age cohort 45 to 59, according to a recent study, work for a different employer from the one who hired them for their first job.[5] Eighty-seven per cent of these men, furthermore, changed occupations during their work careers and 50 per cent work in a community other than the one where they lived at the time of their first job.

Characteristics of Mobile Workers

Young workers are more mobile than old workers. All relevant studies appear to verify the conclusion that the older a person becomes the less likely he is to make a voluntary job shift. The inverse correlation between mobility and age is not very difficult to understand. The initial entrance

---

[2] Bureau of the Census, "Labor Force," *Current Population Reports,* Series P-50, No. 70, February, 1957.

[3] Samuel Saben, "Geographic Mobility and Employment Status, March 1962–March, 1963," *Monthly Labor Review,* August, 1964.

[4] Samuel Saben, "Occupational Mobility of Employed Workers," *Monthly Labor Review,* June, 1967, p. 31.

[5] Herbert Parnes, Belton Fleisher, Robert Miljus, and Ruth Spitz, *The Pre-Retirement Years: A Longitudinal Study of the Labor Market Experience of the Cohort of Men 45–59 Years of Age* (Columbus: Center for Human Resource Research, The Ohio State University, 1968), p. 165.

into labor force activity by many young persons is a haphazard affair. The first job seldom turns out to be exactly what the beginner has in mind. Ambitions are likely to be at a peak in the early years of an individual's working life, and it is not highly probable that a starting job will bear much resemblance to ultimate ambitions or even appear to point in the direction of these ambitions. Relatively unencumbered by family responsibilities, the younger worker is not especially reluctant to leave a job and strike out in search of something else. Also contributing to high job mobility among the young is the fact that quite frequently the first jobs held consist of part-time work while the job holder is attending school. The very nature of such employments occasions a great deal of job shifting.

With the growth of family responsibilities and the accumulation of the perquisites that attend long service with a firm, the worker becomes less inclined to move. Much of the occupational advancement that occurs today takes place within a firm as workers move gradually upward on the occupational ladder. It is not surprising, then, that the older worker is less inclined to make a job change that might involve starting all over again. In any event there is usually some risk involved in changing jobs, and older workers are less likely to assume these risks voluntarily.

A study of geographic mobility substantiates the relationship between age and mobility described above.[6] Responses of interviewees drawn from a national sample indicated that among heads of families aged eighteen to twenty-four, 40 per cent moved to the areas where they now live within the last five years. Of those aged sixty-five or over, only 4 per cent moved to their present area within the past five years. Occupational as well as geographical mobility is most pronounced among younger persons. Twenty-three per cent of employed persons aged 20–24 changed occupations between January, 1965, and January, 1966.[7] After age 34 the rate dropped sharply.

The evidence relative to sex differentials in mobility is conflicting. Most studies indicate that female mobility, whether measured as a movement from one job to another or one occupation to another, is less than male mobility.[8] Some evidence suggests, however, that women with long and continuous work experience have approximately the same mobility rates as men.[9] Women are apparently less likely to change occupations when they change jobs but they are as likely as men to change industries.[10]

---

[6] U.S. Department of Commerce, Area Redevelopment Administration, *The Geographic Mobility of Labor* (Washington, D.C.: U.S. Government Printing Office, 1964).

[7] Samuel Saben, "Occupational Mobility of Employed Workers," *loc cit.*, p. 31.

[8] See e.g. Samuel Saben, "Occupational Mobility of Employed Workers," *loc cit.*, p. 32.

[9] Herbert S. Parnes, *Research on Labor Mobility* (New York: Social Science Research Council, 1954), pp. 109–116.

[10] *Ibid.*, p. 115.

In 1955 about the same proportion of whites and non-whites in urban areas had more than one job.[11] In rural areas, however, non-whites had a higher mobility rate due largely to the fact that non-white workers in rural areas are concentrated in seasonal or casual types of work which involve frequent changes of employers. There is some evidence to the effect that a higher proportion of white males than non-white males make job shifts that require changes in the county or state of residence. A large proportion of the white workers who move long distances for work-related reasons are moving to take jobs that have already been obtained, whereas non-whites are much more likely to be moving to look for work.[12]

Recent studies of inter-county mobility show that the highest rates of migration are found among employed persons, college graduates, and professional workers.[13] About two-thirds of all men who moved between March, 1962, and March, 1963, were employed at the beginning of the period. The rate of migration, however, was about twice as high among unemployed as employed workers. About half of all migrants reported that they moved for job-related reasons.

Occupational and Industrial Aspects of Mobility

It is important to know the direction as well as the amount of worker movement. Should it be found that workers cross industrial and occupational boundaries with ease this would not necessarily prove that the movement is in response to wage pulls. On the other hand, reluctance by workers to take jobs in different industries or occupations would be strong evidence that the capacity of wage differences to stimulate worker movement is limited to the orbits of narrowly circumscribed non-competing groups. The conclusions relative to occupational and industrial aspects of mobility listed below are based upon data taken from a number of recent studies of labor mobility.[14]

1. A considerable amount of job shifting by workers involves simultaneous changes of employer, occupation, and industry. A number of different

---

[11] Bureau of the Census, "Labor Force," *Current Population Reports,* Series P-50, No. 70, February, 1957, p. 4.

[12] U.S. Department of Commerce, Area Development Administration, *Negro-White Differences in Geographic Mobility* (Washington, D.C.: U.S. Government Printing Office, 1964).

[13] See, for example, *Manpower Report of the President* (Washington, D.C.: U.S. Government Printing Office, 1965), pp. 147–149.

[14] A. Parnes, B. Fleisher, R. Miljus, and R. Spitz, *op. cit.,* H. Parnes, *Research on Labor Mobility,* Lowell E. Galloway, *Interindustry Labor Mobility in the United States, 1957 to 1960* (Washington, United States Government Printing Office, 1967), *Mobility and Worker Adaptation to Economic Change in the United States* (Washington: U.S. Department of Labor, Manpower Research Bulletin No. 1, 1963), *Wages and Labor Mobility* (Paris: Organization for Economic Cooperation and Development, 1965), Samuel Saben, "Occupational Mobility of Employed Workers," *Monthly Labor Review,* June, 1967.

TABLE 11

OCCUPATIONAL MOBILITY RATES* BETWEEN JANUARY, 1965, AND
JANUARY, 1966, OF EMPLOYED PERSONS BY AGE, SEX, AND COLOR,
JANUARY, 1966

AGE	ALL PERSONS		WHITE		NON-WHITE	
	Men	Women	Men	Women	Men	Women
Total, 18 years and over	9.9	6.9	9.6	6.8	12.4	7.1
18 and 19 years	31.7	29.0	31.8	28.3	(†)	(†)
20 to 24 years	28.5	14.9	28.4	14.4	29.2	19.0
25 to 34 years	13.8	8.5	13.5	8.3	16.8	9.7
35 to 44 years	7.4	5.3	7.2	5.5	9.5	4.3
45 to 54 years	5.2	4.7	5.1	4.8	6.6	3.8
55 to 64 years	3.8	2.4	3.8	2.6	3.7	1.2
65 years and over	2.7	1.8	2.7	1.6	3.5	(†)

* Proportion of persons employed in both January, 1965, and January, 1966, who had a different occupation in January 1966.
† Rate not shown where base is less than 100,000.
Source: *Monthly Labor Review*, June, 1967, p. 34.

studies substantiate this proposition. It is not possible to estimate accurately how much of the total movement involves this three-way change and undoubtedly the amount is subject to many influences. During a war period, for instance, such complex job shifts might be expected to occur more frequently than in peacetime. Some indication of the amount of complex job shifting that occurs is provided by data derived in a 1965 study. Seventy per cent of the men and 75 per cent of the women who changed occupations between January, 1965, and January, 1966, also changed the industry in which they were working.[15]

2. When changing jobs, workers are more likely to change their industries than their occupations and, further, are more likely to change occupations than to move to another geographical area.

3. Movement from firm to firm seems to occur least often among professional workers and most often among unskilled workers.

4. Geographic mobility among professional and technical workers is greater than among workers in the other major occupational groups. Mobility among farm laborers is also above average in this respect.

5. Certain types of workers are more likely to remain within an occupation when job shifts are involved. Among those showing strong occupational attachments are professional workers, skilled workers, and female clerical workers.

---

[15] Saben, "Occupational Mobility of Employed Workers," *loc. cit.,* pp. 37–38.

6. As noted above, older persons with extended work experience are likely to have made at least one change in occupation during their work careers.

7. The quantity of interindustry job changes is significant. A major study of this type of job shift found that about one worker in four had a different industrial attachment in 1960 than in 1957.[16]

Reasons for Worker Mobility

Among workers there are many who for various reasons are quite immobile and not apt to make job changes unless forced to do so. There is also a group with high mobility that accounts for a large percentage of all movement that occurs. As has been noted, younger workers tend to predominate among the very mobile. Between the extremes there is a large group of workers who will make job shifts in certain circumstances. Although it is not possible to come up with a precise grading system to classify the work force as a whole in terms of inclination to move, it does seem apparent that enough job changing occurs to satisfy the conditions of the competitive market theory of labor supply.[17]

A crucial analytical problem is that of identifying the motives of those who take new jobs. If workers accept jobs because of considerations other than wages, there is no basis for assuming a causal relationship between labor mobility and wage rates within firms. If the reverse is true, an opposite conclusion is at least possible.

Economists have more or less bypassed the question of ultimate motivation. They assume simply that a rational person will prefer a higher profit to a lower profit or a higher wage to a lower wage with all other considerations equal. The equality of the other considerations, however, is itself a subjective evaluation. Different individuals will make different job choices because their judgments of the non-monetary considerations are different. One of the shortcomings of contemporary wage analysis is the absence of a technique to weigh the influence of non-economic considerations in job choice. What this means is that analysis of the motivations of job changers rests upon loose indicators rather than upon intensive psychological probing. One other caution must be expressed. By a process of selective emphasis and de-emphasis, the relation between wages and worker mobility can be minimized or maximized. There is much evidence on both sides of the

---

[16] Lowell E. Galloway, *op. cit.,* p. 29.

[17] It is not necessary for the total labor force to be mobile in order that wage differences be reduced to a point at which they can be attributed to differences that are inherent in jobs. So long as a sufficiently numerous fringe of workers responds to wage differentials by leaving the lower for the higher paying jobs there will be a tendency for differences to diminish and the movement of labor can be accorded recognition as an important influence in wage determination.

question, and final judgment should be made on the basis of all rather than on partial evidence.

Less oriented to wages than to other considerations are the job-seeking activities of persons who have become involuntarily unemployed. The unemployed person probably has some minimum wage figure in mind. Any job that pays at or above the minimum is likely to be accepted. The psychological, social, and economic pressures that weigh upon an unemployed person in our society are strong forces in motivating a person to move from unemployed to employed status as quickly as possible.

The most important consideration in a theory of labor supply is the voluntary movement that occurs. When persons change jobs because they want to rather than because they have to, are they motivated primarily by a desire to increase their incomes? An affirmative answer would seem to imply that workers have knowledge of working conditions and pay levels at numerous places of employment and that they shop around and make the best selection among available job openings. Actually, many workers do not have accurate information concerning wages paid by other firms. Reynolds, in his New Haven study, asked workers to judge their wages as fair or unfair. The percentage of workers in low wage plants who regarded their wages as fair was just as large as that of workers in high wage plants who regarded their wages as fair.[18] Workers were also asked where they would look for work if they were out of a job. Most respondents did not mention a specific place; and, of those who did, about half mentioned plants where they had worked previously. The over-all conclusion drawn was that "workers are poorly informed about job opportunities."[19]

Few labor market students will quarrel with the conclusion that among voluntary job changers there are many who have meager market information. Furthermore, there are many whose job shifts must be attributed to non-wage considerations such as dissatisfaction with working conditions, personal gripes, or dislike of the work. These facts would appear to be strong evidence that wages exert only a minimal influence on worker mobility. Worker responses to hypothetical questions also indicate that the link between job mobility and wage differentials may be weak. In his study of the "reluctant job changer," Parnes asked workers in his sample if they would accept a job offer from another company to do exactly what they were now doing for thirty cents an hour more pay. A very large majority of the respondents answered "no" or qualified their answers.[20]

---

[18] Lloyd G. Reynolds, *The Structure of Labor Markets* (New York: Harper & Row, Publishers, 1951), pp. 213, 214.

[19] *Ibid.*

[20] Herbert S. Parnes, "Workers' Attitudes to Job Changing: The Effect of Private Pension Plans," in Gladys Palmer *et al., The Reluctant Job Changer* (Philadelphia: University of Pennsylvania Press, 1962), pp. 61–65.

The studies cited above and numerous others suggest that the factors motivating worker mobility are complex. When attention is shifted from the individual worker to aggregate labor supply, however, an accumulation of empirical data suggests very strongly that mobility is more closely related to conditions of employment than to anything else. Studies by different authors who used different methodologies and types of data all support the conclusion that the mobility rate will rise when there is a rise in the rate at which employment opportunities are appearing.[21] Whether the question investigated is movement to a single state such as California, national patterns of mobility, movement of inactive persons into active labor force status, or movement of agricultural workers to urban employments, the most significant variable affecting the rate of movement appears to be employment expansion.

How can all of this be squared with the neoclassical theory of labor supply which posits a relationship between wage differences and movements of labor? A careful statement of orthodox theory can show that there is no inconsistency between the findings described above and labor supply theory.[22] Let us restate the basic proposition of the theory: over the long time period, assuming all else equal, it can be predicted that labor will tend to apportion itself in accordance with the relative wage advantages of the various employments. Orthodox theorists do not deny that factors other than wages can be important determinants of labor supply, and they point out that the utility of the theory is limited to providing gross predictions over long time periods. There should be little argument with traditional theory thus described, but the findings of empirical labor market studies raise serious questions about its utility for analyzing problems generated in a dynamic labor market. Defenders of the orthodox theory, however, do not totally lack empirical evidence to support their arguments. Some examples are listed below:

1. A number of studies have shown that a large percentage of persons who voluntarily change jobs improve their income by doing so.

2. The geographical population movements that have occurred in the past two decades are movements from areas of relatively low to relatively high earnings opportunities. Whatever the underlying reasons for these

[21] See, for example, Cicely Blanco, *The Determinants of Regional Factor Mobility* (The Hague: Drukkerj Passmans, 1962), Part 1; Margaret S. Gordon, "Immigration and Its Effects on Labor Force Characteristics," *Monthly Labor Review,* May, 1959, pp. 492–501; Larry Sjaastad, "Occupational Structure and Migration Patterns," *Labor Mobility and Population in Agriculture* (Ames, Iowa: Iowa State University Press, 1961), chap. 2; Richard C. Wilcock and Irvin Sobel, *Small City Job Markets* (Urbana, Ill.: Institute of Labor and Industrial Relations, University of Illinois, 1958).

[22] Simon Rottenberg, "On Choice in Labor Markets," *Industrial and Labor Relations Review,* January, 1956.

movements, they are what one would expect to find by weighing the economic considerations alone.

3. Some workers do shop around and select among the best of the available jobs. This is not an uncommon procedure among professional workers, and it is the typical procedure for recent college graduates. The fact that many others do not explicitly shop does not mean that they are immune to the pulls of a higher wage. A worker hears about a better paying job and he makes inquiries which lead to his being hired. This is a common occurrence; and, though no shopping is involved, the job movement nonetheless is in response to a wage differential.

4. There can be little question that in periods of tight labor supply the connection between wage rates and labor supply is direct and immediate. During the wage control periods of World War II and the Korean War many employers were aggressive in their efforts to win permission to pay higher wages. High wages were of crucial importance to firms for retaining and recruiting workers. The practice of circumventing wage controls by liberal upgrading policies and payment of bootleg wages was not unusual.

5. As noted above, about half of all heads of families who had migrated to another county of residence reported "job related" factors as their reason for moving. (This, of course, is indirect evidence since "job related" can be a reference to factors other than wages.)

Summary: Labor Supply

Our problem has been that of identifying the forces that influence relationships between wage rates in different places of employment. Many workers do not make job changes and thus are not really in the active labor market. Nevertheless, a considerable amount of job shifting does occur. This amount seems to be sufficient in a quantitative sense to redress the balance of labor supply available to higher paying as against lower paying employments.

The evidence is mixed on the question of whether the bulk of the job-to-job movement is influenced primarily by wage rate differentials. The two polar positions—(1) labor supply is totally independent of wage rates and (2) labor supply is totally dependent upon wage rates—are equally untenable. Labor mobility is obviously affected by many considerations, and wage rates must be included among these.

The ultimate influence of labor supply upon relative wage rates is vague for a number of reasons. (1) Supply is not the only variable that affects wages, and it is difficult to disentangle the supply from the other influences. (2) Supply can be manipulated by institutional devices such as union restrictions against free entry to an occupation or community patterns of discrimination against minority groups,[23] and it is impossible to know what the precise conditions or effects of labor supply would have been in the absence of restrictions. (3) Over-all labor supply conditions can change quickly as the economy or an industry or a firm moves from one level of economic activity to another, whereas wage rates usually adjust slowly to such economic changes. To these factors must be added the realities of the processes of wage determination. A surfeit of labor in a given labor market area might have no effect upon wage rates because a union will not let the rates drop or a firm doesn't want to reduce wages. In the former case, there may or may not be employment effects. In the latter instance, the firm might have a variety of reasons for staying with a policy of paying higher wages than are called for by pure supply considerations.

Given a sufficient period of time without disturbances such as war or major technological change, the general direction of gradual worker movement probably would be from the lower to the higher paying occupations, industries, and firms, and this movement would ultimately have the effect of equalizing rates except for differences attributable to hazard, working conditions, skill requirements, etc. Disturbances, however, are a characteristic feature of our economy. Our progress is from one short run period to another, and an understanding of wage rate relationships as they exist from year to year depends as much upon a knowledge of the disturbances as it does upon an understanding of what would occur in their absence. It is necessary to understand both the mechanics and the limitations of demand and supply analysis. In the previous chapter and so far in this chapter, concentration has been upon the theory and its limitations. In the next section there will be an examination of the characteristics of wage structures.

WAGE STRUCTURES

The wage rates paid to drill press operators vary widely even within the same local labor market area. The rate for the highest-paid operator might be thirty cents per hour, or even more, above the rate received by the lowest-paid operator. Statistical averages computed from a survey of all drill press rates within an area are different from the averages found in other regions. No matter what type of comparison is made, significant differences are usually found.

---

[23] Various data suggest that black workers are less likely than whites to make favorable moves with the result that socio-economic disparities between the two groups widen over the course of a working life. Results of one study suggest the presence of a systematic tendency for blacks to be shifted toward the low earnings level industries. Herbert S. Parnes, *et al., The Pre-Retirement Years: A Longitudinal Study of the Labor Market Experience of the Cohort of Men 45–59 Years of Age,* p. 167; Lowell E. Galloway, *op. cit.,* chap. 6.

The fact of a difference requires no involved explanation. It has already been noted that there are frictions and imperfections in the labor market. These factors are sufficient as explanations of the mere existence of wage differences. The size of the differences is less easily explained, however. Can prevailing wage rate disparities be attributed in totality to market frictions and imperfections or is something more basic involved? The examination of wage differentials that follows will be directed toward answering this question and also toward the general problem of understanding the processes of wage determination.

Occupational Differentials

Skilled workers in a plant are usually paid substantially more than unskilled workers. This fact accords with what would be the common expectation. In terms of an economic analysis, the differentials can be attributed to the relative scarcity of skilled workers and to the character of their production contribution, which reflects the results of long and specialized training. An hour's worth of skilled labor is more productive than an hour's worth of unskilled labor and hence should be more highly remuncrated.

An examination of the size of the skilled-unskilled differential reveals several interesting developments that might require additional explanation. The most striking feature of occupational wage relationships is the long-term trend toward a narrowing of the differential between skilled and unskilled classifications. On the average, skilled rates were about double the unskilled rates at the beginning of the century. By 1947 this difference had been reduced by half.[24] There has been some variation in the trend from region to region and from industry to industry, but there is no question about the over-all trend direction.

A number of explanations of what has occurred can be suggested. Several students of the problem attach considerable importance to the influence of cyclical variations in business conditions. In terms of percentages, occupational wage differentials tend to narrow in prosperity and to widen during depressions. Wage rates for unskilled workers are apparently more sensitive to changing business conditions and show larger increases in prosperity and greater declines during depressions than do skilled wages.[25] The long run trend toward a narrowing of occupational differentials, then, might be a result of legislative developments that since 1930 have cushioned the fall of

---

[24] Harry Ober, "Occupational Wage Differentials," *Monthly Labor Review,* August, 1948, pp. 129, 130.

[25] An analysis of the relationship between occupational earnings and education supports this thesis. During years of strong price inflation tendencies, the average wages of occupations requiring less than a college education rose more rapidly than the wages of occupations requiring one. When inflationary pressures diminished, the reverse was true. Alan L. Sorkin, "Occupational Earnings and Education," *Monthly Labor Review,* April, 1968, pp. 6–9.

TABLE 12

RELATIONSHIPS BETWEEN EARNINGS OF SKILLED AND
UNSKILLED OCCUPATIONS IN MANUFACTURING,
SELECTED PERIODS, 1907–1947, BY REGION
(*Average earnings for representative unskilled
earnings* = 100)

REGION	OCCUPATIONAL INDEX	
	MEDIAN	RANGE (*middle half of all indexes*)
United States:		
1907	205	180–280
1918–19	175	150–225
1931–32	180	160–220
1937–40	165	150–190
1945–47	155	145–170
Northeast:		
1907	200	175–245
1918–19	165	150–235
1931–32	175	155–215
1937–40	(*)	(*)
1945–47	155	145–175
South:		
1907	215	195–235
1918–19	195	175–230
1931–32	190	165–235
1937–40	(*)	(*)
1945–47	170	150–195
Middle West:		
1907	190	170–250
1918–19	175	145–235
1931–32	170	150–215
1937–40	(*)	(*)
1945–47	150	140–165
Far West:		
1907	185	165–200
1918–19	170	160–195
1931–32	160	145–170
1937–40	(*)	(*)
1945–47	145	140–165

* Regional data for 1937–1940 period insufficient to warrant presentation of separate regional indexes.
Source: *Monthly Labor Review,* August, 1948, p. 130.

unskilled wages during depression periods. The NIRA codes established wage floors in certain industries during the early New Deal period; and, subsequently, minimum wage legislation has supported the wage levels of the lowest-paid workers. The high levels of prosperity that have prevailed since 1940, furthermore, should have been accompanied by a decline in the skilled-unskilled differential according to the above explanation; and this is what has occurred in fact.

Among the other factors that have been important in reducing the differential are the restriction of immigration and the extension of public education. Both of these developments have lowered the supply of persons who compete for the unskilled jobs. The spread of industrial unionism which has strengthened the relative bargaining power of the unskilled workers and the common practice of bargaining for wages on a cents-per-hour basis have probably been other factors that have contributed to narrowing the unskilled-skilled wage differential.[26] The restiveness of the skilled workers in a number of the industrial unions and the recent tendency of craft workers to break away from industrial unions and establish their own collective bargaining units are facts that are consistent with this hypothesis. Finally, emphasis should be placed upon the effects of a changing technology. The number of jobs that involve hard physical labor and nothing more has diminished significantly. The relatively unskilled jobs have been mechanized to a considerable extent. The unskilled worker is more efficient and hence more highly paid than in past periods.[27]

Recent evidence suggests that the long period of narrowing differentials in pay between skilled and unskilled jobs may be over. According to successive studies of the Bureau of Labor Statistics, the differential in manufacturing industries declined from 105 per cent in 1907 to 80 per cent in 1931–1932, 55 per cent in 1945–1947, and 37 per cent in 1953. The most recent study shows that the differential in 1967 was about at the 1953 level.[28] As a result of the shifts in the character of the demand for labor described in earlier chapters and the increasing attention being paid to occupational wage relationships in collective negotiations, it is not at all unlikely that the years ahead may witness some widening of the skilled-unskilled differential.

Apart from the historical trend in occupational differentials, available data make several other observations possible.[29] The size of the skilled-unskilled differential depends upon the job requirements of an industry. When the skill requirements are not especially high and the unskilled workers perform heavy or unpleasant work, the differential will be small. Examples of such industries are soap manufacturing, leather tanning, and

---

[26] When wage increases are granted on a cents-per-hour across-the-board basis, the percentage differential between the highest and lowest wages in a firm will diminish, of course. Thus, if ten cents an hour is granted to both the $1.00 per hour worker and the $2.00 per hour worker, the money differential will remain constant, but the percentage differential will be reduced.

[27] For a detailed analysis of the skilled-unskilled differential see Melvin W. Reder, "Wage Differentials: Theory and Measurement," *Aspects of Labor Economics* (Princeton, N.J.: Princeton University Press, 1962), pp. 258–276.

[28] Donald J. Blackmore, "Occupational Wage Relationships in Metropolitan Areas," *Monthly Labor Review,* December, 1968, p. 36.

[29] Ober, *loc. cit.*

copper alloying. In industries that require highly skilled workers or where the unskilled work is light in character, the wage rate spread is large. Examples here are tool and die job shops and the garment industries.

The skilled-unskilled wage differential varies considerably by region. The differential is greatest in the South where the supply of unskilled labor is relatively large and the degree of industrialization is less than that in other regions. Skilled rates in the South are only slightly lower than those of some other regions, but unskilled rates are considerably lower.[30]

Geographic Wage Differentials

On the average, wage rates in the United States are lowest in the South and highest in the Far West. A statement of averages, however, conceals a confusing set of irregularities in regional wage relationships. It is a gross oversimplification, for instance, to speak of a southern or a western or a New England wage rate. Rates tend to be higher in the Northwest than in California and higher in the Boston area than in Maine. Within regions and from city to city there are many divergences from the over-all pattern of regional differences. Similarly, there are divergences by occupation and by industry. Investigations have shown that in some industries there is no

TABLE 13

AVERAGE STRAIGHT-TIME HOURLY EARNINGS FOR SELECTED PLANT
OCCUPATIONS BY REGION, 1967

OCCUPATION	REGION			
	Northeast	South	North Central	West
Maintenance and Toolroom				
Carpenters	$3.30	$3.30	$3.58	$3.54
Electricians	3.46	3.47	3.73	3.77
Machinists	3.49	3.50	3.67	3.78
Mechanics, automotive	3.33	3.04	3.46	3.74
Painters	3.18	3.24	3.58	3.59
Tool and diemakers	3.55	3.56	3.92	3.95
Custodial and Material Movement				
Janitors, porters and cleaners	2.13	1.65	2.30	2.30
Laborers, material handling	2.59	2.01	2.73	2.91
Order fillers	2.60	2.08	2.77	2.88
Truck drivers	3.22	2.49	3.21	3.37
Truckers, forklift	2.82	2.32	2.93	3.02

• Source: U.S. Department of Labor, *Handbook of Labor Statistics, 1968*, Table 90.

---

30 *Ibid.*

South-non-South differential. Furthermore, where there is a large differential, variations in wages among southern firms in the industry may be as large as the average South-non-South difference.

The most outstanding difference between wage rates in the South and in other regions appears to be in the lower wage brackets. Table 13 shows average hourly earnings for selected skilled and unskilled job classifications by broad regional breakdown. Earnings in the relatively unskilled jobs are clearly lower in the South than in the other regions. For most of the skilled classifications, the differentials are small; and, in a number of cases, earnings in the South are equal to or higher than those in other regions.

No conclusive explanation of regional wage differences has yet appeared. Part of the diversity in prevailing regional patterns can be attributed to the different wage policies of multi-regional firms. Some firms adhere to a policy of paying the same wage rates regardless of the location of a plant. Others have a practice of paying prevailing local rates, while still others peg their wage schedules at a level slightly above local area rates.

The basic explanation of South-non-South differences can probably be made in demand and supply terms. Despite the large amount of population out-migration from the South, the birth rate continues to result in a supply of labor that is high relative to the demand. Much southern industry is located in small towns, and recruitment of a labor force in a rural area is usually possible at rates lower than those prevailing in large urban centers. For the rural resident, the alternative to a plant job is farm labor where average earnings are very low. Only a small differential above farm labor rates is necessary to attract him to plant employment.

During the present century there has been little change in the South-non-South wage differential. Some evidence suggests that the South may have improved its relative position between 1929 and 1947 but there has been comparatively little change since then.[31] Forces that might have reduced the differential such as capital inflow and population out-migration have apparently been offset by factors such as the high rate of national population increase and the flow of unskilled labor from agriculture to urban labor markets in the South.

Industrial Wage Differentials

There is, of course, overlap in occupational, regional, and industrial wage differentials. Highly remunerated occupations are likely to be found in high wage industries, and a heavy incidence of high wage industries within a geographical region will tend to pull up the general level of wages in that region. Nevertheless, it is fruitful to look at wages from different perspectives. Analysis of industrial wage differentials involves an emphasis

---

[31] H. M. Douty, "Wage Differentials: Forces and Counter Forces," *Monthly Labor Review,* March, 1968, p. 79.

upon factors that are different, to an extent, from those that are emphasized in regional or occupational wage analysis. By looking at wages in different ways, the full range of complexities and influences is brought into sharper focus.

In the United States wage rates in certain industries are relatively high regardless of the location of the production facilities. Automobile, aircraft, and petroleum refining are high wage industries. Cotton textiles, leather products, food canning, and tobacco are among those industries where wages are relatively low.

The following conditions are frequently cited as likely to be present when high wages or earnings characterize an industry: (1) Labor costs are a low percentage of total production costs or income from sales; (2) the capital investment per worker is large; (3) the value added by manufacturing per wage earner-hour is high; (4) employment in an industry has been expanding rapidly; (5) skill requirements are high.[32] Professor Slichter observed some tendency for unskilled average hourly earnings to be low when the percentage of women workers in an industry is high.[33] A possible reason is the simple fact that women are available for work at lower wages than men. In those employments where women are doing semi-skilled or skilled work, managements are probably reluctant to pay male common labor as much or more than semi-skilled or skilled female labor. In industries such as textiles, both male and female members of a family can take jobs, and this probably has an effect upon the supply price for males.

In recent years there has been much interest in the problem of variations of wage structures from industry to industry. Over a long period, wages in one industry change at different rates and by different amounts than in others. What accounts for these variations? There is no over-all consensus in this matter, and different writers have emphasized different variables in their attempts at explanation.

Dunlop places great stress upon productivity changes. Some industries in a given time period will have above average increases in productivity, and others will be below average in this respect. Industries with the above average productivity gains should be expected to be those where wages and salary rates show the largest increases; the reverse is to be expected in the low productivity industries.[34] Apart from productivity, Dunlop cites the following as being of fundamental importance: changes in output, proportion of labor cost to total outlay, competitive conditions in the product market, and changing skill and occupational content in the industry.[35]

---

[32] See, for example, Sumner Slichter, "Notes on the Structure of Wages," *Review of Economics and Statistics,* February, 1950, pp. 80–91.

[33] *Ibid.,* p. 85.

[34] John T. Dunlop, "Productivity and the Wage Structure," in *Income Employment, and Public Policy* (New York: W. W. Norton & Company, Inc., 1948), p. 346.

[35] *Ibid.,* p. 360.

When these fundamental items change in directions that are favorable to the firm, wage increases become possible; the greater the increase the greater the possible wage change.

How is a variation, such as an increase in productivity, translated into higher wages? Dunlop suggests several ways. Workers on incentive can be expected to capture small gains in productivity that arise from minor changes in method and machinery.[36] When substantial gains in productivity occur, the workers' bargaining representative is likely to insist that the gains be allocated among all the workers in the bargaining unit. Furthermore, rapid increases in productivity are likely to be accompanied by large increases in employment within an industry. In order to attract new workers to an industry, wages must be sufficiently high to lure them away from other employments.

Garbarino retains the emphasis upon productivity as a source of possible wage gains but adds additional factors in explanation of how higher wages actually materialize.[37] In the long run, differential changes in output per man-hour are found from industry to industry. An increase in output per man-hour is described as a permissive factor—one that makes wage changes possible. Positive factors are those that determine what will happen to wages within the range established by permissive factors. The positive factors are (1) the degree of concentration of production within an industry (a high degree of concentration means that firms in the industry are more likely to retain the gains of productivity rather than lose them to consumers, competitors, or suppliers) and (2) the degree of union organization. A high degree of organization is construed as likely to lead to a diversion of productivity gains to labor. Thus, an industry where wages are increasing at an above average rate is likely to be one where output per man-hour has increased materially, production is concentrated among a few firms, and the workers are highly organized.

Ross and Goldner believe that variations in interindustry wage structures have been relatively small since 1933. According to their measurements of changes in straight-time average hourly earnings between 1933 and 1946 in 50 industries, 35 industries deviated from the average increase by less than ten cents.[38] From this they conclude that the strongest influences on wages

---

[36] *Ibid.*, p. 344.

[37] Joseph W. Garbarino, "A Theory of Interindustry Wage Structure Variation," *Quarterly Journal of Economics*, May, 1950, pp. 282–305.

[38] Arthur M. Ross and William Goldner, "Forces Affecting the Interindustry Wage Structure," *ibid.*, p. 280. According to several studies, the industry rankings in terms of average wages paid have been rather stable since 1899. Those industries that ranked low in terms of level of wages paid at the beginning of the century, in general, rank low today. Conversely, the high wage industries of fifty years ago are the high wage industries today. Thus even though there has been diversity in patterns of wage changes among industries, the over-all interindustry wage structure appears to have remained stable. See Donald E. Cullen, "The Interindustry Wage Structure, 1899–1950," *American Economic Review*, June, 1956, pp. 352–369.

have been those operating through the economy generally rather than those that have affected individual industries in different degrees. In general they found that earnings increased most rapidly (1) where employment expansion was greatest, (2) in industries with oligopolistic market structures, and (3) among industries where union organization occurred after 1933.' "New unionism (that is, unionization) has been a source of relative wage advantage during the 1933–46 period whereas continuing unionism has not."[39] Ross and Goldner admit an inability to determine which of the three influences (unionization, employment change, and oligopolistic market structure) is the primary cause of interindustry wage variations. Unionism, they conclude, is a necessary but not a sufficient condition for larger than average increases in earnings.[40]

The studies cited advance three explanations of wage relationships among industries. They have some points of similarity but differ in certain respects and especially with reference to the importance of union pressures. Other studies using different analytical methods and testing various hypotheses have failed to clarify the issue to any significant extent. Levinson, for example, computed correlation coefficients between changes in earnings and selected variables in nineteen manufacturing industries for the period 1947–1958 and found no significant relationship between year-to-year changes in earnings and percentage changes in output, production worker employment, or productivity.[41] On the other hand, he found an interrelationship, particularly after 1951, between hourly earnings, profit levels, and industry concentration ratios. In a more recent study, Levinson examined the wage experience of six West Coast industries in detail and concluded that economic factors, internal union politics, and "pure union power" were all important factors affecting the relative movements of wage and fringe benefits.[42] The findings of his study, however, cast doubt on the validity of the general proposition that a combination of oligopolistic product markets and strong union power yields the more favorable increase in earnings since the largest increases occurred in those industries functioning in competitive product markets. Levinson's data suggest that the key to the relationship between product market structure and wage changes is the ability of new firms beyond the jurisdictional control of the union to

[39] Ross and Goldner, *op. cit.,* p. 267.
[40] *Ibid.,* p. 281.
[41] Harold M. Levinson, "Postwar Movement of Wages and Prices in Manufacturing Industries," Study Paper No. 21 prepared in connection with the *Study of Employment, Growth, and Price Levels* for the Joint Economic Committee of the Congress of the United States, January 30, 1960.
[42] Harold M. Levinson, *Determining Forces in Collective Bargaining* (New York: John Wiley and Sons, Inc., 1966), pp. 264–269. See also Bruce T. Allen, "Market Concentration and Wage Increases: U.S. Manufacturing, 1947–1964," *Industrial and Labor Relations Review,* April, 1968, pp. 353–365 for a study that suggests that the relationship between market concentration and high wage increases may be spurious.

enter the industry. When such entry is difficult, the union is better positioned to press for larger wage adjustments. The accumulation of data and the numerous analyses that have been made, in other words, have yet to materialize in a definitive statement of industry wage differences. Similarly, no final conclusion concerning the relative importance of "market" versus "non-market" forces can be persuasively defended.[43]

Wage Differences in Local Labor Markets

In local labor markets one might logically expect to find a pronounced tendency toward an equilibrium in which workers at nearly identical jobs receive nearly identical pay. The fact is, however, that surprisingly large wage differentials for similar jobs in local areas seem to persist in the long run. Despite the apparent illogic of local area wage differentials, they can probably be explained more satisfactorily than the other types of differences noted, possibly because local labor markets are more amenable to observation. Factors that contribute to the durability of local wage rate differences are discussed below:

1. As already noted, labor markets are characterized by frictions and imperfections. Lack of information about job openings and prevailing wage rates and the reluctance of many workers to make job shifts are partially responsible for the failure of wage differentials to narrow as rapidly as they otherwise might.

2. Within local areas, different firms are faced with different competitive situations in the product market. Because of better management, greater engineering ingenuity, or monopolistic advantages, some firms are able to pay higher than average wages and do so either because they want to or are forced to. A successful firm that happens to have a high wage structure is not likely to jeopardize its success by attempting to realign its wage system to take advantage of favorable labor supply conditions. Many firms, furthermore, are caught between industry and area wage pulls. In certain industries, such as automobile or steel manufacturing, the industry influence is clearly dominant. Consequently, firms in these industries can easily be out of line in terms of prevailing area rates.

An assumption frequently made is that occupational wage dispersion in local markets is a result solely of interestablishment wage differences. A recent study, however, indicates that wage differences within establishments also contribute to the dispersion.[44] This is more so in the case of

---

43 For interesting, if inconclusive, statements concerning the relative importance of market and non-market forces see Reder, *op. cit.*, pp. 276–298 and the comment by Donald E. Cullen, pp. 311–317 of the same volume.

44 H. M. Douty, "Sources of Occupational Wage and Salary Rate Dispersion within Labor Markets," *Industrial and Labor Relations Review*, October, 1961, pp. 67–74.

office clerical jobs than of manual jobs in manufacturing, but even for the latter class of occupations intra-establishment variations account for a significant degree of the wage dispersion in local labor markets.

3. Part of the observed differences in local wage rates can be attributed to the technical problems of statistical measurement. The welder in plant *A* may be earning twenty cents per hour less than the welder in plant *B*, but his job may be substantially different despite the similarity of job title. More careful wage surveys might eliminate part of this discrepancy, but it is doubtful that it can be totally eliminated. It is quite probable that when extreme differences are observed in local wage comparisons—the highest-paid worker in a job class earning perhaps 25 per cent to 50 per cent more than the lowest-paid worker—the job performances are also very different.

4. What is commonly regarded as a local labor market is usually a grouping of distinct, albeit overlapping, markets. Residents of a city's west side might have strong preferences for employment in their own section of the city. The same might be true of residents of certain neighborhoods. Nationality, racial, or religious groups might cluster about certain employments. The availability of transportation facilities can influence the dimensions of a labor market. The shapes and characteristics of labor markets within an over-all local area are constantly changing, but it is unusual for the dimensions of a political subdivision and the labor market to be co-extensive. Supposed wage differences in local labor markets might actually be differences between, rather than within, market areas.

5. There is no labor market as such for many semi-skilled occupational classifications. An employer who needs a class *C* assembler does not try to hire someone who is able to show specific experience as a class *C* assembler. Most likely he will transfer or promote someone within the plant. If this is not possible, he will attempt to hire someone who has qualifications such as dexterity and speed rather than experience or training. This means that the semi-skilled worker is often not able to sell his services on the basis of an occupational skill that can be differentiated from others. When unemployed he becomes part of a pool of available factory labor, and local employers hire from this pool.[45] Once hired, the semi-skilled worker is fitted into one of numerous possible job slots in the plant. His wage rate is determined less by his occupational qualifications than by the relationship of his job to key jobs in the plant wage structure. Thus, what is likely to be found in wage comparisons is a wide spread in wage rates for semi-skilled job classifications, for the plant's internal wage structure, rather than the labor market, is responsible for the specific job rate being what it is. Less

---

[45] Robert L. Raimon, "The Indeterminateness of Wages of Semiskilled Labor," *Industrial and Labor Relations Review,* January, 1953, p. 193.

area wage spread should be expected in the case of skilled or key job classes where there is an active and recognizable labor market for persons qualified to hold such jobs. At least one wage student has noted a greater uniformity in the wage rates of the skilled workers.[46]

Five factors have been suggested here as being basic to an explanation of wage differentials in local labor market areas. They are (1) frictions and market imperfections, (2) the different competitive situations in which firms find themselves, (3) difficulties of statistical measurement that probably result in some overstatement of wage differences, (4) a looseness in the definition of local labor markets, and (5) the failure of the market to differentiate very precisely among semi-skilled occupational categories. These are broad and general factors. A more exhaustive explanation of local wage differentials would mention other items such as racial and sex differentials and certain details of hiring and job-seeking practices.[47]

WAGE DETERMINATION WITHIN THE FIRM

Assuming for the time being that we are dealing with non-union firms, the typical situation is one where the firm has some degree of discretion in establishing a wage level. It must be decided whether the company will seek to pay the lowest of possible wage rates or whether, for one of a number of reasons, it will pitch its wage structure at some level above the feasible minimum. Whatever the decision in this respect, the discretion of the firm is ultimately limited on the one hand by a wage floor that might be established by law, prevailing social standards, or labor supply conditions and on the other by the fact that some high wage level will involve costs that are inconsistent with the economic ambitions of the firm.

Apart from the matter of relating a wage structure to wage levels that prevail outside the firm, there is the further problem of achieving satisfactory internal wage relationships. What wage relationships should be established among the different job classes within the firm? In medium sized and large firms this problem might involve a comparison or ranking of anywhere between hundreds and literally thousands of job classes.

Whether the problem is that of relating the wage schedule to prevailing market levels or that of balancing internal wage relationships, the basic goal of the firm's wage policy is to achieve the production of goods and services at a cost that makes a satisfactory profit possible. In many cases this makes

---

[46] *Ibid.,* p. 185.

[47] See Richard A. Lester, "A Range Theory of Wage Differentials," *Industrial and Labor Relations Review,* July, 1952, pp. 483–500, and W. Rupert Maclaurin and Charles A. Myers, "Wages and the Movement of Factory Workers," *Quarterly Journal of Economics,* February, 1943, pp. 262–264.

the internal rate determinations as important as the external comparisons. If poorly planned, the in-plant wage relationship can easily develop into an administrative atrocity that causes a degeneration of worker morale and results ultimately in a low level of productivity with a dangerously high labor cost per unit of output.

Part of the internal wage problem of the firm stems from the fact that the marketplace provides little or no information that is relevant to the larger number of jobs within the plant. In larger establishments especially, there are many jobs that consist of a grouping of duties that is dictated by the technology and work processes within the plant. There is no labor market for these jobs in the sense that there is a labor market for bricklayers, or tool and die makers, or stenographers. The obvious wage standards for what might be called local plant jobs are the in-plant relationships between these and certain key or standard-setting jobs. Wage setting for the bulk of the jobs within a plant, consequently, is performed by the administrative process of ranking or comparing the content of jobs.

The absence of a labor market wage comparison for local plant jobs can be overstressed. Despite the fact that many semi-skilled jobs require no specific experience and can be filled by upgrading common labor or by hiring from a general pool of available labor, there is usually a certain earnings expectation that predominates in a labor market area. The earnings expectation of the semi-skilled worker may be less specific than that of the skilled worker and may spread over such a range that the employer is provided with a broad leeway for making administrative wage determinations. Nevertheless, at a given time there is some level of expectations that sets limits to the employer's discretion. So long, however, as administrative wage determinations are not grossly inconsistent with prevailing wage expectations, rates within the plant can be structured primarily in terms of in-plant imperatives as determined by technological and work process considerations.

Evaluating Jobs

The comparison of jobs within the firm for wage determination purposes may be accomplished in a very informal manner or by quite elaborate techniques. In recent years formal systems of job evaluation have been widely used. Although much variation can be found in the details of job evaluation practices, most of the systems in current use are classifiable as one of several basic types.

The "job ranking system" is one of the simplest forms of job evaluation. Here jobs are simply ranked in order of importance. Usually a few key jobs are selected and other jobs are ranked in terms of their relationships to the key occupations.

Under the "job classification system," job levels or classifications are established on the basis of a prior analysis of the work being performed. Individual jobs are then fitted into one of the classifications.

When a "point system" is used, each job is graded in terms of a number of elements such as skill, effort, responsibility, hazard, and the like. The job is credited with points for each of the elements used in the system, and the total of such points establishes the relative ranking of the job.

One of the most elaborate of job evaluation techniques is the "factor comparison system." A number of factors are selected and certain key jobs are ranked in terms of each factor. By a somewhat involved system of weighing and comparing, all other jobs are appraised in terms of the key jobs and a total monetary wage scale for each job is determined.[48]

Job evaluation only ranks jobs. Some process for transplanting the rankings into money wage rates must be selected by the firm. In simple systems community wage comparisons are obtained for a few key jobs, and other jobs are assigned money wage rates on the basis of an evaluated relationship to the key jobs. Another approach is to establish minimum and maximum money rates and to fit the various jobs into this predetermined range. A common procedure is to use the device of a wage curve to show the relationship between the values of the job evaluation system and a selected standard such as current rates paid by the firm or prevailing community rates. Such a comparison can serve as a guide to the firm in establishing absolute money values for the various labor grades.[49]

Our concern here is less with the details of job evaluation systems than with the implications of such systems for wage determination within the firm. In this respect a number of points can be made. (1) Job evaluation is an administrative procedure for ranking jobs and, thus, for determining the relative remuneration for different jobs. Although deference to the labor market may be made in the selection of rates for key jobs or in the selection of a general wage level, a strict adherence to job evaluation procedures means that an administrative process replaces the labor market as the determinant of which jobs receive the higher wage rates. (2) Job evaluation is nothing more than a systematic method of making judgments. When judgments are involved there is room for wage decisions that may

---

[48] For a more detailed description of job evaluation systems, see Jay L. Otis and Richard H. Leukart, *Job Evaluation* (Englewood Cliffs, N.J.: Prentice-Hall, Inc., 1954), Part 2, or John A. Patton and Reynold S. Smith, *Job Evaluation* (Homewood, Ill.: Richard D. Irwin, Inc., 1950), chaps. 2 and 3.

It has been observed that the principal differences in job evaluation systems can be accounted for on two bases: (1) the consideration of the job as a whole *v.* the consideration of the job by parts or elements and (2) the evaluation of each job against other jobs *v.* the evaluation of each job against a previously prepared rating scale. C. H. Lawshe and G. A. Satter, "Studies in Job Evaluation," *Journal of Applied Psychology,* June, 1944, p. 189.

[49] Otis and Leukart, *op. cit.,* chap. 13.

run counter to what the industrial engineer considers sound principles of job evaluation. A technological change that lowers the skill requirements of a job, for instance, should result in a downgrading of the job's evaluation. Downgrading is not always feasible, however; and this is especially true when a union represents the workers. In some instances it may be far more feasible to change the job evaluation system than to institute large-scale changes in job relationships. In recent years, as automatic processes have diluted the skill content of some jobs, there has been a tendency to give greater weight to the responsibility factor and less to the skill factor in job evaluation procedures. Job evaluation, thus, is not a science but a technique subject to many qualifications. It is likely to be most effective when changes in technology are minor in nature and slow in occurrence and least effective when change is abrupt and large-scale. (3) Job evaluation or some similar technique is an almost inevitable development when work processes necessitate hundreds or thousands of job classes within a firm. Understanding wage determination in such a situation requires an understanding of plant technology and the relationship of key jobs to a family of related jobs. It is also essential that the effects of changed technology be understood as influences upon the process of administrative, as well as economic, wage determination.

Earnings Variations within Firms

We have already noted that workers within the same local labor market area who perform approximately the same work are frequently remunerated in different amounts. A fact that is often overlooked is that within the same firm there may be impressive variations in earnings among workers that cannot be explained by differences in money wage rates alone.

A substantial amount of labor is performed under pay systems that are based upon effort rather than the amount of time worked. Many types of incentive systems are used in plant work, while commission plans are quite common in retail and wholesale sales. In the absence of worker collusion, widespread variations in earnings are likely to be found among workers when incentive or commission plans are in effect.

In incentive or commission pay systems, the wage determination process centers about the establishment and policing of standards. Theoretically, an incentive system standard is constructed so that a normal or average worker will be able to earn some specified percentage above a base rate. A number of difficult problems attend the standard-setting procedure, however.

First, "normal" is a question-begging concept, and the matter of who is normal and what is normal output is rarely settled to everyone's satisfaction. Significant variations in the specification of "normal" output can be found from firm to firm. Second, the re-establishment of standards after technological change has occurred is likely to be attended by conflicting positions relative to the details of change. Third, the question of what happens when and if workers develop work methods to "beat" the standard is difficult to resolve without running into morale problems. These points are raised as examples of additional complexities that arise in wage determination when incentive systems are used. An incentive plan that has been in operation over a period of time is likely to be a mixture of incentive plan theory plus concessions necessary to insure the acceptability of the plan among workers.

Once regarded as an employer technique to get more work for less pay, incentive plans have become increasingly popular among workers as evidenced by numerous instances where incentive pay plans are willingly accepted in operations that are machine—rather than worker—paced. At one time, employers sought and workers resisted the use of incentive pay systems. Presently there is much evidence that the historical attitudes are being reversed.

The important point for this analysis is that an explanation of the level of earnings under incentive pay systems requires an understanding not only of the technical features of plans but the effects of environmental and administrative influences as well. Average earnings in two different plants that use the same incentive pay system may show astounding variation.

Variations in the earnings of workers performing similar operations within a firm are also found when time rates are in effect. Administration of rate range systems, special premium pay arrangements, and slight variations in pay specifications are factors, among others, that account for earnings differences that sometimes reach substantial proportions.[50]

Worker earnings, then, may vary widely within firms and from firm to firm for reasons that are unrelated to the economic forces of demand and supply. Some part of the observed variation in earnings and labor costs must be attributed to differences in wage administration practices.

SUMMARY

In this chapter, a number of factors that thus far have been but imperfectly incorporated into a general explanation or theory of wages have been examined. Aspects of the labor market, mobility characteristics of workers, the details of regional, industrial, occupational, and local wage differentials, and influences that operate within firms are conditioning factors in wage determination that must be grafted into a pure demand and supply analysis

---

[50] For an analysis of the economic implications of a wage range structure for clerks in retail food distribution see Walter A. Fogel, "Job Rate Ranges: A Theoretical and Empirical Analysis," *Industrial and Labor Relations Review*, July, 1964, pp. 584–597.

before a wholly satisfactory explanation of wages can be formulated. The details of wage determination are better understood today than at any time in the past; the systematization of such details that is essential for sophisticated wage generalizations continues to be a baffling problem.

QUESTIONS

1. What factors make it difficult to define the dimensions of a labor market area?

2. The evidence as to whether or not job movement by workers is motivated by wage differences is conflicting. What evidence suggests that workers change jobs primarily to make more money? What evidence suggests a contrary conclusion?

3. The wage structure of the United States is characterized by occupational, geographical, and industrial differentials. Describe the basic factors that appear to account for the persistence of each of the three types of differentials.

4. A survey of occupational wage rates within a local labor market area will usually reveal the existence of a wide range of rates. How can such differences be explained?

5. In order to understand how wages are determined in a large plant it is necessary to know something about the plant's technology and administrative wage practices. Explain the meaning of the foregoing statement. Does the statement imply that "economic forces" are not important? What is the significance of the statement in terms of a theory of wage determination?

6. Over the course of a working life, it is highly probable that a person will change his occupation and his industry of employment and will move from one geographical area to another. What challenges are posed for our educational system by these characteristics of a contemporary work career?

SELECTED READINGS

DOUTY, H. M. "Wage Differentials: Forces and Counterforces," *Monthly Labor Review,* March, 1968, pp. 74–81.

PALMER, GLADYS L., PARNES, HERBERT S., WILCOCK, RICHARD C., HERMAN, MARY W., and BRAINERD, CAROL P. *The Reluctant Job Changer.* Philadelphia: University of Pennsylvania Press, 1962.

PARNES, HERBERT S., FLEISHER, BELTON M., MILJUS, ROBERT C., and SPITZ, RUTH S. *The Pre-Retirement Years: A Longitudinal Study of the Labor Market Experience of the Cohort of Men 45–59 Years of Age.* Columbus, Ohio: Center for Human Resource Research, The Ohio State University, 1968. Chap. 5.

REDER, MELVIN W. "Wage Differentials: Theory and Measurement," *Aspects of Labor Economics.* (National Bureau of Economic Research, Special Conference Series, No. 14.) Princeton, N.J.: Princeton University Press, 1962, pp. 257–317.

REYNOLDS, LLOYD, and TAFT, CYNTHIA. *The Evolution of Wage Structure.* New Haven, Conn.: Yale University Press, 1956.

ROTHSCHILD, K. W. *The Theory of Wages.* Oxford: Basil Blackwell, 1956. Chaps. 3, 6.

CHAPTER 14

Unionism and Wages

IN THE IMMEDIATELY PRECEDING CHAPTERS LITTLE MENTION WAS MADE of the union influence in wage matters. This omission was deliberate. In order to simplify the introductory analysis of wage determination, the question of the union impact was reserved for separate discussion.

In the present chapter there will be a consideration of several facets of unionism and wages. What do unions attempt to do in the wage area? Is there some identifiable union wage goal? Do the labor union arguments for higher wages amount to a consistent expression of a specific wage philosophy, or are such arguments essentially opportunistic? The bulk of the chapter will be devoted to an analysis of the impact of the union upon wage structures and income distribution. Has the behavior of large and potent labor organizations had a significant effect on forms of wage payments, various wage relationships, and the share of the total national income that goes to labor?

These questions, and particularly the latter, have been much debated in recent economic literature. In some respects the impact of the union is obvious. In others it is subtle and perhaps negligible. As usual, no final answers can be given to the problems raised. The nature of the issues will be presented, and what is apparently the current consensus will be noted.

UNION WAGE POLICY

All things considered, the broadest explanation of union wage policy is that it is designed to promote the economic welfare of the membership. This generalization, however, begs many questions. Are unions unmindful of the employment effects of their wage policies? Who decides how to promote welfare and under what pressures are the decisions made? Are some factors typically more important than others in the formulation of union wage policy? Unless these questions are answered the statement that unions attempt to promote employee welfare provides little insight into the specifics of union wage behavior.

Union Wage Rationalizations

Over the years, a variety of slogans and arguments have been used by labor spokesmen to justify a general policy favoring higher wages and wage increases in certain economic contexts. A detailed examination of these pronouncements would not be overly helpful for an understanding of union wage actions. It has long been noted that what unions say about wage matters is less pertinent to an understanding of their behavior than what they do.

Apart from slogans such as "fair wage," "living wage," and "social wage," unions have relied upon various arguments in their appeals which are often as much directed to the membership and the general public as to the employer. The "purchasing power" argument is designed to show that high wages are good for the economy as well as for workers. If producers cannot sell their products, unemployment rises, profits disappear, and major social problems develop. When workers are adequately paid, they are able to purchase the output of a highly productive economic system, and the undesirable consequences of a decline in sales do not occur. The purchasing power arguments enjoyed some currency in the 1920's and acquired an intellectual respectability as a result of the Keynesian impact upon economic thought in the 1930's. In an economy depressed much below full employment levels an argument that tied the appeal for higher wages to the health of the economy as a whole was bound to enjoy a widespread popularity. In the years immediately following World War II, much was made of the "ability to pay" thesis. Business firms, it was alleged, could afford to grant wage increases without raising product prices, since profits were sufficiently high to absorb wage boosts. A "cost-of-living" argument became popular during the Korean War period. It was maintained that workers should not suffer a deterioration in living standards simply because the commodities that workers bought had jumped in price. When living costs rose, pay raises sufficient to maintain prevailing real wages should be forthcoming. Cost-of-living clauses designed to accomplish just this were incorporated into many collective bargaining agreements during the inflation of the early fifties.

The difficulty with these and similar arguments is that they all have reverse counterparts. Cost of living, for instance, can fall as well as rise; and a completely consistent position in this respect involves an acceptance of the risk of wage declines. Most cost-of-living agreements, however, establish floors below which further living cost drops are not matched by wage deductions. Strict adherence to an ability-to-pay doctrine would require a substantial amount of deference to inability to pay. Even the purchasing power thesis can be used as an argument against wage boosts when consumer goods are in short supply and price inflation is incipient or has already occurred.

Complete consistency in the use of these arguments by labor organizations would result in quite restrained wage policies, often requiring a stabilized or even a reduced money wage rate for the workers. Such consistency, however, would be inconsistent with broader goals and purposes of unions. Underlying the wage behavior of many labor organizations is the belief that unions can and should divert more of the total national income into the labor sector. In practice this means a constant and often aggressive effort to achieve wage improvements. The various wage arguments, consequently, are essentially opportunistic and take their coloration from the economic context in which they are broached.

Despite the inconsistencies in union wage rationalizations and despite the sloganlike character of many of the pronouncements, the union arguments cannot be dismissed as totally meaningless. In given situations these pronouncements may constitute highly effective tactics. It is less important, perhaps, to note that labor's use of the cost-of-living doctrine has not been completely consistent than it is to realize that the argument bore fruit by way of an important addition to the wage section of collective bargaining agreements. Wage statements, furthermore, are effective in stimulating union members to support their organization in its wage controversies. Finally, it should be noted that the various arguments are called upon for yeoman service in the public relations fight that frequently accompanies the bargaining in critical wage negotiations. If union pronouncements are opportunistic, the same might be said of the arguments made by management spokesmen. Such arguments may be unrelated to the final agreements reached, but it is important to have a good case to present to the public.

Hypotheses of Union Wage Policy

Labor students have long sought to develop generalized explanations of union wage behavior. In recent years two substantially different formulations have attracted much attention. One approach places the major emphasis upon political considerations. The other insists that wage determination under trade unions is most fruitfully analyzed in economic terms.

Professor Arthur Ross's work is one of the more carefully drawn political analyses.[1] He argues that the trade union is a political agency operating in

[1] *Trade Union Wage Policy* (Berkeley, Calif.: University of California Press, 1948).

an economic environment with the central objective of institutional survival and growth. To be successful the union leadership must reconcile pressures exerted by the rank and file, the employers, other organizational levels of the union, other unions, and the government. Union wage policy, consequently, should be regarded as a technique for dealing with the pressures that must be contained if the union as an institution is going to survive and flourish. This does not mean that economic considerations such as product sales volume and amount of unemployment are unimportant. But it does appear to mean that economic forces exert less influence upon union wage decisions than is popularly supposed. Such forces constitute, at best, a degree of influence that is secondary to the political imperatives involved in the life of the union organization.

Specifically, Ross contends that the compelling influences in wage determination under collective bargaining flow from "orbits of coercive comparison." When a union, for instance, bargains on a regional or national level, wage policy must be designed to avoid the charge that the national union is discriminating in favor of some locals. Similarly in the case of the multi-plant company, the wage bargain is influenced by the fact that workers in one plant will inevitably make comparisons with the wages received by the employees in the other plants of the firm. When there is intra- or inter-union rivalry, the rival leaders will make intensive efforts to outdo each other or to avoid being outdone in the matter of obtaining wage benefits.

These examples are sufficient to illustrate the political nature of union wage policy. Union leadership, according to this approach, is less concerned with the maximization of labor income than it is with striking wage bargains that will satisfy the people who must be satisfied. Ross argues, further, that it is usually impossible for the union to give serious consideration to the employment effects of its wage demands. There are several reasons for this. The typical wage bargain covers only a small segment of the economy and, except in very unusual cases, the employment effect of a wage increase is not predictable. The wage-cost-employment level relationship is too vague to provide the union leader with any sort of workable standard for formulating a specific wage policy. All in all, then, what are commonly regarded as the economic factors play less part in the determination of union wage policy than does a package of relationships that can be described as the political context in which the union functions.

In contrast to the political argument, Professor John Dunlop has contended that wage determination under collective bargaining is best analyzed in terms of an assumption of income-maximizing behavior on the part of unions.[2] Various alternatives are open to the union. It may shoot for ex-

[2] *Wage Determination Under Trade Unions* (New York: Augustus M. Kelley, 1950).

tremely high wages, for instance, regardless of the employment consequences, or it may seek to set wages at a point that will yield the largest
amount of employment for the membership. Probably the most suitable
generalization that can be made is that the union attempts to maximize the
wage bill for the total membership, although in instances some members
may be favored at the expense of others. Whatever the "membership function" may be in a given case, the union leadership does attempt to maximize
the income of the members involved. At the national level, where the influential "key" wage bargains are struck, union leaders are knowledgeable
in an economic sense; and when they formulate their wage demands they
do consider costs, prices, product market competition, and other pertinent
economic variables.

Can these two conflicting hypotheses be reconciled? If not, which is the
more appropriate in analyzing union wage behavior? An obvious answer
is that union wage behavior is conditioned by both economic and political
factors. Both writers quoted above admit this, although each minimizes the
importance of one factor.

In the actual play of collective bargaining there is much evidence to
support the "political" analysis. Inter- and intra-union rivalries and other
similar pressures explain a great deal of what occurs. This theory, however,
is essentially a short run explanation. Over a period of time the political
goals of the union must be compatible with the employer's ability to pay.
It is the economic factors that ultimately set the boundaries within which
political wage maneuvering can occur.

Against the contention that union leaders do not consider the employment effects of their wage demands can be cited the fact that unions have
explicitly considered the employment problem in numerous instances.[3] The
idea that labor leaders typically disregard the unemployment possibilities
of unwise wage demands might stem from the facts of the post-World War
II economic context. In a situation in which there was little unemployment,
the notion that a specific union wage policy might cause some workers to
lose jobs could be established analytically but was empirically testable only
in a few exceptional cases. Faced with the facts of obvious prosperity most
unions followed wage policies that were seemingly uninfluenced by fears
of economic catastrophe. The elements of a special situation, however,
cannot be extrapolated to show that in all cases and at all times unions are
unmindful of the employment effects of their wage demands.

It has been noted that neither the economic nor the political hypothesis
explains specific union wage policies. Both theories are very general and

---

[3] See George P. Shultz and Charles A. Myers, "Union Wage Decisions and Employment," *The American Economic Review*, June, 1950, pp. 362–388.

consequently are compatible with almost any kind of wage policy.[4] A union that is seeking to maximize the income of its members, for example, may select one of many possible policies. The precise nature of the choice cannot be predicted from the mere knowledge that the union is seeking to maximize a wage bill. There may be a significant difference between a policy that will actually maximize membership income and one that the union leader *believes* will maximize income. A knowledge of how and to what extent a union's wage policy is influenced by political and economic considerations will provide some insights into the wage behavior of the organization. Given the present state of our data, a theory that lays claim to more than this is too ambitious.

Numerous difficulties attend the development of a broad single explanation of union wage policy. From union to union, differences in ideological orientation, leadership-membership relations, and the economic health of the industry or firm involved may be so vast that uniformities in a basic matter such as wage policy are oftentimes less striking than the dissimilarities. To speak of "union wage policy" without further differentiation is to engage in a very high level of abstraction. Students of labor organizations have long recognized that there are non-income objectives of union wage policy and that these objectives vary among unions.[5] Wage bargains of some local unions are closely controlled by national organizations, whereas other locals are relatively free to make their own arrangements. In industries such as steel, automobiles, meat packing, electrical manufacturing, and others, a key wage bargain struck by the union and a prominent firm establishes the tone and frequently the details of the agreements reached elsewhere in the industry. Certain unions are imaginative and experimental in their wage policies while others are quite conservative.

This rather incomplete catalogue of complexities is sufficient to illustrate the difficulties of developing a satisfactory generalized explanation of union wage behavior. Such behavior is conditioned by a host of details that are not easily incorporated into a clearly delineated political or economic hypothesis. There are economic limitations upon union wage policy. Within these limitations the wage policy that will be operative in a given case can be uncovered only by close observation of the actual situation.

---

[4] M. W. Reder, "The Theory of Union Wage Policy," *Review of Economics and Statistics,* February, 1952, pp. 34–45.

[5] See John Dunlop, *op. cit.,* pp. 46–50. During organizational campaigns the union wage statement is designed to appeal to potential union members by proving that the union will provide immediate material benefits. Not infrequently in such situations management will make wage offers designed to prove the opposite. Parts of union wage policy are concerned with the control of working conditions. Premium pay arrangements of one sort or another penalize the employer for work done at unusual times such as Sundays, holidays, or late hours. Other types of non-income objectives can be cited, and together they constitute a consequential element of the wage programs of labor organizations.

THE UNION IMPACT ON WAGE STRUCTURES

There may be some question as to how union wage objectives are best described, but there is little doubt that unions believe that their objectives can be achieved. In this and the following section, the nature of the union impact on wages will be examined. Where have the unions been effective and where ineffective? Precisely what have they managed to accomplish in the wage sphere? The discussion of the impact on wage structures will be in two parts. The first will deal with wage structures within the firm and the second with broader wage relationships.

Internal Wage Structures

Nowhere is the impact of the union so evident as in the wage structure of the firm. Our concern here is not with wage levels but with methods and forms of wage payments and occupational wage relationships. Few collective bargaining agreements will fail to provide clear cut examples of union influence in these areas.

The fact of union influence does not mean that all labor agreements will have similar wage clauses. Marked dissimilarities will be found in the methods of payment favored by different unions. The United Automobile Workers, for instance, has consistently opposed incentive pay plans. The Steelworkers, The Amalgamated Clothing Workers, and others have held opposite attitudes, while some unions, such as the Machinists and the Garment Workers, have been ambivalent in respect to incentive payments.[6] Differences in union attitudes toward incentive plans have been ably analyzed by Professor Sumner Slichter.[7] The important point in this discussion is that whatever the attitude, unions, by and large, have had considerable success in imposing their preferences upon employers.

Forms of payment further illustrate the union influence. The prevalence of paid vacations, paid holidays, night shift differentials, premium pay for work in prescribed periods, severance pay, call-in pay, and other fringe items must be attributed in large part to union pressure. Employers, in many cases, have made these fringe item concessions willingly, but the initial and the continuing pressure for the expansion of "non-wage" benefits has a union source. Welfare and pension plans and, more recently, supplemental unemployment compensation plans are additional examples of the importance of union influence.

---

[6] The Machinists Union has a constitutional clause against piecework, yet many of its members are on some form of piecework. The Garment Workers Union has switched its position on piecework several times.

[7] *Union Policies and Industrial Management* (Washington, D.C.: The Brookings Institution, 1941), chap. 10.

Worker benefits can take many forms. The value of all benefits, for instance, can be lumped together and granted as a straight wage payment. For a variety of reasons American labor unions have chosen to seek a package that includes many security and welfare items. Once again it should be emphasized that employers have not always opposed these items. But it is doubtful that forms of payment for work would be nearly so varied as they are, had the labor unions chosen otherwise.

Developing appropriate wage rate relationships for occupational classifications within a plant is always a vexing problem. Labor organizations have sought and frequently have won the right to bargain over these relationships. Somewhat suspicious of formal systems of job evaluation,[8] unions either regard the results of an evaluation as a take-off point for bargaining or seek to participate actively in the evaluation program itself.

In many cases the union influence on internal wage rate relationships has been salutary. Because of union pressures managements have been forced to look more closely at their wage structures. Troublesome intra-plant inequities have been eliminated; and, not infrequently, orderly wage schedules have replaced erratic and sometimes chaotic conditions. In the basic steel industry, for example, a far-reaching adjustment of internal plant wage structures was accomplished in 1947 and 1948, after two years of study and joint negotiations by the United Steelworkers of America and most of the firms in the industry. Wage structures in steel had "grown up" erratically over the years, and wage rate inequities constituted a major proportion of the alleged grievances. Aware of the troublesome situation, twelve major steel companies established the Cooperative Wage Study in 1943 to determine what corrections were needed. A manual developed by the Cooperative Wage Study became the basis of negotiations between U.S. Steel and the union. After two years of almost constant bargaining the negotiating groups agreed to a wage classification in which all jobs were placed in one of thirty-two classes. Descriptions were worked out for some 25,000 jobs in fifty plants. About 160,000 U.S. Steel employees were affected. Subsequently other companies adopted similar plans so that currently approximately 90 per cent of all steel employees are covered by the same job classification system. The wage rate inequity program in the steel industry may rightly be regarded as a tremendous accomplishment of collective bargaining.

Occasionally, union pressure on internal wage structures has a discordant effect. Overly zealous in their efforts to increase wage rates whenever possible, some union leaders can be held responsible for the distorted wage relationships that develop when inadequate attention is paid to the con-

---

[8] Research Department, International Association of Machinists, *What's Wrong with Job Evaluation* (Washington, D.C., 1954).

sistency of wage rates among the various job classes. Situations can be uncovered where the earnings of incentive-rated workers have fallen grossly out of line with the time-rated skilled workers or where historical wage relationships between production and craft maintenance workers have undergone drastic change to the extreme dissatisfaction of the latter group. On the whole, however, the union influence has contributed to orderliness and consistency in plant wage relationships.

External Wage Structures

"External wage structures" refers here to the occupational, regional, and industrial wage differentials described and analyzed in the last chapter. The extent to which the efforts of organized labor have modified such differentials is vague. Available data are imprecise and, among the many forces that influence wage relationships, it is difficult to pinpoint any one as most responsible for what changes have occurred. The predominant, though not unanimous, opinion of wage students is that collective bargaining has had only a minor effect upon these differentials. Some doubt that there has been any effect at all. This conclusion, if valid, runs counter to what is probably the general belief. Year after year unions have been successful in winning increases in money wages. Logically one might suppose that this would affect not only the share of the national income that accrues to labor but the various wage differentials as well. The question of labor's total share will be examined in the next section. In the remaining part of the present section the structural relationships will be considered.

1. *Occupational Differentials.* In the last chapter it was noted that occupational wage differentials measured in percentage terms have shrunk measurably in the past several decades. Immigration restrictions, the influence of cyclical variations in business, and the fact that unskilled workers have become less unskilled were suggested as factors that might be responsible for the relatively large gains made by those holding the less skilled jobs. Since 1930 the bargaining strength of labor unions has increased considerably. Can any part of the wage differential shrinkage be attributed to the exercise of this strength?

A popular practice in recent years has been for unions to seek across-the-board increases on a uniform cents-per-hour basis. (When all workers in a firm are given the same cents-per-hour increase, the percentage differential, of course, will diminish.) Part of the answer as to why this has occurred can be found in government policy.[9] Permissible wage increases under the Little Steel Formula during World War II, for instance, had to be granted

---

[9] H. M. Douty, "Union Impact on Wage Structures," *Proceedings of the Industrial Relations Research Association,* December, 1953, p. 69.

as uniform cents-per-hour adjustments.[10] Apart from government wage policy, the union practice of bargaining for across-the-board increases may have stemmed from leadership preoccupation with matters other than wage rate relationships and also to a feeling that uniform wage increases would be the most feasible way of achieving equity for the lower income workers in a period of inflation.

We have spoken of "union wage policy," but it should be emphasized that there has been considerable variation in the policies and experiences of different unions relative to occupational wage changes. In the early post-World War II years, severe reductions in the pay differences between certain skilled craft groups and the unskilled groups occurred as a result of collective bargaining practices in the radio and electronic, automobile, meat packing, and brewery industries, among others.[11] Examples of situations where pay spreads were maintained can be found in the industrial chemical, steel, electric utility, and petroleum industries.

It has been noted that in industries where significant compression of occupational differentials has occurred, skilled craft workers have been aggressive in seeking more influence in the determination of union wage policy. In a number of cases, open revolts against the union leadership have occurred. New York City subway motormen, for example, temporarily broke away from the Transport Workers Union and conducted a successful strike in protest against the wage levelling that had occurred in their industry. In industries where the skilled-unskilled pay differential has been maintained, no similar restiveness has characterized the skilled craft groups.[12]

Most of the unions affected have responded in one way or another to the internal pressures described above, and more deference is currently being given to the special wage claims of the skilled workers. As noted in the last chapter, there has apparently been little change in the skilled-unskilled differential during the past decade; and a greater awareness on the part of the union leadership of the internal union problems generated by a continuing shrinkage in the differential may have contributed to the stability.

Long run population and technological factors together with the special influences of cyclical variations in business are probably the most important forces accounting for changes in occupational wage relationships. On balance, the union impact has contributed to the narrowing process. The

---

[10] During the Korean War period the Wage Stabilization Board imposed no restrictions on the method of distributing permissible wage adjustments among the eligible workers.

[11] Arnold R. Weber, "The Craft-Industrial Issues Revisited: A Study of Union Government," *Industrial and Labor Relations Review,* April, 1963, pp. 395–398.

[12] *Ibid.,* p. 396.

occupational wage experience varies among unions, however, and in some cases historical differentials have been successfully maintained.[13]

2. *Geographical Differentials.* Wide geographical wage differences have long persisted. There is much variation, however, in the size of differences from industry to industry, firm to firm, and occupation to occupation. Union policy avowedly has been to eliminate geographical differences in the case of inter-regional industries. Firms in low wage areas enjoy a competitive price advantage that can prove detrimental to wage standards achieved elsewhere. Labor unions, consequently, have sought to equalize wages by bringing the low paying areas up to the levels established in other regions.

In a few industries such as basic steel and flat glass, union efforts succeeded in eliminating geographical wage differences. In the bulk of industries, however, union progress has been slow, and wage differences have diminished slowly or not at all. It has been observed that highly favorable conditions have been present in those cases where labor union goals have been achieved.[14] In basic steel, for instance, the workers are strongly organized, there is a high degree of industrial concentration, and southern plants are subsidiaries of northern companies. When there are many small producers and workers are incompletely organized, the job of equalizing wages is considerably more difficult for labor organizations.

It can be concluded that regional wage differences persist despite the intentions of unions because, on the whole, labor organizations have not been sufficiently strong to eliminate them. The forces that have been operative in response to relative economic advantages—for example, migration of labor from South to North and movement of industry in the reverse direction—have had some leavening effect. These forces together with the impact of unionism and government wage legislation account for what reduction of regional wage differences has occurred. The high birth rate in the South which replenishes labor supply, the rural location of much southern industry, and the yet incomplete industrialization of the region are factors that have continued to depress area wage rates in the face of all counteracting influences.

What will occur in the future depends upon which of the forces mentioned above predominates. The efforts of labor unions to organize southern workers have been only mildly successful so far. The unique social condi-

[13] In his study of wages at the McCormick Works of the International Harvester Company for the period 1858 to 1959, Ozanne failed to find evidence of a long run narrowing trend in occupational differentials. He did find that skilled differentials were as much influenced by union policies and prevailing notions of equity as they were by general conditions of labor supply. Robert Ozanne, "A Century of Occupational Differentials in Manufacturing," *Review of Economics and Statistics,* August, 1962, pp. 292–299.

[14] Lloyd G. Reynolds and Cynthia H. Taft, *The Evolution of Wage Structure* (New Haven, Conn.: Yale University Press, 1956), p. 183.

tions of the South, determined employer opposition, and unfavorable state labor legislation have constituted effective barriers against unionization. Despite all this there is a general expectation that it is only a matter of time until the degree of unionization in the South is on a par with that achieved elsewhere. If this occurs it is very likely that there will be a narrowing of geographical wage differences.

3. *Industry Differentials.*   Wage rates and average hourly earnings are higher in some industries than in others. Opinions vary as to whether unionism can be accorded any credit for the differences. A search of the literature will provide the reader with any conclusion he desires: strong unions have improved the relative wage status of the workers in some industries; unions haven't changed the situation much one way or the other; and unions have actually prevented wage levels in strongly organized industries from rising as much as they would have under non-union conditions. The predominant opinion seems to be that unions have had some influence but less than is generally supposed.

An attempt will be made here to summarize the reasons underlying the conclusion that union influence has been minimal, rather than to trace the logic of many individual arguments. The available evidence is hardly conclusive. If the case against union influence is less than fully convincing, it should be kept in mind that the opposite case is no stronger.

1. One group of arguments might be summarized as the permissive approach. When worker earnings in an industry are high or are increasing at an above average rate, economic circumstances that make the high earnings possible can usually be identified. High—or relatively high—wages are usually found where business earnings are also high, and exceptionally good earnings records are usually found in high productivity industries or industries where production is concentrated in a few firms. This argument leaves some room for a union influence. If productivity or degree of concentration produces high business earnings, strong unionism may be the force that siphons part of this income to the workers. It is not unusual to find situations where high productivity, industrial concentration, and strong unions are all present and where it is not immediately obvious which factor is responsible for high wages. The permissive argument stresses the forces that make for business earnings as the more fundamental. Labor unions may play a part in the allocation of earnings, but the earnings must be there in the first place.

2. Numerous attempts have been made to measure union wage influence from both inter- and intra-industry standpoints. From his intensive examination of most of the major studies, Lewis concludes that apart from

periods of rapid inflation the effect of unionism on the average wage of all non-union workers has been on the order of 10 per cent.[15] The sense of the various studies seems to be that unions are capable of affecting relative wages in a way that is favorable for union members but that the degree of union influence has varied considerably over time and among industries. A union influence of more than 25 per cent on relative wages appears to be unusual, however.

Unions obviously do have some effect on wages, and if the net result on industry differentials is minimal some cancelling-out force must be present. Several suggestions have been made along this line. Wage increases obtained in strongly organized industries are usually generalized beyond that industry. Employers elsewhere often grant the same or similar increases because they want to or because they have to. In the latter case the pressure may have a manpower source—higher wages being necessary to attract or keep workers—or wage adjustments may be granted to keep a union at bay. More important, perhaps, is the contention that organized workers suffer less wage decline during depressions, since unions are somewhat effective in resisting pay cuts, but that non-union workers catch up in a relative sense during prosperity when employers voluntarily raise wages in order to attract labor supply.

3. The final argument to be summarized here is that during inflationary periods unions have actually kept wages in certain industries from rising as high as they otherwise might have.[16] Briefly, it is contended that in the presence of a strong union employers are restrained from raising both wages and prices when inflationary pressures are strong. The reason is the fear that prices will eventually fall and the firm will then be saddled with exceptionally high wage costs without the support of a high price level. Rather than face this eventuality, employers choose to exercise moderation in product price setting and thereby remove a union argument for higher wages. The evidence for this argument is that in 1946 and 1947 prices in industries such as autos and steel were substantially below the levels that the market would have sustained. A widespread gray market flourished in steel, and "new-used" cars sold for prices much above the list price of new cars. Obviously then, producers could have sold their outputs at higher prices.

This argument is highly conjectural, but if it is valid it is quite significant. If unions do, in fact, exert a suppressing influence on price during inflation-

---

[15] H. G. Lewis, *Unionism and Relative Wages in the United States* (Chicago: The University of Chicago Press, 1963), chap. 5.

[16] See Albert Rees, "The Economic Impact of Collective Bargaining in the Steel and Coal Industries during the Postwar Period," *Proceedings of the Industrial Relations Research Association,* December, 1950, pp. 203–212.

ary periods the burden of blame for excessive price rises cannot be placed upon the unions. This question will be examined in greater detail in the following chapter.

Summary

The strongest union impact on wage structures is found within the firm where labor organizations, by and large, have been successful in affecting the form, content, and occupational relationships of internal wage structures. External to the firm, the union influence has been weaker. To the extent that unions have affected occupational wage relationships, they have contributed to the narrowing of the skilled-unskilled differential. In a few instances, however, labor organizations have been responsible for the maintenance of historical differences. For the most part geographical differences have been immune to union efforts to eliminate them, although several examples of union success in this respect can be cited. The union impact upon interindustry differentials is vague, but the preponderant opinion is that the influence has been minor.

All of this does not necessarily amount to an argument against unionism. There are many non-wage dimensions to union goals, and not a few labor students believe that these are the most important by far. Furthermore, what unions have been able to do in the past does not conclusively establish what they will be able to accomplish in the future. Finally, it should be noted that the study of the union impact on wage structures is only at a beginning stage. Whether further research substantiates or contradicts the conclusions stated above remains to be seen.

THE UNION IMPACT ON WAGE SHARES

In their *Dynamics of Industrial Democracy,* Golden and Ruttenberg wrote that a prime objective of collective bargaining is "the redistribution of the proceeds of production."[17] Labor spokesmen have more or less assumed that such a redistribution would follow naturally from the ability of unions to insist upon higher money wage rates. When the employer who would prefer to pay $2.00 is forced by union pressure to pay $2.10, it would seem logical to conclude that workers own a larger share of the national income than would have been the case in the absence of unionism.

Unions, of course, have been able to win higher money wages for their members; but this is not the same as a larger share of the national product. If wage increases are accompanied by proportionate increases in profits,

[17] Clinton S. Golden and Harold J. Ruttenberg, *The Dynamics of Industrial Democracy* (New York: Harper & Row, Publishers, 1942), p. 151.

rents, and interest, recipients of wages enjoy no relative gain. The ability of organized labor to redistribute the national income in the favor of labor has been called into question in recent years. In the following sections relevant evidence will be presented, and the union impact on distributive shares will be analyzed. There are differences of opinion among professional economists concerning this matter, and the entire question cannot be regarded as conclusively settled.

The Statistical Evidence

Most of the serious analyses of the labor union effect upon distributive shares are based upon national income data.[18] Statistics of national income show, among other things, the total income distributed within an economy in a given time period, and this at the same time is a measure of the final value of all goods and services produced in the period. If the reader will visualize the geographical vastness of the United States, the multitudes of industries and types of work that are performed, and the many ways in which a person can receive income, some notion of the problem of accumulating income statistics can be conceived.

Two basic problems surround the development of a statistical series of national income. The first centers upon the definition of "income." It can be defined in many ways; the final measures that are derived depend to a great extent upon the definition that is accepted in the first instance.[19] The second problem grows out of the difficulties of data collection. Measures of wages and salaries, corporate income, rent, and interest are not simply "available." The data must be collected, and the collection problem is formidable. The fact that national income statistics are published should not be interpreted to mean that the definition and collection problems have been solved. Some of the definition problems have been resolved by admittedly arbitrary decisions and, because of data collection problems, certain components of the statistical total are less reliable than others.

This is not meant to impugn the value of the income statistics that are currently available in the United States. The development of these data constitutes an amazing statistical accomplishment, and it is difficult to see how intelligent economic policy could be formulated without them. Never-

---

[18] "Distributive shares" refers here to wage and salary income, income of unincorporated enterprises, corporate profits, rental income, and interest income. Total national income is broken down into the shares of these five broad functional classes in the income data presented by the United States Department of Commerce.

[19] Simon Kuznets, whose name is closely associated with the development of national income concepts, has noted that "all national income estimates are appraisals of the end products of economic systems rather than colorless statements of fact; and like all appraisals, they are predetermined by criteria that are at worst a matter of chance, at best a matter of deliberate choice." *National Income and Its Composition, 1919–1938* (New York: National Bureau of Economic Research, 1941), Vol. I, p. 3.

theless, there is a lack of precision that minimizes their value for certain analytical purposes. This caution should be kept in mind in an analysis of the union effect on distributive shares. Available statistics are probably sufficiently reliable to support broad conclusions modestly stated. More affirmative conclusions usually rest upon the preconceptions, values, or analytical ingenuity of the author rather than upon unimpeachable statistical information.

The farther one reaches into the past, the less reliable are the data for an analysis of the union impact upon wage shares. Since mass unionism in the United States occurred after 1930 and since the estimates of national income presented by the Department of Commerce date from 1929, our analysis will neglect the earlier years. If labor organizations are capable of redistributing the proceeds of production to a significant degree, evidence of this capacity might be expected to turn up in the period of labor's greatest strength.

Table 14 shows compensation of employees as a percentage of national income for selected years. In the past several years, employee compensation has been about twelve percentage points higher than it was in 1929. Since the 1929 figure is apparently representative of the 1920 decade, can it be concluded that labor organizations have been successful in accomplishing a redistribution of national income? To answer this question, it is necessary to turn to more refined data than those shown in Table 14.

In the usual analysis of income distribution by broad economic function, national income is divided into the shares received as interest, rent, corporate profits, income of unincorporated enterprises, and employee compensation. An interesting feature of the statistical record is that the percentage rise in employee compensation since 1929 is approximately equal to the combined decline in the interest, rent, and unincorporated enterprise shares. In recent years, corporate profits expressed as a percentage of national income have remained at about the 1929 level.

The distribution of income among functional classes is influenced by structural changes in the economy. If, for example, employees in industry A average \$2.00 per hour while employees in industry B average \$1.50, the labor share of national income will increase if the long run trend is toward an expansion of employment in A and a decline in B. Important among the structural changes that have occurred since 1929 have been the increase in government employment and the decline in the relative significance of unincorporated enterprises resulting largely but not exclusively from the decline in the number of farming enterprises. A popular estimate is that approximately half of the rise in the employee compensation share of national income stems from this structural change. The relationship, if any, between the rise in employee compensation and the decline in interest and

TABLE 14

NATIONAL INCOME AND COMPENSATION OF EMPLOYEES, SELECTED YEARS, 1929–1967
(*Billions of Dollars*)

YEAR	NATIONAL INCOME	COMPENSATION OF EMPLOYEES	COMPENSATION AS PER CENT OF INCOME
1929	87.8	51.0	58.7
1932	42.5	31.0	72.9
1933	40.1	29.5	73.5
1935	57.0	37.3	65.4
1937	73.6	47.9	65.1
1938	67.5	44.4	66.5
1940	72.7	48.1	63.8
1941	104.7	64.7	61.8
1942	137.6	85.2	61.9
1943	170.3	109.5	64.3
1945	181.2	123.1	67.9
1947	197.1	128.7	65.3
1949	216.1	140.8	65.1
1950	239.9	154.3	64.3
1951	277.0	180.4	65.0
1952	290.9	195.4	67.2
1953	305.0	209.0	68.5
1954	301.7	207.5	68.8
1955	330.2	223.8	67.8
1956	349.3	241.7	69.2
1957	363.9	254.6	70.0
1958	367.4	257.1	70.0
1959	399.6	278.4	69.7
1960	417.1	293.7	70.4
1961	426.9	302.2	70.8
1962	455.6	323.1	70.9
1963	478.5	340.3	71.1
1964	518.1	365.7	70.6
1965	564.3	393.8	69.8
1966	620.8	435.6	70.2
1967	652.9	468.2	71.7

Source: United States Department of Commerce.

TABLE 15

NATIONAL INCOME SHARES BY FUNCTIONAL CLASS, 1929 AND 1960
(*Percentages of National Income*)

FUNCTIONAL CLASS	1929	1960
Employee Compensation	58	70
Corporate Profits	12	11
Unincorporated Enterprises	17	12
Interest and Rents	13	7

Source: United States Department of Commerce. The percentages presented here have been rounded.

rent has yet to be satisfactorily explained.[20] In any event, it seems clear that unions have not been able to gain a significant share of national income at the expense of corporate profits.

Numerous studies bear out this latter conclusion. Year-to-year fluctuations in the relationship between employee compensation originating in the private sector of the economy and corporate profits have occurred; but these appear to be best accounted for by cyclical movements of economic conditions, with the employee compensation share rising in depression and falling in prosperity.[21]

The changes that have occurred in the distribution of income among functional classes between 1929 and the present time, thus, seem to be best explained by changes in the structure of industry and cyclical variations in business conditions. A negative verdict against the influence of collective bargaining pressure can be reached by a process of elimination. In the private sector of the economy where wage bargaining is operative, there has been little shift in income distribution. Factors other than unionism seem to account for what shift has occurred. There is little or no residual to be credited to the influence of collective bargaining.

The possibility still remains that within the private sector of the economy, union workers have gained at the expense of non-union workers. We have already noted that the influence of unionism on interindustry wage differentials is vague. Douglas, who studied the statistical evidence for the period 1890–1926, and Ross and Goldner, who examined data for 1933–1946, reached substantially the same conclusion. New unions are able to win appreciable wage gains, but thereafter the rate of gain enjoyed by union members is not significantly higher than that of non-union workers.[22] Levinson believes that between 1933 and 1952 collective bargaining was a factor in obtaining greater wage increases for union workers than those obtained in the non-union sector of the economy.[23] He expresses pessimism, however, concerning the capacity of collective bargaining power to accomplish any fundamental long run readjustments in the distribution of income.[24] Kerr states flatly that "Labor's share of income, industry by

---

[20] For an analysis of the shifts in the shares received by the several functional classes see Walter S. Measday, "Labor's Share in the National Income," *Quarterly Review of Economics and Business,* August, 1962, pp. 25–33.

[21] See Edward F. Denison, "Distribution of National Income," *Survey of Current Business,* June, 1952.

[22] Paul Douglas, *Real Wages in the United States, 1890–1926* (Boston: Houghton Mifflin Company, 1930), p. 562; Arthur M. Ross and William Goldner, "Forces Affecting the Interindustry Wage Structure," *Quarterly Journal of Economics,* May, 1950, p. 267.

[23] Harold M. Levinson, "Collective Bargaining and Income Distribution," *American Economic Review,* May, 1954, p. 311.

[24] *Ibid.,* p. 316.

industry, has fared no more favorably in unionized industries than in non-union."[25] Additional writers could be cited on this question but at no gain in clarification. On the basis of available evidence, doubts can be voiced as to the success of collective bargaining power in winning a larger relative share of income for labor as a whole or for unionized industries as against non-union industries.

Analysis of the Union Impact on Wage Shares

If the labor unions that have been successful in winning higher money wage rates have been unsuccessful in increasing labor's share of total income at the expense of profits, the reason must lie in an ability of management to recoup the revenues that are paid out in the form of higher wages.

The firm faced with higher wage costs may select any one or any combination of several alternatives. By introducing efficiencies and cost-saving devices, expenses may be decreased to the extent that the labor cost of a unit of product is no higher than it was prior to the wage boost. In this case, profit per unit of sales will be unaffected by the higher wage rates, for unit wage costs remain constant. The ultimate effect of higher levels of efficiency will differ among firms. A firm, for instance, might discover that the same volume of output can be produced with a smaller number of workers. If part of the work force is eliminated the net result can be that profits remain constant, the total wage bill remains constant, the employed workers have higher money wage rates, and some part of the firm's labor force must seek work elsewhere.

Unemployment, however, is not inevitably associated with a rise in money wage rates. The firm achieving efficiencies might choose to produce a larger output with the existing body of workers. This choice is feasible if the state of demand for the product is such that the larger volume will find buyers. Whether a firm can sell a larger output depends upon what it has to sell as well as the general condition of business. It also depends upon product price, and this suggests another path by which the firm may recoup its profit position.

A firm may attempt to shift higher wage costs to the consumer by raising prices. The probabilities of successfully making such a shift depend, for one thing, upon the elasticity of demand for the product. When the demand for a product is relatively inelastic the amount that can be sold is independent of price within rather broad limits. Products without close substitutes and regarded as necessities by consumers will have inelastic demands. A ten or twenty per cent rise in the price of bread, milk, or gasoline will not affect the sales of these products to a significant extent. A sudden twenty per cent

---

[25] Clark Kerr, "Trade Unionism and Distributive Shares," *American Economic Review*, May, 1954, p. 288.

increase in the price of jewelry, automobiles, residential dwellings, or train fares, however, may very well result in a large drop in sales. Wage boosts, then, are less easily passed on in the form of higher prices when product demand is elastic.

The ease of shifting higher costs into higher prices also depends upon income elasticity of demand. The nature of income elasticity of demand can be clarified by noting, simply, that more $3,000 automobiles will be sold when worker earnings average $2.00 per hour than when the average is $1.00. It is quite probable, in fact, that more than twice as many cars will be sold at the higher earnings figure. Through larger sales volume and higher product prices, profits that suffer from cost increases are restored or even expanded in a period of rising incomes.

The above explanations are simplified, of course. Many additional factors condition the ability of a firm to adjust to higher wage costs. When wages constitute a small percentage of total costs, the adjustment problem is easier than when wages are a high percentage of total costs. When the product market is highly competitive, wage boosts are less easily passed on to the consumer than when markets are monopolistic. In expanding industries characterized by high productivity, rising wages can be accommodated with greater facility than in declining industries. The fact that profits as a whole have not diminished relative to wages does not mean that all firms have fared equally well. Some firms have been driven to the wall by high labor costs, while others have been able to increase prices to the extent that much more than the original wage increase was recovered.

The changing level of national income is probably the most important conditioning factor in the relationship of the labor and profit shares. Labor unions are most successful in winning money wage increases during periods of rising income. When national income increases it is quite probable that the supply of money is increasing at a faster rate than the supply of goods. This is because the banking system is generating new money in response to a demand created by optimistic business expectations. The velocity of money will also increase. Consumers and business firms keep their money for shorter periods before spending it. When the amount of money in circulation and the rate of money use increase at a greater rate than the output of goods, there is a pressure that forces prices to rise. The firm enjoying good sales volume and higher profits is not apt to jeopardize its fortunes by taking a strong stand against wage demands. The worker possessed of a higher money income seeks to buy more goods, but he finds that prices have risen. The over-all result is a wage-price spiral in which wages chase but never quite catch prices. The question of whether high wages cause high prices or vice versa will be considered in the next chapter. Here it is sufficient to note that, though unions are able to influence the level of money wage rates, they have little or no influence over the processes by which management as a whole is able to maintain the size of profits.

The spokesmen for organized labor who have specified a larger share of national income as a goal of the union movement probably visualize a high wage–low profit situation as an ultimate ideal. Our analysis suggests that a high wage–low profit economy may be impossible so long as a system of free markets exists. The same conditions that make high wages possible insure the fact of high profits.

We have already noted that the wage and salary share of national income tends to be highest in depression periods. When national income falls, prices, profits, and wage rates all decline, but the drop in wage rates is apparently less precipitous. This was the case in the early 1930's when organized labor was not an especially potent force in the economy. A stronger labor movement may be able to slow down the rate of wage decline in depression even more and so increase the labor share in a period of low national income. There is, thus, the paradoxical situation in which organized labor may be most effective in enlarging the wage share of national income in times of high unemployment and low money wage rates and least able to influence the labor share during prosperity when money wage rates are high.

It should be stressed again that logical arguments about the inability of organized labor to influence the share of income that goes to workers are not proof of the inability. The proof depends upon evidence; and although available data appear to support the logic, the fact remains that national income statistics are imprecise in numerous ways. It is also necessary to note that although the wage and profit shares have not changed much in a relative sense, both have increased significantly in absolute terms. Finally, the point should be made that although some spokesmen for organized labor have specified a larger share of national income as a labor goal, most union leaders who negotiate over wages are concerned with the specific income and employment problems of their members rather than with abstractions such as "labor's share." Just as the business firm plans its course of action in terms of its problems and self-defined goals, the typical union negotiator maps his wage strategy in terms of a narrow sphere of interest.

SUMMARY

In this chapter we have considered union wage policy and the union impact upon wage structures and distributive shares of national income. Because union wage goals vary widely depending upon the union and the economic context in which it functions, they are not easily described. Broadly speaking, however, the wage goals may be summarized as the maximization of membership welfare although the methods of achieving this are sometimes dictated by the internal politics of the labor organization. The union impact upon wage differentials and income distribution is probably weaker than has been commonly supposed. A more penetrating impact in these areas may be impossible so long as product markets remain relatively free. Specific unions can and have been successful in raising the relative income status of their memberships. On the whole, however, the relationship between the employee compensation and profit shares of national income has been remarkably constant in periods of peace and prosperity. The cyclical fluctuations of business conditions appear to be the most important influence on the relationships between shares of income over an extended period.

QUESTIONS

1. Is trade union wage policy best explained by a "political" or by an "economic" analysis? What evidence suggests the importance of political factors? What evidence suggests that unions are interested in maximizing the wage bill?

2. In what ways have labor organizations influenced the wage structures of the business firms with which they bargain?

3. Occupational, industrial, and geographical wage differentials were analyzed in Chapter 12. Has trade unionism had a significant effect on the character of these differentials?

4. Many economists have reached the conclusion that the power of unions as expressed in collective bargaining has had little influence on the share of the national income that goes to labor. What evidence supports this conclusion?

5. Labor unions have obviously increased money wage rates. How do you explain the fact that this increase in money wage rates seems not to have increased labor's share of the national income?

6. In the over-all wage area, where has the union impact been the strongest, and where has it been weakest?

SELECTED READINGS

DUNLOP, JOHN T. *Wage Determination under Trade Unions.* New York: Augustus M. Kelley, 1950.

KERR, CLARK. "Labor's Income Share and the Labor Movement," in George W. Taylor and Frank C. Pierson (eds.). *New Concepts in Wage Determination.* New York: McGraw-Hill Book Company, 1957. Chap. 10.

LEWIS, H. G. *Unionism and Relative Wages in the United States.* Chicago: The University of Chicago Press, 1963. Chaps. 3–5.

PHELPS-BROWN, E. H. *The Economics of Labor*. New Haven, Conn.: Yale University Press, 1962, pp. 184–193.

REES, ALBERT. *The Economics of Trade Unions*. Chicago: The University of Chicago Press, 1962. Chaps. 3, 4.

REYNOLDS, LLOYD G., and TAFT, CYNTHIA. *The Evolution of Wage Structure*. New Haven, Conn.: Yale University Press, 1956. Part 1.

ROSS, ARTHUR M. *Trade Union Wage Policy*. Berkeley: University of California Press, 1948.

CHAPTER 15

Inflation and Wages

WAGES, WHICH CONSTITUTE INCOME FOR WORKERS, ARE COSTS FOR EM-
ployers. During the depression period of the 1930's, the attention of government policy-makers as well as of professional economists was focused
primarily on the income aspect. If worker incomes could be increased by
appropriate monetary and fiscal policies, the aggregate demand for goods
and services would also increase. A rise in effective demand, by stimulating
the business community's expectations of profitable operations, would result
in expansion of employment and investment. Investment expenditures, in
turn, would cause employment to rise even more.

The theoretical support for this reasoning was supplied by John Maynard
Keynes in his *General Theory of Employment, Interest, and Money.* Keynes
attempted to show that sporadic wage cuts (cost savings) would only
engender an employer's expectation of further cuts. Such an expectation
could nullify the possibility of an employment increase, since both consumption and investment expenditures could be postponed and made on more
favorable terms after the expected wage cut was realized.[1] Savings in labor
costs, furthermore, might be more than offset by declines in product demand because individual workers would have less income to make purchases. Keynes believed that a "once and for all" wage cut applied
universally so as to create a favorable cost-price relationship might result
in an expansion of employment. Such a general readjustment of costs and

---

[1] *The General Theory of Employment, Interest, and Money* (New York: Harcourt,
Brace & World, Inc., 1936), chap. 19.

prices, however, could not be expected to occur automatically and would be extremely difficult to impose by administrative flat. From a policy standpoint, it would be more feasible to concentrate upon manipulating income than to depend upon wage and price flexibility for a restoration of high employment levels.

The depression bias in economic thought survived the depression. Although unemployment disappeared during the war there was widespread fear that the cessation of hostilities would witness a renewed period of economic distress. Postwar planners, for the most part, concentrated upon the problem of maintaining high levels of income and employment.

Analytical accuracy, of course, is more easily achieved with the benefits of hindsight than when one must rely upon foresight. Nevertheless, there were numerous indications that the immediate postwar years would be characterized by strong consumer demand, high employment levels, and pressures upon commodity prices. Consumer durable goods were in very short supply, potential buyers held large volumes of cash and other liquid assets, and the banking system was heavily loaded with the assets essential for a credit expansion. With the termination of price controls in 1946 the inflationary pressures were unleashed. The postwar price spiral commenced.

Paralleling the price rise was a series of well publicized wage adjustments that started with the eighteen and a half cents "first round pattern" negotiated in the steel industry in the early months of 1946. It was almost inevitable that many observers would impute a cause and effect relationship to the wage-price spiral. Labor spokesmen contended that higher wages were justified because of higher prices. Management spokesmen countered with the reverse argument. More sophisticated analysis eventually demonstrated that both arguments were incomplete.[2]

The postwar price experience has had an impact upon economic thought, and interest in the cost implications of negotiated wage increases has been revived. One analyst has summarized the problem succinctly: "If output per man hour rises by roughly 2 per cent a year, wages cannot go up year after year by, say, 10 per cent."[3] Numerous observers, impressed with the power of organized labor, have concluded that the eventual result of union wage policy can only be unemployment or inflation. If unions continue to negotiate annual wage increases beyond amounts warranted by productivity gains, unemployment will occur as marginal costs are forced above marginal productivity. This result can be averted if the monetary authorities create the money necessary to support the higher wage levels. Such a course, how-

---

[2] See Walter A. Morton, "Trade Unionism, Full Employment, and Inflation," *American Economic Review,* March, 1950, pp. 13–39.

[3] Gottfried Haberler, "Wage Policy, Employment, and Economic Stability," chap. 2 in David McCord Wright (ed.), *The Impact of the Union* (New York: Harcourt, Brace & World, Inc., 1951).

ever, avoids unemployment by creating a price inflation. The more pessimistic opinion is that strong trade unions are incompatible with a free price system.[4] Others believe that appropriate monetary policy or self-imposed restraints by labor leaders will be sufficient to avoid fulfillment of the dire predictions of the pessimists.

Is it possible to have full employment and a stable price level in an economic system where strong labor unions are free to push for higher wages? The question is a fundamental one. Strong labor unions are here to stay. In the absence of far-reaching interferences with free collective bargaining and the price system, wage rates in the important American industries will be established through collective negotiations. If negotiated wage rates are too low, there will be difficulty in maintaining the sales volume essential for full employment. If wage rates are too high, either inflation or unemployment will eventually show up. Excessive price and employment fluctuations in the United States will affect not only internal welfare but the viability of most of the major trading nations as well. The over-all problem, consequently, has international ramifications.

This chapter will be devoted primarily to an examination of the issues posed above. Aspects of post-World War II inflation will be examined in order to clarify the nature of the broader problem. The issues will then be considered more generally.

THE POSTWAR INFLATION

In a dynamic economy, price movements occur constantly. At any given time it is likely that some prices will be moving up, others will be moving down, and still others will be stable. If the net effect of these diverse movements is an increase in the general or average level of prices, a price inflation is taking place. Not all price inflation has serious consequences. Thus, a gradual secular rise in prices can be anticipated as a by-product of industrial growth. Even in a period of general price stability, a monthly measure of prices would be expected to show an increase in some periods and a decline in others. The type of inflation with which we are concerned here is a *persistent* upward movement in the *general* level of prices that creates financial problems for a significant number of individuals and business firms as well as for the several levels of government.

Upward price movements affect different persons in different ways. Those who are able to adjust their incomes with relative facility may suffer little or

---

[4] Henry C. Simons, *Economic Policy for a Free Society* (Chicago: The University of Chicago Press, 1948), chap. 6; Charles E. Lindblom, *Unions and Capitalism* (New Haven, Conn.: Yale University Press, 1949).

no loss. Persons in fixed or partially fixed incomes will, of course, suffer a deterioration in living standards. Pensioners are especially vulnerable, because, more often than not, they are unable to make the adjustments required to maintain the real value of their money incomes. Debtors reap an advantage inasmuch as they are able to meet their contractual obligations with dollars of deflated value. Creditors absorb the loss that is counterpart to the debtors' gain. This last point, incidentally, illustrates the unsettling potential of large-scale price movements. Individuals and business firms hesitate to make long-term commitments when the ultimate burdens of the commitment are liable to differ substantially from those assumed in the original agreement. If price movements are known in advance they can be discounted, but the attempt to discount throws a speculative cast over economic transactions. Individuals purchase real estate less because of need than because "this is a good time to buy." Business firms accumulate abnormally sized inventories in hopes of making an "inventory profit." Inflation is a self-feeding process. When the value of money falls relative to the value of goods, there is a rush to convert liquid into non-liquid assets. This, in turn, lowers the relative value of money even more, and the cycle continues. Inflation may also cause a serious deterioration in a nation's international trade balances. Once relatively immune to this type of problem, the United States has become more sensitive to it as a result of continuing balance of payments difficulties.

This brief description of the effects of inflation is included here to illustrate the unsettling nature and over-all undesirability of large-scale price movements. Extremes in price instability are incompatible with a free market economy, and those who judge unions as potentially responsible for price instability are led naturally to the conclusion that unions are incompatible with a free market economy.

Price and Wage Movements, 1945–1955

For analytical purposes, the post-World War II years will be divided into three periods. Between 1945 and 1955 there were many forces that contributed to price inflation, and there appears to be a strong consensus that negotiated wage increases were contributory rather than initiating factors. Between 1955 and 1958 a modest rise in the price level occurred in circumstances that lend some support to the "cost-push" thesis. From 1958 to mid-1965, prices remained stable, but unemployment was persistently high.

Table 16 shows recent price movements in the United States as measured by the Bureau of Labor Statistics Consumer Price Index. Between 1945 and 1955 the index moved upward by approximately 45 per cent. The rise was not evenly spaced throughout the ten year period, however. Slightly more than two-thirds of the price advance occurred between 1945 and 1948. From 1948 to 1950 there was over-all price stability. Prices then rose abruptly until 1952, at which time a new period of stability commenced. Only minor variations were recorded in the index between 1952 and 1955.

TABLE 16

CONSUMER PRICE INDEX, UNITED STATES AVERAGE, 1940–1955

YEAR	1947–49 = 100	1935–39 = 100	YEAR	1947–49 = 100	1935–39 = 100
Annual Average			Annual Average (cont.)		
1940	59.9	100.2	1948	102.8	171.9
1941	62.9	105.2	1949	101.8	170.2
1942	69.7	116.6	1950	102.8	171.9
1943	74.0	123.7	1951	111.0	185.6
1944	75.2	125.7	1952	113.5	189.8
1945	76.9	128.6	1953	114.4	191.3
1946	83.4	139.5	1954	114.8	191.9
1947	95.5	159.6	1955	114.5	191.4

Source: *Monthly Labor Review.*

The movement of straight-time average hourly earnings of production workers in manufacturing industries is shown in Table 17. Between 1945 and 1955 the average almost doubled.[5] The average, of course, hides differential rates of increase among the component industries in manufacturing and shows nothing of the movements in non-manufacturing. The over-all wage movement in manufacturing was not atypical, however. Average

---

[5] This should not be interpreted to mean that the worker in 1955 was twice as well off as in 1945. Three separate factors operated to cancel out part of the real value of the rise in hourly wage rates. As personal income goes, the tax bite increases at a progressive rate because of the rate structure of the federal personal income tax. *Take-home pay,* thus, is crucially affected by a factor that is independent of the wage bargain struck between employer and employee. *Real wages,* or what the worker can buy with his paycheck, depends upon the size of the check *and* commodity prices. Almost half the value of the rise in average rates between 1945 and 1955 was wiped out by price rises. *Gross earnings* depend upon the number of hours worked as well as the hourly rate. The length of the average work week dropped sharply when the war ended, and this was reflected in large decreases in gross earnings. Despite the rather large wage rate increases negotiated in 1946, gross weekly earnings were lower than in 1945 because of the effect of fewer working hours. Part of the argument for pay increases in 1946 was based upon the necessity of maintaining a wartime level of earnings with a peacetime level of hours. This, it was alleged, was essential for the maintenance of high employment; and on the basis of this argument a few unions made wage demands of as much as thirty cents per hour.

TABLE 17

STRAIGHT-TIME AVERAGE HOURLY EARNINGS, PRODUCTION WORKERS IN MANUFACTURING INDUSTRIES

| PERIOD | MANUFACTURING | | DURABLE GOODS | NON-DURABLE GOODS |
	Amount	Index 1947–1949 = 100		
Annual Average				
1941	$0.702	54.5	$0.770	$0.625
1942	.805	62.5	.881	.698
1943	.894	69.4	.976	.763
1944	.947	73.5	1.029	.814
1945	.963	74.8	1.042	.858
1946	1.051	81.6	1.122	.981
1947	1.198	93.0	1.250	1.133
1948	1.310	101.7	1.366	1.241
1949	1.367	106.1	1.434	1.292
1950	1.415	109.9	1.480	1.337
1951	1.53	118.8	1.60	1.43
1952	1.61	125.0	1.70	1.49
1953	1.71	132.8	1.80	1.56
1954	1.76	136.6	1.86	1.61
1955	1.82	141.3	1.93	1.65

Source: *Monthly Labor Review*, April, 1956, p. 503.

hourly earnings in bituminous coal mining, for instance, rose from $1.24 in 1945 to $2.48 in 1953. In the same period, earnings in Class 1 steam railroads moved from $0.95 to $1.87.[6] In most of American industry, wage rates rose by impressive amounts.

As noted, the price spurt occurred by way of two distinct jumps, each of which was followed by a stable price plateau. The nature of the wage increases that were responsible for the rise in average hourly rates can be summarized briefly.

The first round of postwar wage adjustments was hammered out in a strike-charged atmosphere. Between November of 1945 and October of 1946, strikes occurred in General Motors, General Electric, Westinghouse, the steel industry, the meat packing industry, the non-ferrous metals industry, the bituminous coal mines, the railroads, and the maritime industry. The steel industry settlement of eighteen and a half cents per hour is generally regarded as the pattern-setting agreement of 1946, although similar settlements had been reached several weeks earlier at Ford and Chrysler. Between V-J Day and May of 1946, the steel pattern was put into effect in

[6] Leo Wolman, "Wages in the United States, since 1914," *Proceedings of the Industrial Relations Research Association*, December, 1953, p. 44.

plants covering about one-fourth of all manufacturing workers. In some types of manufacturing, the wage increases were much smaller, about one-fifth of all factory workers receiving no increases at all. The average increase in manufacturing was about fourteen and a half cents. In non-manufacturing, the typical wage increase was closer to ten cents than to the eighteen and a half cents steel pattern.

The conjuncture of strikes, large wage adjustments, and large price increases centered much attention on the inflationary potential of union wage policy. Outwardly at least, the wage-price tie seemed very apparent. The steel increase was negotiated while wage and price controls were still in effect. Steel industry officials contended that a wage boost was impossible unless the government would approve an increase in the price of steel. The final result was not only an eighteen and a half cent wage increase, but a $5.00 per ton increase in the price of steel. As the wage adjustments spread, product prices rose generally. For 1946 the Consumer Price Index showed an average of 83.4 (1947–1949 = 100) as compared to the 1945 average of 76.9.

Second- and third-round wage negotiations in 1947 and 1948 established wage adjustment patterns of fifteen cents and about twelve cents an hour, respectively. Although key labor-management settlements exerted a strong influence in these years, there was much variation from the so-called "patterns." This was especially true in 1948. Prices meanwhile continued to climb, and the Consumer Price Index average for 1948 reached 102.8.[7]

The immediate postwar inflation came to a halt in 1949. Prices dropped slightly and collective bargaining took place in a context of economic recession. Unemployment jumped from 1.8 million in the last quarter of 1948 to over 4 million in July, 1949. The workers who received wage increases were fewer in number than in prior postwar years, and the money gains were smaller. In collective bargaining many unions concentrated

---

[7] One of the outstanding developments in contractual wage agreements in 1948 was the General Motors–United Automobile Workers agreement. The bargainers negotiated a two-year agreement providing for an immediate wage increase of eleven cents an hour and an additional three cents effective in May, 1949. Eight cents of the eleven-cent adjustment was granted to compensate for cost-of-living changes since 1940. Quarterly adjustments in the cost-of-living allowance were to be based upon changes in the Bureau of Labor Statistics' Consumers Price Index. An additional one cent was to be added or subtracted for every 1.14 change in the index. No limit was placed upon upward cost-of-living wage adjustments, but downward adjustments were limited to five cents below the original pay level. The three cents was described as an "annual improvement factor." The improvement factor was designed to channel to the workers the gains from an estimated 2 per cent annual increase in productivity. The reasoning was that such increases were not inflationary, since they reflected an increase in output. Both the cost-of-living and the improvement-factor clauses were to be widely adopted within several years.

upon welfare items, and the pattern for the year was defined by the upsurge in negotiated pension and insurance programs.[8]

Inflationary pressures reappeared as hostilities broke out in Korea in June, 1950. Between June and December, 1950, the general price level advanced by about 5 per cent. Prices continued to move up sharply until March, 1951. By that time direct price controls were in effect, and although the upward surge was not halted the rate of advance was slower.

Wages were also placed under control in January, 1951, and, like prices, were not decontrolled until March, 1953. Under standards established by the Wage Stabilization Board, wage increases were approved if justified on a cost-of-living or inequity basis.[9] Other standards for wage increases were developed during the course of the program, but the larger number of adjustments were made on the aforementioned bases.

The momentum of the Korean inflation burned out before the demise of the wage and price control program. Following decontrol there was little change in the average price level through 1955. Wage bargaining between 1953 and 1955 produced a series of settlements that are not easily defined in terms of an over-all pattern. The picture was characterized by a spottiness that reflected the uneven nature of the prevailing prosperity. On the whole, unemployment was high, prices were stable, and modest wage gains were achieved.

Causes of the Immediate Postwar Price Rise

According to the classical explanation of inflation, the immediate cause of a price rise is an expansion of income relative to the supply of goods. The relationship may be clarified if the reader visualizes two distinct flows,

---

[8] The most important influence in the establishment of the 1949 "pension pattern" was probably the report of a special three-man panel appointed by President Truman to investigate the union-management dispute in steel. The report recommended against a general wage increase but came out in favor of company-financed pension and health benefits. Many of the key wage bargains during the year were shaped by these recommendations.

The panel members, Carroll Daugherty, Samuel Rosenman, and David Cole, in recommending against a wage increase, noted that the cost of living had been stable, that steel workers had fared well in getting money wage increases since 1939, and that an increase in steel would be used as a pattern for other industries with dislocating effects for the economy as a whole.

On the matter of pensions, the panel observed that social insurance and pensions should be considered part of the normal cost of doing business. Such benefits were necessary to "take care of temporary and permanent depreciation in the human machine."

[9] Establishments that had not granted wage increases of 10 per cent between January, 1950, and the date of control were permitted to grant the difference between 10 per cent and the amounts given. Thereafter, additional cost-of-living increases were permissible to the extent that the cost of living increased. Inequity increases were approved when establishment wage rates were out of line with prevailing industry or area levels.

one of money and one of economic goods. In Period 1 a price level is established as the money income is expended to purchase the available goods. Assume that in Period 2 the volume of money doubles while the flow of goods remains constant or changes only slightly. Unless the new money is neutralized by some device, a vastly enlarged money supply will be used to bid for an unchanged quantity of goods. Sellers are able to raise prices because buyers attempt to outbid each other in the scramble for the available goods. Prices, in short, are pulled up by the strength of demand.

One of the important economic debates that has developed in recent years concerns the adequacy of the traditional explanation of inflation for the experience since 1945. Specifically, it has been contended that prices can be pushed up by rising costs as well as pulled up by intensity of demand. The cost-push thesis will be analyzed at a later point. In the remainder of this section, the immediate postwar price rises will be examined to determine whether the traditional monetary theory of inflation provides a reasonably good explanation of what occurred.

According to classical theory, a fundamental explanation of a specific inflation experience requires an analysis of the forces that create imbalance between supply of goods and effective demand. An argument that places blame upon union wage policy, thus, must demonstrate that such policy is responsible for the imbalance. Since no level of costs can produce a higher general level of prices unless consumers are willing and able to support the higher price level, the argument centers upon the effective demand for goods.

Three positions can be posited relative to the wage-price relationship following V-J Day: (1) wage increases were responsible for the rise in effective demand and hence for the price rise; (2) wage increases were not responsible; and (3) wage increases were only partly responsible. It is necessary to examine the economic context of the period to determine which of these propositions is the most accurate.

1. *The Demand for Physical Goods.*   At the start of 1947 there were about 4 million more families in the United States than at the time of Pearl Harbor. Between the two dates the number of automobiles had declined by 2 million. Similar statistics can be cited for many other commodities. Production of consumer goods had been drastically limited during the war; and households were anxious to replace worn-out refrigerators, furniture, stoves, tires, clothes, and many other items.

Household consumers were not alone in their thirst for goods. Business enterprises wanted to make large investment expenditures to replace worn plant equipment and to expand production facilities. Federal government spending, although much below the wartime rate, continued to be high compared to former peacetime levels. State and local governments increased their spendings as school construction, road building, and other war-delayed projects were undertaken. Adding to the pressures that were building up for a domestic buying spree was the fact that foreign governments were anxious to make purchases in the United States. Faced with the devastation of war and a shortage of food, many nations looked to the productivity of the American economy for sustenance until their own economies returned to working order.

In summary, the over-all demand picture was characterized by an intense desire to buy on the part of household consumers, business firms, and foreign customers. While there was substantial diminution in the spending of the federal government, public expenditures remained sufficiently high to aggravate an already unbalanced relationship between supply and demand for goods.

2. *The Effective Demand for Goods.*   Individuals, business firms, and government units rarely own all the economic goods they would like to have. Effective demand, or the ability to translate a want into a purchase, is limited by current disposable income and accumulated savings. The desire for physical goods after V-J Day was unusually strong because of a backlog of pent-up demands. To what extent were potential buyers in a position to make their demands effective?

Corporate and personal income had been exceptionally high during the war. Part of the income had been absorbed by taxation, but substantial residues were in the form of savings. Total gross savings for the period 1940–1945 came to 233.7 billion. Of this amount, 57 per cent was in the form of personal savings, 12 per cent was undistributed corporate profits, and 31 per cent was made up of capital consumption allowances and other forms of saving.[10]

In a given year the bulk of consumption is financed out of current income rather than past savings. Those who forecasted postwar unemployment visualized an extensive decline in aggregate current income. This decline did not materialize. Disposable personal income—total income accruing to persons after taxes—was $151 billion in 1945 and $158 billion in 1946. (By way of contrast, the figure for 1939 was $70.2 billion.) As an aggregate, consumers had both the desire and the wherewithal to buy.

3. *The Supply of Goods.*   The Federal Reserve Index of Industrial Production (1947–1949 = 100) moved from 58 in 1939 to a war-year peak of 127 in 1943. Owing to withdrawals from the labor force, a shortening of the work week, and some production delays as facilities were con-

---

[10] Lester V. Chandler, *Inflation in the United States, 1940–1948* (New York: Harper & Row, Publishers, 1951), p. 78.

verted to peacetime output, there was a postwar drop in the Index to 107 in 1945 and to 90 in 1946. Even in these last two years, however, the volume of industrial production was over 150 per cent of the prewar volume. Furthermore, a much higher proportion of total output became available for civilian uses as government spending declined.

An output increase of this size is impressive, but for purposes of inflation analysis it must be related to a number of other magnitudes. By 1945 disposable income was more than twice the 1939 figure, and the amount of money in circulation was three times as large.[11] Thus, although output was high relative to former peacetime periods, it was low relative to the purchasing power that rested in the hands of buyers.

In 1945 the relationship between the national capacity to produce goods and the desire and ability to buy goods was unbalanced to the degree necessary for a classical case of inflation. A vigorous and fundamental attack upon the problem would have involved a program to limit the further creation of money while the inflationary dollars were being mopped up through taxation.

For a number of reasons such a program was not undertaken. The list that follows enumerates steps that might have been taken but were not. The reader must keep in mind the prominent feelings of the time, however. Because there was a widespread fear of unemployment, there was a natural hesitancy to take steps that might conceivably have reduced work opportunities.

1. The wartime wage and price controls that were lifted in 1946 might have been continued. There was much popular pressure against controls, and both labor and management lent their voices to the clamor for repeal. Only a very firm government stand could have carried the day for control extension. The government wavered, however, and, as controls were progressively weakened, abandonment of the program became the only feasible choice.

2. The high tax rates on corporate and personal income might have been continued with only minor modifications until the postwar economic situation was clarified. Such a course would have been politically unpopular. Furthermore, the fear of unemployment led to a widespread conclusion that business firms and individuals should be allowed to keep more of their

---

11 Between 1939 and 1945 the quantity of money in circulation (demand deposits and currency and coins in circulation) rose from about $33 billion to $99 billion. The increase was due, for the most part, to the manner of financing war deficits. Unable to obtain the amounts necessary to pay for the war by taxation and non-bank borrowing, the federal government sold securities to commercial banks who paid by creating demand deposits for the government. Failure to pay for more of the war costs by taxation and non-bank borrowing guaranteed some degree of inflation after the war.

incomes on the assumption that this would stimulate consumption and investment spending. The Revenue Act of 1945 provided tax savings for both business firms and individuals.

3. The United States Treasury and the Board of Governors of the Federal Reserve System might have taken steps necessary to curb an expansion of money supply through commercial bank lending. For reasons that have been well detailed in recent economic literature this course was not followed, and the total money supply increased by $9 billion between 1945 and 1948.[12]

The facts of the postwar situation argue loudly for the conclusion that a price rise was highly probable even in the absence of the successful union pressure for higher wages. In the face of the strong effective demand for the limited output of the American economy, it is hard to postulate a stable price level after 1945. This is especially so in view of the failure of the government to address its policy against the various inflationary forces. As Morton has suggested, we gave up hope of reducing the quantity of money or lowering the rate of spending by drastic taxation and tried to stop the price rise "by exhorting and threatening labor and business."[13] This led to the belief that the price level is caused by the character of wage bargains and directed attention away from the more basic matters of the quantity and velocity of money.

The explanation of the postwar price rise must be found in a multiplicity of causes. In view of this fact, can any blame be placed upon trade union wage policy? In retrospect, it seems safe to conclude that union wage demands were contributory rather than initiating factors. Wage demands may have contributed to inflation in three ways: (1) Higher wages involve at least a temporary reallocation of income among income recipients. Postwar increases in the total wage bill transferred income from dividend, rent, and interest recipients to wage earners. It is possible that the marginal propensity to spend was higher among the wage earners, but this is by no means a certainty. Whether wage earners spent the marginal increments of their incomes faster than non-wage earners would have spent the same income is conjectural. Nevertheless, it is a possibility. (2) To the extent

---

[12] The Treasury wanted to keep the interest burden of the national debt from increasing and wanted to prevent a decline in the value of government securities held by financial institutions and others. In order to keep the interest rate low, it was necessary for the Federal Reserve to stand ready to support the price of government issues. A drop in the market price of governments would have amounted to a rise in the interest rate, because new issues would have been unmarketable except at more favorable rates of return for the buyer. Federal Reserve readiness to support government securities meant that the commercial banks that were heavily loaded with such paper were insured adequate reserves for an expansion of loans to their customers. Low interest rates, thus, were inconsistent with the ability to control an expansion in money supply.

[13] Morton, *op. cit.*, p. 15.

that higher wage demands forced some employers to borrow funds for payroll purposes, the wage adjustments were inflationary. Some employers, finding their cash balances low, were forced to borrow from commercial banks. The banks created new money in the form of demand deposits and thus the money pressure against the supply of goods was increased. (3) Trade union wage demands gave business firms an excuse for raising prices. In the immediate postwar years there was a high degree of price consciousness among consumers, and there is much evidence that many prices were below the levels that the market would have supported.[14] A policy of exhortation, in other words, worked to some extent. Price increases were generally timed so as to appear in the aftermath of wage negotiations. Wage increases could then be cited as a reason for price increases.

With the perspectives provided by the passage of time, most economists —at least most vocal economists—have concluded that union wage policy was not primarily responsible for the immediate postwar price movements.[15] Nevertheless, the experience of these years has created a legacy of fear to the effect that labor unions can and might upset our market economy.

THE UNION THREAT TO ECONOMIC STABILITY

Several aspects of collective bargaining in the postwar world have aroused fears relative to the capacity of organized labor to threaten the going price system. One is the mere fact of union power. Successive demonstrations of labor organizations demanding and winning wage increases in the face of employer opposition have led many observers to conclude that there is no effective barrier against economically unwise wage demands. The realities of union power together with a union philosophy of more and more wages, outwardly at least, suggest the possibility of continuous cost-price distortions.

Another development that has had a strong influence upon recent economic analysis was the 1955–1958 "creeping inflation." In many respects

[14] This price consciousness did not take the form of consumer resistance to higher prices. The situation is probably best described as one where price setters were concerned with the public relations impact of their price policies. Business firms and labor unions took great pains to prove that they were not responsible for the price rise that was occurring.

[15] Professor Gottfried Haberler, who has been critical of union wage policies, listed the aggressive union wage demands as being probably fourth in importance among the factors responsible for the postwar price inflation. The first three were (1) the large increase in the stock of money and liquid resources which occurred during the war, (2) the large pent-up consumer and investment demand, and (3) the large export surplus financed by foreign aid and the use of gold and foreign-held dollar balances. "Cures and Causes of Inflation," *Review of Economics and Statistics,* February, 1948, p. 10.

the price upsurge that began in the middle of 1955 is different from the two earlier postwar inflations. The degree of inflation was relatively modest, amounting to a 6 per cent increase in the Bureau of Labor Statistics Consumer Price Index between early 1956 and late 1958, as compared to the 35 per cent and 11 per cent rises in 1945–1948 and 1950–1951 respectively. Although there was an excess of aggregate demand in the earlier inflations, there was an excess of capacity in many industries after 1955. By the middle of 1957—before the start of the 1957–1958 recession—manufacturers were operating at about 83 per cent of capacity. Thus, a rise in prices and a growth in excess capacity occurred simultaneously, a phenomenon not easily explained by the classical demand-pull analysis of inflation. Along with these developments, there occurred an increase in wages that was larger than the growth of productivity. From 1955 to 1957, an index of manufacturing wages per hour changed from 129 to 142 (1950 = 100) while an index of manufacturing productivity per hour, using the same base year, moved from 112 to 115.[16]

From these data, many economists have been able to derive a cost-push inflation explanation which identifies union wage policy as a continuing threat to price stability. The nature of the threat may be clarified if its dimensions are examined separately. Gross national product represents the money value of the goods and services produced in a specified time period. Let us assume that from one period to another there is no change in the gross national product, that all factors of production including labor are fully employed, and that the supply of money remains constant. If organized labor as a whole is able to win a general wage increase in this setting, labor will have more income (and more claims to goods and services), and other income recipients will have less. For business firms, costs will rise and profits will shrink. Some firms will be unable or unwilling to continue operations at the new cost-price relationship, and many firms will find it advantageous to release marginal workers. This oversimplifies the totality of the adjustments that will occur.[17] The situation can be summarized, however, by noting simply that the lower level of business income will probably not sustain the pre-wage-increases volume of employment. Some business firms will be squeezed to the extent that they can no longer afford to employ the same number of workers.

Let us now remove the assumption of a constant money supply. In the present era many of the western nations have committed themselves to

---

[16] Lowell E. Gallaway, "The Wage-Push Inflation Thesis, 1950–1957," *American Economic Review,* December, 1958, p. 967.

[17] Where product demand is inelastic, for instance, prices can be raised; but this simply shifts the burden of adjustment to those industries where product demand is elastic. Consumers who spend more of their income for the first group of products will have less to spend for the second group.

maintaining full or high employment within their economies, and a major technique for full employment maintenance is increasing the quantity of money by monetary and fiscal policies. By decreasing the cost of loan funds and by governmental deficit spending, the volume of money and possibly the rate of money use can be manipulated so that effective demand and business expectations combine to create a high employment economy. This, at least, is the hope of many students of the business cycle.

In terms of our present discussion, the significance of the full employment commitment is that it can become a commitment to support whatever wage level is negotiated. If we start with a fully employed economy and posit, say, a 10 per cent wage increase, unemployment can be prevented by the creation of the money supply necessary to finance the increase. Since output cannot be increased significantly—the factors of production being fully employed—the rise in the quantity of money relative to the quantity of goods will force prices upward. Employment will be maintained, but only by way of a price inflation.

The consequence of excessive wage increases, then, is either unemployment or inflation. In order to clarify the issue, the nature of the alleged union threat has been painted above in rather bold strokes. Three basic points have been made: (1) labor organizations have sufficient power to secure the wage goals they establish; (2) if these goals are too high they will cause unemployment or inflation; and (3) the political commitment to full employment makes inflation the likelier possibility in the short run time period.[18] Whether organized labor does constitute this type of threat to economic stability is a question of both fact and probability. In the following subsections we shall examine some of the facts and some of the arguments.

Is the Threat of Unionism Exaggerated?

The issues we are examining revolve about general wage and price movements. A single union may negotiate higher wage rates without serious employment and price effects, since there is enough give in the economic system to absorb a certain amount of cost and price manipulation. Where there are many unions negotiating over wages on an annual or biennial basis, however, labor costs can become higher throughout the economy within a relatively short time period. Even when wage patterns are less distinct than in the postwar years, many wage agreements are imitations of the contracts negotiated by prominent corporations and unions. Non-union

---

[18] For a more detailed description of these consequences see William G. Bowen, "The Dilemma Model of the Inflationary Process," *The Wage Price Issue* (Princeton, N.J.: Princeton University Press, 1960), chap. 3. Bowen's analysis, on the whole, is critical of the "dilemma model."

employers, furthermore, are not always able to remain aloof in the face of upward wage movements. To forestall the unionization of their own workers and to retain adequate work forces, such employers may be forced to take account of union-inspired wage rises.

One other preliminary point must be made. Our concern is with an economy of full or nearly full employment. When resources are idle, higher wages and expansion of money supply may have a revival effect upon a depressed economy. A wage policy that is correct for a depression period, however, may be seriously in error when there is little room for expansion in economic activity.

Those who are inclined to minimize the wage impact of organized labor believe that only a minor fraction of the wage movements that have occurred can be attributed to union pressure. Orthodox economic analysis teaches that wages are determined by the relative strengths of demand for, and supply of, labor. Unions do not control the demand for labor and in most cases have little influence upon supply. According to this argument, wages rise when labor demand is high, and it is the demand factor rather than unionism that is responsible for the wage changes.[19]

Several types of evidence are cited to support this thesis. Comparisons can be made between wage changes of organized and unorganized workers. In this respect it is noted that average annual earnings of unorganized domestic workers were 2.72 times as large in 1948 as in 1939. In the same period, earnings of the heavily organized automobile workers became only 1.98 times as large as they had been.

It has also been alleged that large industrial unions have actually kept wages from rising as high as they might have risen if there had been no unions.[20] The logic underlying this conclusion apparently rests upon two distinct propositions. One is that employers, fearing that unions will resist wage cuts in the future, hesitate to raise wages to a level warranted by the need for labor when product demand is strong. Thus, by introducing a downward inflexibility into wage movements, labor organizations are inadvertently responsible for stronger employer opposition to upward movements. The second proposition is that the practice of negotiating wages on an annual basis creates a time lag in the adjustment of wages to prices. When business conditions improve, unions are prevented from

---

[19] For an extended presentation of this line of argument see Milton Friedman, "Some Comments on the Significance of Labor Unions for Economic Policy," chap. 10 in D. M. Wright (ed.), *The Impact of the Union* (New York: Harcourt, Brace & World, Inc., 1951) and C. L. Christenson, "Variations in the Inflationary Force of Bargaining," *American Economic Review,* May, 1954, pp. 347–366.

[20] See Albert Rees, "The Economic Impact of Collective Bargaining in the Steel and Coal Industries During the Postwar Period," *Proceedings of the Industrial Relations Research Association,* 1950, pp. 203–217, and "Postwar Wage Determination in the Basic Steel Industry," *American Economic Review,* June, 1951, pp. 388–404.

exerting prompt pressure for wage changes by commitments that are tied to contract expiration dates. In the absence of unions, wages would start to climb as soon as demand for labor intensified.

The argument is not that unions are totally incapable of affecting wages. Rather it is alleged that only those unions able to protect themselves against the economic forces of demand and supply are in a position to achieve wage improvements that hold up over time. Certain unions have been able to limit the entry of would-be practitioners to an occupation. Thus, craft unions that charge high initiation fees and otherwise restrict the number of workers are capable of raising the real income of members. They accomplish this by keeping the supply of labor below the quantities that would normally be drawn to an occupation by the promise of high rewards. Contrariwise, the large industrial unions in the automobile, steel, electrical manufacturing, rubber, and other basic industries have, at best, a weak control over labor supply in their industries.

When demand for labor is relatively inelastic—that is, when a higher price for labor will have only minor effects upon the demand for labor— the labor union is well placed strategically to exert pressure for wage gains. Demand for labor is likely to be more inelastic when the particular labor skill is highly essential to the production of the final product and when the fraction of total cost accounted for by the labor power in question is relatively small.[21] These conditions are generally satisfied in the case of highly skilled craft workers, and local unions of such workers are able to do an effective job of winning higher wages in the long run.[22]

The industrial unions generally regarded as strong bargainers are less fortunate in this respect. Initially they may win impressive wage gains, since the demand for labor is usually inelastic in the short run. Over time, however, employment in the industry will shrink if the wage gains are "too large." The rise in wage costs may stimulate the substitutions of machinery for labor, and any management attempt to raise prices may lead consumers to turn to substitutes for the product in question. In the basic mass production industries, consequently, where labor costs are high relative to total costs and where labor is vulnerable to the threat of technological unemployment, the long run demand for labor is elastic. This fact checks the power of labor organizations to affect wage levels.

Professor Milton Friedman, who has been one of the strongest proponents of the analysis presented here, believes that the problem is not so much that strong unions will produce inflation as that inflation will produce strong

---

[21] Friedman, *op. cit.,* p. 207. Friedman's analysis utilizes the theory of joint demand developed by Alfred Marshall in his *Principles of Economics* (8th ed.; New York: The Macmillan Company, 1920), pp. 385, 386.

[22] For a critical appraisal of this point see Lloyd Ulman, "Marshall and Friedman on Union Strength," *The Review of Economics and Statistics,* November, 1955, pp. 384–401. See also Friedman's reply, pp. 401–407 of the same publication.

unions.[23] When inflation occurs, wages rise generally. The wage rises occurring through the media of labor unions are highly publicized, and unions tend to get credit for what actually should be attributed to the forces of inflation. As a result, the hold of the union upon its members is strengthened. The danger of this situation may be that the political power of labor will increase as union strength grows. The economic forces that limit the capacity of monopolistic unions to impose inflation upon the entire economy might then be counteracted by labor control over government monetary and fiscal policies.[24] With the right combination of economic and political power, unions might become more formidable threats to a free market economy.

Another argument that minimizes the importance of union wage policy as an inflation stimulant is based upon an intensive examination of economic variables in different sectors of the economy. First, it should be noted that prices and wages in the American economy have come to have upward flexibility and downward rigidity. Because of administered product prices and negotiated labor prices, a deficiency in aggregate demand usually will not result in price declines while an excess of aggregate demand will obviously produce a price rise. One analyst has compared the situation to a ratchet. Each higher wage and price level becomes a floor from which later increases take off.[25] Maladjustments of wages and prices, furthermore, tend to be corrected by upward adjustments of the wages and prices that are out of line rather than by a mutual adjustment to a common center.

Applying this analysis to the 1955–1957 situation, it is found that there was a boom in capital goods but a slump in autos, housing, and other consumer-goods industries. Thus, there was a shift in the composition of demand. Aggregate demand was stable, but it was "dynamically stable." Through its influence on prices of crude and intermediate materials, the boom in the investment-goods industries produced higher costs in the industrial sectors suffering from deficiency of demand. In competitive sectors of the economy, the rising costs tended to be absorbed, but in many industries they were passed on in the form of markups. The wage experi-

---

[23] Friedman, "Some Comments on the Significance of Labor Unions," *op. cit.*, p. 231.

[24] There has been much controversy over the question of whether unions can be designated as monopolies in the same sense as business firms. Although there are obvious differences between labor unions and corporations, a union may nevertheless be regarded as a monopoly if a narrow criterion is used. This criterion is the ability to force wages to a level higher than what would be established under competitive conditions of wage determination. It seems obvious that proponents of the arguments detailed above are using the term "monopoly" in this narrow sense.

[25] Charles L. Schultze, *Recent Inflation in the United States* (Study Paper No. 1 prepared for the Joint Economic Committee, Congress of the United States [Washington, D.C.: U.S. Government Printing Office, 1959]), p. 10.

ence was similar. Wage increases granted in the excess demand sectors of the economy tended to spread to the other sectors.

This analysis of the post-1955 price rise identifies the initiating cause of the inflation as a shift in the composition of demand.[26] An excess demand in a particular industry produced a general price rise because of the downward rigidities in both wages and prices. Thus, it is concluded, the inflation was due neither to an autonomous cost push nor to an aggregate excess of demand. Since any inflation is normally characterized by wage increases that outstrip productivity gains, the fact that this occurred after 1955 proves nothing about the basic causes of inflation.

An Opposite Viewpoint

The belief that unions have only a minor influence on wage and price movements has a considerable amount of support. Numerous wage students, however, hold an opposite opinion.

So long as wage increases exceed the gains in physical productivity, either inflation or unemployment must eventually occur. Productivity measured in terms of output per man hour increases, perhaps, by 2 or 3 per cent yearly. Wage increases of this size appear quite modest when measured against some of the gains negotiated in recent years.

Those who fear that unionism is an inflation-producing force doubt that unions will limit their wage goals to the annual 2 or 3 per cent required for price stability. A 2 per cent wage increase (four cents an hour for the $2.00 per hour worker) is not likely to satisfy the union member who wants to know what he is getting for his union dues. Competitive rivalries among labor leaders, furthermore, lead to efforts to win spectacular contracts. Add the general union philosophy of more and more wages to these factors of union politics and the outlook is one of labor costs rising faster than physical output.

The conclusion that unions have had little wage influence has been challenged. Doubts have been expressed, for instance, that employers hesitate to raise wages of union workers because of the fear that the union might oppose future wage cuts.[27] Wage cuts, it has been noted, are likely to cause trouble even when workers are non-union. Workers are able to withhold efficiency when dissatisfied with wages or working conditions, and employers know that dissatisfaction is expensive in terms of labor cost.

[26] For an extended development of these points see Schultze, *op. cit.* For a description of an empirical test that lends support to the "composition of demand" hypothesis, see W. G. Bowen and S. H. Masters, "Shifts in the Composition of Demand and the Inflation Problem," *American Economic Review,* December, 1964, pp. 975–984.

[27] Sumner H. Slichter, "Do Wage Fixing Arrangements in the American Labor Market Have an Inflationary Bias?" *ibid.,* May, 1954, p. 331.

Wage slashes in other words are not easily effectuated in the cases of either organized or unorganized labor. The contention that union opposition to wage cuts is a force limiting wage increases, consequently, is of limited validity.

Skepticism has also been expressed over any attempt to measure union influence by comparing movements of money wages in highly organized industries with movements in poorly organized industries, since such comparisons do not show how much union wages have influenced wages in non-union sectors of the economy.[28] In periods of economic expansion when unions are gaining members and winning large-scale increases they exert a powerful influence on the wages in non-union plants. Simple statistical comparisons fail to reveal the full impact of the union at the very time when union influence is strongest.

Part of the fear of the inflationary potential of unionism can be traced to the belief that we are on what Professor Hicks has called a "labor standard."[29] Under the gold standard, high prices caused by a cost rise in one nation would be followed by a fall in export volume and an expansion of imports. Money would then flow from the high-price to the low-price economies. The contraction of money supply in the relatively high-price economy would cause unemployment and deflation, thus purging the system of excessive costs and bringing cost-price relationships back into line.

Today nations are no longer willing to let domestic prices be totally tied to levels dictated by international competition. Tariffs, import quotas, foreign exchange restrictions, and other devices are used to insulate domestic prices and domestic employment levels from foreign influence.

The depression experience of the 1930's created an enduring fear of unemployment; and, as already noted, there is a general commitment in the United States to prevent mass unemployment by positive policy. This commitment tends to remove the threat of unemployment as a corrective for excessive wage increases. Thus, instead of being in a period during which wages are determined by the level of prices, we may be in a period during which prices are determined by the wage level. Once a wage level is negotiated, a strict adherence to the high employment commitment leaves the monetary authorities with little choice but to create the money necessary to support the negotiated wages. With no market corrective available, the more pessimistic viewpoint is that an unchecked union pressure must necessarily lead to inflation unless and until there is general revolt against hurtful price rises. The wage-price experience in recent years provides a good illustration of the relationships discussed above.

---

[28] *Ibid.,* pp. 334–337.
[29] J. R. Hicks, "Economic Foundations of Wage Policy," *The Economic Journal,* September, 1955, pp. 389–404.

A Decade of Contrasts: 1958–1968

Between 1958 and 1965, there was a small decline in the wholesale price index and only a modest rise in the Bureau of Labor Statistics Consumer Price Index. The larger part of the price increase in consumer goods, furthermore, was accounted for by a rise in the price of services where the influence of unionism is slight. The index for consumer durables was barely above the 1958 level.

The condition of price stability was associated with general prosperity except for a slight slowdown in economic activity during 1960 and 1961. An otherwise bright economic picture, however, was marred by a persistently high level of unemployment. During the 1958–1963 period, the unemployment rate ranged from 5.3 to 6.8 per cent of the labor force, and while some improvement occurred during 1964 and 1965 the rate remained above the 4 per cent which had been adopted as an "interim target" for the national administrations' anti-unemployment efforts.

In terms of the variables under consideration here, the years 1966 through 1968 contrast sharply with the 1958–1965 period. The annual average rate of unemployment fell to 3.8 per cent in 1966 and continued downward so that by the end of 1968 the rate was 3.3 per cent, the lowest level recorded since the tight labor supply conditions of the Korean war period in the early 1950's. The rate of the price rise accelerated, however. Consumer prices, which had been rising at a rate of approximately one per cent per year between 1958 and 1965, rose by just under three per cent in 1966 and 1967 and by over four per cent in 1968.

In the stable price-high unemployment years (1958–1965), the relationship between productivity gains and employee compensation gains was such that unit labor costs were fairly stable.[30] In the rising price-low unemployment period (1966–1968), the percentage increase in average hourly employee compensation was substantially above productivity growth resulting in relatively large increases in unit labor costs.

New questions have been raised as a result of the post-1958 developments and concern over union wage pressures has become mixed with a number of associated concerns. Earlier in this chapter it was noted that should a public commitment be made in favor of full or high employment, the government would have no choice other than sanctioning negotiated wage increases by creating the monetary conditions necessary to underwrite the increases. Totally apart from the question of wage adjustments, however, the full or high employment commitment implies a government reaction to unemployment that courts the danger of price inflation. If, in fact, price

---

[30] Jerome Mark and Martin Ziegler, "Recent Developments in Productivity and Unit Labor Costs," *Monthly Labor Review*, May, 1967, p. 28.

TABLE 18

PRICE INCREASES DURING PERIODS OF HIGH EMPLOYMENT

PERIOD	AVERAGE UN-EMPLOYMENT RATE (*per cent*)	PERCENTAGE INCREASE PER YEAR	
		Consumer Price Index	Wholesale Price Index
January 1947–January 1949	3.8	5.5	5.7
September 1950–November 1953	3.2	3.2	1.3
May 1955–September 1957	4.1	2.4	2.8
July 1965–December 1967	3.9	2.9	1.5
January 1968–April 1969	3.6	6.5	4.3

Sources: Department of Labor, and *Economic Report of the President,* 1968, p. 97.

stability is incompatible with a satisfactory employment level, some choice must be made concerning the relative social merits of various combinations of inflation and unemployment. Should we opt for price stability and a chronic unemployment rate of five to six per cent of the labor force or a four per cent unemployment rate with perhaps a creeping inflation or a three per cent rate together with a rapid inflation?[31]

The economic situation at the end of the 1960's forced the painful wage-price employment dilemma to the forefront once again. Until the mid-sixties union wage pressures were dampened by the combination of price stability and unemployment that prevailed. The ensuing inflation, induced to a large extent by the fiscal policy associated with the national administrations commitment to a major military effort in Viet Nam, witnessed a renewal of wage cost-push pressures which were easily translated into price increases in a permissive economic environment.

In this context, it is appropriate to review the recent efforts to confront the general problem of price inflation through a novel income policy popularly referred to as the "wage-price guidepost."

---

[31] In a number of recent analyses, the so-called "Phillips Curve" has been used to study the relationship between changes in money wages and unemployment. From his study of different historical periods, Phillips concluded that an unemployment rate of about five per cent is necessary in Britain to hold wages constant. A. W. Phillips, "The Relation between Unemployment and the Rate of Change in Money Wage Rates in the United Kingdom, 1861–1967," *Economica,* November, 1958, pp. 283–299. Applying Phillips' analytical technique to United States data, Samuelson and Solow conclude that something on the order of a five to six per cent unemployment rate is required to keep annual wage increases within the limits of the typical 2.5 per cent annual productivity increase in the United States. They also suggest that achieving the output level necessary to reduce the unemployment rate to three per cent would require a four to five per cent increase annually in the price index. The authors caution that their conclusions are only best guesses. For one thing, the points in their scatter diagram are rather widely dispersed. Paul A. Samuelson and Robert M. Solow, "Analytical Aspects of Anti-Inflation Policy," *Proceedings of the American Economic Association,* May, 1960, pp. 177–194.

THE PRODUCTIVITY GUIDEPOST

A good deal of attention has been focused on the idea of meshing wages and productivity changes as a result of the recommendations made in the 1962 report of the Council of Economic Advisers.[32] In that report and in subsequent reports until 1968, the council noted that the national rate of productivity change was an important benchmark for non-inflationary wage and price behavior. Although the council's "guidelines" provided for flexibility, the general recommendation called for wage increases in line with national productivity changes and stability for industry prices.

A number of serious problems, most of which the council recognized, would attend any serious effort to implement the recommendations. One of these involves the concept of productivity itself. As used in economic analysis, "productivity" is the ratio of output to any or all units of input used in production. Both output and input can be defined in a number of different ways, however; and rather wide variations in the productivity record for a given time period can be found depending upon the set of definitions used.[33] Output, for example, can be measured gross or net of capital consumption; and military outlays can be treated as "final goods" or as "intermediate goods." Input can be measured in terms of total input or in terms of a single factor of production or some combination of factors with or without some type of weighting for the factors. Thus, the average annual percentage rate of change in productivity for the private domestic economy for the period of 1889–1953 can be identified as 1.0 or 2.3 or a number of intermediate points within this range depending upon the measure of productivity used.[34]

The most commonly cited measures of productivity relate output to man-hours worked. The use of the quantity of man-hours in deriving an index of productivity should not be interpreted to mean that labor power is necessarily a cause of whatever output changes occur. A rise in productivity may reflect technological improvement, more efficient management, the reduction of unit overhead costs as a result of increased output in the firm, and many other factors. The fact that a productivity increase is de-

[32] *Economic Report of the President* (Washington, D.C.: United States Government Printing Office, 1962), pp. 185–190.

[33] A number of good discussions of this aspect of productivity data are available. See, for example, John W. Kendrick, "Productivity, Costs, and Prices," chap. 2 in *Wages, Profits, Prices and Productivity* (New York: The American Assembly, Columbia University, 1959); Kendrick, *Productivity Trends in the United States* (Princeton, N.J.: Princeton University Press, 1961), chaps. 1, 2; Solomon Fabricant, "Which Productivity? Perspective on a Current Question," *Monthly Labor Review,* June, 1962, pp. 609–613.

[34] Solomon Fabricant, "Meaning and Measurement of Productivity," in J. Dunlop and V. Diatchenko (eds.), *Labor Productivity* (New York: McGraw-Hill Book Company, 1964), p. 15.

scribed statistically as the change in output associated with an input of labor indicates nothing about the cause of the change.

Even when productivity is defined in terms of labor inputs, the results are influenced by the choice of measures. Bureau of Labor Statistics data, for instance, measure output changes on the basis of production worker man-hours. Thus, the recent decline in the ratio of production workers to all employees in manufacturing may introduce an upward bias in the BLS data. On the other hand, BLS data measure man-hours worked on the basis of man-hours paid for, which means that time spent on vacations and holidays is included in the derivation of productivity. The average annual change in productivity between 1948 and 1957 is 3.1 if computed on the basis of man-hours paid for but is 3.6 per cent if computed on the basis of man-hours actually worked. This very incomplete description of the technical aspects of productivity measurement suggests that available data, at best, provide loose standards for wage adjustments.

Another problem in the use of a productivity guide concerns the appropriate time interval over which productivity trends should be measured. Annual rates of growth in output per man-hour are 2.4 per cent if measured from 1909 to 1960, 3.0 per cent for the time period 1947 to 1960, and 2.6 per cent for the 1954 to 1960 interval.[35] Very short time intervals may give excessive weight to the influence of business cycles on productivity, whereas very long periods would reflect the influence of events long past and no longer relevant. Although it seems clear that some period of intermediate length would be most appropriate for deriving a wage adjustment criterion, selection of a base date would be a troublesome problem, since man-hour output can fluctuate, and has fluctuated, widely from year to year.[36]

Still another problem is created by the need for flexibility. Recognizing the need for variations from its basic recommendation, the Council of Economic Advisers specifically noted that it was suggesting a guide rather than a rule. Two types of desirable flexibility were noted. One was the freedom to readjust the proportions of labor and non-labor shares of the product of particular firms or industries to the extent that this could be accomplished without affecting the general price level. The other involved the need for some degree of wage and price leeway in specific situations. Thus, where wages in an industry were too low to attract sufficient labor and where wage rates were exceptionally low compared to wages enjoyed elsewhere by similar labor, wage increases could exceed the general guide rate. On the price front, the council suggested that product prices might be

---

[35] *Economic Report of the President,* 1962, p. 186.
[36] See Clark Kerr, "The Short Run Behavior of Physical Productivity and Average Hourly Earnings," *Review of Economics and Statistics,* November, 1949, p. 301.

expected to rise when the level of profits was insufficient to attract the capital required to finance a needed expansion in capacity or when costs other than labor costs had risen. Although the council's efforts to reconcile the general guideposts with equity considerations were laudable, the operational problem involved making some fine distinctions for which the guidelines provided little guidance. When, for example, was the level of profits insufficient to attract the necessary amount of capital to an industry?

A final problem to be discussed here, and one which the Council of Economic Advisers neglected to consider sufficiently, was that of winning labor and management acceptance of the philosophy expressed in the guidelines for wages and prices. In effect, the recommendation of the council amounted to an effort to make national economic policy a relevant variable in the collective bargaining process. But, as Rothbaum has pointed out, no labor-management consensus or commitment preceded the council's pronouncement, and the responsibility that the government assigned to the bargaining process increased with no equivalent increase in the authority of the bargaining parties.[37]

As noted above, the guideposts were presented in the 1962 annual report of the Council of Economic Advisers. The two general guides for non-inflationary behavior were described as follows:

> The General guide for non-inflationary wage behavior is that the rate of increase in wage rates (including fringe benefits) in each industry be equal to the trend rate of over-all productivity increases. General acceptance of this guide would maintain stability of labor cost per unit of output for the economy as a whole—though not of course for individual industries.

> The general guide for non-inflationary price behavior calls for price reduction if the industry's rate of productivity increase exceeds the over-all rate —for this would mean declining unit labor costs; it calls for an appropriate increase in price if the opposite relationship prevails; and it calls for stable prices if the two rates of productivity increase are equal.[38]

The general guides presented in 1962 were made more specific in 1964 when a definite figure was identified in the Annual Report as a measure of acceptable wage increases.[39] This measure was the five-year moving average of increases in output per man-hour in the private economy. For any given year, thus, the acceptable wage increase would be the average per cent gains in output per man hour for the previous five. Use of a five-year moving

---

[37] Melvin Rothbaum, "Economic Dilemmas of Collective Bargaining," *The Annals of the American Academy of Political and Social Science*, November, 1963, p. 100.

[38] *Economic Report of the President, 1962*, p. 189.

[39] *Economic Report of the President, 1964*, p. 114.

average was justified as a means of moderating the effect of cyclical changes in productivity.

The 1966 experience illustrates the problems associated with the selection of what was, essentially, an arbitrary grouping of years. The calculation of the moving average for 1966 indicated an acceptable average wage increase of 3.6 per cent, as against the 3.2 per cent guidepost for 1965. In 1966, however, the economy was operating at close to full capacity and the Council of Economic Advisers concluded that wage increases of 3.6 per cent would turn out to be higher than the productivity increase for that year. The Council, consequently, recommended 3.2 per cent guidepost for 1966, an action that turned an already negative labor union attitude toward the guideposts into one of outright hostility.

In 1967, the Council failed to identify a specific figure for wage increases since the cost of living had turned upward and a wage adjustment limited to the productivity gains would have resulted in a decline in real income for workers. Instead the Council recommended restraint to the extent that wage increases would be something less than the total of the productivity trend plus the rise in consumer prices. In 1968, the Council of Economic Advisers again failed to identify a specific figure for wage changes but recommended instead, that these changes be below the 5.5 per cent average increases in wages and benefits that had occurred in 1967. While these actions were widely interpreted as an abandonment of the guideposts, both the 1967 and 1968 Annual Reports reaffirmed the productivity principle as the only valid standard for non-inflationary wage increases. The new national administration that assumed office in 1969, however, expressed itself as opposed to the guidepost approach, thus putting to rest, for the time being at least, the experiment with a national incomes policy.

What was the impact of the guideposts? If the standard for judgment is the productivity trend, then the guideposts experiment must be written off as a failure since labor organizations, particularly after 1965, demanded and generally won wage gains of a larger amount. There is some evidence, however, that the guideposts may have been a moderating influence upon union wage gains in several industries. A number of studies conclude that increases in average hourly earnings during the "guidepost period" were somewhat below what might have been predicted on the basis of various characteristics of the economy. The evidence is not conclusive but it does suggest the possibility, at least, that the guideposts had a mild dampening effect on the rise of wage costs.[40]

---

[40] John Sheahan, *The Wage Price Guideposts* (Washington, D.C.: The Brookings Institute, 1967), chap. 7.; George L. Perry, "Wages and the Guideposts," *The American Economic Review,* September, 1967, pp. 75–82; *The Wage-Price Issue: The Need for Guideposts,* Joint Economics Committee, Congress of the U.S. Ninetieth Congress, second session, January 31, 1968, pp. 3–7.

The Wage Policy Problem

By "wage policy" we mean a deliberate effort to accomplish a specific social goal through control of some aspect of wages. The concentration in this discussion has been on inflation, and this leads to the obvious question of wage policy for inflation control.

Before discussing this matter we should note that an analysis of wage policy could be oriented toward problems such as the following:

(1) Allocation of economic resources through consumption control. An underdeveloped or a planned economy might adopt a policy of low real wages in order to free factors of production for development of a capital goods industry.

(2) Encouragement of worker mobility toward some employments and away from others. A nation faced with labor shortages in certain regions or industries and labor surpluses elsewhere might attempt to encourage the movement of labor by establishing wage premiums in the areas of shortage.

(3) Accomplishment of social welfare goals. In the United States, for example, existing minimum wage legislation expresses a philosophy that all who work are entitled to no less than a specified minimum reward.

The inflation problem is selected for emphasis here on the assumption that inflation may be a more pervasive problem in the years ahead than other wage-related matters that could call for policy development. This may prove to be an unrealistic assumption, and undoubtedly there will be times when other wage problems come strongly to the fore. The widespread concern about the threat of inflation in the United States, however, suggests that most wage policy discussions in the near future will be related to price stability considerations.

Given a general aversion to direct wage and price controls and the slimness of the possibility of developing a broad consensus concerning wage-price-profit relationships, there is little likelihood that a workable wage policy can emerge in any context outside of emergency conditions. We have already noted the technical problems that would be associated with the use of a productivity guideline as well as the considerable range of opinion among professional economists concerning cause and effect in the several post-World War II inflations. When these considerations are added to what a former president of the American Economic Association called the "sheer ignorance" that surrounds such a subject such as the wage-price-employment relationship,[41] it is not very realistic to hope for the degree of co-operation among the interest groups who must co-operate in order to

---

[41] Edward S. Mason, "Interests, Ideologies, and the Problem of Stability and Growth," *American Economic Review*, March, 1963, p. 2.

underwrite the success of public wage policy. The steel industry price crisis of 1961 is instructive in terms of what is likely to occur when a direct threat to price stability materializes. In that situation, President Kennedy argued against the necessity of an increase in the price of steel on the basis of a particular set of economic data. Industry spokesmen challenged his conclusions with a completely different body of data. The two arguments skirted each other with no real confrontation occurring.

The totality of the uncertainties surrounding the wage-price relationship and the predictable differences in the reactions of various interest groups to any specific wage-price crisis would appear to argue that an effort to promulgate a general wage-price policy is premature. To achieve what it considers an optimal wage-price relationship, the national administration will probably have to rely upon exhortation with monetary and fiscal controls as a second line of defense. Effective use of monetary and fiscal measures, however, might force the painful choice between price stability and low unemployment. Should a serious inflationary threat materialize, it may prove to be impossible to avoid this choice unless there is a greater virtuosity in the use of fiscal and monetary tools than has hitherto been displayed.

QUESTIONS

1. Was the wage-price spiral that occurred immediately after World War II a cause or effect of inflation?

2. What combination of factors was responsible for the price rises that occurred between 1945 and 1955?

3. In what ways were the inflations of 1946–1948 and 1955–1957 different?

4. If wages increase at a faster rate than productivity in a fully employed economy the result must be inflation or unemployment. Explain this statement.

5. In an analysis of the wage-price problem, what is the significance of the national commitment to a high employment economy?

6. According to some analysts, we can have relatively full employment and an annual increase of four to five per cent in the consumer price index or price stability and an unemployment rate of five to six per cent or some intermediate combination of unemployment and price inflation. If this is, in fact, the nature of our choice, which of the possibilities would you argue for?

7. From 1962 to 1968, the Council of Economic Advisers recommended guideposts for non-inflationary wage and price behavior. What are the prospects for success of a guidepost approach to inflation control?

SELECTED READINGS

The American Assembly, Columbia University. *Wages, Prices, Profits, and Productivity*. New York, 1959.

Bowen, William G. *The Wage-Price Issue*. Princeton, N.J.: Princeton University Press, 1960.

Friedman, Milton. "What Price Guideposts?" in Schultz, George P. and Aliber, Robert Z. (eds.) *Guidelines, Informal Controls, and the Market Place*. Chicago: The University of Chicago Press, 1966, pp. 17–39.

Samuelson, Paul A., and Solow, Robert M. "Analytical Aspects of Anti-inflation Policy," *American Economic Review*, May, 1960, pp. 177–194.

Schultze, Charles L. *Recent Inflation in the United States*. Washington, D.C.: United States Government Printing Office, 1959.

Sheahan, John. *The Wage-Price Guideposts*. Washington, D.C.: The Brookings Institute, 1967.

Solow, Robert M. "The Case against the Case against the Guideposts," in Schultz, George P. and Aliber, Robert Z. (eds.), *Guidelines, Informal Controls, and the Market Place*. Chicago: The University of Chicago Press, pp. 41–54.

Rees, Albert. *The Economics of Trade Unions*. Chicago: The University of Chicago Press, 1962, Chap. 5.

PART FIVE

LABOR LAW

CHAPTER 16

THE DEVELOPMENT OF COLLECTIVE BARGAINING LAW

ABOUT FOUR DECADES AGO, A FAIRLY COMPREHENSIVE KNOWLEDGE OF labor law could be acquired by a close reading of not many more than twenty-five leading court decisions. At the present time the orders and decisions of the National Labor Relations Board issued pursuant to the administration of the Wagner and Taft-Hartley Acts fill more than 150 thick volumes. These orders and decisions constitute only a fraction of the total documentation of contemporary labor law. More striking, perhaps, than the volume are the twists and turns that have characterized the law in its several stages of development. The law as it relates to labor organizations and conditions of work has been a subject of controversy for a century and a half. The details of the controversy have changed, but the basic issue has remained substantially the same: who shall have the power to control the conditions and terms of employment in a capitalistic society?

Our analysis will be concerned primarily with three broad questions: (1) What have been the characteristic features of the evolving law at different times? (2) Why has the evolution taken the path that it has? (3) What is the probable future direction of labor law? These questions are posed not only because they are basic to a comprehension of what has happened and what is happening but also because they permit a relatively simple ordering of the confusing details of law. The finer details we shall leave to the legal experts. The presentation that follows will focus upon the broad features of a changing and often uncertain public policy toward a complex social issue.

By "collective bargaining law" we mean the law as it relates to the labor-management relationship. Various approaches might be followed in a description of collective bargaining law. We could, for example, trace the evolution of the complicated present-day instruments of law from the relatively simple law of the early nineteenth century by emphasizing the factors responsible for the transition of simple law to complex law. Another possibility is to order the history of public policy into stages characterized by different governmental attitudes toward labor unions. This is a common approach, incidentally, and the succession of attitudes toward unionism is usually described as (1) hostility, (2) toleration, (3) encouragement, and (4) control. Both approaches will be followed to some extent, but the discussion will be oriented primarily around the concepts of property ideology and power alignments within society.

UNIONS AS CONSPIRACIES

"We find the defendants guilty of a combination to raise their wages." This jury verdict in 1806 terminated the first labor conspiracy case in the United States.[1]

George Pullis and seven other shoemakers residing in Philadelphia had been charged with (1) conspiring "to increase and augment the prices and rates usually paid and allowed to them . . . and unjustly to procure great sums of money for their work and labor . . . to the damage, injury, and prejudice of the masters employing them and of the citizens of the commonwealth generally"; (2) endeavoring "to prevent by threats, menaces, and other means, other artificers, workers, and journeymen in the . . . occupation from working but at certain large prices . . ."; and (3) "unlawfully, perniciously, and deceitfully designing to form . . . into a club . . . and agree that none of the said conspirators . . . would work for any master or person who should employ any artificer, workman, or journeyman . . . who would break any of the said unlawful rules, orders, or bye-laws." Briefly, these shoemakers had struck for higher piece rates, had sought to keep other shoemakers from working at the old rates, and had agreed to blackball, both economically and socially, those workers who would not join their organization.

The alleged misconduct would hardly be sufficient pretext for hailing anyone into court today unless attended by additional circumstances such as violence, property damage, or undue coercion.[2] Even in 1806, as a matter of fact, Pullis and his associates had broken no statutory law. Neither the federal Congress nor the state legislature in Pennsylvania had passed any

---

[1] John R. Commons and his associates were unable to uncover any record of earlier labor conspiracy cases. *A Documentary History of American Industrial Society* (Cleveland, Ohio: The Arthur H. Clark Co., 1910), III, 15–17.

[2] Under the Labor-Management Relations Act of 1947, it is an unfair (illegal) practice for unions to coerce employees who choose not to form, join, or assist labor organizations.

laws that made a strike for higher wages illegal. The defendants were being tried for violations of the common law.

Common law consists of the accumulated decisions of judges who have ruled on issues to which no statutory laws apply. Over the years as precedents pile upon each other, principles emerge which are specific in the sense that they can be given literary formulation but at the same time are vague in terms of applicability to new situations. In the case of the Philadelphia shoemakers, the prosecutor reached back into Anglo-Saxon law and came up with the criminal conspiracy doctrine.

There are several basic strands from which the conspiracy doctrine is woven. One of the most fundamental is that a combination of persons has a power to inflict harm that an individual does not possess. In the words of a New York court, "A combination of men is a very serious matter. No man can stand up against a combination. He may successfully stand up against a single individual, but when his foes are combined and numerous he must fall."[3] From this doctrine of the power of numbers comes the corollary belief that action that is legal when taken by an individual may be illegal when performed by a group. In the Philadelphia shoemakers case the prosecution took pains to make the point that as individuals men had the right to put whatever price they liked upon their labor. "But when they associate, combine, and conspire to prevent others from taking what they deem a sufficient compensation for their labour and when they undertake to regulate the trade of the city, they undertake to regulate what interferes with your rights and mine."

Other features of the conspiracy doctrine can be summarized briefly. If the purposes for which men combine are illegal, the very act of combining is illegal, regardless of whether steps have been taken to accomplish the purpose. Individual acts which may be legal in and of themselves become illegal when performed by a combination with an illegal purpose. A final strand to the doctrine is that all who combine to effectuate an illegal purpose are responsible for the acts carried out by any member of the combination.[4]

The prosecution and the defense—both did an excellent job of presenting their arguments, incidentally—clashed on two basic points: (1) Was the English common law of conspiracy applicable in the state of Pennsylvania? (2) Was a strike for higher wages an illegal conspiracy? In charging the jury, the judge answered both questions. "A combination of workmen to raise their wages may be considered in a twofold point of view: one is to benefit themselves, the other is to injure those who do not join their

---

[3] *People* v. *Wilzig*, 4 N.Y. Crim. 403 (1886).

[4] For a more detailed discussion of the conspiracy doctrine, see Alpheus T. Mason, *Organized Labor and the Law* (Durham, N.C.: Duke University Press, 1925), chaps. 1–4.

society. The rule of law condemns both." Thus instructed, the jury returned its finding of guilty.

In the next thirty-five years, labor organizations were to run up against the conspiracy doctrine on a number of occasions. Some courts continued to apply the rule suggested by the Philadelphia shoemakers case that unions were illegal per se. Others, less willing to go this far, found evidence of conspiracy in the means used by striking workers or in the ends pursued by labor combinations.

Early clashes of interest between employers and employees occurred as product markets were expanding from local dimensions to nationwide scope. Workers, pursuing what they perceived to be their legitimate wage interests, ran into opposition from cost-conscious employers who feared higher wages would weaken their capacities to compete with producers in distant areas. The exertion of strike pressures raised novel questions of law in the United States and, as controversies were steered to the courts, workers found themselves fighting on unfavorable terrain.

A number of factors made anything other than anti-union verdicts improbable at this time. Democracy had only a precarious foothold in the new nation. The idea that society was made up of hierarchical orders in which every man found his appointed place was widespread. Leaders tended to view democracy as freedom for individuals to pursue their own interests within a basically laissez-faire setting of commerce and finance.[5] In this environment, the unenfranchised and numerically few city workers were unimportant in a power sense until well into the nineteenth century.

Laborers who went on strike were attacking the employer's right to use his property without interference; and, as legal scholars have made clear, property received extreme protection under the law during the first century of the nation's existence.[6] Judges drawn from the propertied classes were not likely to sympathize with labor aspirations when their own backgrounds were heavily influenced by a philosophy that had no place for interferences with the "natural laws" of economics.[7] Some students of labor imply that the decisions in the early conspiracy cases were little more than bald reflections of the courts' servitude to property interests.[8] Others question

---

[5] Joseph Dorfman, *The Economic Mind in American Civilization* (New York: The Viking Press, 1946), Vol. I, Preface.

[6] Francis S. Philbrick, "Changing Conceptions of Property in Law," *University of Pennsylvania Law Review,* May, 1938, pp. 723, 724.

[7] The record of the Philadelphia shoemakers case is full of references to Adam Smith's *Wealth of Nations* and the laws of competition that regulate market price.

[8] See Elias Lieberman, *Unions before the Bar* (New York: Harper & Row, Publishers, 1950), chaps. 1 and 2; and Charles O. Gregory, *Labor and the Law* (New York: W. W. Norton & Company, Inc., 1946), pp. 18, 19.

so simple an interpretation.[9] Regardless of the precise facts of law that led to the judgment of unions as conspiracies, the power lineup and prevailing conceptions of property were bound to result in unfavorable court attitudes toward unionism at the time. Unions were new and disturbing factors in the economic situation; the law characteristically accommodates to new pressures slowly. The early labor organizations were simply not strong enough to press successfully a philosophy that was at odds with the dominant property ideology.

Commonwealth v. Hunt

The decision in the 1842 *Commonwealth* v. *Hunt* case is generally regarded as one of the landmarks in the history of American labor law. In his opinion, Chief Justice Shaw of the Supreme Judicial Court of Massachusetts declared that ". . . a conspiracy must be a combination of two or more persons, by some concerted action, to accomplish some criminal or unlawful purpose, or to accomplish some purpose not in itself criminal or unlawful by criminal or unlawful means." The power of a labor organization, Shaw noted, could be used for honorable as well as for pernicious purposes. The doctrine that the actions of labor combinations were illegal per se was explicitly rejected.

The ruling in *Commonwealth* v. *Hunt*, which had been anticipated in earlier court decisions, did not end the usage of the conspiracy doctrine in labor cases. Henceforth, however, the legality of union actions depended upon the legality of the ends sought by labor organizations or of the means employed to accomplish the various union objectives. As the courts of the several states applied this common law doctrine to specific cases, there was much divergence in the tenor of the decisions from court to court. The legality of ends and means still depended essentially on the economic, political, and social philosophies of those empowered to judge. Thus, after 1842, as before, the law remained vague and uncertain. Some courts, for instance, were able to find that a closed shop was a lawful objective and that a strike for a closed shop, consequently, was legal. Others reached an opposite

---

[9] Pound believes that the courts, the legislatures, and doctrinal writers of necessity had to test the applicability of the common law to American conditions with respect to numerous points of law. The fact that this was thoroughly accomplished in three-quarters of a century he regards as a tremendous accomplishment. Pound also asserts that the taught traditions of law have been much more significant than the economics of time and place. He cites the fact that "captains of industry" have had as much cause of complaint in the slowness of law as have laborers. Roscoe Pound, *The Formative Era of American Law* (Boston: Little, Brown and Company, 1938), pp. 20, 21, 82–90.

conclusion. The legality of the activities of a union man depended to a not inconsiderable extent upon where he happened to live.[10]

The notion that unions as such were illegal conspiracies could not survive in an era when economic and social forces spurred workers to organize and protest. Successive economic panics led many to conclude that the natural laws of economic competition were not nearly so beneficient as the philosophers contended. An extensive protest literature, some of it quite radical in tone, jousted vigorously with the accepted canons of property rights. Political and economic action by workers grew in volume and effectiveness. The nation was still predominantly rural and would remain so for many years. The amount of urban employment increased materially, however, and the spread of the franchise gave labor a degree of power that was recognizably greater in 1842 than it had been in 1806.

The *Commonwealth* v. *Hunt* decision can be summarized as a mild relaxation of an extreme doctrine of the inviolability of employer property rights. The ruling was also a recognition of the fact that the right of group action could not be denied to a single group in a nation where concerts of pressure had become commonplace. The slight break in the conspiracy doctrine, however, did not strip the courts of the power necessary to constrain union action when such action was at variance with the economic philosophy of a particular court.

THE INJUNCTION IN LABOR DISPUTES

Apart from the application of conspiracy doctrine to labor disputes there was little development of labor law until the last two decades of the nineteenth century. Until that time the labor movement was small and not particularly successful. Those who molded the law were preoccupied with more pressing matters.

At the century's close organized labor was contending more forcefully with capital, and the question of the rights of each party was thrust into prominence. When the self-defined objectives of labor collided with the interests of business, whose rights would give way, and to what extent? The judiciary continued to be the branch of government that sought to resolve this question. Efforts of the legislative and executive branches in this respect were few, weak, and ineffective.

By the 1880's most courts had come around to the position that certain of the more direct pressures of labor organizations, such as strikes for

---

[10] For a summary of conflicting state policies, see Gregory, *op. cit.*, chap. 3. See also Edwin E. Witte, *The Government in Labor Disputes* (New York: McGraw-Hill Book Company, 1932), chap. 3, for a discussion of the varying legal theories that the courts developed in cases involving the legality of union actions.

higher wages, were lawful. There was less unanimity when the goals were a degree more remote from an objective that would obviously benefit the workers. Thus, a strike for a closed shop was lawful in some jurisdictions, unlawful in others. The same was true for organization strikes, boycotts, and picketing.[11]

The technique by which the courts exercised their control over labor organizations changed from the conspiracy trial to the injunction. The injunction was first employed in connection with labor disputes during the 1880's, but not until the experience of the 1894 Pullman Strike was the potency of this legal weapon fully revealed.

The injunction is an order issued by a court to stop an action that promises to result in irreparable damage to property when the situation is such that no other adequate remedy at law is available to protect the interests of the injunction-seeking party. Employers and judges were quick to learn that the injunction was an ideal technique to protect business interests in the course of labor disputes. Its impact was quick and effective. In comparison, the conspiracy trial before a jury could be a prolonged affair, and there was always the possibility that the jury might not convict or that the penalty imposed would be light.

The judicial application of the injunction procedure in American labor disputes aroused not only labor but many objective students of the law. "Government by injunction" became a political issue after 1895, and both the Democratic and Republican parties repeatedly proposed corrections of what were obvious abuses. The objections to anti-labor injunctions centered upon several categories of alleged abuse.[12] These will be discussed separately.

1. *Injunction Procedure.*[13]   Briefly, the injunction procedure in labor dispute cases was as follows: The complainant—usually the employer but

---

[11] The attitudes of the courts in New York State are usually cited as examples of the more liberal legal viewpoint during this period, whereas the decisions of the Massachusetts courts are frequently quoted as illustrative of the conservative approach. In the former state the courts generally decided that the pressure actions of unions were lawful despite the economic harm that they might inflict upon others, unless the conduct encompassed categories of action such as assault or trespass which are illegal in themselves. In Massachusetts the judges generally held that the harm inflicted upon the economic interests of employers was unlawful unless justified by a purpose that was legal. "Legal justification" is a vague concept, however, and a majority of the judges took a narrow view of what constituted just cause. In the case of *Vegelahn* v. *Guntner* (167 Mass. 92, 44 N.E. 1077, 1896) the Massachusetts Supreme Court ruled against the union in a split decision. Both the minority and majority opinions were based upon the "just cause" theory. See Gregory, *op. cit.,* chap. 3; and Witte, *op. cit.,* pp. 50–52.

[12] The best full-length critique of the labor injunction is that by Felix Frankfurter and Nathan Greene, *The Labor Injunction* (New York: The Macmillan Company, 1930).

[13] For a full discussion of injunction procedure, see Witte, *op. cit.,* chap. 5.

occasionally a worker or a stockholder—appeared in court and filed a complaint that set forth the nature of the property threat and concluded with a request for relief. Usually a *temporary restraining order* was requested to halt the threatened action until the case could be heard. Shortly afterwards a preliminary hearing was held, after which the judge decided whether to issue a *temporary injunction*. Finally, after a trial, a decision was made as to whether a *permanent injunction* should issue.

A number of complaints were made about the unfairness of this procedure. A court order requiring a cessation of strike activity can easily be the blow that breaks a strike. The issuance of *ex parte* (without a hearing) temporary restraining orders frequently meant that the backbone of a strike was broken before labor had had the opportunity to appear in court and present its case. It was not unusual for the temporary restraining order to be prepared by the complainant's attorney and issued by a court as a matter of course. In a number of instances, several different courts could have jurisdiction, and the complainant would select the judge known for his anti-union views. In the preliminary hearing, the judge determined all questions of fact and law. Usually there was no oral examination of witnesses, and the proceedings amounted to a clash of contradictory affidavits. The total effect, then, was to give employers a procedure that could forestall union pressure activities for a considerable time. Failure to comply with temporary restraining orders and injunctions meant running the risk of being held in contempt of court. Compliance, on the other hand, meant a waiting period of many months before the matter came to trial. Even when labor unions won such trials and temporary injunctions were removed the victory was usually pyrrhic. The issue in dispute long since had been won by the employer.

2. *The Concept of Property.*   Historically, the court injunction had been a device to prevent damage to property in situations where an award of money damages would be an inadequate remedy. A legitimate use of the injunction in a labor dispute, thus, might occur in a situation where strong evidence indicates the likelihood of destruction of expensive machinery by the workers. Most labor disputes, however, are peaceful and unattended by evidence that the strike or boycott or picketing activity constitutes a threat to the employer's physical facilities. Instead of conceding that injunctions could not be legitimately issued in a majority of labor disputes, many judges took it upon themselves to define "property" in such a way that even non-violent pressure activities might be enjoined. "Property," in short, came to be regarded as "a right to do business." This was an ingenious manipulation of language that brought practically all pressure activities of labor groups into the orbit of judicial power. By supplementing

the concept of property with the intangible notion of business expectations, the judiciary handed American business firms an ideal technique for crushing the strikes and other activities that were essential to union success.

Of course, not all judges issued injunctions with such alacrity. Nevertheless, after the use of injunctions in labor disputes became firmly established by precedent, it was not a difficult matter for a party interested in curbing union activities to secure a temporary restraining order. With the threat of a contempt citation hanging over their heads, union leaders had little choice but to call off their strikes, boycotts, and picket lines.

3. *The Scope of Injunctions.*   One of the bitterest of labor complaints was leveled against "sweeping" or "omnibus" injunctions. Many court orders contained phrases such as "all persons whomsoever," "in any manner," or some variation of these. The significance of such phraseology was that a single court order could blanket an entire community during a labor dispute and prevent not only the actions that threatened to damage property but all peripheral actions that are the usual concomitants of strike situations. This was quite counter to historical injunction usage which limited a court enjoiner to specific individuals and specific acts. In labor dispute cases, the traditional narrow scope of the injunction was frequently replaced by a buck-shot-like order that made even remote expressions of sympathy for strikers liable to contempt citation.

The restraining order issued by Judge James Wilkerson of the federal district court in Chicago during the railroad shopmen's strike of 1922 is one of the most sweeping on record. Picketing was prohibited as were strike meetings, communications by strike leaders, and being unnecessarily in the strike vicinity. Encouragement of strikers by letter, telegram, telephone, word of mouth, oral persuasion, and newspaper interview was enjoined along with acts such as jeers, entreaties, argument, persuasion, or rewards to induce employees of the struck railways to cease work. This is only a partial listing of actions forbidden by the Wilkerson order, but it is sufficient to illustrate the character of the sweeping injunction.[14]

Employers, the Judiciary, and the Injunction

We have examined the nature of the labor injunction and some of the complaints against the courts in their injunction-issuing capacities. A broader implication of "government by injunction" will now be considered.

In the course of a labor dispute a union attempts to achieve its objectives by inflicting economic damage upon the employer. The employer, of course,

---

[14] For the text of the Wilkerson restraining order, see Frankfurter and Greene, *op. cit.,* Appendix 4.

seeks to avoid being damaged, and in so doing he may inflict serious damage upon the union as an institution and the workers as individuals.[15]

The nature and the amount of economic damage that unions and employers should be allowed to inflict upon each other is an important question of public policy. In recent years a variety of limitations have been placed upon the pressure activities of both labor and management. Regardless of what one thinks of the wisdom of these limitations, at least they represent the thinking of federal and state legislators and, somewhat less directly, that of the voting population. Until the passage of the Norris-LaGuardia Act of 1932, however, the allowable area of economic conflict was undefined by legislative action and only vaguely defined by court dicta. We have already noted that the courts in some states were relatively tolerant of union activities, whereas in others a quite conservative view was held. In few instances, however, were there clear cut criteria of what would or would not be accepted as lawful by the courts.

On the whole, the judiciary was inclined to be sympathetic toward the right of management to do business without interference from employees. Contrariwise, the courts were not especially impressed by the fact that workers had a property right in the freedom to exert pressure to improve their lot.

The situation, then, was one in which business and labor organizations disputed frequently by exerting the power that inheres in the pressure activities of each group. Business, however, having access to judicial aid, had, at the same time, access to a share of public power that was denied to the unions. Labor attempted to rectify this situation by political action; and, as we shall see, these efforts bore little fruit until the important developments of the 1930's.

THE SHERMAN AND CLAYTON ACTS

In 1890 Congress passed the Sherman Anti-Trust Act. The law makes illegal trusts and conspiracies that restrain interstate commerce and forbids persons to monopolize trade or commerce among the states. The Attorney General is given power to start criminal proceedings or to obtain court injunctions against violators. Persons who believe they have been injured by violations have the right to initiate civil suits for triple damages against those who violate the act.

---

[15] Physical violence, whether attributable to union or management, is illegal, just as it would be illegal apart from a labor dispute. The concern here is solely with economic damage, such as a union interference with production by withholding labor supply or an employer's efforts to replace striking workers and thus undermine the organization representing the strikers.

The Sherman Act is a paragon of brevity. It turned out, in fact, to be too brief; after its passage, no one seemed quite sure of its exact intent. This was unfortunate for the cause of unionism. Many opportunities arose for the federal courts to interpret the law, and a number of these interpretations erected serious barriers against the organizational and bargaining efforts of labor.

The question of whether Congress intended the Sherman Act to apply to the activities of unions became a subject of bitter controversy. The law itself is silent on this point, but the congressional debates that preceded enactment suggest that coverage of labor organizations was not intended.[16] After eighteen years, during which time the lower federal courts showed a lack of unanimity on the issue of coverage, a case involving a labor union and the Sherman Act reached the Supreme Court.

The Danbury Hatters Case[17]

In 1902 the United Hatters Union (AFL) called a strike against Loewe and Company, one of the few unorganized firms in the hat manufacturing industry. The union also initiated a boycott against Loewe. Dealers were warned against handling the company's products, advertisements were run in newspapers and trade journals, and the general co-operation of union people throughout the country was sought. The boycott was apparently successful, and the firm estimated its losses at $88,000. Spurred on by the American Anti-Boycott Association, Loewe filed an action against the union in the United States district court, alleging a violation of the Sherman Act and claiming triple damages of $240,000.

The case moved through the echelons of the federal court system several times, and the upshot of the matter was a Supreme Court decision of 1908 that the Sherman Act applied to unions. A further decision in 1915 upheld the ruling of a circuit court that a combination and conspiracy in violation of the Sherman Act had been proved and that the individual members of the union were jointly liable for the money damages awarded.[18]

Three aspects of the Danbury Hatters case alarmed union people. (1) The Supreme Court ruling that unions were covered by the Sherman Act meant that an entirely new area of legal danger had been opened. (2) Since

---

[16] For opposing views on this point, see Edward Berman, *Labor and the Sherman Act* (New York: Harper & Row, Publishers, 1930), Part I, and Mason, *op. cit.,* chaps. 7, 8.

[17] *Loewe* v. *Lawlor,* 208 U.S. 274 (1908).

[18] *Lawlor* v. *Loewe,* 235 U.S. 522 (1915). The homes and bank accounts of 186 workers had been attached since 1903. The American Federation of Labor staged a "Hatter's Day" appeal for funds, and the proceeds were used to pay the judgment and thus save the homes of the workers involved. The payment was made in 1917, some fifteen years after the strike against Loewe and Company had been instituted.

a boycott which had the effect of reducing the volume of interstate flow of goods had been judged as a restraint of trade in violation of the Sherman Act, there was the possibility that the same reasoning might be applied to the strike weapon. (3) The liability of individual union members for damages would very likely serve to intimidate workers in the future and thus strengthen the hands of employers relative to unions.

The decision in *Loewe* v. *Lawlor* together with the rather drastic antiunion ruling in *Gompers* v. *Buck Stove and Range Company* spurred union leaders to seek legislative redress against the onslaught of the federal courts.[19]

The Clayton Act

In 1906 the AFL submitted a Bill of Grievances to the President and to Congress. Among other requests, labor asked for exemption of unions from Sherman Act prosecutions and relief from court injunctions. Nothing came of this and other efforts to influence federal legislation until 1914, when a relatively liberal Congress during the Wilson administration enacted the Clayton Act.

Only two of the Clayton Act's twenty sections deal with labor. The larger part of the Act consists of a variety of provisions that supplement the Sherman Anti-Trust Act. Despite numerous actions taken against business under the latter law, the continuing movement toward business mergers and the prevalence of monopolistic practices demonstrated the inadequacies of the Sherman Act. The Clayton Act and the Federal Trade Commission Act passed a month earlier were designed to make government control over undesirable business practices more effective.

Sections 6 and 20 of the Clayton Act deal with the grievances of labor. Since later court interpretation turned upon the wording of these sections, parts of both are quoted below.

> Section 6: . . . the labor of a human being is not a commodity or article of commerce. Nothing contained in the anti-trust laws shall be construed to forbid the existence and operating of labor . . . organizations . . . or to forbid or restrain individual members of such organizations from lawfully carrying out the legitimate objects thereof; nor shall such organizations, or the members thereof be held or construed to be illegal combinations or conspiracies in restraint of trade under the anti-trust laws.

---

[19] *Gompers* v. *Buck Stove and Range Company*, 221 U.S. 418 (1911). The American Federation of Labor had placed the name of the stove company on the "We Don't Patronize" list published in its magazine, the *American Federationist*. The company sought and the District of Columbia court granted an injunction against further publication of the company's name in the list on the ground that such a publication was an illegal secondary boycott. Gompers and other labor leaders were found guilty of contempt of the injunction decree and sentenced to prison terms. They avoided serving the terms only because the Supreme Court reversed the jail sentence on the basis of a legal technicality.

Section 20: . . . no restraining order or injunction shall be granted by any court of the United States . . . in any case between an employer and employees, or between employees, or between persons employed and persons seeking employment, involving or growing out of a dispute concerning terms or conditions of employment, unless necessary to prevent irreparable injury to property, or to a property right, of the party making the application, for which injury there is no adequate remedy at law.

And no such restraining order or injunction shall prohibit any person or persons, whether singly or in concert, from terminating any relation of employment, or from ceasing to perform any work or labor, or from recommending, advising, or persuading others by peaceful means to so do; or from attending at any place where such persons may lawfully be, for the purpose of peacefully . . . persuading any person to work or abstain from working; or from ceasing to patronize or to employ any party to such dispute, or from recommending, advising, or persuading others by peaceful and lawful means to do so; . . . or from peaceably assembling in a lawful manner and for lawful purposes; or from doing any act or thing which might lawfully be done in the absence of such dispute by any party thereto. . . .

Leaders of organized labor were jubilant after the passage of the Clayton Act. Samuel Gompers went so far as to hail the Act as "labor's Magna Charta." Those who reflected more soberly were not convinced that unions had really won anything. Their reflections proved to be accurate.

Duplex v. *Deering*[20]

An important Supreme Court interpretation of the labor provisions of the Clayton Act was made in a case involving the International Association of Machinists and the Duplex Printing Press Company. Of the four firms that manufactured printing presses at the time, Duplex was the only one not operating under an agreement with the Machinists Union. Because of the lower wage scale and poorer working conditions prevailing at Duplex, this company enjoyed a cost advantage over its competitors. Under pressure from the three organized firms, the union sought to organize Duplex. A strike was called, but practically none of the Duplex employees responded. The union then instituted a series of actions that brought a variety of pressures to bear against the company. Customers were warned not to purchase the Duplex press. A trucking company was warned to expect trouble if it transported the presses. Repair shops were notified that they should not repair Duplex products, and an exposition company was threatened with a strike if it displayed any of the firm's exhibits.

The company sought an injunction to prevent the union from interfering with the sale, cartage, and installation of its products. After a hearing a United States district court vacated a temporary injunction. The case went

[20] 254 U.S. 443 (1921).

to a circuit court on appeal where the court relied upon Section 20 of the Clayton Act to affirm the denial of the injunction. The case then moved on appeal to the Supreme Court.

In denying an injunction, the lower courts had interpreted Section 20 according to the apparent intent of Congress. This section, it will be recalled, provided that no injunctions were to be issued by the federal courts in cases growing out of disputes over terms and conditions of employment unless necessary to prevent irreparable damage to property. The Duplex case certainly grew out of a dispute over terms of employment; and, so far as the evidence went, the boycott was peaceful, and no threat of irreparable damage to property existed. The situation seemed to fit exactly what Congress had had in mind when Section 20 was written.

The Supreme Court, however, was of a different opinion; and in a split decision the lower courts were overruled. Since part of the union argument was based upon Section 6 of the Clayton Act, it was necessary for the court to note that this Section had not removed unions from the control of the Sherman Act. Conceding that labor was not an article or commodity of commerce, Judge Pitney's decision pointed out that this did not mean that the actions of labor organizations could not be in restraint of trade. Nothing else in the section, furthermore, exempted unions from Sherman Act prosecutions. A close reading of Section 6 will show that the court was accurate. The wording provides that the "*lawful* carrying out of *legitimate* objects" is not to be construed as a violation of the anti-trust act, but it hardly required an act of Congress to make this point. Section 6 turned out to be high-sounding phraseology and little else.

The Supreme Court interpretation of Section 20 is more controversial. The decision that an injunction could be issued rested on the fact that the court was unwilling to accept anything other than a very narrow definition of "employer and employee." Since none of the persons engaged in the sympathetic strikes or boycotts were employees of the Duplex Company, no employer-employee relationship existed, and an injunction could legitimately be issued. The circuit court had reasoned that the prohibition against injunctions extended to all disputes between employers and employees regardless of whether the employees actually worked for the employer involved. This construction of Section 20 was unacceptable to the Supreme Court.

The significance of the Supreme Court interpretation is that it demonstrated the unwillingness of that body to recognize the legitimacy of union interests in non-union employments. Since attempts to organize non-union employees not infrequently involved placing pressures upon the employer that stemmed from sources other than his immediate employees, the decision was a heavy blow against the organizational efforts of labor unions.

In a sharply worded dissent Justice Brandeis took issue with the reasoning of the majority. Brandeis pointed out the obvious fact that the employees of the three organized printing press manufacturers had a close and immediate interest in working conditions at Duplex. Unless union standards could be imposed at the latter firm, the gains achieved at the other firms would be threatened. Admitting that the union-management struggle might involve danger to the community at large, Brandeis insisted that it was the function of the legislature rather than of judges to establish the limits of "permissible contest." Furthermore, he alleged, there is always a presumption that when the legislature passes a law it has the intention of changing a situation that existed prior to the law's enactment. The majority interpretation of Section 20 meant, in effect, that the pre-Clayton Act situation relative to court issuance of injunctions was untouched by the language of Section 20.[21]

The Legal Aftermath of the Sherman Act

The conservative tone which characterized judicial control of union activities was amplified by the *Duplex* v. *Deering* decision. Underlying the strained and often tortuous logic of the courts was the simple fact that the Supreme Court majority and most of the state courts were unwilling to sanction a conception of labor union rights that was to become commonplace within a generation. Unions as such were legal bodies, and certain of their more direct pressures against employers were legal if not carried on in a context of violence. This much had been established, but beyond this labor organizations could point to few improvements in their legal status. As the decade of the twenties unfolded, numerous labor disputes ended in the courts and gave the judges an opportunity to elaborate and extend the rules of law laid down in prominent cases such as *Loewe* v. *Lawlor* and *Duplex* v. *Deering*.

A legal dilemma that was bound to appear in the wake of the Danbury Hatters decision revolved about the strike weapon. If a secondary boycott was an illegal restraint of trade under the Sherman Act, could not the same judgment be rendered in connection with strikes? The likelihood of this possibility was enhanced by the fact that the purpose of an organizational strike is precisely the same as the purpose of the Danbury Hatters boycott. It is simply another technique for getting at the same thing—organization

---

[21] Actually, the union legal position deteriorated somewhat as a result of the Clayton Act. Under the Sherman Act only the government could sue for an injunction to prevent a violation of the law. Section 16 of the Clayton Act provided that "any person, firm, corporation, or association shall be entitled to sue for and have injunctive relief in any court of the United States having jurisdiction over the parties, against the threatened loss or damage by a violation of the anti-trust laws. . . ."

of non-union workers. If successful, the organizational strike will be just as effective as a secondary boycott in preventing the interstate movement of goods.

A dilemma, however, was created by the generally established legality of certain categories of strikes such as those for higher wages by the immediate employees of an employer. Since a strike for higher wages may have just as much of an impact on the interstate movement of goods as an organizational strike, a logical extension of the Loewe v. Lawlor rule would have been to judge practically all strikes, regardless of purpose, as violations of the Sherman Act. This position, which if enforced could have meant the end of unionism in the United States, was politically impractical, and the Supreme Court avoided making such an extension in United Leather Workers v. Herkert.[22]

The mere reduction of the supply of an article to be shipped in interstate commerce was considered to be an indirect and remote obstruction to commerce and hence not a violation of the Sherman Act.

In the second of two cases involving the United Mine Workers of America and the Coronado Coal Company, however, the Supreme Court found that a strike was a violation of the Sherman Act.[23] The decision was based upon testimony that the subjective intent of the union had been to prevent the interstate movement of coal and upon the fact that the volume of coal produced by the Coronado mines was a substantial share of total coal output.

The Coronado decision, though consistent with the ruling in Loewe v. Lawlor, nevertheless meant that the law in relation to union activities had degenerated to a new level of confusion. The basic intent of any strike is to achieve objectives such as higher wages, improved working conditions, or organization of non-union workers. It is obviously also the intent of the union to interfere with the production and sale of the employer's product since this is the means by which the strike weapon exerts a pressure. For the Supreme Court to rule that some strikes were illegal restraints of trade and others were not meant only that the judiciary was using the Sherman Act to suppress in a selective way those union tactics of which it disapproved.

One additional example will be sufficient to illustrate how conservative court attitudes inhibited labor union actions in the period under consideration. The Supreme Court decision in the Bedford Stone case[24] has been described as "the capstone of the long development in the application of the Sherman Act to labor."[25] Here the Court held that the action of the

---

[22] 265 U.S. 471 (1924).
[23] 259 U.S. 344 (1922).
[24] 274 U.S. 37 (1927).
[25] Berman, op. cit., p. 179.

Journeymen Stone Cutters Association of America was an undue and unreasonable restraint of trade. The union had issued a notice directing its members to refrain from working on stone that had been cut by men working in opposition to the union. To bring pressure upon stone companies that were hiring non-union labor, building projects were interrupted by strikes in various parts of the country. Justice Brandeis in his dissent pointed out that the workers had simply refused to set stone purchased from noncomplying companies. There had been no trespass, violence, breach of contract, or intimidation. Although the union contended that its sole purpose was to organize workers, the court held that this objective was sought by the illegal means of restricting interstate commerce.

The Courts and Picketing Activity

For many years there was little judicial agreement on the lawfulness of peaceful picketing. In the early years of this century one federal court held, "There can be no such thing as peaceful picketing any more than there can be chaste vulgarity or peaceful mobbing or lawful lynching. When men want to persuade they do not organize a picket line."[26]

The supreme courts of the various states which had ruled on the question before 1920 were about evenly divided, half upholding the sentiment expressed in the above paragraph and the others espousing an opposite viewpoint.

In the American Steel Foundries case, the Supreme Court ruled that in the event of a strike it was lawful for former employees to have a single representative at each entrance and exit to the employer's plant to announce the strike and to persuade peaceably those working to join them. Pickets would have the right of "observation, communication, and persuasion"; but these actions might not be libelous, abusive, or threatening. In addition, pickets had to approach individuals singly.[27]

The Steel Foundries case, which soon became the leading case in the law of picketing, was interpreted by other courts to mean that the designation of the number of pickets and the manner in which they should conduct themselves had to vary with the circumstances in each case. As Professor Gregory has noted, there was a strong implication in the American Steel Foundries decision that picketing could be forbidden or restrained and that its toleration was a matter of legislative or judicial grace.[28] Generally speaking, mass picketing or picketing that intimidated or was characterized by misrepresentation was illegal, whereas a mild form of peaceful persuasion was legal.

---

[26] *Atchison Co.* v. *Gee*, 139 Fed. 582 (1905).
[27] *American Steel Foundries* v. *Tri-City Trades Council,* 257 U.S. 194 (1921).
[28] Gregory, *op. cit.,* p. 338.

The validity of "stranger picketing," that is picketing by persons who were not employees of the picketed establishment, was accorded a varied treatment during this period. Some courts declared such conduct illegal and others regarded all peaceful picketing as lawful.[29]

THE COURTS AND PRO-UNION LEGISLATION

Judicial control over union activities is exercised through equity proceedings, interpretations of legislative intent, and judgments rendered on the constitutionality of laws that regulate the labor-management relationship. The results of the first two processes in the period that extended roughly from 1880 to 1930 were discussed above. The present section will deal with prominent decisions of constitutionality during the same period.

Adair v. *United States*[30]

The Erdman Act, passed by Congress in 1898, was concerned primarily with the establishment of mediation and arbitration processes in the railroad industry.[31] Labor relations had been quite stormy on the railways, and it was the congressional hope that the formal establishment of voluntary mediation and arbitration procedures would remove the weaknesses of earlier legislation and lead to labor-management peace.

Section 10 of the Erdman Act contained a provision that forbade employers to require as a condition of employment that workers agree not to become members of a labor organization. Such agreements, known as "yellow dog contracts," were used extensively in the coal fields and were not uncommon in other industries. Section 10, which also forbade management to threaten a worker with loss of employment or to unjustly discriminate against him because of his membership in a labor organization, was received with understandable enthusiasm by the railway unions.[32]

The constitutionality of Section 10 was tested in the case of *Adair* v. *United States*. Justice Harlan, who wrote the majority decision, posed the issue as follows:

> May Congress make it a criminal offense against the United States—as by the 10th section of the Act of 1898 it does—for an agent or an officer of an interstate carrier, having full authority in the premises from the carrier, to discharge an employee from service simply because of his membership in a labor union?

---

[29] *Ibid.*

[30] 208 U.S. 161 (1908).

[31] For a history of early railway labor legislation, see Leonard A. Lecht, *Experience Under Railway Labor Legislation* (New York: Columbia University Press, 1955), chaps. 1, 2.

[32] Violations of Section 10 were misdemeanors punishable by fines of from $100 to $1,000.

Two major questions were analyzed in the opinion: (1) Was Section 10 of the Erdman Act inconsistent with the Fifth Amendment of the Constitution, which declares that no person shall be deprived of liberty or property without due process of law? (2) Could the legislative authority to enact Section 10 be found in the congressional power to regulate interstate commerce?

On the first question Justice Harlan declared that employees had the right to quit the service of employers for any reason whatever and that employers, for any reason, had the right to dispense with the services of employees. "In all such particulars the employer and the employee have equality of right, and any legislation that disturbs that equality is an arbitrary interference with the liberty of contract which no government can legally justify in a free land."

In regard to interstate commerce, Harlan went on to state that any rule prescribed by Congress for the regulation of commerce must have real or substantial relation to or connection with the commerce regulated. "But what possible legal or logical connection," he asked, "is there between an employee's membership in a labor organization and the carrying on of interstate commerce?" On both counts, then, the court majority could find no constitutional basis for the anti-yellow dog proviso in Section 10 of the Erdman Act.[33]

The Adair decision was important in a number of respects. So long as the Supreme Court adhered to the pronounced concept of the labor-management contract the constitutional outlook for legislation favorable to unions would be dim. The narrow definition of interstate commerce, furthermore, denied to Congress the use of an important avenue for the regulation of economic life. These aspects of the Adair case should be kept in mind when later developments in the law of collective bargaining are considered in the next chapter.

The precedent set in *Adair* v. *United States* was used by the Supreme Court to declare unconstitutional an anti-yellow dog contract law passed by the State of Kansas.[34] Just as the due process clause of the Fifth Amendment was found to prevent Congress from interfering with freedom of contract, the court found that the Fourteenth Amendment set similar limits to the rights of state legislatures. The ultimate blow to the hopes of organized labor for legal relief against the yellow dog contract came in 1917 when the Supreme Court ruled that these contracts might be protected by the

---

[33] Justice McKenna, who dissented, noted that a provision of law which would prevent, or tend to prevent, "the stoppage of every wheel in every car of an entire railroad system" had an obvious influence on interstate commerce. Justice Holmes made the point that Congress had the right to restrain liberty of contract if it felt that such restraint was justified on an important ground of public policy.

[34] *Coppage* v. *Kansas*, 236 U.S. 1 (1915).

injunction.[35] Union organizers who sought to organize workers in defiance of such injunctions could be found in contempt of court.

Truax v. Corrigan[36]

In 1913 the state of Arizona enacted a law forbidding the issuance of injunctions in disputes between employers and employees. The law specifically forbade injunctions against "peacefully persuading any person to work or to abstain from working; or from ceasing to patronize. . . ." The Arizona provision was somewhat similar to Section 20 of the Clayton Act and, unlike the Supreme Court in *Duplex* v. *Deering*, the Arizona State Supreme Court had upheld the validity of the law.

A restaurant owner whose business had suffered because of vigorous picketing by a cooks and waiters union started an action alleging that the law in question violated the Fourteenth Amendment which forbids states to take property without due process of law or to deny a citizen the equal protection of the law. The case eventually reached the Supreme Court on appeal.

Chief Justice Taft wrote the majority opinion. After listing the details of the picketing action and the effects of this action upon the plaintiff, he concluded that any law which made such wrongs lawful deprived the owner of the business and premises of his property without due process of law.[37] He also found that the law constituted class legislation, since it granted immunity to one class at the expense of another. This, Taft felt, ran counter to the equal protection clause of the Fourteenth Amendment.

Truax v. *Corrigan* was a five-to-four Supreme Court decision. Justice Holmes in his dissent stated that "legislation may begin where an evil begins. If as many intelligent people believe that there is more danger that the injunction will be abused in labor cases than elsewhere I can feel no doubt of the power of the legislature to deny it in such cases. . . ." The following portion of Holmes' dissent is especially noteworthy:

> There is nothing I more deprecate than the use of the Fourteenth Amendment beyond the absolute compulsion of its words to prevent the making

---

[35] *Hitchman Coal and Coke* v. *Mitchell*, 245 U.S. 229 (1917).

[36] 257 U.S. 312 (1912).

[37] Justice Taft's description of the picketing action was as follows: "The libelous attacks upon the plaintiffs, their business, their employees, and their customers and the abusive epithets applied to them were palpable wrongs. The patrolling of defendants immediately in front of the restaurant . . . and within five feet of plaintiff's premises . . . the attendance of the picketers at the entrance to the restaurant and their insistent and loud appeals all day long . . . the threats of injurious consequences to future customers . . . were an unlawful annoyance. . . . It was compelling every customer or would-be customer to run the gauntlet of most uncomfortable publicity, aggressive and annoying importunity, libelous attacks, and fear of injurious consequences. . . ."

of social experiments that an important part of the community desires, in the insulated chambers afforded by the several states, even though the experiments may seem futile or even noxious to me and to those whose judgment I most respect.

SUMMARY: THE REPRESSIVE ERA

The period before 1880 can be described as one of legal hostility toward organizations of workers. Although there was an admission that unions as such were lawful, the narrow view of the legitimacy of union objectives nullified the practical importance of this admission in many legal jurisdictions.

After 1880, the courts adopted a somewhat more tolerant attitude toward unions. On the whole, however, the judiciary, while admitting the lawfulness of a narrow range of union tactics and goals, continued to suppress many of the attempts of labor to achieve a power position that would have removed the disparity of bargaining strength between employer and employee.

In the "repressive era" (1880 to about 1930), collective bargaining law was judge-made law for the most part. An overall summary of the law's character is difficult because so many courts had a hand in shaping and defining the legal rules. The overlapping jurisdictions of local, state, and federal courts produced a wide range of attitudes that extended from tolerance to extremes of intolerance. Probably the most accurate generalization that can be made is that striking and boycotting activity by the immediate employees of an employer for recognized objectives such as higher wages and shorter working hours were lawful so long as the activities were carried on peacefully and moderately. Sympathy strikes, organizational strikes, strikes for a closed shop, secondary boycotts, and mass picketing were likely to incur judicial disfavor.

The history of the injunction during the repressive era illustrates two important aspects of labor law: (1) the processes by which the law is administered are frequently as important as the letter of the law; (2) the establishment of basic policy, a function supposedly reserved to the legislative branch in the American democracy, can be and has been performed by one or another of the non-legislative branches. Between 1880 and 1930, the courts, in effect, legislated a conception of property rights that was not inherently a part of competitive free enterprise.

The attempt by Congress to control the growing power of large aggregates of capital was interpreted by the courts so as to create a series of legal barriers against unionism which were rather apart from anything the Congress had had in mind when the Sherman Anti-Trust Law was passed.

Efforts of the legislative branch of government to favor unionism did not survive the test of constitutionality, and this fact serves as a further example of the dominant position of the courts before the 1930's.

We have been examining the details of the collective bargaining law that developed during the post-Civil War industrial revolution. The economy of the nation changed from one dominated by agriculture and commercial enterprise to one dominated by industrial activities. In this era the economic philosophy that prevailed among the groups sufficiently powerful to translate philosophy into policy was one that brooked only a minimum of interference in business activities by either the government or non-business groups. The same property ideology that supported the free issuance of injunctions in labor disputes led to the special definitions of "restraint of trade" and "due process of law" that favored management over union interests. All of this reflected a philosophy that assumed that the best of all economic worlds would result if economic activity were subject to marketplace rather than man-made restraints.

These generalizations need qualification, of course. When the excesses of business became apparent, legislative checks such as anti-monopoly rules were imposed. The court that eventually ruled that only "unreasonable restraints of trade" by business were illegal under the Sherman Act, however, developed no equivalent rule of reason for the actions of labor unions.[38]

Insofar as the law was concerned, the tactical position of management was superior to that of labor because the management philosophy was more readily transformed into legal power in a particular labor dispute. By suing for injunctions or by initiating court tests of interpretation and constitutionality, management was able to force a labor dispute into the orbit of judicial power, where, as we have seen, the courts' philosophies correlated closely with those of management. Labor, on the other hand, could only petition the legislative or administrative branches for a redress of legal grievances. By comparison, this was an inefficient process; and it certainly provided no relief in the course of a specific dispute. From two standpoints then—the dominating property ideology and the ability to call the power of government into play in a favorable way—the forces of management enjoyed an advantage over those of labor.

---

[38] In the Standard Oil and American Tobacco cases of 1911, the Supreme Court ordered the dissolution of the oil and tobacco trusts as unlawful combinations under the Sherman Act. In these cases the court expressed the opinion that only unreasonable restraints of trade were prohibited by the law. Such a doctrine, of course, provided the court with a great deal of flexibility for subsequent interpretations of the Sherman Act.

A NEW ERA IN LABOR-MANAGEMENT LAW: THE BEGINNINGS

In the 1930's the law of collective bargaining changed significantly and became much more favorable toward labor unions. It would be misleading, however, to suggest that any single year marked the change in legal direction. Historical phenomena rarely occur so spontaneously that no forerunners can be found. A study of the court decisions cited above and many others delivered during the same period will show that few were unanimous. Some of the Supreme Court decisions that most restricted unions, furthermore, overruled opposite verdicts of the lower courts. In their dissenting opinions Justices Holmes and Brandeis were setting the stage for a reversal of the law's direction. All that was necessary for the actual reversal was a change in the general climate of opinion; and, when such a change occurred, the dissenting voices of the pre-1930 era provided both encouragement and logic for those burdened with the task of writing new meaning into the federal Constitution.

As we have seen, the few attempts made by the legislative branch of government to formulate a statutory law of labor relations before 1930 were emasculated by the courts. The major exception to this statement is the development in the railroad industry. The quasi-public nature of the industry,[39] the establishment of rate regulation under the Interstate Commerce Commission, and the history of turbulent labor relations on the railways served to focus a congressional interest in that industry. Successive attempts to develop a satisfactory labor law culminated in the Railway Labor Act of 1926 which became the basis of an enduring code for the railway labor-management relationship.

The Railway Labor Act attempted to resolve the problems of a single industry and for this reason cannot be considered a part of the more general overhauling of labor law that commenced several years later. Forerunners of a number of the features of later legislation, however, can be found in the Railway Labor Act.

In the railway law, representatives of labor and management co-operated in writing a piece of legislation that established adjustment, mediation, arbitration, and emergency boards for processing the various types of disputes that might arise. One of the more significant sections provided that for purposes of the act the parties had the right to designate their respective representatives without "interference, influence, or coercion"

---

[39] In *Munn* v. *Illinois* the Supreme Court ruled that when private property is devoted to public use it is subject to public regulation, 94 U.S. 113 (1876).

by the other party. A court test arose when the management of the Texas and New Orleans Railroad disregarded this provision by ignoring the long-established Brotherhood of Railroad Clerks and forming a company union. In the case of *Texas and New Orleans Railroad* v. *Brotherhood of Railroad Clerks*, the Supreme Court upheld the validity of an injunction obtained by the union to prevent the company from interfering with the right of the employees to select their own representatives.[40]

An earlier Supreme Court might have found little difficulty in declaring that the law interfered with the constitutional rights of the defendants. The Supreme Court in 1930, however, rejected the appeal to the principle declared in *Adair* v. *United States*. The Railway Labor Act of 1926, according to the opinion, did not interfere with the carrier's normal right to hire and fire.

The carrier had no right to interfere with the constitutional rights of employees to select their own representatives and hence could not complain of the statute on constitutional grounds. The phraseology and the general tenor of the decision suggested an imminent basic change in the Supreme Court's attitude toward the relative legal rights of employees and employers.

The Norris-LaGuardia Act

The relief from the court injunction that organized labor had sought for so long was provided in 1932 when Congress passed and President Hoover signed the Norris-LaGuardia Anti-Injunction Act. The mistakes of earlier legislation were avoided. Congress intended that the power of the federal courts to issue injunctions in labor dispute cases be closely circumscribed, and the law was carefully designed to accomplish this objective.

1. *The "Labor Dispute" Definition.* The definition of a labor dispute in Section 20 of the Clayton Act was not crystal clear, and the courts eventually decided that the term applied only to disputes between an employer and his immediate employees. In the Norris-LaGuardia Act a labor dispute is defined so as to include "any controversy concerning terms or conditions of employment, or concerning the association or representation of persons in negotiating, fixing, maintaining, changing, or seeking to arrange terms or conditions of employment *regardless of whether or not the disputants stand in the proximate relations of employer and employee.*" (Italics added.)

Labor unions had been pressing for years to have such a broad legal definition of a labor dispute accepted by the lawmakers. This, of course,

---

[40] 281 U.S. 548 (1930).

was the only conception of a dispute that made sense to organized labor. Much of labor's pressure activities had been directed against non-union employers or unorganized workers because the growth and success of Unionism depended so obviously upon what occurred in these non-union employments. Legal sanction of the broad definition of a dispute opened organizing possibilities that had hitherto been limited by the refusal of judges to acknowledge the union concern with non-union labor.

In a series of cases the Supreme Court validated the broad definition of a labor dispute.[41] The court ruled, in effect, that injunctions could not be issued against striking, boycotting, or picketing activity simply because no members of a union were employees of the firm against whom these pressures were directed.

2. *The Issuance of Injunctions.* The Norris-LaGuardia Act does not deny the federal courts the power to issue injunctions in the course of labor disputes. It does, however, prohibit the issuance of injunctions against a number of specified actions; and it defines very carefully those circumstances in which injunctions or temporary restraining orders might be issued.

Federal courts are prohibited from enjoining strikes; payment of strike benefits; picketing (unless attended by fraud or violence); peaceful assembly by those involved in a labor dispute; boycotts; and advising, inducing, or otherwise causing the above acts. The effect of the decision in the Hitchman case (p. 455 above) was nullified by a provision that denied the federal courts the use of the injunction to enforce yellow dog contracts.

Under the Norris-LaGuardia Act, injunctions may be issued in the following circumstances: (1) Unlawful acts have been threatened and will be committed unless restrained. (2) Unlawful acts are being committed and will continue unless restrained. (3) Substantial and irreparable damage to the complainant's property will occur. (4) Greater injury will be inflicted upon the complainant by the denial of relief than will be inflicted upon the defendant by the granting of relief. (5) The complainant has no adequate remedy at law. (6) The public officials charged with protecting the complainant's property are unable or unwilling to furnish adequate protection.

The complainant who seeks an injunction must make every reasonable effort to settle the dispute by negotiation or with the aid of available government machinery. He must comply with any legal obligations that may pertain to the dispute in question. Temporary restraining orders are not to be effective for more than five days, and a sufficient bond must be posted to recompense those who may suffer loss because of an erroneous issuance

---

[41] See *Senn* v. *Tile Layers Protective Union*, 301 U.S. 468 (1937); *Lauf* v. *E. G. Shinner and Co.*, 303 U.S. 323 (1938); *American Federation of Labor* v. *Swing*, 312 U.S. 321 (1941); *New Negro Alliance* v. *Sanitary Grocery Co.*, 303 U.S. 552 (1938).

of a court order. Blanket or omnibus injunctions are circumscribed by the requirement that notice of a hearing must be given to all persons against whom relief is sought.

3. *The Policy Declaration.*   The Norris-LaGuardia Act contains an interesting declaration of public policy. The law declared as the public policy of the United States that workers should have full freedom of association, self-organization, and designation of representatives of their own choosing. Workers should have the right to negotiate the terms and conditions of employment and should be free from interference or coercion in the exercise of concerted activities for the purpose of collective bargaining. The act does nothing to provide positive implementation of the rights declared; but the forthright statement by Congress is worth noting at this point, for it suggests a new attitude toward unionism that was emerging as a concomitant of economic depression. The implementation was to come in a totally separate piece of legislation several years later.

The Norris-LaGuardia Act can be summarized as a change in the rules of the game. Before its passage, the law as administered by the courts tipped the scale in management's favor in the course of labor disputes. Now the government was to stand aside and let the disputants compete on even terms—even, that is, so far as the favors of the law were concerned. The new law did little to minimize conflict nor did it positively encourage unions. It simply removed a legal impediment that had created an almost automatic disadvantage for labor organizations when they joined for battle with management.

The Norris-LaGuardia Act affected procedures in the federal courts only. The passage of the law, however, spurred a number of states to enact similar laws. By 1941, twenty-four states had anti-injunction acts, most of which were modeled closely after the federal law. In the remaining states, the courts were free to follow their historical practices relative to the issuance of injunctions in those disputes that fell within their jurisdictions.

SUMMARY

Throughout the nineteenth century, the law as it applied to the labor-management relationship was shaped by the courts. The law was conservative in tone and reflected the prevailing philosophy of property rights. The conspiracy doctrine, though modified over the years, was interpreted by the courts so as to make illegal many of the pressure activities of labor organizations. In the latter part of the century the injunction began to be applied freely in labor disputes; and, again, unions were put at a disadvantage in their frequent clashes with employers. The legal difficulties of labor were compounded by court interpretations of the Sherman Anti-Trust Act;

and political efforts to achieve redress, though outwardly successful in the Clayton Act of 1914, were nullified by court interpretations of that law during the 1920's. Thus, for more than a century, organized labor found the law hostile to its pretensions, and as a result the power balance was usually tipped toward the side of management during conflict situations.

The Railway Labor Act of 1926, which provided that workers could select their own bargaining representatives without interference or coercion, was an early forerunner of a new era in which the legal position of organized labor would be improved by dramatic proportions. In the Norris-LaGuardia Act of 1932, labor was finally granted its long-sought relief from court-issued injunctions; and as the depression experience modified the property ideology, the stage was being set for legislation that was to give positive encouragement to unionism and collective bargaining.

QUESTIONS

1. What legal philosophy relative to property rights was expressed by the conspiracy doctrine and by the relatively free issuance of injunctions during labor disputes?

2. From the standpoint of the development of labor law, what was the significance of *Loewe* v. *Lawlor* (the Danbury Hatters case)?

3. Describe the ostensible purposes of Section 6 and 20 of the Clayton Act. How were these sections interpreted by the Supreme Court in *Duplex* v. *Deering?*

4. How do you explain the relatively conservative character of collective bargaining law throughout the nineteenth century and the first three decades of the twentieth century?

5. What was the significance of the decision in *Texas and New Orleans Railroad* v. *Brotherhood of Railroad Clerks?*

6. How was a labor dispute defined in the Norris-LaGuardia Anti-Injunction Act? Why did Congress define "labor dispute" so broadly?

7. According to the provisions of the Norris-LaGuardia Act, under what conditions could an injunction be issued by a federal court during a labor dispute?

SELECTED READINGS

BERMAN, EDWARD. *Labor and the Sherman Act.* New York: Harper & Row, Publishers, 1930.

COMMONS, JOHN R., and GILMORE, EUGENE A. "The Philadelphia Cordwainers," *A Documentary History of American Industrial Society.* Cleveland: The Arthur H. Clark Co., 1910. III, 59–248.

FRANKFURTER, FELIX, and GREENE, NATHAN. *The Labor Injunction.* New York: The Macmillan Company, 1930.

MILLER, GLENN W. *American Labor and the Government.* Englewood Cliffs, N.J.: Prentice-Hall, Inc., 1948. Chaps. 6, 7.

WITTE, EDWIN E. *The Government in Labor Disputes.* New York: McGraw-Hill Book Company, 1932. Chaps. 3–7.

CHAPTER 17

The Development of Collective Bargaining Law—Continued

THE NATIONAL LABOR RELATIONS ACT OF 1935 (THE WAGNER ACT) was the most important piece of collective bargaining law enacted during the 1930's. It was a revolutionary law in several respects. The dominance of common law in the field of labor relations was ended, and the long-time legal disadvantages suffered by organized labor were replaced by a number of positive advantages.

The Wagner Act was a product of its time. It could not have been enacted before the 1930's, nor could the same law be passed today. Basically, the act favored unions by stripping away from employers the right to use a variety of anti-union pressures. The organizational and bargaining rights granted to employees were nothing new. Theoretically, at least, labor had possessed these rights in some degree since *Commonwealth* v. *Hunt*. The denial to employers of the right to combat, interfere with, and defeat unionism, however, was new. Whereas, historically, the question of worker unionization had been decided by a contest of strength, the new law made it a matter of worker decision. The worker's decision, furthermore, was not to be influenced overtly or otherwise by anything the employer said or did.

THE BACKGROUND

Fundamental institutional changes (and the change in the law of collective bargaining must be placed in this category) do not come about because of personal whims and rarely occur because of random accidents. They reflect, rather, far-reaching changes that have occurred in the over-all environment of a society. The broad economic and social milieu and the immediate legislative background of the Wagner Act will be examined in the next two sections.

The Economic and Social Background

The environmental factor of overwhelming importance during the 1930's was, of course, the economic depression. The breakdown of the economy destroyed a popular faith in the man of business and his philosophy of economics. Virtues such as "rugged individualism" and "thrift" became hollow-sounding platitudes when stripped of the rewards that supposedly flowed from their practice. New phrases—"the forgotten man," "a new deal," "try something"—had a mass appeal that a conservative administration could neither counter nor emulate. In the 1932 presidential election Roosevelt defeated Hoover with a plurality of almost 7 million votes. Only Pennsylvania, Delaware, Connecticut, Vermont, New Hampshire, and Maine failed to go Democratic.

The election of 1932 was a mandate for social and economic experimentation. The voices that would have effectively opposed experimentation at some earlier date had become weak, defensive, and discredited. Substantial sections of the business community, in fact, were not at all averse to the idea of government aid. Thus, the property ideology that had defended the economy against the inroads of government and labor crumpled, and the way was open for the reform and recovery measures of the New Deal.

The political power position of organized labor had never been more favorable. The heretofore politically powerless labor movement suddenly found itself with a voice in government councils, but this was not because of any sudden upsurge in labor strength. The unions, in fact, were quite debilitated; and, on the whole, the labor leadership was unimaginative. It required several years of mass unemployment before many of the union spokesmen were able to shed the Gompers philosophy of voluntarism and realize that positive help from the government was not only desirable but necessary. In the first instance, then, it was government friendliness rather than inherent union strength that accounted for the labor influence in the legislative halls.

The Wagner Act must be viewed as part of a more general effort to meet the problems of a depressed time. The conditions that spawned the CCC, PWA, TVA, AAA, and other New Deal measures also gave birth to the strongest pro-union piece of legislation in the nation's history. Those who opposed such measures wielded relatively little influence in a period when the vast majority was eager to "try something."[1]

The Legislative Background

The basic principles of the Wagner Act can be enumerated as follows: (1) workers had the right to decide for themselves whether they wanted to form unions; (2) workers were to select their own bargaining representatives; (3) employers were not to interfere with these rights; (4) employers must recognize and deal with the representatives selected by their employees.

These rights had been asserted by sundry government bodies on a number of occasions.[2] Except for the temporary conditions of World War I and the special situation on the railroads, such assertions were in the nature of obiter dicta or recommendations, especially insofar as the employer obligations were concerned. In the Wagner Act, however, the statement of the principles was less equivocal than on past occasions, and the administrative and enforcement mechanisms were relatively effective.

The immediate forerunner of the Wagner Act was part of a law that was addressed primarily to the problem of bolstering business confidence. Title I of the National Industrial Recovery Act of 1933 provided that firms within an industry might get together and draw up codes of "fair competition." This last phrase was a euphemism for a package of monopolistic practices. The government, in effect, agreed to price fixing and other economic arrangements that would ordinarily have been prohibited by the anti-monopoly laws. The hope was that an easing of the rigors of competi-

---

[1] The interpretation of New Deal economics generally, and Franklin D. Roosevelt's economic philosophy specifically, has changed in the course of years. Opponents of the New Deal argued that the program was socialistic, while supporters alleged that it was a planned effort to save capitalism. In recent times the early charge of socialism has evaporated, and a common assertion is that the New Deal had little philosophical direction and Roosevelt knew little of economics. For an analysis of these points and a conclusion that quarrels with both the "myth" of Roosevelt omniscience and the "overly critical reaction" of present day historians, see Daniel R. Fusfeld, *The Economic Thought of Franklin D. Roosevelt and the Origins of the New Deal* (New York: Columbia University Press, 1956).

[2] Bernstein has counted ten instances in which the rights of employees to associate and designate their representatives had been asserted by government bodies. These were the *Commonwealth* v. *Hunt* decision, the 1894 report of the Strike Commission, the Clayton Act, the 1915 report of the Commission on Industrial Relations, the decisions of the National War Labor Board, the American Steel Foundries decision, the rulings of the Railroad Labor Board created by the Transportation Act of 1920, the Railway Labor Act of 1926, and the Norris-LaGuardia Act. He also counts ten instances in which government bodies stated that employers should not interfere with these rights and five occasions on which the responsibility of the employer to deal with worker representatives was declared. Irving Bernstein, *The New Deal Collective Bargaining Policy* (Berkeley: University of California Press, 1950), pp. 18–22.

tion would create a favorable climate for expansion in a volume of business activity that had reached disastrous lows.[3]

The collective bargaining section of the NIRA was a concession granted to labor in a law that was otherwise concerned with improvement of business conditions. Hammered out against the opposition of the National Association of Manufacturers, Section 7(a) of the act provided that all codes were to grant employees the right to organize and bargain collectively through representatives of their own choosing, free of interference or coercion from the employer; that employees were not to be required to join company unions or to refrain from joining or assisting labor organizations as a condition of employment; and that employers were to comply with certain maximum hours and minimum wage prescriptions.

Title I of the NIRA did not work out in practice. The codes governing industrial economic conditions developed into administrative monstrosities, and Section 7(a) raised more questions than it answered. The language of this section proved to be especially ambiguous insofar as the status of company unions was concerned. The combination of employer opposition, inadequate authority vested in the boards that supervised the section, and wavering support by the executive branch limited the effectiveness of 7(a).

The coup de grâce for the entire NIRA experiment was provided by the Supreme Court in the Schecter case when a unanimous court declared that Title I was an unconstitutional delegation of legislative power to the President and that it regulated business transactions that were not part of interstate commerce.[4]

Even before the Schecter case ruling, supporters of collective bargaining legislation had been working to produce a labor law that was less ambiguous and more forceful than 7(a). After several false starts and much political infighting, Congress passed the Wagner Act in 1935. Industry spokesmen had opposed the bill vigorously, but the capacity of industry to defeat pro-labor legislation was on the wane at this time. Although the act was unquestionably favorable towards unionism there was some fear in labor circles that industrial unions might benefit at the expense of craft units. On the whole, however, labor had fought for the Wagner Act, and the passage constituted a substantial legal victory for organized labor.

THE DETAILS OF THE WAGNER ACT

The Wagner Act was not a complex piece of legislation. Its purpose—basically, the encouragement of collective bargaining—was limited in scope;

---

[3] For a summary of the background and purposes of the NIRA, see Basil Rauch, *The History of the New Deal* (New York: Creative Age Press, 1944), pp. 72–80.

[4] *Schecter Poultry Corporation* v. *United States*, 295 U.S. 495 (1935).

and the mechanics of effectuating the purpose were left, for the most part, to a specially created administrative agency. By 1947 when the act was superseded by the Taft-Hartley Act, court interpretations and administrative rulings had produced a quite involved legal instrument. Some of the complexities will be noted at a later point. In this section, the major features of the law will be summarized.

Policy Declaration

The policy of the United States was declared to be that of eliminating obstructions to the free flow of commerce by encouraging the practice and procedure of collective bargaining. Obstructions were identified as the denial by employers of the right of employees to organize and as employer refusal to accept the procedures of collective bargaining. Such employer behavior burdened commerce in two ways. First, it led to strikes and industrial unrest which interfered with the physical movement of goods. Second, the inequality of bargaining power between employer and employees aggravated business instability by depressing wages and thus burdened and affected the flow of commerce.

The heavy emphasis upon interstate commerce in the policy declaration was obviously made in anticipation of a court test of constitutionality. In their forthright statement of the relationship between collective bargaining and interstate commerce, the authors of the act, in a way, were pre-arguing the case before the Supreme Court.

Rights of Employees[5]

Section 7 of the Wagner Act read as follows: "Employees shall have the right to self-organization, to form, join, or assist labor organizations, to bargain collectively through representatives of their own choosing, and to engage in concerted activities for the purpose of collective bargaining or other mutual aid or protection."

Section 8 sought to effectuate the right declared in Section 7 by identifying five types of unfair employer practices. These were as follows:

1. *To interfere with, restrain, or coerce employees in the exercise of the rights guaranteed in Section 7.* This first unfair practice was a catch-all type of prohibition. Interference, restraint, and coercion were not defined, and it fell to the National Labor Relations Board to work out the precise content of these terms on a case-by-case basis.

---

[5] The protections of the Wagner Act accrued only to those workers covered by the terms of the act, of course. Excluded from coverage were those subject to the Railway Labor Act, agricultural employments, domestic service, family employments, and those whose work could not be interpreted as being in interstate commerce.

2. *To dominate or interfere with the formation or administration of any labor organization or to contribute support to it.* The reference here, of course, was to the company union. Henceforth, the long-practiced employer technique of combating unionism by establishing a company-supported worker organization was to be proscribed.

3. *By discrimination in regard to hire or tenure of employment, to encourage or discourage membership in any labor organization.* Since in a closed shop agreement an employer is actually encouraging membership in a labor organization, a proviso was added that removed closed shop agreements from the general prohibition of encouragement or discouragement.

4. *To discharge or otherwise discriminate against an employee because he has filed charges or given testimony under the act.*

5. *To refuse to bargain collectively with the representatives of his employees.* The fifth unfair practice was important in a critical way, since it made refusal to recognize and deal with employee representatives an illegal action. The employee protections asserted in the four other unfair practices would fall short of effectuating the purposes of the act if employers remained free to refuse recognition to unions, for ultimate recognition in such a case would still require a contest of strength. The Wagner Act, it should be emphasized, was not designed to eliminate all strikes; but it was designed to eliminate strikes over the question of union recognition. Thus, the fifth unfair practice granted to unions as a legal right an objective for which they had striven for over a century.

The Representation Question

When a question of union representation arose, the National Labor Relations Board was empowered to settle the question either by a secret ballot of the employees or by some other suitable method. Representatives selected for collective bargaining purposes by a majority of the employees in an appropriate unit were to be the exclusive representatives of *all* the employees in the unit. This meant that the selected union had the obligation to bargain not only for union members but for non-members as well, including those who had opposed the choice of the union.

The NLRB was given the duty of deciding in each case whether an appropriate unit for effectuating the purposes of the act would be an employer unit, craft unit, plant unit, or some subdivision thereof. This particular provision, like most of the others, was not spelled out in detail and proved troublesome over time. Proponents of craft unions were fearful that the board would favor industrial unions and vice versa. At various times the board came under criticism from both the AFL and the CIO for allegedly favoring one or the other in its interpretation of "appropriate unit."

Administrative and Enforcement Procedures

The act created a three-man National Labor Relations Board to be appointed by the President with the advice and consent of the Senate. The board was given the authority to make, amend, and rescind such rules and regulations as were necessary to carry out the provisions of the act. As noted above, the board was empowered in Section 9 to establish procedures for the settlement of questions of representation, and in Section 10 it was empowered to prevent persons from engaging in the unfair labor practices enumerated.

When a charge of an unfair practice was made against an employer, the board or an agent of the board was to hold hearings to determine whether the employer was, in fact, guilty of a proscribed practice. Upon a finding of a violation, the board could issue a cease and desist order and take other affirmative action to effectuate the policies of the act. The board, for instance, could order an employer to reinstate an employee with back pay if it found that the employee had been discharged because of union activity.

The board itself was not given the power to enforce its orders. It was, instead, empowered to petition the United States circuit courts when legal enforcement became necessary.

THE CONSTITUTIONALITY OF THE WAGNER ACT

The Tenth Amendment to the federal Constitution provides that the powers not delegated to the United States by the Constitution nor prohibited by it to the states are reserved to the states respectively or to the people. Since the Constitution does not grant the federal government specific power to regulate collective bargaining, the right to enact such regulatory legislation, if it exists at all, must be found in the powers expressly granted. As noted above, Congress relied upon the commerce clause to justify the enactment of the rules of the Wagner Act.

Section 8 of Article 1 of the Constitution, which enumerates positive powers of Congress, includes, without elaboration, the statement that Congress shall have power "to regulate Commerce with foreign nations, and among the several States, and with the Indian Tribes." Ever since the Constitution went into effect, political and economic interest groups have disagreed about the precise meaning of the commerce clause. In the words of an authority who has played no small part in the development of American constitutional law, "The history of the commerce clause, from the pioneer efforts of Marshall to our own day, is a history of imposing artificial patterns upon the play of economic life whereby an accommodation is achieved between the interacting concerns of states and nation."[6] During most of the nineteenth century, the preoccupation of the Supreme Court was with the restrictive use of the commerce clause. In this period the basic problem that faced the court was the extent to which the commerce clause restricted state control over the interstate transportation of goods and state taxation of business enterprise.[7] After 1890, as economic relationships became more complex, the clause developed as an affirmative instrument for the promotion and encouragement of interstate commerce.

The enormous growth of commerce that started in the latter part of the nineteenth century created conditions that led to positive measures of control over the processes and conditions of commerce. As federal regulatory law developed, the Supreme Court was called upon to interpret and apply many of the provisions of the law. There is much that is confusing in the history of the court's interpretation of the commerce clause. Underlying the details of the law, however, is the simple fact that the long-run direction of Supreme Court philosophy has been from a conservative position to a relatively liberal one.

The main issues of contention in the conflict over the constitutionality of the Wagner Act involved two partly separate and partly related strands in the historical interpretation of the commerce clause. One centered upon the definition of interstate commerce. As the federal government established rules governing commercial relationships through legislation such as the Interstate Commerce and Sherman Anti-Trust Acts, the need for greater

---

[6] Felix Frankfurter, *The Commerce Clause* (Chapel Hill, N.C.: University of North Carolina Press, 1937), p. 21.

[7] Under the Chief Justiceship of John Marshall, Supreme Court interpretations of the commerce clause expanded the power of the federal government at the expense of the states. The basic theme underlying commerce clause interpretations during the Marshall period was that the clause restricted the power of the states even in the absence of national legislation and that the court had the power to express the nature of the limitations of the authority of the states in the area of interstate commercial relationships. See *Gibbons* v. *Ogden*, 9 Wheat 1, 1824; *Brown* v. *Maryland*, 12 Wheat 419, 1827; *Willson* v. *The Black-Bird Creek Marsh Company*, 2 Pet. 245, 1829. The court under Taney derived another implication from the commerce clause and tended to deny that the mere existence of the clause tended to limit state power. The commerce clause was an authority for Congress to act, but in the absence of action the dormant clause did not constitute a limitation upon the states. See the *License Cases*, 5 How. 504, 1847; and *Cooley* v. *Board of Wardens of the Port of Philadelphia*, 12 How. 299, 1851. During Waite's tenure as Chief Justice, controversies tended to turn, as Frankfurter describes it, "on matters of more or less, on questions of degree, on knowledge of governing facts or a perception of their significance." For an analysis of court interpretation of the commerce clause during the nineteenth century, see Frankfurter, *op. cit.*

precision in the legal definition of interstate commerce became apparent. The limits of the power of Congress to regulate commerce had not been precisely defined, and until such boundaries were established there would be uncertainty about the constitutionality of the regulatory laws.

As early as 1871 the Supreme Court had ruled that interstate commerce could begin even before a commodity crossed the borders of a state. "Whenever a commodity has begun to move as an article of trade from one state to another, commerce in that commodity between the States has commenced."[8] An important unanswered question at the beginning of the period of positive commercial legislation involved the manufacturing process. Economic goods, of course, are not in interstate motion during the manufacturing period. What occurs during the production period, nevertheless, can affect commerce in many ways. A legal definition of interstate commerce so contrived as to include the manufacturing process would greatly expand the power of Congress, whereas an exclusion of manufacturing would deny the Congress regulatory powers over a crucially important part of the economy.

The early Supreme Court answer to this question was that manufacturing was distinct from commerce and hence not subject to the powers exercised under the commerce clause.[9] This position was reaffirmed in numerous decisions, although in a 1922 case the elements of a broader definition were voiced. In *Stafford* v. *Wallace* the court ruled that a regulation of certain practices of meat packers was a constitutional exercise of the power to regulate commerce.[10] The stockyards, according to the decision, were not places of rest or final destination. They were "but a throat through which the commerce flows." This ruling did not overturn the position that manufacturing was distinct from commerce, but it did contain the seeds of a new approach.

The second strand in the legal development under discussion concerns the relationship between legislative encouragement of collective bargaining and the constitutional rights of employers. A law that enlarges the rights of one group abridges those of another. When participation in union activity becomes a right protected by law, the right of an employer to select and retain a work force solely on the basis of his personal preferences is limited to an important extent. In *Adair* v. *United States*, discussed in the last chapter, the Supreme Court ruled that a provision of law denying a railway the right to discharge an employee because of union membership was unconstitutional. Such a provision, according to the decision, was an arbitrary interference with the employer's freedom of contract. In the later

[8] *The Daniel Ball,* 10 Wall. 557 (1871).
[9] *United States* v. *E. C. Knight Co.,* 156 U.S. 1 (1895).
[10] 258 U.S. 495 (1922).

Texas and New Orleans Railroad case, however, the court elevated the right of employees to have representatives of their own choosing above the right of employers to discriminate against employees because of union sympathies. The Railway Labor Act of 1926, according to the Supreme Court, did not interfere with the normal employer right to hire and fire. It simply prevented the employer from interfering with the constitutional rights of employees to exercise their choice in the matter of union representation.

Both legal points discussed above came to a head in the determination of the constitutionality of the Wagner Act. Congress had used the power of the commerce clause to enlarge the right of employee association at the expense of employer rights to combat association. The act was clearly intended to apply to manufacturing employments. The bold intent of the law, in effect, forced a Supreme Court clarification of the definition of interstate commerce as well as a clear-cut court statement concerning the powers of the legislative branch to redress the relative rights of employer and employee.

National Labor Relations Board v. *Jones and Laughlin Steel Corporation*[11]

The constitutionality of the Wagner Act was decided in a context of crisis. The Supreme Court had invalidated the NIRA, the Agricultural Adjustment Act, and a number of other important New Deal measures. There was fear in administrative circles that the Wagner Act and the Social Security Act of 1935 would meet the same fate. After his re-election in 1936, President Roosevelt took the initiative and sent a proposal to Congress for a reorganization of the Judiciary.

The most controversial aspect of the President's recommendations was that the number of judges in all federal courts be increased when incumbents over seventy years of age did not retire. The new justiceships in the Supreme Court, however, would be limited to six.

It was no secret, of course, that the Judiciary Reorganization Bill was aimed at offsetting the power of a conservative court majority. At the time, four Justices—Van Devanter, Sutherland, McReynolds, and Butler—were regarded as conservatives, whereas three—Brandeis, Stone, and Cardozo—were classed as liberals. Chief Justice Hughes and Justice Roberts were described as "roving" conservatives who might join with the liberals on some issues. The significance of the Supreme Court composition was that the conservatives needed only the vote of Hughes or Roberts to become a majority, whereas the liberals needed the votes of both. Although it is true

---

[11] 301 U.S. 1 (1937).

that the court (in the Schecter case) was unanimous in ruling that the NIRA was unconstitutional, the relatively consistent disagreement between the conservatives and the liberals brought to public attention what constitutional scholars had known for a long time: the Constitution is a flexible document, and its provisions are subject to differing interpretations.

The administration's court proposal was received with mixed reactions by Congress, and before long the President's own party was deeply divided by the issue. Undeterred by the failure of the Democrats to provide him with strong backing, the President continued his efforts to offset what he described as a "horse and buggy" definition of interstate commerce. In the meantime, many of the important employers in the nation were ignoring the provisions of the Wagner Act. They had been advised by the Liberty League's committee of prominent lawyers that the act was unconstitutional. Unable to achieve the bargaining rights that the law had promised, a number of unions had initiated strikes and some of these employed the "sit-down" technique. It was in this context that the Supreme Court heard the arguments on the constitutionality of the Wagner Act.

To the surprise of many observers, the court found in *National Labor Relations Board* v. *Jones and Laughlin Steel Corporation* that the Wagner Act was constitutional. The decision was five to four with Hughes and Roberts joining the "liberals" to make up the majority.

Justice Hughes, who wrote the majority opinion, rejected the company contention that employees engaged in manufacturing were not subject to federal regulation under the commerce clause.

> The fundamental principle [he wrote] is that the power to regulate commerce is the power to enact "all appropriate legislation" for its "protection and advancement" . . . to adopt measures "to promote its growth and insure its safety" . . . "to foster, protect, control, and restrain." . . . That power is plenary and may be exerted to protect interstate commerce "no matter what the source of the dangers that threaten it." . . . Although activities may be intrastate in character when separately considered, if they have such a close and substantial relation to interstate commerce that their control is essential or appropriate to protect that commerce from burdens and obstructions, Congress cannot be denied the power to exercise that control. . . . The fact that the employees here concerned were engaged in production is not determinative.

Addressing himself to the facts of the immediate case, Hughes wrote that

> the stoppage of those operations [steel production] would have a most serious effect upon interstate commerce. In view of the respondent's far flung activities, it is idle to say that the effect would be indirect or remote. . . . When industries organize themselves on a national scale, making their relation to interstate commerce the dominant factor in their activities, how

can it be maintained that their industrial relations constitute a forbidden field into which Congress may not enter. . . . We have often said that interstate commerce is a practical conception. It is equally true that interferences with that commerce must be appraised by a judgment that does not ignore actual experience. . . .

The question of the law's interference with the right of an employer to conduct his business without arbitrary restraint was treated with relative dispatch. The Supreme Court cited the Texas and New Orleans Railroad case and repeated the argument of that decision. The act did not interfere with the employer's normal right to select or discharge employees. Under the cover of such a right, however, the employer might not intimidate or coerce employees with respect to their self-organization and representation.

The Significance of the Decision

The immediate significance of the Jones and Laughlin decision and a series of other decisions handed down the same day was the revelation that the administration of the Wagner Act would not be hamstrung by an unsympathetic judiciary.[12] Quite apart from the field of industrial relations was the fact that the broadest definition of interstate commerce yet written by the Supreme Court expanded the powers of the federal government to regulate economic life by an unmeasurable but obviously significant degree. The clear-cut statement that henceforth the Supreme Court would not seek to determine whether the site of an action was local or interstate but would seek to weigh its impact upon commerce meant, in effect that only very local economic activities were beyond the potential reach of federal law.

The liberal turn in the tenor of Supreme Court decisions removed the urgency from the question of court reform, and the court reorganization bill eventually passed was a much modified version of the administration's original proposal. The extent to which the well publicized crisis affected the Supreme Court decision cannot be known with certainty. The common law is that the Supreme Court follows the election returns. Like many maxims, this one is only partially true. It would be more accurate to say that the judiciary cannot remain permanently insulated from the currents that sweep a time. Frankfurter has observed that "more than any other branch of law, the judicial application of the Constitution is a function of the dominant forces of our society."[13] In the midst of an economic depres-

---

12 See *National Labor Relations Board* v. *Friedman-Harry Marks Clothing Co.*, 301 U.S. 58; *Associated Press* v. *National Labor Relations Board*, 301 U.S. 103; *Washington, Virginia and Maryland Coach Co.* v. *National Labor Relations Board*, 301 U.S. 142; *National Labor Relations Board* v. *Fruehauf Trailer Co.*, 301 U.S. 49.

13 *Op. cit.*, p. 3.

sion, the electorate was quite ready to accept a government-fostered program that would have been unconstitutional when measured by the legal standards of an earlier day.

The question involved in the constitutional crisis of the middle thirties was not whether the Supreme Court would adapt to the new forces afoot but how soon it would adapt. In this respect part of the significance of the President's reform proposals is generally missed. The law is usually slow in adapting to the needs of a time; and this is not always unwholesome, because the "drag" may serve to winnow out the extremities of measures conceived in haste and emotion. In a period of great stress, however, the slowness of law is especially annoying; and Roosevelt's proposals reflected impatience at a time when speed and maneuverability seemed to be imperative. The widespread condemnation of the reorganization bill—many liberals joined in this condemnation—was primarily a response against the means suggested. An equally important point, however, is that the administration was not content to remain passive in the face of judicial conservatism. This distinguishes the 1930's from earlier legal eras when the court was able to control the character of collective bargaining law. A "horse and buggy" definition of interstate commerce was obsolete; and the administrative branch of the government demonstrated that it intended to make an aggressive use of whatever powers it had, in order to insure the updating of Supreme Court philosophy.

THE WAGNER ACT EXPERIENCE

The Wagner Act was in effect for twelve years. By and large, the objectives of the law were accomplished. Millions of workers were given the opportunity to express themselves in the matter of union preference, and collective bargaining flourished under the government-sponsored protections. At no time, however, were employer spokesmen completely happy with the requirements of the law or the manner in which it was being administered.

The Employer Reaction

Marking, as it did, such an abrupt change in the rules of collective bargaining, the law was a bitter pill for employers to swallow. Until the matter of constitutionality was decided, many employers blatantly refused to abide by the legal requirements. As bargaining relationships matured, there was some softening of opposition; but at all times there was a hard core of hostility. This was particularly true in geographical areas that had been touched only lightly by union organization. In the South and in rural communities, many employers continued to dodge the obligations of the Wagner Act long after the majority of the employers in industrial urban areas had accepted the facts of a new legal situation.

The number of unfair labor practice charges filed by unions in the last two years of the Wagner Act period was almost as large as any other two year total in the twelve year span. In August, 1947, when the Wagner Act was replaced by the Taft-Hartley Act, more than 2,000 unfair practice complaint cases were pending.

The Administrative Experience

The technical aspects of the law proved to be troublesome. The Wagner Act experience should be disenchanting to anyone who believes that a legal code of collective bargaining can be established by a few directives broadly stated. *Collective bargaining* is a loose phrase that covers a complicated mosaic of relationships and pressures. Even though the purpose of the law was a simple one, the National Labor Relations Board found it necessary to erect a rather massive structure of rules and regulations in order to answer the staggering variety of questions that arose.

Numerous concepts such as "bargaining in good faith," "appropriate unit," and "interference and coercion" had to be defined and developed. Problems such as the limits that might be placed upon an employer's right to express himself, the rights of craft workers in an industrial unit, the voting privileges of workers on strike, and the right of one union to challenge another had to be resolved.

The point that should be emphasized is that no set of definitions or answers is uniquely correct. NLRB policy was in a constant state of evolution during the life of the Wagner Act. At no stage of the evolution was the board free from criticism, and the volume of employer complaint was on occasions swelled by attacks emanating from both the CIO and the AFL.

Changes in personnel brought men with different philosophies onto the board, and the interpretation of the law became slightly more conservative during the later years. The board, in the early period, tended to show a bias in favor of broad industrial units which were more to the liking of the CIO than the AFL; and some of the hastily trained—and poorly paid—field examiners lacked an objectivity that would seem to have been desirable. These faults were overstressed by critics of the act, however. The charge that the board was biased can be traced largely to its critics' refusal to acknowledge the legitimacy of the law which established it. The Wagner Act was a pro-union piece of legislation. The mere process of putting it into effect involved setting limits upon employers that would naturally be interpreted as a bias by those out of sympathy with unionism. On the whole, the law was well administered, and early faults noted by employers were removed to an extent that aroused a considerable amount of labor criticism.

In a twelve year period, the NLRB closed over 43,000 cases involving complaints of unfair employer practices and 57,000 cases involving questions of union representation. This record would have been impossible if all cases had gone through formal hearing procedures. In order to streamline the administrative process and cut down the always large backlog of cases, the board encouraged the practice of informal settlements whenever feasible. About 90 per cent of all unfair practice cases and 75 per cent of representation cases were closed before formal action.

Between 1936 and 1947 the board conducted 36,969 elections and cross-checks.[14] In some 30,000 of these instances, the workers chose to be represented by a union and in the remaining cases voted against union representation. CIO affiliated unions won 13,837 elections and crosschecks, AFL affiliates won 12,353, and unaffiliated unions won 3,920.

Remedial action ordered by the board when employers were found guilty of unfair practices included the award of over $12 million in back pay to 40,691 workers. Employers were required to post notices that unfair practices would be terminated in 8,156 cases, and 1,709 company unions were disestablished. More than 75,000 workers found to have been discriminatorily discharged were reinstated.

Summary: The Wagner Act

The years during which the Wagner Act was in effect were also the years in which the membership and power of unions enjoyed the greatest growth in all of American history. The extent to which a favorable legal climate was responsible for union growth cannot be determined accurately. It is quite likely that unions would have flourished even without the Wagner Act. The major contribution of the law is probably the fact that orderly processes were provided for an expression of worker preference. In the absence of the Wagner Act, the expression of worker preference for or against unions would have occurred in a context of violence much greater than that which materialized. Even with the law on the books, unions, too, often, had to win bargaining rights by a militant show of strength.

It is always difficult to anticipate the historical verdict of the future. In the opinion of this writer, the significance of the Wagner Act eventually will be construed in terms of a contribution to social stability during a period of fundamental institutional change. The transition from a condition of predominantly unilateral to predominantly collective determination of the terms and conditions of employment occurred in a remarkably short

---

[14] A question of representation could be decided either by an election or by a check of union membership cards against a payroll list. In the later years of the Wagner Act, elections came to be used exclusively.

time in the United States. The fact that this transition occasioned as little social upheaval as it did must certainly be attributed in part to a law which accurately reflected the requirements of stability by providing a technique for the resolution of a controversial question.

In the short run, the Wagner Act was, and will continue to be, judged in terms of administrative efficiency, individual instances of bias or bad judgment, and the validity of the general philosophy of legal encouragement of unionism. In the longer run, as suggested above, the verdict will probably be that it was the right law at the right time. The replacement of the Wagner Act with a much different law came about not because of the failures but rather because of the successes of the Wagner Act. With equality of bargaining power a reality in most of the significant areas of American economic life, new problems developed, and the need for a new legal framework appeared. Whether the new framework erected is sound or otherwise is a question that will be considered in the following chapter.

THE SHERMAN ACT AGAIN

At a time when the law veered so sharply in the direction of union encouragement, a continuation of Sherman Act prosecutions along the lines suggested by *Duplex* v. *Deering* and the Coronado Coal case could have created a major legal inconsistency. The assumption underlying the Wagner Act was that collective bargaining was a workable method for the determination of terms and conditions of employment. In order for bargaining to succeed, however, it was necessary for both sides to be free to disagree and to resort to the lockout or the strike when peaceful negotiations proved to be fruitless. Under the rule of the Coronado case, however, the right to strike was sharply circumscribed, since an intent to interfere with the interstate movement of commodities could usually be found whenever the judiciary was inclined to find it. The right to strike has always been subject to some limitations, of course; but the limitations imposed by the Sherman Act, as construed by the Supreme Court decisions of the 1920's, raised—and left unanswered—the question of the legality of any union pressure that interfered with the physical movement of goods destined for out of state markets. No one had the temerity to suggest that almost all strikes were violations of the Sherman Act, though it was not really clear why they were not.

No Supreme Court decisions involving Sherman Act prosecutions of unions were handed down in the New Deal period until 1940. Then, when such a case did come before the court, there was a great deal of curiosity about how the conflicting philosophies of the Wagner and the Sherman Acts would be reconciled. In a series of three important decisions, the

Supreme Court, in effect, overruled the restrictive cast of all earlier cases involving labor unions and narrowed the range of union liability to a very special circumstance.

The new relationship between union pressure activities and the limitations imposed by the Sherman Act was spelled out in *Apex Hosiery Company* v. *Leader*,[15] *United States* v. *Hutcheson*,[16] and *Allen Bradley Company* v. *Local Union No. 3, IBEW*.[17] Taken together, these decisions can be summarized as follows: union activities are not to be construed as violations of the Sherman Act unless the union works in combination with business groups to suppress competition. The differences between the earlier and later Supreme Court positions can be suggested by noting simply that the earlier court resolved any doubts concerning the intent of Congress against the interests of labor unions, whereas the later court did exactly the opposite. Thus, the legal pendulum swung from a position where the Supreme Court came perilously close to construing almost all strikes as Sherman Act violations to one where unions enjoy an almost total immunity from anti-trust charges. An important exception to organized labor's exemption from the anti-trust laws, however, was identified in a 1965 decision. In *United Mine Workers* v. *Pennington*, the Supreme Court held that a union forfeits its exemption from the anti-trust laws when it is clearly shown that it has agreed with one set of employers to impose a certain wage scale on other bargaining units.[18] The court noted that a union might conclude a wage agreement in a multi-employer bargaining unit without violating the anti-trust laws and that the same union, might, as a matter of its own policy, seek the same wage from other employers. When there exists a labor management agreement to prescribe labor standards outside the bargaining unit, however, the anti-trust exemption is lost.

CHANGES IN THE LAW OF PICKETING

Developments in the law of picketing, although somewhat confusing, further illustrate the changes that occurred in the character of collective bargaining law after 1930. In the earlier conservative interpretations of the law, courts were reluctant to tolerate "stranger" picketing and, more often than not, found some basis for denying picketing rights even when the line was manned by those with a close and direct interest in the issues at stake. In 1940, however, the Supreme Court bluntly declared that peaceful picketing

---

[15] 310 U.S. 469 (1940).
[16] 312 U.S. 219 (1941).
[17] 325 U.S. 797 (1945).
[18] *United Mine Workers of America* v. *Pennington*, 381 U.S. 657.

was a form of free speech.[19] State legislatures, consequently, were prohibited by the Fourteenth Amendment from enacting laws that interfered with picketing, for this would be the equivalent of a denial of free speech without due process of law.

The court subsequently retreated from this doctrine by identifying situations in which picketing might be enjoined and, thus, tacitly admitted the dubiety of the equation between picketing and free speech.[20] These retreats did not overturn the free speech doctrine, but they did limit its applicability. Even as modified, however, the new approach was a far cry from an earlier situation wherein the legality of picketing depended largely upon the tolerance of a judge.

SUMMARY: THE WAGNER ACT ERA IN LABOR LAW

Changes in the law of collective bargaining before the 1930's can be summarized as changes in the degree of judicial toleration of union activities. In the 1930's the changes were of kind as well as of degree. The broad character of the developments in the New Deal period are outlined below.

The Statutory Influence in Labor Law

Long a result of judicial decision, the law became more statutory in origin during the period under consideration. Thus, the character of collective bargaining law came to depend less upon the philosophies of a very select group of persons and to depend more upon the broad play of forces that shape the results of the legislative process.

In the Norris-LaGuardia Act, the power of the judiciary to control collective bargaining relationships was sharply curtailed; in the Wagner Act, the Congress established a national labor policy that was different in spirit and intent from the common law of earlier periods. Even where the Supreme Court continued to make basic law, as in the Sherman Act and picketing law interpretations, the decisions tended to reflect the pro-union climate established by the legislative branch of government.

While the federal courts came to be less prominent in the law-making process, the New Deal era marks the beginning of the influence of the "quasi-judicial" administrative agency. The Wagner Act was little more than a bare framework, and it fell to the National Labor Relations Board

---

[19] *Thornhill* v. *Alabama*, 310 U.S. 106 (1940).

[20] For a survey of the decisions marking the Supreme Court's retreat from the Thornhill doctrine see *International Brotherhood of Teamsters, Local 695* v. *Vogt, Inc.*, 354 U.S. 284 (1957).

to determine what the law meant in specific instances. True, the board was limited by the general purpose of the law; but within this limit there was considerable room for discretion. In the Wagner Act and the succeeding Taft-Hartley period, the personnel composition of the administrative agency has been one of the most important influences in the shaping of labor law.

The Emphasis upon Equality of Bargaining Power

The framers of the Wagner Act sought to remove the "inequality of bargaining power between employees who do not possess full freedom of association or actual liberty of contract and employers who are organized in the corporate or other form of ownership association." The concept of equal bargaining power was not defined, but it is probable that the law's authors had in mind a situation in which neither labor nor management could arbitrarily impose its will on the opposite party. The desirability of equal bargaining power rests upon two assumptions. One is that in the usual instance labor and management representatives sitting across the table from each other will be able to come to agreement. The second is that the agreements reached will probably be beneficial to the economy as a whole as well as to labor and management. There was nothing in the Wagner Act to insure that these assumptions would be borne out in practice. This point should be underscored. The entire mechanism of the act was designed to lead management and union representatives to a bargaining conference and to insist that they negotiate in good faith. After this point the law imposed no further obligations on the negotiators. One key to an understanding of the Taft-Hartley Law, incidentally, is that it represents a weakening of faith in the aforementioned assumptions.

Recognition of Worker Interdependence

In the last chapter, we saw how the courts repeatedly refused to admit that persons who worked for an employer might have a legitimate concern about the wages and working conditions at other places of employment. Existing law, in this respect, was backward looking. One of the outstanding aspects of modern industrialism is the increasing degree of interdependence that is imposed upon persons who are far removed from each other in a geographical sense. So far as unionism was concerned, the law made it difficult to protect the gains won from organized employers against the competition of non-union goods.

The broad definition of a labor dispute written into the Norris-LaGuardia Act, the general encouragement of unionism in the Wagner Act, and the new interpretations of the Sherman Act had the effect of reversing the traditional legal antagonism toward expressions of mutuality of interest by employees of different employers. In *American Federation of Labor* v.

Swing, Justice Frankfurter wrote that "a state cannot exclude working men from peacefully exercising the right of free communication by drawing the circle of economic competition so small as to contain only an employer and those directly employed by him."[21] Frankfurter's phrasing is apt. The legal developments of the period under consideration brought the law more into accord with the realities of the times by expanding the "circle of economic competition."

The Ideology of the Law

The Wagner Act was the product of a depression period and reflected the intellectual changes that were wrought by the depression. The inability of labor unions to win a more favorable legal position before the 1930's was due essentially to the prevailing philosophy of the sanctity of business property which is often summarized by the phrase, "laissez-faire." Labor unions were unable to mount a successful attack upon the prevailing legal philosophy in a period when the courts were the dominant institution in the shaping of the law because the courts were instrumental in the establishment and protection of the very philosophy that the unions had to attack.

The depression changed the situation in several respects. First, the executive and legislative branches of the government became aggressive in promoting positive measures of economic welfare. Those who sought to revamp the character of labor law were provided with promising new avenues for the exercise of influence. Second, the sanctity of business property was tarnished by the fact of business failure. It was one thing to defend going notions of freedom of contract and due process of law when these notions were built into an economic system that worked. In a crumbling economy, however, few were likely to be impressed by the idea that the federal government lacked the power to repair the damage. Laissez-faire philosophy, of course, had been modified by positive government action before 1930; but the sequence of measures undertaken after that date marked the most pronounced and prolonged effort of the federal government to influence the course of economic events in the entire peacetime history of the nation.

The developments of the 1930 era modified the earlier property ideology to the extent that a fundamental change in labor law became possible. This was a necessary condition for the appearance of a new law. The actual law had to be written, fought through the legislature, and defended against the inevitable challenge of constitutionality. These were matters of tactics, however, and the point has already been made that the tactical position of

---

[21] 312 U.S. 321 (1941).

the proponents of a pro-union law was much improved by the fact that the legislative and executive branches were sympathetic.

Thus, a law that was different from earlier labor law in a revolutionary way could be enacted because of far-reaching changes that had occurred in the ideology of property and in the power of various pressure groups. As further changes in ideology and power positions presented themselves, it could be expected that the law of collective bargaining would change again.

QUESTIONS

1. What were the basic purposes of the Wagner Act? Describe the provisions of the law that were designed to effectuate these purposes.
2. The Wagner Act could not have been passed before the 1930's, and the same law could not be enacted today. Explain why this is so.
3. What was the broad significance of the Supreme Court decision in *National Labor Relations Board* v. *Jones and Laughlin Steel Corporation?*
4. Describe the Supreme Court interpretation of the commerce clause in the Jones and Laughlin case. How did this differ from earlier interpretations?
5. During the New Deal era how did the Supreme Court apply the provisions of the Sherman Act to the activities of organized labor?
6. Summarize the broad character of the developments in labor law during the New Deal period.

SELECTED READINGS

BERNSTEIN, IRVING. *The New Deal Collective Bargaining Policy*. Berkeley: University of California Press, 1950.

BAKKE, A. WRIGHT, KERR, CLARK, and ANROD, CHARLES W. (eds.) "Unions as Economic Monopolies," *Unions, Management, and the Public*. 3rd ed. New York: Harcourt, Brace, and World, 1967, pp. 644–672.

COHEN, SANFORD. *Labor Law*. Columbus, Ohio: Charles E. Merrill Books, Inc., 1964. Chap. 8.

DULLES, FOSTER RHEA. "The New Deal," *Labor in America*. New York: Thomas Y. Crowell Company, 1949. Chap. 15.

GREGORY, CHARLES O. *Labor and the Law*. 2nd rev. ed. New York: W. W. Norton & Company, Inc., 1958. Chaps. 9–12.

MILLIS, HARRY A., and BROWN, EMILY CLARK. *From the Wagner Act to Taft-Hartley*. Chicago: The University of Chicago Press, 1950. Part 1.

CHAPTER 18

The Taft-Hartley Era

IN THE PRESENT PERIOD, WHICH WE SHALL CALL THE TAFT-HARTLEY ERA, collective bargaining law has reached a high point of complexity. A mere study of the Taft-Hartley Act of 1947 and the Labor-Management Reporting and Disclosure Act of 1959, for instance, will not provide us with sophisticated insights into the nature of the law. Only a handful of close observers have an intimate knowledge of these statutes as they are interpreted and administered by the National Labor Relations Board. The basic Wagner Act policy of union encouragement has been replaced by a somewhat ambivalent combination of union encouragement and union control; and, to a greater extent than ever before, the government is engaged in policing the bargaining process and the bargaining contract.

A thorough analysis of the Taft-Hartley era cannot be made within the limits of one chapter, but it is possible to indicate the nature of the law in a summary treatment. The discussion here will be concerned primarily with the transition from the Wagner to the Taft-Hartley era, the prominent characteristics of the law in the present period, and the significance of these characteristics.

FROM THE WAGNER ACT TO THE TAFT-HARTLEY ACT

After 1936, organized employer groups, such as the National Association of Manufacturers, carried on a continuous propaganda battle against the

Wagner Act. This effort was eventually rewarded in 1947, by which time
the momentum of New Deal liberalism was largely spent and the climate
of public opinion was ready to support some control over the behavior of
unions. Long before 1947, however, the character of the Taft-Hartley Act
was being anticipated by legal movements that were occurring outside of
the federal government.

Developments in State Labor Legislation

In 1937, five states passed labor relations acts modeled closely after the
national law. Like the parent status, these "Baby Wagner Acts" sought to
guarantee that employees might organize and bargain collectively with
employers and to prohibit employers from prejudicing these efforts by
exerting job controls and other pressures.[1] The difference between the
federal and state laws, of course, was that the former law applied to those
whose employments involved an interstate movement of goods or services,
whereas the state acts covered employees whose work was intrastate in
nature.

After 1939, several of the state laws were amended so that they became
less concerned with protecting the workers' right to organize and more
concerned with protecting the individual worker, the employer, and the
public against certain forms of union pressure. New laws passed by Michigan, Minnesota, Kansas, Colorado, and Delaware continued the growing
emphasis upon the restriction of union conduct.

Generalizations about the state labor relations acts are difficult to make,
since the laws differed considerably in detail. By 1947, a few had remained
fairly close to the Wagner Act model, several had combined the Wagner
Act protections with a variety of union regulations, and the most restrictive
consisted almost entirely of an array of union limitations. The Delaware
Union Regulation Act of 1947 can be cited as an example of an extremely
restrictive act. Strikes were made unlawful unless approved by a majority
vote of the employees, the secondary boycott was illegalized, picketing was
made subject to close regulation, unions were required to submit detailed
information about their internal affairs, and union contributions to political
campaigns were prohibited. A variety of unfair employee practices was
proscribed, but there was no mention of unfair employer practices. The
purpose of the Delaware law, in short, was to regulate unions. It contained
no hint of an interest in equalizing bargaining power between employer
and employee.

In addition to these omnibus-type laws, there was a widespread movement in the states to regulate specific types of union conduct and activity

---

[1] The states were Utah, Wisconsin, Massachusetts, New York, and Pennsylvania.

through single-purpose legislation.[2] The laws dealt with subjects such as the closed shop, the check-off, boycotts, picketing, jurisdictional disputes, and strikes. The trend toward passage of union limitation legislation advanced with an accelerated momentum and reached a climax in 1947. In that year, ten states passed anti-boycott laws, nine sought to regulate picketing, ten removed or limited the right to strike in the public utilities, and seven banned strikes by public employees. All in all, twenty-eight states enacted laws in 1947 that dealt with the conduct and organization of unions. By 1948, thirteen states had prohibited the closed shop, and several others had made the closed shop conditional upon the voted approval of a stipulated majority of the employees to be covered by the contract.

The rash of state labor legislation, which rested upon premises fundamentally different from those of the Wagner Act, appeared as unions were growing in membership and power. Business and agricultural interests, uneasy about the show of union strength, appealed to the state legislatures where their protestations received a favorable reception. Stymied in their attempts to change the Wagner Act, the various anti-union groups were more successful when they turned to the rural-dominated state legislatures.

The union limitation laws were spotty in a geographical sense. The highly industrialized states of Illinois and Ohio enacted practically no legislation dealing with unions, while many of the agricultural states, where unionism was almost non-existent, pushed through some of the more severe anti-union measures. In the South especially, the quantity of labor union legislation that appeared was impressive. The areas where unions had only tenuous footholds were bracing themselves in anticipation of future organizational drives.

Many of the state laws were of questionable constitutionality, and the courts frequently invalidated them.[3] Thus the branch of government most antagonistic toward union actions in an earlier period became the branch that set limits upon the statutory statements of anti-union sentiment after 1937.

The Economic and Social Background of Taft-Hartley

In order for a Wagner Act to be passed it was first necessary for something to occur that would lower the prestige of American businessmen and bring

---

[2] For a summary of these developments in state labor law see Sanford Cohen, *State Labor Legislation, 1937–1947* (Columbus: Ohio State University Bureau of Business Research, 1948). A one chapter summary can be found in Harry A. Millis and Emily Clark Brown, *From the Wagner Act to Taft-Hartley* (Chicago: The University of Chicago Press, 1950), chap. 9.

[3] See *Alabama State Federation of Labor* v. *McAdory*, Alabama Supreme Court, May 1944; *Stapleton* v. *Mitchell*, U.S. District Court of Kansas, 1945; *American Federation of Labor* v. *Bain*, Oregon Supreme Court, 1940; *American Federation of Labor* v. *Reilly*, Colorado Supreme Court, 1944.

to political power and influence persons who would have the inclination to produce a pro-union piece of legislation. Similarly, the passage of a Taft-Hartley Act required that the business community regain a favorable public relations position at the expense of organized labor and that a Congress willing to listen to management spokesmen be seated in Washington. Elements of management had long sought to have the Wagner Act amended, but it was not until 1947 that events transpired so as to create an environment in which important changes in national collective bargaining law became highly probable.

Responsibility for the conservative turn in federal labor-management law must be apportioned among labor, the government, and management. Union membership grew from 3.6 million in 1935 to 14 million in 1947. It was almost inevitable that a growth of this size would be attended by incidents which would turn a certain amount of public sentiment away from organized labor. The frequency of jurisdictional disputes, the occasional examples of coercive picketing, the well publicized work stoppages during the war, irregularities in the internal affairs of some unions, and the failure of the CIO and the AFL to accommodate their differences are examples of factors that destroyed some part of the general sympathy for unionism. Such incidents were cumulative in their effect upon popular thinking, but in themselves they do not account for the character of the law that was eventually ground out by the legislative mill. By the end of World War II many students of labor law had come to believe that the Wagner Act needed changes. The suggested amendments consisted of proposals such as requiring union representatives to bargain in good faith and prohibiting unions from seeking to organize employers who were required by law to negotiate with another union. If the transition from a war to a peace economy had occurred with little labor-management strife, it is possible that changes in labor law would have been limited to a handful of admittedly necessary Wagner Act amendments. The collective bargaining turbulence of the 1945–1946 period, however, was annoying to a nation eager to resume its peacetime ways. Probably more than anything else, the postwar strike wave was responsible for the growth of a feeling that "something ought to be done about labor unions."

The failure of the government to exercise firm leadership in directing the economy to a peacetime footing was partly responsible for social confusion and, consequently, for the strike outburst that was symptomatic of the confusion. These points have been dealt with elsewhere in this volume. It is sufficient to note here that the government in the immediate postwar period failed to elicit a labor-management compromise that might have served as an equivalent of the various compromises that underwrote the wartime wage and dispute control program.

After V-J Day the power position of management was stronger than it had been for fifteen years. The liberal reform spirit of the New Deal era was gone, and the popularity of organized labor had reached a low point. Unions suffer a disadvantage in that they, rather than management, issue the actual strike call, and the usual tendency is for the public to place the blame for strikes upon unions. Thus, during the war it appeared to be management that was keeping at the job while workers were striking, and after the war it still seemed to be the labor organizations that were breaking the peace.

In this context, management was assured of a favorable reception for its legislative program. It should be stressed that management groups were not of one mind in respect to labor law. The proposals of the Chamber of Commerce, for instance, were substantially milder than those of the National Association of Manufacturers.[4] With minor exceptions, however, it was the more restrictive program of the NAM that was enacted into law.

To summarize, part of the labor-management power struggle since 1935 has consisted of efforts by each party to turn the federal labor law in its own favor. Despite intensive efforts by employer associations, management had little success until 1947. By this time, however, significant changes in popular attitudes and group power relationships had occurred; the election of a conservative Congress in 1946 provided the business group with an avenue for an effective exercise of its power.

The Legislative Background of the Taft-Hartley Act

From 1935 to 1947, 169 bills concerned with national labor policy were introduced in Congress.[5] Some of these dealt with single issues, others prescribed a wholesale revision of the Wagner Act. With the exception of the War Labor Disputes Act of 1943, no major piece of collective bargaining law was enacted prior to the Taft-Hartley Act. The continuing volume of proposals, however, was indicative of a growing impatience with labor-management strife and also revealed the increasing popularity of the feeling that new legislation should impose restraints upon labor organizations. After the 1946 elections returned congressional majorities for the Republican party, it was evident that important changes would be made in labor law. The political victors insisted that their victory was a mandate to take steps to equalize the power of labor and management, and equalization had come to mean a restriction of union power.

House and Senate committees began hearings on a new labor law in January and February, 1947. The House committee alone accumulated

---

[4] Clark Kerr, "Employer Policies in Industrial Relations, 1945–1947," in Colston Warne (ed.), *Labor in Postwar America* (Brooklyn: Remsen Press, 1949), chap. 3.

[5] Millis and Brown, *op. cit.*, p. 333.

nearly 4,000 pages of testimony and heard 130 witnesses. Bills from both committees when reported to their respective bodies occasioned extended and caustic debate. The signs were quite clear, however, that the new law would be more to the liking of management than of labor. In both the Senate and the House, the bills passed with more than enough votes to override the anticipated veto of President Truman.

Many differences between the House and Senate bills had to be ironed out in conference. Throughout the various stages of the legislative process, the House of Representatives had shown itself to be the more vindictive body. In the public press, the House bill was often referred to as a "tough" bill, whereas the Senate proposals were described as "mild." These are relative terms, of course; and union spokesmen found little to their liking in either bill. One of the signs of the times, however, was the total inability of organized labor to stem a movement that was leading to a law which it did not want.

In conference, it was the Senate version that prevailed with only a few exceptions. The great prestige of Robert A. Taft, the Senate committee chairman, was probably the most important factor accounting for the Senate "victory." Among the House bill provisions that were eliminated were limitations on industry-wide bargaining, a ban on mass picketing, and a detailed regulation of internal union affairs.

The House approved the conference measure by a vote of 320 to 79, with 217 Republicans and 103 Democrats in favor of the bill, and 66 Democrats, 12 Republicans and 1 American Labor party member in opposition. In the Senate the vote was 54 to 17 for passage with 37 Republicans and 17 Democrats voting in favor and 15 Democrats and 2 Republicans opposed. Thus, although the sentiment for the Taft-Hartley Law was stronger among Republicans, a majority of the Democrats in both houses supported the measure.

President Truman's veto was easily overridden in both houses, and the measure became law. Labor's last efforts to save the situation consisted of a deluge of mail supporting a veto. Rallies were staged throughout the country, and labor representatives moved to Washington en masse. All this was to no avail. Labor influence was at a low ebb in Congress; and, as things stood, it was the legislative branch that was in a position to shape the character of labor law.

A SUMMARY OF THE TAFT-HARTLEY LAW

The Taft-Hartley Law does not lend itself to easy summary. It is a sprawling piece of legislation—about three and one-half times the page length of the Wagner Act—and provisions that might be interrelated in their effects upon bargaining relationships often appear in sections that are ostensibly separate. Many of the provisions, furthermore, are vague; and their meanings depend more upon the interpretations of the National Labor Relations Board than upon the wording of the statute. It is important for the student of labor law, nevertheless, to be familiar with the basic features of the Taft-Hartley Law. In this section, the major provisions will be summarized and, when appropriate, compared with the earlier Wagner Act.

The National Labor Relations Board

Under the Taft-Hartley Law the three man National Labor Relations Board was enlarged to five members. A new office, that of general counsel of the board, was created, and the general counsel was given final authority to investigate charges and issue complaints of unfair practices. Under the earlier law this authority rested in the hands of the board.

The new division of functions was a response to complaints that the board had acted as a prosecutor, judge, and jury in the Wagner Act period. In a technical sense this was true, but this has been the typical procedure in government administrative agencies. In any event, Congress responded to the complaints by creating a new office and establishing a division of functions. The board now sits as a type of court that hears appeals on decisions made on unfair labor practice charges and representation cases.

Rights of Employees

Section 7 of the Wagner Act, which is a statement of employee rights, is reproduced below. The portion in italics was added by the Taft-Hartley Act.

> Employees shall have the right to self-organization, to form, join, or assist labor organizations, to bargain collectively through representatives of their own choosing, and to engage in other concerted activities for the purpose of collective bargaining or other mutual aid or protection, *and shall also have the right to refrain from any or all of such activities except to the extent that such rights may be affected by an agreement requiring membership in a labor organization as a condition of employment as authorized in Section 8(a) (3).*[6]

Under the Wagner Act, an employee, of course, had the right to refrain from union activity. In 1947, however, Congress felt that there was a sufficient cleavage of interest between workers and the union leadership to warrant an explicit statement of a right that had been implicit in the Wagner

---

[6] The reference to the authorized exception in Sec. 8(a)(3) concerns those situations where a union shop is in effect.

Act. Evidence of this congressional attitude can be found at a number of points in the Taft-Hartley Law.

Unfair Employer Practices

The first, second, fourth, and fifth unfair employer practices enumerated in the Wagner Act (See p. 466) are repeated verbatim in the Taft-Hartley Act. The third is changed in one significant respect. Under the Wagner Act, employers were forbidden to encourage or discourage membership in a labor union by their hiring or tenure policies. Union security provisions such as a closed shop agreement, however, were not to be construed as illegal encouragements of unions. This policy is amended by the Taft-Hartley Act to the extent that closed shop agreements are now invalid.

Less extreme forms of union security such as the union shop are permitted. Even when a union shop is in effect, however, an employer may not discriminate against a non-union worker if (1) membership in the union is not available to the employee on the same terms and conditions applicable to other members and (2) an individual's membership is terminated for reasons other than failure to pay regular dues or initiation fees.

Unfair Union Practices

The Taft-Hartley Act redresses the union-management balance of power in two ways. First, it reduces somewhat the legal limitations placed upon employers by the Wagner Act; and secondly, it places a number of positive restrictions upon unions. Following the lead set by several of the state labor relations acts, the framers of the Taft-Hartley law identified a variety of unfair practices of unions and their agents, and they established procedures for preventing such practices. The unfair union practices are extremely involved, and an attempt to summarize runs the danger of over-simplification. In essence, however, unions are forbidden to coerce employees who do not want to join a union, to force employers to pressure workers into joining a union, to force an employer to discriminate against an employee whom the union refuses to admit to membership, to refuse to bargain collectively with the employer, to engage in certain types of secondary boycotts,[7] to charge excessive initiation fees when union membership is compulsory because of a union shop agreement, and to force an employer to pay for services not performed.

Miscellaneous Section 8 Provisions

The listing of unfair labor practices of unions and employers is found in Section 8 of the law. The section contains two other important subsections.

---

[7] The problem of the secondary boycott will be discussed below. See pp. 502-504.

One, the so-called "free speech" clause, provides that an expression of opinion about unions or unionism is not to be considered evidence of an unfair labor practice unless the expression contains a threat of reprisal or force or a promise of a benefit. It is lawful, then, for an employer to tell his workers that he doesn't like unions; it is an unfair practice if he couples this remark with a threat to discharge those who join a union or with a promise to raise wages if workers reject a union.

An understanding of this clause requires some background knowledge of the first unfair employer practice listed in the Wagner Act and repeated in Taft-Hartley. Employers are forbidden to interfere with, restrain, or coerce workers in their choice of bargaining representatives. Early interpretations of the clause under the Wagner Act administration frequently held that mere expression of an opinion by an employer constituted coercion. This led to complaints that constitutional rights of free speech were being violated, and Supreme Court decisions showed some sympathy with complaints of this nature. Over time, the position of the Wagner Act Board came to be approximately that of the free speech provision written into the Taft-Hartley Act.

The practical importance of the free speech clause varies with time and place. Where local unions are strongly entrenched, workers are not likely to be influenced by employer statements about unionism. In weak locals or in situations where a union is attempting to organize a new local, an opinion of an employer might have a coercive effect, even though no explicit threat is made. The dividing line between coercion and non-coercion is quite thin, and administration of such a provision can be difficult. NLRB interpretations of the employer speech clause have varied over time. In the period when the appointees of President Eisenhower dominated the board, employers were permitted wide latitude. The board held, for example, that employer appeals to racial prejudice or prophecies of unemployment if a union won an election were non-coercive. Since 1962, when NLRB rules on employer speech were affected by the philosophies of President Kennedy's appointees, board policy has been less permissive. Material misrepresentations of fact by employers as well as pessimistic predictions of the economic consequences of a union election victory have been held to be unfair labor practices.

The final subsection in Section 8 conditions the processes of collective bargaining in several important ways. Briefly, parties to an agreement are forbidden to terminate or modify the agreement unless (1) a written notice is given to the other party sixty days before the contract expiration date, (2) offers are made to the other party to meet and confer for the purpose of negotiating a new contract, and (3) notice of the existence of a dispute is given to the Federal Mediation Service within thirty days of the time that the aforementioned notice is made. No strikes or lockouts are to occur for a period of sixty days after the notice to the employer or until the contract expiration date, whichever occurs later. An employee who engages in a strike within this sixty day period loses the protections of the Taft-Hartley Act. This means that he cannot file a complaint of an unfair labor practice or vote in a union representation election.

Representatives and Elections

Section 9 deals in a rather detailed manner with bargaining units and representation elections. Under the Wagner Act, Section 9 was relatively brief and was concerned primarily with establishing procedures for resolving questions of representation. This basic purpose is carried over to the Taft-Hartley Law; but the discretion of the NLRB is limited in numerous ways, and the regulations surrounding representation elections are much more involved. Only one of the important parts of Section 9 will be singled out for comment at this point.

Section 9(b)(2) represents a victory for the craft unions, who contended throughout the Wagner Act period that the NLRB was biased in favor of industrial units. Under this section, the board may no longer decide that a craft unit is inappropriate for purposes of collective bargaining on the ground that a different unit has been established by a prior board determination unless a majority of the craft workers vote against separate representation. This provision has made it possible for many units of craft workers in factories to sever themselves from broad industrial units and to set up their own bargaining groups. The net result has been a certain amount of "Balkanization" of bargaining units. Many employers who formerly negotiated with only one or two union groups now find that they must negotiate with as many as a dozen groups.

In interpreting Section 9(b)(2), the NLRB, after 1954, relied upon its ruling in the American Potash case for two basic tests when resolving severance issues: (1) the employees involved must constitute a true craft or departmental group, and (2) the union seeking to carve out a craft or departmental unit must be one which has traditionally devoted itself to the special problems of the group involved.[8] In 1967 the Board made a comprehensive review of its policies relative to craft severance from established units and concluded that the *American Potash* doctrine was too rigid. Under the new policy adopted, the Board evaluates all relevant considerations. The significance of the new approach is that the NLRB now exercises discretionary authority in craft severance cases and, in some situations, will rule against such severance even when the two tests under American Potash are met.[9]

---

[8] *American Potash and Chemical Corp.,* 107 NLRB 1418 (1954).

[9] *Twenty-Second Annual Report of the National Labor Relations Board* (Washington: U.S. Government Printing Office, 1968), pp. 49–55.

Prevention of Unfair Labor Practices

One of the most important tasks of the NLRB is the prevention of unfair labor practices. When an employee, an employer, or a union files a charge of an unfair practice at the regional office of the NLRB, the following sequence of actions is set in motion:

1. An official of the board investigates the charge.[10] During the investigation an attempt is made to settle the issue informally.

2. If the charge is neither settled nor dismissed as unfounded, a formal hearing is held, and the testimony is reduced to writing and filed with the NLRB.

3. After reviewing the testimony, the board may either dismiss the charge or issue a cease and desist order. The board may also take other affirmative action, such as ordering the reinstatement of an employee with or without back pay.

The controversial aspect of this part of the law stems from several important changes in procedure written into the act by Congress. The board now has the option of requesting a federal district court to enjoin an alleged unfair labor practice. If the charge involves a secondary boycott and there is "reasonable cause" to believe that the charge is true, the appropriate officer of the board is directed to petition a federal district court for an injunction or a temporary restraining order. Secondary boycott charges, furthermore, are given priority over all other board cases.

Miscellaneous Provisions

The features of the Taft-Hartley Act discussed above are found in Title I, which is an amendment of the Wagner Act. The remaining titles deal with a miscellany of subjects and have no particular relationship to any part of the earlier Wagner Act. The more prominent of these remaining sections are listed below:

Title II. Title II consists of a number of sections dealing with conciliation procedures and national emergency disputes. This phase of the law was discussed in Chapter 10.

Title III. This title is a catch-all section of the law in which a number of miscellaneous restrictions are imposed upon labor organizations and, to a lesser extent, upon management. It is made unlawful for an employer to pay anything to a representative of his workers. Secondary boycotts are

---

[10] In the Taft-Hartley Act, the word "board" is frequently used to refer to the office of the general counsel and the regional offices, as well as the five man National Labor Relations Board.

declared to be unlawful, and employers are given the right to sue in any district court of the United States for the recovery of any losses sustained as a result of secondary boycotts. Labor organizations, like corporations, are forbidden to make contributions in connection with national elections, and government employees are forbidden to engage in strikes.

THE LABOR-MANAGEMENT REPORTING AND DISCLOSURE ACT OF 1959 (THE LANDRUM-GRIFFIN LAW)

The Taft-Hartley Act remained practically intact for twelve years. This was due less to the inherent strengths of the law than to the existence of a political stalemate that prevented the enactment of new legislation. Throughout the twelve year period, organized labor pressed for a return to the spirit if not the letter of the Wagner Act. Business spokesmen opposed all changes except those that would have placed additional restrictions upon unions. The national administration proposed "corrective" amendments from time to time but failed to push for any significant change in the law. These conflicting pressures mirrored the divisions of opinion in Congress; and, as a result, all proposals for new labor law were bogged down in the legislative process.

By 1959 the stalemate evaporated. The union corruption uncovered by congressional investigations and a general feeling that union power was contributing to economic instability made some type of legislation almost inevitable.

The legislative situation that developed was roughly parallel to what had occurred before the passage of the Taft-Hartley Act. A final House bill was much tougher in terms of union restrictions than the Senate bill. This time, however, the House bill prevailed for the most part. The political situation called for some type of legislation, and those in favor of a milder law were unwilling to chance the risk of being held responsible for the failure of any law to pass. The bill that emerged from the Senate-House Conference Committee was approved by a vote of 95 to 2 in the Senate and 352 to 52 in the House.

The Landrum-Griffin Law of 1959 covers many subjects. The first five titles deal with union reform and provide, among other things, for periodic secret elections of union officers, free speech and assembly rights of rank and file union members, and detailed financial reports by union organizations. Members of the Communist party and persons convicted of specified crimes are barred from union office until five years after termination of party membership or five years after the end of imprisonment for the crimes listed in the law. (Titles I through V are summarized in Chapter 6 above.) Title VII contains amendments to the Taft-Hartley Law. The discussion below will deal with several of these amendments.

The Problem of the Legal No-Man's Land

Section 14(b) of the Taft-Hartley Act reproduced below is one of the more controversial sections of a controversial law.

> Nothing in this Act shall be construed as authorizing the execution or application of agreements requiring membership in a labor organization as a condition of employment in any state or territory in which such execution or application is prohibited by state or territorial law.

As noted in Chapter 8, closed shops are invalid under the Taft-Hartley Law, but union shops and other union security agreements are permissible. Section 14(b) makes it possible for state governments to enact legislation that prohibits union shops, maintenance of membership agreements, and other arrangements for compulsory union membership.

To understand the full import of 14(b) it is necessary to review some elementary but fundamental aspects of American constitutional law. Article 6 of the Constitution provides that the Constitution and the laws of the United States enacted in pursuance of the Constitution shall be the supreme law of the land. The Tenth Amendment reserves to the states all powers not expressly prohibited to the states and those not expressly delegated to the national government. Taken together, these two provisions mean that where the national government has authority to legislate, the laws passed by Congress are supreme, and no state may legislate to contravene such laws. In Section 14(b) of the Taft-Hartley Act Congress left an opening for those states that might decide to enact stricter union security laws than Congress itself saw fit to impose. In the absence of this permissive section, the power to pass laws governing union security agreements would have been pre-empted by the national government.

The history of state behavior under Section 14(b) was discussed in Chapter 8 and need not be repeated here. There is another significant facet of this particular provision, however. Whatever one may think of the wisdom of 14(b)—and this, of course, will be conditioned by what one thinks of union security clauses—Congress at least spelled out clearly the demarcation between federal and state authority to legislate. Elsewhere in the law Congress was less careful; in numerous areas the boundary line between federal and state authority became hazy. Many students of labor law regarded the prevailing confusion as little less than a constitutional crisis.[11]

As we have seen in earlier chapters, American labor law evolved as a result of judicial decisions that were rendered primarily in connection with

---

[11] See, for example, Paul R. Hays, "Federalism and the Taft-Hartley Act: A Constitutional Crisis," *Proceedings of the Eighth Annual Meeting of the Industrial Relations Research Association* (1955) and Archibald Cox, "Federalism in the Law of Labor Relations," *Harvard Law Review*, 1954.

private suits for damages or injunctions. Regulation of such matters as strikes, boycotts, and picket lines was carried on by the states for the most part. The Jones and Laughlin decision in 1937 expanded the power of the national government in the field of labor relations, but since the Wagner Act was directed mainly at unfair practices and representation cases, the potential for a national-state collision of authority was hidden for a time. From 1937 to 1947, the states continued to exercise their traditional authorities over many aspects of the labor-management relationship. The broad purposes of the Taft-Hartley Act, however, touch in one way or other upon most of those areas in labor law that historically have been within the province of state power. Since Congress failed to provide any guides as to how the new law should be imposed upon the maze of pre-existing state law, it was not immediately clear what areas of labor relations the national government had or had not pre-empted.

Briefly, the problem may be stated as follows: under the broad definition of interstate commerce that the federal courts have upheld, only very minor aspects of labor relations are beyond the potential reach of national regulation. This potential power of the national government, however, does not automatically exclude the states from controlling labor relations. The state governments lose their power only when Congress *uses* its power by enacting laws that explicitly or implicitly prohibit state action. A difficulty arose from the fact that neither the letter of the Taft-Hartley Law nor the spirit of its administration was sufficiently clear so that the pre-empted areas could be known precisely.

Some clarification has been achieved as a result of Supreme Court rulings. A state, for example, may not interfere with an employee's right to engage in concerted activity for the purpose of collective bargaining as guaranteed by Section 7 of the Taft-Hartley Law. In *International Union of Automobile Workers* v. *O'Brien*, the Supreme Court held that the right to strike in support of lawful collective bargaining demands is subject only to the limitations written into the federal law.[12] A Michigan labor mediation law attempted to regulate strikes by requiring strike votes and imposing a number of other conditions. The O'Brien decision held that this law was unconstitutional, since the State of Michigan had attempted to limit a right guaranteed by federal law.

In the Garner case, the Supreme Court held that a state court was without power to enjoin an action that might be construed as an unfair labor practice under the national law.[13] In this instance, a Pennsylvania court had issued an injunction against secondary picketing. Since this was a practice that conceivably could have come to the NLRB for a ruling, the

---

[12] 399 U.S. 454 (1950).
[13] *Garner* v. *Teamsters Local Union 776*, 336 U.S. 485 (1953).

Supreme Court held that the state court had no power to issue an injunction against the union.

These and other decisions rendered by the federal courts have provided some of the guidance that Congress neglected to provide. The legal situation, however, remains confused. Whether an action constitutes an unfair labor practice is not always self-evident, nor can it always be known whether some of the fringe pressures exerted by labor and management are violations of the employee rights guaranteed by Section 7. As a consequence of the prevailing confusion, too much litigation time is spent merely to ascertain what the state governments may or may not regulate. The area of unknown jurisdiction has been called a "legal no-man's land" where the ultimate authority to control cannot be forecast with confidence.

Another no-man's land problem developed as a result of National Labor Relations Board administrative determinations on the question of jurisdiction. Under the law, the NLRB can assert its jurisdiction almost as broadly as it chooses, since some link to interstate commerce can be found in all but a handful of peculiarly local enterprises. Since 1950, the practice of the NLRB has been to determine jurisdiction on the basis of a pre-established set of standards, and these standards have removed a large number of employees from the coverage of the law.[14] This means that many employees formerly protected by federal law against unfair labor practices have lost these protections as well as the right to use NLRB facilities for the determination of representation questions.

A question that arose from this situation was whether the states could act in those areas where the NLRB refused to assert jurisdiction. Section 10(a) of the Taft-Hartley Act, incidentally, provided that the board could cede jurisdiction over certain cases to state labor agencies when state law was not inconsistent with federal law. In *Guss* v. *Utah Labor Relations Board*, however, the Supreme Court ruled that no state could take jurisdiction in a labor case that fell within the authority of the NLRB unless the national agency formally ceded jurisdiction to the state in accordance with Section 10(a) of the Taft-Hartley Act.[15] Since no states had laws that were entirely consistent with the national law, the decision meant that employees could not be covered by any labor relations law in those instances where the NLRB refused to assert jurisdiction.

To rectify the situation, Congress could have required the board to assert its jurisdiction to the fullest extent; it could also have provided that dispute cases be ceded to state labor agencies even though the laws administered by these agencies were in some respects inconsistent with federal

---

[14] See the *Twenty-Third Annual Report of the National Labor Relations Board* (1959) for the existing jurisdictional standards.
[15] 353 U.S. 1 (1957).

law. In the Landrum-Griffin Law the latter course was selected. The law provides that the jurisdictional standards prevailing on August 1, 1959 are to be maintained. The NLRB need not assert jurisdiction over workers not covered by these standards, and the state governments are permitted to take jurisdiction when the board refuses to do so. Thus, the NLRB now has the authority to cede jurisdiction for many employees of smaller firms to the state governments where, on the whole, the labor laws are less encouraging to collective bargaining than is the federal law.

The Secondary Boycott Problem

The secondary boycott has long been the source of some of the most difficult problems in American labor law. After the Danbury-Hatters case (1908) and until the passage of the Norris-LaGuardia Act, secondary boycotts were generally treated either as violations of the Sherman Anti-Trust Act or as illegal behavior under the common law. The broad definition of a labor dispute written into the Norris-LaGuardia Act, the equation of picketing with free speech (secondary picketing is one form of the secondary boycott), and a tendency by the courts to recognize a unity of interests among employees of different employers made lawful many of the secondary pressures that had previously been illegal.

The trend toward a liberalization of secondary boycott law started by the Norris-LaGuardia Act was reversed by the Taft-Hartley Law. Section 8(b)(4)(A) of the latter law made it an unfair labor practice for a labor organization or its agents

> to engage in, or to induce or encourage the employees of any employer to engage in, a strike or a concerted refusal in the course of their employment to use, manufacture, process, transport or otherwise handle or work on any goods, articles, materials, or commodities or to perform any services, where an object thereof is: forcing or requiring any employer or self-employed person to join any labor or employer organization or any employer or other person to cease using, selling, handling, transporting, or otherwise dealing in the products of any other producer, processor, or manufacturer, or to cease doing business with any other person.

Beneath this tangle of legal verbiage is the simple fact that Congress intended to make many of the traditional secondary pressures of labor unions unfair practices to be prevented by the remedial powers of the NLRB. In one of the first cases decided by the NLRB under the Taft-Hartley provision, the board ruled that Section 8(b)(4)(A) was aimed "at eliminating all secondary boycotts. . . ."[16] Since the board had also ruled that Congress did not intend to interfere with the right of a labor

---

[16] *Matter of Wadsworth Building Company, Inc.*, 81 NLRB, No. 127.

organization to take primary action[17] much of the ensuing history of administration of the secondary boycott clause was concerned with the problem of distinguishing between primary and secondary pressures.[18]

Eventually, labor organizations managed to uncover some loopholes in the law and thus to avoid the full impact of the secondary boycott limitation.[19] A prominent type of secondary pressure, for example, is the so-called "hot cargo" boycott in which workers refuse to work on "unfair" goods. Under Section 8(b)(4)(A) it would have been an unfair labor practice for union officers to encourage a group of employees to cease working on materials coming from a non-union plant. There was nothing in the law, however, to prevent an employer from *voluntarily* agreeing not to handle certain products. By negotiating hot cargo contracts with employers, many unions, particularly the Teamsters, managed to circumvent the legal prohibition against secondary pressures.

After about ten years of administrative and court rulings on hot cargo agreements, the Supreme Court held that hot cargo contracts were permissible but that a union could not induce employees to engage in concerted activities to enforce such agreements.[20]

Another loophole resulted from the language of the law which prohibited unions from encouraging a *concerted* refusal by employees to engage in secondary pressures. In the International Rice Milling Case, a labor organization maintained a picket line against a primary employer. When non-union truck drivers of a secondary employer approached the plant, the pickets persuaded them to not make a pick up of the plant's product. The Supreme Court ruled that the picket line behavior was legal, since the pressure was exerted against *individual* workers of a secondary employer and, thus, did not constitute an attempt to encourage a *concerted* refusal to perform work.[21]

The Landrum-Griffin amendments to Taft Hartley are aimed specifically against the loopholes described above. Section 8(b)(4)(A) was amended to make it an unfair labor practice for a union or its agents to induce any *individual* employee to engage in secondary pressures. Voluntary labor-management hot cargo contracts are declared to be unfair labor contracts as well as unenforceable and void.

---

[17] *Matter of Pure Oil Company*, 84 NLRB, No. 47.

[18] See the Annual Reports of the NLRB for a history of the board's struggle with this problem.

[19] For a summary of the legal situation relative to secondary boycotts just prior to the amendment of the Taft-Hartley Act see Melvin J. Segal, "Secondary Boycott Loopholes," *Labor Law Journal,* March, 1959. See also Segal, "Differences among Secondary Boycotts and the Taft-Hartley Act," *Wayne Law Review,* Spring, 1959.

[20] *Local 1976, United Brotherhood of Carpenters* v. *NLRB*, 357 U.S. 93, 1958.

[21] 341 U.S. 665, 1951.

The Landrum-Griffin Law, thus, continues the legal tendency to narrow the circle of permissible economic conflict between employers and labor. Since secondary boycotts are used mainly as organizational weapons, the effect of the law will probably be that of making it somewhat more difficult for unions to organize the unorganized.

Although the major Taft-Hartley loopholes were closed by the Landrum-Griffin amendments, administration of the secondary boycott clauses continues to be troublesome. Recent cases, for example, have involved differentiating secondary employers who are neutrals from those who act as "allies" of a primary employer involved in a labor dispute, and determining the status of picketing at locations where a primary employer's products are used.[22] In the latter case, a union is engaged in an unfair secondary boycott if its picketing does not meet the requirement that it have a reasonably direct effect on the primary employer and that it not be designed to inflict general economic injury on the business of neutrals. Thus, the old problem of distinguishing between primary and secondary pressures is still very much alive.

Economic Strikes and the Right to Vote

Section 9(c)(3) of the Taft-Hartley Act provided that workers on strike who were not entitled to reinstatement were not eligible to vote in representation elections. Under the earlier Wagner Act interpretations, striking employees retained their voting rights in representation elections. At a later time, both strikers and their replacements were given voting rights. Under the Taft-Hartley Act, if a specific job of a striking worker was given to a replacement, the discharged striker lost his vote to the replacement. Unions expressed the fear that in periods of high unemployment, employers would take advantage of this part of the law to eliminate unionism from their plants.

The Landrum-Griffin Act amends the Taft-Hartley clause so as to provide some protection against the possibility of using the representation election during a strike as a "union busting" device. The law now reads as follows: "Employees engaged in an economic strike who are not entitled to reinstatement shall be eligible to vote under such regulations as the Board shall find are consistent with the purposes and provisions of this Act in any election conducted within twelve months after the commencement of the strike."

---

[22] *Twenty-Second Annual Report of the National Labor Relations Board,* (Washington, D.C., U.S. Government Printing Office, 1968), pp. 120–123.

Statutory Control of Picketing

The Landrum-Griffin Act adds a seventh unfair union practice to the list in Taft-Hartley. The practice outlaws picketing in special circumstances. Picketing is an illegal practice when the purpose is to force an employer to recognize or bargain with an uncertified union[23] or to force employees to select an uncertified union as bargaining representative in the following situations:

1. Where an employer has already lawfully recognized another union and a question of representation cannot properly be raised.[24]

2. Where a representation election has been conducted by the NLRB within the preceding twelve month period.[25]

3. Where the picketing has been conducted without a petition for a representation election having been filed within a reasonable period of time not to exceed thirty days from the commencement of the picketing. Nothing in subparagraph (c) of this section of the act, however, is to be construed as prohibiting picketing for the purpose of truthfully advising the public of a non-union operation unless such picketing has the effect of causing an employee of another employer to respect the picket line.

The main purpose of the picketing limitation summarized above is to preserve the integrity of the election machinery of the National Labor Relations Board by controlling the pressures that can be exerted by minority unions. Prior to the Landrum-Griffin Law, it was possible for a union to engage in organizational picketing in circumstances in which the employer, under the law, could not have granted the right of recognition. In subparagraph (c), however, Congress recognized that unions have a legitimate interest in protecting work standards by disseminating publicity about non-union employers. The attempt to distinguish between "recognitional" and

---

[23] "Uncertified" means that the union has not been certified by the NLRB as the exclusive bargaining representative of a unit of employees. Certification is achieved as a result of a representation election in which the union receives a majority of the votes cast by employees in a proposed bargaining unit.

[24] Under the contract bar doctrine of the NLRB, the existence of a valid bargaining contract bars a challenging union from raising a question of representation until the contract expiration date. When a contract is written for a two-year period, the NLRB has regarded the contract as a two year bar against a competing union and in some circumstances has permitted the contract bar to operate for a longer period.

[25] Section 9(c)(3) of the Taft-Hartley Act prohibits an election for a twelve month period after a prior election. The Landrum-Griffin provision cited above means that a union may not picket for recognitional or organizational purposes, even though the union involved was not a party to the prior election.

"informational" picketing has produced some knotty administrative problems. Picketing frequently has both recognition and information objectives.
When both elements are present should picketing be banned in accordance
with the first part of subparagraph (c) or permitted in accordance with
the second part? The NLRB has already moved through several positions
on this question and, at the time of this writing, appears to be giving
precedence to the informational objective.

THE BROAD CHARACTERISTICS OF THE TAFT-HARTLEY ERA

The temptation to get entangled in the details of the Taft-Hartley and
Landrum-Griffin Acts is very strong, for many of the provisions have
interesting and disputative aspects. Often, though, the controversies that
occur fail to go beyond the details. It is understandable that the interests
of management and labor are directed primarily at the specific impacts of
certain clauses in the law. For the student of the law, however, there is a
more fundamental question. What is the character of the law as a whole?
This question was more easily answered in the pre-Taft-Hartley periods.
The subtle and frequently conflicting details of contemporary labor law
are not easily disentangled to facilitate a broad perspective. An attempt
will be made here to suggest some of the broader features although the
reader is cautioned that these are opinions with which others may differ.

A Lessening Emphasis on Equalizing the Bargaining Power of Labor

There is little or no emphasis in the Taft-Hartley Act and the various
state labor relations acts on the necessity of increasing the bargaining power
of labor to a point of equality with that of management. There is a tacit
assumption, in fact, that both labor and management are giants. Equality
of bargaining power, therefore, is considered to be less important than the
consequences of the labor-management contention. It is not difficult, indeed,
to find a strong implication in the law that labor has not only achieved
an equality in its bargaining position but has arrived at a superior position
and that the power inherent in labor unions must be restrained according
to the legislative conception of the public interest. This feature of the law
amounts to a substantial modification of the basic premise in the Wagner
Act.

A Tendency to Narrow the Area of Employer-Employee Relations

In Chapters 16 and 17 we noted that the Norris-LaGuardia and Wagner
Acts reversed a judicial philosophy that was reluctant to admit a unity of

interests among employees of different employers. An important characteristic of present day law is the reappearance of a tendency to limit the permissible boundaries of overt labor-management conflict to an area that encompasses no more than an employer and his immediate employees. This tendency was especially marked in the rash of state labor legislation that appeared before 1947; within the Taft-Hartley and Landrum-Griffin Acts it is expressed in the secondary boycott provisions.

A Concern for Protecting the Worker from the Union

In a period when both state and national legislative bodies are reacting against the power of organized labor, it is to be expected that the law will attempt to provide some protection for workers against unions. One of the most prominent of the legislated protections has been the prohibition or limitation of union security agreements. Other examples of provisions designed to protect the worker against unions are found in Sections 7 and 8 of the Taft-Hartley Act where rights to be free from union coercion and to refrain from union activity are explicitly stated. The same law also provides workers with various methods of repudiating the union leadership. The national emergency strike procedures, for instance, give workers an opportunity to accept the employer's last offer, which is tantamount to an opportunity of voting no confidence in the union leadership. In Titles I through V of the Landrum-Griffin Law, concern for the rights of the union member is expressed through a control of various aspects of internal union affairs.

A Concern with the Rights of the Public

One of the most important premises of contemporary labor law is that the processes and results of collective bargaining should be subject to more control in the public interest. The Wagner Act made no mention of a need for public protection. It was simply assumed that encouragement of union-management bargaining would directly benefit the public by contributing to the maintenance of purchasing power and by resolving the industrial conflict over the right to organize. The Taft-Hartley Law and miscellaneous state laws question the basic Wagner Act assumption that strong unions and collective bargaining are inherently beneficial. Experience during the war and postwar years convinced many that the power of labor could be used to the disadvantage of the public and that it was necessary, consequently, to curb this power with a variety of restrictions.

The most obvious example of the concern with public rights is found in the emergency dispute provisions. In addition, most of the unfair practices listed in Taft-Hartley amount to an indirect protection of the public against an unrestrained exercise of labor union power.

The Growing Role of Government

Today, to a greater extent than ever before, the government is involved in the details of collective bargaining. The attempt to protect labor against management, management against labor, and the public and workers against both, necessarily requires a surveillance of the content, processes, and results of bargaining.

Since the time of the conspiracy trials, the government, in one way or another, has been involved in the labor-management relationship. Until recently, however, the concern of government bodies was with relatively broad problems. What was an illegal conspiracy? When should injunctions be issued? Under what circumstances was a strike a violation of the Sherman Act? To some extent during the Wagner Act era and to a very large extent in the Taft-Hartley era, the attentions of the government have been directed to the sometimes very petty details of the labor-management relationship. A typical set of contemporary legal problems might be cited for comparison with the problems stated above. Does the use of foul language constitute coercion? How many hours should elapse between the time an employer makes an anti-union speech and the time set for a representation election? Should slowdowns and temporary work stoppages during negotiations be interpreted as bargaining without good faith? With the proliferation of administrative and court decisions, the law has tended to become an elaborate code of behavior that has thrown a legalistic cast over the small details of bargaining.

The eventual result of this growing attention to details may be weak rather than strong law. Whatever value judgments one may have about labor law during the repressive era, it was strong law accomplishing its purposes with relative effectiveness. Today labor law runs the danger of becoming a brittle instrument of public policy. In attempting to control too much, the law invites labor and management to seek legal favors as an alternative to resolving problems through the bargaining process. Thus, a law ostensibly devised to encourage bargaining has an opposite effect in many instances.

The Effects of the Taft-Hartley Law

The effects of the Taft-Hartley Law are difficult, and perhaps impossible, to measure. The first angry cry by unions that the "slave labor law" would destroy labor organizations is wide of the mark, but so is the contention that the law is nothing more than a slight corrective of those Wagner Act features that had overly favored unions.

What is reasonably obvious at the present time is that the power of the more powerful labor organizations has been little affected by the law. Unions such as the Steelworkers or the Teamsters, strong in numbers and financially secure, are able to circumvent the disadvantages imposed by law with a high degree of success. Unions functioning in industries or regions that are largely non-union are in a less fortunate position, however. The "free speech" rights of employers, the "one year bar rule" (a union losing an election cannot petition for another twelve months), and the more conservative administration of the law are barriers that make organization of the unorganized much more difficult than was the case before 1947. Many unions, in short, found themselves faced with a Taft-Hartley Act before they were in a position to take advantage of the Wagner Act. The major victims of the Taft-Hartley era have been the weak rather than the powerful unions.

The processes and results of collective bargaining have been affected in numerous ways, and many of these were noted in the course of this chapter. When the union-management bargaining relationship is a healthy one—that is, when each party recognizes and respects the legitimate aspirations of the other—the provisions of law are relatively inconsequential. The unfair practice features of the act come into play only when charges are filed; and the essence of a satisfactory bargaining relationship is that problems, even difficult problems, are worked out through the bargaining mechanism.

Frequent assertion of legal rights by either labor or management is a symptom of an unsatisfactory relationship. It is tantamount to an admission that the parties are unable to resolve their own problems or that they are willing to forsake bargaining when a more favorable result becomes possible by invoking legal processes.

One weakness of present-day law is that it tempts labor and management to "win" by adding the power of government to their own power. An element of hope for the future may be that both bargaining parties will become aware of the illusory nature of such victories. A solution imposed by force rarely reaches the fundamentals of a problem.

SUMMARY

The twelve-year experience under the Wagner Act represented the high point of legal encouragement of unionism in the United States. To a considerable extent the objectives of the Wagner Act were achieved; and, as a result, some parts of this law became obsolete. Amendment of the Wagner Act, however, occurred less in response to a need to take account of the changed character of the labor-management relationship than to the post-World War II strike wave. In 1947, the Taft-Hartley Act placed a number of restrictions upon the pressure tactics, goals, and internal affairs of labor organizations. Although the details of the Taft-Hartley Act satisfied neither labor nor management, a political stalemate inhibited the amendment of the law until 1959. By that time the accumulated disclosures of union corruption facilitated the passage of the Labor-Management Reporting and Disclosure Act. Parts of this law were directed toward union reform and parts toward amendment of the Taft-Hartley Act. These latter amendments, for the most part, continued the conservative trend in labor law that had been initiated by the state governments and given additional impetus by the Taft-Hartley Act.

QUESTIONS

1. What social and economic factors facilitated the passage of the Taft-Hartley Act?
2. How do you explain the inability of labor to prevent the passage of a law that it did not want?
3. How did the fundamental premises of the Wagner Act differ from those of the Taft-Hartley Act?
4. Were the Taft-Hartley and Landrum-Griffin Acts necessary? Would you recommend that they be changed in any way?
5. What future developments in labor law do you anticipate?

SELECTED READINGS

COHEN, SANFORD. *Labor Law.* Columbus, Ohio: Charles E. Merrill Books, Inc., 1964. Chaps. 9, 10, 16, 17, 18, 20.
COX, ARCHIBALD. *Law and the National Labor Policy.* Los Angeles: Institute of Industrial Relations, University of California, 1960.
MILLIS, HARRY A., and BROWN, EMILY C. *From the Wagner Act to Taft-Hartley.* Chicago: The University of Chicago Press, 1950. Parts 2 and 3.
WELLINGTON, HARRY W. *Labor and the Legal Process.* New Haven: Yale University Press, 1968. Part 3.

CHAPTER 19

The Law of Wages and Hours

How many hours should people work, and how much should they receive for working? For a large majority of persons in the labor force, these questions are resolved by collective negotiations, by civil service pay scales, or by the forces of demand and supply that are expressed in the labor market. Wage and hour legislation seeks to answer the same questions for the economically more depressed persons in the labor force. Apart from war emergencies when special controls have been established to enforce wage ceilings, wage and hour legislation has been designed to establish minimum standards.

At the present time the legal minimum wage that may be paid to persons covered by federal law is $1.60 per hour; for those persons covered by state law the legal floor is usually lower than this—in some cases substantially lower.[1] In view of current price levels these standards are not overly impressive, but the purpose of minimum wage law is not to guarantee high wages. The purpose, in fact, is only broadly described in the various wage statutes, and the common definitional denominator that would win general acceptance is probably no more specific than that minimum wage law should prevent the payment of very low wages. There is rarely unanimity as to what constitutes a "very low wage," and the legal floor that prevails at a given time is less the result of some ideal standard scientifically derived than it is a reflection of the varying strengths of political pressure groups.

---

[1] For certain groups covered by federal law, the legal minimum is less than $1.60 per hour. See page 521 below.

In this chapter we shall examine three of the more important problems that have been or are associated with the development of wage and hour law. These are in turn (1) the constitutionality of wage and hour law, (2) the problem of legal standards, and (3) the economic advisability of wage and hour law.

WAGE AND HOUR LAW AND THE CONSTITUTION

Legal regulation of wages is by no means a modern phenomenon. During the mercantile era, wage control was a characteristic feature of economic life in the developing nation states. Wage regulations as well as other government controls were swept away as detailed government intervention in economic life was replaced by the practice of laissez-faire during the late eighteenth and the nineteenth centuries. By the end of the latter century, however, pressures were being exerted in many nations for the establishment of wage floors. Whatever the merits of free labor markets, its had become obvious that some of their consequences could not be squared with concepts of social justice. The play of market forces often led to sweatshop working conditions with long hours at very low pay. New Zealand adopted minimum wage legislation in 1894, and many nations soon followed; by the 1920's the United States was almost the only major industrial and commercial nation without some type of protective wage law.

Within the United States, a federal minimum wage law was finally enacted in 1938. This law and the wage laws of numerous states came after decades of effort, most of which was expended to convince the Supreme Court that a minimum wage law did not violate constitutional precepts of freedom of contract. The history of the legal evolution is complex, and any attempt to make sense out of Supreme Court vicissitudes will fail unless the basic question of Supreme Court philosophy is kept in mind. The Supreme Court —or at least a court majority—was reluctant to modify the philosophy of economic individualism that had predominated in the nineteenth century. It is significant that federal minimum wage law as well as other federal welfare legislation first appeared during the depressed years of the 1930's when the economic environment itself argued strongly for a more flexible interpretation of the Constitution.

Regulation of Working Hours

Apart from occasional suggestions that working hours should be shortened to offset the employment effect of automation, little has been heard in recent times about hours of work as a social problem. The eight-hour day, generally regarded as workable and equitable, has become standard practice in most American industries. Throughout most of the nineteenth century and the first thirty years of the twentieth, however, the "hours of work" question was one of the sore points in labor-management relations. According to the 1909 Census of Manufacturers, less than 8 per cent of wage earners worked in establishments where the eight hour day prevailed. About three-fourths of all wage earners worked from fifty-four to sixty hours per week and over half a million worked in establishments where even longer hours prevailed.[2]

Legislative efforts to limit hours of work began in the 1840's. The first laws sought to protect women and children from the deleterious effects of exceptionally long hours and were usually ineffective because of inadequate enforcement and legal loopholes. After the Civil War, especially during the later years of the century, more effective laws were drawn, and the question of the constitutionality of maximum hour legislation was raised in numerous court cases.

Until the 1930's, most protective labor legislation in the United States was passed by state governments acting under the authority of the broad police power. The main challenge to these laws came in the form of allegations that basic individual rights guaranteed by the federal Constitution were being infringed.

There has always been an aura of vagueness about the police power of the states. As Freund notes, this is partly due to the fact that the power is not a fixed quantity but rather an expression of social, economic, and political conditions that varies as these conditions vary.[3] The police power, according to one description, aims directly at securing and promoting the public welfare, and it does so by restraint and compulsion.[4] Elsewhere, it is described as the general power to legislate in order to regulate the conduct and relations of members of society.[5] The police power, then, is the broad power of the states to correct what a consensus regards as an evil, by placing restraints upon the agents and processes of the purported evil. The power cannot be defined by drawing up neat categories of what it is and what it isn't, because the categories themselves will change over periods of time.

Since an exercise of the police power involves placing restraints upon individuals, it is almost inevitable that such an exercise will inspire a challenge to the authority of the state legislative body. In the case of maximum hour legislation, employers generally challenged the constitutionality of

---

[2] John R. Commons and John B. Andrews, *Principles of Labor Legislation* (New York: Harper & Row, Publishers, 1916), p. 200.

[3] Ernst Freund, *The Police Power* (Chicago: Callahan, 1904), p. 2.

[4] *Ibid.*, p. 3.

[5] Owen J. Roberts, *The Courts and the Constitution* (Cambridge, Mass.: Harvard University Press, 1951), p. 37.

the regulatory laws on the following bases: (1) employers and employees were being deprived of their rights under the Fourteenth Amendment; (2) maximum hour legislation did not obviously promote the public welfare; (3) maximum hour legislation often amounted to an unreasonable, and hence unconstitutional, classification. Before examining the actual cases in which these issues were decided, let us analyze each allegation briefly.

1. Originally passed to protect the rights of former slaves, the Fourteenth Amendment came to be, by judicial interpretation, one of the strong supports of economic individualism. As in other areas of economic life where the state sought to regulate business conduct, employers looked to the Fourteenth Amendment for protection against maximum hour legislation.

The amendment provides that no person may be deprived of life, liberty, or property without due process of law. Since freedom of contract is a property right, the usual allegation was that a maximum hour law impaired the property of both employers and employees in that neither party remained free to contract for hours longer than the statutory maximum.

2. In some cases, the plaintiffs charged and the courts upheld the contention that prevailing hours of work were not obviously harmful and that they were correct in that they reflected the economic forces of demand and supply. To seek to control hours of labor by law was to interfere with the natural laws of economics.

3. Many of the laws enacted by the states singled out women or special groups of male workers for protection. In such cases, it was frequently charged that the laws were based upon an arbitrary classification of persons and hence denied equal protection of the law to all.

Only thinly hidden by the veneer of legalistic arguments was the fact that differences over hours regulation amounted to a clash of opinion over social versus individual values. The federal Constitution provides certain protections for individuals against government action; but the protections are not absolute, and their characteristics change with the passage of time. In a series of cases the Supreme Court was called upon to decide whether a state legislature, acting in response to the desires of its electorate, could legitimately set limits to the number of hours that employers and employees might agree upon. The legal evolution can best be described through references to a select number of key decisions.

Muller v. *Oregon*[6]

As noted above, much of the early hour legislation was pointed toward the protection of women and minors. There was no serious question about

---
[6] 208 U.S. 412 (1908).

the right of a state to regulate working hours of children, but the power to protect female workers in a similar fashion was established less readily.[7]

Proponents of working hour limitation for women received strong encouragement from the United States Supreme Court decision in *Muller* v. *Oregon*. Oregon had passed a law in 1903, prohibiting the employment of women for more than ten hours per day in mechanical establishments, factories, or laundries. When a case under the law reached the Supreme Court on appeal, the plaintiff cited the three arguments listed above (p. 514). These arguments were countered by briefs prepared by Miss Josephine Goldmark of the National Consumers League and Mr. Louis Brandeis. The briefs constituted a new type of legal pleading that relied less upon principles of law than upon an accumulation of economic and sociological data. The "Brandeis brief" attempted to prove with statistical and other evidence that long working hours had harmful effects upon female health.

The Court took cognizance of these arguments, noting that "since healthy mothers are essential to vigorous offspring, the physical well-being of women becomes an object of public interest. . . ." It was not improper, according to the opinion, to place women in a class apart from men for purposes of protective legislation.

In 1915, the Supreme Court upheld a California law that set eight hours as the maximum work day for women.[8] By this time it had become rather firmly established that state governments could use their police powers to limit working hours of women to "reasonable" amounts.

Holden v. *Hardy*[9]

The conflict over the constitutionality of maximum hour legislation for men involved, once again, the clash between the exercise of the police power to promote the social welfare and the individual right to contract for the disposal of labor power. The first Supreme Court support of hours regulation for men came in the *Holden* v. *Hardy* case where the issue was a law limiting hours of work in dangerous occupations.

Utah had established eight hours as the maximum daily work to be permitted in mines and smelters. The court upheld the statute, noting that the law is a progressive science and that certain classes of persons engaged in dangerous or unhealthful occupations were in need of protections not deemed essential when the Constitution was adopted. The legislature of Utah had judged certain occupations to be detrimental to the health of employees, and the Supreme Court was willing to accept the legislative judgment as long as there were reasonable grounds for believing that the judgment was accurate.

[7] See *Ritchie* v. *People*, 155 Ill. 98 (1895).
[8] *Miller* v. *Wilson*, 236 U.S. 373.
[9] 169 U.S. 366 (1898).

Lochner v. *New York*[10]

A close study of this decision will be fruitful for the student of labor law, for the different philosophical positions are clearly stated in the majority and minority opinions. A New York law had established a ten-hour maximum day for bakers. In a five to four decision the Supreme Court held that the law was invalid.

In his opinion, Justice Peckham wrote that bakers as a class were equal in intelligence and capacity to men in other trades and were able to assert their rights without the protecting arm of the state. Bakers were in no sense wards of the state, and the trade of bakers had never been regarded as unhealthy. Since public health or welfare bore only a most remote relation to the statute, the law could not be regarded as a valid exercise of the state police power. "There is," Peckham wrote, "no reasonable ground for interfering with the liberty of person or the right of free contract by determining the hours of labor in the occupation of a baker."

Three justices dissented by arguing that it was not the function of the court to render judgment on the wisdom of legislation. As long as there was a doubt as to the constitutional validity of a statute, the doubt must be resolved in favor of the statute. The state of New York had concluded that bakers needed protection, and the court, according to the dissent, should accept that conclusion.

In a separate dissent, Justice Holmes maintained that the constitution was not intended to embody the economic theory of laissez-faire. Reasonable men might disagree as to whether the law was a proper health measure, but this had nothing to do with "the right of a majority to embody their opinions in law."

Bunting v. *Oregon*[11]

By the time of the Bunting case, the Supreme Court had looked with favor upon state regulation of working hours for certain classes of workers and had disapproved of regulation for other classes. As yet no case involving a general limitation of working hours had been heard by the court, although the Lochner ruling suggested that such a law would not be upheld as valid. It must be remembered, however, that *Lochner* v. *New York* was a five to four decision characterized by vigorous dissents. In *Bunting* v. *Oregon* a general hours limitation law came before the Supreme Court for the first time.

An Oregon law limited the hours of work in mills and factories to ten hours a day and provided that three additional hours might be worked if

---

10 198 U.S. 45 (1905).
11 243 U.S. 426 (1917).

the overtime was paid for at a rate of one and one-half times the regular hourly rate. After rejecting the contention that the law was a regulation of wages rather than hours, the court ruled that the law did not transcend constitutional limits. By 1917, then, a legal evolution had culminated in a Supreme Court attitude that accepted the right of a state government to limit hours of work in non-hazardous occupations for men as well as for women.

Minimum Wage Regulation

An interesting social history could be written around the theme of the five to four Supreme Court decision. Many crucial questions have been decided by the vote of the odd judge, and in the case of minimum wage legislation this was certainly true. In 1923, five Supreme Court justices voted against a minimum wage law, and four voted in favor. The constitutionality of state minimum wage legislation was finally settled in 1937, when the majority and minority voting positions were reversed.

The Supreme Court was more reluctant to accept wage regulation than hour limitation, possibly because government control of price strikes more obviously at the core of a basic laissez-faire principle than does a regulation of working hours. Justice Sutherland, in the Adkins decision, made just this point when he noted that a regulation of hours leaves the parties free to adjust any additional burdens thrown upon an employer by making wage changes.

In 1912 and 1913, nine states passed laws that regulated rates of pay for women and minors. The laws reflected a growing awareness that a large proportion of these wage earners were receiving shockingly low pay. The stated purpose in most of the laws was to protect the health and morals of female wage earners.

Adkins v. *Children's Hospital*[12]

The first Supreme Court test of a state minimum wage law came in 1917 in the *Stettler* v. *O'Hara*[13] decision when an Oregon minimum wage law for women reached the court on appeal. The court split four to four, and this had the effect of sustaining the ruling of the Oregon Supreme Court which had upheld the law. No decision was written in the Stettler case.

A District of Columbia minimum wage law came before the Supreme Court in 1923 and was held to be unconstitutional in a five to four decision. Between 1917 and 1923, the court had become more conservative as a re-

---

[12] 261 U.S. 525 (1923).
[13] 243 U.S. 629.

sult of new appointments. One of the new conservatives, Justice Sutherland, wrote the opinion in *Adkins* v. *Children's Hospital.*

The main points in the opinion were: (1) the statute was a price-fixing law confined to adult women, who were as capable of contracting for themselves as men; (2) the wages fixed had no necessary relationship to the capacity or earning power of the employee; (3) the standards furnished for the guidance of the wage-fixing board were vague; (4) female morality rested upon other considerations than wages, or at least the relationship between the two factors could not be standardized; (5) the law compelled an employer to pay a fixed amount but required no service or equivalent value from the employee.

In his dissent Chief Justice Taft noted that low-paid workers did not enjoy an equality of bargaining power with employers and out of necessity were prone to accept "pretty much anything that is offered." Taft suggested that a minimum wage statute might not be an effective remedy to correct the evils of sweatshop wages, but he did not believe that it was the function of the court to hold legislative acts invalid because they were passed to carry out unwise economic views. Justice Holmes also dissented and pointed out that the statute did not compel anybody to pay anything. It simply forbade employment at rates below those fixed as the minimum requirements of health and right living.

The Adkins decision established the precedent that minimum wage laws were unconstitutional; in subsequent court rulings the laws of several states were invalidated by the Supreme Court, lower federal courts, and state courts. The movement for minimum wage legislation, thus, came to a halt in the 1920's.

Morehead v. *New York ex rel Tipaldo*[14]

By 1933, interest in minimum wage legislation had revived. Wages had fallen to extremely low levels under the impact of economic depression, and there was some feeling that higher wages would help to restore prosperity. The Adkins decision contained a strong suggestion that a wage law would be upheld if there were some relationship between the minimum wage established and the actual value of service rendered. The National Consumers League had worked out a model bill designed specifically to meet the objections raised by the Supreme Court; and in 1933 seven states passed new minimum wage laws, most of them based upon the Consumer League model.[15]

---

[14] 298 U.S. 587 (1936).

[15] The ultimate acceptance of the minimum wage principle was due in large part to the unceasing efforts of the National Consumers League. Far too frequently the League has failed to receive full credit for its part in promoting social welfare legislation.

In the Morehead case the Supreme Court ruled—five to four again—that a New York law was not distinguishable from the one struck down in the Adkins case and that the principle stated in the latter case was still binding. The law invalidated in *Adkins* v. *Children's Hospital* used as a standard a wage adequate to supply the necessary cost of living to maintain women workers in good health and to protect their morals. The New York law defined an oppressive wage as one containing two elements: (1) less than the fair and reasonable value of the services rendered, and (2) less than sufficient to meet the minimum cost of living. The majority opinion held that the second point was the same as the standard established in the earlier District of Columbia case, and the fact that the New York law had added another standard was not sufficient to distinguish the cases.

West Coast Hotel v. *Parrish*[16]

One year after the Morehead decision the Supreme Court ruled that state minimum wage laws for women were constitutional. Justice Roberts, who had voted against the New York law, reversed his position in the West Coast Hotel case; and, thus, after some twenty years of litigation a court majority voted to sustain minimum wage legislation. Ordinarily the Supreme Court seeks to avoid reversing earlier opinions even when reversal is in order. By noting slight distinctions between a present and past decision, for instance, the effect of a reversal can be achieved without the form of a reversal. The court didn't bother to do this in *West Coast Hotel* v. *Parrish*. The Adkins decision was explicitly overruled.

In his opinion, Chief Justice Hughes wrote that if the protection of women is a legitimate end of the exercise of state power, the requirement of a minimum wage payment was an admissible means to that end. He found the fact that a class of workers was being exploited because of a weak bargaining position to be a compelling consideration.

Many states proceeded to enact minimum wage laws after the West Coast Hotel decision. A few extended wage protection to men, but the large preponderance of state wage regulation laws, even at the present time, are confined to specified classes of women workers.

Federal Wage and Hour Law

The first general attempt by the federal government to set wage minima and hour maxima collapsed in 1935 when the NRA experiment was invalidated in the Schechter Poultry case.[17] A second attempt in 1938 survived a test of constitutionality three years later, and federal wage and hour law has continued in effect since then.

---

[16] 300 U.S. 379, 1937.
[17] 295 U.S. 495.

Between 1935 and 1941, there had occurred the sweeping change in court philosophy that so enlarged the scope of the commerce clause in the federal Constitution. In 1935, the Supreme Court was unwilling to relax the position that production was distinct from commerce and hence immune from controls established under the authority of the commerce clause. By 1941, this principle had been seriously weakened in a series of decisions that began with *Jones and Laughlin* v. *National Labor Relations Board.* The Fair Labor Standards Act of 1938 was enacted under the authority of the commerce clause. When the law was challenged in 1941, the Supreme Court was able to brush aside the old distinction between manufacturing and commerce by noting that Congress might regulate intrastate activities where they have a substantial effect upon interstate commerce.[18] The phrase "production for commerce," according to the opinion, embraced those cases where the manufacturer had a normal expectation that some part of his output would later move in interstate commerce.

The validation of federal regulation of wages and hours in the Darby decision ended the long fight over the right of both state and national government to exert controls in these areas. With the basic question of constitutionality settled, problems in the wage and hour field assumed new forms, which we shall examine in subsequent sections.

WAGE AND HOUR STANDARDS

The Fair Labor Standards Act—commonly known as the *Wage and Hour Law*—was enacted in 1938 and amended significantly in 1949, 1955, 1961, and 1966. The original act established a twenty-five cents an hour minimum wage for covered employments and provided for a gradual increase to a forty cents minimum. The 1966 amendment, which established currently prevailing wage standards provides a $1.60 hourly minimum for persons covered by the law prior to the amendment and a lower rate for those brought under FLSA protection for the first time by a significant extension in coverage. Scheduled increases will revise the standard of the newly covered to $1.60 by February, 1971. Protection under the minimum wage law was extended to farm employees for the first time by the 1966 amendment but the language of the law restricts such protection to employees of large farms.[19] Table 19 shows minimum wage standards enacted in 1966 with the effective date of scheduled increases.

---

18 *U.S.* v. *F. W. Darby Company*, 312 U.S. 100, 1941.
19 Karen S. Koziara, "The Agricultural Minimum Wage: A Preliminary Look," *Monthly Labor Review* Sept., 1967, pp. 26–29.

TABLE 19

FEDERAL MINIMUM WAGE STANDARDS

EFFECTIVE DATE	MINIMUM HOURLY WAGE FOR OLD COVERAGE*	MINIMUM HOURLY WAGE FOR NEW NON-FARM COVERAGE	MINIMUM HOURLY WAGE FOR NEW FARM COVERAGE
February 1, 1968	$1.60	$1.15	$1.15
February 1, 1969	1.60	1.30	1.30
February 1, 1970	1.60	1.45	1.30
February 1, 1971	1.60	1.60	1.30

* "Old Coverage" refers to persons covered by the law prior to the 1966 amendments.

The FLSA does not limit the number of hours that employees may work, but it does require payment at the rate of one and one-half times the regular rate for overtime work. Under the 1938 law, forty-four hours per week at straight-time rates was permitted. After two years this was scaled down to forty hours. For employees brought under the coverage of the law in 1966, overtime pay at time and one-half was required after 44 hours during the first year of coverage which began February 1, 1968, after 42 hours during the second year, and after 40 hours thereafter. In addition to the wage and hour standards, the FLSA established a number of child labor regulations.

In 1963 the so-called "equal pay" amendment was added to the FLSA. The purpose of the amendment is to prohibit the payment of lower wages to women in covered employments than are paid to men for doing the same work. The amendment consists of two parts, the first of which provides that an employer cannot discriminate on the basis of sex alone in the payment of wages. The second specifies that labor organizations must not attempt to cause an employer to discriminate in the payment of wages on the sex. The amendment became effective as of June 10, 1964, except for employees covered by a union-management agreement. For the latter, the effective date of the amendment was June 10, 1965, or the contract expiration date, whichever came first.

Other Federal Legislation

In addition to the general regulation of wages and hours accomplished in the FLSA, the federal government has enacted controls that apply to select industries and to special groups of workers. Two of the more important of these laws are the *Davis-Bacon Act* of 1931 and the *Walsh-Healey Public Contracts Act* of 1936.

The Davis-Bacon Act applies to all construction contracts in excess of $2,000 to which the United States or the District of Columbia is a party.

The act requires the payment of a minimum wage to all laborers and mechanics employed by contractors or subcontractors on federal government construction contracts; but, unlike the FLSA, the law states no specific minimum. The Davis-Bacon Act authorizes the Secretary of Labor to determine the prevailing area wage rate for each class of workers to be employed on a project. The rate found to be prevailing becomes the legal minimum that a contractor may pay to his employees.

The Walsh-Healey Act regulates the minimum wages paid by employers who contract with a federal government agency to manufacture or supply articles that exceed $10,000 in value. As in the case of the Davis-Bacon Act, no minimum wage is stated, and special procedures are provided for a wage determination by the Secretary of Labor. Wage determinations under the Walsh-Healey Act are made on an industry or partial industry basis and are issued by the Secretary of Labor at the conclusion of a hearing held to receive evidence of prevailing minimum wages within an industry. Industry minimums usually exceed the statutory minimum set by the FLSA, and where this is the case the Walsh-Healey wage determination prevails. Where prevailing industry minimums are lower than the standard of the FLSA, however, the employer is not absolved of his obligations under the Wage and Hour Law.

The overtime provisions of the Walsh-Healey Law also differ from those in the FLSA. The latter law requires payment at the rate of time and one-half for all hours over forty in a work week. Under Walsh-Healey, premium pay is required after eight hours a day *or* forty hours a week, whichever results in the higher weekly pay.

State Wage and Hour Legislation

In thirty-six states, the District of Columbia, and Puerto Rico, some type of minimum wage law is currently in effect. In nine of these jurisdictions, minimum wages are established for specific industries or occupations by wage boards; and in the others they are established by statute or partially by statute and partially by wage boards. In seven states, the laws provide protection only for women and minors. Twenty states at the present time have "equal pay" laws which specify that there shall be no discrimination between male and female workers when the job requirements are the same.

The statistical enumeration in the above paragraph overplays the importance of prevailing state minimum wage regulation. In several states the laws are not in operation, and in a number of others the minimums have become obsolete. South Dakota, for example, provides for a minimum wage of $17 a week for workers in small communities. Laxity in enforcement and light penalties for non-compliance further diminish the importance of the wage regulations in many of the states. In about a dozen states, however, the minimums set by statute or wage board are $1.40 an hour or higher, and the protection, thus, approximates the standard of the federal law. At the time of this writing three states provide wage minimums that are higher than the federal standard of $1.60.

Forty-six states, the District of Columbia, and Puerto Rico place limitations upon the working hours of female employees; and about a dozen states provide for some type of hour regulation for males. The variations in these laws do not permit an easy summary, and like the state wage laws they range in character from the meaningless to the relatively adequate.

Problems in Wage and Hour Law

The problems that have arisen from our experience with wage and hour law in the United States have been technical and political in character. Wage structures are complex, and the process of tailoring a general statute to fit the multitude of existing wage relationships necessitates hundreds of administrative decisions. Political considerations complicate the tailoring process. Wage and hour legislation is no more immune from political pressures than is collective bargaining law; much of the energy once devoted to challenging the constitutionality of the law is now devoted to limiting the effectiveness of existing wage and hour legislation.

The character of the technical problem can be illustrated by examining some of the definitional questions that have arisen in the FLSA experience. The 1938 law provided that hours worked beyond the statutory maximum were to be paid for at the rate of one and one-half times the regular rate. Apart from a few special circumstances, however, the statute did not indicate what was to be included in the computation of hours worked. Were rest periods and coffee breaks part of the work day? Did the work day start when an employee punched the time clock or when he actually picked up his tools? What about time spent in the work place traveling to and from the actual job site? By itself, this last question prompted an administrative crisis and led to the special act of Congress, known as the *Portal to Portal Act* of 1947.

In a series of cases arising out of disputes over work practices in mining industries, the Supreme Court had ruled that underground travel time must be counted as time worked for statutory overtime provisions.[20] In the Mt. Clemens Pottery Case, the Supreme Court extended the doctrine to workers in other types of employment. According to the ruling, time spent in walk-

---

[20] *Tennessee Coal, Iron, and Railroad Co.* v. *Muscoda Local No. 123*, 321 U.S. 590, 1944; *Jewell Ridge Coal Corporation* v. *United Mine Workers of America*, 325 U.S. 161, 1945.

ing from the plant gate to the work bench and in other preparations for work had to be included in overtime computations.[21]

The Mt. Clemens decision encouraged a flood of "portal to portal" suits that involved an estimated $5 billion in back pay awards. Congress reacted quickly by concluding that the Supreme Court had wandered far from the initial intentions of the FLSA. The Portal to Portal Act of 1947 made "preliminary" and "postliminary" activities non-compensable except for situations where custom, practice, or contract had provided for compensation. The act also stipulated that in cases where employers had relied upon administrative rulings to make their overtime computations, such a reliance was to be considered a defense against liabilities under the FLSA, the Walsh-Healey Act, and the Davis-Bacon Act. In cases where employers had acted in good faith, courts were given the discretion to disallow or diminish damages under the FLSA.

Another complexity in overtime pay computation has resulted from the growing prominence of negotiated pay premiums. Bargaining contracts frequently provide premium pay for hours worked beyond eight a day, or for work on week ends and holidays. If "regular rate of pay" under FLSA is so defined as to include these premiums, the employer's legal obligations relative to overtime pay will be greater, of course, than if the premiums are excluded. There is, furthermore, the question of whether the special premiums should be regarded as offsets against the overtime pay requirements of FLSA. Administrative and court interpretations relative to overtime pay computations wavered back and forth until 1949, when amendments enacted by Congress eliminated the possibility of "overtime on overtime." The technicalities are complex; but, generally speaking, the current law provides for exclusion of premium payments in the computation of the regular rate and for crediting premiums earned toward the employer's obligations under the FLSA.

The solutions reached in the "portal to portal" and "overtime on overtime" experiences were not entirely divorced from political considerations, but the problems have been described here primarily to illustrate the technical complexity of wage and hour law. The political cast of the law becomes more apparent when the basic problems of coverage and benefits are considered.

The FLSA applies to workers who are engaged in commerce or the production of goods for commerce. Coverage under the FLSA is less extensive than under the National Labor Relations Act, since the latter law may be applied to activities which merely *affect* commerce. Under the Wage and

---

[21] *Anderson* v. *Mt. Clemens Pottery Co.*, 328 U.S. 680, 1946. The Supreme Court ruled out compensation for inconsequential time spent in preparatory activities by citing the *de minimis* principle: the law does not concern itself with trifles.

Hour Law, the fact that an employee's work affects commerce in some way is not sufficient in itself to provide him with the benefits of the law. His own work—and not the business of the employer—must be involved in commerce directly or in the production of goods for commerce, if he is to be eligible for the minimum wage and overtime pay guarantees of the act.

The phrase "production of goods for commerce" is vague, and the coverage of the act depends to a considerable extent upon its interpretation. In the 1938 act, employees were deemed to be engaged in the production of goods for commerce if they worked on any process "*necessary* to the production thereof." When the 1949 amendments were being considered, proponents of a more liberal law sought to extend coverage to *all* employees of an employer engaged in commerce or the production of goods for commerce. If adopted, this proposal would have narrowed substantially the differences in coverage between the Labor Relations and the Wage and Hour Laws. A coalition of southern Democrats and Republicans resisted this move and countered with a suggestion to limit coverage to those engaged in occupations *closely related* and *indispensable* to the production of goods for commerce. In the final compromise, the phrase adopted was "*closely related* and *essential* to the production of goods for commerce." The effect of the "closely related and essential" test has been to deny the benefits of the law to a number of persons in occupational categories that had been covered between 1938 and 1949.

Coverage under the FLSA was expanded in 1961 under an amendment which established "enterprise coverage" as an additional test for determination of eligibility under the law. Under enterprise coverage, every employee of a business is covered if that business has some employees who meet the individual coverage test described above and the business falls into one of the categories enumerated in the law. Under the 1966 amendments, employees of an enterprise are covered if the business has some employees who meet the individual coverage test described above and has an annual gross volume of sales of $250,000. Enterprise coverage has also been extended, without a dollar volume test, to employees of laundry and dry cleaning establishments, construction enterprises, and to non-federal hospitals, nursing homes, private and public elementary and secondary schools, and institutions of higher education. Employees not working for enterprises as defined above and not specifically exempted remain subject to the individual coverage tests.

In addition to those groups who do not receive the protections of the Wage and Hour Law as a result of the special definition of interstate commerce, certain occupational groups are specifically exempted. The overtime and minimum wage provisions do not apply to executives, administrators, professional employees, outside salesmen, employees of certain retail and service establishments, employees of certain laundries and cleaners, most agricultural employees, taxicab operators, and several other occupational groups.

A number of employee groups are covered by the minimum wage sections of the law but are exempt from the overtime provisions. These include, among others, dairy farm employees, employees of fish canneries, and employees of carriers subject to regulation by the Interstate Commerce Commission. Workers engaged in agricultural processing and seasonal workers are partially exempt from the overtime provisions. The Wage and Hour Law is also limited in its application to certain miscellaneous categories of workers. The Wage and Hour administrator, for example, may grant authority for the payment of subminimum wages to learners, apprentices, messengers, and handicapped workers. Newspaper delivery boys are exempt from the minimum wage, overtime, and child labor regulations of the law.

Certain elements in this hodge-podge of exemptions, such as the apprentice exemptions, can be justified; however, coverage or non-coverage is best explained by the relative strengths of various interest groups in Congress. As we have seen, the reach of the law has been both contracted and expanded at various times during the history of the federal minimum wage experience. Under the enterprise coverage test, initiated in 1961 and amended in 1966, significant expansion in FLSA coverage has occurred.[22]

THE ECONOMIC ADVISABILITY OF MINIMUM WAGE LAW

From state to state, the observer will find only minor differences in the declared purposes of minimum wage statutes. The phraseology varies, but the goal is usually described as the elimination of "oppressive wages," "unfair wages," or "unreasonable wages." In the federal statute, where the policy declaration was related to interstate commerce for constitutional purposes, the expressed goal is to prevent the instrumentalities of commerce from being used to perpetuate subminimal living standards and otherwise to unburden commerce from the effects of substandard working conditions. The philosophy that is inherent in the minimum wage laws can be paraphrased as follows: the community refuses to condone the payment of real wages below a specified level. Subminimum wages should be prohibited to protect the worker directly involved and to protect the standards of the more adequately paid worker from the competitive advantage enjoyed by the low wage employer.

---

[22] Edward C. Martin, "Extent of Coverage under FLSA as Amended in 1966," *Monthly Labor Review,* April, 1967, pp. 21–24.

The assumption underlying minimum wage legislation, of course, is that a legal wage floor will accomplish the purpose described. The economic analysis of minimum wage legislation has been concerned, for the most part, with the realism of this assumption.

The analysis of minimum wage legislation takes essentially the same form as the analysis of any other wage change that is artificially imposed. For the employer, the first effect is an increase in the amount of his money wage costs. Where the employer adjusts to a legal minimum wage by simply raising the wages of the subminimal workers to the statutory requirements, the total cost of the adjustment is determined by the number of workers affected and the difference between the legal minimum and the pre-existing wage level. In those cases where the employer attempts to maintain his occupational wage structure, the cost of adjustment may be substantially greater, since wage increases will have to be given to the more highly paid as well as to the low-wage workers.[23] In either case, the economic position of the firm has changed, and the reaction may take any one of the forms noted in Chapter 13 where the effects of collectively bargained wages were analyzed.

Briefly, the possible employer reaction to higher money wage levels may consist of any one or some combination of the following: (1) absorption of the increase out of profits, (2) passing the costs on to the consumer if the market will bear such a shift, (3) substituting machine power for labor power, (4) offsetting the cost increase by becoming more efficient, (5) discharging marginal workers whose employment cannot be maintained at the higher wage level, (6) ceasing to do business altogether.

Which of these possibilities is the most likely will depend upon the circumstances surrounded a specific minimum wage adjustment.[24] An increase in the present Wage and Hour minimum of $1.60 an hour to $1.70 would be more easily absorbed out of profits or offset by efficiency changes

---

[23] Studies by the U.S. Department of Labor show that the southern lumber and the fertilizer industries adjusted to the seventy-five cent minimum that went into effect in 1950 by raising substandard wages to exactly seventy-five cents. The result was to compress the earnings range of workers in these industries. Countrariwise, the large concentration at the seventy-five cent level did not occur in the men's dress shirt and nightwear industry where the piece rate changes made to enable the subminimum worker to earn seventy-five cents an hour also benefited the faster workers. *Monthly Labor Review,* October, 1953, pp. 1077–1081; August, 1951, pp. 166–170; January, 1951, pp. 33–37.

[24] The debate among economists over minimum wage legislation is essentially a debate over which of the alternatives noted is the most probable consequence of minimum wage law. If the assumption is made that the labor and product markets are competitive, the marginal productivity analysis can be used to show that a minimum wage law must inevitably lead to unemployment. Proponents of minimum wage law challenge the conclusion that is based upon these assumptions and are generally more sanguine about the possibilities of the fourth reaction outlined above. For a critical appraisal of minimum wage legislation see George Stigler, "The Economics of Minimum Wage Legislation," *American Economic Review,* June, 1946, pp. 358–365.

than an increase to $2.00. Substitution of machinery for labor, which might not be feasible in the face of a five cent an hour rise in wage costs, might become feasible in the event of a seventy-five cent increase. Whereas the employment effect of a modest change in the legal minimum would be extremely difficult to anticipate, a present minimum of $2.50 would unquestionably result in some unemployment.

The results of the minimum wage experience in the United States are hard to judge because so many variables other than changing legal wage standards have affected the economic environment within which the businessman makes his decisions.[25] The forty cent per hour minimum established by the 1938 Fair Labor Standards Act did not become fully effective until 1945, and by that time war-induced price and wage changes had made the legal standard obsolete. The seventy-five cent minimum went into effect on January 1, 1950; and within several months a prolonged inflation began. The subsequent price rise not only ate away much of the protection afforded by the minimum wage but also facilitated the process of shifting the cost of the adjustment to the consumer.

A comprehensive Department of Labor study was made of the economic effects of the $1.00 per hour minimum wage requirement established in 1955.[26] The results of this survey of low wage industries are by no means clear, a point that is substantiated by the opposed conclusions that have been derived from the data.[27] On the one hand, the department admitted that some loss of employment did occur as a result of the $1.00 minimum wage; on the other, it reported that the amount of labor displacement was relatively small. Most employers, when faced with higher labor costs, reviewed their operating procedures and took some action to offset the increased costs. Primary emphasis appeared to be on improvement of machinery and facilities. Although mechanization resulted in labor displacement in some cases, this was not the typical result.

The seriousness of the employment impact varied by industry. Thirty-three per cent of the employers interviewed in the seamless-hosiery mills reported discharges due to the increase in the minimum wage, whereas only 2 per cent of the employers in the fertilizer and footwear industries

---

[25] For an attempt to measure the impact of a proposed minimum wage law under a severe set of limiting assumptions see Maurice Benewitz and Robert E. Weintraub, "Employment Effects of a Local Minimum Wage," *Industrial and Labor Relations Review,* January, 1964, pp. 276–288. See also John M. Peterson, "Research Needs in Minimum Wage Theory," *Southern Economic Journal,* July, 1962, pp. 1–9, for a discussion of the deficiencies in existing minimum wage studies.

[26] "Plant Adjustments to the $1.00 Minimum Wage," *Monthly Labor Review,* October, 1958, pp. 1137–1142.

[27] See, for example, Benewitz and Weintraub, *op. cit.,* pp. 279–280, and Richard E. Lester, *Economics of Labor* (New York: The Macmillan Company, 1964), pp. 510–527.

reported such discharges. Changes in aggregate employment ranged from a 15 per cent decrease in the sawmill industry to a slight increase in the processed waste mills in the first two years after the imposition of the $1.00 minimum. Undoubtedly, however, factors other than the minimum wage influenced the variation in employment.

The debate over the economic wisdom of minimum wage legislation is a continuing one. To date, the dire predictions of large-scale unemployment and economic dislocation have not materialized. In part, this is due to the fact that the legal standards have fallen short of guaranteeing a wage necessary to meet the costs of a minimum family budget for decent living. As long as the minimum wage laws do nothing more than "tidy up the ragged lower edge of the wage structure"[28] the probability of such laws' creating serious economic problems will be small and limited to marginal firms and marginal workers. It may be unrealistic, however, to expect more than this from minimum wage legislation. Low wages are found in the highly competitive and relatively inefficient industries. Although a minimum wage law can limit the degree of worker exploitation in some of these industries, it is not addressed to the fundamental causes of low wages. In the long run, a meaningful improvement in the living standards of the low-wage worker can come about only from productivity improvement in the low-wage industries or worker movement to areas of greater economic promise.

SUMMARY

Progress in wage and hour legislation in the United States was tied up with questions of constitutionality for many years. Originally the state and federal courts took the position that such legislation interfered with an individual's freedom to contract. This position was gradually relaxed, and by 1917 the Supreme Court had held that a state government could limit the hours of work of men and women in non-hazardous as well as hazardous occupations. The courts were more reluctant to accept the legal validity of minimum wage legislation; and not until 1937, and after much legal conjecture by the courts, were such laws accepted as a valid exercise of the police power of the states. The federal Fair Labor Standards Act was enacted in 1938 under the authority of the commerce clause and sustained by the Supreme Court in 1941, thus ending a long fight over the right of both state and national governments to exercise controls in the wage and hour areas.

---

[28] Lloyd G. Reynolds, *Labor Economics and Labor Relations* (Englewood Cliffs, N.J.: Prentice-Hall, Inc., 1954), p. 665.

The Fair Labor Standards Act originally established a twenty-five cent per hour minimum wage, and successive amendments of the law have increased the federal minimum to $1.60 an hour. More than half the states have established legal minimum wages, but in many cases the minima have become obsolete and afford little protection to workers.

The economic advisability of minimum wage legislation has been a controversial issue, and opponents of such laws have argued that they will cause unemployment. Because of the difficulty of separating the effects of a minimum wage law from other variables affecting employment, available data provide no conclusive answer to the question. The aggregate level of unemployment, however, does not appear to have been seriously influenced by the wage minimums that have been established. The main effect of the laws has probably been that of providing a small measure of protection to workers in the low wage industries. It may be unreasonable, however, to expect more than this from minimum wage legislation, since such legislation is not addressed to the fundamental causes of low wages.

QUESTIONS

1. Describe the original Supreme Court objection to the regulation of working hours. What legal reasoning did the court use as it shifted to an acceptance of such regulation? Cite the leading cases in which the court upheld the constitutionality of the regulation of working hours.
2. Compare the Supreme Court decisions in *Adkins* v. *Children's Hospital* and *West Coast Hotel* v. *Parrish*.
3. In your opinion, have the minimum wage levels established by the Fair Labor Standards Act been too low, too high, or just about right? Defend your position.
4. Obtain a copy of your state minimum wage law. Describe the coverage and the standards established. Do you regard your state law as adequate?
5. What basic arguments are usually raised against protective wage legislation? Does the available evidence support or reject these arguments?
6. Is it possible for a minimum wage law to be too high? Explain.
7. The 1963 "equal pay" amendment to the FLSA requires that women be paid the same as men when the job requirements are equal. In your opinion, will the amendment have any consequences other than an increase in female wage rates?
8. What special problems, if any, are involved in bringing farm employees under the coverage of the federal minimum wage law?

SELECTED READINGS

CHRISTENSON, CARROL L., and MYREN, RICHARD A. *Wage Policy under the Walsh-Healey Public Contracts Act: A Critical Review*. Bloomington, Indiana: Indiana University Press, 1966.

COHEN, SANFORD. *Labor Law*. Columbus, Ohio: Charles E. Merrill Books, Inc., 1964. Chaps. 2–5.

LESTER, RICHARD A. *Economics of Labor*. New York: The Macmillan Company, 1964. Chap. 16.

MILLIS, HARRY A., and MONTGOMERY, ROYAL E. *Labor's Progress and Problems*. New York: McGraw-Hill Book Company, 1938. Chaps. 6, 9.

STIGLER, GEORGE. "The Economics of Minimum Wage Legislation," *American Economic Review,* June, 1946, pp. 358–365.

PART SIX

THE PROBLEM
OF ECONOMIC
INSECURITY

CHAPTER 20

Approaches to Economic Security

TWENTIETH CENTURY MAN, WITH ALL HIS SCIENTIFIC AND SOCIAL KNOWL-
edge, has not been able to eliminate the economic insecurity that has
plagued mankind through the ages. Part of the present-day problem results
from the uneven distribution of the resources of the world. In the underdeveloped areas, touched only lightly by industrialization, the economic
burden is almost the same as it has been for centuries. Malnutrition, poverty, and disease produce an insecurity that is but partly described by
statistics of high infant mortality rates, short life expectancy, and extremely
low per capita income. In the technologically advanced nations, economic
insecurity takes new forms that reflect the influence of the very industrialization that has been responsible for the rising living standards enjoyed in the
past 150 years. In addition to the historical causes of major economic
dislocation—war, plague, flood, drought, etc.—the industrial society is
forced to address itself to such problems as mass unemployment, industrial
injury, and a variety of insecurities that are associated with old age.

From a labor market standpoint, economic insecurity may result from
certain major interruptions in the earning power of an individual or from
the fact that a person is denied, for one reason or another, access to the
range of job opportunities that are open to others. Historically, public policy
in the United States has been preoccupied with the first of the causes
described above and long standing programs provide some degree of protection for employed persons who suffer loss of income from experiences
such as industrial injury, job loss, or forced retirement due to age. These

programs are clearly inappropriate for those whose labor market participation is sporadic and ineffective and, in recent years, novel and experimental efforts have been instituted in an effort to relieve the insecurity of those who subsist on the margin of the labor market, if, indeed, they participate in the market at all.

SOCIAL SECURITY

The concept of social security has acquired a number of different meanings. In the broadest sense it is descriptive of the total goal of economic security and of all positive efforts to achieve this goal. Under this conception, measures such as farm price supports, aid to education, school lunch programs, and TVA can be regarded as means to the end of social security. In the popular sense, the term "social security" is frequently used as a synonym of the old age insurance section of the Social Security Act of 1935. Thus, retired persons drawing benefits under the act usually refer to their "social security checks." Among many students of labor legislation in the United States, "social security" has come to have a more specific connotation. It is *the objective or goal of easing the economic burdens caused by industrial injury, unemployment, old age, disability, and, to a lesser extent, medical expense.* In this chapter, we shall follow this last usage.

Social security is a goal that can be approached by different paths. The characteristics of the paths that are most appropriate at any time are determined, to a large extent, by the nature of the forces that are responsible for insecurity. One writer has described the social security of the pioneer as "the musket hanging over the fireplace." This is a far cry from the comprehensive and technically involved present-day programs, but it is well to keep in mind that only a hundred years or so separate the "musket" and the contemporary approaches to security. In the United States, systematized efforts to deal with economic insecurity have occurred only in the present century—for the most part within the past forty years. The major technique used has been social insurance. For areas of insecurity beyond the reach of the social insurance programs, both the federal government and the states have relied primarily upon public assistance. The basic characteristics of these techniques are described below.

Public Assistance

Public assistance has been defined as *financial aid extended to needy persons in their own homes or places of residence.*[1] As an approach to

---

[1] Hilary Leyendecker, *Problems and Policy in Public Assistance* (New York: Harper & Row, Publishers, 1955), p. 2.

economic security, it is relatively new. For more than a hundred years, aid to the needy in the United States was patterned after one or more features of the Elizabethan poor laws. Relief was considered to be primarily a local responsibility, the main cause of personal destitution was thought to be the shortcomings of the individual in need, recipients of aid were stigmatized as paupers, and the public or private poorhouse was the usual fate of the destitute. There was strong opposition to outright money grants to needy persons, since it was thought that such persons were more likely to squander the money for non-essentials than to make an intelligent disposition of the funds. As late as 1929, institutional care was the typical method of providing poor relief in rural communities. Non-institutional relief had come to be more widely used in the larger cities since expanding populations made it difficult to provide institutional facilities to accommodate all the needy.[2]

The beginnings of public assistance programs, as we know them today, occurred in the early years of the present century. Until the 1930 depression, however, state and local assistance was meager and ineffective.

The large-scale destitution in the 1930's forced a reconsideration of fundamental tenets of poor relief philosophy. Reliance upon the local units of government was unrealistic when such units were unable to meet the costs of providing basic services. At a time when the local units were being deluged by claims for relief, the mainstay of local government revenues, the property tax, was producing a sharply declining yield. The widely held notion that indigency was primarily a result of personal shortcomings was also shaken. A "personal" theory of poverty did not sit well in a society where economic distress was so widespread.

The federal government assumed major responsibility for public aid during the 1930's. Federal grants to the states for general public assistance began in 1932, and federal work programs were started in 1933. After the Social Security Act was passed in 1935, the federal government withdrew its financial aid for general public assistance and provided grants-in-aid to the states for the assistance of special categories of needy persons. Work programs for the unemployed were maintained and not completely terminated until 1943. The assistance programs initiated by the Social Security Act have been continued and liberalized substantially since 1935. The various programs, although administered by the state governments, remain strongly influenced by the characteristics of the categorical grants-in-aid.

The public assistance titles of the Social Security Act of 1935 are devices that enable the federal government to use its resources to aid the states in establishing and maintaining programs for the relief of the needy aged; the blind; dependent children; and, since 1950, the permanently and totally disabled. Primary responsibility for starting and developing a program rests

---

[2] *Ibid.,* p. 37.

with the individual state government, but a state that wants to receive federal funds must devise a plan that meets certain conditions stipulated in the federal law.[3] The conditions imposed by federal law leave the state much leeway for decisions as to administrative techniques, eligibility, and amounts of aid to be granted. The state programs, consequently, differ considerably, especially in the matter of maximum payments.

The formula for federal participation has been changed a number of times, but the principle that the federal government will pay a specified proportion of the cost of assistance and administration has been retained. The different formulas in effect for aid to the aged and the blind since 1935 are outlined below:

1935   One-half of individual grant up to a maximum of $30 per month. (Under this formula, the federal government paid $15 to a state granting a $30 pension. States granting larger pensions would still receive $15 grants-in-aid, whereas states with smaller maximums would receive one-half of the amounts granted.)

1939   One-half of the individual grant up to a maximum of $40 per month.

1946   Two-thirds of the first $15 of the average monthly payment and one-half of the remainder up to an average monthly grant of $45.

1948   Three-fourths of the first $20 of the average monthly payment one-half of the remainder up to a maximum of $50 per month.

1950   Four-fifths of the first $25 of the average monthly payment, one-half of the next $10, and one-third of the remainder up to a maximum of $50 per month.

1952   Four-fifths of the first $25 and one-half of the remainder up to a maximum of $55 per month.

1956   Four-fifths of the first $30 of the average monthly payment and one-half of the remainder up to a maximum of $60 per month.

---

[3] In order to qualify for federal grants-in-aid a state plan must meet the following requirements, among others: (1) the plan must be state-wide in operation; (2) the state must participate in the plan financially; (3) a single state agency must administer or supervise the administration of the plan; (4) information about recipients of assistance must be restricted except for closely circumscribed conditions of access; (5) opportunities for a hearing must be provided for claimants whose applications for assistance are denied; (6) reports required by the Social Security Administration must be submitted; (7) in determining need, the state agency shall take into consideration the income and resources of the claimant except for the exemption of $50 a month of earned income by the blind; (8) states may not provide more than one form of public assistance to a person concurrently. State plans may not include age requirements of more than sixty-five years in the old age assistance program, citizenship requirements barring a citizen of the United States who is otherwise eligible for aid, and residence requirements more restrictive than the maximums stated in the Social Security Act. The Supreme Court decision in *Shapiro* v. *Thompson*, April 21, 1969, nullified one year residency requirements for public assistance in a number of states. In a 6–3 decision the Court ruled that state laws conditioning public assistance on one year's residence within a state violated the Fourteenth Amendment's equal protection clause by infringing on the constitutional right to travel.

1958 Four-fifths of the first $30 of the average monthly payment and 50 to 65 per cent of the remainder up to a maximum of $65 per month.
1961 Four-fifths of the first $31 of the average monthly payment and 50 to 65 per cent of the remainder up to a maximum of $66 per month.
1962 Twenty-nine dollars of the first $35 of the average monthly payment and 50 to 65 per cent of the remainder up to a maximum of $70 per month.
1965 Thirty-one dollars of the first $37 of the average monthly payment and 50 to 65 per cent of the remainder up to a maximum of $75 per month.[4]

The reader will note the change in the character of the formula that occurred in 1958. Until that time the same formula for federal participation applied to all states. Since that date the federal share has been more liberal for the poorer states. For states with lower per capita incomes the federal share of the "remainder" is equal or close to 65 per cent, whereas the share for states with higher per capita incomes is equal or close to 50 per cent. The new formula, in other words, represents an attempt to equalize the benefit structure among states by redistributing costs on the basis of ability to pay.[5]

In 1965, Congress provided, in Title XIX of the Social Security Act, for grants to states for medical assistance. This title established a single medical assistance program to replace the separate programs for meeting costs of medical care under the different assistance categories. Under Title XIX, all persons receiving assistance for basic maintenance under the several public assistance titles must be included in the new programs. States may also include in their programs persons who are able to provide for their own maintenance but whose income and resources are not sufficient to defray their medical care costs.

When the Social Security Act was passed in 1935, there was a widely held belief that the public assistance features of the law would decline in importance over time. The logic was that the social insurance programs

[4] States with a medical assistance program under title XIX of the Social Security Act may apply, as an alternative to the above formula, the federal medical assistance percentage (as promulgated for the State by the Secretary of Health, Education, and Welfare) to total money payments to recipients if this procedure yields more Federal funds than the regular formula. The medical assistance matching formula varies with state per capita income and ranges from 50 to 83 per cent of state payments.

[5] The federal share of the remainder equals 100 per cent minus the state per cent which is derived by dividing the square of the state per capita income by the square of the national per capita income and multiplying by 50 per cent. For a complete description of the formula see the 1958 statistical supplement of the *Social Security Bulletin*. See also Robert J. Myers, *Social Insurance and Allied Government Programs* (Homewood, Ill.: Richard D. Irwin, Inc., 1965), pp. 16–20.

would become increasingly effective as more persons established their eligibility for benefits; simultaneously, the end of the depression would witness a large decline in the number of those made destitute by lack of employment opportunities. Although coverage under the social insurance programs has been expanded and the depression ended long ago, the number of persons receiving public assistance and the amounts paid for assistance benefits have remained high. When the Social Security grants-in-aid began in 1936, about 1.1 million persons received aid under the provisions of the Old Age Assistance program. In 1967, an average of about 2.1 million aged persons received assistance grants each month. Total expenditures for old age assistance were $155 million in 1936 and over $2 billion in 1967.

Among the several programs, expansion, measured in terms of aid recipients, has been greatest in the Aid to Families with Dependent Children category. In 1940, there were 1.3 million recipients of such aid. By 1967 the number had increased to 5.3 million. The continuing importance of public assistance has led to a re-evaluation of the economic security problem and generated severe criticism of the public assistance technique. Various alternatives which have been suggested are discussed at a later point in this chapter.

Social Insurance

The social insurance programs currently in effect in the United States represent attempts to deal with various causes of economic insecurity by providing insurance against them. In practice, the programs differ considerably from commercial insurance, but they retain enough of the insurance idea to be basically different from public assistance. Possibly the best way to describe the social insurance method is to compare it with both public assistance and commercial insurance.

Under public assistance, payments to individuals are made because of *demonstrated need;* under social insurance, payments are made because of *presumptive need.* Assistance grants, in other words, are given to persons who can demonstrate to an appropriate government agency that they lack sufficient means to meet basic living requirements. The assumption underlying social insurance is that persons in certain categories—e.g., the unemployed, the aged—are very likely to need money income, and a person who has established his eligibility for insurance benefits is not required to show a condition of need.

Benefit levels under public assistance are determined on an individual basis, whereas benefits under social insurance are based upon assumptions of average need. The assistance recipient gets a money payment that is larger or smaller depending upon his over-all economic condition. Under social insurance, benefit standards are established so as to provide what are assumed to be the minimum needs of persons in specific categories. Persons in quite different economic circumstances, then, might receive equal benefits.[6]

Payments under social insurance are made to individuals as a matter of right, since the beneficiary must meet pre-established requirements to be eligible for payments. The requirements may consist of contributions deducted from pay, as in the case of Old Age and Survivors Insurance, or a work history of covered employment, as in the case of unemployment compensation. In either situation, the individual has a right to a benefit because of his own or his employer's contribution to an insurance fund. Payments under public assistance, as already noted, are made solely because of established need. One of the strongest arguments for expansion of social insurance, incidentally, is that the earned benefit removes the stigma of charity so frequently associated with the assistance payment.

The extent to which social insurance approximates the methods of private commercial insurance provides a good measure of the difference between assistance and social insurance. The purposes of social and commercial insurance are sufficiently different, however, so that some departure from strict insurance principles is essential if the goals of social insurance are to be served. It is not inaccurate, then, to think of social insurance as a halfway point between the public assistance and private insurance approaches to security.

Private insurance is based on the assumption that the occurrence of various hazards can be predicted with a reasonable degree of accuracy. With accuracy in prediction it becomes possible for large numbers of persons to insure against a hazard by paying premiums that amount to only a small fraction of the loss caused by the eventuation of the hazard. Thus, you may be able to buy $20,000 worth of fire insurance for $100 because experience shows that only one out of perhaps 200 houses will suffer fire damage each year.

Social insurance attempts to provide insurance against economic hazards and is similar to commercial insurance in that it tries to cover the losses of the few by contributions from the many. The parallel between the two types of insurance cannot be carried too far, however. There is a qualitative difference in the risks to which each is addressed; and since one pur-

---

[6] There are a number of exceptions to the general principle stated above. The great leveller in public assistance is the existence of a maximum benefit. Since persons need not be totally destitute to qualify for the maximum payment, individuals with different degrees of need will receive maximum, and hence equal, benefits. Contrariwise, some deference to need is made in certain of the social insurance programs. The unemployment compensation laws in a number of states, for instance, provide additional benefits to unemployed persons with dependents.

pose of social insurance is to provide a minimum of income to those who are most likely to need it, the relationship between size of premium and size of benefit usually is more favorable for the low-income worker.[7]

A number of technical differences between private and social insurance can be identified, but it is sufficient to note here that there is a looser relationship between premiums and benefits under social insurance, that participation in social insurance is compulsory for those covered by the law, and that the risks covered by social insurance are not easily predicted in most cases. The details of the individual social insurance programs will be examined in the next two chapters.

Proposals for Income Guarantees

The architects of the American social security system visualized the social insurance programs as the major line of defense against poverty with public assistance serving as a backstop to alleviate the needs of those not covered by insurance. As noted above, it was anticipated that the role of public assistance would dwindle over the years as more and more persons established their eligibility under the insurance programs.

The original hope, unfortunately, has not been realized. Although social insurance has made significant contributions to the economic well being of millions of persons it has proved to be a leaky defense against poverty. The major reason perhaps, is that large numbers of the present day poor participate sporadically in the labor market and, thus, are unable to establish eligibility for social insurance benefits. A second reason is that benefit levels under social insurance, particularly for the aged, are often inadequate and persons with no income other than their insurance benefits frequently fall into a poverty status.

The anticipated decline in the role of public assistance has simply not occurred. Total expenditures under public assistance were about $1 billion in 1940 and over $5 billion in 1969. During these years, assistance recipients under all programs rose from 4.6 million to over 8 million persons. Experience under the different programs has varied considerably, however. The number of persons receiving Old Age Assistance grants, for example, has remained relatively constant while the number receiving help under the Aid to Families with Dependent Children category has grown substantially.

The expansion of public assistance has been associated with a rising level of criticism of its effectiveness as an anti-poverty measure. The major attacks against the system have expressed concern about the mounting burden

---

[7] For a good discussion of the differences between private and social insurance see Myers, *op. cit.,* pp. 6–10.

of welfare costs, inequities in the assistance program, and aspects of the administrative process.

The dimensions of the assistance burden can be suggested by recent New York City experience which, although extreme, is illustrative of the general problem in larger metropolitan centers. The welfare budget in New York City is $1.4 billion. About one million persons are on the welfare rolls and an average of 14 thousand persons are added to the rolls each month.[8]

Inequities in the public assistance program include the range of benefit levels among states ($8.40 per month for a needy child in Mississippi as against $60.75 in New York), the limited reach of assistance (only about a fourth of those with incomes below the poverty line receive assistance benefits), and the level of benefits which usually fall well below a minimum subsistence budget. On the administrative side, 90 per cent of the 50,000 case workers engaged in the administration of public assistance have had no training in social work.[9] Most of the case worker's time is spent in determining the eligibility of assistance claimants and investigating the behavior of aid recipients. His case load is heavy, his pay relatively low, and his relationship with the client more in the nature of an adversary than a social worker.

The obvious shortcomings of public assistance have led to a host of proposals for substitute arrangements. Those that have attracted the most attention are various plans for income guarantees which would use the federal personal income tax as a device for paying subsidies to poor households.

A confusing variety of "negative income tax" plans have been presented, but all specify a minimum income level to be guaranteed to every family with the minimum adjusted according to family size. On the basis of information submitted on a tax form, families would be differentiated as those with "positive incomes" and those with "negative incomes" or incomes below a designated limit. Families in the first group would make tax payments to the government as they do now while the second group would receive payments from the government.

Certain of the proposed plans provide for a full guarantee of a specified income level while others would guarantee a fractional amount. If, for

[8] Julius Horwitz, "In One Month, 50,000 Persons Were Added to the City's Welfare Rolls," *The New York Times Magazine,* January 26, 1969, p. 22. In 1967, Congress "revolted" against the rising level of expenditures under the program of Aid to Families with Dependent Children by enacting a number of restrictive amendments. The most important of these were a freeze on federal grants and a provision to force AFDC parents to take jobs or training that would qualify them for jobs. Under the freeze, the federal government will provide support only to a proportion of the children under age 18 within a state, that proportion being determined by the proportion supported under AFDC during a 1968 base date period.

[9] Clair Wilcox, *Toward Social Welfare,* (Homewood, Illinois: Richard D. Irwin, Inc., 1969), p. 218.

FIGURE 23

TOTAL PAYMENTS TO PUBLIC ASSISTANCE RECIPIENTS

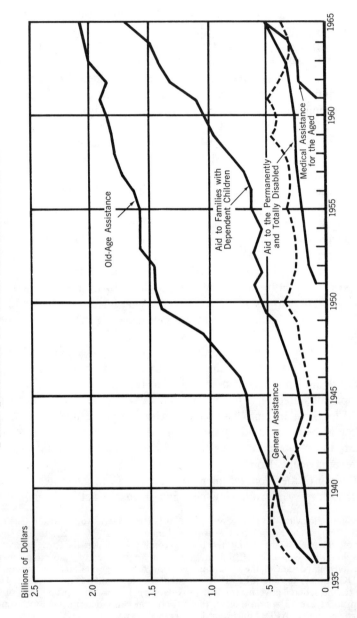

Source: U.S. Department of Health, Education, and Welfare

example, the income level for a family of four is set at $3000 per year, the full guarantee plan would provide whatever subsidy necessary to bring family income to $3000. A family with no income at all, thus, would receive a payment of $3000. Under the fractional proposals, the maximum subsidy would be less than the designated upper limit of the range of poverty incomes. In this case the family of four with no other income might receive a maximum payment on the order of $1500.

The plan proposed by Professor Edward Schwartz is a widely publicized version of a fully guaranteed minimum income.[10] Schwartz who argues that the right to a livelihood should be regarded as a basic constitutional right, suggests different possible standards for incomes guarantees ranging from $3000 a year to $5000 with some variations from these standards on the basis of family size. Under the $3000 annual guarantee, a family of four with no other income would receive the full amount. If the family had $1000 of other income, the allowance would drop to $2399 making total family income equal to $3399. With $2000 of other income the allowance drops to $1699 and continues to decline until "other income" reaches the range $4000–4499. At this point the allowance becomes zero but the family would pay no tax. Beyond $4500, the regular tax rates would become effective.[11]

To illustrate the character of fractional guarantee plans, two out of the many versions will be described briefly at this point.

Under Professor Milton Friedman's negative income tax proposal the amount of subsidy is derived on the basis of a relationship between the total of a tax reporting unit's exemptions and deductions under the federal personal income tax and the unit's gross taxable income.[12] In cases where exemptions plus deductions exceed taxable income, the reporting unit would receive a subsidy equal to 50 per cent of the difference. Thus, in the case of a family of two parents and two young children the value of exemptions and deductions would be $3000.[13] If the family has no income, the subsidy would be half of the deficit or $1500. If the same family has an income of $1000, the deficit would be $2000 and the subsidy would be $1000. Total family income, thus, would be $1500 in the first example and $2000 in the second.

Professor James Tobin's scheme for income supplements is similar to Friedman's in that it retains the fractional guarantee principle but different

---

[10] Edward E. Schwartz, "A Way to End the Means Test," *Social Work,* July, 1964, pp. 3–12.

[11] For another version of a fully guaranteed minimum income plan see Robert Theobold, *Free Men and Free Markets* (New York: Clarkson N. Potter, 1963).

[12] Milton Friedman, *Capitalism and Freedom* (Chicago: The University of Chicago Press, 1962), chap. 12.

[13] The family in the example could claim four exemptions at $600 each, and a standard deduction of $300 for the person filing the return plus $100 for each additional person in the household.

in that payments are based upon flat allowances rather than the value of unused deductions and exemptions in the income tax.[14] Under his proposal, each person in a tax reporting unit would be eligible for an allowance of, say, $400. Using, once again, the example of a four person family, allowances would total $1600 and this would be the family income, if it had no other source of support. Up to a point income earned would be offset against the allowance at a flat rate of 33⅓ per cent. Thus, if earnings were $1000, one-third of this amount would be offset against the allowance and total family income would be $2667. Under the facts of our example, the value of the allowance would become zero when family income reaches $4800. After $4800, no allowances would be paid but the initial allowance of $1600 would continue to be offset against the 33⅓ per cent tax due on other income. At a point slightly above $6000 of annual income, the regular schedule of tax rates would apply.

Pros and Cons of the Negative Income Tax

Usual arguments in favor of a negative income tax are that income would be transferred to all poverty families instead of the 25 per cent now assisted, that a simple income test of poverty would replace the demeaning means test, and that a single program would replace the maze of programs now operating under public assistance.

A basic problem associated with all minimum income guarantees, as Hildebrand has noted, is how to relate earned income to the guaranteed amount.[15] The large number of negative income tax proposals extant, in fact, reflect the efforts of different people to wrestle with this very problem.

When the guarantee level is relatively high, as in the Schwartz plan, a high offset, or reduction in the allowance, must be applied when income is earned to avoid the problem of paying subsidies to those not in a poverty status. Schwartz accomplishes this through effective "tax" rates of 60 to 70 per cent on the first several thousand dollars of earned income. This approach, however, raises the serious question of work disincentive: a nonworking person would receive a payment of $3000 while a person earning $1000 at a job would have a total income of $3,333. To remove the disincentive, it would be necessary to permit the worker to keep a larger part of his earnings without offset against his subsidy but this would accentuate the problem of limiting payments to those below the poverty line. The Tobin plan, through the relatively low 33⅓ per cent offset rate, reduces

---

[14] James Tobin "On Improving the Economic Status of the Negro," *Daedalus,* Fall, 1965, pp. 878–898.

[15] George H. Hildebrand, *Poverty, Income Maintenance, and the Negative Income Tax* (Ithaca, N.Y.: New York State School of Industrial and Labor Relations, 1967), p. 44.

the disincentive to work, although it becomes necessary under his scheme to extend the subsidy well into the range of non-poverty incomes.

Questions about the money cost and the general effectiveness of the negative income tax have also been raised. The estimate of cost for the Schwartz plan with a full guarantee of $3000 of income per family unit each year is $11 billion. The Friedman and Tobin plans would cost considerably less but under their fractional guarantees, many families would remain in poverty status. It is doubtful that they could fully replace the public assistance programs and one of the purported advantages of the negative income tax, consequently, would be lost.

Many who are skeptical about the viability of a cash transfer through a negative income tax argue for a reconstruction of the public assistance system. With nationally standardized minimum payments, a uniform and simplified means test, and federal support for general rather than categorical assistance, it is contended that the assistance system could be made viable without the complications of leakages to the non-poor that might plague the operations of a negative income tax.

QUESTIONS

1. List the differences between the public assistance, social insurance, and private insurance approaches to economic security.

2. What are the major flaws of the public assistance program? In what ways, would a negative income tax be superior to public assistance as a mechanism for transferring income to the poor?

3. Assume that the head of a family of four receives $2500 per year under a negative income tax plan. He receives an offer of part-time work that would pay $1000 a year. Under the tax plan, however, this would reduce his subsidy by $500 making his total income $3000. In your opinion would the individual accept or refuse the job offer?

SELECTED READINGS

HILDEBRAND, GEORGE H. *Poverty, Income Maintenance, and the Negative Income Tax.* Ithaca, New York: New York State School of Industrial and Labor Relations, 1967.

TOBIN, JAMES. "Raising the Incomes of the Poor" in Gordon, Kermit (ed.). *Agenda for the Nation.* Garden City, New York: Doubleday and Co., Inc. 1968. Chap. 3.

WILCOX, CLAIR. *Toward Social Welfare.* Homewood, Illinois: Richard D. Irwin, Inc., 1969. Chaps. 6, 14, 15.

CHAPTER 21

Social Insurance Programs

IN THIS AND THE FOLLOWING CHAPTER, THE NEED FOR THE SEVERAL social insurance programs will be analyzed and the details of the programs presented. The Workmen's Compensation and Unemployment Compensation laws will be treated in the present chapter.

INDUSTRIAL INJURY

The worker of today is far less likely to be injured on the job than was his predecessor of fifty or even twenty-five years ago; yet about 2 million disabling work injuries occur each year. In 1963, 1.9 million of these injuries resulted in temporary total disability, 84,000 in permanent impairment and 14,000 in death.[1] The extent of work injury can be statistically dramatized in numerous ways, but perhaps one example will suffice. During the three year Korean War period, a total of 34,000 soldiers were reported killed or missing in action. In the same years over 48,000 civilians were killed on the job.

Work injury data are too fragmentary to permit an accurate computation of the total money loss involved. The size of the national loss, however, was suggested by the Secretary of Labor when he pointed out that work injuries in 1955 had resulted in a loss of 193 million man-days of output—enough

---

[1] "Preliminary Estimates of Work Injuries in 1963," *Monthly Labor Review,* May, 1964, p. 530.

to produce 100 million refrigerators, or 26,000 jet bombers, or a million six-room houses.[2] Man days of disability resulting from work injuries in 1963 were the equivalent of a year's full-time employment for about 550,000 workers.

Prevention is the ideal answer to the problem of industrial injury, and in the past fifty years much progress has been made in this direction. According to Bureau of Labor Statistics data, the injury frequency rate—the average number of disabling injuries for each million man-hours worked—has declined in manufacturing employments from 42.2 in 1926 to about 12 in recent years. As encouraging as this record may be, the frequency rate is still much above the level of five which many safety engineers consider good.

What is sometimes referred to as the "safety movement" began in the United States in the early years of the present century. Since that time non-profit organizations, such as the National Safety Council, and many progressive leaders in the ranks of industry and labor have worked diligently to make work less hazardous. Since 1911, when the "Wisconsin Plan" was enacted, about thirty-five states have enacted legislation giving a state agency flexible powers to develop and issue regulations in the field of industrial health and safety. The record of the state agencies is mixed, however; and although effective work has been done in some jurisdictions, the old problem of the underpaid, understaffed, and sometimes politically corrupt inspection bureau has minimized the contribution to safety in a number of the states. Eleven states make no provision at all for factory inspection.

Accomplishments in the area of industrial safety have been considerable, but much remains to be done. It is not likely that work accidents and occupational diseases will ever be eliminated *in toto*, however. This fact leads to the question of what social provision should be made for those who suffer income loss and incur medical expense as a result of a work-produced disability.

The Origin of Workmen's Compensation Laws

Workmen's compensation is the branch of social insurance that attempts to provide protection against loss from industrial injury or occupational disease. Although it is the oldest form of social insurance in the United States, workmen's compensation has not been studied as intensively as the other types.[3] In recent years, however, the defects of prevailing compensa-

---

[2] U.S. Department of Labor, Bureau of Labor Statistics, *The President's Conference on Occupational Safety* (Bulletin 187), p. 4.

[3] The relative neglect of the workmen's compensation laws may have been due in part to the fact that the attentions of persons interested in social security were drawn to the exciting developments in the area of unemployment compensation and old age insurance that occurred during the 1930's.

tion procedures have become more manifest, and students of social insurance have redirected their attentions to this problem area.

Before the enactment of the workmen's compensation laws, the recourse of the worker injured on the job was to file suit against the employer unless the latter voluntarily agreed to recompense him. Voluntary settlements were rare, however, since the common law had developed in such a way as to give the defendant in the industrial injury suit the more favorable legal position.

Under the common law, the employer or master was responsible when injury to others resulted from his personal negligence. The doctrine of *respondeat superior* also placed the burden of responsibility upon the employer when injury to third persons resulted from the negligence of his workers, since, theoretically, at least, the master controlled the acts of his employees. Changes in the common law that occurred during the nineteenth century made it much more difficult to prove negligence on the part of the employer and also made the rule of *respondeat superior* inapplicable to a large number of employees. The changes consisted of three common law principles that were sufficiently developed by the year 1900 to provide employers with strong defenses against claims for compensation. These were (1) the fellow servant doctrine, (2) assumption of risk, and (3) contributory negligence.

The employer, thus, was not liable if injury resulted from the negligence of a fellow worker of the injured employee, or if the injured person had voluntarily taken a job that was known to be dangerous, or if the injured worker was himself wholly or partly responsible for the accident that had occurred. Under the common law, then, it had become extremely difficult for injured workers to receive compensation in a period when rapid industrialization was accompanied by a significant increase in the amount of work injury and when employers were much less concerned with the prevention of accidents than they are today.

The obvious inequities of the law resulted in a search for remedial measures. Between 1895 and 1910, most of the states enacted some type of employer's liability law; and in 1908 the federal *Employer's Liability Act* was passed to provide protection for employees of common carriers engaged in interstate commerce. These laws differed in detail, but they can be summarized as a modification of the common law in favor of the employee.[4]

---

[4] Indiana, for instance, made contributory negligence on the part of the plaintiff an affirmative defense to be pleaded and proved by the employer. Ohio adopted a rule of proportional negligence under which the relative negligence of employer and employee was to be determined and the amount of damages was to be adjusted according to the proportion of negligence attributed to the employer. For a summary of the state employers' library laws see Walter A. Dodd, *Administration of Workmen's Compensation* (New York: The Commonwealth Fund, 1936), pp. 13–16.

Although an improvement over the earlier common law, the employer liability acts were unsatisfactory as solutions to the problems, since it remained necessary for employees to resort to court action and to prove fault on the part of the employer.

By 1916, thirty-one states and the federal government had appointed fact-finding bodies to study the effectiveness of employer's liability and to make legislative recommendations. The sense of the various studies was that (1) injured workers received inadequate compensation, (2) the legal processes operated so slowly as to impose serious hardship upon the injured and their families, and (3) the law requiring a show of fault bred antagonism between employer and employee.[5]

The widespread awareness of the inadequacies of the employers' liability laws contributed to the success of a movement to deal with the problem of industrial injury in a fundamentally different way. In the four-year period starting with 1910, twenty-two states enacted workmen's compensation laws. Subsequently the remaining jurisdictions passed similar laws, so that at the present time all fifty states and Puerto Rico have some form of compensation law.[6] Civil employees of the federal government and public employees of the District of Columbia are covered by the Federal Employees' Compensation Act; and another national law, the Longshoremen and Harbor Workers' Compensation Act, covers longshoremen in the United States and private employees in the District of Columbia.[7]

Workmen's compensation differs from the law of employer liability in several important respects. Under the former type of law, an injured employee is considered to have a right to compensation regardless of who is at fault in a particular accident. As a matter of public policy, the cost of compensating the employee is placed upon the employer, not because the latter is negligent, but because industrial injury is considered to be a social cost properly borne by industry. Another important difference centers upon the philosophy of benefit amounts. Under workmen's compensation, the money award to the injured employee does not depend upon the judgment of a court but is determined by a fixed scale of benefits. How much a worker gets depends on the degree of disability suffered and the amount previously earned by the injured employee. These and other aspects of the workmen's compensation laws will be examined in greater detail in the following section.

---

[5] *Ibid.*, pp. 16–26. Investigators in New York State found the following record of compensation to dependents of married men killed in work accidents in Erie County in 1907 and 1908: nothing in thirty-eight cases, $100 or less in nine cases, $101 to $500 in thirty-four cases, $501 to $2,000 in fourteen cases, and over $2,000 in eight cases. These data are representative of the findings in other states.

[6] The last state to enact a workmen's compensation law was Mississippi in 1948.

[7] The coverage of longshoremen by federal rather than state law resulted from a Supreme Court decision that barred longshoremen from state coverage.

The Details of Workmen's Compensation Laws

The compensation laws of the various jurisdictions differ considerably in their technical characteristics and in the amount of protection provided for the injured. In the following subsections the more important characteristics of the laws will be summarized.

At the present time, the workmen's compensation laws are elective in twenty-four states and compulsory in the others. The federal laws are compulsory. In the states where the law is elective, employers have the privilege of refusing to be covered by the law. Usually the elective laws deprive the employer choosing non-coverage of his common law defenses in the event of a damage suit.[8]

Insurance Features. With only minor exceptions, workmen's compensation benefits in the United States are financed exclusively by employers. The state and territorial jurisdictions, again with rare exceptions, require that employers demonstrate their capacity to meet the obligations that may arise under the compensation laws. This requirement may be met by insuring with a state fund or with a private carrier, or by furnishing proof of ability to self-insure. Seven states and Puerto Rico maintain exclusive state funds, which means that in these jurisdictions covered employers have no option other than that of insuring with the state fund. Eleven states maintain competitive funds, whereby employers may meet their legal obligations by insuring either with the state fund or with private carriers, or by carrying their own insurance. States other than those with exclusive or competitive funds require that the insurance obligation be met through private insurance or self-insurance.

All but four states now operate "subsequent injury funds" to encourage employers to hire workers who have sustained a previous permanent injury. When such an employee suffers a new injury, he is compensated for the disability resulting from the combination of injuries. The subsequent or second injury fund, in such cases, pays all of the award except that part attributable to the last injury. The method of financing subsequent injury funds varies among the states. In a few cases it is supported by general

---

[8] The elective law is a legacy of the early constitutional history of workmen's compensation legislation. In *Ives* v. *South Buffalo Railway Co.* (201 N.Y. 271, 1911), a New York court ruled that a compulsory law was invalid as a violation of the due process clause of the state and federal constitutions. Lawmakers in other states, fearing that a compulsory law in their own jurisdictions would meet the constitutional fate, turned to the elective form of statute. In 1917, the United States Supreme Court upheld a compulsory law as a valid exercise of the state policy power. (*White* v. *New York Central R.R. Co.*, 243 U.S. 188, 1917.) Thus, the original justification for the elective law has been removed, but the political influence of employer groups has resulted in the retention of such laws in approximately half the jurisdictions.

appropriations. In other states assessments are made against workmen's compensation insurance carriers or employees.

The penalties for not insuring differ considerably among the states. A common penalty is to make the employer liable to suit with his common law defenses abrogated. In a majority of the jurisdictions, fines and prison terms of varying degrees of severity may be imposed.

Insurance rate making for workmen's compensation is an involved process, but the end result is a classification manual that stipulates separate rates for the industries or occupations covered by law.[9] Under merit rating procedures, the individual enterprise may enjoy a downward adjustment of rates or, conversely, suffer an upward adjustment, depending upon the relationship between the claims experience of the enterprise and the average experience of the industry to which it belongs.

Cash Benefits.   Compensable injuries are classed in one of four categories, for purpoes of benefit determination. These are:

1. Temporary total disability
2. Permanent total disability
3. Permanent partial disability
4. Fatal injury

Once it is determined which of these categories is relevant in a particular injury case, the amount and duration of weekly benefits is given by the benefit formula established in the laws of the various jurisdictions. The factors usually included in these formulas are listed below:

1. *The worker's average wage.*   In most of the jurisdictions, compensation is limited to a specified percentage of the average wage of the victim. Among the jurisdictions these range from 55–90 per cent, but the large majority of the laws stipulate 60 or 66⅔ per cent as the maximum proportion of a wage that may be awarded as a benefit.

2. *A weekly maximum and minimum.*   Regardless of the earnings of a claimant, he cannot receive more than a maximum nor less than a minimum payment stated in the law. In a large number of states, the maximum benefit payable is below the amount necessary to provide the worker the percentage of wage loss that is supposedly protected. In 1968, 13 states paid maximum benefits of $60 or more, 13 paid $50 or more, and the others paid less than $50. These figures do not include allowances for dependents that are incorporated into some of the state programs.

---

[9] The classifications and rates for an individual state can be found in the insurance manuals prepared by the various state commissions.

3. *The benefit period.* In slightly more than half the jurisdictions, the laws specify some maximum period beyond which payments cease in the case of temporary total disability. In the other jurisdictions, benefits may be paid for the full period of disability. For permanent total disability, benefits are paid for life in approximately half the states. In the others benefits are limited by specifying the time for which benefits will be paid or the maximum amount payable. The time limits range from 300 to 550 weeks and the monetary limits from $10,000 to $30,000.

Injuries in permanent partial cases are classed as schedule or non-schedule injuries. The former category includes cases in which there is a readily identifiable loss of part of the body; in such situations the benefit period is set forth in a schedule. In Indiana, for example, loss of a hand qualifies a worker for 200 weeks of benefits, a thumb 60 weeks, an index finger 40 weeks, the sight of one eye 150 weeks, etc. Non-schedule injuries are those less readily classed in terms of severity such as back injuries, headaches, and nervous disorders. In non-schedule cases the benefit period is usually set by administrative determination.

4. *Number of dependents.* In cases of fatal injury, benefits are usually liberalized if there is more than one dependent. Some states give deference to dependents by increasing the maximum payment. Others enlarge the benefit period. The usual specification in this respect is that death benefits will be paid during the period of widowhood or to children until they reach the age of eighteen. In non-fatal injuries, fourteen states provide additional benefits if the disabled person has dependent children.

Occupational Disease. With the sole exception of the Massachusetts law, no state law originally provided compensation for occupational disease. Gradually, as effective political opposition to such coverage diminished, the various jurisdictions amended their laws to provide protection against those diseases that arise out of the course of employment. In thirty states there is "blanket" or full coverage of occupational disease, and in twenty states there is "schedule coverage" or a listing of specific diseases that are compensable.

As noted, the original preoccupation of workmens compensation insurance with physical injury on the job was later expanded so as to include occupational diseases. At the present time, the "frontier" issue is coverage for mental or emotional disorders caused by conditions of employment. While the principle of compensation for mental impairment arising out of and in the course of employment is not yet well accepted, state courts, in several recent instances, have upheld claims of this nature. In one case, an ironworker who saw a co-worker fall to his death was awarded compensation for a psychoneurotic reaction that interfered with his ability to work. In another, a worker who suffered a mental breakdown when he was unable to keep up with the tempo on the assembly line was awarded compensation on a temporary disability basis. These, and a few similar cases, are scattered instances of judicial sympathy with occupationally induced mental disorder. In a number of states, however, the courts have ruled against similar claims.[10]

Rehabilitation. In industrial injury situations, rehabilitation may involve either medical or vocational rehabilitation. Approximately half the jurisdictions in the United States have some type of rehabilitation provisions in their workmen's compensation laws; but these provisions, apparently, are poor indicators of what is actually being done in the various states. According to recent studies, some states whose statutes do not mention rehabilitation are administering successful rehabilitation programs, whereas others with statutory provisions have no programs in operation.[11]

Issues in Public Policy

Most state legislatures meet every other year, and these biennial sessions generally produce many amendments to the workmen's compensation laws. Despite this legislative attention, certain weaknesses persist in the workmen's compensation statutes and inhibit the achievement of a satisfactory degree of security for the industrially injured.[12]

The cash benefit amounts constitute the most glaring deficiencies in the workmen's compnesation programs. In 1968, twenty-four states provided for maximum weekly benefits of $50 or less. Nine of these allowed maximum awards of less than $40. The failure of benefits to keep pace with inflated wage and price levels means that the injured worker is having a smaller proportion of his wage loss replaced. The laws are supposedly designed to offset approximately two-thirds of the wage loss, but the disabled worker is fortunate if he currently receives compensation equal to 40 per cent of his regular wage. Benefits under workmen's compensation are tax-free and a measure of the true income loss suffered by the indus-

10 *Monthly Labor Review,* April, 1968, III–IV.

11 Earl F. Cheit, "Medical Rehabilitation for Injured Workers," *Monthly Labor Review,* November, 1962, p. 1214.

12 For a collection of good discussions dealing with contemporary public policy issues in the area of occupational disability see Earl F. Cheit and Margaret S. Gordon (eds.), *Occupational Disability and Public Policy* (New York: John Wiley & Sons, Inc., 1963).

trially injured requires a comparison between cash benefits and after-tax earnings. So measured, the disparity between pre-injury and post-injury income is narrowed somewhat; but it is not at all unusual to find that the person receiving workmen's compensation is forced to apply for public assistance in order to make ends meet.

Benefits under workmen's compensation are not only low, but they are uneven from jurisdiction to jurisdiction. Workmen's compensation is the only major type of social welfare legislation in which the federal government does not co-operate in some way with the states. The resources of the federal government, thus, are not available to subsidize the state programs, nor is the federal government in a position to insist upon satisfactory benefit and administrative standards. The legislative bodies in the various states, then, subject to no pressures other than those applied by local lobbies, have produced laws that range from the relatively adequate to those that must be judged as unsatisfactory when measured by any reasonable set of standards.

Maximum weekly cash benefits for a worker with temporary total disability are $113 in Alaska, $160 in Arizona, $60 in Minnesota, and $44 in South Dakota. The permanently and totally disabled person may receive benefits for life in Colorado, but a similarly disabled person in Vermont is limited to 330 weeks of benefits. Depending upon his state of residence, the injured worker may receive full medical benefits regardless of the duration of treatment, or he may be limited in some cases to periods of less than six months.

Those who pioneered in the field of workmen's compensation believed that establishment of the principle of liability without fault and provision of modest but certain benefits would minimize the amount of litigation surrounding the compensation of the industrially disabled. This hope has not been realized; and, if anything, there has been a continuing rise in the amount of litigation. A number of different factors contribute to this result. The cost of compensation is borne by the employer; thus, he has a vested interest in contesting awards that may lead to an increase in his insurance premiums. Although benefit levels have remained low, many of the jurisdictions provide full medical care to the injured, and the medical costs associated with a serious injury can involve substantial sums. Employees have developed a legal aggressiveness in asserting their rights, as have the labor organizations that are in a position to hire the specialized legal talent that is becoming a requisite for any party involved in a contested case. Apart from the roles of the parties directly involved, the legal technicalities and medical complexities of workmen's compensation law contribute to the frequency of contests before the administrative commissions and appeals to the courts. In the matter of medical diagnosis, for instance, it is not always a simple matter to determine whether a disability has arisen "in the course of employment," nor is it easy to measure the extent of disability caused by, say, a sore back or partial loss of hearing.

The three issues identified above—inadequate cash benefits, uneven benefits, and increasing litigation—do not exhaust the list of problems that currently beset the administration of workmen's compensation law. Very few of the laws emphasize rehabilitation, and often the full contribution that medical science is able to make to the restoration of the broken body is simply not made. Mention should be made, also, of the poor quality of administration that frequently characterizes workmen's compensation. These laws cover an area of great legal and medical complexity, but the salaries paid to administrative personnel are not sufficient to attract persons with adequate training or to retain those who have developed proficiency through experience.

The shift from the common law and employers' liability philosophies to the workmen's compensation approach marked a great social advance.

There is danger of retrogression, however, unless the present-day laws are revised to make them more effective instruments of public policy. The most pressing need is that of enlarging the cash benefit awards, but the above discussion suggests that a more fundamental overhauling may be in order.

UNEMPLOYMENT

Unemployment is often described as that situation wherein a person willing to work, able to work, and seeking work is unable to find work. Few members of the labor force can boast of never having been unemployed, and even in the high prosperity years enjoyed in the post-World War II era unemployment has been a persistent and troublesome problem.

Unemployment may result from many different causes, some of these more serious in their social consequences than others. Least serious of all, probably, is the unemployment resulting from so-called "frictions" in the labor market. Even in good times, the worker who loses a job usually takes from several days to several weeks to find another. In the interim, he suffers an income loss that might have been avoided if more efficient techniques existed for matching available jobs and available workers. The unemployment that results from cyclical changes in business conditions, laborsaving changes in production methods, or consumer shifts in product preference may create serious economic and social problems. In the past several decades, much attention has been devoted to these problems by social scientists and government policy-makers. Although our knowledge of cause and effect has been advanced, there is still a good deal of uncertainty in the matters of diagnosing, preventing, and dealing with unemployment caused by the inherent instability and the dynamic movements that characterize the American economy.

Unemployment remains a pervasive problem—sufficiently so as to warrant the more detailed analysis that will be made in a later chapter. Our attention at this point will be centered upon the social insurance method that has been developed to offset the income loss suffered when unemployment occurs.

Unemployment Compensation

The philosophy underlying unemployment compensation can be stated simply. The bulk of the unemployment that occurs in the United States is caused by forces that are beyond the control of the individual worker. Since it is attributes of the economy rather than attributes of the individual that cause jobs to disappear, it is less than just for those who become unemployed to bear the full burden of a total wage loss. A system of unemployment compensation seeks to spread the cost of unemployment by building up money funds that can be drawn upon to offset part of the wage loss of out-of-work persons. The person losing a job, thus, is able to pay for basic necessities and ward off destitution while he searches for another position.

Before the passage of the Social Security Act of 1935, there was no social admission that the community had a responsibility to maintain some part of the income of the unemployed. Persons out of work had no claim upon the goods and services produced by the employed factors of production until or unless they qualified for poor relief. The difference between industrial injury and unemployment in this respect might be noted. In the pre-workmen's compensation era the employer was responsible if it could be established that industrial injury resulted from his negligence. Before the unemployment compensation laws were passed, however, neither the employer nor the community as a whole assumed responsibility for wage loss occasioned by unemployment.

The Origin of the Unemployment Compensation Program

Like much of the existing welfare legislation in the United States, the unemployment compensation program was born in the 1930 depression era. In 1934, a *Committee on Economic Security* was established by presidential executive order.[13] The function of the committee was "to study

---

[13] The committee consisted of the Secretary of Labor, the Secretary of the Treasury, the Attorney General, the Secretary of Agriculture, and the Federal Emergency Relief administrator. Three subordinate agencies were established to assist the committee. These were the Advisory Council on Economic Security, consisting of persons outside the government; the Technical Board on Economic Security, consisting of specialists within the government; and the executive director and his staff.

the problems relating to economic security and to make recommendations, both for a long-time and an immediate program of legislation which would promote economic security for the individual."[14] The recommendations of the committee became the basis of the Social Security Act of 1935.

The development of social insurance in the United States lagged behind the developments in many of the European nations, and the Committee on Economic Security was able to study the experiences under the different unemployment insurance schemes that had been attempted in Europe.[15] Against the advantage of being able to draw upon the experiences of other nations was the disadvantage of having to develop a comprehensive plan of compulsory unemployment insurance in one stroke, and this no other nation had attempted to do. The plan that finally emerged was shaped in part by the necessity of political compromise, the preference of the Treasury Department for a particular type of financing, the problems posed by the Constitution, and the pressure for getting something done quickly. The characteristics of the adopted plan will be detailed in the following section.

The Federal-State Relationship

The Social Security Act does not create a system of unemployment insurance, but it contains a tax feature that makes it highly advantageous for the state governments to establish programs designed to provide cash payments to involuntarily unemployed workers. The act levies an excise tax equal to 3.1 per cent of payroll on employers of four or more persons.[16] If employers are paying taxes to finance unemployment compensation

---

[14] *Social Security in America* (Social Security Board Publication No. 20 [Washington, D.C.: U.S. Government Printing Office, 1937]), p. iii.

[15] A number of European cities experimented with plans to subsidize trade union unemployment funds. The most widely copied of these was the plan adopted in Ghent, Belgium in 1901. The Ghent plan provided direct subsidies to union members under the administration of a communal unemployment fund. The first national compulsory system was established in Great Britain in 1911. At first it applied to only six industries, but by 1920 it had been extended to cover almost the entire wage-earning population. The Great Britain plan featured a national pooling of risks. In contrast to this, the German system adopted in 1927 allowed a regional pooling of risks. The experience under these various systems suggested the need for a wide pooling of risks, especially during periods of serious unemployment. For descriptions of these early foreign programs, see *Social Security in America*, chap. 2, and Harry A. Millis and Royal E. Montgomery, *Labor's Risks and Social Insurance* (New York: McGraw-Hill Book Company, 1938), pp. 122–137.

[16] In 1936 the tax was equal to 1 per cent of the total wages of employees in covered employments. This was increased to 2 per cent in 1937 and to 3 per cent in 1938. In 1939 the law was amended so that the tax was placed only on the first $3,000 of an employee's annual wage. In 1954, another amendment made the tax applicable to all employers of four or more workers. This means that employers are subject to the tax if they employ four or more workers during one day in each of twenty different weeks. Prior to this latter amendment the tax was levied on employers of eight or more persons. In 1961, the tax rate was increased to 3.1 per cent.

laws in their own states, the larger part of their federal tax obligation can be "offset" or deducted. Until 1961, the law provided that an employer could offset 90 per cent of the 3 per cent federal tax by his state tax payments. The provisions of the law relating to the size of the tax offset remained unchanged when the federal tax was increased in 1961 to 3.1 per cent of payroll. The tax offset feature amounts to an inducement to the states to enact unemployment compensation laws, since they receive no direct benefits from the revenues of the federal payroll tax unless they do.

A state law must comply with conditions stipulated in the Social Security Act before employers within that state become eligible for the tax offset. The money collected by the state must be paid to the United States Secretary of the Treasury for deposit in an unemployment trust fund, all monies withdrawn from the fund must be used to pay benefits to unemployed workers, and a state must not deny benefits to an individual if he refuses to accept a job under specified conditions.[17]

State governments receive federal funds to administer their unemployment compensation acts. Payment of such funds depends upon a certification by the Secretary of Labor that the state law has met certain standards such as making statistical reports that the federal government may require, using the money for a "proper and efficient" administration of the state law, and providing a fair hearing for claimants who have been denied compensations.[18]

Apart from the specifications described above, the content of a state unemployment compensation law is determined by the state legislative body. There are large differences, consequently, in the details of these laws from state to state.

Details of the State Unemployment Compensation Acts

Coverage. An unemployed worker is not eligible for unemployment insurance benefits unless certain qualifying tests are met. Some of these tests are personal, involving the work experiences of the individual. The impersonal tests consist mainly of *size of firm* and occupational qualifications.

1. *Size of firm.* The federal Unemployment Tax Act levies a payroll tax on all employers of four or more persons, and twenty-five states have laws which apply to employers of this size. Three states cover firms with three or more workers, and twenty-two cover all employers of one or more. All states allow employers with fewer than

---

[17] See Sec. 3304(a)(5) of the Internal Revenue Code of 1954.
[18] See Title III of the Social Security Act, as amended, for a full statement of the law as it covers grants to the states for unemployment compensation administration.

the specified number of workers to elect to have them covered under the state law.

2. *Excluded employments.*   The federal payroll tax does not apply to a number of occupations or types of work, and most states exclude these same employments from coverage under their unemployment compensation acts. The most prominent of the excluded employments are agricultural labor, domestic service in homes, work in non-profit organizations, and self-employment. The federal tax is not levied upon the payrolls of state or local governments, since the federal government does not have the constitutional power to tax the state governments or their instrumentalities. A number of states, however, have brought all or some part of their employees under the coverage of their acts by voluntary action. Under arrangements which the Secretary of Labor has made with each state, unemployment compensation rights have been extended to federal employees.[19] An unemployed federal worker is now entitled to unemployment compensation in the amounts and under the conditions specified in the unemployment compensation law of the state in which he last worked. The federal government makes direct payments to the states to cover the costs of such compensations.

3. *Qualifying work experience.*   An individual must have a work experience to be eligible for benefits. Persons who attempt to enter the labor market for the first time and are unable to find jobs do not qualify for benefits, nor do those who seek jobs unsuccessfully after extended absences from labor force activity.

All states require that an individual must have earned a specified amount of wages or must have worked a specified length of time in a base period. A number of states have both earnings and working time requirements, but there is little uniformity in these requirements among the states. There is, in fact, a good deal of variation in the definition of the base period.

The earnings requirement is usually expressed as a flat amount or as a multiple of the weekly benefit amount. There are other details, such as requirements that an individual earn a specified minimum in the quarter of the base year in which his earnings were highest, or that he earn wages in a specified number of quarters in the base year. The basic purpose of these various requirements is to insure that only those workers who are regular members of the labor force qualify for unemployment compensation benefits.

4. *Disqualification from benefits.*   The unemployment compensation systems in the states are designed to provide cash payments to the involuntarily unemployed. Many types of job loss are not included in

---

[19] These arrangements were authorized by Public Law 767, Eighty-third Congress.

this category, and workers who are otherwise eligible for benefits may be disqualified because of the circumstances surrounding the loss of a job. A person, for example, who quits his job without "good cause" or "just cause" will be disqualified, although it should be added that the definition of these terms varies considerably in the different state laws. The penalty for quitting without good cause also varies. In some states, benefit rights are postponed for the duration of the unemployment, whereas in others they are postponed for a specified number of weeks. Persons who leave a job voluntarily and without good cause may also suffer a reduction of benefits. Discharge for "misconduct in connection with work" may lead to disqualification and benefit limitations similar to those for voluntary quitting.

Persons must be able to work and must be available for work in order to qualify for unemployment compensation benefits. As with the other features of unemployment compensation laws, the meaning of these tests is different from state to state. Women who are unable to work because of pregnancy are usually disqualified, as are those who are unable to work because of illness or disability.

To prove availability, the unemployed person must register at a local office of his state employment service, and he must not refuse an offer of "suitable work." The suitable work provision is difficult to administer and is one of the more controversial features of unemployment compensation law. Consider the following questions by way of example. Should a tool and die maker be required to accept a job as a janitor? Should a person who had been earning $2.00 an hour be required to accept a job at $1.25? How far should a person be required to travel in order to take a job offer? Since many of the state laws do not contain a precise definition of suitable work, the administrative agency has considerable leeway in answering questions such as these. The amount of disqualification that occurs, consequently, depends upon administrative philosophy, although not infrequently the state courts have been called upon to clarify the meaning of suitable work.

One additional—and important—source of disqualification should be noted. Persons whose unemployment is due to a labor dispute are not eligible for benefits, and in almost all the states the ineligibility lasts as long as the labor dispute is in progress.

In recent years there has been a tendency for the states to enact tighter disqualifying provisions and for the administrative bodies to apply these provisions more rigorously. This tendency will be examined at a later point.

Benefit Payments. As a first step in the collection of benefits, the unemployed worker must file a claim at the local office of his state employment service. If he has the qualifying work experience and if he is not disqualified for one of the reasons discussed above, he will receive a cash benefit after a one-week waiting period.[20]

The amount and the duration of benefits are determined exclusively by the states. The different formulas used are complex and quite varied, but all use the worker's wages in a defined base period as the starting point in the computation of benefits. Most of the states use a formula under which benefits are determined on the basis of wages earned in the quarter of the base year in which the worker's wages were highest. In Arizona, for example, the worker's weekly benefit is equal to one twenty-fifth of the wages earned in the highest quarter of the base year, but in no event will he receive less than $10.00 nor more than $50.00. All states specify minimum and maximum benefit amounts payable. In the past few years, a number of states have provided higher benefits for claimants with dependents.

All states except Montana provide benefits for partial unemployment. Partial benefits usually consist of the weekly benefit amount for total unemployment less the wages earned during the week with an allowance of a stated amount for earnings from odd jobs and other sources.

The unemployed worker may receive anywhere from a maximum of twelve to a maximum of thirty-nine weeks of benefits depending upon his state of residence. Thirty-nine states provide twenty-six weeks of benefits. In seven states, all qualified claimants are eligible for the maximum number of benefit weeks specified in the state law, whereas in the other states the duration of benefits depends upon base period earnings or length of time worked in the base period.

Financing Unemployment Benefits. In all but three jurisdictions, unemployment benefits are financed by employer contributions.[21] Until relatively recently, the standard rate of contribution was 2.7 per cent of payroll. (This percentage is the result of offsetting 90 per cent of the 3 per cent federal payroll tax.) With only a few exceptions, the employer's contribution was based on the first $3,000 paid to an employee in a calendar year. In recent years and for various reasons this pattern has been changed in a number of states. As of 1969, more than half these states had contribution rates of more than 2.7 per cent of covered payroll, and twenty-two had higher tax bases than the $3,000 specified in the federal Unemployment Tax Act.

In all states, employer contributions are pooled. This money, collected by the states, is sent to the Secretary of the Treasury, who deposits it in an unemployment trust fund. Each state has a separate account which consists of the contributions made by the states plus interest earned. Apart from

---

[20] As of 1969, all states except Connecticut, Delaware, Maryland, and Nevada required a waiting period of one week.

[21] Alabama, Alaska, and New Jersey collect employee as well as employer contributions.

the amounts necessary to meet current withdrawals for benefit payments, the funds are invested in government obligations. Money may be withdrawn by a state as needed, but only for the purpose of paying benefits to unemployed workers.

All the state laws have an experience rating feature which makes it possible for an employer to achieve substantial tax reductions. The purpose of experience rating procedures is to measure each employer's experience with unemployment or with benefit expenditures. If relatively few employees of an employer have filed claims for benefits and received payments, the employer's contribution rate is adjusted downward. In several jurisdictions, an extremely favorable employment experience may absolve the employer from all state payroll tax obligations.[22]

Extended Unemployment Benefits. In two recent recessions, federal enactments made it possible for the states to extend the period of unemployment benefits for unemployed persons who had exhausted their entitlements under state programs. The Temporary Unemployment Compensation Act of 1958 permitted states signing agreements with the United States Secretary of Labor to pay extended benefits to individuals who had exhausted their benefit rights under state law. Effective during the period June, 1958, to June, 1959, the law provided for extensions equal to 50 per cent of the regular entitlement. In Pennsylvania, thus, where the maximum benefit period was thirty weeks, claimants could qualify for an additional fifteen weeks. Sixteen states participated fully in TUC, and some 1.6 million unemployed persons received more than $470 million in extended benefits. The program was financed out of federal general revenue funds through loans to the participating states. Repayment could be made either directly by the states or by reduction in the federal tax offset of employers effective January 1, 1963, in those cases where the states failed to make direct repayment by the end of 1962.

The Temporary Extended Unemployment Compensation Act of 1961 was effective from April, 1961, to June, 1962, and differed in several respects from the 1958 law. Compensation payable was equal to one-half the regular entitlement, but the total of regular plus extended benefits was limited to thirty-nine weeks of payment. The federal government assumed full responsibility for financing the program. To cover the cost of the extended benefits, all employers were assessed an additional 0.4 per cent of covered payrolls during 1962 and 1963. This particular method of financing was used to induce more states to participate; and, in fact, all states did

---

[22] The systems used for measuring employment experience are quite technical, but the various formulas used are all designed to measure the basic variable of the individual employer's experience with unemployment.

elect to participate in the program. About 2.7 million persons received $770 million in extended benefits.

In addition to these programs, five states enacted exclusively state extended benefit programs during the 1958 recession, and eight subsequently enacted laws providing for an automatic triggering of benefit period extensions when insured unemployment within the state exceeds a specified rate.

Issues in Public Policy

Since 1935, the unemployment insurance system in the United States has been improved in many ways. Coverage has been broadened, benefits have been raised, and the benefit duration period has been lengthened. Despite an undeniable amount of progress, unemployment insurance, like workmen's compensation, is beset with various problems.

One of the continuing areas of controversy involves the adequacy of the benefit. Ideally, the benefit amount should be high enough to prevent undue economic hardship but not so high as to produce a disincentive to work. In the absence of some social consensus on what is implied by "undue hardship" and of firm data on the size of the differential required to avoid disincentives, it is not surprising that the issue of benefit adequacy has been and continues to be controversial.

The general conclusion of what is, perhaps, the most comprehensive analysis yet made of benefit adequacy was that benefits, on the whole, were adequate for single workers without dependents and for working wives but were inadequate for male heads of families who were the only income earners in the family.[23] For this latter group, benefits were found to be insufficient for meeting basic non-deferable consumption needs such as food, housing, clothing, and medical care. An important recommendation of the study, and one that has been made repeatedly by close students of unemployment compensation, is that the maximum benefit amount in every state should equal at least 50 per cent of the state's average gross covered wage.

Since over half the states have benefit maximums of $50 or less, it is obvious that a large number of the insured unemployed are not recovering half of their gross wages. Although the general picture is one of inadequate benefits, certain areas of progress should be noted. Eighteen states now have "flexible maximums." In these states, the maximum benefit is usually defined as 50 per cent of the average weekly wage in covered employment and is automatically adjusted on the basis of annual or semiannual computations of wage levels within the state. Another spreading practice is that of paying

---

[23] Joseph M. Becker, *The Adequacy of the Benefit Amount in Unemployment Insurance* (Kalamazoo, Mich.: The W. E. Upjohn Institute for Employment Research, 1961). The study was based upon samples drawn from seven labor markets and was restricted to claimants who had been unemployed for six weeks or more.

higher benefits to persons with dependents. Eleven states currently follow this practice. Recent extensions in the duration of benefit weeks are also noteworthy. Forty states now provide a maximum of twenty-six weeks of benefits, and some movement toward a thirty-nine week benefit period is detectable.

The mention of benefit duration raises a second issue for public policy. Unemployment insurance was originally conceived as a program for alleviating the economic burden of short-term unemployment. Gradually, however, benefit duration has been extended so that the original general practice of providing sixteen weeks of benefits has changed to a general practice of providing benefits for twenty-six weeks. Ten states have already gone beyond the twenty-six week standard, and we have already described the temporary extensions resulting from federal legislation in 1958 and 1961.

This movement has been, more or less, by drift without adequate consideration of alternatives or consequences. Changing unemployment compensation from a program of short-term to middle- or long-term income protection raises questions of financing, of tax rate disparities between states with the more liberal programs and those lagging behind, of eligibility tests for the long-term unemployed, of co-ordination of unemployment compensation with anti-unemployment programs, and others. The function of unemployment compensation should be periodically reexamined, of course, in the light of prevailing characteristics of unemployment. There may be a danger, however, in superimposing new burdens on the going system without such a reexamination.[24]

Another problem that merits attention is the tendency for the letter and the administration of the state unemployment compensation laws to take forms that make it easier to disqualify workers from benefit payments. Tightening of the disqualification provisions has been done by various devices such as changing the definition of "suitable work"; limiting the acceptable reasons for voluntary quits; and, in a few cases, placing upon the claimant the burden of proof that he is actively seeking work. To some extent, a general tightening of the unemployment compensation laws can be justified as necessary to minimize the amount of malingering,[25] but

---

[24] The Temporary Unemployment Compensation Act of 1958, for example, left a burdensome legacy of debt for the participating states. That experience, as well as the one in 1961, raises questions concerning the use of this method for income protection in recession situations. See Harry Malisoff, *The Financing of Extended Unemployment Insurance Benefits in the United States* (Kalamazoo, Mich.: The W. E. Upjohn Institute for Employment Research, 1963).

[25] One estimate is that from 10 to 15 per cent of all beneficiaries in the course of a year of normal unemployment draw some benefits to which they are not legally entitled but that these improper payments do not constitute more than 2 to 3 per cent of all benefit payments. An improper claim is defined as one that would not be paid if the unemployment compensation agency had all the relevant facts. It is not necessarily a fraudulent claim. See Joseph M. Becker, "Twenty-Five Years of Unemployment Insurance," *Political Science Quarterly,* December, 1960, p. 494.

many students of the system would agree with the statement made several years ago that there has been "a distressing increase in bases for disqualification of workers with adequate employment histories."[26]

Negotiated Unemployment Benefit Plans

Collective bargaining has been responsible for some dramatic developments in unemployment insurance since 1955. In June of that year, the United Automobile Workers and the Ford Motor Company negotiated a *supplemental unemployment benefit* plan, which set the pattern for other industries. Shortly afterwards, a similar scheme was adopted at General Motors; and by October, 1955, more than 800,000 workers in the automotive and allied industries were covered by S.U.B. plans. Important firms outside the automotive industry that have negotiated S.U.B.-type agreements since 1955 include Continental Can, American Can, Libbery-Owens-Ford, Pittsburgh Plate Glass, Allis Chalmers, United States Rubber, and the major steel producers.[27]

These plans are frequently described as guaranteed annual wages, but this is a misnomer.[28] The wage guarantee arrangement, as exemplified by the well known experiments at Hormel, Nunn Bush, or Procter & Gamble, typically guarantees a specified number of paychecks or weeks of work during a year. The employer's liability may be rigidly defined, or it may be vague; but the essential feature is a commitment to provide a given amount of employment or income each year. Shorter-term guarantees of daily, weekly, or monthly pay are quite common in collective bargaining

---

[26] Herman M. Somers and Anne R. Somers, "Trends and Current Issues in Social Insurance," *Monthly Labor Review,* February, 1957, p. 167.

[27] For a description of the development and extent of later SUB plans see Joseph Becker, *Guaranteed Income for the Unemployed: The Story of SUB* (Baltimore: The Johns Hopkins Press, 1968), chap. 2.

[28] Part of the tendency to class S.U.B. as a form of the guaranteed annual wage can be traced to the immediate history of S.U.B. The original proposals of the auto workers union were closer to the usual wage guarantee than was the final agreement. Spokesmen for the auto workers were among those making reference to a guaranteed annual wage. (See Nat Weinberg, "Discussion of the Economics of the Guaranteed Wage," *Proceedings of the Seventh Annual Meeting of the Industrial Relations Research Association,* 1954, pp. 186–192.) In addition to this, the matter of the guaranteed annual wage has been topical since 1943. In that year the United Steel Workers made a proposal for a guaranteed annual wage in the steel industry. When management rejected the proposal, the resulting dispute came before the War Labor Board. The board denied the union request but recommended that the President appoint a body to study the matter of annual wage guarantees. A board was appointed, and the report, generally referred to as the Latimer Report, was completed in 1947 (*Guaranteed Wages: Report to the President* [Washington, D.C.: U.S. Government Printing Office, 1947]). In addition to being an excellent history of business firm experience with guaranteed wage plans, the report suggested that wage guarantees might be helpful in promoting economic stability but they were not panaceas. The steelworkers sought again—unsuccessfully—to negotiate a guaranteed annual wage in 1951, and numerous other unions have expressed interest in wage guarantees.

agreements.[29] The S.U.B. plans provide no such guarantees. They attempt rather to supplement the unemployment compensation checks of the laid-off worker so as to maintain his income at a specified percentage of his regular take-home pay.

The various S.U.B. plans are similar in broad outline, different in detail. All require an employer contribution to a reserve fund. In most the contribution is based upon the number of employee hours worked and varies from three to seven cents an hour in the different plans. Most plans stipulate a maximum size for the employer reserve fund. Once the maximum is reached, further employer contributions are limited to the amounts necessary to maintain the fund at the specified level.

The supplementary unemployment benefit plans attempt to guarantee that workers who are laid off will receive a percentage—usually 60 to 80 per cent— of their gross pay. Part of the income lost during unemployment is made up by the benefit provided under the state unemployment compensation law. The difference between the unemployment compensation benefit and the total benefit figure stated in the union-management agreement is the sum that the employer must pay to the unemployed worker.[30]

S.U.B., then, is uniquely related to unemployment compensation. With minor exceptions, an employee must be eligible for unemployment compensation payments under a state law in order to be eligible for S.U.B. payments from his employer. The amount the worker receives is a residual that is determined by subtracting his unemployment compensation benefit from the amount expressed in the S.U.B. plan that covers him.

The different S.U.B. plans provide benefits for various maximum periods with fifty-two weeks being the usual maximum although some of the more liberal plans provide benefits for a longer period. Since few of the state unemployment compensation laws grant benefits after thirty weeks of unemployment, the lengthier S.U.B. arrangements usually provide for an increase in the supplementary benefit payment after unemployment compensation ceases.

The employer's liability under S.U.B. is limited to the amount of money in the reserve fund. In order to protect the fund against rapid depletion, each plan provides for a downward scaling of benefits when the money in the fund falls to slated percentages below the maximum level.[31]

[29] See "Daily, Weekly, and Monthly Guarantees" Appendix Vol. 4 to *Report of the Presidential Railroad Commission* (Washington, D.C.: U.S. Government Printing Office, 1962), pp. 313–321.

[30] The S.U.B. plans, however, specify a maximum award that may be granted as an S.U.B. benefit. It is possible that some of the highly paid workers will not receive the percentage of take-home pay that is specified under a plan even when unemployment compensation and S.U.B. payments are totaled.

[31] For a detailed description of the experience under S.U.B. see Joseph Becker, *op. cit.*

In the late 1960's, S.U.B. plans covered over two million workers. Sixty-three per cent of those covered were members of the Auto Workers and Steel Workers unions and another 28 per cent were members of the Garment Workers, Electrical Workers, and Rubber Workers unions.[32] Although S.U.B. has spread to a number of new industries, the overall growth in coverage in recent years has been small.[33]

QUESTIONS

1. What shortcomings in the common law of employer liability encouraged the passage of workmen's compensation legislation?

2. How did the state workmen's compensation laws attempt to rectify these shortcomings?

3. If you were testifying before the appropriate committee of your state legislature, what recommendations would you make relative to your state unemployment compensation law?

4. Private insurance can be purchased as protection against a variety of economic risks. Why in the case of unemployment has it been necessary to rely upon *social* rather than *private* insurance?

5. Examine a copy of your state unemployment compensation law. Describe the coverage limitations, the necessary qualifying work experience, and the amount and duration of benefit payments.

6. Assume the following situation. A worker enters an elevator in his place of employment. The elevator becomes stuck between floors for a period of several hours. As a result of the experience the worker suffers a mental breakdown and is unable to work. In your opinion, should this situation be treated as compensable under the workmen's compensation law in your state?

SELECTED READINGS

CARLSON, VALDEMAR. *Economic Security in the United States.* New York: McGraw-Hill Book Company, 1962.

LARSON, ARTHUR. "Compensation Reform in the United States," in Earl F. Cheit and Margaret Gordon (eds.). *Occupational Disability and Public Policy.* New York: John Wiley & Sons, Inc., 1963. Chap. 1.

MYERS, ROBERT J. *Social Insurance and Allied Government Programs.* Homewood, Ill.: Richard D. Irwin, Inc., 1965. Chaps. 12, 13.

WILCOX, CLAIR. *Toward Social Welfare.* Homewood, Ill.: Richard D. Irwin, Inc. 1969. Chap. 7.

---

[32] Joseph M. Becker, "Private Supplementation of Public Unemployment Benefits" in Sar Levitan, Wilbur Cohen, and Robert Lampman (eds.), *Toward Freedom from Want* (Madison, Wisconsin: Industrial Relations Research Association, 1968), pp. 105–132.

[33] *Ibid.,* p. 106.

CHAPTER 22

Social Insurance Programs—
Continued

THIS CHAPTER EXTENDS THE ANALYSIS OF ECONOMIC SECURITY PROGRAMS begun in the last chapter to the social security provisions for the aged and the disabled. The analysis is restricted to those labor considerations that relate to interruptions of individuals' earning power, and also to these problems as they exist in the United States.

SECURITY FOR THE AGED

Many of the problems besetting the aged in our society have been intensified by various aspects of present-day life. Along with the advances in medical science that have increased average life expectancy, changes have occurred in our social and economic arrangements that, on the whole, make adjustments to the problems of old age more difficult. Our society, for example, has become less rural, more urban. On the farm, where economic activities are ordered around the family unit, the aged are able to contribute technical skill and know-how long after the decline in strength requires a tapering-off of their physical contribution to the work. In the rural society, furthermore, the family usually consists of a large kinship group. The young, middle aged, and old remain parts of an integrated economic and social unit in which status and privileges increase with age. The farm family, typically, is larger than the urban family; and a large number of children by itself constitutes a type of security for the aged.[1]

In modern urban life there has been a strong tendency for the family to become what sociologists call the extreme conjugal family type. When a male city dweller speaks of his family he is usually referring to his wife and his children and not to his parents, brothers, or sisters. As Wilbert Moore notes, the conjugal family involves a radical separation of the generations and of adult brothers and sisters.[2] "Old people have no definite claim upon an extended kinship group for support and social participation. The primary obligation of each brother and sister is to his or her own family and the same is true for married children."[3]

This means that persons must depend more and more upon their own resources for psychological and economic security in their old age. Frequently the necessary resources are far more than aged persons are able to command. Our concern here is primarily with economic insecurity, although caution should be expressed against an expectation that adequate social provision for the economic needs of the aged will solve all the problems of this group. Our knowledge of the old age problem has been much advanced in recent years by contributions that have come from disciplines and specializations such as economics, sociology, psychology, gerontology, political science, architecture, and demography; these contributions suggest that the problem goes beyond simple economic dimensions.

One explanation of the growing concern with the aged is provided by population statistics: the relative number of persons aged sixty-five and over has increased by dramatic proportions since the turn of the century. In 1900, one out of every twenty-five persons was over sixty-five years of age. In 1960 the proportion was one out of eleven. Between 1950 and 1960, the total population of the United States increased by 18 per cent while population aged sixty-five and over increased by 35 per cent. Several factors account for this change in the age structure. (1) Average life expectancy has increased. In 1900 the chances of a newborn male child living to age sixty-five were approximately four out of ten. In 1960 the chances were six and one-half out of ten. For female infants, the odds changed from four out of ten in 1900 to almost eight out of ten in 1960. (2) The birth rate declined steadily from 1915 to the start of World War II. The combination

---

[1] See T. Lynn Smith, "The Aged in Rural Society," in *The Aged and Society* (Madison, Wis.: Industrial Relations Research Association, 1950) for a good description of the position of the aged in a rural society. Smith notes, incidentally, that the urban influence has extended to the rural areas of our economy and that there has been a strong tendency for elderly farm people to leave the farm and take up residence in the towns and cities along the Pacific and Gulf coasts.

[2] Wilbert E. Moore, "The Aged in Industrial Society," *ibid.*, p. 35.

[3] *Ibid.*

of a longer life span and a declining birth rate results, of course, in an increase in the average age of the population. (3) The decline in the amount of immigration since the 1930's has reduced the relative number of younger people. During the large-scale immigration of the 1910–1914 period, 95 per cent of the immigrants were under forty-five years of age.

Present projections of the Bureau of the Census indicate the number of persons aged sixty-five and over will grow at a faster rate than total population until 1975. Between 1960 and 1970, the projections indicate a 17.5 per cent increase in the number of those sixty-five and over as compared to a 15.7 per cent growth for total population. Between 1970 and 1975 the two rates will be about equal with an 8.2 per cent growth projected for the aged and 8.1 per cent for total population. According to the projection, population aged sixty-five and over—16.6 million in 1960—may reach a figure of 21 million by 1975.

The Economic Problem of the Aged

Persons who reach age sixty-five can expect, on the average, to survive for twelve more years. For many of the aged, this fact means that more than a decade of life can be anticipated in which the need for income is likely to outstrip the capacity to earn income. This, in essence, is the economic problem of a large proportion of our aged population.

Ideally, a person should provide for his needs during old age by accumulating savings during the course of his working life, but a large percentage of the aged do not have the savings necessary to maintain themselves at what might be considered a bare but adequate level of living. A 1963 survey of the aged reported that 10 per cent of all aged couples and 25 per cent of the non-married aged had no income-producing assets at all.[4] A substantial percentage of those with some income from dividends, interest, or rent received less than $140 a year from these sources. In the United States we have traditionally extolled the virtues of thrift and hard work and have assumed that economic security would follow from their practice. We now recognize, however, that a person might work hard and live modestly and still fail to accumulate the savings essential for old age security. Many exigencies beyond the control of the individual may occur during a lifetime of work to eat up whatever savings have been made. The most prominent among these are unemployment, medical expense, death of the family breadwinner, and price inflation. Whatever the reasons, a majority of the persons who reach retirement age find themselves unable to depend upon their private resources for support.

At a time when so much is heard of retirement and pensions, it is surprising to learn that a substantial number of persons aged sixty-five and

---

[4] "Assets of the Aged in 1962," *Social Security Bulletin,* November, 1964, p. 3.

over receive all or an important share of their income from employment. Earnings from employment constitute 32 per cent of the aggregate income of the aged and, for this group, rank second to pensions in importance as an income source.[5] Labor force participation rates for those over sixty-five are 28 per cent for men and 10 per cent for women. For the sixty-five to sixty-nine age bracket, the rates are 40 per cent for men and 18 per cent for women.

The occupational pattern for older workers is different from that of the population as a whole. About 13 per cent of the aged in the labor force are farmers, whereas only 7 per cent of the total labor force is in farming. Operatives make up 17 per cent of the total labor force, but only 9 per cent of those over sixty-five are operatives. Almost half the employed male persons over sixty-five are self-employed as compared with 15 per cent of the total labor force. These differences are explained in part by the fact that many of the older workers, once retired from their earlier employment, move into activities such as small-scale proprietorships and custodial work. Aged workers, also, are more likely to be attached to declining occupations such as farming than are younger persons in the labor force.

Older persons work because they have to and quite often because they want to, but sooner or later the period of labor force activity ends for most. A recent survey of working persons who were about to retire showed that poor health was the most prominent cause of the imminent retirements. The employer's compulsory retirement policy was also an important cause. Only 5 per cent of those interviewed indicated that they planned to retire in order to enjoy more leisure time.[6]

Although employment continues to be an important source of economic security for the aged, the long run trend in the labor force participation rate for older workers has been downward. In 1890, about 70 per cent of all men over sixty-five were in the labor force, whereas only 28 per cent of this age group are in the labor force today. The explanation of the trend direction can probably be found in the combined facts of the growing practice of compulsory retirement and the shrinkage of opportunities in farming and other areas of self-employment. Thus, concurrent with a large growth in the absolute number of older persons, there has been a decline in the relative amount of labor force opportunities for the aged worker.

[5] About 40 per cent of the aggregate income of persons sixty-five and over comes from retirement programs, 32 per cent from employment earnings and 15 per cent from assets. The remainder comes, for the most part, from public assistance, veteran's benefits, and contributions of relatives. Lenore A. Epstein, "Income of the Aged in 1962," *ibid.*, March, 1964, p. 7.

[6] Erdman Palmore, "Retirement Patterns Among Aged Men," *ibid.*, August, 1964, p. 6.

Technically speaking, an unemployed person is a member of the labor force and not retired, but for aged persons the line between unemployment and retirement is thin. Once he loses a job, the older worker usually finds another only with great difficulty and after an extended period of unemployment. Since many business firms refuse to hire persons over forty-five, the plight of the worker over sixty-five is easily imagined. This problem, incidentally, applies with equal force to professionals or executives.[7] The older white collar worker, no less than the blue collar one, has difficulty in finding a job after he becomes unemployed.

To summarize the economic problem of the aged we can note the following points: (1) While average life expectancy is increasing, the employment opportunities for older workers are shrinking. Most persons would prefer to continue working after age sixty-five, but compulsory retirement policies and poor health force many into a retired status. (2) The older worker is vulnerable when unemployment hits. Once unemployed he finds another job with difficulty, if at all. (3) Only few persons are able to draw upon savings during retirement. Children of aged parents, furthermore, are frequently unable to furnish the amounts and types of support that older persons must have.

SOCIAL SECURITY PROGRAMS FOR THE AGED

Two distinct programs to benefit the aged were created by the Social Security Act of 1935. Old Age, Survivors, Disability, and Health Insurance (OASDHI) utilizes the social insurance method, whereas Old Age Assistance (OAA) uses the public assistance technique.

The national programs for helping the aged originated in the 1930 Depression when the plight of older persons was extraordinarily serious. The programs survived the depression and, since 1939, have been strengthened considerably. The significance of the latter fact is that the goal of economic security for the aged has become entrenched as a part of national policy. In our social security programs we have systematized the techniques for siphoning some part of the annual national income to those older persons whose economic contribution has diminished or ceased.

Since the main features of OAA were described in Chapter 20, the discussion below will be concerned with OASDHI.

---

[7] In 1956 the National Conference of Forty Plus Clubs was organized "to enlarge the employment opportunities for executives and professional men over 40," *New York Times,* August 30, 1956, p. 27.

Old Age, Survivors, Disability and Health Insurance[8]

OASDHI, the only part of the Social Security Act of 1935 operated exclusively by the federal government, was amended significantly in 1939, 1950, 1952, 1954, 1956, 1958, 1961, 1965, and 1967. As a result, the present law bears little resemblance to the original. Like the other social insurance programs in the United States, OASDHI is technically complex. A detailed consideration of the technicalities is beyond the scope of an introductory analysis, and the description that follows will be limited to the prominent characteristics of the present law.

Coverage.   Originally, only industrial and commercial employees were covered by OASDHI, but today over 90 per cent of all gainfully employed persons are under the federal old age insurance system. The bulk of the group still not covered consists of certain very low income farm workers, and domestic employees. Federal civilian employees and railroad workers who are under their own public retirement systems are excluded from coverage as are employees of Communist-front or Communist-action organizations registered under the Internal Security Act of 1950. Coverage is possible but not compulsory for state and local government employees and employees of non-profit organizations. Apart from these and a few other groups, coverage is compulsory.

Benefit Eligibility.   Benefits are paid at retirement to persons who are *fully insured*. Persons are fully insured if they have a total of forty quarters (ten years) of coverage or if they have at least one quarter of coverage for every year since 1950 and before age sixty-five (sixty-two in the case of women).[9] Persons measuring coverage on the basis of the second of the alternatives must have a minimum of six quarters to be fully insured. The

---

[8] Before 1956, the old age pension section of the Social Security Act was abbreviated as OASI (Old Age and Survivors Insurance). The 1956 amendments provided benefits for certain totally disabled persons, and the abbreviation was changed to OASDI (Old Age, Survivor's, and Disability Insurance). The 1965 amendments added health insurance benefits for older persons and the designation was changed to OASDHI. To simplify the discussion reference will be made here only to OASDHI even though this designation is technically incorrect for the years before 1965.

[9] A quarter is a three month period ending March 31, June 30, September 30, or December 31. A quarter of coverage for the wage earner is a calendar quarter during which he received at least $50 in covered employment.

Since the insurance system was inaugurated in 1935, the 1950 date in the second alternative may be puzzling. The date is explained by the fact that a "new start" became necessary after the 1950 amendment. Coverage was extended significantly by the 1950 and later amendments, and older persons among the newly covered would not have been able to establish their eligibility for benefits under the existing rules. To remedy this situation, an alternative method of achieving fully insured status was provided; and since it would have been unfair to make full insurance available to the newly covered groups on terms more liberal than those applicable to persons already covered, the new rules were extended to all.

1965 amendments made it possible for women born in 1895 or earlier and men born in 1892 or earlier to qualify for monthly payments of $35 with only three quarters of coverage.

Those who are fully insured become eligible for retirement benefits at age sixty-five or, on a reduced basis, at age sixty-two.[10] To receive benefits, insured individuals must cease working to the extent that they earn no more than $1,680 per year.[11] After age seventy-two, the earnings limitation is removed.

Benefits to survivors become payable if the deceased was *currently insured*. The current insurance status is achieved if a person had six quarters of coverage in the thirteen quarters prior to the quarter in which death occurred.

Benefit Amounts. Different types of benefits are payable under OASDHI, but all of these bear a relationship to the *primary benefit*. The primary benefit, in turn, depends upon the size of the average monthly wage of the insured.

The derivation of the average monthly wage is a complex affair, but for our purposes it is sufficient to say that it is equal to earnings in covered employment after 1950 divided by the number of months after 1950 in which a person might have been in covered employment. Time spent in non-covered work, thus, will reduce the size of the average monthly wage. Most persons, however, are entitled to "drop out" a total of five years in which there was no covered employment or in which income from covered employment was low. Periods of total disability may also be excluded from the average monthly wage computation. The maximum earnings creditable for social security are $3,600 for 1951–1954, $4,200 for 1955–1958, $4,800 for 1959–1965, $6,600 for 1966–1967, and $7,800 for 1968 and after.

As noted above, an individual's primary benefit is based upon his average monthly wage as computed. Under the current benefit schedule, there is a minimum primary benefit at age 65 of $55 for a person with an average monthly wage of $74 or less. Technically, the maximum primary benefit is $218 per month for a person with an average monthly wage of $650, but it will not be possible for anyone to qualify for a pension of this size for

---

[10] Originally benefits were only payable at age sixty-five. A minimum retirement age of sixty-two was established for women in the 1956 amendments, and a similar provision for men was enacted in the 1961 amendments. Neglecting some of the complications, the basic rule is that the monthly benefit is reduced by 5/9 of 1 per cent for each month prior to the recipient's sixty-fifth birthday that the benefits begin.

[11] Retirees earning more than $1,680 per year are subject to a reduction of $1.00 in benefits for each $2.00 of earnings over $1,680 and up to $2,880. One dollar in benefits is withheld for each $1.00 of earnings over $2,880. Benefits, however, are not withheld for any month in which the beneficiary has wages of $140 or less.

many years to come. At the present time, the maximum benefit is about $140 for a person with an average monthly wage of about $400. Secondary or dependents' benefits are determined by the nature of the dependency relationship and the size of the insured person's primary benefit. Table 20 shows basic retirement and survivors' benefits for various levels of average earnings.

TABLE 20

EXAMPLES OF MONTHLY OASDHI PAYMENTS

AVERAGE YEARLY EARNINGS AFTER 1950*	$899 OR LESS	$1800	$3000	$4200	$5400	$6600	$7800
Retired worker—65 or older / Disabled worker—under 65	55.00	88.40	115.00	140.40	165.00	189.90	218.00
Wife 65 or older	27.50	44.20	57.50	70.20	82.50	95.00	105.00
Retired worker at 62	44.00	70.80	92.00	112.40	132.00	152.00	174.40
Wife at 62, no child	20.70	33.20	43.20	52.70	61.90	71.30	78.80
Widow at 62 or older	55.00	73.00	94.90	115.90	136.20	156.70	179.90
Widow at 60, no child	47.70	63.30	82.30	100.50	118.10	135.90	156.00
Disabled widow at 50, no child	33.40	44.30	57.60	70.30	82.70	95.10	109.20
Wife under 65 and one child	27.50	44.20	87.40	140.40	165.00	190.00	214.00
Widow under 62 and one child	82.50	132.60	172.60	210.60	247.60	285.00	327.00
Widow under 62 and two children	82.50	132.60	202.40	280.80	354.40	395.60	434.40
One child of retired or disabled worker	27.50	44.20	57.50	70.20	82.50	95.00	109.00
One surviving child	55.00	66.30	86.30	105.30	123.80	142.50	163.50
Maximum family payment	82.50	132.60	202.40	280.80	354.40	395.60	434.40

* Generally, average earnings are figured over the period from 1950 until the worker reaches retirement age, becomes disabled, or dies. Up to 5 years of low earnings can be excluded. The maximum earnings creditable for social security are $3,600 for 1951–1954; $4,200 for 1955–1958; $4,800 for 1959–1965; and $6,600 for 1966–1967. The maximum creditable in 1968 and after is $7,800, but average earnings cannot reach this amount until later. Because of this, the benefits shown in the last two columns on the right generally will not be payable until later. When a person is entitled to more than one benefit, the amount actually payable is limited to the larger of the benefits. In 1969, the Nixon administration proposed a ten percent increase in the rates shown above.

Financing. OASDHI is financed by a payroll tax shared equally by employer and employee. The tax is levied only on the first $7,800 of annual income. The tax on self-employed persons is higher than the employee's tax but lower than the combined tax on employer and employee. The current tax and scheduled increases are shown in Table 21. The amounts shown as contributions for hospital insurance are payroll taxes added by the Medicare program enacted in 1965. The details of the hospital insurance program are described at a later point in this chapter.

Issues in Public Policy

Despite unquestionable improvements in our social security programs for the aged, certain basic problems remain.

TABLE 21

CONTRIBUTION RATE SCHEDULE FOR OASDHI

YEAR	FOR RETIREMENT, SUR-VIVORS, AND DISABILITY INSURANCE BENEFITS	FOR HOSPITAL INSURANCE	COMBINED RATE
	Percent of covered earnings* for employee and employer, each		
1968	3.8	.60	4.40
1969–70	4.2	.60	4.80
1971–72	4.6	.60	5.20
1973–75	5.0	.65	5.65
1976–79	5.0	.70	5.70
1980–86	5.0	.80	5.80
1987 and after	5.0	.90	5.90
	Percent of covered earnings* for self-employed		
1968	5.8	.60	6.40
1969–70	6.3	.60	6.90
1971–72	6.9	.60	7.50
1973–75	7.0	.65	7.65
1976–79	7.0	.70	7.70
1980–86	7.0	.80	7.80
1987 and after	7.0	.90	7.90

* Annual contribution base is $7,800 beginning in 1968.

1. *Are Benefits Adequate?* There is a good deal of evidence that they are not. A comprehensive survey of the aged population in the United States found that 44 per cent of the married and 58 per cent of the non-married OASDHI beneficiaries had inadequate incomes in 1962.[12]

A large number of beneficiaries have little cash income besides their benefits. According to the recent study, one-third of the non-married beneficiaries had additional income of less than $150 per year, and one-fifth of the couples had less than $300.[13] Those also drawing payments from private pension plans were relatively well off, but this group constituted only 4 per cent of the total OASDHI beneficiaries. Furthermore, 17 per cent of the couples and 29 per cent of the non-married persons with both private pension and OASDHI incomes had less than the amount necessary for the "modest but adequate" budget of the BLS. Very few of those who depended

---

[12] Lenore A. Epstein and Janet H. Murray, *The Aged Population of the United States,* Part 2 (Washington, D.C., U.S. Government Printing Office, 1967). The standard for adequacy in this study was the Bureau of Labor Statistics estimate of the cost of a modest but adequate level of living. In 1962 prices this amount was $1,800 per year for the non-married aged person and $2,500 for the aged couple.

[13] *Ibid.*

580 <i>The Problem of Economic Insecurity</i>

TABLE 22

SIZE OF MONEY INCOME BY OASDI BENEFICIARY STATUS
FOR UNITS AGED 65 AND OVER
(Percentage Distribution by Income Interval, 1962)*

TOTAL MONEY INCOME	MARRIED COUPLES†		NON-MARRIED MEN		NON-MARRIED WOMEN		
	OASDI Benefi-ciaries	Non-benefi-ciaries	OASDI Benen-ciaries	Non-benefi-ciaries	OASDI Beneficiaries‡		Non-benefi-ciaries
					Retired	Widowed	
Number (in Reporting on Total ..... thousands):	3,743	1,120	1,490	803	1,912	1,502	2,543
income ...	3,289	932	1,384	685	1,690	1,325	2,192
Total per cent	100	100	100	100	100	100	100
Less than $1,000	4	10	26	46	36	44	65
1,000–1,499 ...	9	12	32	13	23	27	14
1,500–1,999 ...	15	11	14	10	17	16	7
2,000–2,499 ...	16	5	13	6	9	6	4
2,500–2,999 ...	14	6	6	3	5	2	2
3,000–3,999 ...	16	12	5	4	4	2	3
4,000–4,999 ...	11	10	2	4	2	1	1
5,000–9,999 ...	12	24	2	12	4	2	2
10,000 and over	3	11	(§)	1	(§)	1	(§)
Median income	$2,710	$3,580	$1,375	$1,135	$1,300	$1,105	$755

* Excludes beneficiaries who received their first benefit in February, 1962, or later.
† With at least one member aged sixty-five or over.
‡ The retired women receive benefits based on their own wage record, regardless of eligibility as widows; the widowed receive benefits based on the husband's wage record.
§ Less than 0.5 per cent.
Source: *Social Security Bulletin*, March, 1964.

upon public assistance to supplement their OASDHI benefits had as much income as the BLS budget requires.

The average monthly OASDHI benefit in recent years has been under about $95. This figure will be higher in the future as more persons with higher average monthly wages retire. A larger proportion of those retiring, furthermore, will be drawing benefits from private pension plans. The general economic outlook for the aged population is bleak, however. One half of all families headed by a person over sixty-five are poor, according to the 1964 report of the Council of Economic Advisers, and foreseeable improvements in our social security system are not likely to reduce this fraction significantly.

2. *Financing Security for the Aged.*   In the immediate future, Congress will probably continue to hold the position it has maintained relative to

OASDHI financing since 1935: the system should be self-supporting. The money to pay benefits, thus, will have to come from the tax payments of employees, employers, and the self-employed. Since 1935, the amounts collected in taxes have exceeded the amounts paid in benefits, and a reserve of some 23 billion dollars has been built up. Eventually, as the number of retired persons increases, the annual income may be less than sufficient to pay total annual benefit claims; but it is difficult to know when such a relationship between income and benefits will materialize as a persistent condition of the system. Much depends upon what Congress does by way of changing benefit amounts and tax rates; if there is no change in the law, the system will be self-supporting for a number of additional decades.[14] At that time, the American people will have to reach a decision about future financial arrangements—if one has not already been reached—and it is entirely possible that some part of the cost will eventually be borne by the federal Treasury.

Financing has been a controversial matter throughout the history of OASDHI. The debate has centered over issues such as pay-as-you-go versus reserve financing, the regressivity of the payroll tax, and the economic effects of a large reserve. The existing system is well established, however; and it is unlikely that the basic framework will be changed, although changes in the benefit formula and tax rates will undoubtedly occur.

The debate over the *money* costs has tended to veil a more important consideration: the real cost of an old age insurance system. Regardless of what techniques are used to finance benefits, the food, clothing, utilities, and other commodities used by the aged must come out of current production. The real burden of a social insurance program for the aged, consequently, is measured by the amount of goods and services that the productive sector of the economy relinquishes to the economically inactive aged. Although there is little evidence that the real cost of OASDHI has been especially burdensome so far, the rapid increase in the number of the aged has raised fears about the future weight of the burden.

Population projections indicate that there will be a 32 per cent increase in the number of persons aged sixty-five and over between 1960 and 1975. Labor force projections indicate an increase in the size of the labor force

---

[14] Whether the system will be self-supporting by the turn of the century will depend upon the accuracy of the actuarial cost estimates that have been made. Intermediate, high, and low cost estimates have been made; and if the experience is close to the intermediate estimate, the system will continue to be self-supporting. Under the low cost estimate, the trust fund will build up rapidly and will amount to more than $255 billion by the year 2000. Under the high cost estimate, the trust fund will be exhausted by that time. The extremity of the range suggests the difficulties associated with actuarial analysis of a social security system. See Robert J. Myers, "Old-Age Survivors and Disability Insurance: Financing Basis and Policy under the 1961 Amendments," *Social Security Bulletin,* September, 1961, pp. 12–19.

over the same years of approximately 27 per cent. Each active member of the labor force, thus, will be supporting a slightly larger number of the inactive aged. An estimate of the precise weight of the burden requires assumptions concerning the length of the future work week, future labor force participation rates of the aged, unemployment rates, and productivity changes. Assuming reasonably full employment and no dramatic changes in working hours, support of the inactive aged at prevailing living levels would appear to involve no net increase in the economic burden. Output per man-hour increased by 50 per cent between 1947 and 1960, and an assumption of at least an equal increase between 1960 and 1975 is not particularly bold. Productivity growth, thus, should be more than sufficient to absorb the increased real costs that will be associated with an increase in the relative size of the aged population.

A more serious question of burden is raised if a social decision is made in favor of improving the living levels of the aged. According to one estimate, an annual fund of $13.3 billion would be necessary to raise the income of the aged to the level required by the Bureau of Labor Statistics standard described above.[15] This amount is about 2 per cent of 1963 gross national product and is almost equal to total current benefit disbursements from the OASDHI trust fund.

3. *Declining Employment Opportunities for the Aged.* When an aged person continues to work beyond the usual point of retirement, advantages accrue to society as well as to the individual. For society, the advantage is the obvious one of having a productive contributor to economic output rather than an inactive consumer of the output of others. The individual, at the same time, usually earns an income that is substantially above what he would receive if retired. Among the aged, in fact, those who continue to work are, on the average, better positioned financially, by far, than those who have dropped out or who have been forced out of employment. A large number of the aged, furthermore, prefer work to retirement. For many, including the wealthy, retirement turns out to be a bore, and the feeling of participating in something important is lost when employment ties are cut. Employment today, it has been noted, carries with it so many opportunities for leisure that the leisure of retirement loses some of its attractiveness.[16]

Unfortunately, it is becoming increasingly difficult for older persons to continue on the job. Compulsory retirement policies of employers force many into retirement at age sixty-five; and, in a labor market characterized

[15] Herbert E. Striner, "The Capacity of the Economy to Support Older People," in Harold L. Orbach and Clark Tibbits (eds.), *Aging and the Economy* (Ann Arbor: University of Michigan Press, 1963), p. 21.

[16] Sumner Slichter, "Retirement Age and Social Policy," in *The Aged and Society* (Madison, Wis.: Industrial Relations Research Association, 1950), p. 109.

by persistent unemployment, older persons who lose jobs are frequently unable to find new employment. In reference to this latter situation, a recent government report noted that "It would be unrealistic not to recognize that a significant group of older workers, particularly the 55 to 64 age group, once displaced, will remain permanently unemployed. . . . They will still be able and willing to work, yet forced by technological change, skill obsolescence, lack of education, absence of demanded skills, and the shortness of their future years into early uncompensated retirement."[17]

Many older workers enjoy the protection of seniority rights against job loss during employment cutbacks. Seniority, however, offers no protection when entire departments or plants are shut down; and, in a context of rapid technological change and much industrial relocation, such shutdowns occur frequently.

Once unemployed, the older person is discriminated against by business employing practices. The reasons usually cited to justify the discrimination are preferences for promoting from within the firm, the superiority of younger workers, problems posed by pension plans, and the difficulty of finding suitable job assignments for newly hired older workers when a strict seniority system governs promotions.[18] There is also a widely held belief that the job performances of the aged are inferior to those of younger persons; and although this is true to some extent and in some occupations, the differences are frequently exaggerated.[19]

Labor force participation rates of the aged have been declining, and the outlook is for a further decline. For males sixty-five and over, the rate was 32 per cent in 1960, and had dropped to 26.9 per cent by 1965. A further decline to about 23 per cent is anticipated by 1975. In the absence of a direct and effective attack against the various factors that are discouraging the employment of older persons, a growing proportion will become completely dependent upon retirement income.

The 1961 amendments of OASDHI permitting men to retire at age sixty-two on a reduced scale of benefits encourages earlier retirement and represents one response to the employment problems of older persons. The possibility of getting a retirement income at an earlier age will provide some relief for the distressingly large number who have found that they are too old to work but too young to retire. The relaxation of the limitations upon employment earnings of OASDHI beneficiaries, on the other hand, makes it

---

[17] Subcommittee on Employment and Manpower of the Committee on Labor and Public Welfare, United States Senate, *Toward Full Employment: Proposals for a Comprehensive Employment and Manpower Policy in the United States* (Washington, D.C.: U.S. Government Printing Office, 1964), p. 70.

[18] Margaret Gordon, "The Older Worker and Hiring Practices," *Monthly Labor Review*, November, 1959, pp. 1198–1205.

[19] U.S. Department of Labor, Bureau of Labor Statistics, *Comparative Job Performance by Age* (Bulletin No. 1273, February, 1960).

possible to supplement the benefits more substantially through part-time work and, thus, encourages labor force activity beyond age sixty-five.

Private Pension Plans

Retired persons drawing benefits from both OASDHI and private pension plans are relatively well off among the retired aged. One analyst, in fact, has described such persons as constituting an "elite" of the retired. At the present time, about 55 per cent of all employees are covered by private retirement plans and over two million persons are now drawing benefits from such plans.

The number of persons under private pension plans has expanded rapidly since 1950 when only half a million persons were covered. A number of factors are responsible for the expansion, but a large part of the impetus can be traced to the following:

1. The emphasis upon fringe benefits that developed as a consequence of the World War II wage freeze.

2. The 1946 pension agreement between the United States government and the United Mine Workers, when the mines were under government control. (The agreement provided a $100 a month pension at age sixty-two for every miner who had been a member of the union for twenty or more years.)

3. The recommendation of the President's Steel Industry Board during the 1949 dispute that the United Steel Workers and the steel producers negotiate a pension plan.

4. The decision of the federal courts in the Inland Steel case that pensions are within the area of compulsory bargaining. (This made refusal to bargain over pensions an unfair labor practice under the Taft-Hartley Act.)

5. The pattern-setting effects of the 1949 pension agreements in the automotive and steel industries.

Most of the persons covered by private schemes are under plans that have been negotiated through collective bargaining. The variations in the negotiated plans are too detailed to permit simple summary. The larger number of plans are "non-contributory," but some require contributions from the employee as well as the employer. Most are funded but a substantial number are financed on a pay-as-you-go basis, which means that benefits will be paid only so long as the firm remains solvent. The plans may or may not provide for vesting. (Vesting is a guarantee that the employee will not lose that part of his pension equity based upon employer contributions should he terminate employment before retirement.) Under some plans, retirement is voluntary, whereas other stipulate a compulsory retirement age.

Certain recent trends in the private pension area are relevant to a discussion of the security of the aged. One is the growth in the number of "involuntary retirement plans" or those that make retirement mandatory at a given age. We have here, then, one more factor that is making it increasingly difficult for the older person who would prefer to remain economically active. Another important development is the spreading popularity of the early retirement provision. In the larger plans negotiated through collective bargaining, provision for early retirement benefits is now the prevailing practice.[20] The usual stipulation in these plans is that a worker has to have ten to fifteen years of service and be fifty-five or sixty in order to qualify for an early retirement benefit. A number of the plans have recently liberalized the eligibility requirements for workers affected by a permanent plant shutdown, and some encourage early retirement in such situations through liberalization of benefits.

Coverage under private pension plans is still increasing but at a decreasing rate.[21] A large proportion of those presently not included in such plans work in industries characterized by high labor turnover or short duration jobs. One close student of private pension plans argues that even 20 years from now, about 25 per cent of the working population will not be covered by private plans.[22] These persons will have to rely entirely on the social security system for their retirement income.

SECURITY FOR THE DISABLED

We have examined the problems of insecurity caused by unemployment, industrial injury, and old age. There remains for consideration the economic insecurity caused by sickness and non-work-connected injury.

The disabled person may run into a double-sided economic hazard. On the one side there is the possibility of economic loss resulting from inability to work. On the other, there is the added burden of medical costs. The absence of a comprehensive program of social insurance against these hazards is explained, in part, by the effective political opposition that has been mobilized against it and, in part, by the rapid growth of voluntary health

---

[20] Joseph Krislov, "Employee Benefit Plans, 1954–1962," *Social Security Bulletin,* April, 1964, p. 20.

[21] Robert Tilove, *"The Impact of Social Insurance on the Development of Private Benefit Plans,"* in William Bowen, Frederick Harbison, Richard Lester, and Herman Somers (eds.) *The American System of Social Insurance* (New York: McGraw-Hill Book Company, 1968), chap. 7.

[22] *Ibid.,* p. 192.

insurance. Between 1942 and 1961, hospital coverage under voluntary health insurance plans increased from about 20 million persons to more than 135 million. In 1969, enrollment in Blue Cross Hospital Service Plans alone was more than 71 million.

In recent years there has been a growth of support for a more active government role in the health field. Prominent among the factors responsible for this have been the rising costs of medical care, the incomplete character of the protection provided by many of the voluntary plans, and the large increase in the number of retired persons who incur added medical expense at a time when their incomes fall off sharply.

Income Protection for the Disabled

Originally, the Social Security Act of 1935 made no provision for the payment of cash benefits to the disabled. Since 1950, however, the federal government has matched state public assistance grants for the totally disabled; and in 1956 the Old Age and Survivors Insurance title of the act was amended to provide benefits to totally disabled persons. Under OASDHI, a disabled worker may be eligible to receive monthly payments if he had a total of at least twenty quarters of coverage out of the forty quarters immediately preceding the time of disability.[23] Benefits are determined on the same basis as they are for those who reach the retirement age of sixty-five. Under the 1956 provision, a disabled worker could qualify for monthly payments if his disability made it impossible for him to engage in any substantial economic activity and if there was an expectation that the condition would last indefinitely or until death. The 1965 OASDHI amendments liberalized this provision by making it possible for disabled workers to qualify for benefits if their disabilities are expected to last for at least twelve months. Determinations of disability are made by state agencies subject to review by the Social Security Administration.

Four states have enacted laws providing cash payments for temporary disability resulting from illness and non-occupational injury. The federal government has established a similar system for the railroad industry.

Rhode Island pioneered in the field of compulsory disability compensation when it enacted a disability benefit law in 1942. The Rhode Island plan aroused much interest, and for a time it appeared that disability compensation laws would spread rapidly among the states. Actually, only three other states have followed Rhode Island; but the three together with Rhode Island include about 25 per cent of all industrial and commercial employees in the United States.

---

[23] Persons under 31 years of age may qualify for disability benefits after shorter periods of coverage.

Rhode Island was one of a handful of states that had levied a tax on employees as well as employers for the purpose of financing unemployment benefits. The disability provision has been financed by diverting the employee tax from unemployment benefit purposes to a fund for paying disability benefits. The tax has varied but most recently has been 1 per cent of the first $3,600 of annual wages. Coverage is the same as that under the state unemployment compensation law, and the system is otherwise integrated with unemployment compensation. The person who becomes disabled must file a claim at the public employment office. The claim includes information from the claimant's physician about the nature of the disability. A medical claims examiner then reviews the claim and determines the number of weeks that the disability is likely to last. The maximum duration of benefits is twenty-six weeks in a benefit year, and benefits are computed in the same manner as they are for unemployment compensation.

The other states that have enacted disability benefit laws are California in 1946, New Jersey in 1948, and New York in 1950.[24] Payments for sickness benefits in the railroad industry began in 1947, the result of an amendment of the railroad unemployment insurance system enacted by Congress in 1946. There are numerous minor and a few major differences in the details of the disability payment laws. Only the more prominent variations will be noted here.[25] The Rhode Island plan is an exclusive state scheme, and no provision is made for private insurance. California, on the other hand, permits employers to exercise an option in this respect. A California employer, if the majority of his employees approve, may elect to have private insurance against disability. The cost to employees must be no greater than that under the state fund; and the benefits of the private plan must, in some respect, be more liberal than those granted by the state system. A unique feature of the New Jersey statute is that both employees and employers pay taxes to finance benefits. In Rhode Island and California the system is financed exclusively by taxes levied on employee wages. New York, alone among the four states, has modeled its law after the state workmen's compensation law, and the system in that state is administered by the state workmen's compensation board rather than by the agency administering unemployment compensation.

Social Security and Medical Care

The Committee on Economic Security, whose recommendations underlay the 1935 Social Security Act, made a general statement in favor of a

---

[24] Puerto Rico enacted a temporary disability insurance law in 1968.

[25] For a detailed description of the state disability benefit laws see Robert J. Myers, *Social Insurance and Allied Government Programs* (Homewood, Ill.: Richard D. Irwin, Inc., 1965), chap. 14.

compulsory national health insurance system. Congress, however, did not act upon this suggestion in the 1935 law. In ensuing years, the social controversy over medical care was largely over the pros and cons of a national insurance system. Since 1960 the debate has switched from the yes-or-no issue of the earlier years to one over the form of federal participation in a health care program. Specifically, the question has been over the relative merits of the public assistance as against the social insurance method. On the whole, those who formerly opposed federal involvement in the medical care area now favor the public assistance approach, whereas those who have long favored a national health insurance plan have supported the social insurance method.

The legislative history since 1960 has reflected the relative political power of the partisans of each position. The Kerr-Mills Act of that year was a public assistance measure. Under that law, federal grants were made available to the states for the first time to enable them to provide medical assistance to low income, aged persons who were not receiving old age assistance. Under Medical Assistance for the Aged (the Kerr-Mills Law) the states determined whether persons sixty-five or over had insufficient resources and income to meet medical care costs. The federal share of amounts expended by the states to defray the medical costs of eligible persons ranged from 50 to 80 per cent under a formula based largely on per capita income.[26]

Critics of the public assistance approach drew heavily upon the first three years of experience under Kerr-Mills to substantiate their case for a social insurance measure. The main arguments were (1) only twenty-eight states had MAA plans in operation by August, 1963, and the larger number of these were ineffective; (2) the Kerr-Mills program had been used to finance benefits for persons previously eligible for relief under other programs; and (3) the superior ability of the wealthier states to generate matching funds had resulted in an inequitable distribution of MAA funds contrary to the intent of Congress. In reference to the third point, it was noted that five states—California, Massachusetts, New York, Michigan, and Pennsylvania—had received 88 per cent of all MAA funds distributed from the start of the program through December 31, 1962, although these states contained only 32 per cent of the nation's elderly people.

The effectiveness of the political opposition to a social insurance program of medical care for the aged was smashed by President Lyndon Johnson's landslide election victory in 1964, and in July, 1965, "medicare" became a part of the national system of social security. The details of the medicare program are described below.

---

[26] For a description of the legislative history and the basic provisions of the Kerr-Mills Law see *Social Security Bulletin,* November, 1960, pp. 5–15.

Basic Plan. Under the 1965 health measure, as amended in 1967, medical insurance for persons aged 65 and over is provided by a basic plan and a supplemental plan. The basic plan automatically covers everyone over 65 except for certain classes of aliens and federal employees eligible for government health insurance under another law. The benefits provided by the basic plan are financed by increases in the Social Security payroll tax (see Table 21).[27]

Benefits under the basic plan include hospitalization of up to 90 days in each period of illness, nursing home care of up to 100 days after a stay of at least three days in a hospital, home nursing of as much as 100 visits a year by nurses or technicians, and outpatient diagnostic services provided by hospitals. Hospitalized patients pay the first $40 of hospital costs, and those staying over 60 days pay an additional $10 per day up to the 90 day limit. Nursing home care is provided without charge for the first 20 days after which the patient pays $5 for each day up to the 100 day limit. Charges for diagnostic studies are $20 of the charge for each diagnostic study plus 20 per cent of the charges above $20. The basic insurance plan covers the full costs of home nursing visits.

Supplementary Plan. Insurance under the supplementary plan is available on a voluntary basis to those who enroll and pay monthly premiums of $3. The federal government will match these premiums with funds appropriated from general tax revenues. The insurance supplements the basic plan by covering most other major medical expenses except for dental services, medicines, and drugs. Benefits under both the basic and supplemental plans became available on July 1, 1966.

As noted in Chapter 20, the 1965 amendments to the Social Security Act consolidated a number of pre-existing programs of medical assistance into a single and separate program. At the date of this writing about 40 states have adopted the new medical assistance or "medicaid" plans. Medicaid is, of course, a public assistance approach to medical care and should not be confused with "medicare" which is a form of social insurance.

Persons eligible for medicaid include those eligible for public assistance and, at the option of the state, persons able to provide for their own maintenance but whose incomes and resources are inadequate to defray medical expenses. To qualify for federal grants-in-aid, a state medicaid program must offer welfare recipients inpatient and outpatient hospital services,

---

[27] The cost of benefits for persons not covered by OASDHI was met by appropriations from general tax revenues. Eligibility for those attaining age 65 was established after three quarters of coverage. In subsequent years, the eligibility requirement is gradually scaled upward each year until the requirements eventually reach the regular insured status requirement.

laboratory and X-ray services, nursing home care for adults, and physicians' services. Other items of medical services are optional with the states.

Expenditures under medicaid expanded beyond expectations and the 1967 amendments to the Social Security Act incorporated limits to the federal matching formula. After July, 1968, states were limited in setting income levels (income eligibility levels for medicaid assistance) for federal matching purposes to 150 per cent of the payment level under the program of Aid to Families with Dependent Children. The percentage after calendar year 1969 drops to 133⅓ per cent. Under the 1967 amendments, states may impose deductables or other cost-sharing provisions for hospital care which they were not originally permitted to do.

QUESTIONS

1. What aspects of modern life have intensified the economic problems of the aged?

2. Many older persons resist retirement. How do you explain this resistance?

3. Explain the difference between the money costs and the real costs of the OASDHI benefits for the aged.

4. Opposition to the use of the social insurance method for providing medical care has been quite strong in the United States. In this respect, the United States' experience has been different from that of most other major industrial nations. How would you explain the difference of attitudes in the United States from those in the other nations?

SELECTED READINGS

COHEN, WILBUR J. "Economic Security for the Aged, Sick, and Disabled: Some Issues and Implications" in Levitan, Sar., Cohen, Wilbur, and Lampman, Robert (eds.) *Towards Freedom from Want*. Madison, Wisconsin: Industrial Relations Research Association, 1968, pp. 63–87.

EPSTEIN, LENORE. "Income of the Aged in 1962," *Social Security Bulletin,* March, 1964.

ORBACH, HAROLD L., and TIBBITS, CLARK (eds.). *Aging and the Economy.* Ann Arbor: University of Michigan Press, 1963.

TURNBULL, JOHN G. *The Changing Faces of Economic Insecurity*. Minneapolis, Minn.: The University of Minnesota Press, 1966. Chap. 3.

WILCOX, CLAIR. *Toward Social Welfare*. Homewood, Ill.: Richard D. Irwin, Inc., 1969. Chap. 8.

CHAPTER 23

The Unemployment Problem

IT IS NOT NECESSARY TO BELABOR THE POINT THAT ECONOMIC SECURITY for the typical worker depends, in the last analysis, upon steadiness of employment. For the unemployed person, a social insurance benefit is a temporary stopgap, at best. Few workers are in a position to maintain their living standards for any length of time when their regular job incomes cease.

Despite the general conditions of prosperity that have prevailed since the end of World War II, unemployment has proved to be a persistent and stubborn problem. Between 1948 and 1965, the unemployment rate was typically above 4 and frequently over 5 per cent of the labor force. Between 1966 and the date of this writing, the rate has been less than 4 per cent but even in this period, particular population subgroups have been beset by joblessness at a rate well above the national average. "Prosperity unemployment" has posed novel challenges for a nation conditioned by the 1930 experience to associate serious unemployment with general economic depression. The dimensions of the contemporary problem and the efforts to deal with it will be examined below. Before turning to these matters, however, we must consider the problem of identifying the unemployed.

UNEMPLOYMENT STATISTICS

Outwardly, at least, the job of counting the unemployed does not appear to be especially troublesome. A person is either working or not working, and to assign him to one or the other of these categories would seem to be

591

a simple matter. The reader may find it worthwhile, however, to refer to the discussion of labor force statistics in Chapter 2, since the problem involved in counting the unemployed is identical to the problem of counting the total number of persons in the labor force. In any statistical enumeration, the answers derived are shaped, in part, by decisions made before the counting process begins. There are many ways to define unemployment, and the basic statistical data that are currently available are conditioned by the particular definition used by the Bureau of the Census.

Monthly Estimates of Unemployment

The Census Bureau in its labor force statistics divides all persons over sixteen years of age into two categories: persons in the labor force and those not in the labor force. Persons in the labor force are classed either as employed or unemployed. The total number of persons counted as unemployed will vary depending upon the precise definition of two statistical borderlines. One is the line between unemployment and "not in the labor force," and the other, the line between employment and unemployment. Fortunately for the cause of labor force statistics, the employment status of some persons is clear cut and easily ascertained. The number of marginal situations, however, is sufficiently large so that the total of the unemployed can be affected by the placement of the "borderline." Since the late 1930's, when concepts similar to those now in use were first introduced, the definition of unemployment has been altered several times. The latest changes made in 1967 tend to reduce somewhat the number of persons counted as unemployed.

Census Bureau statistics of unemployment are derived from a monthly sample survey of households.[1] Unemployed persons are those civilians who had no employment during the survey week, were available for work and (1) had engaged in specific job seeking activity within the past 4 weeks, (2) were waiting to be called back to a job from which they had been laid off, or (3) were waiting to report to a new job within the following 30 days.

Prior to the 1967 changes, there was no time period specified for a jobless person's latest work seeking activity. Furthermore, persons who indicated that they would be looking for work except for their belief that no work was available are now excluded from the count of unemployed whereas they were included before 1967. As suggested above, these and other changes in the definition of unemployment, have moved the statistical borderlines to eliminate from the count of the jobless several categories of non-workers that had previously been classified as unemployed.

One of the most controversial issues in the area of labor force statistics concerns the classification of part-time workers. (The Census Bureau con-

---

[1] Census Bureau estimates of labor force size and unemployment are based upon a monthly sample taken during the week that includes the twelfth day.

siders all persons who work thirty-five or more hours during the survey week to be full-time workers. Those who work one to thirty-four hours are classified as part-time.) A person who has done as little as one hour of work for pay during the survey week is counted as employed rather than unemployed. Thus, in a period of declining economic activity when there is a large increase in the amount of part-time work, the figure of total unemployment will understate the actual amount of job loss that is occurring.

Since the Census Bureau presents the number of part-time workers as a subclassification of the number of employed persons and, in fact, presents a detailed breakdown of reasons for working part-time, a question might be raised about what the difference is between calling part-time workers employed or calling them unemployed.[2] Anyone who is interested can examine the statistics and discover how many among the employed are working less than full-time and why they are working less than full-time.

One answer to the question raised above is that persons usually draw inferences about the seriousness of unemployment from the single figure that is published for total unemployment and rarely examine the detailed breakdowns of labor force statistics. Among the special interest groups in the nation, there are those who favor quick government action when unemployment begins to rise and those who would be far more cautious insofar as government intervention is concerned. From a strategic standpoint, the political positions of these groups are stronger or weaker depending upon the size of the figure published for total unemployment. Thus, the way in which the Census Bureau defines unemployment has important political implications.

A single statistical series cannot show everything, and we have seen that the Census Bureau's concept of unemployment emphasizes the fact of active job seeking. Although the data are reasonably good indicators of gross employment trends, recent research findings suggest that they may have shortcomings as a guide for full employment policies. The calculations of Strand and Dernburg, for example, indicate that during the period 1953–1962 the loss of 100 jobs was associated with a reduction of about fifty persons in the size of the measured labor force.[3] As unemployment rose, in other words, large numbers of persons became discouraged and withdrew from active labor force activity. In periods of serious unemployment, there may be a significant gap between measured labor force and

---

[2] Part-time workers are classed according to their usual status at their present jobs (full-time or part-time) and by their reasons for working part-time. The reasons are further subclassified as "economic" and "other." Economic reasons include slack work, material shortages, repairs to plant, and inability to find full-time work. "Other" reasons include labor disputes, bad weather, and no desire for full-time work.

[3] Kenneth Strand and Thomas Dernburg, "Cyclical Variation in Civilian Labor Force Participation," *Review of Economics and Statistics,* November, 1964, pp. 378–391.

what the size of the labor force would be given full employment conditions. A program to achieve full employment, thus, will fall short of the desired result if it derives its job targets from the unemployment rate shown in the monthly estimates.[4]

BES Unemployment Data

A second major source of information about employment trends is a variety of statistics published by the *Bureau of Employment Security* in the Department of Labor.[5] The state government agencies operating unemployment insurance laws and public employment offices are required to submit reports to the Bureau of Employment Security as one condition of receiving federal funds for administrative purposes. These reports are the source of the employment data presented by the BES. Several types of data published by the BES have been used as indicators of unemployment. Each is described briefly below.[6]

Active File Data. When a person seeks a job through a public employment office his application is placed in an "active file." There it remains until the individual is placed in a job or until the application is cancelled on the assumption that he has found a job or is no longer seeking a job. The active file can be regarded as a rough indicator of employment trends since it is reasonable to assume that worker use of the public employment service will be heavier when unemployment rises, and vice versus. For a number of reasons, however, the active file cannot be used as an accurate indicator of the amount of unemployment. Workers have not developed the habit of relying extensively upon the public employment service. Those workers filing claims for unemployment benefits must register for work, but

---

[4] In order to present more incisive data on selected social, demographic, and economic characteristics of the labor force, the U.S. Department of Labor now publishes periodic special reports based on supplementary questions included in the schedule used for the monthly labor force survey. Certain of those reports have presented detailed data on the employment problems of particular population sub-groups and, thus, are valuable supplements to the basic statistics of employment and unemployment.

A major gap in the data required for a full assessment of the condition of the labor market has been the absence of information on job vacancies. In a January, 1969, announcement, the U.S. Department of Labor revealed plans for a monthly survey of job opportunities in 50 metropolitan areas. For a discussion of the problems associated with a measurement of job vacancies, see *The Measurement and Interpretation of Job Vacancies* (New York: National Bureau of Economic Research, 1966).

[5] At the time of this writing the Bureau of Employment Security is being reorganized and will probably have a new name when the reorganization is completed.

[6] A good analysis of the usefulness and shortcomings of BES data can be found in Herbert Parnes, "Unemployment Data from the Employment Security Program," in National Bureau of Economic Research, *The Measurement and Behavior of Unemployment* (Princeton, N.J.: Princeton University Press, 1957).

a significant proportion of the labor force is not covered by the state unemployment compensation laws. Furthermore, there are some doubts about the accuracy of the data in the active files. As Herbert Parnes notes, the function of the employment service is to find jobs for people, not to develop unemployment statistics.[7] The amount of validation of the active file data that takes place varies from state to state and even among local employment offices within a state.

Claims Data. Claims filed by workers for unemployment benefits are another source of information about unemployment. The first claim filed by a newly unemployed person is called an *initial claim;* the total initial claims filed during a week show how many workers covered by unemployment insurance have recently lost jobs. A *continued claim* is filed on a week by week basis after the initial claim has been made, and the total continued claims indicate the number of persons covered by unemployment insurance who have been unemployed for one or more weeks.

The value of claims data lies in their timeliness, for they are published within one week after a claim has been filed; also, they are available on state, regional, and local bases, as well as for the nation as a whole. The inexperienced analyst, however, should be cautious about drawing conclusions from data on claims for unemployment benefits. Not only is coverage under unemployment compensation limited, but the limitations vary in different states. Thus, the compensation laws of the states would have to be examined carefully before inferences could be drawn from a state-by-state comparison of benefit claims. Claims data, also, do not show the amount of unemployment that is occurring among workers who are ineligible for unemployment benefits because of inadequate work experience; among workers who have exhausted their benefit rights; and among those who, for one reason or another, do not file claims for benefits although they are eligible to do so.

Local Area Estimates. The only regularly available estimates of local area unemployment are those made by public employment office labor market analysts and published by the Bureau of Employment Security.[8] The estimates are derived from statistics of insured unemployment adjusted to take into account non-insured unemployment and other factors affecting area unemployment totals. On the basis of the estimates, the BES classifies 150 major production and employment centers each month according to reported labor supply conditions. The classifications range from Group *A* areas (over-all labor shortage with an unemployment rate of less than 1.5 per cent) to Group *F* areas (substantial unemployment with an unemploy-

---

[7] *Ibid.,* p. 126.
[8] See the BES publication, *Area Trends in Employment and Unemployment.*

ment rate of 12 per cent or more). In addition to the major area classification, the BES maintains a list of smaller areas with an unemployment rate
of 6 per cent or higher. Areas with heavy unemployment that has persisted
for some time are classified as having "substantial and persistent" unemployment.

At one time, the basic purpose of the area estimates was to aid local
employment offices in the planning of their activities. At the present time,
however, the BES classification is an important criterion in the determination of an area's eligibility for assistance under the 1961 Area Redevelopment Act as well as other federal programs.

The accuracy of the area estimates depends, to a considerable extent,
upon the caliber of the labor market analyst in the local public employment
office. A number of observers believe that the data, on the whole, are too
crude to serve as criteria for determinations on area assistance.[9]

Summary: Unemployment Statistics

If a government program to deal with unemployment is to have adequate
direction, the following questions must be answered accurately: How much
unemployment is occurring, where is it occurring, and what groups are
most seriously affected? Taken together, the available statistical materials
will provide the analyst with a broadly accurate picture of the total situation, but more refined data would be helpful for programmatic purposes.
Desirable supplements to the currently available statistics would include
measures of the impact of unemployment on the labor force activity of
the population and more accurate indicators of local area unemployment.

TYPES OF UNEMPLOYMENT

The person who wants a job and cannot find one is not apt to be impressed
by the fact that his unemployment is due to seasonal rather than frictional
causes or to frictional rather than cyclical causes. For purposes of understanding and dealing with unemployment, however, it is necessary to
differentiate the causes. Unemployment may result from any one of several
distinct causes, and remedies that are appropriate in certain situations may
be ineffective in others.

For purposes of distinguishing the causes of unemployment, the following
terminology will be used: (1) *normal unemployment* subclassified into
seasonal and short run frictional categories, (2) *cyclical unemployment,* and

---

[9] See, for example, Joseph C. Ullman, "How Accurate are Estimates of State and
Local Unemployment?" *Industrial and Labor Relations Review,* April, 1963, pp.
434–452.

(3) *long run frictions* subclassified into technological and structural categories. Structural unemployment will be further broken down into a number of subtypes.

Normal Unemployment

The word "normal" is used to describe certain types and amounts of unemployment that occur as normal consequences of the workings of our economy. Unlike the other types, normal unemployment is not indicative of any serious economic malfunction.

Some unemployment will occur each year because of seasonal influences upon economic activity. Several different types of seasonal effects can be identified:

1. Weather conditions affect the physical production of many goods and services. Thus, in outdoor activities such as building construction, Great Lakes shipping, agriculture, or logging, the number of persons employed will be much larger in summer than in winter.

2. The demand for certain commodities fluctuates periodically by significant amounts. Sales of ice cream, soft drinks, beer, bathing suits, and sun glasses, for example, are up in summer, down in winter. The reverse is true for protective footwear, coats, ice skates, and heating fuel. With the seasonal changes in the demand for such products, there is, of course, a seasonal variation in the number of job opportunities. Other economic phenomena that occur periodically, and so affect consumer buying patterns and employment, are style changes and new model innovations. Periodic ups and downs in employment can also be expected to occur as a result of holiday buying habits.

3. Some unemployment results from periodic fluctuations in labor supply. The most important variation here occurs at the beginning of the summer when the size of the labor force is swelled by the millions of students who seek summer jobs and the recent graduates who are looking for steady employment. Until these persons find jobs they are counted as unemployed.

Seasonal variations in unemployment, then, can be attributed to periodic contractions in job opportunities caused by weather conditions, periodic changes in the demand for certain types of commodities, and periodic fluctuations in the number of job seekers.

Seasonal unemployment is difficult to measure because the amount that will materialize in a given year is affected by many factors. Seasonal fluctuations, for instance, are less pronounced in periods of high employment than during depressions. When jobs are easily available, those persons in seasonal employment—such as the construction worker, the seaman on the

Great Lakes freighter, and the dairy plant worker—are able to find other jobs to carry them through the slack season, and high school and college graduates are more easily absorbed into the labor force. Although the amount of seasonal unemployment may vary from year to year, the broad rhythm of seasonal swings tends to repeat itself. Peaks in seasonal unemployment usually occur in February and June, whereas the low points are reached in May and October. When seasonal unemployment is expressed as a percentage of total industry unemployment, the highest percentages are generally found in construction and agriculture, and the lowest are in durable goods manufacturing, trade, finance, and service. In 1960, for example, over a third of all unemployment in construction and agriculture was attributable to seasonal factors, whereas only 10 to 15 per cent was seasonal in the other industries named.[10] Seasonal factors are also responsible for a large part of the unemployment suffered by new entrants into the labor market.

For the economy as a whole, seasonal unemployment does not constitute a pressing or serious problem, and little social policy has been developed to cope with such unemployment. Public employment offices help to locate seasonally displaced persons in new jobs, and many of the seasonally unemployed are able to depend upon the support of the unemployment compensation benefit. In specific industries where seasonal unemployment has been serious, the primary responsibility for coping with the problem has rested on the shoulders of the firms and workers involved.

In a study published in 1931, Edwin S. Smith found that many business firms had made quite extensive efforts to reduce their seasonal variations in labor requirements.[11] Among the techniques found to be effective in individual circumstances were energetic sales efforts in the dull season, creation of out-of-season uses for products, product diversification, and manufacturing in advance of orders. Numerous cost advantages accrue to the firm as a result of employment regularization. Production on small and irregular lots in the off season tends to involve high costs; workers who are laid off during the dull season may not return when they are needed; many costs, such as executive salaries, continue regardless of the level of output. In addition to these factors, recent developments in law and collective bargaining make unemployment a direct expense for the employer. Prior to these developments, the only direct costs of unemployment for the employer were the clerical costs incurred as a result of layoffs. Today, the merit rating provisions of unemployment compensation laws cause payroll taxes to be higher for the employer who offers irregular employment. Severance pay and supplemental unemployment benefit provisions in labor-

---

[10] Subcommittee on Economic Statistics of the Joint Economic Committee, Congress of the United States, *Unemployment: Terminology, Measurement, and Analysis* (Washington, D.C.: U.S. Government Printing Office, 1961), p. 82.

[11] *Reducing Seasonal Unemployment* (New York: McGraw-Hill Book Company).

management agreements associate the level of unemployment among a firm's employees with costs that vary directly with the level. There is little evidence, however, as to whether these direct costs have induced employers to regularize employment.

In those cases where the employer cannot or will not regularize employment, the burden of adjustment must be assumed by the worker. The obvious and quite common solution for the worker associated with a seasonal industry is to dovetail his usual occupation with out-of-season work. The feasibility of this solution depends, of course, upon the availability of other work. Even during prosperity, off-season work is not a realistic prospect for workers in certain situations. In a one-industry town, other jobs may simply not exist for the person who is unable to leave his area of residence. In those large metropolitan areas where economic activity is dominated by one industry, the other industries may not be able to absorb persons made unemployed by a large seasonal layoff in the dominant industry. Some workers, furthermore, tend to remain idle during off seasons because of occupational immobility.

Unemployment compensation, as we have already noted, removes some of the sting of seasonal unemployment; but coverage limitations deny this protection to certain groups, such as agricultural workers, who are especially vulnerable. Unemployment compensation, incidentally, may actually discourage some seasonally unemployed persons from seeking off-season work. For instance, a construction industry truck driver might earn $3.00 an hour or $120 for a forty-hour week. If, during the winter layoff, he can do no better than, say, $1.50 an hour as a cab driver or a semi-skilled plant employee, his weekly earnings for forty hours are $60.00. When income taxes are withheld and other deductions made, his take-home pay is between $40 and $45. It is understandable, perhaps, that he will prefer a $30 to $35 unemployment benefit check over the alternative of working forty hours for an extra $10 of take-home pay.

Seasonal unemployment can be reduced to an extent, but is is doubtful that it can be eliminated. As long as the economy is generally prosperous, the burden of seasonal unemployment will be relatively light. Thus, the most effective thing that can be done to minimize the losses caused by seasonal unemployment is to deal energetically with the unemployment arising from other causes.

Normal unemployment also occurs as a result of labor market frictions. A considerable amount of milling around goes on in the labor market; and, at any given time, there are as many as 2 million persons who are in the process of changing jobs or looking for a first job. Even when the number of job openings and the number of job seekers are in balance, it takes time for the available workers to be matched with the available jobs.

As is the case with seasonal unemployment, frictional unemployment is difficult to measure. If defined, somewhat arbitrarily, as unemployment with a duration of less than five weeks, the quantity of frictional unemployment has been stable over time usually amounting to 1.5 to 2 per cent of the labor force.

During the periods of 1946–1948 and 1951–1953, when jobs were relatively easy to find, the amount of unemployment ranged from an annual average of 2.5 to 3.9 per cent of the labor force. It is quite likely that most of this unemployment was a result of seasonal and frictional forces. The percentages represent a degree of unemployment that can be reduced by only minor amounts in a dynamic economy where adjustments of one sort or another are constantly occurring.

CYCLICAL UNEMPLOYMENT

For more than 100 years after Adam Smith wrote his *Wealth of Nations* in 1776, the main stream of economic theory paid little attention to the phenomenon of recurring economic crisis. Unemployment was attributed to mistakes, such as production of the wrong kinds of goods, or frictions which prevented certain necessary adjustments from occurring instantaneously. In either case, unemployment was considered to be a temporary situation which would be corrected by the movement of capital and labor from depressed sectors of the economy to areas of greater promise. A general overproduction of goods was regarded as an impossibility, since it was thought that the act of production generated sufficient income to buy back the product that was produced. If some people saved and thus held unspent income, others would borrow the savings for investment purposes. In this way, the market would be cleared of the goods that had been produced, and, as long as everything produced was sold, there would be no reason for unemployment to appear.

By the end of the nineteenth century, it had become apparent to numerous observers that the up and down movements of business conditions could not be brushed aside this lightly, and many theories have since been advanced to explain recurrent waves of prosperity and depression. The business cycle has been attributed to psychology, monetary factors, over-investment, underconsumption, and saving and investment relationships, among other causes.[12] All the prominent theories provide some insight into

---

[12] A good description of the various business cycle theories can be found in Gottfried Haberler, *Prosperity and Depression* (New York: United Nations, 1946) or in any one of a number of business cycle textbooks. See, for example, D. Hamberg, *Business Cycles* (New York: The Macmillan Company, 1951); Maurice Lee, *Economic Fluctuations* (Homewood, Ill.: Richard D. Irwin, Inc., 1955); Earl Hald, *Business Cycles* (Boston: Houghton Mifflin Company, 1954). For a collection of significant recent writings on various aspects of business fluctuations, see John J. Clark and Morris Cohen (eds.), *Business Fluctuations, Growth, and Economic Stabilization* (New York: Random House, Inc., 1963), Part III, Sections *B* and *C*, and Part IV.

the nature of depression and unemployment, but none is definitive. The explanation of unemployment developed by John Maynard Keynes has won the widest acceptance, and most of the present-day thought relative to elimination of cyclical unemployment has its roots in the *Keynesian* analysis.[13]

The complexities and subtleties of the Keynesian system are not easily reduced to a few summary propositions, but the prominent elements of the analysis can be summarized. The total amount of money that is spent in an economy in a given period, hence the national income for the period is the sum of the amounts spent by consumers, by business for investment, and by the government. Let us assume that at some level of national income, all persons who want jobs at prevailing wage levels are employed. As long as total spending remains at the full employment level, the number of persons working will remain approximately the same. If, however, spending by any of the three sectors in the economy declines, and if there is no compensation for the drop by an increase in spending by the other sectors, national income will fall, and the amount of employment associated with the higher level of national income will drop along with it.

If the assumption is made that government spending is determined by the costs of government functions and does not vary significantly from year to year, the major variables that determine the level of employment are consumer spending and business spending. Some consumers are unable to make ends meet out of current income and must dip into past savings or rely upon outside help. Others are just barely able to pay for their needs out of current income. Still others receive more than they spend. As a group, however, consumers usually spend less than aggregate consumer income. In other words, a positive amount of saving usually occurs each year. Unless business invests an amount of money equal to what consumers are saving, some part of the national inventory of goods and services will remain unsold, and national income will fall.

The relationship between the amounts that the business community plans to invest and the amounts that consumer units plan to save determines income and employment levels. The process by which unemployment actually materializes is easily explained. Let us assume that aggregate savings are high and that aggregate investment is low. In this situation, there will be an increase in business inventories because of lagging sales, and retailers and wholesalers will be placing smaller orders with producers. Producers will need fewer workers, and those who are discharged will necessarily curtail their buying. This, in turn, will lead to further unemployment; and thus, by a cumulative process, national income will become smaller and smaller while unemployment becomes more and more wide-

---

[13] John Maynard Keynes, *The General Theory of Employment, Interest, and Money* (New York: Harcourt, Brace & World, Inc., 1936).

spread. How long will this process continue? At some lower level of national income, the amount that the community attempts to save will be equal to the amount that business plans to invest. At this level, the economy is in an employment equilibrium, and no further decline in employment need occur.

The difference between the older and the newer theories of employment should be noted. The old theory assumed a quantitative identity between savings and investment.[14] If savings were high and investment low, the interest rate or the cost of borrowing money would drop. This would discourage saving and encourage investment, and at some rate of interest the amounts saved and invested would be equal. Such unemployment as existed, then, was attributed to the fact that persons out of work wanted a wage that was higher than the value of their marginal products. These persons were "voluntarily" unemployed. By lowering their wage demands they could find jobs, since at the lower wage their employment would become profitable to employers.

The significance of the interest rate is diminished in the newer analysis. People save money for many reasons, and the rate of interest is by no means the most important among them. Similarly, the amount of investment that occurs is considered to be less dependent upon the price of money than was assumed by the orthodox economists. Decisions to save and decisions to invest are made by different sets of people, and there is no guarantee that the decisions will dovetail. The possibility of disparity in these decisions means that the economy is inherently unstable. When the business community attempts to invest more than is being saved, levels of economic activity will rise until a full employment condition is reached, and then inflation will commence. When the business community attempts to invest less than the amounts that the entire community is attempting to save, there will be a decline in national income and in the amount of employment. A lowering of wage demands by workers is not considered to be a certain cure for unemployment, since employers may hesitate in making employment commitments while costs are falling generally.

The Keynesian analysis is a general attempt to explain the instability of an economic system in which people remain free to make important deci-

---

[14] The "new" economics also assumes a quantitative equality between savings and investment, but the implications are different. Thus, in the short run according to Keynesian economics, savings are equal to investments, even though consumers save more than business firms intend to invest, because business firms hold larger inventories than they anticipated. Business firms have invested unintentionally in inventories that are equal in value to the "excess" savings of the community. In the longer run, efforts to save more than is being invested fail, since the decline in national income and employment that is caused by such efforts makes it impossible for persons to save as much as they had desired. Differences between planned savings and planned investment, then, are eliminated by changes in the level of national income. The orthodox economists assumed that differences between planned savings and planned investments would be eliminated by changes in the rate of interest.

sions. It is not a total explanation of the business cycle. Since the turn of
the century, there have been far-reaching institutional changes in the
United States, such as growth in the importance of large corporations and
labor unions. There has been large-scale technological change. The economy has been shaken by two world wars. There have been several orgies
of speculation. There has been dishonesty in high places. The role of the
United States vis-à-vis the rest of the world has changed in a fundamental
way. All these factors have affected the operation of the economy, including the levels at which it has operated. An understanding of an individual
experience of cyclical unemployment requires an analysis of the specific
economic history of the period. The Keynesian analysis suggests that, apart
from everything else, certain economic relationships are responsible for an
inherent instability in a relatively free market economy. Decisions to save
and invest, however, cannot be assumed to be unaffected by "everything
else"; and the difficulty of sizing up the influence of all the factors that may
be significant has inhibited our capacity to forecast the economic future
with any degree of accuracy.

Demand Unemployment. As noted above, unemployment attributable
in inadequate demand for consumer and investment goods has ordinarily
occurred during the depression phase of the business cycle. The level of
unemployment that persisted between 1957 and 1965, however, has shown
that demand may be inadequate to sustain a desirable level of employment
in an economic context of prosperity. A sharp debate has been waged over
conflicting interpretations of persistent unemployment, but the consensus
among professional economists appears to be that the rate of growth in the
demand for goods was not adequate during the years mentioned to bring
the level of unemployment down to amounts associated with short run
frictional causes. Our experience with persistent unemployment will be
considered in greater detail at a later point in this chapter.

LONG-RUN FRICTIONS

Long run frictional unemployment results when the economy is slow in
adjusting to significant changes in the characteristics of labor supply, labor
demand, or both. In certain of its manifestations, such as the case of technological unemployment, long run frictional unemployment is a by-product
of economic progress. In others, it is associated with flaws in the economic
or social structure. Not infrequently, long run frictional unemployment
grows out of an admixture of causes which are difficult to disentangle for
analytical purposes. The problem is further complicated when cyclical
factors are also operating, as they frequently do. As we shall note in a

later part of this chapter, serious policy issues are created when both frictional and demand forces appear to be present. The discussion that follows below will deal with the nature of the longer run frictions that are currently posing troublesome problems for the American economy.

TECHNOLOGICAL UNEMPLOYMENT

Technology has been described as "accumulated knowledge, techniques, and skills and their application in creating useful goods and services."[15] In twentieth century United States, both accumulation and application have been proceeding at a rapid pace, and living standards have risen amazingly in a remarkably short time period. Whereas technological change has made life more comfortable and interesting for a large majority of the people, it has also been partly responsible for some of the serious economic and social disruptions that have occurred. Industrial progress, for instance, has made it possible to mass produce items that were luxury goods only a short while ago; however, the occasional failure to sell mass output at profitable terms has stopped the wheels of industry almost as effectively as drought, plague, or other natural disasters stopped the producers of the pre-machine age. The inanimate machine, of course, is not responsible for the wholesale cessation of economic activity that was examined earlier under the heading of cyclical unemployment. The accoutrements of the machine age, however —urbanization, the monetary institutions, the patterns of income distribution, the particular consumer and producer psychologies, among others— make up an economic context in which cyclical movements of business are likely to occur.

Technological unemployment is different from cyclical unemployment in that it is a consequence of progress rather than of economic failures. Whenever an important technical innovation occurs, the economic society must adapt to the facts of the new setting. The process of adaptation may result in displacement of workers, since some firms will be unable to survive, and some labor skills will become obsolete. Viewed in this light, a certain amount of unemployment is a price that is usually paid for economic progress. Technological advance makes it possible for economic actors to perform more efficiently, but on occasions it demands different, or fewer, actors.

Technical innovations may create unemployment in two ways. Most directly, a change in machinery or method may so enlarge the productivity of a single worker that fewer workers are needed to satisfy the immediate

---

[15] J. Frederic Dewhurst and Associates, *America's Needs and Resources* (New York: The Twentieth Century Fund, 1955), p. 834.

market demand for a product. The second type of employment effect occurs when a new method, product, or service renders the old forms obsolete. Usually any job loss that is caused by industrial progress is more than counter-balanced in amount by the new opportunities created. The problem is that the displaced workers are not the beneficiaries of the new opportunities in many instances.

When innovation results in the development of new and major industries, the quantitative relationship between jobs eliminated and opportunities created is obvious and requires little analysis. It is not conceivable, for instance, that employment in the buggy and carriage industry could ever have equaled the number of persons who are now employed in the automobile industry and in complementary industries, such as highway construction, oil refining, and rubber tire production. In the direct laborsaving type of innovation, such as a machinery change that reduces the labor input required for a given output, the relationship between jobs eliminated and opportunities created is less obvious. Logically it can be demonstrated that laborsaving machinery does not reduce the total demand for labor, but the argument rests on long run propositions and ignores important frictions that impede the adjustment processes in the labor, capital, and product markets.[16]

Although it can be conceded that technological unemployment is a short run phenomenon, it does not follow that serious hardship will not be endured by those made jobless. In practice, the ability of the technologically unemployed to find new jobs depends upon many of the factors already examined in this and earlier chapters. Technological unemployment is less

---

[16] The economic "proof" that laborsaving machinery does not reduce employment rests on the proposition that total purchasing power is unaffected by the substitution of machines for men. When a product is sold in a competitive market, for example, the introduction of a laborsaving piece of equipment will ultimately result in lower product prices. If a consumer finds that he can purchase for $75 a commodity that had previously cost $100, he may react in any of the following ways: (1) *He might buy more units of the commodity.* If this occurs generally, no employment decline in the industry need occur at all. (2) *He might buy more of some other commodity.* If enough persons react in this manner, employment will fall in the industry where the new equipment has been installed, but there will be an offsetting employment increase in other industries. (3) *He might increase his savings.* A large increase in savings induced by price declines will enlarge the supply of capital funds and possibly stimulate new investment which will open up new jobs. This last proposition assumes, of course, that potential investors will respond favorably to a drop in the rate of interest.

In a non-competitive market situation, the immediate result of an installation of laborsaving equipment is higher profits for the firm. Higher profits might be disposed of in numerous ways such as larger dividends, plant expansion, salary and wage increases, increased advertising expenditures, etc. The point of the analysis in either the competitive or monopolistic case is that the money saved by reduction of labor costs becomes disposable income to other persons, and the actual disposal of the extra income creates about as many employment opportunities as were eliminated by the technical innovation.

serious when the economy is prosperous and the workers displaced are young and mobile. For the individual, the burden of adjustment may be lighter or heavier, depending upon whether the job eliminated called for modest or highly specialized skills. The female textile mill operator, for example, may be perfectly satisfied to move to electronic assembly work; but the professional musician may be less intrigued by the prospect of servicing juke boxes. In short, the person displaced by a machine becomes one job seeker among all other job seekers. Prospects depend—as they do for all the unemployed—upon the general state of business conditions and personal characteristics of the job seeker such as age, sex, race, education, and mobility.

Automation and Technological Unemployment

It is difficult to find a simple, clear-cut statement of what is involved in automation. Automation experts—and there seem to be a surprisingly large number of them for a field that is so young—have not agreed upon a definition of automation, nor is there any consensus as to the significance and scope of what is occurring. An examination of the extensive automation literature, however, suggests that the absence of a common definition is the result of differences in emphasis and terminology rather than of any fundamental disagreement over the content of automation technology.

Of the various descriptions of automation, the one suggested by Baldwin and Shultz is possibly the easiest for the layman to comprehend.[17] According to their description, automation consists of three fundamental developments. One involves the linking together of what had been separate operations into lines of continuous production. This aspect of automation has been variously described as "Detroit automation," "link automation," "continuous automation production," and "transfer machining."

A second development involves the use of electronic equipment to eliminate or diminish the need for human control of industrial processes. The feature common to many automatic control systems is an interdependence of the different phases of a process, or what has come to be called "feedback." Feedback involves the use of an automatic device to correct undesired variations from a pattern.[18] A simple example of feedback is a thermostatic temperature control system. One way to control the temperature of a room is to make a thermometer reading and then to adjust the

---

[17] George B. Baldwin and George P. Shultz, "Automation: A New Dimension To Old Problems," *Proceedings of Seventh Annual Meeting of the Industrial Relations Research Association,* 1954, pp. 115, 116.

[18] For a good description of feedback technology see Arnold Tustin, "Feedback," *Scientific American,* September, 1952, pp. 48–55.

operation of the furnace to correct for any deviation from a desired standard. This arrangement is what engineers call an "open loop system." The control comes from an agent that is outside of the heating system. In a closed loop system, the operation of the system itself feeds back information that automatically sets up corrections when necessary. Thus, a thermostat records the variations from a desired temperature, and the record sets in motion the changes in the operation of the furnace that are necessary to produce the desired result. The operation of the thermostat depends upon the temperature of the room, and the temperature of the room depends upon the operation of the thermostat.[19] The loop is closed, and there is no need for a human operator to intervene in the process.

The third major aspect of automation is what has been called "computer technology." The development of complex computing machines has revolutionized the area of data processing and is affecting the office operation just as fundamentally as transfer machining is affecting the plant.

The application of techniques and instruments that are basic to automation is not limited to highly automatized industries. High speed analogue and digital computers, for example, can be used in any operation where it is advantageous to process large amounts of data in a short time. The significance of this point is that the impact of automation will extend far beyond the much publicized applications of equipment that minimize the need for human physical and mental labor. Not every firm can aspire to have a workerless producing unit, but few industries are likely to remain totally untouched by the new technology.

In any anticipation of future technology, the words "atomic power" must at least be mentioned. The potential impact of atomic power on industrial processes is even more conjectural than the series of scientific developments that we have called automation. The simultaneous development of electronics and atomics, however, cannot help but stir the imagination with a promise of a more abundant economy than man has ever known.

Automation and Unemployment. One might make his way through the entire literature of automation—a substantial undertaking—and emerge with something less than a clear picture of the employment effects of the new technology. At one pole, there are assertions to the effect that the problem of general unemployment from automation "is a non-existent will-o'-the-wisp problem."[20] At the other, it is contended that automation is a

---

[19] In practice, the typical feedback process is far more complex, of course, than the simple thermostatic system described above.

[20] W. Allen Wallis, "Some Economic Considerations," in John T. Dunlop (ed.), *Automation and Technological Change* (New York: The American Assembly, Columbia University, 1962), p. 110.

major factor in destroying over 2 million jobs each year.[21] There is little disagreement, however, on the point that automation is responsible for a large amount of labor market dislocation.

The argument that minimizes the seriousness of automation follows the lines of the traditional analysis of the employment effects of technological change. An example cited recently to show that jobs are created as well as eliminated when automatic pinsetters replace manual pinsetters in bowling alleys, for instance, is no different from those cited before anyone heard of automation.[22] Those who associate automation with more serious employment problems usually use aggregative industry data as well as case studies of individual firms to support their position. Buckingham, for example, has noted that employment of production workers in the electrical industry declined by about 10 per cent between 1953 and 1961 despite a 21 per cent increase in the industry's output.[23] Similar statistics are cited for the instrument production, basic steel, aircraft, soft coal, and railroad industries. There are numerous estimates of the total disemployment resulting from recent increments in productivity, but they vary widely. One, based upon a careful study of the 1947–1959 experience, projects an annual disemployment of at least 200,000 workers per year during the present decade.[24]

Case studies of individual firms usually show that dramatic reductions in labor requirements result from the installation of automated equipment. Frequently, however, actual labor displacement is minimized through transfers, reassignments, or retraining of the workers affected. Contraction of the work force occurs over time as the superfluity of employees is eliminated through normal attrition.[25]

A more direct challenge to the traditional economic analysis of the employment impact of technological change has been made by Killingsworth,

[21] Subcommittee on Employment and Manpower of the Committee on Labor and Public Welfare, U.S. Senate, *Toward Full Employment: Proposals for a Comprehensive Employment and Manpower Policy in the United States* (Washington, D.C.: U.S. Government Printing Office, 1964), p. 16.

[22] Wallis, *op. cit.,* p. 10.

[23] Walter Buckingham, "The Great Employment Controversy," *The Annals of the American Academy of Political and Social Science,* March, 1962, pp. 49, 50.

[24] Ewan Clague and Leon Greenberg, "Employment," chap. 7 in Dunlop, *op. cit.*

[25] See, for example, U.S. Department of Labor, Bureau of Labor Statistics, *Impact of Automation* (Bulletin No. 1287 [Washington, D.C.: U.S. Government Printing Office, 1960]), pp. 77–114.

[26] Charles C. Killingsworth, "Automation, Jobs, and Manpower" (Reprint Series No. 62 [East Lansing: Michigan State University School of Labor and Industrial Relations, 1963–1964]).

who argues that the present-day laborsaving installations are being made in mature rather than adolescent industries.[26] It was one thing, in other words, to introduce assembly line techniques in the automobile industry when

FIGURE 24

INDEXES OF OUTPUT PER MAN-HOUR
Total Private, Farm, and Private Nonfarm Economy, 1909–1965

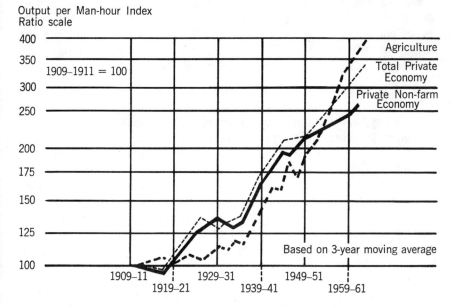

Output per Man-hour Index
Ratio scale

Source: *Technology and the American Economy* (Washington, D.C.: U.S. Government Printing Office, 1966), p. 3.

practically no one owned a car and another to install Detroit automation when there are 40 million registered cars in the United States. The doctrine that "machines make jobs," he argues, had more relevance when the market for mass produced goods was practically untapped.

Concern over the employment impact of technology led to the passage of Public Law 88-444 in August, 1964, authorizing President Johnson to appoint a fourteen member National Commission on Technology, Automation, and Economic Progress. The Commission's report issued in 1966 sided, in general, with those holding a non-alarmist view of technological change.[27] The following points were stressed in the report:

---

[27] *Technology and the American Economy* (Washington, D.C.: U.S. Government Printing Office, 1966).

1. Although there has been some increase in the pace of technological change, the rate of acceleration of productivity growth does not square with the assumption that a veritable technological revolution has occurred. If agriculture is excluded, output per man hour rose at a trend rate of 2 per cent per year before World War II and 2.5 per cent afterward. There has been no sharp break in the continuity of technical progress nor is such a break likely to occur in the next decade.

2. Changes in the volume of employment are governed by three fundamental factors. These are (a) growth of the labor force, (b) the increase in output per man hour of work and (c) the growth of total demand for goods and services. In the late 1950's and early 1960's productivity and the labor force were increasing more rapidly than usual but product demand was not rising at a rate necessary to maintain steady full employment.

3. A considerable amount of worker displacement has occurred through shifts in employment among industries and occupations. Technological change has been a major cause of occupational displacement though not the only one. These changes in the structure of occupational requirements have increased the relative labor market disadvantages of the unskilled and the uneducated.

As noted in the commission's report there is little disagreement over the fact that automation is responsible for a considerable amount of labor displacement. A displaced worker, however, becomes unemployed only if he cannot find another job. The severity of technological unemployment, thus, depends upon the general state of the economy and upon the degree to which other forces are inhibiting an easy re-employment of the displaced. In the 1960's the problem of re-employing the disemployed has been complicated by various structural changes in the economy.

Structural Unemployment

Structural unemployment is the joblessness that results from changes to basic characteristics of an economic structure. Structural unemployment may be produced by changes in the rate of population growth, by variations in the composition of labor demand, or by shifts in industrial location among other causes. The significance of structural change as a factor in the recent United States experience with persistent unemployment has been a much debated subject. At this point the discussion will be limited to a description of the factors that may be contributing to structural unemployment.

Labor Force Growth.   Growth in the size of the labor force was analyzed in the first two chapters of the book, and the details need not be repeated here. Briefly, the outlook is for an annual increment in labor force size of about 1.5 million persons, which is approximately twice the average annual increment during the 1950's. Totalling the number of new entrants to the labor force and the probable amount of technological disemployment, we get a figure of 1.7 million to 2.0 million persons who will be seeking jobs each year. This, of course, will be in addition to the already jobless. It will be necessary, consequently, for the economy to generate close to 2 million new employment opportunities each year simply to keep the unemployment rate from rising.

The Composition of Labor Demand. Changes in both the industrial and occupational structures of the demand for labor have produced employment disadvantages for particular segments of the labor force. During the 1950's, the number of employees in the service industries surpassed those in the goods-producing industries for the first time in our history. Barring unforeseen developments, the gap in labor demand between the two sectors will widen. Although certain types of labor capabilities are easily transferred from one sector to the other, others are not. Qualified office employees, for example, can shift from a goods-producing to a service firm with little difficulty, whereas the unskilled and semi-skilled plant employees frequently cannot. The change in the industrial structure of demand, consequently, is making the re-employment problem of the displaced blue collar plant worker more difficult.

Changes in the occupational composition of demand reflect both the industrial shifts described above and the impact of technological change. Killingsworth has described these changes as a "twist" in the pattern of demand: as a result of automation and other factors, demand is being pushed down for the workers with little training and being pushed up for those who are highly trained.[28] Automation experts are in disagreement about how much upgrading in the demand for labor has been associated with recent technological innovations, and some argue that the need for highly trained as against slightly trained employees has been overplayed.[29] Statistical descriptions of the occupational structure of the labor force, however, show rather conclusively that a combination of factors including the technological has resulted in a rapid rise in the demand for professional and technical personnel and only a moderate rise in the demand for semi-skilled employees. (See Chapter 2.) The twist in the demand pattern, thus, is working to the disadvantage of the insufficiently educated and the mis-educated.

Geographical Factors. Long run frictional unemployment may be produced by uneven rates of economic growth among the regions of the nation,

---

[28] Killingsworth, *op. cit.*
[29] Buckingham, *op. cit.*, pp. 96–100.

TABLE 23

RATE OF GROWTH IN NON-FARM PAYROLL EMPLOYMENT BY REGION,
SELECTED PERIODS, 1947–66

REGION	AVERAGE ANNUAL GROWTH RATE		
	1947–61	1961–65	1965–66
New England	0.8	1.9	3.6
Middle Atlantic	.6	1.8	2.6
East North Central	.9	3.1	4.2
West North Central	1.5	2.4	4.0
South Atlantic	2.3	4.1	4.8
East South Central	1.8	4.0	5.0
West South Central	2.4	3.5	4.4
Mountain	3.6	3.0	4.3
Pacific	3.3	3.6	5.9
Average Growth Rate	1.6	2.9	4.2
Mean deviation	1.0	.7	.7
As per cent of average	62.5	24.1	16.7

Source: *Manpower Report of the President,* 1967, p. 26.

by large-scale industrial relocation, and by continuing conditions of backwardness in certain sections.

Non-farm employment increased by 26 per cent between 1947 and 1962. Among the major regions of the nation, however, the increases ranged from a low of 10 per cent in the middle Atlantic states to highs of 61 per cent and 70 per cent in the Pacific and mountain states respectively. Part of the unevenness of regional employment growth is due to the substantial industrial relocation that has been going on. Dispersion of facilities in the meat packing, automobile production, and rubber tire industries, for example, has resulted in some decline in the relative importance of Chicago, Detroit, and Akron as employment centers. The flight of the textile industry from New England to the South has left a wake of depressed communities in the former area. New patterns of defense spending have favored the development of production centers in the West and particularly in California. The general direction of these and other shifts in the location of industry has been away from the older industrial areas of the nation and toward the newer ones. The result has been an imbalance between labor supplies and demands in the several regions. Since 1962, there has been less disparity in rates of employment growth among regions. In these recent years the substantial overall growth in non-farm jobs has been associated with a pervasive regional expansion in employment and, with the exception of the Middle Atlantic Region (New York, New Jersey, Pennsylvania), differences in regional rates of growth have been relatively small. Uneven employment expansion among regions, thus, has been less significant as a factor in structural unemployment between 1962 and 1970 than it was in 1947–61.

Within the past few years, a good deal of attention has been drawn to the stagnating areas of the economy. Appalachia comes to mind at once in this connection, but there are other areas such as the Upper Peninsula of Michigan, the Ozark Plateau, and the Indian reservations. Unattractive to industry, geographically and culturally isolated, these regions have remained underdeveloped islands in a highly industrialized economy. Most of those unable or unwilling to move are faced with the bleak prospects of subsistence farming or marginal mining work. Unemployment and underemployment are rampant, and the general job outlook will continue to be gloomy unless large-scale efforts at economic development are made. Recent programs in area assistance are described in the following chapter.

VULNERABLE GROUPS IN THE LABOR MARKET

Since 1953, the American economy has suffered three recessions, and after each the unemployment rate remained higher than it had been before the preceding downturn. The level of "prosperity" unemployment, in fact, rose to the extent that the unemployment rate in 1962 (a prosperity year) was as high as it had been in 1954 (a recession year). The concern generated by the persistence of a high level of unemployment has been intensified by the post-1961 experience. In the face of a prolonged prosperity, unemployment continued to hover about a rate of 5 per cent of the labor force until 1965. Since then, the rate has fallen to less than 4 per cent but the national average rate conceals the persistence of high unemployment among particular population sub-groups. Who, then, are the people who have been without jobs in a prosperous economy? Major findings of recent research on this question are summarized below.

Young Workers. Teen-agers have been especially vulnerable to unemployment. During the past ten years, the proportion of teen-agers without jobs has usually ranged between two and three times the average for all workers. For the twenty- to twenty-four-year-old group, unemployment rates have averaged about one and one-half times the national average. While the unemployment rate for all workers was nearly halved between 1961 and 1968, the teen-age rate declined very little. Persons under 25, who constituted 25 per cent of the labor force in 1968, accounted for about 50 per cent of the unemployment.

Many younger persons experience unemployment immediately when they enter into labor force activity. Unemployment rates, for example, are especially high among inexperienced teen-agers looking for summer jobs or

TABLE 24

ANNUAL AVERAGE RATE OF UNEMPLOYMENT
1947–1968

YEAR	UNEMPLOYMENT AS PER CENT OF CIVILIAN LABOR FORCE
1947	3.9
1948	3.8
1949	5.9
1950	5.3
1951	3.3
1952	3.0
1953	2.9
1954	5.5
1955	4.4
1956	4.1
1957	4.3
1958	6.8
1959	5.5
1960	5.6
1961	6.7
1962	5.5
1963	5.7
1964	5.2
1965	4.5
1966	3.8
1967	3.8
1968	3.6

Source: U.S. Department of Labor Bureau of Labor Statistics.

seeking their first full-time jobs after terminating their educations. Within the past several years, however, other factors appear to have affected employment trends among younger persons. In 1963, the number of teen-agers employed in non-farm jobs failed to increase even though the employment of adults in such jobs rose by 1.25 million. Low seniority status, the reluctance of employers to hire persons subject to the military draft, and the decline in the relative number of jobs open to persons with little skill or experience are apparently contributing to the employment difficulties of younger persons.

Older Workers. Unemployment rates among older persons have been only a little higher than the all-worker average, but those who lose jobs tend to remain unemployed for long periods of time. The specific employment problems of the older worker are discussed in Chapter 22.

Non-white Workers. Non-white workers suffer much heavier unemployment than white workers. Unemployment rates for non-whites, about 90 per cent of whom are Negroes, have been about double the rate for whites since 1955. The rate has been particularly high for younger non-white persons. In recent years one out of every four sixteen- to nineteen-year-old non-white boys in the labor force has been jobless.

The differential between white and non-white rates is explained partly by the high concentration of the latter in the less skilled blue collar and service occupations where unemployment occurs frequently. As noted in the 1964 *Manpower Report of the President,* however, the difference between white and non-white unemployment rates is relatively greater in the more skilled occupations. Negroes who have had great difficulty in breaking into the more skilled occupations also experience difficulty in holding on to their jobs once they do break through.

The Negro population has made substantial job gains during the 1960's. Employment of non-white workers rose by 16 per cent as against a 13 per cent rise for whites between 1960 and 1967. Unemployment rates for adult non-white workers, furthermore, have come down substantially in the past decade. No similar progress, can be reported for non-white teen-agers, however, a group that continues to suffer from extremely high unemployment.

Educational Attainment. Inadequate education has become a serious handicap in the job market. The average person now enters the labor force as a high school graduate. Fifty years ago he had no more than an elementary school education.[30] As a result of changes in the occupational patterns of demand for labor and the rise in the general level of educational attainment, those without at least a high school education are under greater and greater disadvantages in the race for jobs.

The education-unemployment relationship in March, 1968, is representative of the pattern in recent years. The 4.9 per cent unemployment rate for those with less than 4 years of high school education, was about double the rate for high school graduates. Only one per cent of the college graduates were without jobs.

UNEMPLOYMENT: INADEQUATE DEMAND OR STRUCTURAL TRANSFORMATION

Two distinct hypotheses have been advanced to explain the persistence of unemployment since 1957 at a level above that which can be attributed

---

[30] Elizabeth Waldman, "Educational Attainment of Workers," *Monthly Labor Review,* February, 1969, p. 14.

TABLE 25

UNEMPLOYMENT RATE FOR NON-WHITE WORKERS AS PER CENT OF RATE FOR WHITE WORKERS 1947–1967

YEAR	UNEMPLOYMENT RATE		NON-WHITE RATE AS PER CENT OF WHITE
	White	Non-white	
1947	3.3	5.4	164
1948	3.2	5.2	163
1949	5.2	8.2	158
1950	4.6	8.5	185
1951	2.8	4.8	171
1952	2.4	4.6	192
1953	2.3	4.1	178
1954	4.5	8.9	198
1955	3.6	7.9	219
1956	3.3	7.5	227
1957	3.9	8.0	205
1958	6.1	12.6	207
1959	4.9	10.7	218
1960	5.0	10.2	204
1961	6.0	12.5	208
1962	4.9	11.0	224
1963	5.1	10.9	214
1964	4.6	9.8	213
1965	4.1	8.1	197
1966	3.3	7.3	221
1967	3.4	7.4	217

Source: U.S. Department of Labor, Bureau of Labor Statistics.

to short run market frictions. One identifies structural changes in the economy as the prime cause of unemployment, whereas the other emphasizes the inadequacy of the aggregate demand for final goods and services.

Structural transformationists identify all the factors discussed above under the heading "long run frictions" as the fundamental causes of persistent unemployment. Thus, the concentration of unemployment among younger persons, Negroes, the relatively uneducated, and blue collar workers are cited as evidence of the "twist" in the labor demand pattern. The rise in the importance of service industries relative to the goods-producing industries and the long term unemployment besetting certain groups in the labor force are also important considerations in the structural thesis. What the structural transformationists are saying, in essence, is that regardless of the conditions of demand for the output of the economy, large numbers of persons will remain out of work because of improper training, age factors, or other reasons that prevent their being hired for available jobs.[31]

---

[31] For a statement of the structural transformation hypothesis see Killingsworth, *op. cit.*

Arguments to support the aggregate demand hypothesis consist, for the most part, of statistical refutations of the structuralist position. If structural unemployment has worsened since 1957, labor force statistics should reveal a relative worsening of unemployment among teen-agers, Negroes, workers in industries being automated, etc.

A number of studies have been made, and all have failed to detect the relative worsening posited by the structural thesis.[32] Unemployment rates among the relatively disadvantaged groups, thus, did not appear to be higher in 1962 or 1963 than they were in the mid-fifties, the relative unemployment rate for blue collar workers has not worsened, and there seems to be little support for the assertion that unemployment has become more concentrated in the technologically vulnerable industries. The conclusion suggested is that there is a gap between potential and actual output and that with appropriate policy to simulate demand, a large part of the prevailing unemployment can be eliminated by closing the gap.

Among economists, a strong consensus has developed in favor of the aggregate demand hypothesis. The argument is not completely conclusive, however. The labor market experience of teen-agers, for one thing, is consistent with the structural hypothesis. The differential between teen-age and adult unemployment rates has been widening and has apparently led to some reappraisal of the measures necessary to accomplish a reduction. The 1965 *Manpower Report of the President*, for example, notes that "the lack of any real accomplishment during the past few years in reducing the differentials is a demonstration of the need for specific remedies to these problems to augment measures to raise the general level of employment."

Undoubtedly a faster growth of aggregate demand would eliminate some part, perhaps a large part, of the prevailing unemployment. The possibility that structural factors are responsible for a significant percentage of the unemployment cannot be written off, however, even though it is difficult to assign a specific weight to the strength of such factors.

QUESTIONS

1. What types of unemployment data are currently available in the United States? Explain the nature of the more important types of unemployment statistics.

2. What is frictional unemployment? Distinguish between short run and long run frictional unemployment.

---

[32] See R. A. Gordon, "Has Structural Unemployment Worsened?" *Industrial Relations,* May, 1964, pp. 53–77; N. J. Simler, "Long-Term Unemployment, the Structural Hypothesis, and Public Policy," *American Economic Review,* December, 1964, pp. 985–1001; L. E. Gallaway, "Labor Mobility, Resource Allocation, and Structural Unemployment," *ibid.,* September, 1963, pp. 694–716.

3. "Technological unemployment is different from cyclical unemployment in that it is a consequence of progress rather than of economic failure." Explain the meaning of this statement.

4. Technological change usually creates at least as many jobs as it eliminates. Does this mean that technological unemployment is not a serious problem?

5. What groups in the labor force have been especially vulnerable to unemployment in recent years? Describe the disadvantages of these groups in the search for jobs.

6. Since unemployment is unemployment, does it make any difference if the cause is structural transformation rather than inadequate demand for goods and services?

SELECTED READINGS

Bowen, Howard R. and Mangum, Garth L. *Automation and Economic Progress*. Englewood Cliffs, N.J.: Prentice-Hall, Inc., 1966.

Manpower Report of the President, Washington, D.C.: U.S. Government Printing Office, January, 1969. Part One.

Marshall, Ray. *The Negro Worker*. New York: Random House, 1967. Chap. 6.

Ross, Arthur (ed.). *Unemployment and the American Economy*. New York: John Wiley & Sons, Inc., 1964. Part II.

CHAPTER 24

Employment Policy

IN THE LAST CHAPTER, CONFLICTING INTERPRETATIONS OF THE PERSISTENT unemployment experience were examined. The employment policy that has evolved in the past several years actually defers to both schools of thought. Measures have been taken to stimulate demand, and a considerable amount of legislation has been enacted to ameliorate the problems of special groups in the labor force.

STIMULATING DEMAND

The essence of the argument supporting government policy to stimulate employment through an encouragement of demand for goods and services is well known to students of macroeconomic principles. The total amount of money that is spent in an economy in a given period, hence the national income for the period, is the sum of the amounts spent by consumers, by business for investment, and by government. If spending by any of the three sectors declines and if there is no compensation by an increase in the spending by the other sectors, national income will fall, and the amount of employment associated with the higher level of national income will drop along with it. The post-1957 experience has shown that even a continuing rise in the total of the expenditures of the three spending groups may be insufficient to maintain a desirable level of employment when the labor force is growing rapidly or when the volume of technological displacement is high. Appropriate public policy, consequently, is to apply monetary and fiscal measures so as to maintain total spending at a level that produces the desired amount of employment.

The main techniques for influencing spending are, as noted above, monetary and fiscal measures. Monetary policy is directed toward changing the cost and availability of credit primarily through measures that affect the size of commercial bank reserves. The instruments of fiscal policy are government purchases of goods and services, transfer payments, subsidies, grants-in-aid, and taxes. Of the two techniques, fiscal policy is the more powerful, since it can be used to affect the incomes of spending units directly, whereas monetary policy is limited to easing access to money. Fiscal and monetary policy are subject to both technical and policy constraints. Technically, for example, it is difficult to know when to impose changes, since economic forecasting continues to be an art even though some degree of progress can be noted in forecasting techniques. Fiscal measures, furthermore, frequently require legislative sanction, and it is not usually possible to achieve the fine inter-governmental co-ordination essential for the most effective use of fiscal policy. On the policy side, fiscal and monetary measures may be constrained by incompatibilities among public goals. Strong fiscal measures to encourage employment, for example, may be inconsistent with the goal of price stability.

From the standpoint of the unemployment experience of the 1960's, the most noteworthy fiscal policy effort has been the tax cut approved in 1964 and effective in 1964 and 1965. As noted in the *Economic Report of the President* for 1965, this was the first time that taxes were cut in the United States for the declared purpose of "speeding the advance of the private economy toward maximum employment, production, and purchasing power." Long urged by the President's Council of Economic Advisers, the tax reduction was supported as a measure necessary to reduce the gap between potential and actual gross national product. (Potential GNP was defined by the Council of Economic Advisers as the output that would be produced if unemployment were reduced to 4 per cent of the labor force).[1] Unemployment dropped from an annual average of 5.7 per cent of the labor force in 1963 to 5.2 per cent in 1964, and a further drop to slightly below 5 per cent occurred in early 1965. Without the tax cut it is likely that there would have been an increase in unemployment instead of the decline of more than half a percentage point.[2]

The post-1965 surge in the American economy has been alluded to at numerous points in this volume. The Vietnam buildup together with strong

---

[1] *Economic Report of the President* (Washington, D.C.: U.S. Government Printing Office, 1965), pp. 81–85.

[2] See *Manpower Report of the President* (Washington, D.C.: U.S. Government Printing Office, 1965), p. 11.

consumer and investment demand pressures pulled the unemployment rate below 4 per cent but induced a rise in retail and wholesale prices. To contain the price pressures, monetary and fiscal policy were redirected toward restraint rather than stimulation of the economy.

ACTIVE MANPOWER POLICY

The phrase "active manpower policy" has been adopted by various federal agencies engaged in the attack against the residue of unemployment that persists under conditions of general prosperity. Although the phrase has been in use for several years, it defies precise definition and a description of the numerous manpower programs initiated since 1961 runs the danger of imputing to the policy more form and direction than actually exists. Perhaps the best way to describe what has occurred is to suggest that emphasis —at least at the present time—should be placed upon the word "active." Activity there certainly has been in the form of a confusing proliferation of programs. Although explicit manpower policy in the United States is young, it has already undergone several changes in orientation with certain programs being downgraded and others elevated in importance.

Mangum has suggested that the members of the labor force might be regarded as queued in order of attractiveness to the employer.[3] As the labor market tightens, employers dip more deeply into the queue for their manpower. Fiscal and monetary instruments are tools designed to increase aggregate demand so as to cause employers to reach farther down the line for their labor. Manpower programs attempt to capacitate those at the rear of the line to compete more effectively for jobs. Certain of the manpower programs attempt to accomplish this by providing training opportunities while others attempt to modernize institutions such as vocational schools and the employment service so as to make them more responsive to the needs of the disadvantaged. The major programs are described in the following sections.

MANPOWER PROGRAMS

Numerous precursors of recent manpower programs can be identified. Major landmarks among these include the Morrill Act of 1862 which

---

[3] Garth Mangum, "The Emergence of a National Manpower Program," in Robert A. Gordon (ed.) *Toward A Manpower Policy* (New York: John Wiley & Sons, Inc., 1967), p. 21.

provided land grants for agricultural colleges, the Smith-Hughes Act of 1917 which instituted a federal-state program of vocational education, the Wagner-Peyser Act of 1933 which created the federal-state employment service, and the Servicemen's Readjustment Act of 1944 more popularly referred to as the GI Bill. In response to the launching of Sputnik by the Soviet Union, Congress passed the National Defense Education Act of 1958 providing fellowships and other federal aid to scientific and technical education. The programs we are concerned with here were responses to the high unemployment rates that persisted after 1957 and the heavy incidence of unemployment among youths, minority groups, the uneducated and un-skilled, and residents of depressed areas. The first of the contemporary programs, that is, those instituted in the early years of the 1960 decade, were preoccupied with the threat of automation related unemployment. As anxieties over automation eased newer programs began to reflect a concern about the social and economic problems of disadvantaged groups in both urban and rural areas.

AREA ASSISTANCE

A particular area may suffer long run economic distress because of geo-graphical isolation, poor resource endowment, depletion of a resource which had served as the base of the region's economy, a flight of industry to other areas, or excessive dependence upon a declining industry. The factors that account for an area's lack of development are usually the same factors that make the location unattractive to new industry. In the absence of new industry, however, the area remains doomed to continued distress. Without outside assistance, economic backwardness attended by a high level of unemployment and underemployment is likely to persist indefinitely.

A program for area assistance was inaugurated in 1961 under the Area Redevelopment Act. The law provided various types of federal help for urban and rural areas with high unemployment. These included loans to create new private enterprises and to expand existing firms in the area; financial aid for improvement of public facilities; and technical assistance for developing new products, markets, or resources or for more effective use of old resources. Some funds were also made available for job retraining programs designed to equip the unemployed with the skills needed by indus-tries in the area.

To be eligible for these benefits, an area had to be designated as a "de-velopment area" by the Secretary of Commerce. The basic test for such a designation was an unemployment rate of 6 per cent (excluding seasonal or temporary unemployment) and an annual average rate of unemployment substantially above the national average.

FIGURE 25

EMPLOYMENT CHANGE IN MAJOR INDUSTRY GROUPS FOR
APPALACHIA AND BALANCE OF U.S., 1950–1960

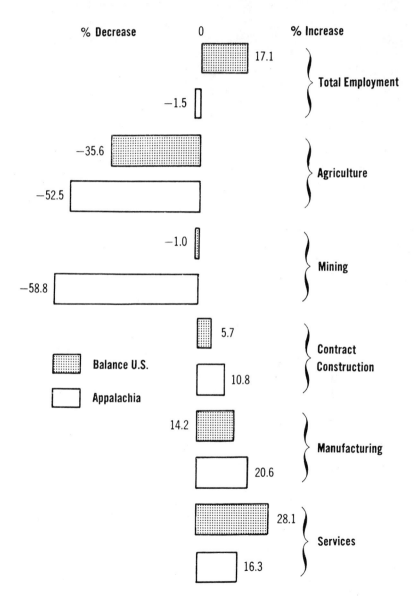

Source: Committee on Education and Labor, House of Representatives, *Poverty in the United States* (April, 1964), p. 179.

The Area Redevelopment Act and the 1962 Public Works Acceleration Act which authorized funds for public works projects in areas with continued substantial unemployment constituted the approach of the Kennedy administration to the area problem.

A frequent criticism of the approach was that federal funds were spread too thin in the effort to assist thousands of communities scattered throughout the United States. The Johnson administration responded to these criticisms by singling out the eleven state regions in the Appalachian Mountain Range of the eastern United States for receipt of massive federal help. Appalachia was selected because it is generally regarded as the most extended rural slum in the nation.

The 1.1 billion Appalachia Aid Law enacted in 1965 is designed to remove the basic economic disabilities of the Appalachian area. The law places heavy emphasis upon ending the isolation of the region through the construction of new highways and access road. Funds are also provided for health and education facilities, land reclamation, mine restoration, and timber development. By the end of fiscal year 1968, almost $600 million had been appropriated with about three-fifths of the total allocated to highway and road construction.

Under the Public Works and Development Act of 1965 five regional commissions have been established to encourage multi-state cooperation in planning and program implementation for depressed areas in the Upper Great Lakes, Ozarks, New England, Coastal Plains and Four Corners (New Mexico, Arizona, Colorado, Utah) regions. The regional commissions have not as yet proved themselves as effective planning units and little development activity has occurred as a result of their efforts.

THE MDTA

Changes in the occupational and industrial patterns of demand for labor have been described at a number of earlier points. As a result of these changes, many persons have found little or no demand for their labor skills, and those without skills face a market of shrinking opportunities. The major government effort to assist the unemployed in adjusting to the changing demand situation is the Manpower Development and Training Act passed in 1962 and amended in 1963, 1965, 1966, and 1968. In its original form, the MDTA concentrated upon unemployed heads of households who had had at least three years of work experience. This emphasis was modified by the several amendments and the present major focus is on providing training for the hard core unemployed.

Under the provisions of the MDTA, cash allowances are paid to trainees who are enrolled either in institutional or on the job training programs. When necessary, basic literacy and "employment orientation" training are provided as supplements to vocational programs. The MDTA also provides funds for pilot or demonstration projects concerned with the problem of hard core unemployment.

According to Department of Labor reports, over 600,000 persons completed training courses during the first six years of MDTA operations and 90 per cent of those who completed institutional training programs obtained jobs within a year.

THE POVERTY PROBLEM

In the early 1960's, America rediscovered poverty. "Rediscovered" is, perhaps, not the appropriate term since few were not aware of the fact that there were poor people in the United States; but a nation that was, on the whole, heady with affluence managed for a considerable time to avoid taking a hard look at its non-affluent population pockets.

A number of developments, not the least important of which was a sudden flow of books and articles about "the other America," pushed the poverty problem to the forefront of the nation's attention. Since then, an intensive examination of the nature of poverty has occurred, and much more is now known about the identity and characteristics of the poor.

The conventional standard being used for identification of the poor is an annual income of $3,000 a year or less. This standard oversimplifies the classification problem, but it is difficult to argue that a boundary of $3,000 overstates the extent of poverty. On the basis of this standard, the pertinent facts of poverty in the United States were summarized in a recent government report as follows: One-fifth of our families and nearly one-fifth of our total population are poor. Twenty-two per cent of the poor are non-white, and nearly half of all non-whites live in poverty. The heads of over 60 per cent of all poor families have only grade school educations.

One-third of all poor families are headed by a person over sixty-five, and almost one half of the families headed by such a person are poor.

Of the poor, 54 per cent live in cities, 16 per cent on farms, and 30 per cent in rural non-farm areas.

Over 20 per cent of all farm families are poor. More than 65 per cent of the non-white farmers live in poverty.

Fewer than half of the poor are in the South, but a southerner's chance of being poor is roughly twice that of a person living in another part of the country.

One quarter of the poor families are headed by a woman, and nearly one-half of all families headed by a woman are poor.

A family headed by a young woman who is non-white and has less than an eighth grade education is poor in ninety-four out of 100 cases. Even if she is white, the chances are eighty-five out of 100 that she and her children will be poor.[4]

An attack upon poverty might be made on the basis of encouraging economic growth in general. If incomes throughout the economy are rising, conceivably the incomes of the poor will also rise. The difficulty with this approach is that the incomes of certain groups of families are, to a considerable extent, isolated from economic growth.[5] This is particularly true for farm families, families headed by a woman, and families headed by an aged person. Even in periods of rapid economic growth, sufficient income does not trickle down to these groups to reduce poverty.

TABLE 26

NUMBER OF POOR HOUSEHOLDS AND INCIDENCE OF POVERTY, 1959 AND 1966

CHARACTERISTICS OF HEAD OF HOUSEHOLD	NUMBER OF POOR HOUSEHOLDS (Millions)*		INCIDENCE OF POVERTY (Per Cent)†	
	1959	1966	1959	1966
Non-farm	11.6	10.3	22.5	17.6
White	9.0	7.9	19.6	15.3
Male head	5.0	3.9	13.4	9.4
Under 65 years	3.3	2.4	10.2	6.8
Aged (65 years and over)	1.7	1.5	34.0	24.7
Female head	4.0	4.0	45.2	37.7
Under 65 years	2.2	2.0	37.8	30.5
Aged (65 years and over)	1.8	2.0	59.3	48.9
Non-white	2.6	2.4	48.9	37.5
Male head	1.4	1.2	39.7	26.9
Under 65 years	1.2	.9	36.7	23.3
Aged (65 and over)	.2	.3	64.4	51.4
Female head	1.1	1.2	69.4	60.8
Under 65 years	.9	.9	68.1	58.8
Aged (65 and over)	.2	.2	76.3	69.9
Farm	1.8	.6	40.9	20.8
White	1.3	.5	34.7	16.9
Non-white	.4	.2	85.0	69.7

* Households are defined here as the total of families and unrelated individuals.
† Poor households as a percent of the total number of households in the category.
Note: Poverty is defined by the Social Security Administration poverty-income standard; it takes into account family size, composition, and place of residence. Poverty-income lines are adjusted to take account of price changes during the period.
Detail will not necessarily add to totals because of rounding.
Source: *The Annual Report of the Council of Economic Advisers,* 1968, p. 143.

---

4 House of Representatives, Committee on Education and Labor, *Poverty in the United States,* pp. 2, 3.

5 For a statistical study that reaches this conclusion see W. H. Locke Anderson, "Trickling Down: The Relationship between Economic Growth and the Extent of Poverty among American Families," *The Quarterly Journal of Economics,* November, 1964, pp. 513–524.

Another approach is to tailor an anti-poverty program to meet the specific problems and conditions of the poor. This approach is embodied in the Economic Opportunity Act of 1964. The program is strongly oriented toward increasing the employability of young persons, but a number of the provisions are addressed to the problems of the adult poor. The major features of the act are summarized below:

The job preparation features of the Economic Opportunity Act are geared primarily to the needs of youths in the sixteen to twenty-one age group. Under the *Job Corps* program, high school dropouts and unemployed youths lacking basic work skills receive basic education and skill training in residential centers. Job Corps enrollees receive a monthly allowance, room and board, health services and work clothing for as long as two years.[6] Under the *Neighborhood Youth Corps* program, enrollees live at home and participate in work-training activities sponsored by non-profit organizations, state agencies, or local government agencies. The *Work-Study Program* provides part-time and summer employment for students who would be unable to enter or remain in college without such help. *Community Action Programs* attempt to help local communities mobilize their resources in fighting poverty. Financial and technical assistance is provided for a wide range of community actions designed to deal with some aspect of poverty. The *Adult Literacy Program* assists adults who are handicapped in their search for work by an inability to read and write English. *Special programs* attempt to aid the poverty-stricken in rural areas. Direct loans to low income farm families, loans to co-operatives serving low income rural families, and special aid for migratory farm workers are the main features of the rural anti-poverty program.

The Economic Opportunity Act establishes a domestic version of the Peace Corps. Volunteers in VISTA (*Volunteers in Service to America*) serve one year assignments in various types of anti-poverty projects. They may, for example, teach in the Job Corps training centers, work in Indian reservations, or participate in Community Action Programs.

PROLIFERATION OF MANPOWER PROGRAMS

Simply to describe the recent developments in American manpower policy has come to be a difficult chore. Programs have proliferated at a confusing rate reflecting, in part, an attempt to design approaches to fit the needs of particular groups among the disadvantaged and, in part, a somewhat frenzied effort to make the various programs more effective. Objectives of

---

[6] Under the Nixon administration the Job Corps has been severely constricted. The new administration argued that the costs of the program were high and that more effective training could be accomplished through other approaches.

the newer programs include improving the delivery of manpower services to the disadvantaged, enlisting the cooperation of the private sector in the anti-poverty fight, and coordinating the efforts of the many agencies now involved in manpower programming. Examples of these activities are described below.

Under the Concentrated Employment Program (CEP), the Department of Labor enters into contracts with local area sponsors for the purpose of developing effective manpower service delivery systems. The broad intent is to enlist the support of local businesses and labor organizations, provide a range of counseling, education, and training services, develop employment opportunities, and provide followup assistance to those placed in jobs. Examples of CEP activities include serving as the manpower (training and placement) component of the Model Cities program in a number of cities and sponsorship of the New Careers Program under which unemployed or underemployed persons are prepared for entry level professional aide jobs with career ladder opportunities.

Under the JOBS program, cooperating private companies provide training and employment to hardcore unemployed persons. The companies bear the normal training costs while costs for supplemental services such as basic education and personnel counseling are borne by the government.

The CAMPS program (Cooperative Area Manpower Planning System) represents an effort to meet the need for better coordination in the manpower field. In the carefully worded prose of the government report, the lack of coordination has been described as follows:

> The need for joint governmental action in providing manpower and related services is obvious. But there has been little precedent. Each agency draws its authority from different legislative acts, each act imposing its own conditions on utilization of funds. Many agencies function through State or local grantees, or both. The timing of each grant has seldom been closely related to that of others, although the state or local programs involved might be interrelated and even interdependent. In established Federal-State programs, a large element of local autonomy has made immediate local response to Federal stimulus unpredictable.[7]

Under CAMPS, area manpower coordinating committees in larger labor markets are charged with the responsibility of drawing up coordinated area manpower plans. At the time of this writing, inadequate funding and staff has limited the effectiveness of the attempt to achieve a unique level of interagency cooperation.[8]

---

[7] *Manpower Report of the President,* April, 1968, p. 196.

[8] The above description of newer directions in the war against poverty are illustrative rather than exhaustive. The reader interested in more detailed accounts is directed to the annual *Manpower Report of the President.* Pages 1–20 of the January, 1969, Report and 193–212 of the April, 1968, Report are especially recommended.

The Experience Under an Active Manpower Policy

It is as difficult to read the record of the national effort to grapple with hardcore unemployment as it is to describe the dimensions of the effort. Thousands of persons have been trained under one program or another and placed in jobs. In a period of strong labor demand, however, it is hard to know how much of the rise in employment is due to the employer's reaching farther down into the queue of job candidates and how much to the capacitation of these standing at the rear of the line. The major failure, perhaps, has been the inability to improve the employment situation of younger persons and particularly negro youths. Other flaws have been an excessive overlap among the programs with resulting inefficiency and waste and the amateur character of local area efforts to manage programs that call for a high degree of sophistication about the job market.

Although the pioneering attempt to devise an active manpower policy has been less than fully successful the various programs, many of them innovative and experimental, have provided a necessary experience for further efforts.[9]

UNEMPLOYMENT AND DISCRIMINATION

On the basis of whatever indicator one chooses to use, Negroes will be found to fare poorest in the labor market. They are the most vulnerable to unemployment, the most afflicted by long-term unemployment, and are effectively barred from practicing in many occupations. In recent years, median wage and salary earnings of non-white workers have been 55 per cent of the earnings of white workers, and the Negro unemployment rate has been more than double the rate for whites.

The differentials are, in part, a result of the poor quality of education that has been available to most Negroes. They also reflect discriminatory hiring and tenure practices. Title VII of the Civil Rights Act of 1964 is addressed to the problem of improving employment opportunities for Negroes through control of discrimination in the labor market.

Title VII, which became effective in July, 1965, forbids employment discrimination on the basis of sex, religion, and national origin as well as race and color. Specifically, employers are forbidden to discriminate in respect to hiring, discharge, wage payments, working conditions, promotional opportunities, and training. It is made unlawful for unions to practice discrimination in membership rules, job referral practices and apprentice-

---

[9] At the time of this writing a series of bills have been prepared which, if enacted, would centralize the existing programs under a single comprehensive manpower program. The Department of Labor is sponsoring such an approach.

ship programs. At the start the law applied only to employers with 100 or more employees and to unions with 100 or more members. In 1968, smaller employers and unions, those with twenty-five or more employees or members, became subject to the provisions of Title VII.

Administration of the Civil Rights Act is the responsibility of a five man Equal Employment Opportunity Commission appointed by the President. When a complaint is filed, the Commission is required by law to attempt to resolve the issue through conciliation. If conciliation fails the complaining party may file a civil action in a federal district court. When a district court finds that an unlawful discriminatory action was intentional, the court is empowered to enjoin the illegal practice, and it may order other remedial measures such as reinstatement and back pay.

In areas where a state or municipal anti-discrimination law exists, the EEOC may take no action on complaints until the state or local agency is notified. If these agencies fail to act within 90 days, the Commission may then exercise authority.

Enforcement procedures under the Civil Rights Act are clumsy and slow. A number of cases, however, have been worked through the courts and several district court decisions have swept away long standing discriminatory practices of both employers and labor organizations. Union discrimination in job referrals and seniority systems which have been utilized as instruments of "a pervasive pattern of discrimination" are among the practices that have been adjudged as violations of the Civil Rights Act.[10]

What might turn out to be the most significant legal attack against discrimination in employment may result, not from an action under the Civil Rights Act of 1964, but, rather from a charge filed under the National Labor Relations Act. Until recently the National Labor Relations Board avoided a direct confrontation with the problem of racial discrimination on the part of unions and employers. In the past several years, the NLRB has adjudicated suits alleging that union discrimination violated the legal obligation of labor organizations to provide fair and equal representation to all persons on a bargaining unit. Until 1969, however, the Board had received no complaints in which an employer's policy of discrimination because of race was alleged to be a violation of the National Labor Relations Act. In a case involving this issue, a Federal Court of Appeals has ruled that racial discrimination is an unfair employer practice in that it interferes or restrains with the discriminated employees' statutory rights to act in concert for their own aid and protection.[11] Should this decision become firmly established

---

10 *Local 53, International Association of Asbestos Workers* v. *Vogler*, C.A. 5, January 15, 1969; *Douglas Quarles* v. *Philip Morris, Inc.* D.C.—E.D. Va., January 4, 1968; *United States* v. *Local 189, United Paperworkers and Papermakers*, D.C.—E.D. La., March 26, 1968.
11 *United Packinghouse Workers* v. *NLRB*, C.A.—D.C., February 7, 1969.

as precedent, racial minorities will have an expeditious legal weapon against employer discrimination.

UNEMPLOYMENT AND A SHORTER WORK WEEK

Until the 1930's, when the forty-hour week and the eight-hour day became typical in American industry, the hours-of-work question had been a prominent social issue. The hours reduction that occurred in that decade fulfilled the hopes of many social reformers and labor leaders and, with some small exceptions, there was little serious clamor for further curtailment of working time. Recently, the interest of organized labor in reduced hours has reappeared, and there is a fairly widespread expectation that the work week or perhaps the work year of the future will be shorter than it is presently.

An important component of the rising standard of living in the United States has been increased leisure time. A nation enjoying productivity gains may elect to have more goods and services or more leisure or some combination of the two. (In certain circumstances, working time can be reduced without loss of production. When hours of work are extremely long, for example, a reduction in hours might result in an actual increase in output.) Within the United States, productivity gains have been taken in the form of increased leisure *and* increased real income. A common estimate is that the division has been about half and half.

The standard work week has remained at forty hours since the middle thirties. Meanwhile, productivity gains have occurred, and the growth of automation promises even more substantial gains for the future. The current demand for a shorter work week seems to be stimulated primarily by the fact that technological improvements are making a shorter week feasible. Now as always, however, the arguments for shorter hours are based partly on the hope that a decrease in working time will be helpful in alleviating unemployment.

Trends in Working Hours[12]

The first standard work day in the United States apparently lasted from sunup to sundown. Agitation for shorter hours continued throughout the nineteenth century, with the result that the ten-hour day and the fifty-eight

---

[12] An excellent survey of the shorter-hour movement can be found in Harry A. Millis and Royal E. Montgomery, *Labor's Progress and Some Basic Labor Problems* (New York: McGraw-Hill Book Company, 1938), pp. 465–488. The summary here has drawn heavily upon this source for factual data.

to sixty-hour week were established in a majority of industries and occupations before 1890. Progress was uneven, however. Hours tended to be longer in the South than in the North, and in rural areas than in industrialized centers. Skilled and organized workers generally worked a shorter week than the unskilled and unorganized. In the steel industry the twelve-hour day prevailed.

Between 1914 and 1920, substantial reductions in working time were achieved. An eight-hour standard was adopted in anthracite coal, slaughtering and meat packing, boot and shoe manufactures, newsprint paper, and the garment trades. By 1919, 48.7 per cent of the wage earners in manufacturing had a basic work week of forty-eight hours or less; 25.8 per cent had full-time weeks of fifty-five hours or more, and 12 per cent worked sixty hours or more. The comparable percentages in 1914 were 11.8, 48.9, and 26.9. For all groups of workers, average weekly hours declined from 58.4 in 1890 to 50.4 in 1920.

The general downward trend in working hours did not continue during the 1920's. Decreases occurred in some industries, increases in others. According to Millis and Montgomery, the dominant trend in manufacturing was a shift from a forty-eight to a fifty-one or fifty-four-hour week. The outstanding single development during the decade was the virtual disappearance after 1923 of the twelve-hour day and the "thirteen out of fourteen days" system in the steel industry.

In one way or another, the fact of economic depression influenced most of the major changes in working hours that occurred during the 1930's. Between 1930 and 1933, working hours fell sharply as a consequence of curtailment of activity by many business firms and also of the widespread practice of work sharing. Many employers and union leaders felt that the limited amount of available work should be divided among as many workers as possible. Work sharing, however, was regarded as a temporary expedient rather than as a forerunner of a long run reduction in work time. A more permanent development during these years, though not so widespread, was the appearance of the five-day week. Quite common by this time in the building trades, the five-day week was also adopted by a number of large manufacturing firms.

The basic achievement after 1933 was the generalization of the forty-hour week. Unlike earlier hour reductions, this was accomplished primarily by legal regulation. The NRA codes of 1933–34 and the Fair Labor Standards Act of 1938 were most important among the factors that led to the eight-hour day and the five-day week, the predominant standards up to the present time. The material increase in working hours that occurred during World War II was a temporary phenomenon that aroused no worker objection, since the overtime hours carried premium pay.

Examples of work weeks shorter than forty hours are still relatively rare. There has been some progress in this direction, however. Since 1953, the International Ladies Garment Workers Union has negotiated reductions in the work week from forty to thirty-five hours for more than 200,000 workers. In most of the major cities, the printing unions have negotiated thirty-six- to thirty-seven-hour weeks. About 30,000 rubber workers in Akron have been on a six-hour day and thirty-six-hour week since the 1930's. Other industries or occupations in which a significant number of persons work fewer than forty hours a week are construction, brewing, baking, newspaper publishing, office work, and municipal administrative and clerical work.

Although the prevalent work week is nominally forty hours, a decline in the amount of time worked has occurred as a result of what might be called fringe reductions. Paid vacations, paid holidays, rest periods, coffee breaks, and paid sick leave amount to a substantial reduction in time actually worked over the course of a year. Items such as these do not show up in statistics of standard working hours, but in a realistic sense they should be regarded as forms of work time reduction.

TABLE 27

AVERAGE WEEKLY HOURS IN MANUFACTURING,
SELECTED YEARS, 1909–1968

YEAR	HOURS	YEAR	HOURS
1909	51.0	1947	40.4
1914	49.4	1949	39.2
1924	43.7	1950	40.5
1930	42.1	1955	40.7
1934	34.6	1958	39.2
1939	37.7	1964	40.7
1941	40.6	1966	41.3
1944	45.2	1968	40.7

Source: United States Department of Labor, Bureau of Labor Statistics.

Arguments for a Shorter Work Week

The shortening of the work week was not easily accomplished. Many labor-management fights have been waged over the hours issue, and we have already noted the controversy that attended efforts to limit working hours by legislation. The arguments advanced to bolster the case for the shorter work week have changed over time. Early arguments stressed the matter of citizenship and health. Shorter hours, it was alleged, were essential so that workers could have the leisure necessary for intelligent citizenship and enjoyment of cultural, social, and family life. In a period when the twelve-hour day was prevalent and work more burdensome than it is today, this was a telling argument. Toward the end of the nineteenth century, a health argument became popular. The spread of the factory system; the rise in the incidence of industrial injury; and literature, such as Josephine Goldmark's pioneering study of the effects of work fatigue, helped to focus public attention upon the hazards of long working hours.[13] Today, we are aware of the fact that worker efficiency improves up to a point as hours are reduced, and that a shorter work period is not inevitably associated with a reduction in output. It seems clear that a ten-hour day is more efficient than a twelve-hour day, and apparently an eight-hour day is frequently more efficient than a ten-hour day. Obviously there is some limit beyond which a reduction in hours will result in a positive loss of output, and there is little evidence that fewer than eight hours of work per day can be justified on the basis of health needs of workers or productive efficiency. In fact, as more and more of our productive processes are becoming machine paced, the relationship between hours worked by employees and efficiency is diminishing. The relevance of the citizenship and health arguments is also limited at the present time, and the justification of a shorter work week is usually expressed in other terms.

Various arguments of a more theoretical cast have been advanced by labor spokesmen to prove the essentiality of a shorter working day. The arguments are similar, but the basic point has been embellished differently over the years. In recent times, major stress has been placed upon the dual need of higher wages and shorter hours to offset the threat to employment posed by technological change and overproduction of goods.

Labor has made much of the underconsumption argument: depressions occur because sales lag, and sales lag because groups with the greatest need do not have adequate purchasing power. A corollary of the underconsumption thesis is that reduction of hours with no curtailment of pay constitutes a promising approach for preventing unemployment. This logic was especially prominent in the 1930's and to some extent was relied upon by proponents of the New Deal hours-limitation legislation.

Most economists have had little sympathy with the notion that an hours reduction is a depression curative. To simplify the presentation, let us eliminate several types of working hour limitations that are not relevant to the discussion. It can be conceded that it is possible to spread *available* employment through hours reduction. The practice of work sharing during

---

[13] Josephine Goldmark, *Fatigue and Efficiency* (New York: The Russell Sage Foundation, 1912).

the depression has been noted, and similar arrangements could be made in the future. Work sharing can be described with equal accuracy as unemployment sharing, however. Neither the total amount of hours worked nor the aggregate income earned is increased by a sharing of available work. There is nothing in the work sharing arrangement, furthermore, that resolves the fundamental causes of depression. We shall also bypass the situation in which increased leisure is made possible by efficiency gains. A work time reduction made in the wake of productivity increases involves no additional costs for the firm. A society fortunate enough to enjoy productivity gains has an opportunity to choose between additional goods and additional leisure, and in certain circumstances a choice of leisure may be helpful in sustaining employment.

Is there any reason to believe that a shorter work week of and by itself will help to sustain the volume of employment? In recent years, most of the persons who have argued the affirmative of this issue have been talking in terms of hours reduction with no reduction in pay. Let us, then, consider this as a possibility.

The broad negative argument against the efficacy of an hours reduction is that such a course of action does not affect the basic causes of unemployment. The simplest point that can be made in the case of cyclical unemployment is that the depression phase of the business cycle has not disappeared over the course of years although daily work hours have fallen from about twelve to eight. Disparities between decisions to save and decisions to invest can occur regardless of the length of the standard work week.

The traditional economic argument against hours reduction as a depression cure can be explained by positing a situation in which hours are cut back from forty to perhaps thirty-five during a period of heavy unemployment. If we assume that there has been no increase in productivity and that take-home pay has been maintained, the immediate effect of such a move is increased production costs. Unless something occurs to change product demand in a way that is favorable to the firm, the individual business firm might find it impossible to sustain the old volume of employment under the new cost conditions. But it is possible that price rises will offset the cost effects of the reduced hours. Thus, when work time is cut and take-home pay maintained, a constant amount of worker income will be bidding against a reduced supply of goods and services. In this situation, prices will rise and workers will have the same money income but lower real income. Workers will also have more leisure, of course, but a swap of real income for leisure can hardly be construed as an improvement in a period of less than full employment. As a final possibility, let us assume that employers seek to maintain existing levels of output by hiring additional workers after hours have been reduced. As long as total output is no larger than it was before the hours reduction, total real income cannot rise. Those who were

The Problem of Economic Insecurity

formerly unemployed will have improved their positions, but those who had been working will have a smaller real income despite the maintenance of money income. In real terms, they will have a smaller share of a total output that will not have changed. The ultimate result in this situation is the same as in the case of work sharing.

Thus, regardless of the merits of the underconsumption argument, it cannot be assumed that a reduction in hours will *necessarily* lead to a redistribution of income and a higher level of aggregate demand. Cause and effect in the economic world are much too involved to warrant the assumption that a change in one variable—hours—will have a single consequence that can be predicted. The above discussion illustrates several possibilities that oppose the conclusion that shorter hours must be associated with an increase in employment.

AFL-CIO economists have proposed, as a device to counter existing unemployment, a gradual reduction in the standard work week to thirty-five hours.[14] The proposal visualizes a maintenance of take-home pay so as to avoid a contraction in aggregate purchasing power and a doubling of the present penalty rates for overtime in order to discourage the use of overtime as a substitute for hiring new workers.

Various objections to the AFL-CIO proposal have been voiced. If the rise in productivity is sufficient to absorb the increase in hourly wage costs, total wages and total production will remain unchanged as a result of the cut in hours. It is not clear, however, why such an adjustment would produce any increase in the demand for labor. A rise in hourly wage rates, furthermore, might accelerate the present rate of substitution of machinery for labor and, thus, aggravate the problem of technological displacement.

A NOTE ON HUMAN CAPITAL AND MANPOWER ANALYSIS

The various employment policies discussed earlier in this chapter are based, at bottom, on the assumption that expenditures for education or training "pay off." Since 1960, a good deal of research has gone into the measurement of costs and benefits of education, training, and other programs designed to improve the economic quality of people. These studies, in turn, are part of a broader concern that has grown up around what has been summarized by the expression "human capital."

Perhaps the best way to show what modern writers mean by human capital is to cite the example used by Professor Theodore Schultz whose

---

[14] For a detailed analysis of the AFL-CIO proposal see Sar Levitan, *Reducing Worktime as a Means to Combat Unemployment* (Kalamazoo, Mich.: W. E. Upjohn Institute for Employment Research, 1964), pp. 14–19.

name is prominently associated with the subject. Suppose, says Schultz, that we had an economy with the land and physical capital that we now have in the United States but that there were no persons who had any on-the-job training or formal schooling. Obviously production would be far below the current output of the United States. Or suppose, less drastically, that human capabilities were what they were in 1929. Even in this case, output would be below the present level. The main point here is that the quality of human resources within a nation is a key factor in the economic growth process.

Several distinctive features of recent history have aroused interest in the subject of human capital. The job of restoring the industrial capacity of Western Europe took less time than most people supposed it would, whereas bringing many of the developing economies to a position of self-support is taking longer than was originally anticipated. Many observers have concluded that the difference in the two situations is the existence of a large stock of human capital—professionals, technicians, skilled crafts-men, managers—in the European countries, compared to the scarcity of such talents in the developing nations. Expanded research in the economics of developing areas has produced specific evidence of the critical impor-tance of human capital in the development process and of the damaging results of the lack of human capital. Various writers, for example, have stressed the special importance of the "creative personality" or the "binding agent," in mobilizing human and material resources.

Recent studies of the growth in economic output of the United States have suggested that some part of the growth has resulted from factors other than quantitative increments in labor and capital inputs. The approach in most of these studies has been to take the economic output of the United States over a given period of time and to associate as much of the increase as possible with measurable inputs such as labor or capital. In his study, *Productivity Trends in the United States,* John Kendrick found that an input index increased at an average rate of 1.9 per cent per annum from 1889–1957, and an output index increased at a rate of 3.5 per cent. The residual, thus, was 1.6 per cent.[15] Others, using different measurement methods, have found residuals that varied somewhat in either direction from Kendrick's findings. Many analysts have concluded that the residual is explained in part by the increased education and training of workers in the recent periods. The human capital stock, in other words, has risen.

Interest in human capital also stems from the national anti-poverty effort. Much of the anti-poverty program is designed to capacitate the disadvan-taged so as to enable them to compete more effectively in the labor market. Given the massive dimension of poverty and the limits on the availability of

---

[15] New York: National Bureau of Economic Research, 1961.

public funds, a good deal of thought has gone into the problem of how to best allocate available resources among the numerous programs and approaches.

Much of the formal analysis of human capital has consisted of efforts to develop data for the guidance of policy decisions. These decisions have been concerned primarily with such questions as how much and what types of investments to make in order to improve the quality of the human agent in the productive process. Investments in human capital might take the form of expenditures to improve health, to relocate unemployed persons, to eliminate illiteracy, etc. The larger part of the recent research, however, has been devoted to the area of education and the discussion here will concentrate upon this aspect.

The investor contemplating an investment in physical capital will relate the costs of the investment to the anticipated returns over the lifetime of the physical unit. *Cost-benefit analysis* of education attempts to follow the same approach for investments in education.

Cost-benefit analysis has been described as a practical way of assessing the desirability of projects where it is important to take a long view.[16] The technique has been used to determine the feasibility of irrigation projects, flood control, inland waterways, road improvement schemes, and other public projects. In the area of education, the cost-benefit approach, as noted above, involves an effort to measure the costs and benefits of investments in education.

One way to study the economic value of education is to compare the lifetime earnings of people with different levels of education. The differences can then be expressed as rates of return on the costs of acquiring the education.

While this approach can be defended as providing a rough and ready measure, it has some obvious difficulties. There is, first, the problem of aggregation. What is true for the individual is not necessarily true for the economy as a whole. For the individual, a college degree may lead to an increase in earning power which can be estimated, more or less, by reference to the earnings of others with a college education. A public investment program which produces a dramatic increase in the number of college graduates, on the other hand, could affect the market value of education and, thus, the lifetime stream of income for the graduates. Other questions that have been raised concern the validity of earnings as a measurement of productivity, the influence of other variables—race, sex, etc.—on earn-

---

[16] A. R. Prest, R. Turvey, "Cost-Benefit Analysis: A Survey," *The Economic Journal,* December, 1965, p. 684.

ings, and the difficulty of imputing a quantitative value to the indirect benefits of a better educated population.[17]

Although the imprecisions of cost-benefit analysis limit its reliability, the method can be useful to policymakers who are aware of the limitations. The Department of Labor, for example, has commissioned pilot studies to compare the costs and benefits of institutional and on-the-job training programs under the Manpower Development and Training Act. Although the studies have admitted data deficiencies, Labor Department officials believe they demonstrate (1) that benefits exceed costs in both programs and (2) that the benefit-cost ratio is more favorable for on-the-job training. (The ratios of benefits to costs shown by the pilot studies are 2.13 to 1 for on-the-job training and 1.09 to 1 for institutional training.)[18]

Another, and quite different, technique for reaching decisions about investments in education is the so-called manpower requirements approach. This approach requires that a forecast be made of future manpower needs classified by occupations. The forecasts may be made on the basis of a projected size of gross national product, anticipated growth of the various industrial sectors, or, in the case of nations with plans for economic development, from the details of the development plan. Future size of occupational stocks is determined by adjusting current stocks for attrition due to deaths and retirements and increments produced by the educational system and on-the-job training. The computed excess of future requirements over future supplies, if any, is then used as a guide for altering the patterns and amounts of investments in education so as to remove the discrepancy. The manpower requirements approach may be used for economy wide or regional manpower planning or, in a more limited way, for planning to remove particular occupational shortages. Analysis, thus, may be made of future requirements and supplies of medical doctors, and educational expenditures adjusted so as to eliminate anticipated deficiencies in this single occupation.

---

[17] For a discussion of these problems see Prest and Turvey, *loc. cit.,* pp. 683–724 and William G. Bowen, *Economic Aspects of Education* (Princeton, New Jersey: Industrial Relations Section, Princeton University, 1964), pp. 13–33.

A major problem in all types of cost-benefit analysis is the selection of an appropriate discount rate. The money benefits from an investment in education accrue over time. The differences between the sum of the benefits and the present value of the sum is the compound discount of the former. ($P = S (1+i)^{-n}$ where P is the present value, S the returns to educational investment over n time periods and i the interest rate). Computation of the present value of a stream of benefits is sensitive to the discount factor selected but the appropriate choice of a factor for public investment is complicated by the constellation of interest rates that one finds in the private sector plus the necessity of making adjustments for various differences between public sector and private sector investments. Prest and Turney, *loc. cit.* p. 697–700.

[18] *Manpower Report of the President,* January, 1969, p. 219.

Major difficulties associated with the manpower requirements method are (1) occupational needs in many areas of activity are not rigidly defined by technology and, thus, are difficult to forecast and (2) for many activities it is difficult to relate occupational needs to specific training programs. In defense of the approach, it can be argued that it is impossible to avoid making decisions about investments in education and, consequently, it is preferable to reach such decisions after the systematic accumulation and analysis of manpower data that is involved in the manpower requirements approach.

CONCLUSION

The main elements of an evolving manpower policy have been described in this chapter. The policy is based upon the assumption that special assistance to disadvantaged groups *and* a stimulation of aggregate demand are necessary in order to reduce unemployment to tolerable levels.

A large number of anti-unemployment measures have been enacted in a short period of time, and one would have to go back to the early years of the New Deal period to find comparable experimentation with social welfare legislation. The word "experimentation" should be emphasized. As a nation, we have had little experience in dealing with the labor market problems that we presently face. Despite the attention that has been lavished on the subject within the past five years, there is considerable uncertainty in the diagnosis of the causes of persistent unemployment, and it is highly probable that the action programs underway will enjoy something less than complete success. Some of the programs will be caught in the crossfire of local politics at the cost of their ultimate effectiveness, and others will be hampered by a lack of expertise in the administration of novel approaches to social problems. Effective co-ordination of the different elements of the national manpower policy has yet to be achieved, and it can be anticipated that a certain amount of intergovernmental power strife will occur as a result of program overlap. Some degree of inefficiency and failure, in other words, may be the necessary price of learning how to deal with contemporary employment problems. It can be hoped that the programs initiated during the sixties will lead to a less troubled labor market in the seventies.

QUESTIONS

1. Many studies of poverty in the United States use a standard of $3,000 or less annual income as a means of identifying the poor. What are the shortcomings of such a standard?

2. The Economic Opportunity Act of 1964 provides funds for local community anti-poverty projects. In your opinion, what would be the most effective way to use such funds in your community?

3. The Peace Corps has had a relatively successful experience in foreign countries. Do you believe that VISTA will be equally successful on the domestic scene?

4. What are the characteristics of a rural slum? What features of our manpower and employment programs are addressed to the problems of the rural slums?

5. Will a shortening of the work week help to sustain the level of employment?

SELECTED READINGS

BAKKE, E. WIGHT. *A Positive Labor Market Policy.* Columbus, Ohio: Charles E. Merrill Books, Inc., 1963.

BOWEN, WILLIAM G. *Economic Aspects of Education.* Princeton, N.J.: Industrial Relation Section, Princeton University, 1964. Pp. 1–38.

DANKERT, CLYDE E., MANN, FLOYD C., NORTHRUP, HERBERT R. *Hours of Work.* New York: Harper and Row Publishers, 1965.

Manpower Report of the President. Washington, D.C.: U.S. Government Printing Office, Annual.

PARNES, HERBERT. *Forecasting Educational Needs for Economic and Social Development.* Paris: Organization for Economic Cooperation and Development, 1962.

The People Left Behind. Report by the President's National Advisory Commission on Rural Poverty. Washington, D.C.: U.S. Government Printing Office, 1967.

SCHULTZ, THEODORE. "Investment in Human Capital," *American Economic Review,* March, 1961. Pp. 1–17.

CHAPTER 25

Conclusion:
The Outlook for Labor
in The United States

IN THE LABOR FIELD, THE SHORT RUN OUTLOOK IS FOR A PERIOD OF POLICY and institutional adjustments to various developments that have occurred since 1945. If, as has been suggested, contemporary history began when the problems which are actual in the world today first took visible shape, then contemporary labor history began in the first years after World War II. At that time, population, technological, and economic movements gave the first signals of what were subsequently to become the prominent social concerns in the labor field; and modern labor history is primarily the story of the adjustment to these developments. Historical time does not fall into neat compartments, of course; and there are current experiences, particularly in industrial relations, that are reminiscent of the 1930's. These, however, are marginal to what have emerged as the major areas of social concern. Two aspects of the postwar economy can be identified as new and important determinants of the direction of public policy for labor problems. One is the existence of an array of national economic goals, each of which may constrain, in greater or lesser degree, the vigor and quality of the policy developed relative to the others. Pursuit of the goal of full employment, for example, is subject to constraints imposed by the goal of price stability. The second aspect is the fact that even in a prolonged economic expansion, unemployment has persisted at a level above that which can be attributed to short run market frictions.

INDUSTRIAL RELATIONS POLICY

In the matter of industrial relations policy, the pre- and postwar eras can be contrasted through key phrases that summarize the significant characteristics of the public policy approaches in the two periods. The 1935 Wagner Act was an exercise in *countervailing power*. The tone of the postwar approach is found in the notion of *wage-price guidepost.*

The underlying assumption of the Wagner Act was that society, as well as workers, would be well served by a strengthening of employee bargaining power. The worker who was fortunate enough to have steady employment in the 1930's usually had little to say about his wages or working conditions; and with wages low and working conditions frequently intolerable, it seemed to many a matter of simple justice to help the worker join with his fellows to face the employer with a meaningful aggregate of power. Apart from considerations of equity, a policy to encourage collective bargaining appeared to make good economic sense. In a badly stalled economy, the purchasing power theory which stressed the importance of high wages in a system where mass consumption was a necessary condition of prosperity was attractive.

Since 1945, the popularity of the economic assumption of the Wagner Act has diminished. Specifically, there has been much questioning of the compatability of the decisions reached through collective bargaining with various national economic goals such as price stability, economic growth, and a viable balance of payments position. Social concern, thus, has shifted from a preoccupation with the equity of the bargaining process to the economic implications of the decisions reached in the private bargains between management and labor.

To state the matter differently, there has been a growth of concern over the possibility that labor-management settlements, however attractive the terms to the bargaining parties, may not be in the public interest. The settlements must be "correct," and the definition of "correct" will vary depending upon the state of the economy. Thus, the elaborate structure of industrial relations law erected since 1935, which is very much concerned with the processes of collective bargaining and very little concerned with the content, has little relevance to the "new" problems in industrial relations.

The idea of a wage-price guidepost, first elaborated in the 1962 report of the Council of Economic Advisers, was a mild effort to guide labor and management toward what are visualized as economic decisions in the public interest. It was also a halting step in the direction of what a number of European nations have called a "national incomes policy" or a policy to make wage and price movements compatible with national economic goals. Although the Nixon administration, which assumed office in 1969, has disdained the use of guideposts, it is unlikely the the new administration will be able to ignore the wage-price problem in the context of an inflated economy.

LABOR MARKET POLICY

The challenge for labor market policy is posed by four major and partially overlapping developments. These are (1) unusually large annual increments in labor force size resulting primarily from the post-1945 rise in the birth rate, (2) a shift in the composition of labor demand which works to the disadvantage of the relatively uneducated and untrained, (3) the emergence of class unemployment in which certain socio-economic groups consistently have a higher than average unemployment experience, and (4) the persistence of poverty in about 20 per cent of all family units even when the economy is enjoying a prolonged expansion.

The debate over the causes of unemployment described in an earlier chapter is, in effect, a debate over the relevance of the four points listed above—and particularly Points 2 through 4—to policy formation. Implicit in the aggregate demand hypothesis is the conclusion that policy appropriate for a condition of mass unemployment is equally appropriate for class unemployment. The structuralist position, of course, is that policy must be devised to deal directly with the specific problems.

The odd feature of the present experience is that despite the strong consensus that has developed in favor of the aggregate demand hypothesis, the most exciting elements of our emerging employment policy are found in those features that are addressed to structural problems. In part, this reflects different evaluation of the character of the unemployment problem among the government agencies. One gets a different picture of the problem, for example, from the Labor Department's report on *Manpower Requirements, Resources, and Utilization,* which is appended to the annual *Manpower Report of the President,* than from the annual *Report of the Council of Economic Advisers,* which is appended to the annual *Economic Report of the President.* Apart from this, there appears to be a lurking fear that the structuralists may have a point despite the logic of the opposite position. The fear may be justified. Recent experience with the problems of poverty has demonstrated that many among the poor are incapable of effective participation in the labor market and require both vocational training and general education to gear them for the world of work.

Subsequent to the tax cut of 1964, unemployment fell to a rate of less than 4 per cent of the labor force and, in recent years, has hovered about a rate of 3.5 per cent. The dangers of inflation, however, have made the debate over aggregate demand versus structural change an academic one since fiscal policy has been redirected toward restraint rather than stimulation of the economy. Until inflationary conditions ease, policy for hard core unemployment will proceed along the lines implied by the structuralist approach.

At the time of this writing, the major challenge for labor market policy is that of making the various training and job placement programs more effective. As noted in earlier chapters, many of the on-going programs have suffered from a lack of expertise, inadequate funding, and poor coordination. Labor market policy, like industrial relations policy is in a state of flux and what emerges will depend to a considerable extent upon the results of the present efforts. The character of the programs underway implies a continuing commitment on the part of the federal government to play a more active role than it has in the past relative to both the provision of adequate employment opportunity and manpower training.

THE PROBLEMS OF UNIONISM

For the labor movement, the contemporary problem is basically that of shaking off the debilitating effects of past successes and reorienting itself to face a variety of novel challenges in an effective way. The specific problems facing organized labor were detailed earlier and can be summarized briefly at this point. They are (1) labor displacement and other problems resulting from technological change, (2) shifts in the composition of labor demand which disfavor the occupational groups from which the larger part of the labor union membership is drawn, (3) the resistance of certain white collar groups to unionism, (4) the general loss of drive within the labor movement, (5) the aging of the labor leadership (6) the restiveness on the part of the rank and file, (7) factionalism among unions, (8) a deterioration of the public image of organized labor, and (9) hostility toward the union movement by minority groups and younger activists.

A listing of the problems may give a distorted picture of the state of affairs, since not all unions are equally affected and since, among those affected, some have made more progress than others in coming to grips with the various challenges. Noteworthy progress has been made, for example, in attracting certain of the professional white collar groups to unionism; and if some of the unions appealing to the white collar workers fail to win mass membership, they can at least take comfort in the fact that their efforts have driven certain of the professional associations to behavior that smacks very much of unionism. Collective bargaining has already proved to be a more effective method of dealing with some aspects of automation-induced problems than many observers supposed it could be, and a number of prominent unions have experienced recent changes in leadership which may lead to some strengthening of the organizations involved.

A pressing and immediate problem of organized labor is that of working out bargaining arrangements and pressure techniques that will prove effective for unions of public employees and at the same time not impose costs and levels of inconvenience that will antagonize the general public. Another major challenge is to soften hostility toward unions on the part of minority group leaders who see the labor organizations as agencies of discrimination.

CONCLUSION

The long run outlook for labor in the United States will depend to a considerable extent upon what eventuates in the course of the short run policy and institutional adjustments discussed above. At the present time, the outlook is for a much heavier reliance upon statute-based programs to deal with employment and other labor market problems and a greater reliance upon non-statutory methods to deal with the more important problems of industrial relations. Organized labor which has historically functioned as a protest movement has come to be, in Barbash's words, "a going concern." The latter is a more comfortable position but it does pose for unions the novel dilemma of how to be innovative, imaginative, and aggressive without jeopardizing their new status.

Index